Straightforward
STATISTICS

To my parents and the four most amazing
guys in my life: Bill, Ted, Tim, and Kingsley.

SAGE was founded in 1965 by Sara Miller McCune to support
the dissemination of usable knowledge by publishing innovative
and high-quality research and teaching content. Today, we
publish more than 850 journals, including those of more than
300 learned societies, more than 800 new books per year, and
a growing range of library products including archives, data,
case studies, reports, and video. SAGE remains majority-owned
by our founder, and after Sara's lifetime will become owned by
a charitable trust that secures our continued independence.

Los Angeles | London | New Delhi | Singapore | Washington DC

Chieh-Chen Bowen

Cleveland State University

Straightforward

STATISTICS

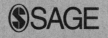

Los Angeles | London | New Delhi
Singapore | Washington DC

Los Angeles | London | New Delhi
Singapore | Washington DC

FOR INFORMATION:

SAGE Publications, Inc.
2455 Teller Road
Thousand Oaks, California 91320
E-mail: order@sagepub.com

SAGE Publications Ltd.
1 Oliver's Yard
55 City Road
London EC1Y 1SP
United Kingdom

SAGE Publications India Pvt. Ltd.
B 1/I 1 Mohan Cooperative Industrial Area
Mathura Road, New Delhi 110 044
India

SAGE Publications Asia-Pacific Pte. Ltd.
3 Church Street
#10-04 Samsung Hub
Singapore 049483

Acquisitions Editor: Vicki Knight
eLearning Editor: Katie Bierach
Editorial Assistant: Yvonne McDuffee
Production Editor: Jane Haenel
Copy Editor: QuADS Prepress (P) Ltd.
Typesetter: C&M Digitals (P) Ltd.
Proofreader: Scott Oney
Indexer: Robie Grant
Cover Designer: Candice Harman
Marketing Manager: Nicole Elliott

Copyright © 2016 by SAGE Publications, Inc.

Printed in the United States of America

Library of Congress Cataloging-in-Publication Data

Bowen, Chieh-Chen.

Straightforward statistics / Chieh-Chen Bowen.

pages cm
Includes bibliographical references and index.

ISBN 978-1-4833-5891-8 (pbk. : alk. paper) 1. Social sciences—Statistical methods. I. Title.

HA29.B7567 2016

519.5—dc23   2015020345

This book is printed on acid-free paper.

Certified Chain of Custody
SUSTAINABLE FORESTRY INITIATIVE
Promoting Sustainable Forestry
www.sfiprogram.org
SFI-01268

SFI label applies to text stock

15 16 17 18 19 10 9 8 7 6 5 4 3 2 1

Brief Contents

Detailed Contents

Preface

In my 20 years of teaching statistics, I have encountered many students who are anxious, confused, and frustrated in their efforts, trying to learn and understand statistics—this was such a contrast to my own experience learning statistics. I loved learning statistics, and I still love using them to extract useful information out of data. Every statistical procedure has a clear structure and a definite purpose. It all seems intuitive and logical to me. I wished I could share my love of statistics and my views on the clear structure and purpose of every statistical procedure with as many people as possible, so I decided to write a book that helps students understand introductory statistics.

I believe that learning statistics is similar to building a Lego project. Lego pieces have a lot in common, allowing them to be connected together. There are special pieces to make particularly interesting shapes, but there are always basic pieces to connect different parts together. Once you learn how to use the basic pieces and how the basic pieces connect together, you can build complicated projects by connecting different parts together. Learning statistics is similar to that. It involves clear understanding of basic terms, theories, formulas, and purposes of statistical procedures. Complicated statistical concepts are simply modifications, extensions, and combinations of basic statistical concepts. In making the journey to learn and understand statistics, the process hopefully gets easier instead of more difficult. By the time you get to more complicated statistical concepts, you should already be well versed in all the basic components. Learning how to use the basic components allows you to connect the different parts together.

Failing to recognize the common components and to make connections from one statistical topic to the next will likely contribute to the anxiety, confusion, and frustration often experienced by those who are trying to learn and understand statistics. I carefully move from one topic to the next, pointing out how the topics are similar, what you should already know, and in what crucial ways the topics are different. Such explicit connection should equip you with the necessary knowledge and assurance to feel confident in tackling a new topic. My intention is to reinforce the accumulative nature of learning statistics. As you work through chapters and gain more knowledge, moving on to the more complicated topics in later chapters should be relatively easy, and hopefully, a piece of cake.

I believe good statisticians can explain statistics in sophisticated terms, but the best statisticians can explain statistics in simple terms. Of course, sophisticated language has its time and place in statistics because it requires very precise language to express definite meanings. However, the language does not need to be sophisticated all the time. Language should be a facilitator for learning statistics instead of a hurdle. My simple and straightforward approach to learning statistics is thus to identify the common components of statistics, and how different topics are connected together, so that it provides a holistic learning experience. To help you with this learning experience, you can test your knowledge with the frequent pop quizzes you will find in all chapters. Also, at the end of the chapters, there is a trove of resources to help you further understand and succeed in mastering the material.

My goal has been to write an introductory statistics book that covers all the important topics in a plain, clear, and straightforward manner, and I hope that with your success, I achieve that goal. This book is designed to help social sciences students who are learning college-level statistics for the first time. With that in mind, the book is presented with a balance between mathematical operations and conceptual explanations. Most important, both the mathematical operations and conceptual explanations are technically accurate.

You need to be an active learner to be successful in a statistics course. Starting on the first day of the class, read the book chapter that is going to be covered in advance, pay attention to the professor's lecture, complete homework assignments on time, form study groups, and, most critically, don't skip any classes. What you get out of a statistics course depends on what you put into it. Learning statistics is a joint effort between the students and the professors. Students need to be prepared to learn, and professors need to provide a straightforward path to help the students reach their goal. This book provides a clear road map for your joint journey.

Instructor Resources

Instructors, visit edge.sagepub.com/bowen for a test bank, PowerPoint slides, additional practice problems, and more.

Acknowledgments

I would like to thank Bill Bowen for faithfully reading every word that I wrote in this book and for offering sincere and constructive comments on the first draft. Thanks are also due to Vicki Knight, SAGE Publisher, and my developmental editor, Jim Strandberg, for believing in this book, providing boundless support and helpful suggestions throughout this process. I am grateful to the many reviewers for their valuable critiques on earlier versions of this book to make it better:

Arin M. Connell, *Case Western Reserve University*

Frederick Drake, *Evangel University*

DeMond M. Grant, *Oklahoma State University*

Dan Ispas, *Illinois State University*

Jitendra M. Kapoor, *Alabama A&M University*

Veena S. Kulkarni, *Arkansas State University*

James H. Lampley, *East Tennessee State University*

Tracey A. LaPierre, *University of Kansas*

James E. Lennon, *New Jersey City University*

Christopher John McKinney, *University of Colorado at Denver*

David M. Mendelsohn, *California State University San Bernardino*

Nyaradzo H. Mvududu, *Seattle Pacific University*

Masaru Teramoto, *University of Utah*

About the Author

Chieh-Chen Bowen is an associate professor in the Department of Psychology at Cleveland State University. She received her PhD in Industrial and Organizational Psychology and a doctoral minor in Statistics from Penn State. She teaches undergraduate and graduate-level Statistics, Personnel Psychology, Job Analysis, and Performance Management. Her research interests are comparing cross-cultural management practices, investigating women's issues in the workplace, and validating personality questionnaires for employee selection. When she is not teaching or doing research, she can be found providing expert witness consulting services to attorneys who are involved in employment discrimination cases. On her days off, she works on figuring out the probability of a black-and-white cat selectively shedding only white fur on a navy blue carpet while shedding only black fur on white ceramic tiles.

Introduction to Statistics

After reading and studying this chapter, you should be able to do the following:

- Define samples and populations
- Define descriptive statistics and inferential statistics
- Define scales of measurement
- Provide two or three examples of each scale of measurement
- Identify numeric characteristics of each scale of measurement

This chapter defines and introduces fundamental statistical terms. Statistics is a science that deals with collecting, organizing, summarizing, analyzing, and interpreting numerical data. It is especially useful when using numerical data from a small group (i.e., a sample) to make inferences about a large group (i.e., a population). Definitions, numerical characteristics, and symbols for samples and populations are clearly presented and explained in this chapter. Scales of measurement are introduced to show how each scale measures and describes different numerical attributes of data. After reading this chapter, you should have learned how to differentiate samples from populations as well as understand specific numerical attributes of scales of measurement.

WHAT IS STATISTICS?

Let me begin this introductory chapter by clearly defining the terms that will be used throughout the book. Examples will be used to illustrate the concepts. **Statistics** is a science that deals with the collection, organization, analysis, and interpretation of numerical **data**.

Data are defined as factual information used as a basis for reasoning, discussion, or calculation, so that meaningful conclusions can be drawn. The use of statistics originated in collecting data about states or communities as administrators studied their social, political, and economic conditions in the mid- to late 17th century. Statistics are used to describe the numerical characteristics of large groups of people. Understanding statistics is useful in answering questions such as the following:

- What kind of data need to be collected?
- How many data are needed to provide sufficient guidance?
- How should we organize the data?
- How can we analyze the data and draw conclusions?
- How can we assess the strength of the conclusions?

POPULATION VERSUS SAMPLE

Learning statistics is very similar to learning a new language. Before you can master a new language, there are basic vocabularies you need to memorize and understand. The basic vocabulary of statistics starts with terms describing the numerical characteristics of a population and numerical characteristics of a sample. A population is defined as the entire collection of everyone or everything that researchers are interested in measuring or studying. A sample is defined as a subset of the population, from which measures are actually obtained. For example, a Midwest urban university wants to gauge students' interest in purchasing a city bus pass as a way of commuting to campus. The population, in this example, is the number of students in the entire student body, $N = 17,894$. N, capitalized, refers to the size of the population; a lowercase n is used for sample size. It would have been extremely time-consuming and very expensive to ask every student in the university his or her interest in purchasing a city bus pass. No matter how hard you try, it is highly likely that there would be some people who simply refuse to answer survey questions.

To obtain information efficiently, the university administration assigned the task to the Student Government Association. This association put a survey on the university website and collected responses from 274 students, sample size $n = 274$. This group of 274 students is the sample where measures were actually obtained. The answers from these 274 students formed the data. Data are the raw material required to run statistical analyses. Collecting and sorting data usually happens before calculating statistics. Both a population and a sample contain numerical attributes that researchers try to investigate. The numerical attributes of a population are called parameters, and they are usually denoted by Greek letters. Numerical attributes of a sample are called sample statistics, and they are usually denoted by ordinary English letters. Table 1.1 shows the basic vocabulary to describe populations and samples. It is important to master the basic vocabulary, so as to make effective and clear understanding of statistical concepts achievable. In this chapter,

TABLE 1.1 The Basic Vocabularies to Describe Numerical Characteristics of a Population and a Sample

MEANING OF THE SYMBOL	POPULATION PARAMETERS	SAMPLE STATISTICS
Mean	μ	$\bar{X}$
Standard deviation	σ	s
Variance	σ^2	s^2
Size, number of observations	N	n

only the meanings of population parameters and sample statistics are covered. The corresponding mathematical formulas will be covered in the following chapters.

DESCRIPTIVE STATISTICS AND INFERENTIAL STATISTICS

Statistical procedures can be generally classified into two categories: (1) *descriptive statistics* and (2) *inferential statistics*. Descriptive statistics are statistical procedures used to describe, summarize, organize, and simplify relevant characteristics of data. They are simply ways to describe and understand the data, but they do not go beyond the data. Mean, standard deviation, and variance are examples of descriptive statistics.

Inferential statistics are statistical procedures that use sample statistics to generalize to or make inferences about a population. As a rule, inferential statistics are more complicated than descriptive statistics, and they will be introduced in Chapter 7 of this book. Such statistical procedures usually require samples to be unbiased representatives of the population. This can be achieved if samples are randomly selected from the population. As there are different ways to slice a pie, there are different ways to sample a population.

SAMPLING A POPULATION

Let's start this section with examples of a population. For instance, all the cars built by an automobile manufacturer, the entire student body in a university, and every citizen in a particular country are all examples of a population. As you can imagine, the number of members in a population can get enormous and become impossible to measure or study. Sometimes, it is simply not feasible to use the population for research purposes. You understand why an automobile manufacturer does not use every car they make to conduct the crash safety test. There would only be crashed cars to sell! Therefore, many times, scientists have to conduct their research with a carefully selected sample. For example, a small number of cars used to conduct a crash safety test, an online survey administrated to evaluate students' preference of living on campus versus off campus, public polling on a politician's popularity, and a phone survey on the most memorable advertisement during a Super Bowl: All of these are examples of conducting research using samples. The reason to use a sample to conduct research instead of using the population is that it is neither possible nor feasible to gain access to every member in the population and have everyone consent to participate in the research. The most obvious difference between a population and a sample is its size. As noted above, remember that a capitalized N is used to refer to the population size and a lowercase n is used to refer to the sample size.

Two basic ways of sampling a population are nonprobability and probability sampling. A *convenience sample* and a *random sample* are an example of each. A convenience sample is one in which researchers use anyone who is willing to participate in the study. A convenience sample is created based on easy accessibility. For example, a student completes a homework assignment on measuring job satisfaction by recruiting her Facebook friends to fill out a job satisfaction questionnaire. Various talent shows (e.g., *American Idol*, *The Voice*, *Dancing With the Stars*, *America's Got Talent*, etc.) on television ask the audience to vote for their favorite contestants, so they can move on to the next level of the competition. A convenience sample is a nonprobability sample because not all members in the population have an equal chance of being included in the sample.

A random sample is an ideal way to select participants for scientific research. A random sample is defined as being one in which every member in the population has an equal chance of being selected. Because of the random nature of the selection process, it creates an unbiased representation of the population. However, this ideal is easier said than done. Can you think of an example of a random sample? This is a question I pose to my students in Introductory Statistics classes. An overwhelming majority of students' answers actually fall in the category of convenience samples, such as exit polling during an election, spot surveying in a shopping mall/library/cafeteria, using students in a class, and so on.

Random sampling does not just happen. It actually requires thoughtful planning and careful execution. How do we select a random sample? I'm glad you asked!

Pop Quiz

1. A human resource manager creates an employee job satisfaction survey and posts the link on the company's website to invite employees to participate in the survey. This manager is likely to get a _____ sample.

   a. convenience

   b. random

   c. probability

   d. population

Answer: a

Random Sampling Methods

There are four commonly used methods to select a random sample: (1) simple random sampling, (2) systematic sampling, (3) stratified sampling, and (4) cluster sampling. The definition of each method and a practical example of each method will be provided in the following subsections.

SIMPLE RANDOM SAMPLING

A simple random sample of a sample size n is created in a way that all samples with the same sample size have the same chance of being selected. A simple random sample has a stronger requirement than a random sample. Each individual is chosen randomly, entirely by chance, and each subset of n individuals has the same probability of being chosen as any other subset of n individuals. Assume, for instance, that a university is considering switching courses from four credit hours to three credit hours and that the university administration wants to seek students' opinions before making such changes. The targeted population is the entire student body in the university ($N = 17,500$). The administration would like to select 2% of the students to participate in a survey ($n = 350$). A simple random sample can be obtained by listing all students' names and giving each a unique identification number ranging from 1 to 17,500. A computer can then be used to randomly generate 350 numbers between 0 and 17,500. This creates a sample. Such a procedure can be repeated many times to create many samples. Any one of these $n = 350$ samples has an equal chance of being selected to participate in the survey.

SYSTEMATIC SAMPLING

A systematic sample is obtained by selecting a sample from a population using a random starting point and a fixed interval. Typically, every "kth" member is selected from the population to be included in the sample. Systematic sampling is still thought of as being random, as long as the interval is determined beforehand and the starting point is selected at random. To choose a 2% systematic sample in our previous example, the university needs to randomly select a number between 1 and 50 as its starting point and then choose every 50th number to be included in the sample. For instance, to create a random sample with 350 students, Number 35 might be randomly chosen as the starting point. The sample is obtained by picking every 50th student after that—meaning that we choose the 85th, 135th, 185th, 235th, and so on until 350 students are obtained in the sample.

STRATIFIED SAMPLING

Stratified sampling works particularly well when there are large variations in the population characteristics. Stratification is the process of grouping members of the population into relatively homogeneous subgroups before sampling. These homogeneous subgroups are called "strata." The strata need to be mutually exclusive: Every member in the population must be assigned to only one stratum. The strata should also be collectively exhaustive—meaning that no member in the population is excluded. A random sample from each stratum is independently taken in the same proportion as the stratum's size relative to the population. These subsets of the strata are then pooled to form a random sample. Therefore, the distribution of the key characteristics is the same as that in the population. For example, there are 60% female students and 40% male students in the university; to create a sample size of 350, a stratified sampling will randomly choose 60% × 350 = 210 female students and 40% × 350 = 140 male students.

CLUSTER SAMPLING

Cluster sampling works best when "natural" grouping (clustering) occurs in the population. Random sampling is conducted to select particular clusters to include in the sample. Once a cluster is selected in the sample, all individuals in the cluster are included in the sample. In the previous university example, there are, say, 900 courses offered in any given semester. A list of all 900 classes could be obtained from the registrar's office. A random sampling procedure is conducted to select 2% of classes to be included in the sample ($n = 18$ classes). Once the 18 classes are selected, every student in each of these classes is included in the sample. In this particular example, students need to be reminded not to answer the survey multiple times if more than one of the classes in which they are enrolled gets selected in the sample.

Although all four random sampling methods are designed to obtain random samples in the university's effort to seek opinions from students, it is important to recognize that not everyone who is selected in the sample completes the survey. A high nonresponse rate ruins the nature of probability sampling, especially when there are systematic differences between students who take time to answer the survey versus students who either neglect or refuse to answer the survey. If you are interested in understanding more about the effects of nonresponse on statistical inferences, you may read Jones's (1996) article on "The Effects of Non-response on Statistical Inference."

Pop Quiz

1. When a large school district randomly selected three classes to conduct a learning environment study, every student in these three classes participated in a face-to-face interview with the school psychologist. This is an example of

   a. simple random sampling.

   b. systematic sampling.

   c. stratified sampling.

   d. cluster sampling.

Answer: d

Scales of Measurement

Researchers study physical or psychological characteristics by measuring them or asking questions about the attributes. In statistics, a variable refers to a measurable attribute. These measures have different values from one person to another, or the values change over time. Different values of a variable provide information for researchers. If there is no variation in the measures, the variable does not contain any information. For example, when I studied the variables that might be related to students' performance in a statistics course, I collected answers to the following questions: student's grade point average (GPA), number of mathematical courses taken at the college level, number of classes missed in the statistics course, number of tutoring sessions attended for the statistics course, and gender. The answers to these questions reflected the attributes of the students, and they usually varied from one individual to the next. I did not have to ask, "Are you currently enrolled in a statistics course?" Enrolling in a statistics course is an unnecessary question because only students who enrolled in a statistics course were selected for this study. A question producing identical answers from everyone provides no information at all. Only when answers to questions change from one individual to the next do they provide information that we do not have before the questions are answered. Variables have different numerical values that can be analyzed, and, hopefully, meaningful information can be extracted from them.

Scales of measurement provide a way to think systematically about the numerical characteristics of variables. Scales of measurement specifically describe how variables are defined and measured. Each scale of measurement has certain mathematical properties that determine appropriate applications of statistical procedures. There are four scales of measurement: (1) *nominal*, (2) *ordinal*, (3) *interval*, and (4) *ratio*. I will discuss them in the order from the simplest to the most complex. Remember that a higher-level scale of measurement contains all the mathematical properties from a lower-level scale of measurement plus something more.

NOMINAL SCALE

In nominal scales, measurements are used strictly as identifiers, such as your student identification number, phone number, or social security number. The numbers on athletes' jerseys, for example, are simply used as identifiers. Among other things, jersey numbers allow referees to identify which player just committed a personal foul so a penalty can be properly assessed. In social sciences and behavioral sciences, nominal variables such as gender, race, religion, social economic status, marital status, occupation, and so on are often included in research. Nominal scaled variables allow us to figure out whether measurements are the same or different. The mathematical property of the nominal scale is simply $A = B$ or $A \neq B$.

ORDINAL SCALE

In **ordinal scales**, measurements not only are used as identifiers but also carry information about ordering in a particular sequence. The numbers are ranked or sorted in an orderly manner such as from lowest to highest or from highest to lowest. For example, the first time you are invited to a friend's house for dinner, at the outset, you need to find the house. Luckily, you have the address. You notice that on one side of the street the house numbers are odd, and on the other side of the street, the house numbers are even. The house numbers either increase or decrease as you walk down the street. Yes! House numbers are arranged in order, and they are ordinal. So you know 2550 is located in between 2500 and 2600. Can you imagine how confusing it would be trying to find a house if house numbers were nominal instead of ordinal? Another example is that at a swimming meet, gold, silver, and bronze medals are awarded to swimmers who finish in first, second, and third place. Although we don't know the time difference between the gold medalist and the silver medalist or the time difference between the silver medalist and the bronze medalist, we are sure that the gold medalist is faster than the silver medalist, and the silver medalist is faster than the bronze medalist.

Likert scales are often used to measure people's opinions, attitudes, or preferences. Likert scales measure attributes along a continuum of choices such as 1 = *strongly disagree*, 2 = *somewhat disagree*, 3 = *neutral*, 4 = *somewhat agree*, or 5 = *strongly agree* with each individual statement. The ratings from Likert scales belong in the category of ordinal scales. We know the rankings of the responses, but we don't know how different they are from one another. For example, Melissa rates her satisfaction with an online purchase she made a week ago: 1 stands for *very unhappy*, and 5 stands for *very happy*. Melissa's answers are reflected by underlined bolded numbers.

	VERY UNHAPPY	SOMEWHAT UNHAPPY	NEUTRAL	SOMEWHAT HAPPY	VERY HAPPY
Quality of product	1	2	3	4	**5**
Delivery time	1	2	3	**4**	5
Competitive price	1	2	**3**	4	5
Customer service	1	2	3	**4**	5

In this particular case, we learn that Melissa is *very happy* with the product quality, *somewhat happy* with the delivery time and customer service, and *neutral* on the pricing. But we don't know how much happier Melissa is with the product quality than with its price. It is not possible to quantify the difference between two numbers from an ordinal scale.

In summary, order contains information. Order gives us the direction of the rankings between two values. The mathematical properties of ordinal scales include everything a nominal scale has (i.e., identifiers) and something more: the direction of the rankings. The mathematical property of the ordinal scale is expressed as if A > B and B > C, A > C.

INTERVAL SCALE

As measurements evolve to be more sophisticated, scientists go beyond merely figuring out the direction of the rankings. Being able to calculate the amount of the difference becomes the primary objective. The interval scale is designed to fulfill that particular objective. Interval scales can be used as identifiers, showing the direction of the rankings and something more: equal units. Interval scales not only arrange observations according to their magnitudes but also distinguish the ordered arrangement in equal units. When measurements come with equal units, they allow us to calculate the amount of difference or the distance between two measurements. Fahrenheit and Celsius temperature scales are two of the most commonly mentioned examples of interval scales, for which equal units exist and zero is an arbitrarily assigned measurement. We know that 0 degrees Celsius equals 32 degrees Fahrenheit. Zero in an interval scale simply represents a measurement.

Equal units have very important implications in statistics. Calculation of means and standard deviations, which are introduced in Chapter 3, require the variables to have equal units. Many measures in social science are interval scales, such as age, test scores, or standardized intelligence quotient (IQ) scores.

Interval scales allow us to do mathematical operations on the amount of difference between two values. The mathematical property of the interval scale is expressed as when A < B < C, the difference between A and C is the sum of the difference between B and A plus the difference between C and B, $(C - A) = (B - A) + (C - B)$, as shown in Figure 1.1.

For example, age is an interval variable. The ages of three siblings in a family are 8, 13, and 17. The age difference between the youngest and the oldest is $17 - 8 = 9$, which equals the sum of the differences between the oldest and the middle one, $17 - 13 = 4$, and between the middle one and the youngest, $13 - 8 = 5$.

RATIO SCALE

The ratio scale is the most sophisticated scale of measurement. The ratio scale contains everything that lower-level scales of measurement have, such as identifiers, direction of rankings, and equal units, but it also has something more: an absolute zero. Absolute zero means that zero is not an arbitrarily assigned number. Absolute zero means a

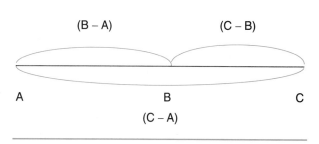

FIGURE 1.1 Calculating Differences Among Three Values of an Interval Scale

complete absence of the attribute that you are measuring. Most physical measurements, such as height and weight, belong in the ratio scales. Income is a good example of a ratio scale in the social sciences. Some of you can easily relate to zero income, which means a complete absence of income.

Absolute zero makes it possible to measure the absolute amount of the variable, and it allows us to compare measures in terms of ratios. This unique mathematical property of ratio scales is expressed as if $A = 2B$ and $B = 2C$, then, $A = 4C$.

After discussing scales of measurement, sometimes students have questions about why exam scores and IQ scores are classified as interval scales instead of ratio scales. Let's discuss the reasons why exam scores and IQ scores are classified as interval scales. The purpose of an exam is to measure your knowledge in a specific topic. The purpose of an IQ test is to measure and quantify intelligence. When an exam or IQ score turns out to be zero, it does not mean that the person completely lacks knowledge or intelligence. There might be other reasons to explain the zero, such as the test is in a language foreign to the test taker, the test taker is provided a wrong scantron for the test, or the test taker marks the answers on the wrong side of the scantron. The point is that exam or IQ scores do not have an absolute zero to show complete absence of the attribute; therefore, they belong in the category of interval scales.

It is useful to summarize all four scales of measurement with their mathematical properties in Table 1.2. This table also illustrates that the higher-level scales of measurement have every attribute that the lower-level scales have, plus something more. It is very common to label variables with nominal or ordinal scales of measurement as categorical variables and variables with interval or ratio scales of measurement as continuous or numerical variables.

 ## Pop Quiz

1. Travel speed is measured by the distance traveled divided by the time traveled. This is an example of a(n)_____ scale of measurement.

   a. nominal

   b. ordinal

   c. interval

   d. ratio

2. The answers to a marital status question are usually married, single, divorced, or cohabiting. This is an example of a(n)_____ scale of measurement.

   a. nominal

   b. ordinal

   c. interval

   d. ratio

Answers: 1. d, 2. a

TABLE 1.2   Mathematical Properties of Scales of Measurement

SCALE OF MEASUREMENT	IDENTIFIER	DIRECTION OF RANKING	EQUAL UNITS	ABSOLUTE ZERO
Nominal	X			
Ordinal	X	X		
Interval	X	X	X	
Ratio	X	X	X	X

VARIABLE CLASSIFICATIONS

There are other ways to classify variables. Some are related to the scales of measurement, but others are related to the research designs. We will cover the essential ones.

DISCRETE VERSUS CONTINUOUS VARIABLES

Discrete variables are made of values that have clear separation from one number to the next. The answers for discrete variables can only be integers (i.e., whole numbers). For example, how many cars do you own? The answer can simply be counted as the number of cars that are registered under your name. The answers are likely to be 0, 1, 2, 3, and so on. You can't own 2.56 cars. The same goes with the answer to "How many pets do you have?" I hope, for your sake, you don't own 2.5 cats. Clearly, nominal and ordinal scales can also be classified as discrete variables.

Continuous variables are composed of values that do not have clear separation from one number to the next. There are numerous possible answers between two adjacent integers for continuous variables. Continuous variables are usually expressed with decimals or fractions. For example, the world record in men's 50-meter freestyle long course swimming was 20.91 seconds in 2013. Official swim time is measured at 100th of a second. Physical measures such as height and weight are similarly continuous variables. As a person who is "vertically challenged" (a politically correct way to say "short"), it is very important for me to list my height with as many numbers after the decimal point as possible given the limits of the rulers with which I am measured. Interval and ratio scales can also be classified as continuous variables.

INDEPENDENT VARIABLES VERSUS DEPENDENT VARIABLES

The distinction between independent variables and dependent variables is very important in experimental research. Generally speaking, there are three different types of empirical research: (1) *experimental*, (2) *quasi-experimental*, and (3) *nonexperimental research*. Experimental research is usually conducted in a tightly controlled environment (i.e., research laboratories). Researchers deliberately choose variables to manipulate at different levels so as to investigate their effects or impacts on variables that researchers are really interested in. The variables that are deliberately manipulated by researchers are called independent variables, predictor variables, or explanatory variables. Dependent variables are what researchers are really interested in studying. Dependent variables are also called criterion variables or response variables. Measuring and/or observing the changes in dependent variables due to the deliberate manipulation of the independent variables is the foundation of experimental research.

For example, researchers might want to study the effect of starvation on the longevity of rats. Researchers select a sample of 20 pairs of newborn rats in a lab. Each pair of rats was from the same mother. The researchers randomly assign one in each pair to the control group and the other to the experimental group. The control group is fed a normal amount of food every day. The experimental group is fed only 40% of the normal amount every day. At the end, researchers compare the life span of rats in the control group versus that of the experimental group. In this experiment, the rats' living environment is strictly controlled and kept constant by the researchers in terms of light, temperature, moisture, and sound. The independent variable is the amount of food provided every day, which is deliberately manipulated by the researchers to set at 100% for the control group versus 40% for the experimental group. The dependent variable is the life span of the rats, which is the focus of this study. Researchers are really interested in finding out how variation in the amount of food intake affects rats' life span by comparing rats in the control group with those in the experimental group.

In summary, experimental research is scientific research that has achieved three important features: (1) control to keep everything else constant, (2) manipulation of the independent variable, and (3) random assignment of research participants to different conditions.

"Quasi" means "almost but not really." Quasi-experimental research has some but not all the features of experimental research. More specifically, if one or more important features are not feasible but others remain intact, the research becomes quasi-experimental. For example, a school wants to test the effects of two instruction methods on sixth graders' science proficiency. One class is assigned to use inquiry through which students are supposed to find answers to their own questions while the instructor helps them design ways to do so. The other class is assigned to use standard lectures to teach science. Let's compare this study with the starvation on rats' longevity study. The school study occurs in a school setting, not a research laboratory. These two groups of students are exposed to the particular instruction methods only during the science course instead of 24 hours a day. Both studies have manipulations on the independent variables. However, in the school study, it is not feasible to randomly assign every student to either the student-centered inquiry or the standard lecture group. This is done by assigning entire classes to either one of the conditions. Thus, we can see that some of the control, manipulation, and random assignments are not achieved in the school study but others remain intact; therefore, the school study is quasi-experimental. The independent variable in this research is the instruction methods, and the dependent variable is sixth graders' science proficiency scores.

Nonexperimental research is composed of studies in which none of the control, manipulation, or random assignment is attempted. Nonexperimental research happens in a natural environment where the research participants' behaviors, thoughts, opinions, interests, or preferences are observed and recorded. Surveys and public opinion polling belong in the category of nonexperimental research, and so do observational studies and cross-sectional studies. For example, when a company wants to know whether its current employees are happy with their work conditions, an employee job satisfaction survey is a proper way to investigate how employees really feel about their current work conditions without any attempt to control, manipulate, or randomly assign employees to any particular condition. There is no real distinction between independent variables and dependent variables. Nonexperimental research is about observing and studying research participants in their natural settings without deliberately controlling the environment or manipulating their behavior or preferences.

There is no one single best way to conduct an empirical study. The selection of research design depends on the purpose of the research. If the identification of a causal relationship is desired, experimental research is more likely to achieve the purpose. The *extraneous variables* that exist with quasi-experimental and nonexperimental research designs will prevent a causal relationship being asserted as a result of the research. The extraneous variables are variables that are not included in the study but might have an impact on the relationship between variables included in the study. Extraneous variables can be attributable to a lack of strict control of environmental variables or individual differences that research participants bring along with them. On the other hand, if participants' behavior in their natural habitat is the focus of the research, nonexperimental research is the right choice.

Pop Quiz

A company wants to study the effect of its compensation (pay) structure on job performance of salespeople. The company randomly chooses three stores to conduct the study. Every salesperson in Store A is compensated with salary, every salesperson in Store B is compensated by sales commissions, and every salesperson in Store C is compensated by a low base salary plus a sales-based bonus. Six months later, job performance is measured and reported.

1. What is the independent variable of this study?

2. What is the dependent variable of this study?

3. What type of research design is used in this study?

Answers: 1. Pay structure, 2. Job performance of salespeople, and 3. Quasi-experimental research design with cluster sampling

REQUIRED MATHEMATICAL SKILLS FOR THIS COURSE

What kinds of mathematical knowledge and skills are required for this statistics course? It is important to know that some basic mathematical knowledge and skills are required to be able to go through this course smoothly and successfully. First, you need to master the order of operations. A statistical formula usually contains multiple parts of different math operations such as addition, subtraction, multiplication, division, exponentiation, and parentheses. Knowing which part of a mathematical operation to do first is the key to arrive at the correct answers. Remember that there is only one correct answer and an unlimited number of wrong answers for a mathematical question. Knowing the order of operations provides a standard way to simplify and find the correct answer to a mathematical equation. There are several priority levels in order of operations shown in Table 1.3. The principle is to perform higher priority operations before moving on to lower priority ones. Many middle school math teachers use the phrase "please excuse my dear Aunt Sally" to help students memorize the order of operations: **P-E-MD-AS**.

The basic principle in order of operations is to perform higher priority operations before lower priority operations. When dealing with many operations at the same level of priority, simplify the operations in the order they appear from left to right. The strict rule of order of operations provides a standard way for everyone to interpret and solve statistical formulas containing complex operations. Therefore, when faced with the operations $8/2 \times 3 - 7$, you will be able to come up with the correct answer (i.e., 5). Order of operations is a fundamental math principle that needs to be strictly followed at all times. If you come up with wrong

TABLE 1.3   Priority Levels in Order of Operations

PRIORITY LEVEL—PERFORM HIGHER PRIORITY OPERATIONS FIRST BEFORE MOVING ON TO LOWER PRIORITY ONES	MATH OPERATIONS	EXAMPLE
1.	*Parentheses*—simplify whatever is inside the parentheses before doing anything else	$(X - 1)$, $(X^2 - 1)$ or $(3 - 1) \times (4 + 2)$
2.	*Exponentiation*	X^2, $\sqrt{x}$ or 8^2
3.	*Multiplication and division*	XY, $\frac{X}{Y}$ or $2 \times 4/5$
4.	*Addition and subtraction*	$X_1 + X_2 + X_3$, $n - 1$ or $5 - 7 + 8$

answers in your statistical exams, quizzes, or homework assignments, then chances are that you have messed up the order of operations somewhere.

Second, you need basic algebra, which involves the ability to solve equations. Solving equations means figuring out a solution set for the equations. A very basic algebraic knowledge is that one linear equation can solve one unknown and two linear equations can solve two unknowns, and so on.

There are two common methods to solve equations: (1) substitution and (2) elimination. Substitution is a way to decrease the number of variables in the equation by replacing one variable with another. You may choose which variable to use in this process.

EXAMPLE 1.1

Solve for X and Y in these two equations:

$$2X + 3Y = 30 \tag{1}$$
$$X - Y = 6 \tag{2}$$

Substitution: From the second equation, we may substitute $X = Y + 6$ and then put that into the first equation: $2(Y + 6) + 3Y = 30$. This equation becomes an equation with only one unknown. Apply the order of operations to simplify the parentheses.

$$2Y + 12 + 3Y = 30$$
$$5Y = 18$$
$$Y = \frac{18}{5} = 3.6$$
$$Y = 3.6$$

Insert the value into Equation 2,

$$X - 3.6 = 6$$
$$X = 9.6$$

Elimination: We manipulate the two equations to get rid of one of the variables and to create a new equation with one unknown. Let's use the same two equations but solve them with elimination this time.

(Continued)

(Continued)

We add Equation 1 to Equation 2 multiplied by 3 (i.e., 3 × Equation 2).

$$2X + 3Y = 30$$
$$+\quad 3X - 3Y = 18$$

$$5X = 48$$

$$X = \frac{48}{5}$$

$$X = 9.6$$

Then insert the value into Equation 2,

$$9.6 - Y = 6$$

$$Y = 3.6$$

Either the substitution or elimination method provides exactly the same solution set to the equations. The ability to solve equations is a necessity in learning the content of this course.

STATISTICAL NOTATION

It is very common to add a set of values in statistics. To make it easier to communicate such a computation, a special notation is used to refer to the sum of a set of values. The capital Greek letter Σ (pronounced sigma) is used for summation. Here is our first summation operation:

$$\sum_{i=1}^{n} X_i$$

This summation operation means to calculate the sum of all values of X, starting at the first value, X_1, and ending with the last value, X_n.

In a summation operation, there are several components. They are clearly explained one by one in the following list.

1. The summation sign, Σ, means performing addition in this operation.

2. X is the variable being added.

3. The subscript i, which is placed next to X, indicates that there are i values of X.

4. There is a starting point and an ending point of the index i. This tells us how many values need to be added. Usually the starting point is $i = 1$, which is placed under the Σ sign, and the ending point is n, which is placed on top of the Σ sign.

$$\sum_{i=1}^{n} X_i = X_1 + X_2 + X_3 + \cdots + X_n$$

Sometimes, for the sake of simplicity, summation is expressed as ΣX.

$$\Sigma X = X_1 + X_2 + X_3 + \cdots + X_n$$

From now on this simple form of symbol (Σ) will express summation. You have to do summation from the first value to the last value given to you in a problem statement. Let's go through several examples of the summation question to get you used to the simple form of Σ.

EXAMPLE 1.2

$X = 3, 5, 7$, and 9. Find ΣX, $(\Sigma X)^2$, and ΣX^2.

There are four values in the X variable in this problem statement. You need to go through all four values in the summation procedure.

$$\Sigma X = 3 + 5 + 7 + 9 = 24$$

$(\Sigma X)^2$ requires knowledge of order of operations. There is addition inside parentheses and exponentiation in this question. Order of operations tells us to simplify whatever is inside the parentheses first. Therefore, you need to figure out ΣX first.

$$(\Sigma X)^2 = (3 + 5 + 7 + 9)^2 = (24)^2 = 576$$

ΣX^2 requires knowledge of order of operations. There is both exponentiation and addition in this problem. Order of operations mandates that the exponentiation has to be done before the addition. Therefore, you figure out the value of each X^2 and then add them up.

$$\Sigma X^2 = 3^2 + 5^2 + 7^2 + 9^2 = 9 + 25 + 49 + 81 = 164$$

It is obvious that the correct order of operations must be followed to arrive at the correct answer. There will be more practices like this in the Exercise Problems.

Pop Quiz

1. $X = 3, 6, 9, 12,$ and 15.
   Find (1) $\sum(X - 9)^2$ and (2) $\sum X^2 - 9$.

Answers: 1. $\sum(X - 9)^2 = 90$,
2. $\sum X^2 - 9 = 486$

EXERCISE PROBLEMS

1. Researchers are studying the effect of texting on driving. College students are recruited to participate in the study. Due to risk of actual driving on the road, researchers decide to conduct the research in a lab with a driving simulator. Students are randomly assigned to one of the two groups: (1) "driving without distraction" or (2) "driving while texting." Driving behaviors are recorded by the simulator, which include maintaining the speed limit and driving within the lane. What type of research is this study? What is the independent variable in this study? What is the dependent variable in this study?

2. Researchers are curious about the gender gap in pay for physicians. An online salary survey is sent out to the members of the American Medical Association with an electronic link. What type of research is this study? What kind of sample is likely to be obtained by this online survey?

3. Solve the following equations:

$$4X + 3Y = 23$$

$$3X - Y = 1$$

4. Where $X = 1, 2, 3,$ and 4, and $Y = 2, 4, 6,$ and 8, compute $\sum XY$ and $\sum X^2 Y^2$.

Solutions With EXCEL Step-by-Step Instructions When Needed

1. The research is conducted in lab with a driving simulator. There are two conditions that are manipulated by the researchers. Research participants are randomly assigned to one of the two conditions. All three important features, namely (1) control, (2) manipulation, and (3) random assignment, are achieved in this study. Therefore, this study is an experimental research design. The independent variable measures the two driving conditions: (1) "driving without distraction" and (2) "driving while texting." The dependent variable measures the driving behavior: maintaining speed and driving within the lane.

2. An online survey does not attempt to control, manipulate, or randomly assign participants to different conditions. Therefore, it is a nonexperimental design. Not all physicians belong to the American Medical Association. Therefore, sending a survey out to its members can reach a sample of physicians. The survey is voluntarily answered by people who received the link. Some physicians would simply ignore the e-mail. It is a convenience sample.

3. There are two equations with two unknowns, X and Y. We can solve these equations by either substitution or elimination.

$$4X + 3Y = 23 \tag{1}$$

$$3X - Y = 1 \tag{2}$$

I choose substitution, based on the second equation, $Y = 3X - 1$. Put this back into the first equation $4X + 3(3X - 1) = 23$. The equation only has one unknown. Simplify the equation,

$$4X + 9X - 3 = 23$$

$$13X = 23 + 3$$

$$13X = 26$$

$$X = 2$$

Insert this answer into the second equation,

$$3(2) - Y = 1$$

$$6 - Y = 1$$

$$-Y = 1 - 6$$

$$-Y = -5$$

$$Y = 5$$

Therefore, the solutions to the equations are $X = 2$ and $Y = 5$.

4. It will be easy to create a table of X and Y to figure what need to be computed to complete the summations.

$$X = 1, 2, 3, \text{ and } 4; Y = 2, 4, 6, \text{ and } 8; \text{ compute } \sum XY \text{ and } \sum X^2 Y^2$$

EXCEL is a great tool to construct such a table to complete the mathematical operations. All instructions regarding EXCEL use Microsoft EXCEL 2010. Most programming of

FIGURE 1.2   Programming *XY* in EXCEL

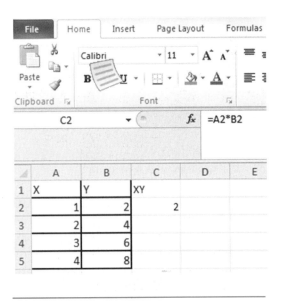

FIGURE 1.3   Programming ∑*XY* in EXCEL

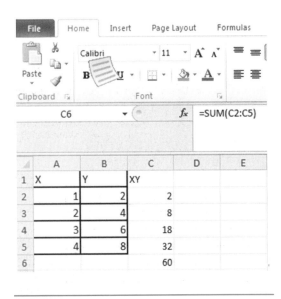

mathematical operations is identical across different versions of EXCEL. However, the graphing functions are likely to vary. EXCEL allows you to program mathematical operation formulas in each column. It is a great skill to have to be able to program operation formulas in EXCEL. Let's start by labeling **C1** as *XY*. According to the question, you need to find ∑*XY*, so you need to create *XY*. Move the cursor to **C2** (Column C, Row 2), and type the formula that you want to create. In EXCEL, a function starts with a "=." EXCEL is based on location of the variable. Therefore, to create the first operation of *XY*, grab the first value of *X* located in **A2** (Column A, Row 2) and the first value of *Y* located in **B2** (Column B, Row 2) to do the multiplication. To create *XY*, simply type "=**A2*B2**" and then hit **enter;** the answer 2 appears as shown in the EXCEL screenshot (Figure 1.2).

The beauty of EXCEL is that once you create a formula for the first value of the variables involved, you may simply copy and paste the formula for the rest of the values in the sequence. Copy and paste can be done by moving the cursor to the lower right-hand corner of **C2** where the formula is successfully created, until a solid + shows up. Hold the left click on the mouse and drag to the last row of the variable, and then let go of the left click. You should see that the formula is copied with all cell references. The formula is performed on the first row of the variables all the way to the last row of the variables. Once all the *XY*s are calculated, simply conduct a summation function in **C6**, "= **sum(C2:C5)**" and hit **enter;** the answer, 60, for ∑*XY* appears as shown in the EXCEL screenshot (Figure 1.3).

EXCEL is great when you have to figure out statistics in a large sample. The other alternative is to simply figure out the answer by hand. First, you need to recognize that $\sum XY$ involves multiplication and addition. The order of operations dictates that multiplication needs to be done first. Therefore, $\sum XY = 2 + 8 + 18 + 32 = 60$.

Next, you need to figure out how to construct a formula for $\sum X^2Y^2$ in EXCEL. $\sum X^2Y^2$ involves exponentiation, multiplication, and addition. Order of operations dictates that exponentiation needs to be done first, next multiplication, and then addition. Each step is shown in a column of the tables in Figures 1.4 and 1.5.

In **D1**, label it as X^2. EXCEL calculates the square by using ^2. In **D2**, the function is "=A2^2," which means grab the first value of X and square it. Hit **enter** and the answer, 1, appears in **D2**. Move the cursor to the lower right-hand corner of **D2** where the formula is successfully created, until a solid + shows up. Hold the left click on the mouse and drag to the last row of the variable, and then let go of the left click. You should see that the formula is copied with all cell references. The formula's operations are performed on the first row of the variable all the way to the last row of the variable. In **E1**, I label it Y^2. The function is "=B2^2," which means grab the first value of Y and square it. Copy and paste the formula to the rest of the Y values as shown in the EXCEL screenshot (Figure 1.4).

Now, the next step to solve this question is to create a formula for the multiplication of X^2Y^2. Label **F1** as X^2Y^2. Move the cursor to **F2**. Type the function "=D2*E2," which means grab the first values of X^2 and Y^2 and multiply them. Copy and paste the function to the rest of the variables. Move the cursor to **F6** and conduct a summation by typing in "=sum(F2:F5)." Hit **enter** and the answer, 1,416, appears as seen in the EXCEL screenshot (Figure 1.5).

FIGURE 1.4   Programming X^2 and Y^2 in EXCEL

FIGURE 1.5   Programming $\sum X^2Y^2$ in EXCEL

Sharpen your skills with SAGE edge!

Visit edge.sagepub.com/bowen for mobile-friendly quizzes, flashcards, videos, and more!

What You Learned

In this chapter, you have learned some of the basic vocabulary of statistics. Three major objectives of statistics are as follows:

1. To describe information contained in a sample

2. To design a sampling process, so that the selected sample is an unbiased representation of the population

3. To make inferences about a population from information contained in a sample

A brief definition of all the statistical terms mentioned in the chapter will be listed in the section "Key Words." You also need to sharpen some basic math skills such as order of operations and basic algebra to be able to follow formulas and solve equations. The correct order of operations is P-E-MD-AS. The two most common methods to solve equations are substitution and elimination.

Note: I have used EXCEL to illustrate the calculation process of some examples in the earlier chapters of this book to offer greater accessibility. Each column of the EXCEL spreadsheet shows a particular step in the order of operations. Using EXCEL clearly shows the step-by-step procedures that lead to the correct answers. EXCEL is also widely available without incurring additional expenses for students. I found EXCEL to be a great teaching tool. When we cover more complicated concepts in later chapters, SPSS will be used as a tool to run analysis as well.

Key Words

Absolute zero: Absolute zero means a complete absence of the attribute that you are measuring. It is not an arbitrarily assigned number.

Cluster sampling: Cluster sampling works best when "natural" grouping (clustering) occurs in the population. Random sampling is conducted to select which clusters are included in the sample. Once a cluster is selected in the sample, all individuals in the cluster are included in the sample.

Continuous variables: Continuous variables are values that do not have separation from one integer to the next. Continuous variables usually are expressed with decimals or fractions.

Convenience sample: A convenience sample is one in which researchers use anyone who is willing to participate in the study. A convenience sample is created based on easy accessibility.

Data: Data are defined as factual information used as a basis for reasoning, discussion, or calculation, so that meaningful conclusions can be drawn.

Dependent variable: A dependent variable is the variable that is the focus of researchers' interests and is affected by the different levels of an independent variable.

Descriptive statistics: Descriptive statistics are statistical procedures used to describe, summarize, organize, and simplify relevant characteristics of sample data.

Discrete variables: Discrete variables are values that have clear separation from one integer to the next. The answers for discrete variables can only be integers (i.e., whole numbers).

Experimental research: Experimental research is usually conducted in a tightly controlled environment (i.e., research laboratories). The three important features in experimental research are (1) control, (2) manipulation, and (3) random assignment.

Extraneous variable: The extraneous variables are variables that are not included in the study but might have an impact on the relationship between variables included in the study.

Independent variable: An independent variable is the variable that is deliberately manipulated by the researchers in a research study.

Inferential statistics: Inferential statistics are statistical procedures that use sample statistics to generalize to or make inferences about a population.

Interval scale: An interval scale not only arranges observations according to their magnitudes but also distinguishes the ordered arrangement in equal units.

Likert scales: Likert scales are often used to measure people's opinions, attitudes, or preferences. Likert scales measure attributes along a continuum of choices such as 1 = *strongly disagree*, 2 = *somewhat disagree*, 3 = *neutral*, 4 = *somewhat agree*, or 5 = *strongly agree* with each individual statement.

Nominal scale: In a nominal scale, measurements are used as identifiers, such as your student identification number, phone number, or social security number.

Nonexperimental research: Nonexperimental research is conducted to observe and study research participants in their natural settings without deliberately controlling the environment or manipulating their behaviors or preferences.

Ordinal scale: In an ordinal scale, measurements not only are used as identifiers but also carry orders in a particular sequence.

Parameter: Parameters are defined as numerical characteristics of a population.

Population: A population is defined as an entire collection of everything or everyone that researchers are interested in studying or measuring.

Quasi-experimental research: Quasi-experimental research has some but not all of the features of experimental research. More specifically, if one or more of the control, manipulation, and random assignment features are not feasible but others remain intact, the research becomes quasi-experimental.

Random sample: A random sample is an ideal way to select participants for scientific research. A random sample occurs when every member in the population has an equal chance of being selected.

Ratio scale: A ratio scale contains every characteristic that lower-level scales of measurement have, such as identifiers, direction of ranking, equal units, and something extra: an absolute zero.

Sample: A sample is defined as a subset of the population from which measures are actually obtained.

Sample statistics: Sample statistics are defined as numerical attributes of a sample.

Scales of measurement: Scales of measurement illustrate different ways that variables are defined and measured. Each scale of measurement has certain mathematical properties that determine the appropriate application of statistical procedures.

Simple random sample. A simple random sample is a subset of individuals (a sample) chosen from a larger set (a population). Each individual is chosen randomly and entirely by chance, and each subset of k individuals has the same probability of being chosen for the sample as any other subset of k individuals.

Statistics: Statistics is a science that deals with the collection, organization, analysis, and interpretation of numerical data.

Stratified sampling. Stratified sampling is the process of grouping members of the population into relatively homogeneous subgroups before sampling. A random sample from each stratum is independently taken in the same proportion as the stratum's size to the population. These subsets of the strata are then pooled to form a random sample.

Systematic sample. A systematic sample is achieved by selecting a sample from a population using a random starting point and a fixed interval. Typically, every "*k*th" member is selected from the total population for inclusion in the sample.

Variable: A variable refers to a measurable attribute. These measures have different values from one person to another, or the values change over time.

LEARNING ASSESSMENT

Multiple Choice: Circle the best answer in every question.

1. A researcher was interested in the sleeping habits of college students. A group of 50 students were selected at random and interviewed. The researcher found that these students slept an average of 6.7 hours per day. For this study, the 50 students are an example of a _____.

    a. parameter

    b. statistic

    c. population

    d. sample

2. A character, usually an unknown numerical value that describes an entire population, is a _____.

    a. parameter

    b. statistic

    c. population

    d. sample

3. What additional characteristic is required on a ratio scale compared with an interval scale?

    a. Whether the measurements are the same or different

    b. The order of the magnitudes

    c. An absolute zero

    d. Scores with equal units

4. For $X = 0, 1, 6, 3$, what is $(\Sigma X)^2$?

    a. 20

    b. 46

    c. 64

    d. 100

5. Gender, religion, and ethnicity are measurements on a(n) _____ scale.

    a. nominal

    b. ordinal

    c. interval

    d. ratio

6. The measure of temperature in Fahrenheit is an example of a(n) _____ scale of measurement.

    a. nominal

    b. ordinal

    c. interval

    d. ratio

7. Which of the following pairs is usually unknown parameters of the population?

   a. M and μ

   b. s and σ

   c. s^2 and σ^2

   d. μ and σ

8. The measure of income is an example of a(n) _____ scale of measurement.

   a. nominal

   b. ordinal

   c. interval

   d. ratio

Free Response Questions

9. $X = 3, 4, 5$, and 7; compute ΣX, $(\Sigma X)^2$, and ΣX^2

10. $X = -3, 0, 1$, and 2; compute ΣX, $\Sigma (X-1)^2$, and $\Sigma X^2 - 3$

11. $X = 3, 4, 5$, and 7; $Y = -1, 0, 1$, and 2; compute ΣXY and $(\Sigma XY)^2$

12. $X = 3, 4, 5$, and 7; $Y = -1, 0, 1$, and 2; compute $\Sigma X^2 Y^2$ and $\Sigma (X-2)(Y-3)$

13. $X = 4, 5, 6$, and 9; $Y = -1, -1, 1$, and 2; compute ΣY^2 and $\Sigma (X-5)(Y+1)$

14. $2X + 3Y = 21$, and $3X - Y = 4$; solve for X and Y

15. $X - 2Y = -8$, and $3X - Y = 6$; solve for X and Y

Summarizing and Organizing Data

After reading and studying this chapter, you should be able to do the following:

- Construct a frequency distribution table with individual values to summarize data
- Create a frequency distribution table with equal intervals to summarize data
- Identify the differences between bar graphs and histograms
- Identify the common distribution shapes
- Define the positively skewed and negatively skewed distributions

WHAT YOU KNOW AND WHAT IS NEW

You learned most of the basic vocabulary for statistics in Chapter 1. You learned how to distinguish between samples and populations, and how to identify the different scales of measurement. You learned the basics of summation notation and refreshed your skills in algebra. You also learned that different scales of measurement come with distinct mathematical attributes. All of these will be extremely useful and will continue to be relevant throughout this book.

One of the main purposes in statistics is to make sense out of large amounts of data. It can be very confusing to encounter a large amount of data without any particular pattern. There are some simple and commonly used methods to make a large amount of data manageable. In

FIGURE 2.1   Unsorted Data

this chapter, we will explore different ways to make sense out of nominal, ordinal, interval, and ratio variables by summarizing and organizing them.

The following three images illustrate why summarizing and organizing help us understand and extract useful information out of data. Data are facts presented in numerical form. Unfiltered or unprocessed data are disorienting and confusing. Data can simply look like an unruly mess such as the big pile of miscellaneous pieces shown in Figure 2.1.

When data are organized or sorted according to a particular pattern, such as by type, we can start to get a rough idea about this pile of miscellaneous pieces. It seems that there are two kinds of pasta: (1) macaroni and (2) shells, and three kinds of snacks: (1) almonds, (2) Wasabi peas, and (3) chocolate-covered espresso beans, as shown in Figure 2.2. Sorting is very useful and commonly used in tracking inventory in retail.

When data are summarized in a way that provides easy-to-process information about the numeric attributes, we can make sense out of them immediately. The following graph provides

FIGURE 2.2   Organized or Sorted Data

the number of pieces in each type. A summary graph might not include all the characteristics of the data such as weight and size of each piece, but it provides meaningful information on the number of pieces in every type as shown in Figure 2.3.

In Figure 2.3, the graph presents a quick and easy way to communicate the quantity of each itemized product. All these three figures together illustrate the reason why it is helpful to organize and/or summarize data. Commonly used methods to organize and summarize numerical data are the main topics discussed in this chapter.

FREQUENCY DISTRIBUTION TABLE

Organizing and summarizing of data can be done in table form. A frequency distribution table lists all values or categories along with a tally count for each value or category in a variable. Distribution is defined as arrangement of values of a variable as they occur in a sample or a population. Both categorical variables (i.e., nominal or ordinal variables) and numerical

FIGURE 2.3   Number of Pieces in Each Type

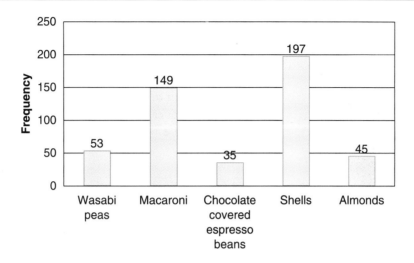

variables (i.e., interval or ratio variables) can be organized in frequency distribution tables (often simply referred to as "frequency tables").

ORGANIZING AND SUMMARIZING CATEGORICAL VARIABLES

When dealing with categorical data (i.e., nominal or ordinal scales of measurement), the process of organizing and summarizing is fairly simple. The observations are organized or sorted into categories, and then the tally count of number of occurrences in each category is reported as **frequency**, which is referred to simply as f in this book. When you add up the fs in each category, the sum of all fs equals the sample size, n. Example 2.1 is used to demonstrate such a relationship between f and n.

EXAMPLE 2.1

You ask 20 people "what kind of job do you do?" The answers turn out to be "truck driver," "retail salesperson," "secretary," "personal assistant," "day care worker," "construction worker," "car wash worker," "server," "bartender," "librarian," "customer service representative," "call center worker," and so on. To organize these answers, you may group similar jobs into occupational categories such as professional, sales, service, clerical, and laborer. Then, you count the number of answers in each occupation category. The results are shown in Table 2.1.

(Continued)

(Continued)

TABLE 2.1   Frequency Distribution Table of Occupations

X (OCCUPATION)	f (FREQUENCY)	RELATIVE FREQUENCY
Professional	3	.15
Sales	6	.30
Service	5	.25
Clerical	4	.20
Laborer	2	.10
Total	**20**	**1.00**

When you add up all the frequencies, 3 + 6 + 5 + 4 + 2, the total frequency equals the sample size, $n = 20$. The last column of the frequency distribution table is called the relative frequency. Relative frequency is the same as proportion and very similar to percentage. It is defined and calculated as the frequency of a category (f) divided by the sample size (n). Based on Table 2.1, we learn that the majority (i.e., 55%) of the 20 people whom you encounter work in either sales or service jobs.

The sum of all relative frequencies should add to 1.00. It is a good way to check the math. If it does not add to 1.00, there are two possible explanations. First, the math is wrong. You need to double-check your calculations. Second, if the answer is .99, 1.01, or something very close to 1.00, it might be due to rounding.

$$\text{Relative frequency (proportion) for a category} = \frac{\text{Frequency of a category}}{\text{Total frequency}} = \frac{f}{n}$$

$$\text{Percentage for a category} = \frac{\text{Frequency of a category}}{\text{Total frequency}} \times 100\% = \frac{f}{n} \times 100\%$$

ORGANIZING AND SUMMARIZING NUMERICAL VARIABLES

When dealing with numerical variables, frequency tables are constructed in a logical way to present the data in an orderly fashion with a reasonable number of categories. An example is used to explain the concepts of "orderly fashion" and "reasonable number of categories."

EXAMPLE 2.2

This shows the number of computer network interruptions per day on a university campus in the month of November.

1 3 1 1 0 1 0 1 1 0

2 2 0 0 0 1 2 1 2 0

0 1 6 4 3 3 1 2 4 0

It is hard to extract useful information by looking at these 30 numbers in a chronological order. Let's rearrange the numbers and put them in a frequency distribution table. The table needs to have a reasonable number of categories, so the table is not too long or too short. When the table is too long, the information is too detailed to be absorbed quickly. When the table is too short, there is not enough distinction among the categories. What is a reasonable number of categories? The answer to that question is based on the capacity of human short-term memory: 7 ± 2. A frequency table with categories between 5 and 9 is reasonable. The short-term memory capacity is defined as the capacity of holding a small amount of information in the brain in an active, immediately available fashion so that we are able to receive, process, and remember the information. According to Miller (1956), the capacity for short-term memory across many different types of stimuli such as words, notes, sounds, or pitches in various laboratory experiments all came to the same magical number seven, plus or minus two.

Next, let's talk about the concept of "orderly fashion." There are many different kinds of "orders." One such kind is ascending order, in which numbers are arranged from the lowest to the highest. Another is descending order in which numbers are arranged from the highest to the lowest.

I generally prefer constructing a frequency table in an ascending order, from the lowest to the highest. To do this in the example of network interruptions, first, you need to identify the minimal value and maximal value. The minimal value is 0, and the maximal value is 6. Using the number of network interruptions as individual categories, thus, you have seven total categories. Tally the count for each category and report it as the frequency for that category. Therefore, when the values of the network interruptions are arranged in an ascending order, lowest to highest, and the frequency of each value is counted, you have constructed a frequency distribution table as shown in Table 2.2a.

When adding up all frequencies, the total is 30. There were originally 30 numbers reported in the month of November, one for each day of the month. Relative frequency (or proportion) is calculated and reported in the third column of Table 2.2a.

(Continued)

(Continued)

TABLE 2.2a Frequency Distribution Table for Daily Network Interruptions on a University Campus in November

X (VALUE)	f (FREQUENCY)	RELATIVE FREQUENCY
0	9	.300
1	10	.333
2	5	.167
3	3	.100
4	2	.067
5	0	.000
6	1	.033
Total	**30**	**1.000**

The sum of all relative frequencies is 1.000. From this table, we learn that about 63% of the time, the network is functioning fairly well with one interruption or no interruptions in a day. Some of you might have noticed that the value 5 is not in the reported daily network interruption data. It is also acceptable to construct the frequency distribution table without the value 5 as shown in Table 2.2b. Because the frequency for the value 5 is 0, it does not affect the frequency count or the calculation of relative frequency. Either Table 2.2a or Table 2.2b is an acceptable way to construct a frequency table for these data.

TABLE 2.2b Frequency Distribution Table for Daily Network Interruptions on a University Campus in November

X (VALUE)	f (FREQUENCY)	RELATIVE FREQUENCY	fX
0	9	.300	0
1	10	.333	10
2	5	.167	10
3	3	.100	9
4	2	.067	8
6	1	.033	6
Total	**30**	**1.000**	**43**

The frequency table summarizes the number of daily network interruptions in ascending order with corresponding frequency. Such an organization makes it easy to calculate the total number of network interruptions in November. Instead of adding 30 numbers ΣX from the first number to the last number, you can use the modified formula $\Sigma X = \Sigma fX$. The frequency table shows every distinct value with number of times it occurs in the distribution. In this example, 0 occurs 9 times, 1 occurs 10 times, 2 occurs 5 times, 3 occurs 3 times, 4 occurs twice, and 6 occurs once. Therefore, you have to multiply the frequency by every distinct value and add them all up. $\Sigma X = \Sigma fX = 0 \times 9 + 1 \times 10 + 2 \times 5 + 3 \times 3 + 4 \times 2 + 6 \times 1 = 43$. There are multiplications and additions involved in ΣfX; the order of operations dictates that the multiplications have to be done before the additions.

It is critically important for any calculation involving a frequency table to incorporate the impact of frequency into the calculation, such as converting ΣX to ΣfX as just discussed above. The rule is to multiply the frequency by the original operation before you add them up. You modify the formula by inserting the frequency, f, between the summation, Σ, and the original calculation.

When dealing with data spanning over a large range, creating a frequency table with **equal intervals** is a good solution. Equal intervals are created by including the same number of values in each interval in a frequency table. We will use a couple of examples to illustrate this process.

EXAMPLE 2.3

Midterm exam scores for 25 students are shown below.

79, 45, 66, 89, 97, 55, 61, 86, 93, 81, 80, 73, 76,

84, 81, 67, 92, 75, 76, 69, 57, 88, 84, 59, 72

Create a frequency table with a reasonable number of categories in an orderly fashion to organize the midterm scores.

It is difficult to get a sense of the distribution of the scores by looking at 25 scores in no particular order. The minimal exam score in this example is 45 and the maximal value is 97. The score range is maximal value minus the minimal value, $97 - 45 = 52$. It is not advisable to create a frequency table using individual values with such a large range in this case. Equal intervals are usually defined over the intervals of 5 or 10 for convenience,

(Continued)

(Continued)

if feasible. To create equal intervals to cover this range of 52, an interval of 10 is appropriate. The lowest interval is between 40 and 49, so it covers the minimal value, and the highest interval is between 90 and 99, so it covers the maximal value. There should not be any overlap between two adjacent intervals. A frequency table with equal intervals is constructed in Table 2.3a for the 25 exam scores.

TABLE 2.3a   Frequency Distribution Table for 25 Exam Scores

SCORE INTERVAL	f (FREQUENCY)	RELATIVE FREQUENCY
40-49	1	.04
50-59	3	.12
60-69	4	.16
70-79	6	.24
80-89	8	.32
90-99	3	.12
Total	**25**	**1.00**

Table 2.3a summarizes and organizes the 25 exam scores with useful insights such as 16% of the students scored below 60, more than 50% of the scores are in the 70s or 80s, and 12% of the scores are higher than 90.

When you are asked to estimate the total exam scores $\sum X$ from the frequency table, you don't know exactly where the score is located within the interval. The best estimate for each interval is the midpoint of the interval, which is defined by the average of the endpoints in the interval, $X_{midpoint} = (\text{low-end value} + \text{high-end value})/2$. When the frequency table consists of equal intervals, the formula for $\sum X$ needs to be modified to $\sum f X_{midpoint}$. The midpoint for the first interval 40–49 is $(40 + 49)/2 = 44.5$. The midpoints are shown in Table 2.3b. The estimated total score is the sum of the midpoint of each interval times its corresponding frequency. Again, multiplication and addition are involved in $\sum f X_{midpoint}$. Multiplication operations have to be done before addition operations. The estimated total exam score for 25 students is 1,872.5. Clearly, this estimated total is slightly different from the $\sum X$ when you calculate the total score by adding the first exam score all the way to the last exam score. However, if you are only presented with a frequency table instead of the list of all exam scores, this estimate provides a quick answer that is very close to the laborious $\sum X$ due to the fact that some numbers in the interval are higher than the midpoint and others are lower than the midpoint. The positive differences and the negative differences might cancel each other out to some extent.

TABLE 2.3b Frequency Distribution Table for 25 Exam Scores With Midpoint of Each Interval

SCORE INTERVAL	f (FREQUENCY)	$X_{midpoint}$	$fX_{midpoint}$
40-49	1	44.5	44.5
50-59	3	54.5	163.5
60-69	4	64.5	258
70-79	6	74.5	447
80-89	8	84.5	676
90-99	3	94.5	283.5
Total	**25**		**1,872.5**

The same principles that were used in constructing a frequency table for discrete variables can also be applied to continuous variables. Continuous variables mean that the observations may take any value between two integers in the forms of fraction or decimal point. It is difficult to obtain precise measures for continuous variables. Therefore, the concept of **real limits** is designed to cover a range of possible values that may be reflected by a continuous measure. The lower limit is the value minus ½ of the unit and the upper limit is the value plus ½ of the unit. Physical measurements, such as height and weight, are continuous variables. For example, when 1 pound is used as a unit to measure a person's weight and John's weight is 180 pounds. The lower limit of John's weight is 179.5 pounds and the upper limit is 180.5 pounds.

Let's apply real limits to height measures in Example 2.4.

You Must Remember This

$$\Sigma X = X_1 + X_2 + X_3 + \cdots + X_n$$

The summation notation requires adding the first value of the variable all the way to the last value of the variable. However, in frequency tables such a long process can be simplified by modifying ΣX to ΣfX. In frequency tables, the frequency for each distinct value is reported. ΣfX is to multiply the frequency with the corresponding value and then add them up. This process effectively considers the impact of frequency in the original mathematical operation. Such a modification of the summation operations in frequency tables will be repeatedly used in later chapters. It is important for you to remember this to master the learning of statistics.

EXAMPLE 2.4

There are 59 students in one of my statistics classes. The shortest student is 57 inches and the tallest is 75 inches. Thus, the range is 18 inches. To create a frequency table with a reasonable number of categories, an equal interval of 3 inches is appropriate. All 59 students' height measures are presented in Table 2.4a.

TABLE 2.4a   Frequency Distribution Table for 59 Students' Height Measures

X (HEIGHT, INCHES)	f (FREQUENCY)	RELATIVE FREQUENCY
57-59	5	.08
60-62	7	.12
63-65	25	.42
66-68	12	.20
69-71	7	.12
72-74	2	.03
75-77	1	.02
Total	59	.99

Based on Table 2.4a, more than 60% of the students are between 63 and 68 inches. The first interval is between 57 and 59 inches with real limits 56.5 and 59.5 inches. The next interval is between 60 and 62 inches with real limits 59.5 and 62.5 inches. Just to make it clear that each interval includes the lower limit but not the upper limit (i.e., lower limit $\leq X <$ upper limit), there is no overlap between two adjacent intervals. You might have already noticed that the total relative frequency adds to be .99. This is simply due to rounding.

To obtain an estimated total height from these 59 students, midpoints need to be calculated. The frequency table with midpoints is shown in Table 2.4b. In a frequency table

TABLE 2.4b   Frequency Distribution for 59 Students' Height Measures With Midpoint of Each Interval

X (HEIGHT, INCHES)	f (FREQUENCY)	$X_{midpoint}$	$fX_{midpoint}$
57-59	5	58	290
60-62	7	61	427
63-65	25	64	1,600
66-68	12	67	804
69-71	7	70	490
72-74	2	73	146
75-77	1	76	76
Total	59		3,833

consisting of equal intervals, the formula for ΣX needs to be modified to $\Sigma fX_{midpoint}$. The estimated total score is the sum of the midpoint of each interval times its corresponding frequency. Again, multiplication and addition are involved in $\Sigma fX_{midpoint}$. Multiplication has to be done before addition. The estimated total height for 59 students is 3,833 inches.

Let's review the process of constructing a frequency table with equal intervals. The key points are summarized below.

1. Identify the minimal and maximal values of the variable. Calculate the range.

2. Choose an appropriate and convenient interval, usually in 5s or 10s if feasible, to construct a frequency table with 7 ± 2 equal intervals.

3. Create the equal intervals in an ascending order.

4. Make sure that there is no overlap between two adjacent intervals. For continuous variables, each interval includes the lower limit but not the upper limit.

Pop Quiz

1. In a statistics class, students' quiz scores on a pop quiz with only four questions are reported in the frequency table below. Use the frequency table to calculate the total quiz score for the class.

X, QUIZ	f (FREQUENCY)
0	2
1	1
2	5
3	8
4	9

What is the total quiz score for the class?
   a. 10
   b. 25
   c. 71
   d. 100

2. Constructing a frequency table with equal intervals of a continuous variable X, each interval consists of the same width. To make sure that there is no overlap between two adjacent intervals, each interval actually includes

   a. lower limit $< X <$ upper limit.
   b. lower limit $\leq X <$ upper limit.
   c. lower limit $< X \leq$ upper limit.
   d. lower limit $\leq X \leq$ upper limit.

Answers: 1. c, 2. b

Graphs

Creating a graph is another common way to organize and summarize data. A well-organized graph can deliver useful numerical information in a quick and easy-to-understand fashion. Two commonly used graphs are (1) bar graphs and (2) pie charts.

BAR GRAPHS AND HISTOGRAMS

When **bar graphs** are used to organize categorical data, the horizontal scale (x-axis) represents the values (or categories) of the variable and the vertical scale (y-axis) represents the frequency or relative frequency of each value. When using the data from Table 2.1 (back on page 30) to construct a bar graph, the result is shown in Figure 2.4a with the x-axis representing occupations and the y-axis representing the corresponding frequency of each occupation.

It is also possible to create a bar graph with multiple sets of bars to represent multiple categorical variables. For example, male and female students' jobs can be reported separately as shown in Figure 2.4b where males' occupations are represented in lighter blue bars and females' occupations are represented in darker blue bars. There is no darker blue bar in the last occupational category, laborer, because there are no females in this category.

Bar charts can also be applied to discrete data. When using data from Table 2.2 (back on page 32) to construct a bar graph, the x-axis represents the number of reported daily network interruptions, and they are lined up from the smallest to the largest value from

FIGURE 2.4a   Bar Graph of Occupational Categories

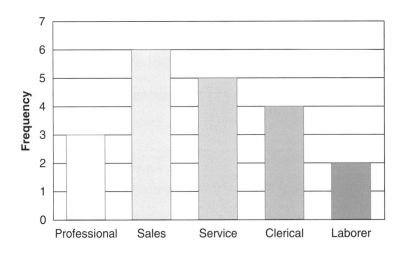

FIGURE 2.4b   Bar Graph of Males' and Females' Occupations

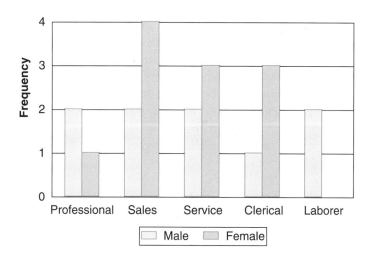

left to right. The *y*-axis represents the corresponding frequency of each value. Frequency can only be integers. There are no valid answers between two integers: (1) *k* and (2) *k* + 1, because the number of daily network interruptions has to be whole numbers. It is not possible to have 2.5 network interruptions. Therefore, the bars are separate from one another, showing a gap in between two adjacent values. In bar graphs, bars do not touch each other (Figure 2.5).

FIGURE 2.5   Bar Graph for the Number of Daily Network Interruptions in November

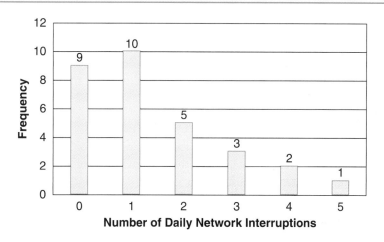

When using a graph to summarize a continuous variable, we need to consider the real limits of the values. Due to the fact that there are numerous possible answers between two adjacent values, there are no gaps between two values. We need to create a new type of graph called the **histogram**. A histogram is defined as a graphical presentation of a continuous variable. The bars of a histogram are of equal width to represent equal intervals of values, and they are touching each other to illustrate that the values are continuous. The difference between a bar graph and a histogram is that the two adjacent bars are touching each other in a histogram but there are gaps between the bars in a bar graph. Bar graphs are used for discrete variables, and histograms are used for continuous variables. The height of the bar represents the corresponding frequency for each interval. Using height measure data in Table 2.4a (back on page 36), we can construct a histogram with 3-inch intervals as shown in Figure 2.6.

FIGURE 2.6   Histogram of 59 Students' Height Measures

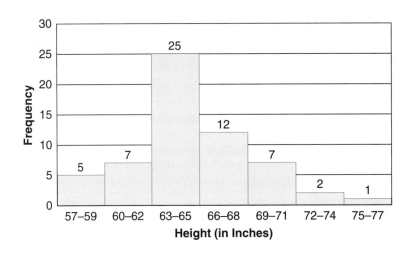

A height measured at 57 inches is actually bounded by a lower limit of 56.5 inches and an upper limit of 57.5 inches. Therefore, the real limits of the interval 57–59 refer to $56.5 \leq X < 59.5$, and the real limits of the next interval 60–62 refer to $59.5 \leq X < 62.5$. Notice that the lower limit is included in the interval but the upper limit is not. Such a rule is to make sure that there are no overlaps between intervals for continuous variables.

PIE CHARTS

A **pie chart** usually depicts categorical data in a circle where the size of each slice of the pie corresponds to the frequency or relative frequency of each category. Pie charts are visually intuitive because the entire circle is 360 degrees. All the categories add to up to 100%, which constitutes the entire 360 degrees. Using the job data in Table 2.1 (back on page 30), a pie chart is constructed in Figure 2.7. It presents a clear image that sales and service job categories cover more than half of the pie, which means more than 50% of respondents hold jobs in these two categories.

Pie charts are extremely popular in presenting reports on budgets, reports on government spending, or TV polling. When used appropriately, pie charts can be a powerful visual aid to present information. The right conditions to use pie charts include (a) the total adds to a meaningful sum, (b) there are no overlaps between categories, and (c) there is a reasonable number of categories. As you can imagine, if the number of categories is more than 10, each pie slice becomes very small. There will be too much information crowded into the pie chart. The disadvantage of a pie chart is that it doesn't present any statistical information other than frequency or proportion.

FIGURE 2.7 Pie Chart of the Occupational Categories

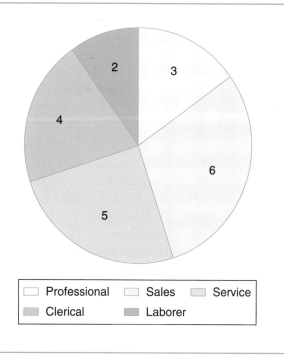

Professional ☐ Sales ☐ Service ☐
Clerical ☐ Laborer ☐

Pop Quiz

1. Which one of the following variables is most likely to use histograms?

   a. Nominal variables

   b. Ordinal variables

   c. Discrete variables

   d. Continuous variables

Answer: d

COMMON DISTRIBUTION SHAPES

A distribution refers to the number of times every value occurs in a sample or a population. In either a bar graph or a histogram when values are lined up from smallest (the left side of the x-axis) to the largest (the right side of the x-axis), the height of the bar represents frequency or relative frequency (i.e., probability) of each value. Such an arrangement shows the shapes of the distribution. Common shapes of distributions include uniform distribution, normal distribution, and skewed distribution.

UNIFORM DISTRIBUTION

In a **uniform distribution**, every value appears with similar frequency, proportion, or probability. Many things have uniform distribution such as dice, coins, and cards. For example, a die has six sides with 1, 2, 3, 4, 5, or 6 dots on each side. The relative frequency or probability of throwing a die and obtaining any of 1, 2, 3, 4, 5, or 6 dots is evenly distributed as 1/6, which is shown in Table 2.5 and Figure 2.8. The probability distribution of the number of dots on a die is called a uniform distribution. A fair die produces the same probability of landing on every side.

TABLE 2.5 Probability of Throwing a Die and Obtaining a Specific Number of Dots

X (NUMBER OF DOTS)	f (FREQUENCY)	RELATIVE FREQUENCY (PROBABILITY)
1	1	1/6 = 0.167
2	1	1/6 = 0.167
3	1	1/6 = 0.167
4	1	1/6 = 0.167
5	1	1/6 = 0.167
6	1	1/6 = 0.167
Total	**6**	**1**

NORMAL DISTRIBUTION

When you throw two dice at the same time and add the number of dots on the dice, the answers will be 2, 3, 4, 5, 6, 7, 8, 9, 10, 11, or 12 dots. The probabilities of obtaining those dots

FIGURE 2.8   Uniform Distribution of Number of Dots on a Die

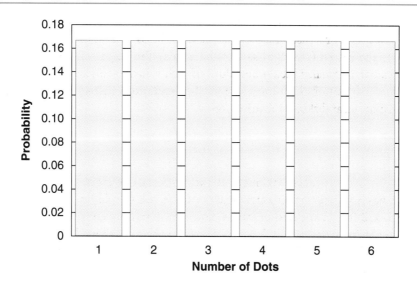

and various combinations for creating the number of dots are listed in Table 2.6. The total probability adds to 1.001 due to rounding. The bar graph of the sum of dots from two dice is shown in Figure 2.9.

TABLE 2.6   Total Number of Dots From Two Dice and the Probabilities

X (NUMBER OF DOTS)	f (FREQUENCY)	PROBABILITY
2 (1,1)	1	1/36 = .028
3 (1,2); (2,1)	2	2/36 = .056
4 (1,3); (2,2); (3,1)	3	3/36 = .083
5 (1,4); (2,3); (3,2); (4,1)	4	4/36 = .111
6 (1,5); (2,4); (3,3); (4,2); (5,1)	5	5/36 = .139
7 (1,6); (2,5); (3,4); (4,3); (5,2); (6,1)	6	6/36 = .167
8 (2,6); (3,5); (4,4); (5,3); (6,2)	5	5/36 = .139
9 (3,6); (4,5); (5,4); (6,3)	4	4/36 = .111
10 (4,6); (5,5); (6,4)	3	3/36 = .083
11 (5,6); (6,5)	2	2/36 = .056
12 (6,6)	1	1/36 = .028
Total	**36**	**1.001**

FIGURE 2.9   Probability of a Specific Number of Dots From Two Dice

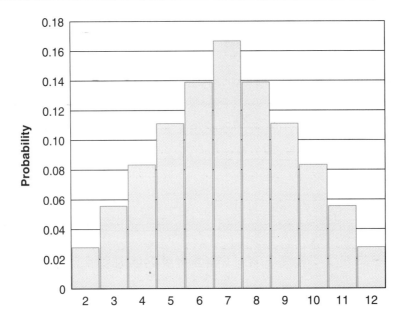

The bar graph shown in Figure 2.9 has the typical characteristics of a **normal distribution**: (a) the distribution peaks at the center, (b) the distribution symmetrically tapers off on both sides and the left side is a mirror image of the right side, and (c) 50% of the distribution is above the mean and 50% below the mean.

Many statistical procedures require that sample data come from a population with a distribution that is approximately normally distributed. A normal distribution is a very important data distribution pattern in statistics. When one examines a distribution from a large sample size, the edges of the histograms are likely to be smoothed out and almost become a curve as seen in Figure 2.10, showing the bar graph of the probability of getting a certain number of heads from 100 coin tosses.

When you trace the outline of the bar graph in Figure 2.10 by connecting the dots on the top of adjacent bars, you create a **line graph**. A line graph is defined as a graph that displays quantitative information with a line or curve that connects a series of adjacent data points. This particular line graph shows a normal distribution curve. A normal distribution curve peaks at the center of the data (i.e., the mean), and then symmetrically tapers off on both sides with 50% of the distribution above the mean and 50% of the distribution below the mean. Draw a line straight through the mean, and the left side and the right side are mirror images of each other as shown in the line graph in Figure 2.11. (The statistical mean will be discussed in detail in Chapter 3.)

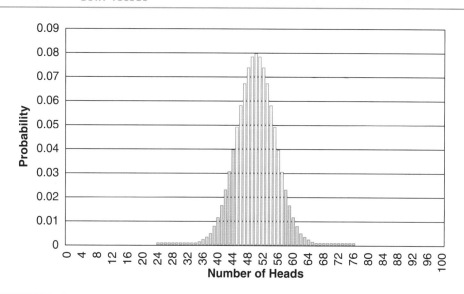

SKEWED DISTRIBUTION

Not all data are normally distributed. A **skewed distribution** happens when values are not symmetrical and they concentrate more on one side than the other. When the distribution mostly concentrates on the left side with a long tail to the right side, it is labeled as **positively skewed** or right skewed as shown in Figure 2.12. For example, income distribution in the United States is positively skewed with a very long tail to the right side. It means that most people earn a modest income while the top 1% is making close to one million.

When the distribution mostly concentrates on the right side with a long tail to the left side, it is labeled as **negatively skewed** or left skewed as shown in Figure 2.13. For example, when students are asked what grades they expect to get on a statistics exam, the majority of the students answer 80s or 90s with very few low scores. The labeling of the skewness depends on the direction of the tail. When the tail points to the high end of the distribution, the data distribution is positively skewed (or right skewed) and when the tail points to the low end of the distribution, the data distribution is negatively skewed (or left skewed).

FIGURE 2.11   Normal Distribution Curve

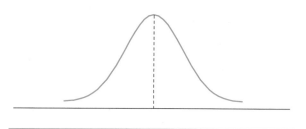

FIGURE 2.12 Positively Skewed or Right-Skewed Distribution

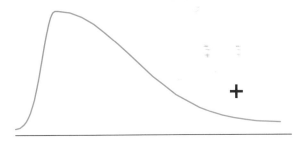

+

FIGURE 2.13 Negatively Skewed or Left-Skewed Distribution

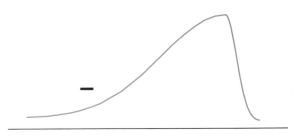

−

EXCEL STEP-BY-STEP INSTRUCTION FOR CALCULATING ΣX FROM A FREQUENCY TABLE AND CONSTRUCTING A BAR GRAPH

To calculate ΣX using a frequency table in EXCEL, we use the network interruption example. First, enter the data showing daily network interruptions in November in EXCEL as shown in Figure 2.14.

The ΣX formula needs to be adjusted to ΣfX using the frequency table. You need to calculate the multiplicative product of the frequency (f) times the value X by moving the cursor to Column C Row 2 (**C2**) and then typing "**=A2*B2**" for the multiplication. All formulas start with "=," A2 is the first value of X, and **B2** is the corresponding frequency. Then hit **enter**. Notice **C2** shows 0, which is the result of **A2*B2** = 0 × 9 as shown in Figure 2.15.

FIGURE 2.14   Network Interruptions Example in EXCEL

	A	B
1	X	f
2	0	9
3	1	10
4	2	5
5	3	3
6	4	2
7	6	1

FIGURE 2.15   Programming fX in EXCEL

| C2 | | | | f_x | =A2*B2 |

	A	B	C	D	E
1	number o	frequency			
2	0	9	0		
3	1	10			
4	2	5			
5	3	3			
6	4	2			
7	6	1			

Then move the cursor to the lower right corner of **C2** until + shows up; then left click and hold the mouse and drag it to **C7**, and then release the mouse. You will see that the rest of the multiplicative products of fX automatically show up in **C3** to **C7**. Now you need to sum up all the fX values from **C2** to **C7**. Move the cursor to **C8**, type "=SUM(C2:C7)." Then hit **enter**. The answer for the total number of network interruptions is 43 as shown in Figure 2.16.

The following graphing instructions apply to Microsoft EXCEL 2010. Graphing functions are likely to vary across different versions of EXCEL. To create a bar graph of daily network interruptions using EXCEL 2010, first highlight the column showing frequency by moving the cursor to **B2**, holding the shift key while moving the cursor to **B7**. Once the frequency numbers are highlighted, click the **Insert** tab on the top of the tool bar; then click on **Column** within the **Charts** section as shown in Figure 2.17.

FIGURE 2.16   Programming ΣfX in EXCEL

| C8 | | | | f_x | =SUM(C2:C7) |

	A	B	C	D	E
1	number o	frequency			
2	0	9	0		
3	1	10	10		
4	2	5	10		
5	3	3	9		
6	4	2	8		
7	6	1	6		
8			43		

Then click on the first option on the left in the **2-D column**, and a bar graph appears. The **Chart Tools** tab shows up. Under **Data**, click **Select Data**. A pop-up window, as shown in Figure 2.18, will show up.

FIGURE 2.17   Finding the Bar Graph Function in EXCEL

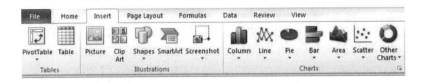

FIGURE 2.18   Identifying the Data Range for a Bar Graph

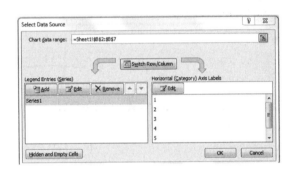

In the **Select Data Source** pop-up window, under **Chart data range,** =Sheet1!$B$2:$B$7 automatically appears in the blank. This means that the data range you want to use to create a bar graph is located in Sheet 1 between Column B, Row 2 and Column B, Row 7. Notice that the **Horizontal (Category) Axis Labels** need to be changed to the values of *X*. Click on **Edit**. A window with **Axis Labels** pops up as shown in Figure 2.19.

Click on the icon to **Select Range** by highlighting *X* values, and =Sheet 1!$A$2:$A$7 automatically appears in the blank as shown in Figure 2.20. This means that the *x*-axis label is located in Sheet 1 between Column A, Row 2 and Column A, Row 7. Then click **OK**.

The bar graph shows up inside Sheet 1 of the EXCEL file as shown in Figure 2.21.

FIGURE 2.19   Axis Labels Window to Allow Editing of Axis Labels

FIGURE 2.20   Customization of Axis Label

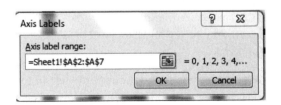

FIGURE 2.21   Bar Graph Created by EXCEL

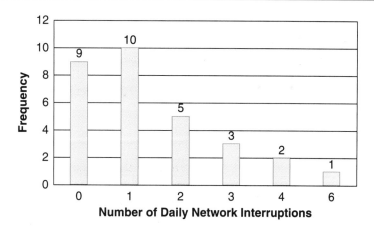

EXERCISE PROBLEMS

1. Here is a list of 20 students' quiz scores. Quizzes are scored based on the number of questions answered correctly. The scores can only be integers.

    5, 3, 4, 4, 4, 3, 5, 2, 5, 5,

    1, 2, 4, 3, 0, 5, 4, 3, 5, 5

    Organize them into (a) a frequency table and (b) a bar graph.

2. The following data are the ages for a random sample of $n = 35$ adult patients who are diagnosed with depression.

    50, 23, 44, 20, 66, 34, 55, 63, 21, 36, 39, 38,

    54, 48, 32, 28, 37, 42, 60, 27, 38, 45, 46, 51,

    49, 58, 57, 62, 26, 35, 45, 29, 43, 55, 32

    Create (a) an appropriate frequency table with equal intervals and (b) a histogram.

3. Based on the frequency table of student loans from a random sample of $n = 32$ students in Table 2.7, create a histogram and comment on the shape of the distribution.

TABLE 2.7   Frequency Table of Student Loans

STUDENT LOAN (IN DOLLARS)	f (FREQUENCY)
Less than 20,000	2
20,000-29,999	4
30,000-39,999	6
40,000-49,999	8
50,000-59,999	6
60,000-69,999	4
70,000 or more	2

TABLE 2.8 Frequency Table of Quiz Scores

QUIZ	f (FREQUENCY)
0	1
1	1
2	2
3	4
4	5
5	7
	20

FIGURE 2.22 Bar Graph of Quiz Scores

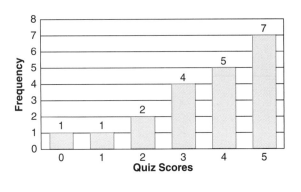

Solutions

1. The minimal value of the quiz scores is 0 and the maximal value is 5. The frequency table can be created using the individual values.

   a. The frequency table of 20 quiz scores is shown in Table 2.8.

   b. The bar graph of the quiz scores is shown in Figure 2.22.

2. The minimal value of adult patients' ages is 20, and the maximal value is 66. The range is 46. Equal intervals of 10 are appropriate in this case. The first interval is 20–29 and the last interval is 60–69. There are no overlaps between two adjacent intervals.

   a. The frequency table of 35 adult depression patients' ages is shown in Table 2.9.

   b. The histogram of adult depression patients' ages is shown in Figure 2.23.

3. The histogram was created based on the frequency table of a random sample of 32 students' loans in Table 2.7. The distribution of student loans peaks at the center and symmetrically tapers off on both sides. The right side is a mirror image of the left side with 50% of the data above the center and 50% below the center. The distribution of student loans has the characteristics of a normal distribution. The histogram is shown in Figure 2.24.

TABLE 2.9 Frequency Table of 35 Adult Depression Patients' Ages

PATIENT'S AGE	f (FREQUENCY)
20-29	7
30-39	9
40-49	8
50-59	7
60-69	4
Total	35

FIGURE 2.23 Histogram of Depression Patients' Ages

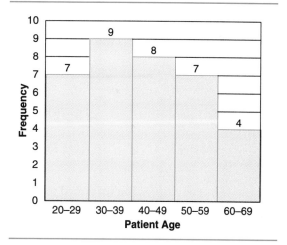

FIGURE 2.24 Histogram of Student Loans

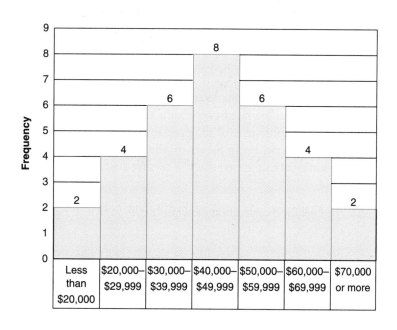

⑤SAGE edge™

WHAT YOU LEARNED

In this chapter, you've learned to construct frequency tables and use graphs to represent data. When constructing a frequency table, here are the keys to success.

1. Identify the minimal and maximal values of the variable. Calculate the range.

2. Construct a frequency table with 7 ± 2 categories. When the range is too large to construct a table with individual values, choose an appropriate and convenient interval, usually in 5s or 10s, if feasible.

3. Create the categories or equal intervals in an ascending order.

4. Make sure that there are no overlaps between any two adjacent intervals. For continuous variables, each interval includes the lower limit but not the upper limit.

In bar graphs and histograms, the graphs consist of bars of equal width. The bar width presents the value or interval. The bar height represents the frequency or relative frequency of each value or interval. Bar graphs are used to organize discrete variables, and histograms are used to organize continuous variables. In pie charts, the graphs consist of different slices. The size of the slice is proportional to the frequency or relative frequency of each category.

Common distribution shapes include uniform distribution, normal distribution, and skewed distribution.

KEY WORDS

Bar graph: A bar graph uses bars of equal width to show frequency or relative frequency of discrete categorical data (i.e., nominal or ordinal data). Adjacent bars are not touching each other.

Distribution: Distribution is the arrangement of values of a variable as it occurs in a sample or a population.

Equal intervals: Equal intervals are created in a frequency table by including the same number of values in each interval.

Frequency: Frequency is a simple count of a particular value or category occurring in a sample or a population.

Frequency distribution table: A frequency distribution table lists all distinct values or categories arranged in an orderly fashion in a table, along with tally counts for each value or category in a data set.

Histogram: A histogram is a graphical presentation of a continuous variable. The bars of a histogram are touching each other to illustrate that the values are continuous.

Line graph: A line graph is a graphical display of quantitative information with a line or curve that connects a series of adjacent data points.

Negatively skewed distribution: When the data points mostly concentrate on the high-end values with a long tail to the low-end values, the distribution is negatively skewed.

Normal distribution: A normal distribution curve peaks at the mean of the values and symmetrically tapers off on both sides with 50% of the data points above the mean and 50% of the data points below the mean. Draw a line straight through the mean, and the left side and the right side are mirror images of each other.

Pie chart: A circular graph that uses slices to show different categories. The size of each slice is proportional to the frequency or relative frequency of each category.

Positively skewed distribution: When the data points mostly concentrate on the low-end values with a long tail to the high-end values, the distribution is positively skewed.

Real limits: Real limits cover a range of possible values that may be reflected by a single continuous measure. The lower limit is the value minus ½ of the unit and the upper limit is the value plus ½ of the unit.

Relative frequency: Relative frequency is defined as the frequency of a particular value or category divided by the total frequency (or sample size). Relative frequency is also called proportion.

Skewed distribution: A skewed distribution happens when data points are not symmetrical, and they concentrate more on one side of the mean than the other.

Uniform distribution: In a uniform distribution, every value appears with similar frequency, proportion, or probability.

Multiple Choice Questions: Choose the best answer in the following questions.

1. A _____ skewness is a distribution with a high concentration of data points at the high end of the distribution and a long tail toward the low end of the distribution.

   a. negative

   b. positive

   c. discrete

   d. continuous

2. A proportion describes the frequency (f) of a category in relation to the total frequency or sample size (n), f/n. It is also called a

   a. frequency.

   b. relative frequency.

   c. cumulative relative frequency.

   d. correlation.

3. The appropriate number of categories in a frequency table is

   a. 5 ± 2

   b. 7 ± 2

   c. 9 ± 2

   d. 11 ± 2

4. What is the sample size according to the frequency table of students' homework grades?

X (HOMEWORK GRADE)	f (FREQUENCY)
0	2
6	4
7	4
8	12
9	14
10	17

   a. 40

   b. 41

   c. 51

   d. 53

5. Calculate the total quiz score from the following frequency table.

X (QUIZ GRADE)	f (FREQUENCY)
0	2
1	4
2	4
3	12
4	14
5	17

a. 15

b. 53

c. 189

d. 193

6. What is wrong with the following frequency table?

X (EXAM GRADE)	f (FREQUENCY)
40-50	2
50-60	4
60-70	4
70-80	12
80-90	4
90-100	7

a. The frequency table does not consist of equal intervals.

b. The number of intervals is too large.

c. The number of interval is too small.

d. There are overlaps between two adjacent intervals.

Free Response Questions

7. There is a small city in Ohio with a population of 179 people and 0.27 miles on a busy interstate highway. It is famous for its speed traps. A speed trap is defined as a section of a road where police, radar, or traffic cameras carefully check the speed of motorists and strictly enforce traffic regulations.

A municipality can intentionally lower the speed limits to catch motorists cruising by without paying attention to the speed signs to boost its revenues. Table 2.10 shows a summary of citation amount intervals and frequency associated with each interval. Use the EXCEL step-by-step instructions to calculate the total dollar amount of the traffic citations in this small city. Create a histogram and comment on the shape of the distribution of traffic citations.

TABLE 2.10   Frequency Table of Traffic Citation Amounts

X (CITATION AMOUNT IN DOLLARS)	f (FREQUENCY)
90-109	12
110-129	53
130-149	104
150-169	290
170-189	405
190-209	852
210-229	907
230-249	981

8. A summary of employees' absenteeism from a local company for the past 12 months is shown in Table 2.11. Absenteeism is defined as days absent with or without excuses. Use the EXCEL step-by-step instructions to

calculate the total number of days absent for all employees. Number of days absent can be expressed as ½ day or ¼ day. Create a histogram of the number of days absent and comment on the shape of the distribution of days absent.

TABLE 2.11   Frequency Table of Days Absent

X (DAYS ABSENT)	f (FREQUENCY)
0-1	329
2-3	342
4-5	198
6-7	60
8-9	13
10-11	3
12-13	2
14-15	1

Descriptive Statistics

After reading and studying this chapter, you should be able to do the following:

- Describe and differentiate among the three common central tendency measures: (1) mode, (2) median, and (3) mean

- Calculate mean from the formula

- Adjust the mean formula when using frequency tables

- Choose the correct formulas to calculate variance and standard deviation in populations or samples

- Adjust the variance and standard deviation formulas when using frequency tables

WHAT YOU KNOW AND WHAT IS NEW

In Chapter 2, you learned to organize and summarize data by constructing frequency tables or graphs to provide useful insights at a quick glance. Different statistical procedures are appropriate for different scales of measurement. Mathematical operations need to be adjusted when using frequency tables. Such adjustments are extremely important to remember and continue to be used in calculating descriptive statistics, which are discussed in this chapter.

In this chapter, you will learn new quantitative terms and formulas, such as *central tendency* and *variability measures* to organize and summarize sample data. There are several different ways to describe the center of a variable. The center of a variable can be a typical value that repeats most frequently or it can be the middle position of sorted values arranged from low-est to highest. It can also be the sum of all values divided by the number of values. There are three common measures of central tendency: (1) mode, (2) median, and (3) mean. You will learn their relative positions in different shapes of distributions. In Chapter 2, you have learned about the shape of a distribution.

Measures of variability quantify the variation or dispersion of values within a variable. Using quantitative terms to organize and summarize variables is an efficient way to communicate numerical attributes of variables among people who understand the definitions of these quantitative terms in addition to frequency tables or graphs. The definitions of these quantitative terms will be clearly explained and illustrated in this chapter. It is also important to link the appropriate central tendency and variability measures with scales of measurement. Frequency tables will be used in calculating measures for central tendency and/or variability.

MEASURES OF CENTRAL TENDENCY

Central tendency is defined as a single number used to describe the center of a distribution. The center of a distribution is usually the most typical or representative value of all the values. There are three measures that are commonly used to represent central tendency: (1) *mean*, (2) *median*, and (3) *mode*. These three common measures for central tendency will be presented in order of mathematical complexity from the simplest to the most sophisticated. Therefore, we will discuss mode first, median second, and mean last.

MODE

The mode is defined as the value or category with the highest frequency in a distribution. It means the value or category that occurs most often. To identify the mode in a distribution, you may do a simple tally count on individual values or look into a frequency table and identify the value with the highest frequency without performing any other mathematical operation. Frequency counts can be applied to all four scales of measurement: (1) nominal, (2) ordinal, (3) interval, and (4) ratio. Let's look at an example.

EXAMPLE 3.1

According to Mosby's Medical Dictionary, family structure is defined as the composition and membership of the family and the organization and patterning of relationships among individual family members. The U.S. Department of Health and Human Services conducted National Health Interview Surveys between 2001 and 2007 among 12,604,000 adults with children below 18 years of age living with them (Blackwell,

2010). The frequency and percentage of family structure is shown in Table 3.1. Based on the table, what is the mode of family structure in the United States?

TABLE 3.1   Frequency and Percentage of Family Structure Based on the National Health Interview Surveys (Number in Thousands)

FAMILY STRUCTURE	FREQUENCY	PERCENTAGE (RELATIVE FREQUENCY)
Nuclear family	4,246	33.7
Single-parent family	2,668	21.6
Unmarried biological or adoptive family	246	2.0
Blended family	1,105	8.8
Cohabiting family	493	3.9
Extended family	3,166	25.1
Other family	680	5.4
Total	**12,604**	**100.5**

The family structure question is answered on a nominal scale of measurement. Mode can be applied to a nominal variable. The category with the highest frequency is nuclear family. Notice that only 33.7% of families belong in this category. In other words, roughly one in three families fits in this traditional family model. The total percentage adds to 100.5 due to rounding.

Mode can be applied to all four different scales of measurement. In the next example, we will demonstrate how mode can be applied to an ordinal scale of measurement.

EXAMPLE 3.2

A middle school conducted an anonymous survey on the occurrences, severity, and types of bullying incidents at school. The answers to the question "How often have you been bullied at school in the past couple of months?" were tallied and reported in Table 3.2. What is the mode of this distribution?

(Continued)

(Continued)

TABLE 3.2 Occurrences of Bullying Incidents at a Middle School

OCCURRENCES OF BULLYING INCIDENTS	FREQUENCY	PERCENTAGE (RELATIVE FREQUENCY)
I have not been bullied at school.	320	65
I have been bullied once or twice.	121	24
I have been bullied twice or three times a month.	25	5
I have been bullied about once a week.	17	3
I have been bullied several times a week.	13	3
Total	**496**	**100**

SOURCE: **Adapted from Rocori Middle School (2014).**

The frequency table reported the occurrences of bullying incidents in five categories. The answers to "How often have you been bullied at school in the past couple of months?" are classified as an ordinal scale of measurement. The answers indicate an increasing level of occurrences of bullying incidents from "not being bullied" to "several times a week." The mode is the category with the highest frequency. The highest frequency is 320. The mode is the value or category with this highest frequency, so the mode is "I have not been bullied at school in the past couple of months." As is indicated by the relative frequency column, 65% of children reported that they were not bullied at school. It was good news that a majority of the students did not have the personal experience of being bullied. The results also indicated that there were 30 students who had encountered regular weekly bullying. The school needs to take action to protect these students, so they don't continue to suffer such mistreatment or abuse at school.

There are two things that you need to know about mode:

1. It can be applied to nominal, ordinal, interval, or ratio data.

2. A data set may have one mode, multiple modes, or no mode. For example, if two values or categories both have the same highest frequency, then the distribution has two modes, which is called a bimodal distribution. When none of the values are repeated in a distribution, or when each value is repeated the same number of times, there is no mode. Usually, it is common to have one mode in a distribution.

MEDIAN

The median is defined as the value right in the middle of the distribution when all values are sorted from the lowest to the highest. Based on the definition, the data need to be sorted. Therefore, they need to have at least ordinal attributes. It is important to note that median can be meaningfully applied to only ordinal, interval, or ratio variables.

The median is a measure of location, which is the midpoint of sorted observed values. Let's clarify the term *right in the middle*. When the sample size, n, is an odd number, there is only one midpoint in the distribution. When the sample size, n, is an even number, there are two midpoints in the distribution. Finding the median involves finding the midpoint(s) of the distribution. This process is illustrated by Examples 3.3 and 3.4.

EXAMPLE 3.3

The following numbers are the fuel efficiency, in miles per gallon, reported by car manufacturers on five new models: (1) 31, (2) 28, (3) 46, (4) 39, and (5) 41. What is the mode and median fuel efficiency of these five models?

These five values all occur once in the sample. There is no mode in this case.

The sample size, $n = 5$, is an odd number. There is one midpoint when sample size is an odd number. However, the values were reported in an arbitrary order, so they need to be sorted first. The sorted values from lowest to largest are as follows: 28, 31, 39, 41, and 46. When n is an odd number, the location of the midpoint is determined by $L = n/2$ rounded up to the next integer. In this example, $L = 5/2 = 2.5$, which rounds up to 3. The third position of the sorted data is the median. The value of the third position is 39. Therefore, the median fuel efficiency for these five new models is 39 miles per gallon.

EXAMPLE 3.4

Let's use the frequency table of the Internet network interruption example in Chapter 2 to illustrate how to figure out the mode and median in a frequency table (Table 3.3a).

The highest frequency is 10, and its corresponding value is 1. Therefore, the mode is 1.

The sample size, $n = 30$, is an even number. There are two midpoints in this sample. The two middle locations are $L = n/2$ and the next location $(L + 1)$. The median is the average of the values in the Lth and $(L + 1)$th locations. Let's identify the two middle

(Continued)

(Continued)

positions, $L = 30/2 = 15$ and $L + 1 = 16$. The values for the 15th and 16th locations are both 1. The median is the average of these two values, $(1 + 1)/2 = 1$. The median for these reported network interruptions is 1.

TABLE 3.3a   Frequency Table for Daily Network Interruptions on a University Campus

X (VALUE)	f (FREQUENCY)	RELATIVE FREQUENCY
0	9	0.300
1	10	0.333
2	5	0.167
3	3	0.100
4	2	0.067
5	0	0.000
6	1	0.033
Total	30	1.000

EXAMPLE 3.5

Another way to obtain the median is by calculating cumulative relative frequency. Cumulative relative frequency is defined as the accumulation of the relative frequency for a particular value together with all the relative frequencies for lower values. It is obvious that cumulative relative frequency only applies to variables with orders (i.e., ordinal, interval, or ratio variables). Median can be identified in a frequency table where the first value has a cumulative relative frequency more than .50. Let's use the network interruptions example with cumulative relative frequency calculated in Table 3.3b.

Median can be identified as the first value with cumulative relative frequency more than .50. In this case, the first cumulative relative frequency more than .50 is .633, and its corresponding value is 1. Therefore, the median is 1. The answer is identical to that of Example 3.4 where two middle points are identified in a sample size $n = 30$. Then the values of two midpoints in positions 15 and 16 are averaged to obtain the median value 1.

TABLE 3.3b Frequency Table for Daily Network Interruptions With Cumulative Relative Frequency

X (VALUE)	f (FREQUENCY)	RELATIVE FREQUENCY	CUMULATIVE RELATIVE FREQUENCY
0	9	0.300	0.300
1	10	0.333	0.633
2	5	0.167	0.800
3	3	0.100	0.900
4	2	0.067	0.967
5	0	0.000	0.967
6	1	0.033	1.000
Total	**30**	**1.000**	

Here is a summary of the steps to identify the median in a distribution. Median can only be obtained in ordinal, interval, or ratio variables.

1. SORT the data from the smallest value to the largest value.

2. If n is an odd number, the location for the midpoint is $L = n/2$, rounded up to the next integer. Identify the median as the value of the Lth location in the distribution.

3. If n is an even number, there are two midpoints in the data. The two midpoints are located in the Lth and the $(L + 1)$th positions. The median is the average of the values at those two middle locations.

4. In a frequency table, the median is the first value with cumulative relative frequency more than .50.

There are three things that you need to know about the median:

1. It can only be applied to ordinal, interval, and ratio data.

2. Its calculation does not involve every value in the variable.

3. It is not affected much by extreme values of the variable. It remains relatively stable even with extreme values in the variable.

MEAN

The **mean** (also referred to as the average or arithmetic mean) is a measure of central tendency that is determined by adding all the values and dividing by the number of values. The formula for the sample mean is $\bar{X} = \dfrac{\sum X}{n}$, and the formula for the population mean is $\mu = \dfrac{\sum X}{N}$.

The common element of the formulas for $\bar{X}$ and μ is $\sum X$. As mentioned in Chapter 1 in the section "Statistical Notations,"

$$\sum X = X_1 + X_2 + X_3 + \cdots + X_n$$

The summation of X, $\sum X$, requires adding all values, from the first value to the last value. The mean is calculated by the sum of all values divided by the number of values, $\bar{X} = \dfrac{\sum X}{n}$ or $\mu = \dfrac{\sum X}{N}$.

Although relative to the mode and the median, the calculation for mean might involve more work, the logic is simple and straightforward. When applying the mean formula using frequency tables where individual values occur different numbers of times, the formula needs to be modified to $\bar{X} = \dfrac{\sum X}{n} = \dfrac{\sum fX}{n}$. Such a modification allows the impact of frequencies to be fully incorporated. The same modification also applies to calculation of the population mean. We will use an example to illustrate this process.

EXAMPLE 3.6

Students' statistics quiz scores are reported in Table 3.4a. What are the mode, median, and mean of the quiz scores?

TABLE 3.4a Students' Quiz Scores

X (QUIZ SCORE)	f (FREQUENCY)	RELATIVE FREQUENCY	CUMULATIVE RELATIVE FREQUENCY
0	1	0.02	0.02
1	2	0.04	0.06
2	2	0.04	0.1
3	14	0.28	0.38
4	15	0.3	0.68
5	16	0.32	1.00
Total	50	1.00	

The highest frequency is 16 in Table 3.4a, and its corresponding value is 5. The mode is 5.

The median on a sample size of 50 is the average of two midpoints in the distribution. The two midpoints are $L = n/2 = 50/2 = 25$ and the next one, 26. A simple way to find the values in the 25th and 26th locations in a frequency table is to add the frequency of the lowest value with the frequency of the next value and repeat this procedure until the summed frequencies reach the targeted numbers. In this example, when you add the first four frequencies, $1 + 2 + 2 + 14 = 19$. The sum of the first four frequencies did not reach the targeted numbers 25 and 26. You have to add the first five frequencies, $1 + 2 + 2 + 14 + 15 = 34$, to reach over 25. The median is the value of the midpoints in the distribution. The corresponding values for the 25th and 26th locations are both 4. The average of the two values is still 4. The median is 4. Also, from the cumulative relative frequency column, it can be readily seen that 4 is the first value with cumulative relative frequency more than .50. The median is 4.

The mean is $\bar{X} = \dfrac{\Sigma X}{n} = \dfrac{\Sigma fX}{n}$. According to the formula, the numerator and the denominator need to be figured out before the division. For the numerator, the order of operations dictates that the multiplication of fX be conducted first. Therefore, the column of fX is added to Table 3.4b. Then at the end, the summation ΣfX is calculated, and the answer is 188. For the denominator, the sample size is 50. The mean is $\bar{X} = \dfrac{\Sigma X}{n} = \dfrac{\Sigma fX}{n} = \dfrac{188}{50} = 3.76$. The rule of rounding in reporting median or mean is to report the answer with one more decimal place than in the original data. Since the original quiz scores are reported as integers, the answer for the mean should be rounded one digit after the decimal point. The mean is 3.8. That is, the students' mean quiz score is 3.8 for this particular quiz.

TABLE 3.4b Students' Quiz Scores With fX Column

X (QUIZ SCORE)	f (FREQUENCY)	fX
0	1	0
1	2	2
2	2	4
3	14	42
4	15	60
5	16	80
Total	50	188

It is important to know which statistical procedures can be appropriately applied to what scales of measurement. Here is a summary table on what measures of central tendency can be appropriately applied to which scales of measurement (Table 3.5).

TABLE 3.5 Summary Table on What Central Tendency Measures Apply to Which Scales of Measurement

CENTRAL TENDENCY	SCALES OF MEASUREMENT			
Mode	Nominal	Ordinal	Interval	Ratio
Median	—	Ordinal	Interval	Ratio
Mean	—	—	Interval	Ratio

Author's Aside

You might have heard of the radio program host Garrison Keillor's famous closing line, "That's the news from Lake Wobegon, where all the women are strong, all the men are good looking, and all the children are above average." Lake Wobegon is a fictional place created by Keillor's imagination. As tempting as it is to wish all students are above average, by now, you should know, if all students are above average, the mean is calculated wrong!

In the following sections, we will discuss calculating mean in different situations that involve slight modification of the mean formula.

Estimating the Mean Using a Frequency Table With Equal Intervals

When observed values cover a wide range, constructing a frequency table with equal intervals makes it more manageable to organize and summarize the values. It will also make reporting the central tendency of the observations easier. As you learned in Chapter 2, in a frequency table consisting of equal intervals, the formula for ΣX needs to be modified to $\Sigma fX_{midpoint}$. Therefore,

$$\mu = \frac{\Sigma fX_{midpoint}}{N} \text{ and } \bar{X} = \frac{\Sigma fX_{midpoint}}{n}.$$

EXAMPLE 3.7

Temperatures vary throughout the day. The highest temperature reached in a day is reported as the daily high. January 2014 was a particularly cold month in Cleveland, Ohio. The recorded daily high temperatures of Cleveland in January in Fahrenheit are listed below.

22, 28, 15, 14, 35, 39, −12, 3, 15, 30, 37, 36, 40, 45, 37, 33,

32, 13, 22, 39, 28, 7, 10, 2, 25, 22, 26, 3, 14, 28, 31

Based on the recorded daily high temperatures of January in Cleveland, what are the mode, median, and mean high temperatures for this month?

There are 31 days in January, and there are 31 daily high temperatures reported. Therefore, these 31 daily high temperatures constitute a population. Deciding whether you are dealing with a population or a sample is critical because it determines which formula is correct.

It is difficult to process quickly the numeric information from a list of 31 daily high temperatures. A frequency table of the temperatures is created to pursue the central tendency measures (Table 3.6a). First, you need to figure out the range, which is obtained by subtracting the minimal value from the maximal value, that is, range = maximal value − minimal value = 45 − (−12) = 57. When the temperature range is 57, equal intervals need to be created to organize the values. Equal intervals of 10 or 5 are usually created for easy calculation. I would use an equal interval of 10 degrees in this example.

TABLE 3.6a Daily High Temperatures of Cleveland, Ohio, in January

X (HIGH TEMPERATURE)	f (FREQUENCY)
(−14) °F-(−5) °F	1
(−4) °F-5 °F	3
6 °F-15 °F	7
16 °F-25 °F	4
26 °F-35 °F	9
36 °F-45 °F	7
Total	31

a. The highest frequency is 9. The corresponding value is 26 °F–35 °F. Therefore, mode = 26 °F–35 °F.

b. The population size is $N = 31$, an odd number; therefore, there is one midpoint in the distribution. The position is $L = N/2 = 31/2 = 15.5$, which rounds up to 16. The value of the 16th location is 26 °F–35 °F; therefore, the median = 26 °F–35 °F.

c. In order to calculate the mean, the midpoint of each interval needs to be estimated. $X_{midpoint}$ = (low-end value + high-end value)/2 are shown in the $X_{midpoint}$ column and $fX_{midpoint}$ is created as the last column in Table 3.6b.

(Continued)

(Continued)

TABLE 3.6b **Daily High Temperatures of Cleveland, Ohio, in January With $X_{midpoint}$ and $fX_{midpoint}$**

X (HIGH TEMPERATURE)	f (FREQUENCY)	$X_{midpoint}$	$fX_{midpoint}$
(−14) °F-(−5) °F	1	(−14) + (−5)/2 = −9.5	−9.5
(−4) °F-5 °F	3	(−4 + 5)/2 = 0.5	1.5
6 °F-15 °F	7	(6 + 15)/2 = 10.5	73.5
16 °F-25 °F	4	(16 + 25)/2 = 20.5	82
26 °F-5 °F	9	(26 + 35)/2 = 30.5	274.5
36 °F-45 °F	7	(36 + 45)/2 = 40.5	283.5
Total	31		705.5

It is easy to see the advantage of choosing an interval of 10 when constructing a frequency table. As shown in the $X_{midpoint}$ column, the difference between the adjacent $X_{midpoint}$ values is 10. The formula for mean, $\mu = \dfrac{\Sigma X}{N}$, needs to be replaced by $\mu = \dfrac{\Sigma fX_{midpoint}}{N}$ in frequency tables with equal intervals. The last column, $fX_{midpoint}$, is created to consider the impact of frequency of each interval. The sum of $fX_{midpoint}$ is calculated at the end of the column.

$$\Sigma fX_{midpoint} = 705.5$$

$$\text{Mean } \mu = \frac{\Sigma fX_{midpoint}}{N} = \frac{705.5}{31} = 22.8$$

The average daily high temperature in Cleveland, Ohio, in January 2014 was 22.8 °F.

Occasionally, some students in my class complain about learning a new formula to estimate the mean in frequency tables with equal intervals. Some argue that they could have got an exact answer for the mean by adding up one by one all 31 daily high temperatures without learning this new $\mu = \dfrac{\Sigma fX_{midpoint}}{N}$ formula. I would agree with this argument *if* the original values are stated in the problem. However, oftentimes, students have to calculate an estimated mean with only the information in frequency tables. Such questions are presented in the section "Exercise Problems" at the end of the chapter. The point of learning statistics is working smart instead of working hard. In my personal opinion, calculating $fX_{midpoint}$ for six intervals is easier than adding 31 individual values one by one.

Weighted Mean

The **weighted mean** is defined as calculating the mean when data values are assigned different weights, w. The formula for weighted mean is $\bar{X} = \dfrac{\sum wX}{\sum w}$. Weighted mean is appropriate when every value in the data is not treated equally. One of the most relevant examples for calculating a weighted mean for students is to show how GPA is calculated. Here is a statement that I have often heard from students: "I got an A in one course and a C from another course, so my average for this semester was a B." Was this statement correct? Not necessarily, as it depends on whether these two courses had the same number of credit hours. If John got an A in a one-credit-hour "American Sign Language" course and a C in a four-credit-hour Behavioral Science Statistics course, then his semester average would be closer to C than B. When calculating GPA, courses with a higher number of credit hours are given more weight than courses with a lower number of credit hours. The credit hours of the courses are the weights that need to be considered. In a four-point system, the grades are worth A = 4, B = 3, C = 2, D = 1, and F = 0 points. Full-time undergraduate students usually take four to six different courses in a semester. Let's demonstrate how to calculate a student's GPA by using an example.

EXAMPLE 3.8

Chris received a B in Abnormal Psychology (3 credit hours), an A in Behavioral Science Statistics (4 credit hours), an A in Rock and Blues (1 credit hour), a C in Psychology of Women (3 credit hours), and a B in Biology (5 credit hours) last semester (Table 3.7a). What was Chris's GPA for last semester?

TABLE 3.7a Chris's Courses, Grades, and Credit Hours

COURSE	X (GRADE)	w (CREDIT HOURS)
Abnormal Psychology	B = 3	3
Behavioral Science Statistics	A = 4	4
Rock and Blues	A = 4	1
Psychology of Women	C = 2	3
Biology	B = 3	5

(Continued)

(Continued)

Let's start by organizing all the courses in a table including the courses, grades, and credit hours.

According to the formula for weighted mean, $\bar{X} = \dfrac{\sum wX}{\sum w}$, the multiplication wX needs to be performed first. Therefore, the column of wX is created in Table 3.7b.

TABLE 3.7b   Chris's Courses, Grades, and Credit Hours With wX Column

COURSE	X (GRADE)	w (CREDIT HOURS)	wX
Abnormal Psychology	B = 3	3	9
Behavioral Science Statistics	A = 4	4	16
Rock and Blues	A = 4	1	4
Psychology of Women	C = 2	3	6
Biology	B = 3	5	15
Total		16	50

Once the column of wX is created, the $\sum wX = 50$ is calculated at the end of the column, which provides the total weighted points earned. Then the value of the total weighted points is divided by the total number of credit hours (the total weight). This division gives the weighted mean, which is 50/16 = 3.125. Again, the rounding off rule states that the answer of a calculation is one more decimal place than in the original data. The original grades are reported as integers. The weighted mean should be reported by rounding off the value to one digit after the decimal point, so Chris's GPA for the last semester is 3.1.

There are three things that you need to know about the mean:

1. It applies to interval or ratio measures that come with equal units.

2. Its calculation involves every value in the variable.

3. Therefore, it is sensitive to the impact of *outliers*.

Outliers are extreme values in a distribution. Outliers usually stand far away from the rest of the data points. They are not representative of the sample or population. In some statistical procedures, outliers can have heavy influences on the results. In central tendency measures, mean is the only one that is heavily influenced by outliers. Mode and median are not likely to be influenced by outliers. We will continue this discussion in a class exercise later in this section.

Based on the rounding off rule, the measures of central tendency should be reported at one more decimal place than in the original data. When the original data report whole numbers, the median and mean are reported by rounding off the values to one digit after the decimal point. The exception is the mode. Mode should be reported as it is in the original data.

Locations of Mean, Median, and Mode in Different Shapes of Distribution

In a normal distribution, the highest frequency is in the middle; then it symmetrically tapers off on both sides. The right side is a mirror image of the left side; thus, mean, median, and mode are located in the same spot, as shown in Figure 3.1.

The mode is the value with the highest frequency, which is at the peak exactly in the middle. The median is the midpoint of the distribution, so it is also precisely in the middle. Because of the symmetrical tapering off on both sides, the values above the mean on the right side compensate for the values below the mean on the left side perfectly. Therefore, the mean stays exactly in the middle as well. In a normal distribution, the mean, median, and mode are located at the same spot, exactly in the middle.

The locations of the mean, median, and mode in skewed distributions are quite different. In a positively skewed (right skewed) distribution, the mode is the value with the highest frequency. This occurs at the peak, which is located to the left side as marked in Figure 3.2. The mean is the arithmetic average of all values and is sensitive to the impacts of outliers. Therefore, the long tail to the right side is pulling the mean toward the tail. The median is in between the mode and the mean.

FIGURE 3.1 Normal Distribution Curve With Mean, Median, and Mode

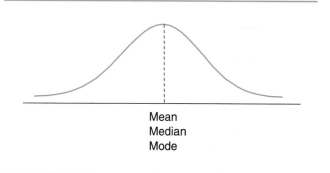

Mean
Median
Mode

FIGURE 3.2 Positively Skewed (Right Skewed) Distribution With Mean, Median, and Mode

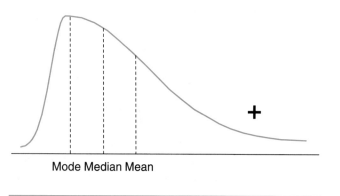

Mode Median Mean

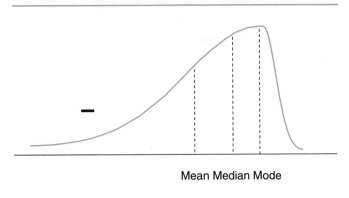

FIGURE 3.3 Negatively Skewed (Left Skewed) Distribution With Mean, Median, and Mode

Mean Median Mode

In a negatively skewed distribution, the peak is located to the right side as marked in Figure 3.3. The peak is the mode, which is the value with the highest frequency. The mean is the arithmetic average of all values and is sensitive to the impacts of outliers. Therefore, the long tail to the left side is pulling the mean toward the tail. The median is in between the mode and the mean.

There are three measures for central tendency. Which measure of central tendency is the best? The answer to that question is not simple. It depends on the shape of the distribution and the purpose for the central tendency.

Use household wealth as an example. Some economic reports state that Americans with the lowest 40% annual income are below the poverty line and carry debts, while the top 1% of Americans control 35.7% of all privately owned wealth in 2010. Based on statements like this, you can imagine that the shape of the household wealth distribution is positively skewed with a very long tail to the right. Consider the following exercises.

1. Collect the household wealth information from everyone in the classroom by handing out a piece of paper and having each student anonymously write down a number that best estimates his or her household wealth. Fold up the paper and submit the number to the instructor. Calculate all three measures of central tendency for the household wealth values.

2. Now imagine that Bill Gates visits your class. Assume that Bill Gates's reported net worth for last year is around 77.3 billion dollars. Include his wealth in the household wealth numbers collected from Exercise 1. Calculate all three measures of central tendency.

Based on the numbers you calculate from Exercises 1 and 2, which measure remains exactly the same, which measure remains fairly similar, and which measure changes dramatically?

In Exercise 1, you collect household wealth information from everyone in the classroom. In Exercise 2, your sample size increases by one, and Bill Gates's household wealth is added to the numbers collected in Exercise 1. The mode is the value with the highest frequency. The mode is not likely to change by including Bill Gates's household wealth in the sample. The answer is that the mode remains exactly the same. The median is the midpoint of the sorted values. By adding one person in the sample, the midpoint might shift by one location. The median remains fairly similar. The mean in the first exercise is likely to be a modest amount, but the mean in the second exercise is likely to jump over one billion dollars. The calculation of the mean requires every value of the variable. It is sensitive to the extreme outliers' influence. For a very brief moment, everyone in the class becomes a billionaire on the calculation of mean. It is clear that such a value is not a typical or representative value of the sample. It is not appropriate to use the mean as a measure of central tendency in this case.

Now you have experienced calculating measures of central tendency with a powerful outlier (i.e., Bill Gates's wealth). You have learned that the mode is usually not influenced by the presence of a powerful outlier. The median might stay the same or shift by one location by adding a powerful outlier in the sample. The mean is highly sensitive to the influence of a powerful outlier. Which one of the measures of central tendency is not suitable in the presence of outliers? The answer is clearly the mean.

 ## Pop Quiz

1. In a negatively skewed distribution, the mean would be

   a. larger than the median.

   b. smaller than the median.

   c. equal to the median.

   d. none of the above.

2. The normal distribution curve is symmetric around which point of the distribution?

   a. mean

   b. median

   c. mode

   d. all of the above

Answers: 1. b, 2. d

MEASURES OF VARIABILITY

Variability describes the extent to which observed values from a variable are dispersed, spread out, or scattered. Basically, variability measures tell us how different individual values are from one another in a sample or a population. As in the case of central tendency, there are three common **variability measures**: (1) range, (2) variance, and (3) standard deviation. These measures of variability involve calculating differences that require an interval or ratio scale of measurement.

RANGE

Range is defined as the difference between the maximal value and the minimal value in observed values of a variable. As stated in the definition, range only takes the two most extreme values in its calculation, so it is highly sensitive to the impact of outliers. It is a simple formula but not particularly useful in describing differences between individual values other than the maximum and minimum. Let's use an example to illustrate this point.

$$Range = Maximal\ value - minimal\ value$$

EXAMPLE 3.9

In a family of five, the ages of these five family members are 17, 22, 26, 48, and 57.

What is the range of this population?

The reason these five numbers are referred to as a population is that there are five members in this family and every member's age is listed in the problem statement. The range is calculated by the formula range = maximal value − minimal value = 57 − 17 = 40.

The range provides a rough but unreliable measure of variability. Statisticians were not satisfied with the results. Therefore, better ways of measuring variation were invented to ensure that two considerations are met: (1) the difference is calculated between each individual value and the mean and (2) every value is considered in the calculation. Variance and standard deviation are developed to provide more precise measures of variability. The formulas for calculating variance and standard deviation are different in a population versus in a sample, so they are discussed in separate subsections.

VARIANCE AND STANDARD DEVIATION FOR A POPULATION

Deviation from the mean is defined as $X - \mu$. Deviation from the mean can be calculated for every value. Then we can sum up all the deviations. Unfortunately, that's where the difficulty occurs. Let's illustrate this difficulty with an example.

EXAMPLE 3.10

In a family of five, calculate the deviation from mean age for all family members: 17, 22, 26, 48, and 57. What is the sum of deviations?

The example lists every member's age, so it is a population. Let's put the calculation process in Table 3.8a. $\mu = \sum X/N = 170/5 = 34$. Deviation from mean is $(X - \mu)$, which is calculated for every value as shown in the column. The sum of deviations is added up at the bottom of the column.

TABLE 3.8a   Ages of Family Members and Deviation From Mean

X(AGE)	X − μ
17	−17
22	−12
26	−8
48	14
57	23
$\sum X = 170$	$\sum(X - \mu) = 0$

The sum of all deviations adds up to 0. This is not a special case. It is a mathematical certainty for every variable. Let's prove this point by breaking up $\sum(X - \mu)$ into $(X_1 - \mu) + (X_2 - \mu) + (X_3 - \mu) + \cdots + (X_N - \mu)$. Let's rearrange this process and present it vertically.

$$(X_1 \quad - \mu)$$
$$(X_2 \quad - \mu)$$
$$(X_3 \quad - \mu)$$
$$\cdots$$
$$+) \quad (X_N \quad - \mu)$$
$$\overline{}$$
$$\sum X - N\mu = \sum X - \sum X = 0$$

The terms to the left of the minus sign become $X_1 + X_2 + X_3 + \cdots + X_N = \sum X$, and the terms to the right of the minus sign become μ times N, that is $N\mu$. Based on the mean formula $\mu = \sum X / N$, therefore, multiply N on both sides of the equation and you get $N\mu = \sum X$. As the last step of the calculation, you get $\sum X - \sum X = 0$.

Now, it is mathematically proven that in every situation the sum of deviations is always 0. This is what I referred to as a difficulty earlier in the subsection. Any mathematical operation that always produces an answer of 0 is not useful in providing any information. The positive deviations completely cancel out the negative deviations. So the sum of deviations concept needs to be adjusted before it can provide useful information. The useful information is the magnitude of deviations. To retain the magnitude but avoid positive deviations perfectly canceling out negative deviations, the negative signs need to be modified. To get rid of negative signs, squaring is a convenient and universal mathematical operation. Therefore, the sum of squared deviations was invented. In short, it is called **Sum of Squares** = **$SS = \sum(X - \mu)^2$**. The mean squared deviation is obtained by dividing the sum of squared deviations by the population size. The mean squared deviation is also called the variance $= \sigma^2 = SS/N$. Once the differences have been squared, they are no longer at the same scale as the original data. Therefore, a square root operation is used to reverse it to the original scale, and it is labeled as the standard deviation. The formula for standard deviation is $\sigma = \sqrt{\text{variance}} = \sqrt{SS/N}$. The standard deviation is the most commonly used measure of variability in statistics.

EXAMPLE 3.11.

Let's continue to use the example of family members' ages in Table 3.8a. What are the variance and standard deviation of the ages?

Based on the formula for $SS = \sum(X - \mu)^2$, the order of operations dictates that the column of $(X - \mu)$ be constructed first; then the column for $(X - \mu)^2$ needs to be created as the squared deviation from mean. Then the sum adds up at the end of the column. A step-by-step calculation process is demonstrated in Table 3.8b.

TABLE 3.8b Family Members' Ages, Deviations, and Squared Deviations

X (AGE)	$X - \mu$	$(X - \mu)^2$
17	−17	289
22	−12	144
26	−8	64
48	14	196
57	23	529
$\sum X = 170$	$\sum(X - \mu) = 0$	$\sum(X - \mu)^2 = 1{,}222$

Once the table is completed, all the numbers needed for the variance and standard deviation are available.

$$\text{Variance} = \sigma^2 = \frac{SS}{N} = \frac{\sum(X - \mu)^2}{N} = \frac{1222}{5} = 244.4$$

$$\text{Standard deviation} = \sigma = \sqrt{\text{variance}} = \sqrt{244.4} = 15.6$$

Based on the round-off rule, the final values for the variability measures are reported at one more decimal place than in the original data. It is important to note that the round-off rule applies to the final answer, not the intermediate numbers in the calculation process; otherwise, rounding errors cumulate throughout the calculation steps. The unit for variance is the square of the unit for the original variable, and the unit for range and standard deviation is the same as the original variable. In the case of ages of family members, the unit for variance is year², and the unit for range and standard deviation is year. The formula for population variance and standard deviation is useful in theory and in explaining the concepts. But, in reality, they are rarely used. This is because the population mean, μ, is usually unknown, and it is almost impossible to obtain measures from every member in the population when the population size is large.

VARIANCE AND STANDARD DEVIATION FOR A SAMPLE

In most cases, not every member in the population is ready or willing to provide information for research purposes. Researchers are glad to use sample statistics to make inferences about the population parameters such as population mean, μ, variance, σ^2, and standard deviation, σ.

Sample mean, $\bar{X}$, is an unbiased estimate of the population mean, μ, and sample variance is also an unbiased estimate of the population variance. The calculation of sample variance follows the same basic principles used in calculating population variance except for a few changes in notation that signify the difference between population parameters and sample statistics. Sample mean is $\bar{X}$, and sample size is n. Because the population mean, μ, is unknown, you must calculate the sample mean, $\bar{X}$, to estimate μ. Continue to calculate the deviation from the mean $(X - \bar{X})$ for every individual X value, and then square the deviation, $(X - \bar{X})^2$, to get rid of the negative signs. Then add up the squared deviations at the end to form the sum of squares, $SS = \sum(X - \bar{X})^2$. Up to this point, the calculations are identical both for a population and for a sample.

$$\bar{X} = \frac{\sum X}{n}$$

$$SS = \sum(X - \bar{X})^2$$

Now, you have to learn the most important distinction between the population variance formula and the sample variance formula. It is called the degrees of freedom, which is calculated as $df = (n - 1)$ for sample variance. The degrees of freedom of a statistical procedure is defined as the number of values involved in the calculation that can be free to vary in the sample. The degrees of freedom are usually determined by these two factors: (1) the sample size (n) and (2) the number of parameters (k) that need to be estimated. When you have to estimate one parameter, you lose one degree of freedom. Therefore, the general rule for determining the degrees of freedom is $(n - k)$. In other words, in the process of calculating variance, sample mean, $\bar{X}$, is used to estimate the population mean. This restricts the calculation of the variance and, accordingly, one degree of freedom is lost. Hence, the degrees of freedom for sample variance are $(n - 1)$. Let's use an example to explain the degrees of freedom concept.

EXAMPLE 3.12

In a sample of four boys, the average height is 69 inches. The heights of three boys are measured at 67, 71, and 72 inches (Table 3.9). What is the fourth boy's height?

TABLE 3.9   Height Measures of a Sample of Four Boys

X (HEIGHT)
67
71
72
$X_4 = ?$
$\bar{X} = 69$

This question illustrates the point that when the sample mean is known, only $(n - 1)$ values can vary freely. Once the sample mean and height measures of the three boys are given, the fourth boy's height is determined. It can no longer freely assume any other value.

Apply the formula $\bar{X} = \dfrac{\Sigma X}{N}$ and plug in the numbers into the formula $69 = \dfrac{\Sigma X}{4}$, therefore, $\Sigma X = 276$.

$$X_1 + X_2 + X_3 + X_4 = 276$$

$$67 + 71 + 72 + X_4 = 276$$

$$210 + X_4 = 276$$

$$X_4 = 276 - 210$$

$$X_4 = 66$$

This example is meant to illustrate that estimating the population mean by calculating the sample mean results in the loss of one degree of freedom. Therefore, only $(n - 1)$ values in the sample can vary freely. Such a restriction applies when calculating a sample variance and standard deviation.

The sample variance is the mean squared deviations, which is the sum of squared deviations divided by the degrees of freedom, $s^2 = \sum \dfrac{(X - \overline{X})^2}{df} = \dfrac{SS}{df} = \dfrac{SS}{(n-1)}$, and the sample standard deviation, s, is the square root of the sample variance $s = \sqrt{\dfrac{SS}{df}} = \sqrt{\dfrac{SS}{(n-1)}}$.

EXAMPLE 3.13

Researchers conducted a pet survey. In a random sample of 40 households, they asked about the number of pets in the house, and the answers are summarized in Table 3.10a. What are the central tendency measures and variability measures for the number of pets owned by this sample of 40 households?

The central tendency measures are mode, median, and mean. The measures of variability are range, variance, and standard deviation.

Mode is the value with the highest frequency; mode = 1.

Median is the midpoint of the data. There are two midpoints in a sample $n = 40$. The two midpoints are $n/2 = 40/2 = 20$th location and the next, 21st loca-

TABLE 3.10a   Number of Pets in a Household

X (NUMBER OF PETS)	f (FREQUENCY)
0	7
1	14
2	13
3	4
4	2
Total	40

tion. The value in the 20th position is 1, and the value in the 21st position is also 1. The average value of these two midpoints is median = 1.

The formula for the mean is $\overline{X} = \dfrac{\sum X}{n}$. In a frequency table, when values occur different numbers of times, the formula needs to be modified to $\overline{X} = \dfrac{\sum fX}{n}$. According to the modified mean formula, the first step is to create the multiplication of fX in the table. Table 3.10a evolves to Table 3.10b. Once the column fX is created, the sum of fX is calculated at the end of the column $\sum fX = 60$.

(Continued)

(Continued)

TABLE 3.10b Number of Pets in a Household With *fX* Column

X (NUMBER OF PETS)	f (FREQUENCY)	fX
0	7	0
1	14	14
2	13	26
3	4	12
4	2	8
Total	40	60

Mean $\bar{X} = \dfrac{\sum fX}{n} = \dfrac{60}{40} = 1.5$. The mean number of pets for each household in this sample is 1.5. Continue on to the measures of variability.

$$\text{Range} = \text{Maximal value} - \text{minimal value} = 4 - 0 = 4$$

You Must Remember This

In Chapter 2, we mentioned the impact of frequency in mathematical operations when using frequency tables by modifying $\sum X$ to $\sum fX$. In Chapter 3, you have learned more mathematical formulas such as mean, SS, variance, and standard deviation. You need to consistently apply the same principle to consider the impact of frequency by multiplying the f with the original formula before you sum up the results, for example, modifying $SS = \sum (X - \bar{X})^2$ to $SS = \sum f(X - \bar{X})^2$.

Both variance and standard deviation start with $SS = \sum (X - \bar{X})^2$. In frequency tables, individual values occur different numbers of times, so the impact of frequency needs to be incorporated. Therefore, the original SS formula, $\sum (X - \bar{X})^2$, is modified to $SS = \sum f(X - \bar{X})^2$. Based on the order of operations in the SS formula, the first step is to create column $(X - \bar{X})$, and the second is to square it to create column $(X - \bar{X})^2$. Remember to incorporate the impact of frequency by creating $f(X - \bar{X})^2$. These computations are shown in Table 3.10c.

At the end of the $f(X - \bar{X})^2$, column the SS adds to $\sum f(X - \bar{X})^2 = 44$.

$$\text{Sample variance } s^2 = \frac{SS}{df} = \frac{SS}{(n-1)} = \frac{44}{39} = 1.1$$

$$\text{Sample standard deviation } s = \sqrt{\text{variance}} = \sqrt{1.1} = 1.0$$

TABLE 3.10c Number of Pets in a Household With $(X - \bar{X}), (X - \bar{X})^2$, and $f(X - \bar{X})^2$ Columns

X (NUMBER OF PETS)	f (FREQUENCY)	$(X - \bar{X})$	$(X - \bar{X})^2$	$f(X - \bar{X})^2$
0	7	$(0 - 1.5) = -1.5$	2.25	15.75
1	14	$(1 - 1.5) = -0.5$	0.25	3.5
2	13	$(2 - 1.5) = 0.5$	0.25	3.25
3	4	$(3 - 1.5) = 1.5$	2.25	9
4	2	$(4 - 1.5) = 2.5$	6.25	12.5
Total	40			44

The result shows that some households have no pets while others may have four pets. The average number of pets per house is 1.5, and the standard deviation is 1.0. Although we know that it is impossible to have 1.5 pets, the mean tells us that on average people have between 1 and 2 pets. Some people have more and others have fewer pets.

The interpretation of mean is intuitive; however, the interpretation of variance and standard deviation requires some effort. It might be helpful to interpret variance and standard deviation when comparing two groups of individuals side by side as shown in the next example.

EXAMPLE 3.14

Assume that a homework assignment is worth 10 points. The instructor separates the male students' homework from the female students' homework grades. The grades are reported in two separate tables. Use the information in Tables 3.11a and 3.12a to compare males' versus females' central tendency measures and variability measures.

Central tendency: mode, median, and mean

The mode of male students' homework grades is 5.

The mode of female students' homework grades is 5.

The median is the average of the two values in the 4th and 5th locations for male students. Both values are 5. Therefore, the median of male students' homework grades is 5.

(Continued)

(Continued)

TABLE 3.11a   Male Students'
              Homework Grades

X (HOMEWORK GRADES)	f
1	2
5	4
9	2

TABLE 3.12a   Female Students'
              Homework Grades

X (HOMEWORK GRADES)	f
3	3
4	4
5	5
6	4
7	3

The median is the value in 19/2 = 9.5 round up to the 10th location. The value is 5. Therefore, the median of female students' homework grades is 5.

The mean formula $\bar{X} = \dfrac{\sum X}{n}$ needs to be modified to $\bar{X} = \dfrac{\sum fX}{n}$ when using frequency tables. According to the modified mean formula, fX needs to be created in the frequency table as shown in Table 3.11b.

TABLE 3.11b   Male Students'
              Homework Grades
              With fX Column

X (HOMEWORK GRADES)	f	fX
1	2	2
5	4	20
9	2	18
Total	8	40

TABLE 3.12b   Female Students'
              Homework Grades
              With fX Column

X (HOMEWORK GRADES)	f	fX
3	3	9
4	4	16
5	5	25
6	4	24
7	3	21
Total	19	95

$$\bar{X} = \frac{\sum fX}{n} = \frac{40}{8} = 5$$

The mean of male students' homework grades is 5.

Apply the same modified mean formula to female students' grades and create the fX column as shown in Table 3.12b.

$$\bar{X} = \frac{\sum fX}{n} = \frac{95}{19} = 5$$

The mean of female students' homework grades is 5.

Both male and female students have identical mode, median, and mean of the homework grades.

Next, let's calculate the variability measures: range, variance, and standard deviation.

The range for male students' homework grades is $9 - 1 = 8$.

The range for female students' homework grades is $7 - 3 = 4$.

TABLE 3.11c Male Students' Homework Grades With $(X - \bar{X}), (X - \bar{X})^2$, and $f(X - \bar{X})^2$ Columns

X (HOMEWORK GRADES)	f	$(X - \bar{X})$	$(X - \bar{X})^2$	$f(X - \bar{X})^2$
1	2	−4	16	32
5	4	0	0	0
9	2	4	16	32
Total	8			64

The calculation process for variance and standard deviation of male students' homework grades is shown in Table 3.11c with $SS = \sum(X - \bar{X})^2$ modified to $SS = \sum f(X - \bar{X})^2$.

$$SS = \sum f(X - \bar{X})^2 = 64$$

$$\text{Variance} = s^2 = \frac{SS}{df} = \frac{64}{(8 - 1)} = 9.1$$

$$\text{Standard deviation} = s = \sqrt{\text{variance}} = \sqrt{9.1} = 3.0$$

The calculation process for variance and standard deviation of female students' homework grades is shown in Table 3.12c with $SS = \sum(X - \bar{X})^2$ modified to $SS = \sum f(X - \bar{X})^2$.

$$SS = \sum(X - \bar{X})^2 = 32$$

$$\text{Variance} = s^2 = \frac{SS}{df} = \frac{32}{(19 - 1)} = 1.8$$

$$\text{Standard deviation} = s = \sqrt{\text{variance}} = \sqrt{1.8} = 1.3$$

(Continued)

(Continued)

TABLE 3.12c   Female Students' Homework Grades With $(X - \bar{X}), (X - \bar{X})^2$, and $f(X - \bar{X})^2$ Columns

X (HOMEWORK GRADES)	f	$(X - \bar{X})$	$(X - \bar{X})^2$	$f(X - \bar{X})^2$
3	3	−2	4	12
4	4	−1	1	4
5	5	0	0	0
6	4	1	1	4
7	3	2	4	12
Total	19			32

The purpose of measuring central tendency is to use one single number to represent the center of the distribution. Central tendency does not provide any information on how individual values might differ. In this example with fictional data, it was designed to demonstrate that two distributions can be very different but all three measures of central tendency can be identical. The distribution of male students' homework grades is very different than that of the female students', but their mode, median, and mean are identical. The differences in distribution are presented in the variability measures. Male students have a range of 8 and female students have a range of 4. Male students have a variance of 9.1 and a standard deviation of 3.0. Female students have a variance of 1.8 and a standard deviation of 1.3. Male students' variance and standard deviation are much larger than female students'. Male students have more extreme scores on both ends and female students tend to have scores near the middle of the distribution. Variance and standard deviation reflect the magnitude of the spread between individual values in the distribution.

As a reminder, when you encounter variance or standard deviation questions, the columns added in the frequency table are created based on the formula $SS = \sum f(X - \bar{X})^2$. Following the order of operations, the first step is to perform the operation inside the parentheses, $(X - \bar{X})$, the second is to perform the exponentiation $(X - \bar{X})^2$, the third is to consider the impact of frequency by modifying $SS = \sum (X - \bar{X})^2$ to $SS = \sum f(X - \bar{X})^2$, and the final step is to add up all the values in the last column to get SS. The added columns document the step-by-step calculation process to reach the final answer.

To make sure all the symbols are clearly stated in measures of variability, here is a summary table (Table 3.13) for all the formulas in either populations or samples.

TABLE 3.13 Summary Table for Statistical Formulas in Populations or Samples

	POPULATION	SAMPLE
Mean (original)	$\mu = \dfrac{\Sigma X}{N}$	$\bar{X} = \dfrac{\Sigma X}{n}$
Mean modified in frequency tables	$\mu = \dfrac{\Sigma fX}{N}$	$\bar{X} = \dfrac{\Sigma fX}{n}$
Sum of deviation	$\Sigma(X - \mu) = 0$	$\Sigma(X - \bar{X}) = 0$
SS (original)	$SS = \Sigma(X - \mu)^2$	$SS = \Sigma(X - \bar{X})^2$
SS modified in frequency tables	$SS = \Sigma f(X - \mu)^2$	$SS = \Sigma f(X - \bar{X})^2$
Variance	$\sigma^2 = \dfrac{SS}{N}$	$s^2 = \dfrac{SS}{(n-1)}$
Standard deviation	$\sigma = \sqrt{\dfrac{SS}{N}}$	$s = \sqrt{\dfrac{SS}{(n-1)}}$

Pop Quiz

1. In the process of calculating the sample variance, the sample mean is used to estimate the population mean. This puts one restriction on the number of values in the sample that can vary freely. Therefore, the degrees of freedom for calculating the sample variance are

   a. n.
   b. $(n - 1)$.
   c. $(n - 2)$.
   d. $(n - 3)$.

Answer: b

BOXPLOT: FIVE-NUMBER SUMMARY

Both central tendency and variation measures reflect well-defined quantitative attributes of variables. A **boxplot** is a useful graphic tool that incorporates some central tendency and some variation measures to report five important quantitative attributes: (1) minimum,

(2) maximum, (3) *first quartile* (Q_1), (4) median, and (5) *third quartile* (Q_3). The graph displays a line starting at the minimum and ending at the maximum (whiskers), and a box somewhere in between the two extreme values bordering on Q_1 and Q_3 with median marked inside the box. A boxplot is also called a box and whisker plot. A boxplot is useful in presenting a majority of data points.

Quartiles are measures of locations. They are labeled as Q_1, Q_2, and Q_3, which divide the data evenly into four groups containing 25% of the data points in each group. Q_2 is the same as the median, which is the midpoint of sorted values. Q_1 is the 25th percentile of the variable, which separates the lowest 25% of sorted values from the rest. Q_3 is the 75th percentile of the variable, which separates the lowest 75% of sorted values from the rest. The difference between Q_3 and Q_1 is labeled as interquartile range $= Q_3 - Q_1$. The interquartile range contains the middle 50% of the data points, which is also the length of the box in the boxplot.

The process of identifying the values for Q_1 and Q_3 is similar to the procedure we used to identify the median. The same procedure can be applied to find a data value for any percentile.

1. Sort the observed values from the lowest to the highest.

2. Identify the location, L, of the kth percentile in the sorted data with sample size n. Calculate $L = \dfrac{k}{100}n$. If the calculated L does not turn out to be a whole number, round it up to the next integer. Identify the value in that location.

3. If L is a whole number, identify the values in the location L, and the next location $L + 1$. Then average the two values to produce the data value for the kth percentile.

4. In addition to identifying the location of a sorted variable for the percentile, you may also use the cumulative relative frequency. Look for the first value with cumulative relative frequency over the particular percentile, that is, .25 for Q_1 and .75 for Q_3.

EXAMPLE 3.15

A survey is conducted, using a Likert scale as discussed in Chapter 1, to ask people to rate the quality of food served in the cafeteria on campus. There are 63 students randomly selected to answer this survey. Response Option 1 stands for *very low quality*, and 5 stands for *very high quality*. The answers are summarized in Table 3.14. Draw a boxplot to include the minimum, Q_1, the median, Q_3 and the maximum of this variable.

The minimal value is 1.

The maximal value is 5.

Q_1 is the 25th percentile: $L = \dfrac{k}{100} n = \dfrac{25}{100} 63 = 15.75,$ which rounds up to 16. The value for the 16th position in the sorted data is 2; therefore, $Q_1 = 2$.

Q_2 (median) is the 50th percentile: $L = \dfrac{k}{100} n = \dfrac{50}{100} 63 = 31.5,$ which rounds up to 32. The value for the 32nd position is 3, therefore, median = 3.

Q_3 is the 75th percentile: $L = \dfrac{k}{100} n = \dfrac{75}{100} 63 = 47.25,$ which rounds to 48. The value for the 48th position is 4, $Q_3 = 4$.

Based on the minimum, maximum, $Q_1, Q_2,$ and $Q_3,$ the boxplot is shown in Figure 3.4.

TABLE 3.14 Quality Ratings of Food in the Cafeteria

X	f
1	7
2	15
3	23
4	13
5	5

FIGURE 3.4   Boxplot for Food Quality Ratings

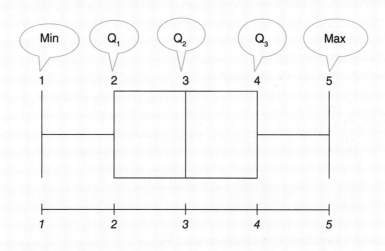

Based on the results of the boxplot, the ratings of the quality of food served in the cafeteria cover the entire range of response options; 50% think it is above average, and 50% think it is below average. Twenty-five percent of students gave the food quality a 4 or better rating and 25% of students gave it a 2 or lower rating. The outcome reflects that the food quality in the cafeteria is okay, but it certainly has room for improvement.

1. Which one of the following measures always provides the range of the middle 50% of the data values?

   a. Range

   b. Interquartile range

   c. Half range

   d. The third quartile

EXERCISE PROBLEMS

1. In a sample of 21 students, homework grades are presented in Table 3.15.

   a. What are the mode, median, and mean of this sample?

   b. What are the range, variance, and standard deviation of this sample?

TABLE 3.15   Homework Grades

X (HOMEWORK)	f (FREQUENCY)
0	2
7	3
8	4
9	5
10	7

2. Based on a biannual alumni survey of a master's program in Industrial and Organizational Psychology at a Midwest urban university, a sample of 42 alumni completed the survey. Their annual salary amounts are summarized in Table 3.16. What are the mode, median, and mean of this sample?

TABLE 3.16   Salary of Industrial and Organizational Psychology Alumni

X (SALARY IN DOLLARS)	f (FREQUENCY)
30,000-49,999	5
50,000-69,999	21
70,000-89,999	10
90,000-109,999	3
110,000-129,999	2
130,000-159,999	1
Total	**42**

3. Rollover accounts for 33% of all passenger vehicle fatalities. Taller and narrower vehicles are more likely to roll over. Rollover ratings are from 1 to 5 stars. The higher the number of stars, the less likely is the SUV (sports utility vehicle) to roll over. The results of rollover ratings conducted by the National Highway Traffic Safety Administration on a sample of 37 used SUVs are presented in Table 3.17a.

a. What are the mode, median, and mean of this sample?

b. What are the range, variance, and standard deviation of this sample?

Solutions With EXCEL
Step-by-Step Instructions

1.a. The mode is the value with the highest frequency, mode = 10.

The median is the midpoint of a sorted variable. When $n = 21$, there is one midpoint. Its position is $(n)/2 = (21)/2 = 10.5$ rounded up to 11. The value for the 11th position is 9; thus, median = 9.

In a frequency table, the mean formula is modified to $\bar{X} = \dfrac{\Sigma fX}{\Sigma f} = \dfrac{\Sigma fx}{n}$. Therefore, a column of fX needs to be created in the frequency table. You may choose to do the frequency table and the calculation process in EXCEL. Enter the homework grades in Column A and the frequency in Column B. You need to calculate the multiplication of the frequency (f) times the grade, X, by moving the cursor to Column C, Row 2 (**C2**) and typing =**A2*B2** for the multiplication. All formulas start with "=," **A2** is the first value of X, and **B2** is the corresponding frequency. Then hit **enter**. Notice **C2** shows 0, which is the result of **A2** × **B2** = $0 \times 2 = 0$ as shown in Figure 3.5.

Then move the cursor to the lower right corner of **C2** until + shows up, left click and hold the mouse and drag it to **C6**, and then release the mouse. You will see the rest of the multiplication operations of fX automatically show up in **C3** to **C6**. Now you need to sum up all the multiplication operations from **C2** to **C6**. Move the cursor to **C7** and type =**SUM(C2:C6)**. Then hit **enter**. The answer for the total homework grades is $\Sigma fX = 168$. In **C8**, type in =**C7/B7** to calculate mean $\bar{X} = \dfrac{\Sigma fX}{n} = \dfrac{168}{21} = 8$. The mean of the homework grades is 8 as shown in Figure 3.6.

TABLE 3.17a National Highway Traffic Safety Administration Rollover Ratings on SUVs

X (NUMBER OF STARS)	f (FREQUENCY)
1	2
2	5
3	14
4	16
5	0

FIGURE 3.5 Programming fX in EXCEL

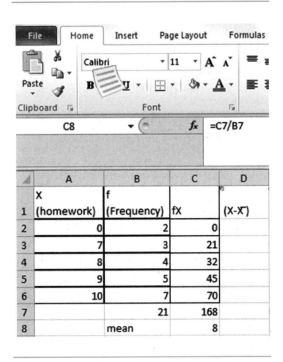

FIGURE 3.6　Programming ΣfX and $\bar{X}$ in EXCEL

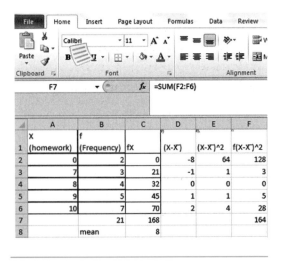

FIGURE 3.7　Programming $SS = \Sigma f(X - \bar{X})^2$ in EXCEL

1.b.　The range is the maximal value – the minimal value = 10 – 0 = 10.0.

The sample $SS = \Sigma(X - \bar{X})^2$ needs to be modified to $SS = \Sigma f(X - \bar{X})^2$ in a frequency table. Based on the order of operations, $(X - \bar{X})$, $(X - \bar{X})^2$, and $f(X - \bar{X})^2$ columns need to be created. In **D1**, label the column as $(X - \bar{X})$. In **D2**, type =A2-C$8, which shows the operation of first $(X - \bar{X})$. The $ in the EXCEL program allows the program to fix the value $(\bar{X})$ in **C8** for the subsequent operations. Therefore, it is possible to copy the operation to produce the rest of $(X - \bar{X})$. Then move the cursor to the lower right corner of **D2** until + shows up; then left click and hold the mouse and drag it to **D6** and release the mouse. You will see the rest of $(X - \bar{X})$ automatically show up in **D3** to **D6**. In **E1**, label the column as $(X - \bar{X})^2$. In **E2**, type =D2^2, which shows the operation of first $(X - \bar{X})^2$. Then move the cursor to the lower right corner of **E2** until + shows up, left click and hold the mouse, and drag it to **E6**; then release the mouse. You will see the rest of $(X - \bar{X})^2$ automatically show up in **E3** to **E6**. In **F1**, label it as $f(X - \bar{X})^2$. In **F2**, type =B2*E2, which shows the operation of first multiplication of $f(X - \bar{X})^2$. Then move the cursor to the lower right corner of **F2** until + shows up, left click and hold the mouse, and drag it to **F6**; then release the mouse. You will see the rest of $f(X - \bar{X})^2$ automatically show up in **F3** to **F6**. In **F7**, type =sum(F2:F6) to obtain $SS = \Sigma f(X - \bar{X})^2 = 164$ as shown in Figure 3.7.

$$\text{Sample variance} = \frac{SS}{(n-1)} = \frac{164}{20} = 8.2$$

Sample standard deviation $= s = \sqrt{\text{variance}} = 2.9$

Based on the round-off rule, the values of sample variance and sample standard deviation are reported at one more decimal place than in the original data.

2. The mode is the value with the highest frequency, mode = $50,000–$69,999.

The median is the midpoint of the distribution. In a sample $n = 42$, the two midpoints are in locations $L = n/2 = 42/2$ = 21st and the next one, 22nd. The value for the 21st position is $50,000–$69,999 and the value for the 22nd position is $50,000–$69,999. The average of these two medians is still $50,000–$69,999.

The mean formula in a frequency table with equal intervals needs to be modified to $\bar{X} = \dfrac{\sum fX_{midpoint}}{n}$. Therefore, the midpoint of each interval needs to be calculated: $X_{midpoint} = $ (low-end value + high-end value)/2. Then, label **D1** as the multiplication of $fX_{midpoint}$. In **D2**, type =**B2*C2**, which shows the operation of first $fX_{midpoint}$. Then move the cursor to the lower right corner of **D2** until + shows up, left click and hold the mouse, and drag it to **D7**; then release the mouse. You will see the rest of $fX_{midpoint}$ automatically show up in **D3** to **D7**. In **D8**, type =**sum(D2:D7)** to obtain $\sum X$ by estimating $\sum fX_{midpoint} = 2939979$ as shown in Figure 3.8. Calculate the estimated $\bar{X} = \dfrac{\sum fX_{midpoint}}{n} = \dfrac{2939979}{42} = 69999.5$.

The estimated mean for alumni annual salary is $69,999.5.

3. The EXCEL procedures for National Highway Traffic Safety Administration rollover ratings are exactly the same as the first Exercise problem regarding homework grades. The step-by-step instructions for EXCEL are not repeated here. Only the answers for the additional columns are shown in Table 3.17b.

FIGURE 3.8 Programming $\bar{X} = \dfrac{\sum fX_{midpoint}}{n}$ in EXCEL

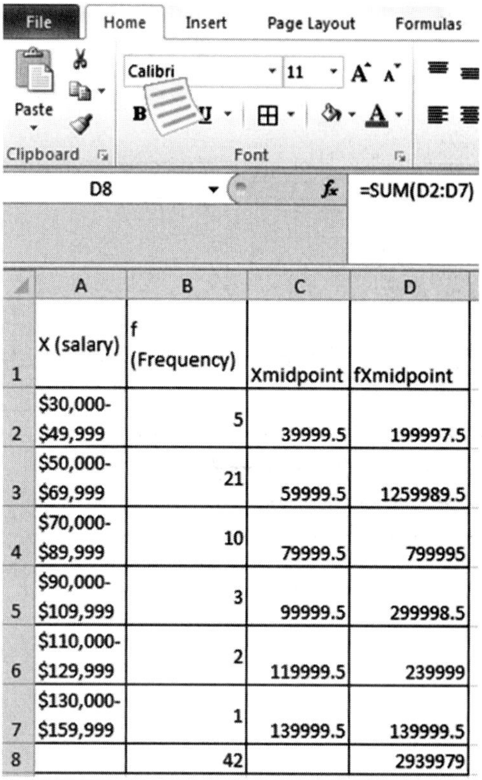

	A	B	C	D
		f		
1	X (salary)	(Frequency)	Xmidpoint	fXmidpoint
2	$30,000–$49,999	5	39999.5	199997.5
3	$50,000–$69,999	21	59999.5	1259989.5
4	$70,000–$89,999	10	79999.5	799995
5	$90,000–$109,999	3	99999.5	299998.5
6	$110,000–$129,999	2	119999.5	239999
7	$130,000–$159,999	1	139999.5	139999.5
8		42		2939979

TABLE 3.17b   Calculations for National Highway Traffic Safety Administration Rollover Ratings on SUVs

X (NUMBER OF STARS)	f (FREQUENCY)	fX	$(X - \bar{X})$	$(X - \bar{X})^2$	$f(X - \bar{X})^2$
1	2	2	−2.2	4.79	9.59
2	5	10	−1.2	1.41	7.07
3	14	42	−0.2	0.04	0.50
4	16	64	0.8	0.66	10.52
5	0	0	1.8	3.28	0.00
Total	**37**	**118**			**27.68**
	$\bar{X}$= 3.2				

a. Mode is the value with the highest frequency, mode = 4.

Median is the midpoint of a sorted variable. When $n = 37$, there is one midpoint which is in the location $L = (n)/2 = (37)/2 = 18.5$ rounded up to 19. The value for the 19th position is 3, so median = 3.

The formula for a mean in a frequency table is modified to $\bar{X} = \frac{\Sigma fX}{n} = \frac{118}{37} = 3.2$. Based on the round-off rule, the mean is reported at one decimal place more than in the original data. The original data are reported as whole numbers; therefore, the mean is reported at one digit after the decimal point.

b. The range = maximal value − minimal value = 4 − 1 = 3. The highest rollover rating can go to 5, but in this sample, no SUV received a 5 rating. The maximal value is 4 and the minimal is 1, thus the range is 3.

The *SS* formula in a frequency table is modified to $SS = \Sigma f(X - \bar{X})^2$. New columns of $(X - \bar{X})$, $(X - \bar{X})^2$, and $f(X - \bar{X})^2$ are created in Table 3.17b.

$$SS = 27.68$$

$$\text{Sample variance, } s^2 = \frac{SS}{(n-1)} = \frac{27.68}{36} = 0.8$$

$$\text{Sample standard deviation, } s = \sqrt{\text{variance}} = \sqrt{0.8} = 0.9$$

⑤SAGE edge™

Sharpen your skills with SAGE edge!

Visit edge.sagepub.com/bowen for mobile-friendly quizzes, flashcards, videos, and more!

WHAT YOU LEARNED

Two major topics were covered in Chapter 3: (1) central tendency and (2) variability measures.

Central tendency is defined as using one single value to represent the center of the data. There are three common measures: (1) mode, (2) median, and (3) mean.

1. Mode is the value with the highest frequency in the distribution.

2. Median is the midpoint of a sorted distribution. Median is not affected much by extreme outliers.

3. Mean is the arithmetical average of all values. The formula for the population mean is $\mu = \dfrac{\Sigma X}{N}$, and the formula for the sample mean is $\bar{X} = \dfrac{\Sigma X}{n}$. When using a frequency table to calculate the mean, the formula needs to be modified to $\bar{X} = \dfrac{\Sigma fX}{n}$ to incorporate the impact of different frequencies on individual values in the table. The same modification also applies to $\mu = \dfrac{\Sigma fX}{N}$. The mean is highly sensitive to the impact of outliers.

Variability measures how dispersed or spread out values are. Variability measures quantify the difference between values in the distribution. Three variability measures are (1) range, (2) variance, and (3) standard deviation.

1. Range is the maximum minus the minimum in the distribution, which is highly sensitive to extreme values.

2. Variance and standard deviation are more reliable and frequently used in further statistical analyses than range. Be careful in choosing the correct formula when calculating variance and standard deviation in a population versus in a sample.

$$\text{Population variance} = \sigma^2 = \dfrac{SS}{N}$$

$$\text{Population standard deviation} = \sigma = \sqrt{\frac{SS}{N}}$$

$$\text{Sample variance} = s^2 = \frac{SS}{df} = \frac{SS}{(n-1)}$$

$$\text{Sample standard deviation} = s = \sqrt{\frac{SS}{df}} = \sqrt{\frac{SS}{(n-1)}}$$

The concept of degrees of freedom is important when calculating sample variance and standard deviation. It will be repeatedly mentioned in other statistical analyses.

When using frequency tables to calculate variance and standard deviation, the formula $SS = \sum (X - \bar{X})^2$ needs to be modified to $SS = \sum f(X - \bar{X})^2$ to incorporate the impact of frequencies. The same modification also applies to population $SS = \sum f(X - \mu)^2$, when using frequency tables.

A boxplot is a graphic tool that effectively depicts the minimum, the maximum, Q_1, the median (Q_2), and Q_3.

KEY WORDS

Boxplot: A boxplot is a graphic tool that presents five quantitative attributes of a sample: (1) the minimum, (2) Q_1, (3) Q_2, (4) Q_3, and (5) the maximum.

Central tendency: Central tendency is defined as utilizing a single value to represent the center of a distribution. There are three commonly used measures for central tendency: (1) mean, (2) median, and (3) mode.

Cumulative relative frequency: Cumulative relative frequency is defined as the accumulation of the relative frequency for a particular value and all the relative frequencies of lower values.

Degrees of freedom: The degrees of freedom in a statistical procedure are defined as the number of values involved in the calculation that can vary freely in the sample.

Mean: The mean is defined as the arithmetic average of all values in a data distribution.

Mean squared deviation: The mean squared deviation is another term for the variance.

Median: The median is defined as the value in the middle position of a sorted variable arranged from the lowest value to the highest value.

Mode: The mode is defined as the value or category with the highest frequency in a data distribution.

Outliers: Outliers are extreme values in a distribution. These are usually far away from the rest of the data points.

Range: The range is defined as the maximum minus the minimum in a variable.

Standard deviation: Standard deviation is a commonly used measure for variability, and it is mathematically defined as $\sigma = \sqrt{\text{variance}}$ for a population or $s = \sqrt{\text{variance}}$ for a sample.

Sum of squared deviations (SS): SS is the acronym for sum of squared deviations, population $SS = \sum(X - \mu)^2$, and sample $SS = \sum(X - \bar{X})^2$. SS is an important step in calculating variance and standard deviation. It is also called sum of squares.

Variability: Variability describes the extent to which observed values from a variable are dispersed, spread out, or scattered.

Variability measures: There are three commonly used measures for variability: (1) range, (2) variance, and (3) standard deviation.

Variance: Variance is a commonly used measure for variability, and it is mathematically defined as the mean squared deviation, population variance, $\sigma^2 = SS/N$, and sample variance $s^2 = SS/(n-1)$.

Weighted mean: The weighted mean is defined as calculating the mean when data values are assigned different weights, w. The formula for weighted mean is $\bar{X} = \dfrac{\sum wX}{\sum w}$.

LEARNING ASSESSMENT

Multiple Choice Questions: Choose the best answer to every question.

1. In a sample where outliers are present, the worst statistical measure to represent the central tendency is
   a. the mean.
   b. the median.
   c. the mode.
   d. all of the above.

2. In a distribution with positive skew, scores with the highest frequencies are _____.

   a. on the high end (right side) of the distribution

   b. on the low end (left side) of the distribution

   c. in the middle of the distribution

   d. represented at two distinct peaks

3. In a frequency distribution, the _____ is the score or category that has the highest frequency.

   a. mean

   b. median

   c. mode

   d. range

4. When there are 12 observations in a small sample, the median is calculated by

   a. the sixth position of an ascending sort of the data.

   b. the average value of the sixth position and the seventh position of an ascending sort of the data.

   c. the sixth position of the data as they were presented without sorting.

   d. the average value of the sixth position and the seventh position of the data as they were presented without being sorted.

5. Mean is an appropriate statistical measure for central tendency for _____ scales of measurement.

   a. nominal, ordinal, interval, and ratio

   b. ordinal, interval, and ratio

   c. both interval and ratio

   d. only ratio

6. In a sample of 45 homework grades, the highest score is 10 and the lowest score is 5. The range for this sample is

   a. 5

   b. 6

   c. 22.5

   d. 23

7. For the scores 3, 3, 5, 7, 14, and 16, what is the correct answer for $\Sigma(X - \bar{X})$?

   a. −6

   b. 0

   c. +6

   d. 160

8. The relationship between variance and standard deviation is that

   a. standard deviation is smaller than variance.

   b. standard deviation is larger than variance.

   c. standard deviation is the square root of the variance.

   d. standard deviation is equal to variance.

9. What is the *SS* for the following sample data: 10, 7, 6, 10, 6, and 15?

a. 60

b. 36

c. 100

d. −25

10. Which of the following statements is correct?

a. The degrees of freedom for sample variance are $n - 1$.

b. The degrees of freedom for population variance are $n - 1$.

c. The degrees of freedom for sample standard deviation are n.

d. *SS* means sum of standard deviations.

11. The round-off rule states that the final values for measures of variation should be reported

a. with the same decimal places as in the original data.

b. with one more decimal place than in the original data.

c. with two more decimal places than in the original data.

d. with three more decimal places than in the original data.

12. In a positively skewed distribution, the mean would be

a. larger than the median.

b. smaller than the median.

c. equal to the median.

d. none of the above.

Free Response Questions

13. In a randomly selected sample of 50 women, shoe sizes are measured and reported in Table 3.18.

a. What are the measures of central tendency for these 50 women's shoe sizes?

b. Based on the mode, median, and mean, make a comment on the shape of the distribution of women's shoe sizes.

c. What are the measures of variability for these 50 women's shoe sizes?

d. Draw a boxplot of these 50 women's shoe sizes.

TABLE 3.18 Women's Shoe Sizes

X (SHOE SIZE)	f (FREQUENCY)
5	2
6	5
7	14
8	16
9	7
10	5
11	1

14. If you think the drive-through service at fast-food restaurants is getting slower, you are not alone. A market research firm found fast-food drive-through time is slower this year compared with last year. Here is a sample of 55 randomly selected

customers and their drive-through time as shown in Table 3.19.

TABLE 3.19 Fast-Food Drive-Through Time

X (SECONDS)	f (FREQUENCY)
61–90	2
91–120	6
121–150	20
151–180	17
181–210	7
211–240	3

a. What are the measures of central tendency for these drive-through times?

b. Based on the mode, median, and mean, make a comment on the shape of the distribution of drive-through time.

Standard Z Scores

After reading and studying this chapter, you should be able to do the following:

- Convert raw scores to Z scores to get measures of the difference of individual values from the mean in units of standard deviation

- Identify unusual values and outliers using Z scores

- Calculate Z scores from populations or samples

- Explain how converting raw scores to Z scores does not change the shape of the distribution

- Apply the empirical rule to connect Z scores with probabilities in special cases

WHAT YOU KNOW AND WHAT IS NEW

You learned measures of central tendency and measures of variability in Chapter 3. Central tendency measures reflect the center of the distribution, and variability measures demonstrate the spread of individual values. Under the normal distribution, the mean is the most commonly used measure for central tendency, and the standard deviation is the most commonly used measure of variability. In the presence of outliers, however, the mean is not a suitable measure of central tendency. Moreover, you learned different formulas for population parameters versus sample statistics. When calculating the sample variance and standard deviation, the degrees of freedom are $df = n - 1$.

In Chapter 4, you will learn to use the mean and standard deviation together to create *Z scores*. Z scores are standard scores that describe the differences of individual values from the mean in units of standard deviation. Two main attributes of Z scores are direction and magnitude. Positive Z scores indicate that the values are above the mean, and negative Z scores indicate that the values are below the mean. The magnitude of a Z score is reflected by the absolute value of the Z score, which determines the distance between the value and the mean. The higher the absolute value, the longer is the distance between the value and the mean. When $Z = 1$, it means that the value is 1 standard deviation above the mean. When $Z = -0.5$, it means that the value is 0.5 standard deviations below the mean. Z scores provide markers to identify the location of every value in the distribution. There are different formulas for population Z scores and sample Z scores, and you will be introduced to those formulas in this chapter.

Standard Z Scores

When you were still in high school, intending to apply to college, you may have taken some standardized tests such as the SAT or the ACT. Did you find the score reports confusing? If you did, you are not alone. Let's take a moment to discuss the makeup of the SAT scores. Once you understand one standardized test, the same principle applies to other standardized tests. SAT scores are reported on a scale from 200 to 800 (with additional subscores we won't go into). The scaled SAT scores are theoretically designed to have a mean of 500 and a standard deviation of 100. However, the mean and standard deviation of the scaled scores in each section do not always turn out to be 500 and 100, respectively, as shown in Table 4.1. Such numbers also vary from year to year. The College Board recorded and analyzed every test taker's score. There were 1,672,395 recorded SAT scores in 2014.

Assume that you received the score report in 2014 with Critical Reading = 640, Math = 590, and Writing = 610 on the SAT. Which section was your strongest compared with other students who took the same SAT exam? The answer is probably not as simple as directly

TABLE 4.1   2014 College-Bound Seniors' Mean and Standard Deviation of Each SAT Section Score

	CRITICAL READING	MATHEMATICS	WRITING
N	1,672,395	1,672,395	1,672,395
Mean	497	513	487
Standard deviation	115	120	115

SOURCE: The College Board (2014). Data retrieved from https://secure-media.collegeboard.org/digitalServices/pdf/sat/sat-percentile-ranks-crit-reading-math-writing-2014.pdf

comparing 640, 590, and 610 and picking the largest value. Don't worry! I am here to help. The answer to this question will be provided in the first example of this chapter after discussing the concept of Z scores.

When you try to compare values from different variables, the original values are not helpful in determining which one is your strongest, even when all three scores are reported on the same scale (ranging from 200 to 800). All subsection scores have their own distributions, as shown in Table 4.1. Their means and standard deviations are different.

Here is another scenario. Assume that you also took the ACT in 2014 and received 28 in English, 29 in Math, 30 in Reading, 29 in Science, and an ACT composite score of 29. According to the ACT Profile Report—National, the mean and standard deviation of the ACT subsection and composite score varied, as shown in Table 4.2.

You know that most colleges only require either ACT or SAT scores. You were probably wondering which set of the test scores has a better chance of getting you accepted in a selective university. The SAT scores were reported between 200 and 800, and the ACT scores were reported between 1 and 36. Clearly, the worst reported SAT scores are higher than the perfect ACT scores. The answer to which test score has a better chance of getting you accepted in a selective university would not be simply picking the higher reported scores between ACT and SAT. In applying to colleges, you especially need to figure out how your performance compared with that of other students who took the exams at the same time. Z scores are the perfect tool to provide answers in such a situation. I bet that you wish you had learned Z scores in high school!

Z scores are standard scores that describe the differences of individual values from the mean in units of standard deviation. As long as the mean and standard deviation are known in a distribution, all original values (also known as raw scores) of a variable can be converted into Z scores. Z scores can be compared on the same yardstick. You may think of the yardstick marked by Z scores as a universal yardstick. All Z scores are reported only as the number of

TABLE 4.2 2014 College-Bound Seniors' Mean and Standard Deviation of Each ACT Section Score and Composite Score

	ENGLISH	MATH	READING	SCIENCE	COMPOSITE
N	1,845,787	1,845,787	1,845,787	1,845,787	1,845,787
Mean	20.3	20.9	21.3	20.8	21.0
Standard deviation	6.6	5.3	6.3	5.5	5.4

SOURCE: The ACT (2014). Data retrieved from http://www.act.org/newsroom/data/2014/pdf/profile/National2014.pdf

standard deviations above or below the mean, without the specific measurement unit. Z scores provide a rule of thumb to identify unusual scores and extreme scores (i.e., outliers). The difference between unusual values and extreme values is that there are about 5% of values considered to be unusual in a distribution but they are known to exist. But extreme values (i.e., outliers) do not always exist in a distribution. If they do exist, less than 1% of the values in a distribution are considered outliers. Outliers have undue influence on the outcomes of statistical analysis. They need to be identified and treated with caution. The rule of thumb is that if a value X converts to a Z score and is more than 2 standard deviations from the mean, $|Z| > 2$, then X is an unusual value. The rule of thumb to identify outliers is stricter. If a value X converts to a Z score and is more than 3 standard deviations from the mean, $|Z| > 3$, then X is an outlier. The Z values between −2 and +2 are ordinary values, as shown in Figure 4.1.

Standard Z scores have three important attributes:

1. The sign + or − describes the score in relation to the mean. All positive Z scores are above the mean, and all negative Z scores are below the mean.

2. The magnitude of the Z score describes the distance between the value and the mean in number of standard deviation units.

3. When transforming all raw scores to Z scores, you are conducting a mathematical operation on the raw values. This mathematical operation does not change the shape of the distribution. The shape of the distribution remains the same as the original distribution. Z scores have mean = 0, standard deviation = 1, and variance = 1.

Z SCORES FOR A POPULATION

The Z-score formula for a population is $Z = \dfrac{(X-\mu)}{\sigma}$, where X is the value of the variable, μ the population mean, and σ the population standard deviation. We get the numerator of the Z formula by calculating the distance between X and μ by doing a simple subtraction $(X - \mu)$.

FIGURE 4.1 Ordinary Values, Unusual Values, and Outliers

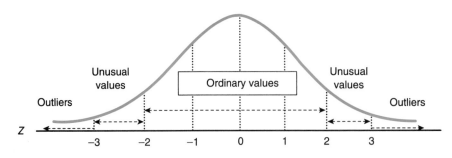

To complete the formula, you use the distance divided by σ. The result of the Z formula generates a standardized measure expressed in units of σ. You need to know the population mean and standard deviation before you can calculate Z scores. The SAT and the ACT are standardized aptitude tests used to predict how high school students will perform in colleges or universities. The testing industry keeps records of scores from millions of students who take the exam annually and routinely reports means and standard deviations in different sections and composite scores and conducts comparisons across different groups. It is feasible to obtain the population mean and standard deviation for standardized tests such as the SAT and ACT.

Z scores can be calculated to show the relative standing of the reported scores. Let me demonstrate the process of calculating Z scores with several examples.

EXAMPLE 4.1

Sarah received a SAT score report. She scored Critical Reading = 640, Math = 590, and Writing = 610 on the SAT. Which section is Sarah's strongest compared with other students who took the SAT exams? According to Table 4.1, SAT scores are normally distributed, and the population mean and standard deviation for SAT Critical Reading are $\mu = 497$, $\sigma = 115$; for SAT Math, $\mu = 513$, $\sigma = 120$; and for SAT Writing, $\mu = 487$, $\sigma = 115$.

Use of Z scores gives a solution to help figure out the relative standing of an individual score within its own distribution. Since Z scores provide a universal yardstick, we can compare individual values of different variables with different distributions.

a. SAT Critical Reading: $\mu = 497$ and $\sigma = 115$

Z score for Sarah's SAT Critical Reading: $Z = \dfrac{X - \mu}{\sigma} = \dfrac{640 - 497}{115} = \dfrac{143}{115} = 1.24$

b. SAT Math: $\mu = 513$ and $\sigma = 120$

Z score for Sarah's SAT Math: $Z = \dfrac{X - \mu}{\sigma} = \dfrac{590 - 513}{120} = \dfrac{77}{120} = 0.64$

c. SAT Writing: $\mu = 487$ and $\sigma = 115$

Z score for Sarah's SAT Writing: $Z = \dfrac{X - \mu}{\sigma} = \dfrac{610 - 487}{115} = \dfrac{123}{115} = 1.07$

(Continued)

(Continued)

Z scores show the exact location of each individual score in each distribution. All three distributions are normal. *Z* scores can place individual scores from different distributions on the same yardstick, as shown in Figure 4.2, where *Z* scores are overlaid with the population mean and standard deviation. All scales are lined up by the mean and equally spaced by the standard deviation. *Z* scores have mean = 0, which is lined up with all other population means; μ and *Z* scores have a standard deviation = 1. Therefore, in a *Z* scale, 1 standard deviation above the mean is expressed as 1, and for other scales, μ + σ; 2 standard deviations above the mean is expressed as 2, and for other scales, μ + 2σ; and 3 standard deviations above the mean is expressed as 3, and for other scales μ + 3σ. Due to the symmetry of the normal distribution curve (i.e., the left side is the mirror image of the right side), the same principle applies to the left side of the curve. That is, in a *Z* scale, 1 standard deviation below the mean is expressed as −1, and for other scales, μ − σ; 2 standard deviations below the mean is expressed as −2, and for other scales, μ − 2σ; and 3 standard deviations below the mean is expressed as −3, and for other scales, μ − 3σ, as shown in Figure 4.2.

FIGURE 4.2   *Z* Scale Overlaid With Population Parameters

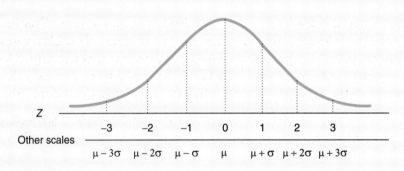

In standardized tests, higher *Z* scores mean better scores. Based on the location of the *Z* scores and the relative standing of the three *Z* scores, 1.24 > 1.07 > 0.64, Sarah's strongest section on the SAT was Critical Reading when compared with other students who took the exams at the same time. The *Z* scores overlaid with the three SAT scales are shown in Figure 4.3.

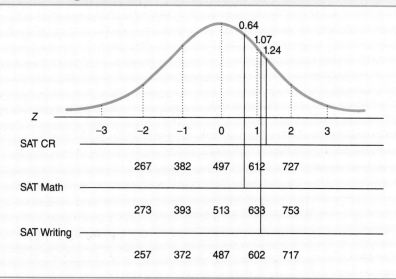

FIGURE 4.3 Locations of Three Calculated Z Scores Overlaid With the Original Scales

NOTE: CR = Critical Reading; SAT = Scholastic Aptitude Test.

Z scores higher than 2 or lower than −2 are considered to be unusual scores. They have a small chance of occurring under normal circumstances. $Z = 2$ translates into the original scale as $\mu + 2\sigma$, and $Z = -2$ translates into the original scale as $\mu - 2\sigma$. In other words, most students' SAT Critical Reading scores are between 267 and 727, SAT Math scores between 273 and 753, and SAT Writing scores between 257 and 717. Scores outside these intervals are considered to be unusual.

Next, let's solve the problem of picking a better-scoring SAT or ACT to boost your chances of getting admitted to a selective university.

EXAMPLE 4.2

Assume that Sarah also took the ACT in 2014. She scored 28 in English, 29 in Math, 30 in Reading, and 29 in Science. According to Table 4.2, the English scores have $\mu = 20.3$, $\sigma = 6.6$; Math, $\mu = 20.9$, $\sigma = 5.3$; Reading, $\mu = 21.3$, $\sigma = 6.3$; and Science, $\mu = 20.8$, $\sigma = 5.5$. Most colleges and universities only require either ACT scores or SAT scores for admission. Which set of scores would be a better choice if Sarah applied to a selective university?

(Continued)

(Continued)

You already learned in Example 4.1 that picking a better score from different sections is not simply picking the higher reported scores. This is true for picking a better score from different exams as well. Otherwise, SAT scores would be higher than ACT scores every time because SAT scores are reported on a range between 200 and 800 and ACT scores are reported on a range between 1 and 36. You learned that you need to convert reported scores to standard Z scores. Again, the Z scale provides a universal yardstick, allowing comparisons of the values of different variables with different distributions.

We already converted Sarah's SAT Critical Reading score to a Z score = 1.24, SAT Math score to $Z = 0.64$, and SAT Writing score to $Z = 1.07$ in Example 4.1. Apply the same formula to convert Sarah's ACT scores to Z scores:

$$\text{ACT English: } Z = \frac{X - \mu}{\sigma} = \frac{28 - 20.3}{6.6} = \frac{7.7}{6.6} = 1.17$$

$$\text{ACT Math: } Z = \frac{X - \mu}{\sigma} = \frac{29 - 20.9}{5.3} = \frac{8.1}{5.3} = 1.53$$

$$\text{ACT Reading: } Z = \frac{X - \mu}{\sigma} = \frac{30 - 21.3}{6.3} = \frac{8.7}{6.3} = 1.38$$

$$\text{ACT Science: } Z = \frac{X - \mu}{\sigma} = \frac{29 - 20.8}{5.5} = \frac{8.2}{5.5} = 1.49$$

Based on the different Z scores from the ACT and SAT, Sarah's SAT Z scores ranged from 0.64 to 1.24 and ACT Z scores ranged from 1.17 to 1.53. Overall, Sarah scored better on the ACT than other students who took the same exams. Submitting ACT score reports instead of SAT would boost Sarah's chance of being admitted by a selective university. The basic principle of comparing the values of different variables with different distributions is to convert the reported scores to Z scores to allow sensible comparisons on the universal yardstick, the Z scale.

Let's consider an example that has less to do with scholastic aptitude.

EXAMPLE 4.3

According to current data from the National Center for Health Statistics, the height of adult women in the United States is normally distributed, with $\mu = 63.8''$ and $\sigma = 4.2''$.

a. What is the Z score for a woman with a height of 5 foot 3 inches?

b. How tall would a woman have to be to reach $Z = 2$?

c. How short would a woman have to be to reach $Z = -2$?

It is necessary to initially convert all numbers into the same unit: inch. As you know, there are 12 inches in a foot.

a. $$X = 5'3'' = 5 \times 12 + 3 = 63''$$

$$Z = \frac{X - \mu}{\sigma} = \frac{63 - 63.8}{4.2} = \frac{-0.8}{4.2} = -0.19$$

An adult woman's height of 5 foot 3 inches puts her at 0.19 standard deviations below the mean.

b. $$Z = \frac{X - \mu}{\sigma}$$

$$2 = \frac{X - 63.8}{4.2}$$

$$8.4 = X - 63.8$$

$$X = 72.2$$

A woman has to be 72.2 inches to reach $Z = 2$.

c. $$Z = \frac{X - \mu}{\sigma}$$

$$-2 = \frac{X - 63.8}{4.2}$$

$$-8.4 = X - 63.8$$

$$X = 55.4$$

A woman has to be 55.4 inches to have a score of $Z = -2$.

As mentioned before, Z scores higher than 2 or lower than -2 are considered to be unusual. Few women are taller than 72.2 inches or shorter than 55.4 inches.

Why Statistics Matter

Children's height and weight measures naturally vary, but at times they can vary quite dramatically. The Centers for Disease Control and Prevention (CDC) has an extensive data bank on health statistics. Children's growth charts on height and weight are part of the health statistics. The CDC publishes growth charts for infants between 0 and 36 months on its website, indicating the normal range of monthly growth. Babies grow at a fast pace within the first few months of birth. That is the reason to have a different growth chart for every month. Boys grow at a different pace from that of girls, so their growth charts are separate. By choosing the correct age and correct sex of the child on the growth charts, you can figure out roughly where a baby stands when compared with other babies of the same sex at the same age. These statistics are especially important to identify early health and growth problems in the instances where the baby's height or weight deviates significantly from the normal range.

EXAMPLE 4.4

A newborn baby boy weighs 7 pounds, 2 ounces and is 21 inches tall. What are the newborn's Z scores in weight and height? Based on the CDC's growth chart for newborn boys, the mean weight $\mu = 3.53$ kilograms and $\sigma = 0.46$ kilograms, and the mean height $\mu = 49.99$ centimeters and $\sigma = 2.47$ centimeters. There are 16 ounces in a pound, 1 ounce equals 28.35 grams, and 1 inch equals 2.54 centimeters.

Height and weight are not only different measures with different distributions; they are also measured and reported by different measurement units. Make sure the correct μ and σ are used in the calculation process.

    a. Z score for weight with all measures converted to grams:

$$7 \text{ lb } 2 \text{ oz} = 7 \times 16 + 2 \text{ oz} = 114 \text{ oz}$$

$$114 \text{ oz} = 114 \times 28.35 \text{ g} = 3{,}231.9 \text{ g}$$

$$3.53 \text{ kg} = 3.53 \times 1{,}000 \text{ g} = 3{,}530 \text{ g}$$

$$0.46 \text{ kg} = 0.46 \times 1{,}000 \text{ g} = 460 \text{ g}$$

$$Z = \frac{X - \mu}{\sigma} = \frac{3231.9 - 3530}{460} = \frac{-298.1}{460} = -0.65$$

b. *Z* score for height with all measures converted to centimeters:

$$21'' = 21 \times 2.54 \text{ cm} = 53.34 \text{ cm}$$

$$Z = \frac{X - \mu}{\sigma} = \frac{53.34 - 49.99}{2.47} = \frac{3.35}{2.47} = 1.36$$

According to the *Z* scores, this newborn boy's weight is 0.65 standard deviations below the mean, and the newborn boy's height is 1.36 standard deviations above the mean. Although height and weight come from different distributions, it is possible to compare the *Z* scores for height and weight. Accordingly, this boy weighs less and is taller than other newborn boys. He is a tall and slim newborn boy.

EXAMPLE 4.5

In a family of five, the family members' ages are 17, 22, 26, 48, and 57. Convert every age into a *Z* score. What are the mean and standard deviation of the *Z* scores?

Since this is a family of five and all five members' ages are reported, it is a population. This example uses the same numbers as in Example 3.9, for which you have already calculated the mean and standard deviation.

$$\mu = \sum X/N = 170/5 = 34$$

$$\sigma = \sqrt{SS/N} = \sqrt{1222/5} = 15.6$$

You have everything you need to convert your raw score (*X*) into *Z* by using $Z = \frac{(X-\mu)}{\sigma}$.

Then you can calculate the mean and standard deviation of *Z* the same way you calculated the mean and standard deviation of *X* (Table 4.3).

Mean of *Z* scores: $\bar{Z} = \sum Z/N = ((-1.09) + (-0.77) + (-0.51) + 0.90 + 1.47)/5 = 0$

$$SS \text{ of } Z = (-1.09)^2 + (-0.77)^2 + (-0.51)^2 + 0.90^2 + 1.47^2 = 5.00$$

Standard deviation of $Z = \sqrt{SS/N} = \sqrt{5/5} = 1$

(Continued)

(Continued)

TABLE 4.3 Family Members' Ages and Z Scores

X (AGE)	X − μ	Z = (X − μ)/σ	(Z − Z̄)²
17	−17	−1.09	1.18
22	−12	−0.77	0.59
26	−8	−0.51	0.26
48	14	0.90	0.81
57	23	1.47	2.16
170	0	0	5.00
ΣX	Σ(X − μ)	ΣZ	Σ(Z − Z̄)²

This example is to demonstrate that when you convert every value in the population into Z scores, the Z scores have mean = 0 and standard deviation = 1. Z scores are customarily calculated to two places after the decimal point to conform to the way Z scores are reported in the Standard Normal Distribution Table, or the Z Table, which will be introduced in the next chapter.

Z SCORES FOR A SAMPLE

Z scores usually refer to populations. However, there are not many population means and standard deviations readily available. When Z scores are calculated for a sample, both μ and σ are unknown, so the Z formula needs to be adjusted to $Z = \dfrac{(X - \bar{X})}{s}$, where $\bar{X}$ is the sample mean, and s is the sample standard deviation. An example should help make this clear.

EXAMPLE 4.6

Alex receives 30 points on the ACT composite score. There are 125 students in her graduating class; their mean ACT composite score $\bar{X} = 22$ and $s = 4.5$. What is Alex's Z score compared with the scores of her graduating class?

$$Z = \frac{X - \bar{X}}{s} = \frac{30 - 22}{4.5} = 1.78$$

Alex's ACT composite score is 1.78 standard deviations above the mean compared with the graduating class in her high school.

The same principle for calculating Z scores for populations applies to Z scores for samples. The attributes of Z scores remain the same. Conducting a Z transformation does not change the shape of the distribution. The shape of the Z-score distribution is the same as that of the original distribution of the raw scores, and the Z-score distribution has mean = 0 and standard deviation = 1.

Let's take a look at calculating Z scores from another perspective, using a different example.

EXAMPLE 4.7

Assume that a happiness study investigates participants' subjective feelings about their work, family, and sense of achievement. In a sample of 200 participants, a happiness score of 66 corresponds to $Z = 1.6$, and a happiness score of 37 corresponds to $Z = -1.3$. What are the mean and standard deviation of the happiness scores for this sample?

One linear equation solves one unknown variable. Two equations can solve two unknowns. First, identify the formula for the Z-score conversion for a sample $Z = (X - \bar{X})/s$. Then list all the numbers given in the problem statement into the formula.

$$Z = \frac{X - \bar{X}}{s}$$

$$1.6 = \frac{66 - \bar{X}}{s} \tag{1}$$

Equation 1 is $1.6s = 66 - \bar{X}$.

$$Z = \frac{X - \bar{X}}{s}$$

$$-1.3 = \frac{37 - \bar{X}}{s} \tag{2}$$

Equation 2 is $-1.3s = 37 - \bar{X}$.

(Continued)

(Continued)

Using the elimination principle, Equation 1 − Equation 2, we get $2.9s = 29$.

$$s = 29/2.9 = 10$$

Putting $s = 10$ back in Equation 1, we get $1.6(10) = 66 - \bar{X}$.

$$\bar{X} = 50$$

The mean for the distribution of happiness scores is 50, and the standard deviation is 10.

EXAMPLE 4.8

Assume that a random sample of five students answer a survey about the number of hours spent studying the night before an exam. The answers are 1, 1, 3, 5, and 5. Convert the hours into Z scores, and calculate the mean and standard deviation for the Z scores.

You need to find out the sample mean and standard deviation to convert X into Z.

$$\bar{X} = \sum X/n = (1+1+3+5+5)/5 = 15/5 = 3$$

$$SS = \sum(X - \bar{X})^2 = (1-3)^2 + (1-3)^2 + (3-3)^2 + (5-3)^2 + (5-3)^2 = 16$$

$$\text{Variance } s^2 = SS/(n-1) = 16/(5-1) = 4$$

$$\text{Standard deviation } s = \sqrt{\text{Variance}} = \sqrt{4} = 2$$

$$Z = \frac{X - \bar{X}}{s}$$

The results of this Z calculation are shown in the fourth column of Table 4.4.

$$\bar{Z} = \sum Z/n = ((-1)+(-1)+0+1+1)/5 = 0$$

Table 4.4 shows the step-by-step process of calculating the mean and standard deviation for the Z scores in Example 4.8.

TABLE 4.4 Step-by-Step Process for Calculating the Mean and Standard Deviation for Z Scores

X (HOURS OF STUDYING)	$(X - \bar{X})$	$(X - \bar{X})^2$	$Z = (X - \bar{X})/s$	$(Z - \bar{Z})^2$
1	−2	4	−1	1
1	−2	4	−1	1
3	0	0	0	0
5	2	4	1	1
5	2	4	1	1
Total		16	0	4
		SS of X		SS of Z

$$SS \text{ of } Z = (-1-0)^2 + (-1-0)^2 + (0-0)^2 + (1-0)^2 + (1-0)^2 = 4$$

$$\text{Variance of } Z = s^2 = SS/(n-1) = 4/(5-1) = 1$$

$$\text{Standard deviation of } Z = \sqrt{\text{Variance}} = \sqrt{1} = 1$$

This example demonstrates that Z scores from a sample have mean = 0 and standard deviation = 1, just as they do in a population.

Pop Quiz

1. For a population with $\mu = 100$ and $\sigma = 10$, what is the X value corresponding to Z = 0.75?

   a. 92.5

   b. 97.5

   c. 105

   d. 107.5

2. What is the measurement unit of Z scores?

   a. The same as the measurement unit of the original scores

   b. The square of the measurement unit of the original scores

   c. The square root of the measurement unit of the original scores

   d. There is no measurement unit for Z scores.

Answers: 1. d, 2. d

EMPIRICAL RULE FOR VARIABLES WITH A NORMAL DISTRIBUTION

A very useful concept to interpret Z scores is the empirical rule. The **empirical rule** states that about 68% of the values fall within 1 standard deviation from the mean, about 95% of the values fall within 2 standard deviations from the mean, and about 99.7% of the values fall within 3 standard deviations from the mean, as shown in Figure 4.4. The empirical rule applies to all normally distributed variables.

FIGURE 4.4 Empirical Rule for Normally Distributed Variables

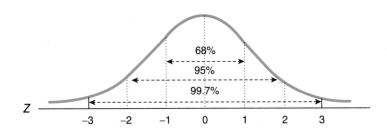

Roughly 68% of the values fall within $-1 \leq Z \leq 1$ or $\mu \pm \sigma$

Roughly 95% of the values fall within $-2 \leq Z \leq 2$ or $\mu \pm 2\sigma$

Roughly 99.7% of the values fall within $-3 \leq Z \leq 3$ or $\mu \pm 3\sigma$

The empirical rule is also called the 68–95–99.7 rule. It helps in interpreting Z scores. Due to the fact that only 5% of the values fall outside 2 standard deviations from the mean, customarily, these 5% are viewed as unusual values. In Example 4.9, we will demonstrate how the empirical rule can help in interpreting Z scores.

EXAMPLE 4.9

In the United States, adult men's height is normally distributed, with $\mu = 5'8''$ and $\sigma = 6''$. What percentage of men are taller than 6 foot 8 inches?

Let's figure out the Z score for $6'8''$ first.

$$\mu = 5'8'' = 5 \times 12 + 8 = 68''$$

$$X = 6'8'' = 6 \times 12 + 8 = 80''$$

$$Z = \frac{X - \mu}{\sigma} = \frac{80 - 68}{6} = \frac{12}{6} = 2$$

The question asks for the percentage of men taller than 6 foot 8 inches, so Z is greater than 2. In a normal distribution, the mean, median, and mode are located at the same spot. Since the distribution is symmetrical around this spot, 50% of the values are above the mean and 50% are below the mean. Together, the values below and above the mean constitute 100% of the values. Another way to say this is that everything under the normal distribution curve is 1, or 100%. According to the empirical rule, 95% of the values fall within $-2 \le Z \le 2$. The area between $Z = 0$ and $Z = 2$ is half of the 95%, due to the symmetry of the normal curve. Therefore, the percentage of men who are taller than 6 foot 8 inches is 100% − 50% − 47.5% = 2.5% (see Figure 4.5). Thus, only 2.5% of adult men are taller than 6 foot 8 inches. You have a small chance of seeing a man taller than 6 foot 8 inches. You may also interpret this to say that a man whose height is greater than 6 foot 8 inches is taller than 97.5% of adult men.

FIGURE 4.5 Applying the Empirical Rule to Interpret Z > 2

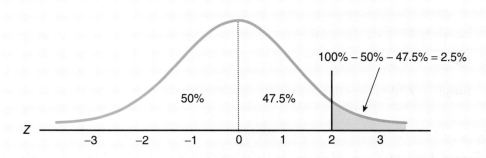

EXAMPLE 4.10

Tim's SAT Critical Reading score is 612. SAT Critical Reading scores are normally distributed, with $\mu = 497$ and $\sigma = 115$. How does Tim's score compare with the scores of other students who took the exams at the same time?

(Continued)

(Continued)

First, Tim's Critical Reading score needs to be converted to

$$Z = \frac{X - \mu}{\sigma} = \frac{612 - 497}{115} = 1.$$

FIGURE 4.6   Applying the Empirical Rule to Interpret $Z > 1$

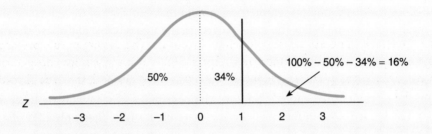

Tim scored 1 standard deviation above the mean. The empirical rule provides a rough estimate of the percentage of students who scored above $Z = 1$ and the percentage of students who scored below $Z = 1$, as shown in Figure 4.6.

The area below $Z = 0$ is 50%. The area between $Z = 0$ and $Z = 1$ is half of the 68% for $-1 < Z < 1$, due to the symmetry of the normal distribution curve: 68%/2 = 34%. Tim's SAT Critical Reading score of 612 was higher than the scores of 84% of the students who took the exams at the same time. However, 16% of the students scored higher than Tim.

To reinforce this calculation process, here is one final example.

EXAMPLE 4.11

In the Ohio Division II high school boys' swimming competitions, the swimmers' times were recorded. The time (in seconds) to complete the 50-yards free style event (known simply as 50-free) was normally distributed, with a mean of $\bar{X} = 25$ seconds and a standard deviation of $s = 2.5$ seconds. Josh swam a time of 20 seconds for the

50-free event. How does Josh's time compare with the times of other Division II high school boys?

The faster the swimmer, the less time it takes to complete the event. First, Josh's 50-free time of 20 seconds needs to be converted to a Z score.

$$Z = \frac{X - \bar{X}}{s} = \frac{20 - 25}{2.5} = -2$$

Josh's time is 2 standard deviations below the mean. The empirical rule provides a rough estimate of the percentage of students whose swim times are above $Z = -2$ and the percentage of students whose swim times are below $Z = -2$, as shown in Figure 4.7.

FIGURE 4.7 Applying the Empirical Rule to Interpret $Z > -2$ or $Z < -2$

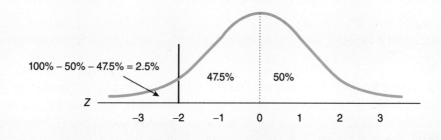

In a sport that is competed in and reported by time, the lower the time, the faster is the speed. Thus, 97.5% of the Ohio Division II high school boys have 50-free times that are slower than Josh's. In other words, Josh's speed in the 50-free is faster than the speed of 97.5% of Ohio Division II boy swimmers. There are still 2.5% of Ohio Division II boy swimmers who can swim faster than Josh.

The empirical rule (68–95–99.7 rule) in normal distributions in combination with the symmetry of the normal distribution curve allows us to use probability to interpret Z scores clearly in special cases. The connection between Z scores and probability will be extended beyond a few special cases such as 68%, 95%, and 99.7% to all values in the next chapter.

Pop Quiz

1. Based on the empirical rule, 99.7% of values are within 3 standard deviations from the mean, $-3 < Z < 3$. What percentage of values fall within $0 < Z < 3$?

   a. 49.9%

   b. 68%

   c. 95%

   d. 99.7%

2. Assume that the scores on a statistics exam were normally distributed. Bianca earned 74 points on the exam. The exam scores had $\bar{X} = 82$ and $s = 8$. What percentage of students scored higher than Bianca?

   a. 16%

   b. 32%

   c. 68%

   d. 84%

EXERCISE PROBLEMS

1. Body mass index (BMI) is a common way to measure the percentage of body fat and screen for obesity. The formula for BMI = Weight (in kilograms)/Height² (in square meters). If you are interested in finding out your BMI, you need to convert your weight to kilograms and your height to meters. Adult women and men have different BMI distributions. Men's BMI is normally distributed, with a mean $\mu = 27.8$ and a standard deviation $\sigma = 5.22$. Women's BMI is also normally distributed, with a mean $\mu = 27.3$ and a standard deviation $\sigma = 7.01$. If a man and a woman both have BMI = 34, compared with people of the same sex, whose BMI is farther from the mean?

2. The distribution of reaction time of adults is positively skewed, with a long tail to the right. In a random sample of 200 adults, a mean of 400 milliseconds is reported. A Z score equal to 2 is reported for a participant with a reaction time of 500 milliseconds.

   a. What is the standard deviation of reaction time in this sample?

   b. If all the reaction times are converted to Z scores, what is the shape of the Z-score distribution?

3. Jimmy scored a 90 on an IQ test. The IQ test scores are normally distributed, with $\mu = 100$ and $\sigma = 10$. How does Jimmy's score compare with the scores of other people who took the same IQ test?

STRAIGHTFORWARD STATISTICS

4. In a hearing test, Mackenzie scores 86.25, and her Z score is 1.75; Michael scores 52.5, and his Z score is –0.5. What are the mean and standard deviation of this hearing test?

Solutions

1. First, convert the original BMI = 34 to Z scores for men and women:

$$\text{Man's } Z = \frac{X - \mu}{\sigma} = \frac{34 - 27.8}{5.22} = 1.19$$

$$\text{Woman's } Z = \frac{X - \mu}{\sigma} = \frac{34 - 27.3}{7.01} = 0.96$$

The man's BMI = 34 converts to Z = 1.19; it is 1.19 standard deviations above the mean. The woman's BMI = 34 converts to Z = 0.96; it is 0.96 standard deviations above the mean. (See Figure 4.8.) Therefore, the man with BMI = 34 is farther from the mean compared with people of the same sex.

2.a. First, identify the formula for the Z-score conversion for a sample, $Z = (X - \bar{X})/s$.

Then list all the numbers given in the problem statement into the formula:

FIGURE 4.8 Locations of Two Calculated Z Scores Overlaid With the Original Scales

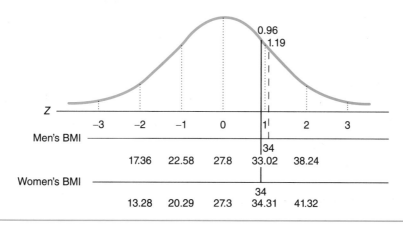

NOTE: BMI = body mass index.

$$Z = 2$$

$$X = 500$$

$$\bar{X} = 400$$

$$s = ?$$

You can solve one unknown with three values in this formula. Plug three values into the formula, and solve the fourth one.

$$2 = \frac{500 - 400}{s}$$

$$2s = 100$$

$$s = 50$$

The standard deviation of reaction time in this sample is 50 milliseconds.

2.b. The shape of the Z-score distribution is the same as that of the original reaction time. It is positively skewed, with a long tail to the right.

3. First, identify the formula for the Z-score conversion for a population $Z = (X - \mu)/\sigma$

Then list all the numbers given in the problem statement into the formula:

$$X = 90$$

$$\mu = 100$$

$$\sigma = 10$$

$$Z = ?$$

$$Z = \frac{X - \mu}{\sigma} = \frac{90 - 100}{10} = -1$$

Jimmy's 90 converted to a $Z = -1$.

According to the empirical rule, the area between $-1 < Z < 1$ is 68%; therefore the area between $Z = 0$ and $Z = -1$ is half of it: $\frac{1}{2} \times 68\% = 34\%$.

Of the people who took the IQ test, 84% scored higher than Jimmy and 16% scored lower than Jimmy, as shown in Figure 4.9.

FIGURE 4.9   Applying the Empirical Rule to Interpret Z > –1 or Z < –1

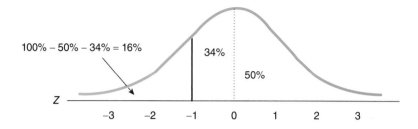

4. One linear equation can solve one unknown variable. Two equations can solve two unknowns. First, identify the formula for the Z-score conversion for a sample, $Z = (X - \bar{X})/s$.

Then list all the numbers given in the problem statement into the formula:

$$\text{From Mackenzie's score, } Z = \frac{X - \bar{X}}{s}$$

$$1.75 = \frac{86.25 - \bar{X}}{s} \tag{1}$$

Equation 1 is $1.75s = 86.25 - \bar{X}$.

$$\text{From Michael's score, } Z = \frac{X - \bar{X}}{s}$$

$$-0.5 = \frac{52.5 - \bar{X}}{s} \tag{2}$$

Equation 2 is $-0.5s = 52.5 - \bar{X}$.

Using the elimination principle, Equation 1 – Equation 2, you can eliminate $\bar{X}$. You get $2.25s = 33.75$.

$$s = \frac{33.75}{2.25} = 15$$

Putting $s = 15$ back in Equation 2, we get $-0.5(15) = 52.5 - \bar{X}$.

$$\bar{X} = 60$$

The mean for the hearing test is 60, and the standard deviation is 15.

Sharpen your skills with SAGE edge!

Visit edge.sagepub.com/bowen for mobile-friendly quizzes, flashcards, videos, and more!

WHAT YOU LEARNED

Chapter 4 focused on Z scores. You learned how to convert raw scores to Z scores using the mean and standard deviation of the distribution. The principles can be applied to populations as well as samples. The distribution of Z scores remains the same shape as that of raw scores. Z scores have a mean of 0 and a standard deviation of 1.

For populations, the Z-score formula is $Z = \dfrac{(X - \mu)}{\sigma}$.

For samples, the Z-score formula is $Z = \dfrac{(X - \bar{X})}{s}$.

In both formulas, there are four values involved: (1) X, (2) Z, (3) the mean, and (4) the standard deviation of the distribution. You may solve one unknown with one equation. Therefore, as long as three values are provided, you can calculate the fourth one.

The empirical rule (68–95–99.7 rule) provides a rule of thumb for connecting Z scores and probabilities for normally distributed variables.

KEY WORDS

Empirical rule: The empirical rule describes the following attributes for variables with a normal distribution: About 68% of the values fall within 1 standard deviation of the mean, about 95% of the values fall within 2 standard deviations of the mean, and about 99.7% of the values fall within 3 standard deviations of the mean.

Z scores: Z scores are standard scores that describe the differences of individual raw scores from the mean in terms of standard deviation units.

LEARNING ASSESSMENT

Multiple Choice Questions: Choose the best answer in every question.

1. For a population with $\mu = 100$ and $\sigma = 20$, what is the X value corresponding to $Z = 0.50$?
   a. 90
   b. 95
   c. 105
   d. 110

2. A sample of $n = 200$ scores has a mean of $\bar{X} = 45$ and a standard deviation of $s = 8$. In this sample, what is the Z score corresponding to $X = 39$?
   a. $Z = 0.75$
   b. $Z = 1.00$
   c. $Z = -0.75$
   d. $Z = -1.00$

3. A sample of $n = 500$ scores are transformed into Z scores. The mean for the 500 Z scores _____.
   a. is 0.
   b. is 1.
   c. is -1.
   d. cannot be determined without more information.

4. Under a normal distribution curve, the area covered by $\mu \pm 2\sigma$ is roughly _____% of the data.
   a. 50
   b. 68

c. 95
d. 99

5. For a sample with $\bar{X} = 36$, a score of $X = 40$ corresponds to $Z = 0.50$. What is the standard deviation for the sample?
   a. 2
   b. 4
   c. 8
   d. 16

6. A sample of $n = 500$ scores are transformed into Z scores. The standard deviation for the 500 Z scores _____.
   a. is 0.
   b. is 1.
   c. is -1.
   d. cannot be determined without more information.

7. In an IQ test with mean = 100 and standard deviation = 15, what score is 1.5 standard deviations above the mean ($Z = 1.50$)?
   a. 100
   b. 115
   c. 122.5
   d. 130

8. In a sample $n = 5$, all the raw scores are converted into Z scores. The first four Z scores are -1.19, -0.69, 0.75, and 1.12. What is the last Z score?

   a. -0.01

   b. -0.10

   c. 0.01

   d. 0.10

9. Which one of the following distributions where $X = 70$ would have the highest Z value?

   a. $\mu = 100$ and $\sigma = 60$

   b. $\mu = 100$ and $\sigma = 30$

   c. $\mu = 100$ and $\sigma = 15$

   d. $\mu = 100$ and $\sigma = 10$

10. Which one of the following distributions with $X = 60$ has the largest Z score?

    a. $\mu = 50$ and $\sigma = 60$

    b. $\mu = 50$ and $\sigma = 30$

    c. $\mu = 50$ and $\sigma = 15$

    d. $\mu = 50$ and $\sigma = 10$

Free-Response Questions

11. In a sample of $n = 150$ high school girls who take a physical fitness test, Megan scores 97.5 and her Z score is 1.5, and Jenny scores 60 and her Z score is -1. What are the mean and standard deviation of this fitness test?

12. Robin scored 40 points on an English test with $\bar{X} = 30$ and $s = 8$. He also scored a 50 on a math test with $\bar{X} = 55$ and $s = 5$. In which subject did Robin perform better than his classmates according to these test scores?

13. According to the College Board, the SAT Critical Reading $\mu = 497$ and $\sigma = 115$, and the SAT Math $\mu = 513$ and $\sigma = 120$. Ted's SAT Critical Reading score is 730, and his SAT Math score is 760. Are Ted's scores considered unusual scores?

14. According to the Institute of Education Sciences, the ACT composite score $\mu = 21.0$ and $\sigma = 5.2$. Hanna's ACT composite score is 29. Is Hanna's score considered an unusual score?

Basic Principles of Probability

After reading and studying this chapter, you should be able to do the following:

- Define probability terms such as simple event, event, and sample space
- Explain the addition rule, multiplication rule, and complementary rule in probability
- Identify and provide an example of a binomial probability distribution
- Explain how to construct a probability distribution table
- Define Z score and explain the relationship between probability and Z score in a normal distribution
- Describe the purpose of using the Z table

WHAT YOU KNOW AND WHAT IS NEW

You learned frequency distribution tables in Chapter 2 as a way to organize and simplify numeric data by listing values in an ascending order and tallying the frequency for each value. You learned to calculate means and standard deviations using frequency tables in Chapter 3. You now understand the importance of considering the impact of frequency when calculating the mean and standard deviation. You learned to transform raw scores to Z scores by using the Z formula and to use the empirical rule to connect Z scores and probability in a few special cases in Chapter 4. The concepts you learned and the skills you mastered in those early chapters are the building blocks of statistics, and they continue to be relevant throughout the rest of this book.

You will learn the basic principles of probability in Chapter 5. *Probability* is a measure to quantify uncertainty. Probability is a new topic, and all the basic terms, such as *simple event*, *event*, and *sample space*, will be clearly defined. The mathematical operations (i.e., *addition rule, multiplication rule, and complementary rule*) for probability will be explained. The same principles for calculating mean and standard deviation from a frequency table can be applied in a probability distribution. You will learn the connection between probabilities and Z scores under a normal distribution. Such a connection facilitates the understanding and interpretation of Z scores.

BASIC TERMS AND MATHEMATICAL OPERATIONS IN PROBABILITY

To understand the basic principles of probability, we need to start with the definitions of terms. It is strange and somewhat ironic that probability, which is a measure to quantify uncertainty, usually makes students *feel* uncertain after learning about this topic. Hopefully, the examples that follow the definitions below will reinforce the meaning of each term and make the learning of this somewhat abstract concept more tangible.

BASIC TERMS IN PROBABILITY

Learning a new mathematical topic, such as probability, is similar to learning a new language. There is a basic vocabulary that you have to know before you become fluent in the language. Understanding and memorizing the vocabulary is the first step to master the language. Here are the basic terms in probability.

Event: An event is defined as a set of outcomes from an experiment or a procedure (i.e., tossing a coin, throwing a die, going through a treatment, having a child, or buying a lottery ticket).

Simple event: A simple event is defined as an elementary event that cannot be broken into simpler parts.

Sample space: A sample space is a complete list of all possible outcomes. The probabilities of all possible outcomes add to 1.

Notations in Probability

P stands for probability.

A or B denotes particular events.

$P(A)$ stands for the probability of Event A happening.

$$P(A) = \frac{\text{Number of ways A happens}}{\text{Total number of all possible outcomes}}$$

Probability is expressed with numbers between 0 and 1, $0 \leq P(A) \leq 1$. When $P(A) = 0$, it means that Event A does not happen, and when $P(A) = 1$, it means that Event A definitely happens. Probability can never be greater than 1 or less than 0. When you answer a probability question with a negative number or a number greater than 1, your calculation is *absolutely wrong*. You have to redo your calculation!

Once you have the basic vocabulary in probability, we can proceed with discussing probability in everyday situations. When expectant parents are anticipating the birth of a newborn, they wonder whether it is a boy or a girl. Most human births are single births, with one baby born per pregnancy. To keep things simple, we are limiting the discussion of probability to single births. The probability of having a boy is roughly .5, and the probability of having a girl is also .5. Let's use b for boy and g for girl. $P(b)$ is the probability of having a boy, and $P(g)$ is the probability of having a girl.

Here are probabilities from one single birth:

$$P(b) = .5$$

$$P(g) = .5$$

$$P(b) + P(g) = 1$$

The probability of having a boy or a girl in a single birth is pretty easy to calculate. There are two possible outcomes, and the sum of these two possible outcomes adds to 1. Having a boy is one possible event, and having a girl is the other possible event. Both events are examples of a simple event that cannot be broken down further. The sample space includes two possible outcomes of having a boy or having a girl. That is easy enough. Let's move on to discuss the probabilities of having two children.

When having two children, the parents might have two boys, two girls, or one boy and one girl. These are events. The event "one boy and one girl" can be broken further into having a boy first and a girl second or having a girl first and a boy second. The other two events (i.e., two boys or two girls) cannot not be broken down any further. Table 5.1 lists the basic probability terms for having two children.

As you can see, the probabilities of having a boy or a girl when having two children are more complicated than the probability of having a boy or a girl when having one child. To calculate the probability of having two children, we need to introduce mathematical operations for the probabilities.

TABLE 5.1　Basic Probability Terms for Having Two Children

PROCEDURE	EVENT	SIMPLE EVENT
Having two children	Two boys	bb
	One boy and one girl	bg, gb
	Two girls	gg
Sample space		bb, bg, gb, gg

MATHEMATICAL OPERATIONS FOR PROBABILITIES

Table 5.1 shows that there are four simple events in the sample space of having two children. We need to calculate the probability of having two boys, $P(bb)$; the probability of having one boy and one girl, $P(bg)$ or $P(gb)$; and the probability of having two girls, $P(gg)$. Calculating these probabilities involves two new probability concepts: (1) *independent events* and (2) *multiplication rule for independent events*. A and B are two **independent events** if the occurrence of one event does not affect the probability of the occurrence of the other event. In the example of having two children, it means that the sex of the firstborn child does not affect the sex of the second child.

The **multiplication rule for independent events** states that when Event A and Event B are independent, the probability of both events happening is $P(AB) = P(A) \times P(B)$.

Let's think about the probability of having two boys. This can only happen when the first baby is a boy and the second baby is also a boy. The probability of the second baby's sex is independent of the probability of the first baby's sex. Thus, the probability of the first baby being a boy is $P(b) = .5$, and the probability of the second baby being a boy is $P(b) = .5$.

Therefore, the probability of having two boys is

$$P(bb) = P(b) \times P(b) = (.5) \times (.5) = .25$$

The probability of having two girls is, similarly,

$$P(gg) = P(g) \times P(g) = (.5) \times (.5) = .25$$

Now, let's figure out the probability of having one boy and one girl. This event can be broken down into two simple events: (1) having a boy first and then a girl (bg) and (2) having a girl first and then a boy (gb). Only one of these two events would occur in any family. We need to calculate $P(bg$ or $gb)$. In general, calculating $P(A$ or $B)$ involves understanding two new probability concepts: (1) *mutually exclusive events* and (1) *Addition Rule 1 of probability.* A and B are **mutually exclusive events** when only one of the events can happen: If one happens, the other does not. They cannot both happen at the same time. There is no overlapping between Event A and Event B. When having one boy and one girl in a family, it means either having a boy first and then a girl (bg) or having a girl first and then a boy (gb), but two such events cannot happen at the same time. Mutually exclusive events are also called **disjoint events**. *Disjoint events* is simply another label for mutually exclusive events. A Venn diagram for events that are mutually exclusive (i.e., disjoint events) is shown in Figure 5.1.

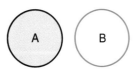

Addition Rule 1 of probability states that when Event A and Event B are mutually exclusive, the probability of either Event A or Event B happening is the sum of the probability of each event, $P(A \text{ or } B) = P(A) + P(B)$.

The event of having one boy and one girl includes two simple events, bg and gb. These two simple events are mutually exclusive because if one happens, the other does not and they can't happen at the same time.

Having a boy first and a girl second: $P(bg) = P(b) \times P(g) = (.5) \times (.5) = .25$

Having a girl first and a boy second: $P(gb) = P(g) \times P(b) = (.5) \times (.5) = .25$

Therefore, the probability of having one boy and one girl is

$$P(bg \text{ or } gb) = P(bg) + P(gb) = .25 + .25 = .50$$

Let's take this one step further and look into the probabilities of having three children. Think of all the possible outcomes of having three children first before worrying about calculating the probabilities. All the possible outcomes are listed in Table 5.2.

As mentioned earlier, the probability of having a boy or a girl in one birth is independent of having a boy or a girl in any other birth.

The probability of having three boys is

$$P(bbb) = P(b) \times P(b) \times P(b) = (.5) \times (.5) \times (.5) = .125$$

The event of having two boys and one girl can be broken down into three simple events, and these events are mutually exclusive: bbg, bgb, and gbb.

TABLE 5.2 Probabilities of Different Numbers of Boys or Girls in a Family With Three Children

PROCEDURE	EVENT	SIMPLE EVENT
Having three children	Three boys	bbb
	Two boys and one girl	bbg, bgb, gbb
	One boy and two girls	bgg, gbg, ggb
	Three girls	ggg
Sample space		bbb, bbg, bgb, gbb, bgg, gbg, ggb, ggg

$$P(bbg) = P(b) \times P(g) \times P(g) = (.5) \times (.5) \times (.5) = .125$$

$$P(bgb) = P(b) \times P(g) \times P(b) = (.5) \times (.5) \times (.5) = .125$$

$$P(gbb) = P(g) \times P(b) \times P(b) = (.5) \times (.5) \times (.5) = .125$$

Therefore, the probability of having two boys and one girl is

$$P(bbg \text{ or } bgb \text{ or } gbb) = P(bbg) + P(bgb) + P(gbb) = .125 + .125 + .125 = .375$$

The event of having one boy and two girls can be broken down into three simple events, and these events are mutually exclusive: bgg, gbg, and ggb.

$$P(bgg) = P(b) \times P(g) \times P(g) = (.5) \times (.5) \times (.5) = .125$$

$$P(gbg) = P(g) \times P(b) \times P(g) = (.5) \times (.5) \times (.5) = .125$$

$$P(ggb) = P(g) \times P(g) \times P(b) = (.5) \times (.5) \times (.5) = .125$$

Therefore, the probability of having one boy and two girls is

$$P(bgg \text{ or } gbg \text{ or } ggb) = P(bgg) + P(gbg) + P(ggb) = .125 + .125 + .125 = .375$$

The probability of having three girls is

$$P(ggg) = P(g) \times P(g) \times P(g) = (.5) \times (.5) \times (.5) = .125$$

The probability of having r number of girls out of n number of children fits a particularly important probability distribution called a *binomial probability distribution*.

BINOMIAL PROBABILITY DISTRIBUTION

A **binomial probability distribution** is a probability distribution applied to variables with only two possible outcomes (i.e., success vs. failure) in each trial. The trials are independent of one another. The probability of a success and the probability of a failure remain the same in all trials. Linking the definition back to our previous example, having a child has only two possible outcomes: a boy or a girl. If you decide to have more children, the outcome of a previous birth will not affect the probabilities of outcomes in the next birth. The probability of having a boy and the probability of having a girl remain the same in all births.

In summary, a binomial probability distribution has the following four requirements:

1. The procedure has a fixed number of trials.

2. The trials are independent events. The probabilities of outcomes in one trial do not affect the probabilities of outcomes in the other trials.

3. There are only two possible outcomes for each trial: (1) success and (2) failure. These are commonly used labels. There is no value judgment involved. The outcomes can be head/tail or boy/girl.

4. The probability of a success and the probability of a failure remain the same in all trials.

Here is the basic notation vocabulary for binomial probability distributions:

S stands for success, and F stands for failure

$P(S) = p$, the probability of success in one trial

$P(F) = 1 - p = q$, the probability of failure in one trial

n = the number of trials

r = the number of successes in n trials

$P(r)$ = the probability of getting exactly r successes in n trials

Binomial probability formula:

$$P(r) = C_r^n \, p^r q^{(n-r)} = \frac{n!}{(n-r)!r!} p^r q^{(n-r)} \quad \text{for } r = 0, 1, 2, 3, \ldots n$$

Let us break the binomial formula down and explain each component.

C_r^n is a mathematical operation to calculate the number of possible ways to produce r number of successes out of n trials,

$$C_r^n = \frac{n!}{(n-r)!r!}$$

C stands for combination

$$n! = n \times (n-1) \times (n-2) \times (n-3) \dots 3 \times 2 \times 1$$

$n!$ is pronounced as "n factorial." It is a mathematical operation calculated as the multiplicative product of all positive integers less than or equal to n. $0!$ is defined as 1. You can calculate the factorial for positive integers. The value can get large pretty quickly. For example,

$$5! = 5 \times 4 \times 3 \times 2 \times 1 = 120$$

$$10! = 10 \times 9 \times 8 \times 7 \times 6 \times 5 \times 4 \times 3 \times 2 \times 1 = 3628800$$

Let's use simple numbers to practice the combination of r successes in n trials, C_r^n. If you produce three successes out of five trials, in how many different ways can it happen?

$$C_3^5 = \frac{n!}{(n-r)!r!} = \frac{5!}{(5-3)!3!} = \frac{5!}{2!3!} = 10$$

Let's apply the binomial probability formula to the example of having three children. The number of girls in a family with three children could be 0, 1, 2, or 3. Let's label having a girl as a success and having a boy as a failure. Again, there is no value judgment. Success and failure are commonly used labels to refer to two possible outcomes of one trial.

The probability of having no girl in three single births:

$n = 3$

$r = 0$

$p = .5$

$q = .5$

$$P(0) = \frac{3!}{(3-0)!0!}(.5)^0(.5)^3 = .125$$

The probability of having one girl in three single births:

$n = 3$

$r = 1$

$p = .5$

$q = .5$

$$P(1) = \frac{3!}{(3-1)!1!}(.5)^1(.5)^2 = .375$$

The probability of having two girls in three single births:

$n = 3$

$r = 2$

$p = .5$

$q = .5$

$$P(2) = \frac{3!}{(3-2)!2!}(.5)^2(.5)^1 = .375$$

The probability of having three girls in three single births:

$n = 3$

$r = 3$

$p = .5$

$q = .5$

$$P(3) = \frac{3!}{(3-3)!3!}(.5)^3(.5)^0 = .125$$

Applying the binomial probability formula, we easily get the probabilities of having no, one, two, and three girls without analyzing and listing the entire sample space. Table 5.3a is the binomial probability distribution table of the number of girls in a family with three children.

If you survey 10 families with three single births, you might not get exactly the same probabilities. The attributes obtained from a small sample size (i.e., $n < 30$) tend to fluctuate a fair amount depending on which families are included in the sample. If you obtain information from

TABLE 5.3a Probability Distribution Table of the Number of Girls in a Family With Three Children

X (NUMBER OF GIRLS)	P(X)
0	.125
1	.375
2	.375
3	.125

every family with three children, you get the probability distribution of the entire population. Probability distributions are used to describe populations. Let's proceed with calculating the population mean, variance, and standard deviation with this example. Here are formulas for the population parameters of a probability distribution.

Population mean for a probability distribution: $\mu = \sum[XP(X)]$.

Population mean is calculated as the sum of the values of X multiplied by its associated probability.

Population variance for a probability distribution: $\sigma^2 = \sum[(X-\mu)^2 P(X)]$.

Population variance is calculated as the sum of squared deviations multiplied by its associated probability.

Population standard deviation for a probability distribution:

$$\sigma = \sqrt{\text{Variance}} = \sqrt{\sum[(X-\mu)^2 P(X)]}.$$

As always, population standard deviation is equal to the square root of the population variance.

The binomial probability distribution is a special probability distribution. The calculation of μ, σ^2, and σ is simplified in a binomial probability distribution.

$$\mu = np$$
$$\sigma^2 = npq$$
$$\sigma^2 = \sqrt{npq}$$

Let's document the step-by-step process by adding columns to Table 5.3a. The new columns are shown in Table 5.3b. According to the order of operations in the formula for $\mu = \sum[XP(X)]$, the multiplication between X and $P(X)$ inside the brackets needs to be done first. Add up every $XP(X)$ to obtain $\sum[XP(X)]$ at the end. According to the order of operations in the formula for $\sigma^2 = [(X-\mu)^2 P(X)]$, three more columns need to be calculated: $(X-\mu)$, $(X-\mu)^2$, and $(X-\mu)^2 P(X)$. Then, every $(X-\mu)^2 P(X)$ is added up to obtain $\sum[(X-\mu)^2 P(X)]$ at the end.

According to Table 5.3b,

$$\text{mean} = \mu = \sum[XP(X)] = 1.5$$

$$\text{variance} = \sigma^2 = \sum[(X-\mu)^2 P(X)] = 0.75$$

$$\text{standard deviation} = \sigma = \sqrt{\text{Variance}} = \sqrt{\sum[(X-\mu)^2 P(X)]} = \sqrt{0.75} = 0.87$$

TABLE 5.3b Mean and Variance of the Probability Distribution of the Number of Girls in a Family With Three Children

X (NUMBER OF GIRLS)	P(X)	XP(X)	$(X - \mu)$	$(X - \mu)^2$	$(X - \mu)^2 P(X)$
0	.125	0	−1.5	2.25	0.28125
1	.375	0.375	−0.5	0.25	0.09375
2	.375	0.75	0.5	0.25	0.09375
3	.125	0.375	1.5	2.25	0.28125
Total		$\mu = 1.5$			$\sigma^2 = 0.75$

These general probability distribution formulas are exactly the same as the formula you learned in Chapter 3 when using a frequency distribution table for a population.

Population mean for a frequency table: $\mu = \sum fX/N$

For every X, the associated probability of X is $P(X) = f/N$; therefore,

$$\mu = \frac{\sum fX}{N} = \sum[XP(X)]$$

For the same reason, $P(X) = f/N$, the population variance for a frequency table:

$$\sigma^2 = \frac{SS}{N} = \sum \frac{f(X - \mu)^2}{N} = \sum[(X - \mu)^2 P(X)]$$

Population standard deviation: $\sigma = \sqrt{\text{Variance}}$

Let's verify the answers calculated from the probability distribution formulas with the simplified formulas from the binomial probability distribution.

$$\mu = np = 3(.5) = 1.5$$

$$\sigma^2 = npq = 3(.5)(.5) = 0.75$$

$$\sigma = \sqrt{npq} = \sqrt{0.75} = 0.87$$

The binomial probability distribution is a special type of probability distribution. Its simplified formulas generate the same answers for μ, σ^2, and σ as a regular probability distribution. Once you replace $P(X) = f/N$, the formulas are mathematically identical to the ones you used in Chapter 3 for the frequency distribution of a population.

Binomial probability distributions have wide application because many things in life can be classified into success or failure. For example, a set of product quality test outcomes can be classified as successes or failures. The probability of success and the probability of failure don't always split evenly at 50:50. Let's go over an example where the probability of success and the probability of failure are not evenly split.

EXAMPLE 5.1

A statistics professor uses quizzes to evaluate students' learning. There are five multiple choice questions in a quiz. Each question has four options: a, b, c, and d. What is the probability of a student simply guessing blindly and getting the answers to four out of the five questions correct?

There are five questions, $n = 5$; the student gets four questions correct, $r = 4$.

The probability of success for each question is $p = 1/4 = .25$.

The probability of failure for each question is $q = 1 - p = .75$.

$$P(4) = C_r^n\, p^r q^{(n-r)} = C_4^5 (.25)^4 (.75)^{(5-4)} = \frac{5!}{(5-4)!4!}(.25)^4(.75)^1 = 5(.25)^4(.75)^1 = .0146$$

As you can tell, blindly guessing four out of the five questions correctly is a low-probability event. This student is very lucky to get such an outcome by guessing blindly. Probability is often linked with being lucky. People have the tendency to think that positive things are more likely to happen and negative things are less likely to happen than the calculated probability. For example, people who buy lottery tickets tend to think that they will be the big winners someday. No one ever wakes up in the morning and thinks that he or she will get into a car accident because of texting while driving. However, the probability of getting into a car accident when driving distracted is much higher than the probability of being the jackpot winner of a lottery. We will learn how to calculate the probability of winning a lottery in the next section.

Pop Quiz

1. Which one of the following is not a required attribute of a binomial probability distribution?

   a. The procedure has a fixed number of trials.

   b. The trials are independent of one another.

   c. There are only two possible outcomes for each trial: success and failure.

   d. The probability of a success is $p = .5$, and the probability of a failure is $q = .5$.

2. When Events A and B are mutually exclusive, what is $P(A \text{ or } B)$?

   a. $P(A) + P(B)$

   b. $P(A) - P(B)$

   c. $P(A) \times P(B)$

   d. $\dfrac{P(A)}{P(B)}$

Answers: 1. d, 2. a

PRACTICAL PROBABILITY APPLICATION: WINNING THE MEGA-MILLION LOTTERY

Newspapers like to headline people winning lottery jackpots with huge payouts. Many people dream about winning lotteries themselves. It is human nature to overestimate the probability of positive events but underestimate the probability of negative events. Although the probability of getting injured or killed in a car accident due to distracted driving is almost 1,000 times higher than the probability of winning a lottery, you hear more people asserting that they will win lotteries than that they will get into car accidents.

Let's apply the basic probability principle to a practical matter: figuring out the probability of winning the jackpot of a lottery. All you have to do is to apply the probability formula:

$$P(\text{Winning the jackpot}) = \frac{\text{Number of ways winning numbers can happen}}{\text{Total number of all possible numbers}}$$

The probability of winning the jackpot formula is exactly the same as

$$P(A) = \frac{\text{Number of ways Event A can happen}}{\text{Total number of all possible outcomes}}$$

Let's demonstrate the process by using several examples.

EXAMPLE 5.2

Ohio's Pick 3 lottery has many different ways of playing. Winning numbers are selected from three sets of one-digit numbers. In a "straight-bet" situation, a player's three-digit number has to match in the exact order as the winning number. What is the probability of winning a straight bet in the Pick 3 lottery?

One-digit numbers range from 0 to 9.

The game is to pick three numbers out of three sets of one-digit numbers.

The probability of picking the first number correctly is 1/10.

The probability of picking the second number correctly is 1/10.

The probability of picking the third number correctly is 1/10.

Players have to match all numbers in the exact order as the winning number.

$$P(\text{Winning Pick 3}) = \frac{1}{10} \times \frac{1}{10} \times \frac{1}{10} = \frac{1}{1000}.$$

The sample space for all possible numbers in a Pick 3 lottery comprises numbers from 000 to 999, that is, 1,000 different numbers. The winning number has to match all three numbers in exact order in a straight bet. There is only one winning number under this rule. Therefore, the probability of winning the Pick 3 is 1/1000.

It is pretty easy to calculate the winning probability for Pick 3 games. Let's look into other popular lottery games with big jackpots. Bigger jackpots often involve more complicated lottery rules. You might have heard that in some lottery rules, the order of numbers does not matter. How will it affect the winning probability when the order of numbers does not matter? We will find out the answer in the next example.

EXAMPLE 5.3

The multistate Mega-Million lottery is a popular lottery that attracts players from multiple states because of its big jackpot prize. It recently changed its rules for winning. Both old rules and new rules are provided for you to calculate the winning probability. Under the old rules, players picked six numbers from two separate pools of numbers: five different numbers from 1 to 56 (white balls) and one number from 1 to 46 (yellow balls). You win the jackpot by matching all six winning numbers in a drawing. The order of numbers does not matter. The new rules state that players may pick six numbers from two separate pools of numbers: five different numbers from 1 to 75 (white balls) and one number from 1 to 15 (yellow balls). What are the probabilities of winning the jackpot under these two different sets of rules?

Under the old rules, let's figure out the following probabilities:

Picking the first number correctly: 1/56.

Picking the second number correctly: 1/55 (The rule states that players must select different numbers, and there are 55 different numbers left after the first one is picked.)

Picking the third number correctly: 1/54 (The rule states that players must select different numbers, and there are 54 different numbers left after the first two are picked.)

Picking the fourth number correctly: 1/53 (The rule states that players must select different numbers, and there are 53 different numbers left after the first three are picked.)

Picking the fifth number correctly: 1/52 (The rule states that players must select different numbers, and there are 52 different numbers left after the first four are picked.)

Once the five correct numbers are picked, the order of the numbers does not matter. There are five different numbers that can be in the first place, four different numbers in the second place, three different numbers in the third place, two different numbers in the fourth place, and one number left in the fifth place. Accordingly, there are $5 \times 4 \times 3 \times 2 \times 1 = 120$ possible combinations of these five numbers in different orders.

Probability of picking the one number from a different pool correctly: 1/46

Only one number is picked from the yellow balls, so you don't have to worry about the order.

Players must pick all six numbers correctly to win the jackpot; therefore, the probability of winning is

$$\frac{5 \times 4 \times 3 \times 2 \times 1}{56 \times 55 \times 54 \times 53 \times 52 \times 46} = \frac{120}{21085384320} = \frac{1}{175711536}$$

(Continued)

(Continued)

The sample space for all possible numbers in a Mega-Million Lottery under the old rules is 21,085,384,320 numbers. Once the correct numbers are picked, their order does not matter. There are 120 different combinations of orders for the first five numbers. Therefore, the probability of winning the jackpot is 120/21085384320, which can be simplified to 1/175711536.

Thus, players have a 1 in roughly 176 million chance of winning the Mega-Million Lottery jackpot under the old rules.

Under the new rules, let's figure out the following probabilities for picking each number correctly:

Picking the first number correctly: 1/75

Picking the second number correctly: 1/74

Picking the third number correctly: 1/73

Picking the fourth number correctly: 1/72

Picking the fifth number correctly: 1/71

Once the five correct numbers are picked, their order does not matter. There are five different numbers that can be in the first place, four different numbers in the second place, three different numbers in the third place, two different numbers in the fourth place, and one number left in the fifth place. There are thus $5 \times 4 \times 3 \times 2 \times 1 = 120$ possible combinations of these five numbers in different orders.

Probability of picking the one number from a different pool correctly: 1/15

Players must pick all six numbers correctly to win the jackpot; therefore, the probability of winning is

$$\frac{5 \times 4 \times 3 \times 2 \times 1}{75 \times 74 \times 73 \times 72 \times 71 \times 15} = \frac{120}{31066902000} = \frac{1}{258890850}$$

The sample space for all possible numbers in a Mega-Million Lottery under the new rules is 31,066,902,000 numbers. Once the correct numbers are picked, the order of numbers does not matter. There are 120 different combinations of orders for the first five numbers. Therefore, the probability of winning the jackpot is 120/31066902000, which can be simplified to 1/258890850.

THE DICE GAME

Probabilities are also commonly applied in dice games. A die is a three-dimensional cube with six sides; *dice* refers to two or more such objects. Each side has a different number of dots ranging from 1 to 6.

EXAMPLE 5.4

When you roll a die, what are the probabilities of getting 0, 1, 2, 3, 4, 5, 6, and 7 dots?

In Chapter 2, we discussed the probabilities of obtaining various numbers of dots by throwing one die, as shown in Table 5.4. It is clear that it is not possible to get 0 dots or

(Continued)

(Continued)

7 dots by throwing a single die. When some events are definitely not happening, their probabilities are 0. Therefore, $P(0) = 0$ and $P(7) = 0$. The rest of the probabilities are $P(1) = P(2) = P(3) = P(4) = P(5) = P(6) = 1/6 = .167$.

TABLE 5.4   Probabilities of Obtaining Various Numbers of Dots by Throwing One Die

X (NUMBER OF DOTS)	PROBABILITY P(X)
1	1/6 = .167
2	1/6 = .167
3	1/6 = .167
4	1/6 = .167
5	1/6 = .167
6	1/6 = .167
Total	1

EXAMPLE 5.5

What is the probability of throwing a single die to get a number smaller than 4 or an odd number?

This is a probability question of either Event A or Event B, expressed as $P(A \text{ or } B)$ or $P(A \cup B)$, or "the probability of A union B." First, we need to verify if Events A and B are mutually exclusive. Event A contains numbers smaller than 4, that is, $\{1, 2, 3\}$; Event B contains odd numbers, $\{1, 3, 5\}$. Event A and Event B are not mutually exclusive. Events A and B overlap with each other. Therefore, we need to introduce the Addition Rule 2 of probability.

> Addition Rule 2 of probability: When Event A and Event B are not mutually exclusive, the probability of either Event A or Event B happening, or both, is the sum of the probabilities of each event minus the probability of the overlap of the two events, $P(A \text{ or } B) = P(A \cup B) = P(A) + P(B) - P(A \cap B)$.

The overlap of the two events is expressed as $P(A \cap B)$, or "Event A intersects Event B." In the example, Event A is a number smaller than 4, $A = \{1, 2, 3\}$, and Event B is an odd number, $B = \{1, 3, 5\}$. The overlap between Event A and Event B is $A \cap B = \{1, 3\}$.

A ∩ B means that both events are true at the same time. The numbers are both smaller than 4 and odd numbers.

A Venn diagram for Events A and B when they are not disjoint is shown in Figure 5.2. The light blue circle with a solid black outline represents the probability of Event A, $P(A)$; the white circle with a black dashed outline represents the probability of Event B, $P(B)$; and the darker blue portion represents the probability of both Events A and B, $P(A \cap B)$.

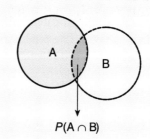

$P(A \cap B)$

$$P(A \cup B) = P(A) + P(B) - P(A \cap B)$$

The reason we subtract the overlap is to eliminate the double-counting, in order to keep an accurate count of all simple events.

Event A = {1, 2, 3}, and its probability is $P(A) = 3/6 = .5$

Event B = {1, 3, 5}, and its probability is $P(B) = 3/6 = .5$

The overlapping part of Events A and B is {1, 3}, and its probability is $P(A \cap B) = 2/6 = .333$. This probability gets counted twice, once with Event A and again with Event B.

$$P(A \text{ or } B) = P(A \cup B) = P(A) + P(B) - P(A \cap B) = .5 + .5 - .33 = .67$$

The probability of throwing a die to get a number smaller than 4 or an odd number is .67.

We can also verify the calculated probability by listing all the simple events in each term.

The sample space for throwing a die is {1, 2, 3, 4, 5, 6}.

Event A covers numbers smaller than 4; A = {1, 2, 3}, and $P(A) = 3/6 = .5$.

Event B covers odd numbers; B = {1, 3, 5}, and $P(B) = 3/6 = .5$.

A ∩ B requires that both Event A and Event B happen at the same time. The numbers need to be smaller than 4 and odd numbers; A ∩ B = {1, 3}, and $P(A \cap B) = 2/6 = .33$.

A ∪ B means that either Event A or Event B happens. The numbers can be smaller than 4 or odd numbers; A ∪ B = {1, 2, 3, 5}, and $P(A \cup B) = 4/6 = .67$.

EXAMPLE 5.6

Use a probability distribution to determine the mean, variance, and standard deviation of the total numbers of dots from throwing two dice.

We discussed the probabilities of obtaining specific numbers of dots by throwing two dice in Chapter 2. The total numbers of dots from throwing two dice and their probabilities are shown in Table 5.5a. These probabilities allow us to put together a **probability distribution** table for the total numbers of dots from throwing two dice. There are three requirements for constructing a probability distribution table:

1. The variable X is a discrete, random, and numerical variable. The number of possible values in X is finite. Each value is associated with a probability.

2. The probability of each value needs to be within 0 and 1, inclusive. This is expressed as $0 \leq P(X) \leq 1$.

3. The sum of the probabilities of all the values is 1. It is expressed as $\sum P(X) = 1$.

TABLE 5.5a   Total Numbers of Dots From Throwing Two Dice and Their Probabilities

X (NUMBER OF DOTS)	P(X) (PROBABILITY)
2 (1,1)	1/36 = .028
3 (1,2), (2,1)	2/36 = .056
4 (1,3), (2,2), (3,1)	3/36 = .083
5 (1,4), (2,3), (3,2), (4,1)	4/36 = .111
6 (1,5), (2,4), (3,3), (4,2), (5,1)	5/36 = .139
7 (1,6), (2,5), (3,4), (4,3), (5,2), (6,1)	6/36 = .167
8 (2,6), (3,5), (4,4), (5,3), (6,2)	5/36 = .139
9 (3,6), (4,5), (5,4), (6,3)	4/36 = .111
10 (4,6), (5,5), (6,4)	3/36 = .083
11 (5,6), (6,5)	2/36 = .056
12 (6,6)	1/36 = .028
Total	**1.001**

The total numbers of dots from two dice could be 2, 3, 4, 5, 6, 7, 8, 9, 10, 11, and 12. When two dice are thrown, the values of the total number of dots are random, discrete, and numerical. The number of possible values is 11. Each value is associated with a probability, and the probability of each value is within 0 and 1. The total probability is $\sum P(X) = 1$. This example fulfills all three requirements of a probability distribution.

The $\sum P(X)$ (or the sum of all probabilities) equals 1.001 instead of 1, which is attributable to rounding.

Population mean for a probability distribution: $\mu = \sum[XP(X)]$

Population variance for a probability distribution: $\sigma^2 = \sum[(X-\mu)^2 P(X)]$

Population standard deviation for a probability distribution:

$$\sigma = \sqrt{\text{Variance}} = \sqrt{\sum[(X-\mu)^2 P(X)]}$$

Let's document the step-by-step process by adding columns to Table 5.5a. The new columns are shown in Table 5.5b. According to the order of operations in the formula $\mu = \sum[XP(X)]$, the multiplication between X and $P(X)$ inside the brackets needs to be

TABLE 5.5b Mean, Variance, and Standard Deviation of the Total Numbers of Dots From Throwing Two Dice and Their Probabilities

X (NUMBER OF DOTS)	P(X) (PROBABILITY)	XP(X)	$(X-\mu)$	$(X-\mu)^2$	$(X-\mu)^2 P(X)$
2	.028	0.056	−5.0	25	0.702
3	.056	0.168	−4.0	16	0.899
4	.083	0.332	−3.0	9	0.750
5	.111	0.555	−2.0	4	0.447
6	.139	0.834	−1.0	1	0.141
7	.167	1.169	0.0	0	0.000
8	.139	1.112	1.0	1	0.137
9	.111	0.999	2.0	4	0.441
10	.083	0.83	3.0	9	0.744
11	.056	0.616	4.0	16	0.893
12	.028	0.336	5.0	25	0.698
Total	1.001	$\mu = 7.0$			$\sigma^2 = 5.9$

(Continued)

(Continued)

done first. Add up every $XP(X)$ to obtain $\Sigma[XP(X)]$ at the end. According to the order of operations in the formula $\sigma^2 = \Sigma[(X - \mu)^2 P(X)]$, three more columns need to be created: $(X - \mu)$, $(X - \mu)^2$, and $(X - \mu)^2 P(X)$. Then add up every $(X - \mu)^2 P(X)$ to obtain $\Sigma[(X - \mu)^2 P(X)]$ at the end.

According to Table 5.5b,

$$\text{mean} = \mu = \Sigma[XP(X)] = 7.0$$

$$\text{variance} = \sigma^2 = \Sigma[(X - \mu)^2 P(X)] = 5.9$$

$$\text{and standard deviation} = \sigma = \sqrt{\text{Variance}} = \sqrt{\Sigma[(X - \mu)^2 P(X)]} = \sqrt{5.9} = 2.4$$

The mean number of dots from throwing two dice is seven, and the standard deviation is 2.4.

Gambling payouts are tied to the probabilities of events. The rule is that the smaller the probabilities, the larger the payouts. That is the reason why throwing two dice landing seven dots will not win any payout.

Probability seems to have a natural affiliation with gambling, such as the lottery and dice games. The application of the probability formula in calculating the probability of winning the Mega-Million lottery jackpot or the dice games shows that the basic principle of calculating the probability of a particular event of interest is to figure out how many ways that event can happen divided by the number of all possible events.

 Pop Quiz

1. Which one of the following attributes is not required for constructing a probability distribution table?

   a. The variable X is a discrete, random, numerical variable. The number of

possible values of X is finite. Each value is associated with a probability.

   b. The probability of each value needs to be within 0 and 1, inclusive. This is expressed as $0 \leq P(X) \leq 1$.

c. The sum of the probabilities of all the values equals 1. It is expressed as $\sum P(X) = 1$.

d. The probability remains the same for every value.

2. What is the probability of throwing two dice to get the total number of dots greater than 4 and odd numbers?

a. .250

b. .333

c. .444

d. .667

Answers: 1. d, 2. c

Linkage Between Probability and Z Score in a Normal Distribution

In a standard normal distribution, the area under the curve of a probability distribution equals 1 because it covers all possible values of Z. When you obtain a specific Z score, you can identify the location of that Z score in the distribution. Using the Z score as a boundary, the area under the curve of a probability distribution can be divided. For example, for Z > 2, the probability $P(Z > 2)$ can be identified. The empirical rule (68–95–99.7 rule) provides a rough linkage between probabilities and Z scores under the normal distribution: 68% of the values are within $-1 \le Z \le 1$, 95% are within $-2 \le Z \le 2$, and 99.7% are within $-3 \le Z \le 3$, as discussed in Chapter 4. We can explore the linkage between probabilities and Z scores in more detail with a probability density function. A probability density function describes the probability for a continuous, random variable to be in a given range of values. When the normal distribution is expressed by Z scores, the probability density function formula is as given below:

$$y = \frac{1}{\sigma\sqrt{2\pi}} e^{-\frac{1}{2}\left(\frac{x-\mu}{\sigma}\right)^2}$$

Under the standard normal distribution, $\mu = 0$ and $\sigma = 1$, the function can be simplified to

$$y = \frac{1}{\sqrt{2\pi}} e^{-\frac{z^2}{2}}$$

$$e \cong 2.71828\ldots$$

$$\pi \cong 3.14159\ldots$$

The formula looks scary, but the good news is that you don't actually have to do any calculation using this formula. Some very considerate and smart people have created the Standard Normal Distribution Table (Z Table) to provide precise linkages between probabilities and Z values, as shown in Appendix A. All you need to do is learn how to use the Standard Normal Distribution Table. Many different ways to present the Z Table have shown up in various statistics textbooks. The Z Table ranges from one to eight pages, with different instructions on how to use it. For this book, I chose to use a two-page Z Table with one page of instructions. The first page of the Z Table consists of positive Z values, and the second page consists of negative Z values. It is important that you follow the instructions on how to use the Z Table. Keep in mind that Z (capital Z) stands for a collection of Z values and z (lowercase z) stands for a particular z value specified in a problem statement.

Here is a list of what you need to know about the Z Table:

1. All Z values are reported to two places after the decimal point, and all probabilities are reported to four places after the decimal point.

2. The column represents Z values to one place after the decimal point, and the row represents Z values' second place after the decimal point.

3. The intersection between the column and the row shows the area to the left of the specified z value or the probability of all Z values smaller than the specified z value, which is expressed as $P(Z < z)$.

4. If the problem statement asks for the probability of Z values larger than the specified z value, which is expressed as $P(Z > z)$, it can be calculated as 1 minus the probability listed in the Z Table.

Once you learn how to use the Z Table, your understanding of the linkage between probabilities and Z scores will go beyond the limited, special Z values as stated in the empirical rule. You will be able to figure out the probability associated with any specified range of Z values. Let's use examples to illustrate the use of the Z Table. You will learn to figure out the probability to the left of a particular z value, $P(Z < z)$; the probability to the right of a particular z value, $P(Z > z)$; or the probability in between two specified z values, $P(z_1 < Z < z_2)$.

EXAMPLE 5.7

Find the probabilities associated with the specified Z values.

a. What is the probability of having a cholesterol level less than 1.53 standard deviations above the mean?

It is important to learn to mathematically express the probability of less than 1.53 standard deviations above the mean as $P(Z < 1.53)$.

Draw and identify this area in the standard normal distribution curve. The drawing does not need to be precise, but it helps identify any additional steps required to figure out the probability (Figure 5.3).

FIGURE 5.3   Using the Z Table to Figure Out $P(Z < 1.53)$

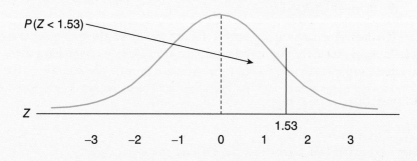

The Z Table provides the probability to the left of the specified Z values. According to the Z Table, $P(Z < 1.53) = .9370$; no additional calculation is needed. The probability of having a cholesterol level less than 1.53 standard deviations above the mean is .9370.

b. What is the probability of being shorter than 0.25 standard deviations below the mean in height?

It is important to learn to mathematically express the probability of being shorter than 0.25 standard deviations below the mean as $P(Z < -0.25)$. Then draw and identify this area in the standard normal distribution curve (Figure 5.4).

FIGURE 5.4   Using the Z Table to Figure Out $P(Z < -0.25)$

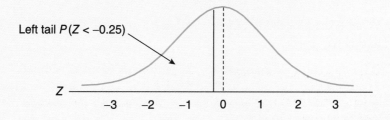

(Continued)

(Continued)

The Z Table provides $P(Z < z)$. Therefore, the answer for $P(Z < -0.25)$ can be found directly in the Z Table: $P(Z < -0.25) = .4013$.

c. What is the probability of scoring higher than 1.78 standard deviations above the mean on the SAT?

The mathematical way to express the probability of a score higher than 1.78 standard deviations above the mean is $P(Z > 1.78)$. Once you have stated this, draw and identify this area in the standard normal distribution curve. The drawing helps you to identify any additional steps required to figure out the probability (Figure 5.5).

FIGURE 5.5   Using the Z Table to Figure Out $P(Z > 1.78)$

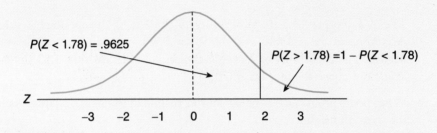

The Z Table provides $P(Z < z)$. It specifies the area to the left of the specified Z value. But Example 5.7c asks for $P(Z > 1.78)$, the area to the right of the z value. The entire area under the curve is 1. Therefore, the area to the right of the z value equals 1 minus the area to the left of the z value; that is, $P(Z > 1.78)$ $= 1 - P(Z < 1.78) = 1 - .9625 = .0375$.

d. What is the probability of being within 0.5 standard deviations of the mean in running speed?

It is important to learn to express the probability of being within 0.5 standard deviations from the mean as $P(-0.5 < Z < 0.5)$. Once you have expressed this, draw and identify this area in the standard normal distribution curve. The drawing does not need to be precise, but it helps identify any additional steps required to figure out the probability (Figure 5.6).

FIGURE 5.6 Using the Z Table to Figure Out $P(-0.5 < Z < 0.5)$

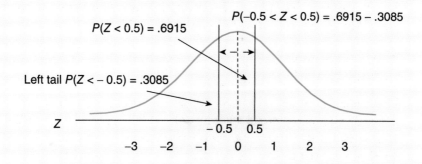

The Z Table provides $P(Z < z)$.

$$P(Z < -0.5) = .3085$$

$$P(Z < 0.5) = .6915$$

Therefore, the area in the middle, $P(-0.5 < Z < 0.5)$, which is the difference between $P(Z < 0.5)$ and $P(Z < -0.5)$, is $.6915 - .3085 = .383$.

You have learned to use Z values to identify probabilities in the previous four examples. In the next three examples, you will learn the same process but from a different perspective. We can use the known probabilities to figure out the Z values.

EXAMPLE 5.8

Find the Z values associated with the specified probabilities.

a. What is the Z value that sets the top 1% apart from the rest of the distribution?

The mathematical way to express the z value that sets the top 1% apart from the rest of the distribution is $P(Z < z) = .99$. Once you have expressed this, draw and identify this area in the standard normal distribution curve. The top 1% refers to the right tail. The probability of a right tail is 1 minus the rest of the distribution. The area to the left of the Z value $= 1 - .01 = .99$. The Z Table

(Continued)

(Continued)

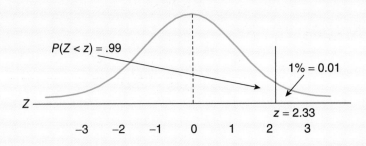

provides $P(Z < z)$; therefore we need to identify a Z value that gives a $P(Z < z)$ as close to .99 as possible. The probability closest to .99 in the Z Table is .9901, and the Z value associated with this probability is 2.33, as shown in Figure 5.7. $Z = 2.33$ sets the top 1% apart from the rest of the distribution.

b. What Z values set the boundaries of the middle 50% from the rest of the distribution?

The mathematical way to express the Z values that set the boundaries of the middle 50% from the rest of the distribution is $P(-z < Z < z) = .50$. Due to the symmetrical attributes of the Z Table, the left side is the mirror image of the right side. The middle 50% sits in the center of the distribution, with 25% above the mean and 25% below the mean. The Z values that set the boundaries have the same magnitude but with different signs—one is positive and the other is negative. Once you have expressed this, draw and identify this area in the standard normal distribution curve (Figure 5.8).

Left tail $P(Z < -z) = .25$

You need to identify a Z value that gives a $P(Z < -z)$ as close to .25 as possible. The probability in the Z Table closest to .25 is .2514, and the Z value associated with this probability is −0.67, as shown in Figure 5.8.

Using the symmetry of the Z Table, you know that the other Z value above the mean is 0.67.

Therefore, the Z values that set the boundaries of the middle 50% from the rest of the distribution are −0.67 and 0.67.

FIGURE 5.8   Using the Z Table to Figure Out $P(-z < Z < z) = .50$

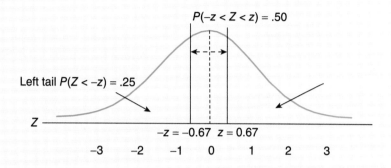

c. What Z value sets the fastest 5% of swimmers' times in a 100-meter freestyle race apart from the rest of the distribution?

It is important to mathematically express the probability correctly. The faster the swimmer, the less time it takes to complete an event. Therefore, the fastest 5% of swimmers' times is at the left tail, $P(Z < -z) = .05$. Once this has been expressed, draw and identify this area in the standard normal distribution curve (Figure 5.9).

There are two probabilities equally close to .05 in the Z Table, .0505 and .0495, and the corresponding Z values are −1.64 and −1.65, respectively. Either answer is fine. However, I recommend using the z value with the larger absolute value to set a higher standard for future statistical testing purposes. Some statistics textbooks even go for interpolation to get a Z value of −1.645 and then round it to −1.65. The top 5% of swimmers' times are faster than 1.65 standard deviations below the mean.

FIGURE 5.9   Using the Z Table to Figure Out $P(Z < -z) = .05$

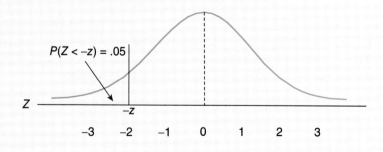

Pop Quiz

1. The connection between the probabilities and Z scores is made possible by

   a. the multiplication rule of probability.

   b. the Addition Rule 1 of probability.

   c. the Addition Rule 2 of probability.

   d. the probability density function.

2. Which one of the following attributes applies to the Z Table?

a. All possible Z values under the normal distribution curve have a probability equal to 1.

b. If you cut the Z Table in the middle, the left side is a mirror image of the right side.

c. $P(Z > z) = 1 - P(Z < z)$

d. All of the above attributes apply to the Z Table.

Answers: 1. d, 2. d

PROBABILITIES, Z SCORES, AND RAW SCORES

You have learned the connection between Z values and probabilities in a normal distribution from the previous section. However, it is unusual to hear someone say that he or she scored 1.57 standard deviations above the mean in a Sociology final exam. The linkage between probabilities and Z scores in a normal distribution needs to be extended further to raw scores to make this connection fully practical and useful. Such a connection between raw scores and probabilities also helps with interpreting raw scores. The connection between raw scores and Z scores is through the Z formulas you learned in Chapter 4. Let's review the Z formulas. Repetition is a good way to learn statistics.

The Z formula for a population is $Z = (X - \mu)/\sigma$. When Z scores are calculated for a sample, both μ and σ are unknown, so the Z formula needs to be adjusted to $Z = (X - \bar{X})/s$. Therefore, the linkage between probabilities and raw scores can be established by a two-step process:

1. Transform raw scores (X) to Z scores by using the Z formula:

$$Z = \frac{X - \mu}{\sigma} \quad \text{or} \quad Z = \frac{X - \bar{X}}{s}$$

2. Use the Z Table to connect the Z scores with probabilities.

Let's use examples to demonstrate this two-step process.

EXAMPLE 5.9

A prestigious college only accepts students with ACT composite scores above the 80th percentile. Assuming that ACT scores are normally distributed with $\mu = 21.0$ and $\sigma = 5.4$, what ACT composite scores are required to get into this college?

This example provides a known probability that directly connects to a Z score via the Z Table. Then through the Z formula, a raw score can be calculated.

Draw and identify this area under the standard normal distribution curve. Based on the Z Table, the 80th percentile means $P(Z < z) = .80$. According to the Z Table, the probability closest to .80 is .7995. The corresponding Z value for .7995 is $Z = 0.84$ (Figure 5.10).

The raw score for $z = 0.84$ can be calculated from the Z formula:

$$Z = \frac{X - \mu}{\sigma}$$

$$0.84 = \frac{X - 21}{5.4}$$

$$X = 25.54$$

The college wants students who score higher than the 80th percentile, that is, higher than the scores of 80% of the students who took the exam. The probability of scoring higher than the 80th percentile is directly linked with a Z score higher than 0.84. Then the Z score links back to the ACT composite score with $\mu = 21.0$ and $\sigma = 5.4$. The raw score is calculated as 25.54. Therefore, students with ACT composite scores of 26 or higher may be accepted by this college.

FIGURE 5.10   Using the Z Table to Figure Out the Z Value for $P(Z < z) = .80$

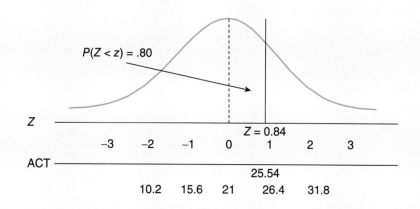

NOTE: ACT = American College Test.

The two-step procedures that link the probabilities with Z scores and link Z scores with raw scores provide the exact location where the value is in relation to the rest of the distribution. This is a good way to interpret raw scores, especially in measures that are not as widely used as standardized exams.

Psychologists and other social scientists constantly develop new measures to quantify social or psychological attributes according to certain rules. In the next example, we will look at a newly developed measure to quantify "life satisfaction."

EXAMPLE 5.10

Satisfaction with life is a subjective feeling that psychologists have tried to measure over the past three decades. Researchers usually ask participants to indicate their level of agreement with statements such as "I feel I can take on anything in life," "I am happy about everything in my life," or "I have a cheerful influence on other people." Assume that life satisfaction scores are normally distributed, with $\bar{X} = 35$ and $s = 8$. What is the probability of randomly selecting an individual whose life satisfaction score is higher than 50?

The question asks for $P(X > 50)$. The raw score 50 needs to be transformed into a Z score. The Z Table provides the probability of Z scores lower than this z score, $P(Z < z)$. Then $P(Z > z)$ can be calculated as $1 - P(Z < z)$. Here is the two-step process.

Step 1.

$$Z = \frac{X - \bar{X}}{s}$$

$$Z = \frac{50 - 35}{8} = \frac{15}{8} = 1.875$$

All the Z values are reported to two places after the decimal point. Therefore, $Z = 1.875$ needs to be rounded off to 1.88.

Step 2. Draw and identify this area under the standard normal distribution curve, $P(Z > 1.88)$ (Figure 5.11).

According to the Z Table, $P(Z < 1.88) = .9699$

$$P(X > 50) = P(Z > 1.88) = 1 - P(Z < 1.88) = 1 - .9699 = .0301$$

FIGURE 5.11 Using the Z Table to Figure Out P(Z > 1.88)

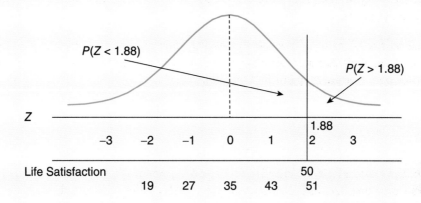

The probability of randomly selecting an individual whose life satisfaction score is greater than 50 is .0301, or 3.01%. This is a small-probability event ($P = .0301$), which means that not many people have life satisfaction scores higher than 50.

Converting raw scores into Z scores provides for easy interpretation of a particular value on the universal yardstick (Z scale). Such a process applies not only to social or psychological measures but also to physical measures such as BMI. The universal yardstick provides a good reference of what is being considered as normal by the society. The ideal of "being normal" usually is expressed by the middle 95% of a distribution.

EXAMPLE 5.11

Adult women's BMIs are normally distributed, with a mean $\mu = 27.1$ and a standard deviation $\sigma = 6.5$. What are the low end and the high end for the middle 95% of adult women's BMIs?

The connection between raw scores and probabilities is indirect. It needs to go through a two-step process. In this example, where the probability is known, you need to figure out the Z scores. First, the connection between the Z score and the probability can be obtained from the Z Table. Second, raw scores can be calculated from the Z formula. Draw and identify this area under the standard normal distribution curve, $P(-z < Z < z) = .95$ (Figure 5.12).

(Continued)

(Continued)

FIGURE 5.12 Using the Z Table to Figure Out $P(-z < Z < z) = .95$

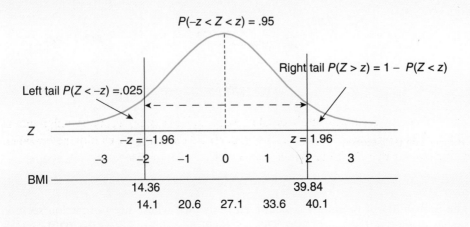

NOTE: BMI = body mass index.

Everything under the standard normal curve is 1, whereby the Z values that separate the middle 95% also divide the two tails evenly.

Left tail $P(Z < -z) =$ Right tail $P(Z > z) = 1 - P(Z < z) = .025$

Therefore, $P(Z < -z) = .025$, and $P(Z < z) = .975$

The Z Table provides $P(Z < z)$; thus, we need to identify a Z value that has $P(Z < -z)$ as close to .025 as possible or a Z value that has $P(Z < z)$ as close to .975 as possible. The Z Table provides $P(Z < -z)$; when the probability is .025, the Z value is −1.96. Or the Z Table provides $P(Z < z)$; when the probability is .975, the Z value is 1.96. The Z values set the boundaries of the middle 95% as −1.96 and 1.96.

Then the raw scores can be calculated from the Z formula. The low end of the middle 95% of adult women's BMI:

$$Z = \frac{X - \mu}{\sigma}$$

$$-1.96 = \frac{X - 27.1}{6.5}$$

$$X = 14.36$$

The high end of the middle 95% of adult women's BMI:

$$Z = \frac{X - \mu}{\sigma}$$

$$1.96 = \frac{X - 27.1}{6.5}$$

$$X = 39.84$$

The low end of the middle 95% of adult women's BMI is 14.36, and the high end is 39.84. This range covers 95% of adult women's BMI. You don't usually meet women with BMI less than 14.36 or higher than 39.84.

Why Statistics Matter

With a preset standard, such as the middle 95% or middle 68%, on the universal yardstick, the Z scale, this approach is widely applied to medical test results such as blood pressure, blood cholesterol level, blood sugar, heart rate, or blood white cell count to flag the test results outside the preset standard for proper treatment.

Pop Quiz

1. Assume that a health insurance company conducted a free health screening for its middle-aged 35- to 65-year-old) customers. During this health screening, the total blood cholesterol was measured for the 2,800 customers who participated. The total blood cholesterol level has $\bar{X} = 216 \, mg/dl$ and $s = 46.5 \, mg/dl$. High total cholesterol is linked to heart diseases. The insurance company decided to use $Z > 1$ as a red flag to send its customers educational information on keeping their cholesterol under control. Above what total cholesterol level would the customers receive this educational information, and what proportion of the customers will receive this information?

(Continued)

(Continued)

Answer:

$Z > 1$ converts to a raw score with $\underline{X} = 216$ mg/dl and $s = 46.5$ mg/dl.

$$Z = \frac{X - \overline{X}}{s}$$

$$1 = \frac{X - 216}{46.5}$$

$$X = 262.5$$

Thus, customers will receive the educational information if their total cholesterol level is higher than 262.5.

$$P(Z > 1) = 1 - P(Z > 1) = 1 - .8413 = .1587$$

Thus, 15.87% of the customers will receive the educational information on keeping total cholesterol under control.

EXERCISE PROBLEMS

1. The Powerball lottery rule states that players may pick six numbers from two separate pools of numbers—five different numbers from 1 to 59 and one number from 1 to 35. You win the jackpot by matching all six winning numbers in a drawing. The order of numbers does not matter. What is the probability of winning the jackpot of the Powerball?

2. The distribution of adult males' BMI is normal, with $\mu = 27.5$ and $\sigma = 6.5$. What proportion of adult males have a BMI between 21 and 41?

3. SAT Critical Reading scores are normally distributed, with $\mu = 497$ and $\sigma = 115$. SAT Math scores are normally distributed, with $\mu = 513$ and $\sigma = 117$. A prestigious university only accepts students who score above the 90th percentile on SAT Critical Reading and SAT Math. What SAT scores are needed to be accepted in this university?

Solutions

1. $P(A) = \dfrac{\text{Number of ways } A \text{ can happen}}{\text{Total number of all possible outcomes}}$

Under the Powerball rule, let's figure out the following probabilities:

Picking the first number correctly: 1/59

Picking the second number correctly: 1/58

Picking the third number correctly: 1/57

Picking the fourth number correctly: 1/56

Picking the fifth number correctly: 1/55

Once the five correct numbers are picked, the order of the numbers does not matter. There are $5 \times 4 \times 3 \times 2 \times 1 = 120$ possible combinations of these five numbers in different orders.

Probability of picking the one number from the second pool correctly: 1/35

$$P(\text{Winning Powerball}) = \frac{5 \times 4 \times 3 \times 2 \times 1}{59 \times 58 \times 57 \times 56 \times 55 \times 35} = \frac{120}{21028021200} = \frac{1}{175233510}$$

The probability of winning the Powerball jackpot is 1 in roughly 175 million.

2. The question asks for $P(21 < X < 41)$. There is no direct connection between raw scores and probability under the normal distribution. The two-step process is needed to solve the problem.

   i. Transform raw scores (X) to Z scores by using the Z formula:

   $$Z = \frac{X - \bar{X}}{s} = \frac{21 - 27.5}{6.5} = -1$$

   $$Z = \frac{X - \bar{X}}{s} = \frac{41 - 27.5}{6.5} = 2.08$$

   ii. Use the Z Table to connect Z scores with probabilities.

   $$P(21 < X < 41) = P(-1 < Z < 2.08)$$

   Draw and identify this area under the standard normal distribution curve, $P(-1 < Z < 2.08)$ (Figure 5.13).

   $P(-1 < Z < 2.08)$ can be calculated as $P(Z < 2.08) - P(Z < -1)$.

   $$P(Z < 2.08) = .9812$$

   $$P(Z < -1) = .1587$$

FIGURE 5.13   Using the Z Table to Figure Out $P(-1 < Z < 2.08)$

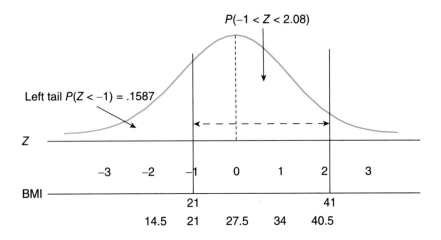

$P(-1 < Z < 2.08)$

Left tail $P(Z < -1) = .1587$

Z

-3   -2   -1   0   1   2   3

BMI

21   41

14.5   21   27.5   34   40.5

NOTE: BMI = body mass index.

$$P(-1 < Z < 2.08) = .9812 - .1587 = .8225$$

The answer is that 82.25% of adult males have a BMI between 21 and 41. This exercise demonstrates that you can figure out the probability within any two specified raw scores by using the two-step process to connect raw scores with Z scores and then Z scores with probabilities.

3. The question asks for the raw score for the 90th percentile on SAT Critical Reading and the 90th percentile on SAT Math.

$$P(Z < z) = .90$$

Draw and identify this area under the standard normal distribution curve, $P(Z < z) = .90$. According to the Z Table, the probability closest to .90 is .8997, which corresponds to $Z = 1.28$ (Figure 5.14).

SAT Critical Reading:

$$Z = \frac{X - \mu}{\sigma}$$

$$1.28 = \frac{X - 497}{115}$$

$$X = 1.28 \times 115 + 497 = 644.2$$

FIGURE 5.14 Using the Z Table to Figure Out $P(Z < z) = .90$

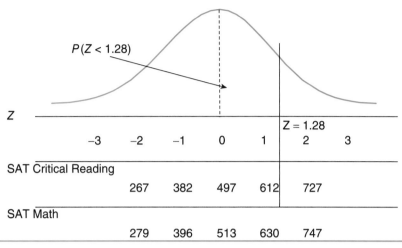

NOTE: SAT = Scholastic Aptitude Test.

SAT Math:

$$Z = \frac{X - \mu}{\sigma}$$

$$1.28 = \frac{X - 513}{117}$$

$$X = 1.28 \times 117 + 513 = 662.76$$

Students need to score 645 or higher on SAT Critical Reading and 663 or higher on SAT Math to be accepted by this university.

Sharpen your skills with SAGE edge!

Visit edge.sagepub.com/bowen for mobile-friendly quizzes, flashcards, videos, and more!

You have learned the basic vocabulary in probability: event, simple event, and sample space. It is important to review the definitions of these terms in the Key Words.

Binomial probability formula:

$$P(r) = C_r^n p^r q^{(n-r)} = \frac{n!}{(n-r)!r!} p^r q^{(n-r)} \quad \text{for } r = 0, 1, 2, 3, \ldots, n$$

Where

p = probability of success in one trial

$q = 1 - p$ = probability of failure in one trial

n = number of trials

r = number of successes in n trials

$P(r)$ = probability of getting exactly r successes in n trials

Binomial probability distribution is a special probability distribution. The calculation of μ, σ^2, and σ in a binomial probability distribution is simplified.

$\mu = np$

$\sigma^2 = npq$

$\sigma = \sqrt{npq}$

Three requirements of a probability distribution are as follows:

1. The variable X is a discrete, random, and numerical variable. The number of possible values in X is finite. Each value is associated with a probability.

2. The probability of each value needs to be within 0 and 1, inclusive. This is expressed as $0 \leq P(X) \leq 1$.

3. The sum of the probabilities of all the values is 1. It is expressed as $\sum P(X) = 1$.

The formulas for calculating the population mean, variance, and standard deviation from a probability distribution are the same as those using a frequency distribution.

Population mean for a frequency table: $\mu = \sum \dfrac{fX}{N}$

For every X, the associated probability of X is $P(X) = \dfrac{f}{N}$; therefore,

$$\mu = \sum \dfrac{fX}{N} = \sum [XP(X)]$$

For the same reason, $P(X) = f/N$, the population variance for a frequency table:

$$\sigma^2 = \dfrac{SS}{N} = \dfrac{\sum f(X-\mu)^2}{N} = \sum [(X-\mu)^2 P(X)]$$

Population standard deviation: $\sigma = \sqrt{\text{Variance}} = \sqrt{\dfrac{\sum f(X-\mu)^2}{N}}$

Three attributes of the Standard Normal Distribution Table (Z Table) are as follows:

1. All Z values are reported to two places after the decimal point, and all probabilities are reported to four places after the decimal point.

2. The column represents Z values to one place after the decimal point, and the row represents Z values' second place after the decimal point.

3. The intersection between the column and the row shows the area to the left of the specified z value, or the probability of all Z values smaller than the specified value, z, which is expressed as

$$P(Z < z)$$

The connection between probabilities and raw scores can be established by a two-step process:

1. Transform raw scores (X) to Z scores by using the Z formula:

$$Z = \dfrac{X - \mu}{\sigma} \quad \text{or} \quad Z = \dfrac{X - \bar{X}}{s}$$

2. Use the Z Table to connect Z scores with probabilities under the normal distribution.

KEY WORDS

Addition Rule 1 of probability: When Event A and Event B are mutually exclusive, the probability of either Event A or Event B happening is the sum of the probabilities of each event: $P(\text{A or B}) = P(\text{A}) + P(\text{B})$.

Addition Rule 2 of probability: When Event A and Event B are not mutually exclusive, the probability of either Event A or Event B, or both, happening is the sum of the probabilities of each event minus the overlapping part of the two events: $P(A \text{ or } B) = P(A \cup B) = P(A) + P(B) - P(A \cap B)$.

Binomial probability distribution: A binomial probability distribution is a probability distribution that applies to variables with only two possible outcomes (i.e., success vs. failure) in each trial. The trials are independent of one another. The probability of a success and the probability of a failure remain the same in all trials.

Disjoint events: Disjoint events are the same things as mutually exclusive events.

Event: An event is defined as a set of outcomes from an experiment or a procedure.

Independent events: Two events A and B are independent when the occurrence of one event does not affect the probability of the occurrence of the other event.

Multiplication rule for independent events: When Event A and Event B are independent, the probability of both events happening is $P(AB) = P(A) \times P(B)$.

Mutually exclusive events: When Event A and Event B are mutually exclusive, it means that only one of the events can happen: If one happens, the other does not.

Probability density function: A probability density function describes the probability for a continuous, random variable to be in a given range of values.

Probability distribution: There are three requirements for a probability distribution:

1. The variable X is a discrete, random, and numerical variable. The number of possible values of X is finite. Each value is associated with a probability.

2. The probability of each value needs to be within 0 and 1, inclusive. This is expressed as $0 \leq P(X) \leq 1$.

3. The sum of the probabilities of all the values equals 1. It is expressed as $\sum P(X) = 1$.

$$\text{Probability of Event A} = P(A) = \frac{\text{Number of ways A can happen}}{\text{Total number of all possible outcomes}}$$

Sample space: A sample space is a complete list of all possible outcomes.

Simple event: A simple event is defined as an elementary event that cannot be broken into simpler parts.

LEARNING ASSESSMENT

Multiple Choices: Circle the best answer to every question.

1. For a normal distribution, $P(Z > 1.5) = .0668$. What is $P(Z < -1.5)$?
   a. .0668
   b. .9332
   c. .9772
   d. .0228

2. What is the answer for $P(Z < 0.25)$?
   a. .25
   b. .75
   c. .5987
   d. -.4013

3. What is the answer for $P(-2 < Z < 1.45)$?
   a. .0963
   b. .9037
   c. .8389
   d. .1611

4. What is the probability that the total number of dots from throwing two dice is eight?
   a. 3/36
   b. 4/36
   c. 5/36
   d. 6/36

5. Which of the following is true?
   a. $P(Z > 2.0) > P(Z > 1.0)$
   b. $P(Z > -2.0) > P(Z > -1.0)$
   c. $P(Z > 0) > P(Z < 0)$
   d. $P(Z < -2.0) > P(Z < -1.0)$

6. What is the answer for $P(-2 < Z < -1)$?
   a. .3413
   b. .4772
   c. .1359
   d. .8185

Free Response Questions: Show step-by step process to obtain the answers.

7. The distribution of adult females' BMI is normal, with $\mu = 27.1$ and $\sigma = 6.5$. What proportion of the adult females have a BMI between 31 and 41?

8. What is the probability of throwing two dice and getting the total number of dots as even numbers greater than six?

9. The Ohio Lottery Classic Lotto's rule stipulates that players may pick 6 different numbers out of 49 numbers. The order of numbers does not matter. You win the jackpot by matching all 6 numbers in a drawing. What is the probability of winning the jackpot of the Ohio Lottery Classic Lotto?

10. A cardiologist studies heart rate variability. Heart rates are normally distributed, with a mean of 68 beats per minute and a standard deviation of 19 among a sample of 100 patients. What is the probability of randomly selecting a patient to obtain a heart rate less than 60?

11. The ACT composite score is normally distributed, with a mean of 21 and a standard deviation of 5.4. What is the ACT composite score that separates the top 30% from the rest of the distribution?

CHAPTER 6

The Central Limit Theorem

After reading and studying this chapter, you should be able to do the following:

- Define sampling error, and explain why it is a frequent, natural occurrence in empirical research
- Identify the principal characteristics of the central limit theorem
- Explain the law of large numbers in calculating probability
- Describe how a Z test is conducted, and interpret the results of a Z test

WHAT YOU KNOW AND WHAT IS NEW

You have learned the connection between raw scores and Z scores via the Z formula in Chapter 4, and the connection between Z scores and probabilities via the Z table in Chapter 5. You knew how to transform a raw score into a Z score, figure out its exact location in the distribution, and figure out the probability of a particular section separated by a specific Z score compared with the rest of the distribution. All of this information continues to be relevant in Chapter 6, where you will learn the most fundamental probability theory, the *central limit theorem*.

In a large population, we can randomly select a sample of n values and calculate the mean of these n values. We can do this again by taking another sample of n values and calculating the mean. The mean we get from the second sample may be very different from the mean from the first sample simply because different values are selected in each sample. The central limit theorem is the theoretical description of the sampling distribution of the mean that teaches us how sample means behave in relation to the population mean, so that we can draw accurate conclusions when conducting hypothesis tests. Hypothesis testing forms the logic of decision-making rules in testing the strength of evidence provided by sample statistics, which is the topic of Chapter 7. This demonstrates the accumulative nature of learning statistics. Concepts that you learned from earlier chapters are necessary and relevant in later chapters. Once you learn the relationship between sample means and population mean, you will learn how to use sample statistics to make inferences about the population parameters. You can calculate the probability of a sample statistic being located within a certain distance from the population parameter. As you will see, Chapter 6 is mostly a logical extension of Chapter 5 with slight modifications.

SAMPLING ERROR

A population is defined as an entire collection of everything or everyone that researchers are interested in studying or measuring. A sample is defined as a subset of the population from which measures are actually obtained. The definitions of samples and population are dealt with in detail in Chapter 1. Such fundamental concepts deserve some repetition. Frankly, repetition is the key to learning statistics. If you have any difficulty in a particular statistical concept the first time you read or hear it, studying it several times will help.

There are many possible samples within a population. No matter how hard you try, how perfectly you plan, and how well you achieve the random sampling, your sample statistics still do not match population parameters exactly. A sampling error is defined as a situation in which a sample is randomly selected and a natural difference, divergence, distance, or error occurs between the sample statistic and the corresponding population parameter. Such differences are really not "errors" because no mistakes are made in the calculation process. They are likely due to random sampling variations. Sample variations are attributed to individual differences from the participants who are included in different samples. There are many kinds of individual differences such as age, height, weight, speed, intelligence, physical strength, artistic skills, creativity, exam scores, and so on. For example, if you randomly select a sample of 25 high school seniors from the population of all high school seniors, you can calculate their mean SAT score. Let's label the mean as $\bar{X}_1$, repeat the procedure to get a second sample of 25 high school students whose mean SAT is $\bar{X}_2$, repeat the procedure to get a third sample of 25 high school students whose mean SAT is $\bar{X}_3$, and you may keep on doing this for k times. These sample means

$\bar{X}_1, \bar{X}_2, \bar{X}_3, \ldots \bar{X}_k$ might not be exactly the same as the population mean. The difference between a sample mean and the population mean is called a sampling error. Sampling errors are unavoidable natural fluctuations due to the fact that different individuals are included in different samples.

If sampling errors always exist, one way or another, the sample statistics are not going to be exactly the same as the population parameters. Why bother to go through all the careful planning and meticulous research designs to ensure the quality of data collection? The key to that question is that sampling errors are random errors. As long as they are random errors, they can be explained by probability theory.

There are many different kinds of errors that can happen when conducting research. Sampling error is just one of them. Besides sampling errors, there are nonsampling errors. Nonsampling errors are mostly avoidable and preventable human errors. Such human errors include survey questions written with ambiguous wording causing different interpretations from respondents, respondents offering socially desirable but not necessarily honest answers, data coding errors, data entry errors, nonresponses, inappropriate statistical analyses, and/or wrong conclusions. Such human errors are not random errors. Nonrandom errors could not be explained by probability theory. Careful planning, meticulous research design, and proper training in statistical analysis are specifically developed to minimize nonsampling errors because nonsampling errors are not fixable or interpretable by probability theory. When a sample contains nonsampling errors, it is inappropriate to use sample statistics to make inferences about the population parameters.

 Pop Quiz

1. Which one of the following sampling procedures makes an effort to minimize nonsampling errors?

    a. TV shows asked the audience to call in to vote for their favorite contestants.

    b. Pollsters asked voters how they cast their ballots at the exit of a voting location.

    c. The ratings collected by ratemyprofessors.com.

    d. University students were assigned a number; then, 10% of the students were selected by a random number generator to provide opinions on the university parking services.

Answer: d

Sampling Distribution of the Sample Means and the Central Limit Theorem

To understand the central limit theorem, you have to assume that a sample of a particular size, n, is randomly selected from a population. Then, the same procedure is repeated k times to create k samples of the same sample size from the same population. To illustrate the process, the outcomes are summarized in Table 6.1.

The sample mean ($\bar{X}$) is calculated for each of the samples. Therefore, we have $\bar{X}_1$ from the first sample, $\bar{X}_2$ from the second sample, and all the way to $\bar{X}_k$ from the kth sample. This hypothetical distribution of all sample means selected from a given population (i.e., $\bar{X}_1, \bar{X}_2, \ldots \bar{X}_k$) is defined as the sampling distribution of the sample means. These sample means might take on different values due to sampling error. When you calculate the mean of all sample means, $\mu_{\bar{X}}$, the answer is the population mean, μ. You can easily calculate the standard deviation of the sample means, which is given a special label, $\sigma_{\bar{X}}$, as the standard error of the mean. The sample means are normally distributed as long as the population is normally distributed. All these characteristics of sample means can be expressed as $N(\mu, \sigma_{\bar{X}})$, which is defined as a normal distribution with a mean of μ and standard deviation of $\sigma_{\bar{X}}$. The standard deviation of all sample means is also called the standard error of the mean. The standard error of the mean is calculated by the population standard deviation divided by the square root of the sample size, $\sigma_{\bar{X}} = \sigma/\sqrt{n}$. Judging by the formula, you can see the larger the sample size, the smaller the standard error of the mean. It demonstrates that using a larger sample size produces a more stable sample mean with less variability and closer to

TABLE 6.1 Randomly Selecting a Sample With n Cases, Then Repeating the Same Procedure k Times

SAMPLING	SAMPLE SIZE	SAMPLE MEAN
Sample 1	n	$\bar{X}_1$
Sample 2	n	$\bar{X}_2$
Sample 3	n	$\bar{X}_3$
Sample 4	n	$\bar{X}_4$
$\vdots$	n	$\vdots$
Sample k	n	$\bar{X}_k$

the population mean. The sampling distribution of the sample means tells us, in theory, if we do repeated random sampling with a particular sample size many times, each sample produces a sample mean. We can understand how sample means behave in relation to the population mean. In reality, the population mean is unknown, and we don't have the time, money, or energy to do repeated sampling an unlimited number of times. Therefore, all we have is the information from one sample. Understanding the sampling distribution of the sample means allows us to use the sample statistic to gain useful insights into the unknown population.

The central limit theorem is a mathematical proposition that describes important characteristics of the sampling distribution of the sample means: distribution shape, central tendency, and variability. The central limit theorem states the following:

1. The sampling distribution of the sample means becomes more and more normally distributed as the sample size increases. When sample size $n > 30$, the sampling distribution of means is approximately normally distributed regardless of the shape of the original population distribution.

2. If the population is normally distributed, the sampling distribution of the sample mean is also normally distributed regardless of the sample size.

3. The mean of all sample means (also called the expected value of the mean) is the population mean, $\mu_{\bar{X}} = \mu$.

4. The standard error of the mean is the standard deviation of all sample means, $\sigma_{\bar{X}} = \sigma/\sqrt{n}$.

In summary, the central limit theorem states that for a sample size $= n$, the distribution of sample means, or $\bar{X}$s, is normally distributed with a mean $\mu_{\bar{X}} = \mu$ and standard deviation $\sigma_{\bar{X}} = \sigma/\sqrt{n}$. This statement is true when the sample size is large, $n > 30$, or when the population is normally distributed. As the sample size increases, the standard error of the mean decreases. In other words, larger samples tend to generate smaller standard errors of the mean; thus, the sample means tend to cluster closer to the population mean than smaller samples. The larger the standard deviation of the population, the larger the standard error of the mean is.

EXAMPLE 6.1

SAT math scores are normally distributed with $\mu = 513$ and $\sigma = 120$. Researchers randomly select a sample with a particular sample size and then repeat the procedure many times. The sample mean is calculated for each sample. The standard error of the mean is the standard deviation of all sample means.

(Continued)

(Continued)

A. What is the standard error of the mean for a sample size of 4?

B. What is the standard error of the mean for a sample size of 25?

C. What is the standard error of the mean for a sample size of 100?

Standard error = $\sigma_{\bar{X}} = \sigma/\sqrt{n}$

A. When $n = 4$, $\sigma_{\bar{X}} = \dfrac{\sigma}{\sqrt{n}} = \dfrac{120}{\sqrt{4}} = 60$

B. When $n = 25$, $\sigma_{\bar{X}} = \dfrac{\sigma}{\sqrt{n}} = \dfrac{120}{\sqrt{25}} = 24$

C. When $n = 100$, $\sigma_{\bar{X}} = \dfrac{\sigma}{\sqrt{n}} = \dfrac{120}{\sqrt{100}} = 12$

There is an inverse relationship between the sample size and the standard error of the mean. As the sample size increases, the standard error of the mean decreases. A small standard error of the mean indicates that the sample means are fairly close to the population mean. The statistics calculated from large sample sizes are more stable and better

Pop Quiz

According to the central limit theorem, which one of the following sampling distributions of the mean might not be normally distributed?

a. When samples of a particular sample size, $n > 30$, are randomly selected from a normally distributed population.

b. When samples of a particular sample size, $n > 30$, are randomly selected from a population that is not normally distributed.

c. When samples of a particular sample size, $n \leq 30$, are randomly selected from a normally distributed population.

d. When samples of a particular sample size, $n \leq 30$, are randomly selected from a population that is not normally distributed.

Answer: d

estimates of population parameters than those from small sample sizes. This is the reason why researchers prefer using sample statistics collected from large sample sizes to small sample sizes in making inferences about the population parameters.

THE LAW OF LARGE NUMBERS

The **law of large numbers** is another probability theorem that describes the relationship between sample means and population means. The law of large numbers describes the results of performing the same experiment multiple times: As the number of trials n approaches infinity, the observed sample mean approaches the population mean. Let X be the number of successes in n independent trials with a probability of success in each trial, p. The population mean is also called the expected value of X, which is expressed as $E(X) = \mu = np$.

Let's use an example to explain the law of large numbers. When you toss a fair coin, the probability of getting a head is .5, and the probability of getting a tail is .5. If you toss 10 coins at the same time, the number of heads you might get is 0, 1, 2, 3, 4, 5, 6, 7, 8, 9, or 10. In any particular trial, you might get 2 heads and 8 tails, or 3 heads and 7 tails. The results might not be split 50–50 as the expected value of heads = np = 10(.5) = 5. That's because you have not done enough trials to come close to infinity. You may continue tossing these 10 coins 100 times, 1,000 times, or 10,000 times. As the number of trials approaches infinity, the observed sample mean approaches the population mean. The law of large numbers is intuitive because it demonstrates, in the long run, that natural fluctuations will even out. Thus, the observed sample mean will equal the population mean (or the expected value) eventually.

The law of large numbers is a simple theorem. Nothing can explain the process better than actually doing such an exercise. Of course, you will not reach the infinite number of trials. However, you will observe the fluctuations through a relatively small number of trials and observe the outcomes over a large number of trials. The last problem in the "Exercise Problems" is a class exercise on the law of large numbers.

The law of large numbers describes the relationship between the sample means and the population mean as which of the following numbers approaches infinity?

a. The number of successes

b. The population mean

c. The number of trials

d. The sample mean

Answer: c

RELATIONSHIPS BETWEEN SAMPLE MEANS AND THE POPULATION MEAN

You learned the Z formula in Chapter 4, allowing you to convert a raw score X to a Z score by using $Z = (X - \mu)/\sigma$. The basic principle of the Z formula is $Z = (\text{raw score} - \text{mean})/\text{standard deviation}$.

Now, you can apply the same principle to convert a sample mean, $\bar{X}$, to a Z value. You learned that the mean of sample means $\mu_{\bar{X}}$ is μ and the standard deviation of sample means, also called the standard error of the mean, is $\sigma_{\bar{X}} = \sigma/\sqrt{n}$, so converting a sample mean to a Z value becomes $Z = (\bar{X} - \mu)/(\sigma/\sqrt{n})$. The Z value provides the exact location of a particular sample mean in the distribution of all sample means. This process allows us to conduct a Z test between a sample mean and the population mean. Z tests measure the difference between a sample statistic and its hypothesized population parameter in units of standard error. Let's use examples to illustrate how to conduct a Z test.

EXAMPLE 6.2

Adult male heights are normally distributed with $\mu = 69$ inches and $\sigma = 6$ inches. What is the probability of randomly selecting a sample of 16 adult males whose mean height is less than 67 inches?

The process of comparing a sample mean to the population mean is slightly different from comparing one individual score to the population mean. According to the question, $P(\bar{X} < 67)$ is the correct mathematical expression. There is no direct connection between $\bar{X}$ and probability, so $\bar{X}$ needs to be converted into a Z value by using $Z = (\bar{X} - \mu)/(\sigma/\sqrt{n})$.

$$Z = \frac{\bar{X} - \mu}{\frac{\sigma}{\sqrt{n}}} = \frac{67 - 69}{\frac{6}{\sqrt{16}}} = \frac{-2}{1.5} = -1.33$$

$$P(\bar{X} < 67) = P(Z < -1.33)$$

Draw and identify this area under the standard normal distribution curve, $P(Z < -1.33)$.

The standard error of the mean = $\sigma/\sqrt{n} = 6/\sqrt{16} = 1.5$ as shown in Figure 6.1 on the adult male height scale.

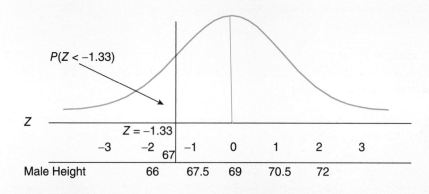

The left tail can be directly obtained from the Z table.

$$P(\bar{X} < 67) = P(Z < -1.33) = .0918$$

The probability of randomly selecting 16 adult males whose mean height is less than 67 inches is .0918 or 9.18%. This example clearly illustrates the differences between what you learned in Chapter 4 converting a raw score X to a Z score by using $Z = (X - \mu)/\sigma$ versus what you learned in this chapter converting a sample mean, $\bar{X}$, to a Z value by using $Z = (\bar{X} - \mu)/(\sigma/\sqrt{n})$. Simply remember that you apply the same principle of calculating the Z score by putting the mean of all the sample means and the standard deviation of the sample means (i.e., the standard error of the mean) in the formula when dealing with comparing a sample mean with a population mean. You should also notice that the standard deviation of all sample means (i.e., the standard error of the mean $\sigma_{\bar{X}} = \sigma/\sqrt{n}$) is much smaller than the population standard deviation, σ.

EXAMPLE 6.3

ACT composite scores are normally distributed with $\mu = 21.0$ and $\sigma = 5.4$. A sample of nine students is randomly selected. What is the probability that the sample mean is greater than 25?

The question asks for $P(\bar{X} > 25)$. There is no direct connection between $\bar{X}$ and probability, so $\bar{X}$ needs to be converted into a Z value by using $Z = (\bar{X} - \mu)/(\sigma/\sqrt{n})$.

$$Z = \frac{\bar{X} - \mu}{\dfrac{\sigma}{\sqrt{n}}} = \frac{25 - 21}{\dfrac{5.4}{\sqrt{9}}} = \frac{4}{1.8} = 2.22$$

Draw and identify this area under the standard normal distribution curve, $P(Z > 2.22)$.

The standard error of the mean $= \sigma_{\bar{x}} = \sigma/\sqrt{n} = 5.4/\sqrt{9} = 1.8$ as shown in Figure 6.2 on the ACT composite scale.

FIGURE 6.2   Using the Z Table to Figure Out $P(Z > 2.22)$

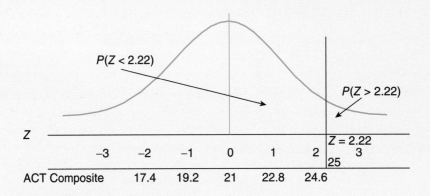

The Z table only provides the area to the left of a particular z value, $P(Z < z)$. The area to the right of that z value can be calculated by $P(Z > z) = 1 - P(Z < z)$.

$$P(\bar{X} > 25) = P(Z > 2.22) = 1 - P(Z < 2.22) = 1 - .9868 = .0132$$

The probability of randomly selecting nine students whose mean ACT composite score is greater than 25 is .0132. This is a low probability occurrence. You might have noticed that it is more common to get an individual ACT score greater than 25 than getting a randomly selected sample of nine students whose sample mean is greater than 25. That is because the standard error of the mean is only 1.8 for a sample of nine students. The sample means are more likely to be clustered around the population mean than individual scores. The difference between 25 and 21 is 2.22 times the standard error of the mean. The linkage between the Z value and the probability tells us that it is an unusual situation. Many medical tests also use the mean and standard deviation to flag unusual situations. In the next example, we will deal with blood cholesterol measures.

EXAMPLE 6.4

The total cholesterol levels for women aged 20 to 30 years are normally distributed with $\mu = 190$ mg/dl and $\sigma = 40$ mg/dl. A sample of 25 women in this age-group is randomly selected. What range of cholesterol scores is expected for the middle 95% of all sample means?

According to the question, $P(X_1 < \bar{X} < X_2) = .95$ is the correct mathematical expression. The connection between sample means and probabilities is not direct. The connection between the Z values and probabilities can be obtained from the Z table. Then, sample means can be calculated from Z values. Draw and identify this area under the standard normal distribution curve, $P(-z < Z < z) = .95$.

You need to identify the middle 95% of the distribution. This question asks you to identify z values from a known probability. The symmetry of the standard normal distribution creates two identical halves. When you cut the normal curve in half at $Z = 0$, the left half is identical to the right half. $P(Z < -z)$ specifies the left tail, which has the same probability as the right tail, $1 - P(Z < z)$. The two tails evenly share the 5% after the middle 95% have been blocked off. Each tail shares $.05 / 2 = .025$ (Figure 6.3).

The Z table provides $P(Z < z)$ for the area to the left of a particular z value. The left tail $P(Z < -z) = .025$ can be directly obtained from the Z table. When you look into the Z table, you find that the z value connected with the probability .025 is $z = -1.96$. Due to the symmetry of the standard normal distribution, the low end of the middle 95% distribution is −1.96, and the high end of the middle 95% is 1.96.

If you insist on going through the Z table to find the high end of the middle 95% distribution without using the symmetry, you may figure out that the right tail is $P(Z > z) = 1 - P(Z < z) = .025$. Therefore, $P(Z < z) = .975$. When you look into the Z table, you find the z value connected with the probability .975 is 1.96.

(Continued)

(Continued)

FIGURE 6.3   Using the Z Table to Figure Out $P(-z < Z < z) = .95$

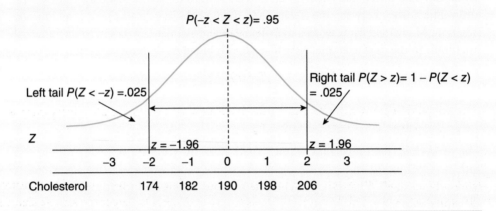

Then, the sample means can be calculated from the Z formula.

The low end of the middle 95% of mean blood cholesterol in a sample of 25 adult women is

$$Z = \frac{\bar{X} - \mu}{\frac{\sigma}{\sqrt{n}}}$$

$$-1.96 = \frac{\bar{X} - 190}{\frac{40}{\sqrt{25}}}$$

$$-1.96 = \frac{\bar{X} - 190}{8}$$

$$\bar{X} = 174.32$$

The high end of the middle 95% of mean blood cholesterol in a sample of 25 adult women is

$$Z = \frac{\bar{X} - \mu}{\frac{\sigma}{\sqrt{n}}}$$

$$1.96 = \frac{\bar{X} - 190}{\frac{40}{\sqrt{25}}}$$

$$1.96 = \frac{\bar{X} - 190}{8}$$

$$\bar{X} = 205.68$$

The low end of the middle 95% of blood cholesterol for a sample of 25 adult women is 174.32 mg/dl and the high end is 205.68 mg/dl.

The Z tests compare an observed sample mean with its known or hypothesized population mean in the units of standard error of the mean, $\sigma_{\bar{x}} - \sigma/\sqrt{n}$. The larger the sample size, the smaller the standard error of the mean. Larger sample sizes produce stable sample statistics, and they tend to cluster closer to the population parameters than smaller sample sizes. That is the reason why sample size is one of the main characteristics of a research study and requires careful advanced planning. If the sample size is too large, it wastes time and resources to collect data. If the sample size is too small, it produces unstable and unreliable statistics that might not be representative of the population parameters.

Social scientists create a standard procedure to test the strength of empirical evidence. For example, the Z tests compare an observed sample mean with its known or hypothesized population mean in the units of standard error. Then, they use the Z table to figure out the probability associated with the calculated Z value. Such a probability forms the basis to evaluate the strength of empirical evidence. Such a standard procedure is discussed in the next chapter: Hypothesis Testing.

Pop Quiz

In the Z formula for an individual raw score X and a Z test for a sample mean, which part of the formula remains the same?

a. Population mean, μ

b. Sample mean, $\bar{X}$

c. Raw score, X

d. Standard error of the mean, $\sigma_{\bar{x}} = \frac{\sigma}{\sqrt{n}}$

Answer: a

EXERCISE PROBLEMS

1. Adult women's BMI is normally distributed with a mean $\mu = 27.1$ and a standard deviation $\sigma = 6.5$.

   a. What is the probability of randomly selecting a group of four women who participate in a nutritional education program and the mean BMI for the sample is less than 25?

   b. What is the probability of randomly selecting a group of 35 women who participate in a nutritional education program and the mean BMI for the sample is less than 25?

   c. Explain the impact of sample size on the results.

2. The SAT verbal score is normally distributed with $\mu = 497$ and $\sigma = 115$. What is the probability of randomly selecting a group of 25 high school seniors to obtain a mean SAT verbal score greater than 450?

3. A businessman just acquired a motor coach. The motor coach has a payload capacity of 13,000 pounds. There are 55 passenger seats and one driver seat inside the coach. Each passenger is allowed to bring a piece of luggage weighing no more than 40 pounds. Adult males' weight is normally distributed with $\mu = 182.5$ and $\sigma = 40.8$, and adult females' weight is normally distributed with $\mu = 165.2$ and $\sigma = 45.6$. Assuming full luggage capacity, what is the highest probability that this motor coach overloads when carrying 55 passengers? *Hint:* Males on average weigh more than females. The highest probability to overload is when the driver is male and all 55 passengers are male.

4. *The law of large numbers class exercise.* In this exercise, students will see the natural fluctuations in a small number of trials. Then, they get to see that when aggregated to a large number of trials, the sample mean approaches the population mean.

   Every student in the class is given the assignment to record the number of heads by tossing 10 coins at the same time. Repeat the process 20 times and report the number of heads for each trial using Table 6.2. Compile the report for the entire class using Table 6.2 in EXCEL. If there are 50 students in the class, you will have $50 \times 20 = 1,000$ repetitions. Calculate the number of heads out of 10 coins with the number of repetitions obtained from the entire class. What is the mean number of heads? How is it compared with the expected value $E(X) = \mu = np = 10(.5) = 5$.

TABLE 6.2 Number of Heads When Tossing 10 Coins at the Same Time

TRIAL	1	2	3	4	5	6	7	8	9	10	11	12	13	14	15	16	17	18	19	20
Student1																				

Solutions

1. Usually, the advertisements of special nutritional programs only show one person's before-and-after pictures to show the dramatic weight reduction. Then, somewhere in a corner, there is a legal disclaimer stating that results are not typical. You should never put too much weight on any result based on a report of $n = 1$. Let's examine the effect of sample size on such comparisons.

  a. The standard error of the mean is $\sigma_{\bar{x}} = \sigma/\sqrt{n}$.

    When $n = 4$, $\sigma_{\bar{x}} = \sigma/\sqrt{n} = 6.5/\sqrt{4} = 3.25$

    According to the question, $P(\bar{X} < 25)$ is the correct mathematical expression. There is no direct connection between sample means and probabilities. The $\bar{X}$ needs to be converted into a Z score by using $Z = (\bar{X} - \mu)/(\sigma/\sqrt{n})$.

    $$Z = \frac{\bar{X} - \mu}{\dfrac{\sigma}{\sqrt{n}}} = \frac{25 - 27.1}{\dfrac{6.5}{\sqrt{4}}} = \frac{-2.1}{3.25} = -0.65$$

    $$P(\bar{X} < 25) = P(Z < -0.65)$$

    Draw and identify this area under the standard normal distribution curve, $P(Z < -0.65)$ (Figure 6.4).

    $$P(Z < -0.65) = .2578$$

FIGURE 6.4 Using the Z Table to Figure Out $P(Z < -0.65)$

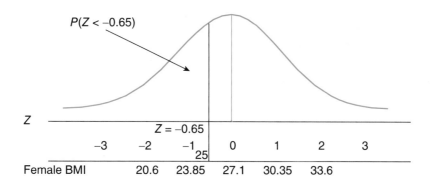

The probability of randomly selecting four women whose mean BMI is less than 25 is .2578 or 25.78%.

b. The standard error of the mean is $\sigma_{\bar{X}} = \sigma/\sqrt{n}$.

$$\text{When } n = 36, \ \sigma_{\bar{X}} = \sigma/\sqrt{n} = 6.5/\sqrt{35} = 1.10$$

The question asks for $P(\bar{X} < 25)$. There is no direct connection between sample means and probabilities. The $\bar{X}$ needs to be converted into a Z score by using $Z = (\bar{X} - \mu)/(\sigma/\sqrt{n})$.

$$Z = \frac{\bar{X} - \mu}{\dfrac{\sigma}{\sqrt{n}}} = \frac{25 - 27.1}{\dfrac{6.5}{\sqrt{35}}} = \frac{-2.1}{1.10} = -1.91$$

$$P(\bar{X} < 25) = P(Z < -1.91)$$

Draw and identify this area under the standard normal distribution curve, $P(Z < -1.91)$ (Figure 6.5).

$$P(Z < -1.91) = .0281$$

The probability of randomly selecting 35 women whose mean BMI is less than 25 is .0281 or 2.81%.

c. Larger sample size leads to smaller standard error of the mean; therefore, it generates a larger absolute value of the calculated Z value. Results that come from larger

FIGURE 6.5 Using the Z Table to Figure Out $P(Z < -1.91)$

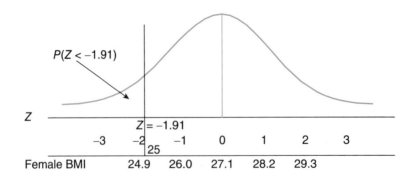

absolute values of Z are more stable and are less likely due to random sample variations. The probability of randomly selecting 4 women with an average BMI of less than 25 is higher than randomly selecting 35 women with such an average BMI. The results with higher probabilities mean that they are more likely to happen due to pure chance.

2. The correct mathematical expression according to the question is

$$P(\bar{X} > 450) = P\left(Z > \frac{\bar{X} - \mu}{\frac{\sigma}{\sqrt{n}}}\right) = P\left(Z > \frac{450 - 497}{\frac{115}{\sqrt{25}}}\right) = P(Z > -2.04)$$

Draw and identify this area under the standard normal distribution curve, $P(Z > -2.04)$ (Figure 6.6).

$$P(Z > -2.04) = 1 - P(Z < -2.04) = 1 - .0207 = .9793$$

The probability of randomly selecting 25 high school seniors to obtain a mean SAT verbal score greater than 450 is .9793 or 97.93%.

3. The payload capacity of a motor coach is 13,000 pounds, assuming full luggage capacity $55 \times 40 = 2,200$. There is $13,000 - 2,200 = 10,800$ pounds payload capacity left to carry 56 people. There are 55 passenger seats and one driver's seat inside the coach. The average male has to weigh more than $10,800/56 = 192.86$ pounds to overload the motor coach. Therefore, the question asks for $P(\bar{X} > 192.86)$. There is no direct connection between sample mean and probability, so the $\bar{X}$ needs to be converted to a Z value.

FIGURE 6.6 Using the Z Table to Figure Out $P(Z > -2.04)$

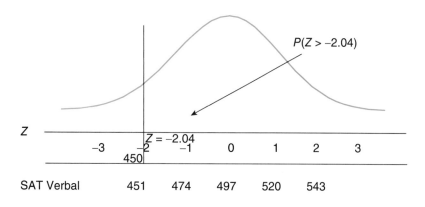

$$Z = \frac{\bar{X} - \mu}{\frac{\sigma}{\sqrt{n}}} = \frac{192.86 - 182.5}{\frac{40.8}{\sqrt{56}}} = \frac{10.36}{5.45} = 1.90$$

$$P(\bar{X} > 192.86) = P(Z > 1.90)$$

Draw and identify this area under the standard normal distribution curve, $P(Z > 1.90)$ (Figure 6.7).

$$P(Z > 1.90) = 1 - P(Z < 1.90) = 1 - .9713 = .0287$$

The probability of the motor coach getting overloaded with 56 males is .0287 or 2.87%, assuming full luggage capacity. On average, females weigh less than males. Therefore, when the motor coach carries both males and females, the risk of overloading is less than .0287.

4. The solution for this question depends on the actual data collected from the entire class.

Here is an example of 25 students who use Table 6.2 to record number of heads when tossing 10 coins at the same time for 20 trials. The results are shown in Table 6.3.

Table 6.3 shows the results of 25 students who recorded the number of heads they got by tossing 10 coins at the same time for 20 trials. Each student's records were merged to create Table 6.3. First, the average number of heads from Student 1's 20 trials of

FIGURE 6.7   Using the Z Table to Figure Out $P(Z > 1.90)$

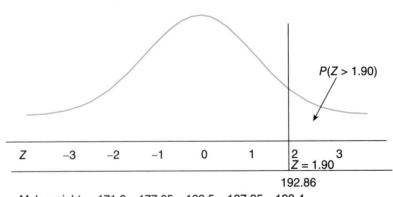

STRAIGHTFORWARD STATISTICS

TABLE 6.3   Twenty-Five Students Toss 10 Coins for 20 Trials

TRIAL	1	2	3	4	5	6	7	8	9	10	11	12	13	14	15	16	17	18	19	20	$\bar{X}$
Student 1	3	6	4	5	8	8	4	6	3	2	9	5	6	4	7	8	2	7	2	7	5.3
Student 2	3	7	4	6	2	8	5	6	7	3	4	7	3	5	6	5	2	7	4	5	4.95
Student 3	3	6	5	4	3	2	8	4	6	5	3	4	7	6	5	2	7	4	6	5	4.75
Student 4	5	6	5	4	5	4	6	4	2	7	4	7	5	6	4	3	2	5	6	4	4.7
Student 5	6	4	7	5	8	8	7	4	7	6	8	6	5	5	7	3	6	9	7	4	6.1
Student 6	5	4	2	8	6	4	8	3	5	2	4	6	4	4	5	2	5	3	4	4	4.4
Student 7	4	3	5	4	3	5	8	8	7	3	4	4	5	6	6	3	7	5	3	7	5
Student 8	3	5	5	7	6	8	2	6	4	6	6	2	7	3	5	8	4	3	4	4	4.9
Student 9	6	7	5	6	5	4	6	4	2	5	4	7	3	2	8	5	2	7	4	2	4.7
Student 10	4	5	6	6	4	6	5	8	5	5	6	6	6	5	2	3	4	5	4	6	5.05
Student 11	5	5	5	7	7	5	6	5	4	5	3	8	6	5	5	5	4	5	6	5	5.3
Student 12	4	4	5	4	5	4	4	3	6	4	5	6	5	5	2	6	4	4	5	7	4.6
Student 13	4	4	6	3	1	5	6	3	4	4	4	5	7	6	2	3	2	4	5	6	4.2
Student 14	6	3	5	7	4	4	5	5	7	7	4	5	4	5	6	7	5	4	5	7	5.25
Student 15	3	4	7	3	6	4	6	5	4	6	6	4	8	4	5	2	7	3	8	4	4.95
Student 16	5	4	2	4	5	4	8	3	5	7	3	4	6	3	4	5	5	4	4	3	4.4
Student 17	5	6	8	7	4	5	5	4	3	5	5	3	4	6	2	4	3	6	6	3	4.7
Student 18	8	3	6	3	4	6	3	4	5	7	6	2	3	8	4	6	7	2	5	4	4.8
Student 19	6	5	5	6	5	5	5	5	7	5	4	5	4	6	4	5	5	5	6	5	5.15
Student 20	6	3	1	6	2	7	4	2	6	2	5	5	5	6	6	4	3	4	8	4	4.45
Student 21	7	5	7	4	6	5	5	5	7	4	4	2	5	4	5	3	6	2	6	5	4.85
Student 22	4	5	6	7	3	8	10	9	4	7	6	5	9	5	8	6	4	10	4	8	6.4
Student 23	7	8	4	5	6	9	10	5	6	3	2	4	6	5	8	9	5	6	7	8	6.15
Student 24	3	2	6	4	4	1	3	5	7	2	4	5	3	4	4	2	6	3	6	4	3.9
Student 25	5	4	4	6	2	5	5	8	4	7	4	5	3	7	5	7	7	4	3	2	4.85
																					4.95

tossing of 10 coins was calculated, and it was 5.3 heads. Then, the mean for every student's 20 trials is calculated and reported in the last column. You can see the variation of number of heads was large for individual trials. It ranged from 1 to 10 heads.

However, when the mean was calculated over 20 trials, it ranged from 3.9 to 6.4. Then, the mean of all 25 students' 20 trials (i.e., effectively, mean for 500 trials of tossing 10 coins) was 4.95, which was very close to $E(X) = \mu = np = 10(.5) = 5$. This process demonstrates that when the number of trials gets larger and larger, the sample mean gets closer and closer to the population mean. If you are not satisfied with this result from 500 trials, you may keep on increasing the number of trials until it approaches infinity. It will take you a long time to get there.

$SAGE edge™

WHAT YOU LEARNED

In this chapter, you have learned the central limit theorem, the law of large numbers, and how to apply the same principle you learned in the Z formula to convert a sample mean to a Z value by using $Z = (\bar{X} - \mu)/(\sigma/\sqrt{n})$ to figure out the exact location of a particular sample mean in the distribution of sample means. The knowledge about how to use the Z Table to connect Z values and probabilities remains important for both Chapters 5 and 6. Overall, you've learned that when you repeat the same random sampling procedure to produce many sample means, the sample means form a normal distribution with a mean of μ and standard deviation of $\sigma_{\bar{x}} = \sigma/\sqrt{n}$ as long as the samples are selected from a normally distributed population or the sample size $n > 30$. Sampling errors produce random errors. As long as the errors are random, the relationship between the sample means and the population mean can be explained by probability theory. The location of the sample mean can be identified exactly in the distribution. The probability associated with the Z value serves as a basis for evaluating the strength of the Z test.

KEY WORDS

Central limit theorem: The central limit theorem states that when the same random sampling procedure is repeated to produce many sample means, the sample means form a normal distribution with a mean of μ and a standard deviation of $\sigma_{\bar{x}} = \sigma/\sqrt{n}$ as long as the samples are selected from a normally distributed population or the sample size $n > 30$.

Law of large numbers: The law of large numbers is another probability theorem describing the relationship between sample means and population means. When the number of trials approaches infinity, the observed sample mean approaches the population mean $E(X) = \mu = np$.

Sampling distribution of the sample means: The sampling distribution of the sample means is defined as the distribution of all sample means from all samples of a particular sample size, n, randomly selected from the same population (i.e., $\bar{X}_1, \bar{X}_2, \bar{X}_3,...$).

Sampling error: A sampling error is defined as when a sample is randomly selected, a natural divergence, difference, distance, or error occurs between sample statistics and population parameters.

Standard error of the mean: The standard error of the mean is defined as the standard deviation of all sample means. Its calculation is the standard deviation of the population divided by the square root of the sample size, $\sigma_{\bar{x}} = \sigma/\sqrt{n}$.

Z test: A Z test measures the difference between a sample statistic and its known or hypothesized population parameter in units of standard error, $Z = (\bar{X} - \mu)/(\sigma/\sqrt{n})$.

LEARNING ASSESSMENT

Multiple Choice: Circle the best answer in every question.

1. IQ test scores are normally distributed with a mean of 100 and standard deviation of 10. What is the probability of randomly selecting an individual with an IQ greater than 130?

   a. .9987

   b. .0013

   c. .9772

   d. .0228

2. Assume that the population of adult heights forms a normal distribution with a mean of 68 inches and a standard deviation of 6 inches. What is the probability of randomly selecting a group of 25 people and their average height is more than 5 feet 11 inches?

   a. .9332

   b. .0668

   c. .9938

   d. .0062

3. In any normal distribution, the middle 50% is bound by _____.

   a. $-.5 < Z < .5$

   b. $-.67 < Z < .67$

c. $-1.5 < Z < 1.5$

d. $-1.67 < Z < 1.67$

4. The standard deviation of all sample means is also called

   a. the standard error of the mean.

   b. the sampling error.

   c. the central limit theorem.

   d. the sum of squared deviations.

5. What is the probability of randomly selecting a sample of $n = 16$ people with an average happiness score greater than 60 when the happiness scores are normally distributed with a $\mu = 65$ and $\sigma = 20$?

   a. .6587

   b. .3413

   c. .1587

   d. .8413

6. The number of days of hospital stay after a particular procedure is a skewed distribution. Researchers randomly select 40 patients after this procedure. Assuming that the sampling process can be repeated many times, the shape of the sampling distribution of sample means is

   a. the same shape as that of the population.

   b. normally distributed.

   c. negatively skewed.

   d. positively skewed.

7. A population is normally distributed with $\mu = 80$ and $\sigma = 8$. The sampling distribution of sample means for sample size $n = 4$ selected from this

population would have a standard error of the mean of ____.

   a. 80

   b. 8

   c. 4

   d. 2

8. Which of the following samples would have the smallest standard error of the mean?

   a. $n = 25$ from a population with $\sigma = 10$

   b. $n = 25$ from a population with $\sigma = 20$

   c. $n = 100$ from a population with $\sigma = 10$

   d. $n = 100$ from a population with $\sigma = 20$

9. A random sample of $n = 4$ scores is obtained from a normal population with $\mu = 20$ and $\sigma = 4$. What is the probability of randomly selecting a sample with a mean greater than 22?

   a. -1

   b. 1

   c. .1587

   d. .3085

10. A sample is obtained from a population with $\mu = 100$ and $\sigma = 10$. Which of the following sample means would produce a Z score closest to zero?

   a. A sample of $n = 25$ with $\bar{X} = 102$

   b. A sample of $n = 100$ with $\bar{X} = 102$

   c. A sample of $n = 25$ with $\bar{X} = 104$

   d. A sample of $n = 100$ with $\bar{X} = 104$

11. What are the Z values that set the middle 99% apart from the rest of the distribution?

    a. $Z < 1.96$

    b. $Z < 2.58$

    c. $|Z| < 1.96$

    d. $|Z| < 2.58$

Free Response Questions

12. A new water taxi has a maximal load limit of 3,200 pounds. Adult males' weight is normally distributed with $\mu = 182.5$ and $\sigma = 40.8$ and adult females' weight is normally distributed with $\mu = 165.2$ and $\sigma = 45.6$. The safety certificate sets the maximum number of people at 16 (including the driver). It is not possible to know how many male and female passengers will get on the water taxi for every trip. On average, males weigh more than females. Therefore, it is prudent to assume that all passengers and the driver are male in this calculation. What is the probability that this water taxi overloads when carrying 15 male passengers and a male driver?

13. An Internet car insurance company advertises that it takes $\mu = 15$ minutes to get an insurance quote to save you money. The company's records show that the standard deviation for the time spent on the site to get insurance is $\sigma = 5$ minutes. The company randomly selects a sample of 16 customers and records their time spent on the site to get their insurance quotes. What is the probability that the sample mean of this randomly selected 16 customers' online time to get an insurance quote is longer than 17 minutes?

14. A food processing company labels the net weight of a bag of frozen chicken vegetable dumplings as $\mu = 16$ ounces. According to the company's records, the standard deviation of the net weights of the frozen chicken vegetable dumplings is $\sigma = 1.5$ ounces. What is the probability of randomly selecting a sample of nine bags of the frozen chicken vegetable dumplings with the average net weights less than 15 ounces?

Hypothesis Testing

After reading and studying this chapter, you should be able to do the following:

- Define the terms *Type I error* and *Type II error*, and explain their significance in hypothesis testing

- Identify and describe the four steps in conducting a hypothesis test

- Explain the importance of the null hypothesis and the alternative hypothesis in conducting a hypothesis test

- Compare and contrast a one-tailed test and a two-tailed test

- Describe the relationship between a significance level and the rejection zone in conducting a hypothesis test

- Explain why rejecting a null hypothesis or failing to reject a null hypothesis are mutually exclusive and collectively exhaustive

What You Know and What Is New

You have learned the connection between probability and the sampling distribution of the mean in Chapter 6. Understanding that connection allows you to compare a particular sample mean with a known population mean when the population standard deviation, σ, is known. In conducting a comparison between a sample mean and a population mean, you have to make a critical judgment on "are they the same or are they different?" Scientists have developed a standardized procedure called *hypothesis testing* to make such a critical judgment.

In this chapter, we will study the rationale and the standard procedure of *hypothesis testing*. Hypothesis testing is a process that researchers use to test a claim for a population. Hypothesis testing usually involves four steps.

Step 1. Start with explicitly stating the pair of hypotheses: the null hypothesis and the alternative hypothesis.

Step 2. Identify the rejection zone for the hypothesis test.

Step 3. Calculate the appropriate test statistic.

Step 4. Make the correct conclusion.

Obviously many basic terms involved in these four steps need to be clearly defined first. These terms may sound very technical, scientific, and unfamiliar; therefore, an analogy to the litigation process will be used to illustrate the hypothesis testing procedure because almost every student seems somewhat familiar with the litigation process due to the popularity of many legal dramas, such as *Law and Order, Boston Legal, CSI*, and *Suits*.

TYPE I ERROR AND TYPE II ERROR

Researchers declare the purpose of conducting research by using the pair of hypotheses. In the language of statistics, the null hypothesis, H_0, is the statement that researchers directly test with empirical data. The null hypothesis is the "no effect" hypothesis. Researchers hope to use data to nullify or reject the null hypothesis. When the null hypothesis is rejected, the researchers turn to the alternative hypothesis. The alternative hypothesis, H_1, states the relationship that researchers are interested in, thus H_1 is also referred to as the research hypothesis. The null hypothesis and alternative hypothesis are *mutually exclusive* statements describing population parameters. "Mutually exclusive" was a key term first introduced in Chapter 5; it means H_0 does not overlap with H_1. Only one of these two statements can be true. When one of them is true, the other is not. In reality, the effect either exists or not. At the end of a hypothesis test, we find out whether the null hypothesis is rejected by the data or not.

You might be confused at this point. Why bother to state a no effect hypothesis and then try to reject it? The reason to use the null hypothesis as the starting point of any empirical study is to assume that the study has no effect unless there is strong evidence to reject or dispute the no effect hypothesis. Such a process is to establish a standard scientific procedure to guard against anyone falsely claiming a treatment effect when such an effect does not exist.

For example, in the wake of the 2014 West Africa Ebola outbreak, many companies claimed that their products can cure Ebola. These products ranged from vitamin C, silver, dark chocolate, cinnamon bark, and oregano to snake venom. The Food and Drug Administration (FDA) and Federal Trade Commission (FTC) had to warn these companies to stop fraudulent claims immediately or face potential legal actions. It is illegal to market dietary supplements claiming to cure human diseases. New drugs may not be legally introduced or delivered into interstate commerce without prior approval from the FDA. FDA approval of new drugs requires vigorous clinical studies to validate their effects. Such a process is designed to protect the general public from falling victim to the modern snake oil scams. Con artists are very skilled at creating fear in order to make a profit. Falsely claimed treatment effects of dietary supplements plague the Internet every day. Some of the false claims include curing cancers, AIDS, and Ebola, reversing the aging process, or losing weight. That is the reason why scientifically proven clinical studies are required to start with the no effect hypothesis; then strong evidence is provided to dispute the no effect hypothesis.

We can further illustrate this point by drawing an analogy to the legal system in the United States. In the legal system, the defendant is presumed innocent (H_0 is true) until proven guilty (reject H_0). In a criminal trial, if there is not enough evidence to convince the jury beyond a reasonable doubt that the defendant committed the alleged crime, the defendant must be found "not guilty" (fail to reject H_0). The starting point of a legal trial is presumed innocence. Presumed innocence is best described as an assumption of innocence that is indulged in the absence of contrary evidence.

Hypothetically, in an extreme case, neither the prosecutor nor the defendant's lawyer offers a shred of evidence to prove or disprove the defendant's guilt. No one in the courtroom has any idea about what happened. In this case, using U.S. legal conventions, the verdict must be "not guilty."

The same logic applies to hypothesis testing. The starting point of a hypothesis test is to assume that the new treatment has no effect (H_0 is true). When no evidence or weak evidence is provided, the default conclusion should be "fail to reject H_0." It is up to the researchers to provide strong evidence to dispute or reject H_0.

The decisions from hypothesis tests can be either correct or incorrect, exactly the same way as the decisions from a jury trial can be just or unjust. Let's use the legal system to examine the possible outcomes of a jury trial. Table 7.1 shows all possible outcomes from different combinations of two possible scenarios of the unknown reality: (1) the defendant did not commit the crime or (2) the defendant did commit the crime and two possible jury decisions: (1) guilty or (2) not guilty.

TABLE 7.1 Possible Outcomes of a Jury Decision

		UNKNOWN REALITY	
		DEFENDANT DID NOT DO IT	DEFENDANT DID IT
JURY DECISION	**GUILTY**	Mistake I	Correct decision
	NOT GUILTY	Correct decision	Mistake II

The cells inside Table 7.1 represent four different combinations of the unknown reality and the jury decisions. The table clearly shows that there are two correct decisions: (1) when the defendant did not commit the crime and the jury found the defendant not guilty and (2) when the defendant actually committed the crime and the jury found the defendant guilty. There are two different types of mistakes. Mistake I is when the defendant did not commit the crime but the jury found the defendant guilty. Mistake II is when the defendant committed the crime but the jury found the defendant not guilty.

Mistakes incur costs to the society and individuals alike. The presumption of the U.S. society is that Mistake I, putting innocent defendants in prison for crimes they did not commit, is a far worse injustice than Mistake II, letting guilty criminals go free. Although the table shows two types of mistakes and two types of correct decisions, fortunately, they are not a 50–50 split. There are quality control standards in the legal system to make sure that the number of correct decisions outweighs the number of mistakes.

Now apply the same logic to hypothesis testing. There are two possible scenarios of the unknown reality: (1) H_0 is true and (2) H_0 is false. There are also two possible research decisions: (1) reject H_0 or (2) fail to reject H_0. Table 7.2 shows all possible combinations of the unknown reality and research decisions.

In Table 7.2, I want to focus on the two types of mistakes: (1) Type I error and (2) Type II error. Type I error is when H_0 is true but the researchers decide to reject H_0. Type II error is when H_0 is false, but the researchers fail to reject H_0. In plain English, a Type I error occurs when the researchers falsely claim that there is an effect when the effect actually does not exist. Type II error occurs when the researchers fail to claim an effect when the effect actually exists.

To ensure the quality of scientific research, scientists collectively agree to keep Type I error under control. In the example of the FDA, the cost of Type I error is to potentially expose the public to useless treatments that might potentially harm their health. Traditionally, the acceptable risk of committing Type I error, α is set to be at a .05 level for psychological and other social scientific research because psychologists and social scientists collectively agree that if 1 in 20 studies generates a bogus effect, it is an acceptable risk. Type II error, on the other hand, does not incur such risk to the public. The

TABLE 7.2 Possible Outcomes of a Hypothesis Test

	UNKNOWN REALITY	
	H_0 IS TRUE	H_0 IS FALSE
REJECT H_0	Type I error	Correct decision
FAIL TO REJECT H_0	Correct decision	Type II error

probability of committing Type II error is called β. Researchers simply fail to claim an effect when an effect actually exists. In such situations, researchers can always start over and conduct more studies later. Sooner or later, someone is going to discover that overlooked effect.

Now, let's discuss the correct decisions. First, when H_0 is true, and the researchers fail to reject H_0, this is a correct decision. The probability of such a correct decision can be calculated as $(1 - \alpha)$. This probability $(1 - \alpha)$ is also called the confidence level, which will be introduced in Chapter 8. Second, when H_0 is false and the researchers reject H_0, it is again a correct decision. The probability of such a correct decision is calculated as $(1 - \beta)$, which is called power. Power is defined as the sensitivity to detect an effect when an effect actually exists. The power of the hypothesis test is the probability of correctly rejecting H_0 when H_0 is false.

Power is an important statistical concept and is influenced by the following three factors:

1. Sample size, n

2. Significance level, α

3. Effect size

Sample size and power are positively correlated. All else being equal, when the sample size is larger, power is bigger. When the sample size is smaller, power is smaller. Large sample size makes a standard error small. When a standard error is small, it is more likely to detect an effect when it actually exists. Sample size is the most influential factor in calculating statistical power because sample size is under the control of researchers. Researchers can plan ahead to figure out how big the sample size needs to be to reach a desirable power level.

Significance level, α, and power are also positively correlated. When α is higher, power is higher. When α is lower, power is lower. The rationale is that when the Type I error is under strict control, the risk of falsely claiming an effect is low; however, the sensitivity to detect an effect is also low. A Type I error is to reject H_0, when H_0 is true. A Type II error is to fail to reject H_0 when H_0 is false. It is obvious that there is a trade-off relationship between the probability of committing a Type I error, α, and the probability of committing a Type II error, β. As one goes up, the other has to come down. Therefore, when α goes up, researchers decide to increase the risk of Type I error; then β will go down, and $(1 - \beta)$ will go up. Just remember that α and β move in opposite directions, but α and $(1 - \beta)$ move in the same direction.

The effect size is positively related with power. The effect size is a standardized measure of the difference between the sample statistic and the hypothesized population parameter in units of standard deviation. Such a standardized measure makes it possible to compare results across different studies. A large effect size means that there is a substantial difference between the sample statistic and the hypothesized population parameter. When standardized effect size is larger, power is bigger. When standardized effect size is smaller, power is smaller. Therefore, a large effect size makes it easy to detect an effect when the effect actually exists. A small effect size makes it difficult to detect such an effect.

A summary table of the probabilities associated with all possible outcomes from conducting a hypothesis test is shown in Table 7.3. The probability of committing a Type I error is α, and the probability of correctly failing to reject H_0 when H_0 is true is $(1 - \alpha)$. As we discussed in Chapter 5, these two events are mutually exclusive and they complement each other because the probabilities of these two events add to 1. Similarly, the probability of committing a Type II error is β and the probability of correctly rejecting H_0 when H_0 is false is $(1 - \beta)$, which is also called the statistical power. The statistical power and the probability of committing the Type II error are mutually exclusive and complementary events. The statistical power is positively correlated with sample size, the probability of committing a Type I error, and an effect size. This section demonstrates the conceptual process of the hypothesis test, so now you are ready to go through the technical steps of actually conducting a hypothesis test in the following section.

Author's Aside

The calculation of power is more complicated than I would like to pursue in an introductory statistics course. If you are interested in calculating power in different situations, you may refer to Cohen (1988) and Park (2010).

Cohen, J. (1988). Statistical power analysis for the behavioral sciences (2nd ed.). Hillsdale, NJ: Lawrence Erlbaum.

Park, H. M. (2010). Hypothesis testing and statistical power of a test. Bloomington, IN: University Information Technology Services, Indiana University. Retrieved from https://scholarworks.iu.edu/dspace/handle/2022/19738

TABLE 7.3   Probability of Type I Error, Type II Error, and Power

	UNKNOWN REALITY	
	H_0 IS TRUE	H_0 IS FALSE
REJECT H_0	α	$(1 - \beta)$
FAIL TO REJECT H_0	$(1 - \alpha)$	β

1. What is the correct definition of Type I error?

   a. Reject H_0 when H_0 is true.

   b. Fail to reject H_0 when H_0 is true.

   c. Reject H_0 when H_0 is false.

   d. Fail to reject H_0 when H_0 is false.

2. What is the correct definition of Type II error?

   a. Reject H_0 when H_0 is true.

   b. Fail to reject H_0 when H_0 is true.

   c. Reject H_0 when H_0 is false.

   d. Fail to reject H_0 when H_0 is false.

3. Which of the following variables is positively correlated with the statistical power?

   a. The probability of committing a Type I error, α

   b. The sample size, n

   c. The effect size

   d. All of the above three variables are positively correlated with the statistical power.

Answers: 1. a, 2. d, 3. d

THE FOUR-STEP PROCESS TO CONDUCT A HYPOTHESIS TEST

Hypothesis testing is a standardized process to test the strength of scientific evidence for a claim about a population. Hypothesis testing involves the following four-step process. All four steps are explained and elaborated in the following sections.

Step 1. Explicitly state the pair of hypotheses.

Step 2. Identify the rejection zone for the hypothesis test.

Step 3. Calculate the test statistic.

Step 4. Make the correct conclusion.

STEP 1. EXPLICITLY STATE THE PAIR OF HYPOTHESES

Hypothesis tests are conducted to test the strength of scientific evidence for a claim about a population. Research purposes are expressed by the pair of hypotheses. H_0 is the "no effect" (null) hypothesis, and H_1 is the research (alternative) hypothesis, which researchers turn to when H_0 is rejected by the data. H_1 states the effect that researchers are interested in. Both hypotheses describe characteristics of the population. Hypothesis tests can be nondirectional or directional. Nondirectional versus directional hypotheses are best illustrated by using an example.

The average IQ score for the general population is $\mu = 100$. If a researcher wants to compare the average IQ of students in a school district to the population mean, the starting point of this comparison should be explicitly stating the H_0: $\mu = 100$. It is assumed that the average IQ score of students in this school district is the same as the population. Then, the alternative hypothesis needs to be stated. Depending on the nature of the comparison, the researchers may use nondirectional hypothesis testing or directional hypothesis testing. Nondirectional hypothesis testing is only interested in whether the sample could come from a population with the hypothesized mean or not, so the alternative hypothesis is H_1: $\mu \neq 100$. A nondirectional hypothesis test is called a two-tailed test.

Directional hypothesis testing, on the other hand, is interested in a particular direction, so the alternative hypothesis could be expressed as either higher or lower than the population parameter, H_1: $\mu > 100$ or H_1: $\mu < 100$. A directional hypothesis test is also called a one-tailed test. Under a one-tailed test, the alternative hypothesis is stated with a direction such as a right-tailed test or a left-tailed test. Which of these tests to use depends on whether the problem statement contains clear direction with key words such as "higher," "increasing," "improving," "lower," "decreasing," or "deteriorating." When the problem statement contains these key words for a particular direction, one-tailed tests are appropriate. To complete the example of the IQ score, here is a list of hypotheses in all possible tests.

Two-tailed test:	H_0: $\mu = 100$
	H_1: $\mu \neq 100$
Right-tailed test:	H_0: $\mu = 100$
	H_1: $\mu > 100$
Left-tailed test:	H_0: $\mu = 100$
	H_1: $\mu < 100$

This list illustrates that H_0 is the "no effect" hypothesis. It states that the average IQ score of students in the school district is the same as the population parameter. Please note that the "=" sign is always in H_0, the null hypothesis.

The alternative hypothesis, H_1, is the hypothesis that researchers turn to when H_0 is rejected. It states that there is some kind of difference between the average IQ scores of students in the school district and the population mean. The nature of the difference depends on whether the test is a two-tailed test, a right-tailed test, or a left-tailed test. H_1 in a two-tailed test states that the average IQ score of students in the school district is not the same as the hypothesized population mean. H_1 in a right-tailed test states that the average IQ score of students in the school district is higher than the hypothesized population mean. H_1 in a left-tailed test states that the average IQ score of students in the school district is lower than the hypothesized population mean.

You might have seen other textbooks list one-tailed tests as H_0: $\mu \leq 100$ and H_1: $\mu > 100$ in a right-tailed test or H_0: $\mu \geq 100$ and H_1: $\mu < 100$ in a left-tailed test, so that all possible outcomes are included in the pair of hypotheses. These kinds of expressions are regarded as outdated. In this book, for the sake of simplicity and clarity, all null hypotheses remain with "=" sign only. It is implied that the single direction sign (> or <) opposite to the H_1 is included in the H_0. For example, a swimming coach is testing the effectiveness of a particular training routine. The purpose of the training routine is to drop swimmers' times and make them swim faster. Therefore, the hypothesis test is set up as a left-tailed test. If the swimmers' times do not change, then we have to conclude that the training routine has no effect (i.e., we fail to reject H_0). Obviously, if the swimmers' times get slower due to the training routine, clearly not the effect intended by the coach, we have to conclude that the training routine has no effect.

STEP 2. IDENTIFY THE REJECTION ZONE FOR THE HYPOTHESIS TEST

As discussed in the previous section, social scientists collectively agree that Type I errors need to be kept under control to protect the general public from falsely claimed effects. The probability to commit a Type I error is α and is the key to establishing the decision rules for the hypothesis test. Therefore, α is also called the significance level. Different α levels may be assigned according to the nature of the research. In a research project with strong theoretical reasoning behind it, or in a project with many similar studies being conducted repeatedly and resulting in consistent findings, a strict standard may apply, such as $\alpha = .01$. In contrast, in a research project of an exploratory nature, without much if any theoretical reasoning to back it up, a weak standard may suffice, such as $\alpha = .10$. Usually for research in social sciences, the default level is $\alpha = .05$.

The significance level helps identify the rejection zone. The rejection zone is bounded by the critical value of a statistic. Once the rejection zone is set, decision rules can be clearly stated. If any calculated test statistic falls in the rejection zone, the decision is to reject H_0. Otherwise, if the test statistic does not fall in the rejection zone, we fail to reject H_0. The term *fail to reject H_0* is a double negative and seems cumbersome. I will explain in more detail why "fail to reject H_0" is preferred to "accept H_0" in Step 4, which is to make the correct conclusion.

Let's continue the previous IQ example to identify the rejection zones assuming $\alpha = .05$. First, we use $\alpha = .05$ to identify the rejection zone for a two-tailed test.

Two-tailed test: H_0: $\mu = 100$

                     H_1: $\mu \neq 100$

Rejection zone: $|Z| > Z_{\alpha/2}$

The rejection zone is specified by the critical value of Z. In a two-tailed test, the significance level, α, is evenly divided into two tails, and the critical value of Z is specified as $Z_{\alpha/2}$. Assuming α = .05, the probability of each tail is α/2 = .05/2 = .025. We can easily identify the left tail $P(Z < -z) = .025$ from the Z Table; the z value is −1.96. Based on the symmetrical nature of the curve, the right tail $P(Z > z) = .025$; the z value is 1.96. Therefore, the best way to express the rejection zone for a two-tailed test is $|Z| > 1.96$, as shown in Figure 7.1.

FIGURE 7.1 Rejection Zone for $|Z| > 1.96$

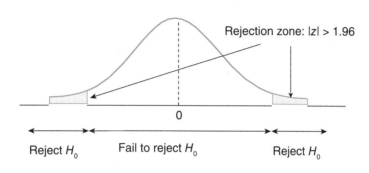

Next, we use α = .05 to identify the rejection zone for a right-tailed test.

Right-tailed test: H_0: μ = 100

H_1: μ > 100

Rejection zone: $Z > Z_\alpha$

In a right-tailed test, the significance level, α, is solely in the right tail. Assuming α = .05, the probability of the right tail is .05. According to the Z table, when the tail probability is .05, the critical value of Z is between 1.64 and 1.65. I prefer to use the more conservative (i.e., a higher standard and more difficult to reach) standard, so I pick the value 1.65. Therefore, the best way to express the rejection zone for a right-tailed test is $Z > 1.65$, as shown in Figure 7.2.

Next, we use α = .05 to identify the rejection zone for a left-tailed test.

Left-tailed test: H_0: μ = 100

H_1: μ < 100

Rejection zone: $Z < -Z_\alpha$

The rejection zone for a left tailed test is $Z < -1.65$, as shown in Figure 7.3.

FIGURE 7.2   Rejection Zone for Z > 1.65

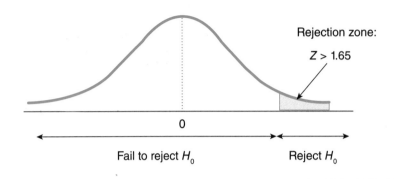

FIGURE 7.3   Rejection Zone for Z < −1.65

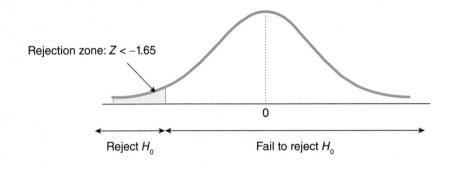

STEP 3. CALCULATE THE TEST STATISTIC

When we use a sample mean, $\overline{X}$, to compare with the population mean, μ, with the population standard deviation, σ, provided in the problem statement, we use the Z formula in Chapter 6 to calculate the test statistic. The calculated Z value is based on the data collected by the researcher. The calculated Z value shows the strength of the evidence in the research.

$$Z = \frac{\overline{X} - \mu}{\dfrac{\sigma}{\sqrt{n}}}$$

We will learn other statistics in the following chapters to deal with different kinds of comparisons. The basic principle of a test statistic is to calculate the difference between a sample statistic and a hypothesized population parameter, and then divide it by the standard error of the statistic.

$$\text{Test statistic} = \frac{(\text{Sample statistic} - \text{Population parameter})}{\text{Standard error of the statistic}}$$

After the four-step hypothesis procedure has been introduced, a few examples will illustrate the process in its entirety.

STEP 4. MAKE THE CORRECT CONCLUSION

After identifying the rejection zone in Step 2 and calculating the test statistic in Step 3, the next step is to compare the calculated value with the rejection zone. If the calculated value falls in the rejection zone, we reject H_0. If the calculated value does not fall in the rejection zone, we fail to reject H_0. In statistics, we prefer to use precise language. The decision made by researchers after conducting a simple hypothesis test is to reject H_0 or fail to reject H_0, and such decisions are mutually exclusive and collectively exhaustive. This means that the two decisions (1) "reject H_0" and (2) "fail to reject H_0" could not be true at the same time, and they cover all possible outcomes.

Let's discuss the difference between "accept H_0" and "fail to reject H_0." The analogy of the legal system helps illustrate the distinction. In the legal system, there are two possible outcomes from a jury decision: (1) "guilty" or (2) "not guilty." "Not guilty" is also a double negative phrase but there is no movement to change "not guilty" to a simple phrase "innocent" anytime soon. To be clear, "not guilty" is not the same as "innocent." "Not guilty" simply means there is not enough evidence to convince all jury members that the defendant has committed the crime beyond a reasonable doubt. "Innocent" is an affirmative statement that the defendant did not commit the crime and "innocent" belongs in a subcategory of the "not guilty." However, "innocent" and "not guilty" are not 100% synonymous. In some cases, a highly suspicious defendant may be found "not guilty" because a key piece of evidence was thrown out by the judge, a key eyewitness went missing, the police mishandled the evidence, the murder weapon was never found, or a brilliantly convincing alternative story was argued by the defense lawyer. These are just some examples of why "not guilty" is not the same as "innocent."

Now let's apply the same principle to hypothesis testing in scientific research. "Fail to reject H_0" simply means that there is not enough evidence to support the claimed effect. "Accept H_0" is an affirmative statement that there is no effect and "accept H_0" belongs in a subcategory of the "fail to reject H_0." I want to emphasize the key point that "fail to reject H_0" is not the same as "accept H_0." I summarize all the legal decisions and research decisions in Table 7.4.

TABLE 7.4 Mutually Exclusive and Collectively Exhaustive Decisions

	ONE FEASIBLE OUTCOME	THE ONLY OTHER FEASIBLE OUTCOME
JURY DECISIONS	Guilty	Not guilty
RESEARCH DECISIONS	Reject H_0	Fail to reject H_0

Here is a real-life example to illustrate why this seemingly trivial distinction might have major consequences. A few years ago, I attended a research presentation made by a job candidate seeking a tenure-track position at a university. The candidate presented his research to the faculty members in the department where the hiring decision was going to be made. The candidate's research topic was on spatial orientation. According to the previous literature, spatial orientation is an ability that consistently shows significant gender differences. After his presentation, I asked, "Did you find any gender difference in your study on spatial orientation?" He answered, "There were no gender differences in my study." The answer would have been much better if he said, "There was not enough evidence to support the claim that gender differences existed in my study." "There were no gender differences in my study" is the "accept H_0" answer. "There was not enough evidence to support the claim that gender differences exist" is the "fail to reject H_0" answer. The fail to reject H_0 answer is logically and technically superior to the accept H_0 answer. The job candidate's research was not focused on gender differences, and the research design was not conducive to show whether they existed or not. There simply was not enough evidence on gender differences in his study. Being able to answer questions correctly during a job interview might have a big impact on the hiring decision.

Let's move on to more specific examples of how the four-step hypothesis test works in action.

EXAMPLES OF THE FOUR-STEP HYPOTHESIS TEST IN ACTION

The four-step hypothesis test is a standard scientific approach to test the significance of the empirical evidence on a claim about a population. Such a four-step hypothesis testing process will be useful not only in this chapter but also in all of the later chapters. Let's go through the four-step process by using a couple of examples.

EXAMPLE 7.1

A standardized IQ test is known to be normally distributed and has $\mu = 100$ and $\sigma = 10$. There is a common belief that students in wealthier school districts tend to have higher IQ scores. A researcher randomly selects a sample of 25 students from wealthy school districts. The average IQ of this sample is $\overline{X} = 103$. Conduct a test to verify if the average IQ score for students from wealthy districts is higher than 100, assuming $\alpha = .05$.

We are going to use the four-step hypothesis testing process to answer this question.

Step 1. State the pair of hypotheses.

Based on the problem statement "If the average IQ score for students from wealthy districts is higher than 100," the problem indicates a directional hypothesis. The key word "higher IQ scores" indicates a right-tailed test. The alternative hypothesis, H_1, is $\mu > 100$. Then H_0 covers the equal sign, $\mu = 100$. It is important to point out that the research interest is to compare the average IQ score of students from wealthy districts to the general population mean. The research interest is not to compare the sample mean of the 25 students to the general population mean. Thus, the hypotheses must be phrased to describe the "research population," which refers to all students in wealthy districts.

H_0: $\mu = 100$

H_1: $\mu > 100$

Step 2. Identify the rejection zone for the hypothesis test.

We know this is a right-tailed test from Step 1. When the tail probability is .05, according to the Z table, the Z value is 1.65. The rejection zone for the right-tailed test is $Z > 1.65$. It is clear and useful to draw a simple normal curve with the rejection zone shaded as shown in Figure 7.4.

FIGURE 7.4   Rejection Zone for $Z > 1.65$ for Example 7.1

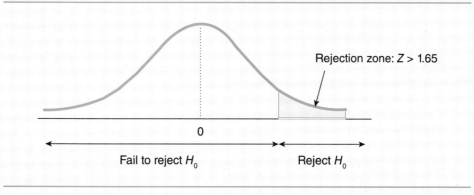

Rejection zone: $Z > 1.65$

0

Fail to reject H_0

Reject H_0

(Continued)

(Continued)

Step 3. Calculate the test statistics.

The problem statement asks for a comparison between students in wealthy districts and the general population mean with a known σ. Therefore, the Z test is the correct statistic to accomplish this purpose. It is easy to list all the numbers stated in the problem statement, so as to separate out what we know and what we need to figure out.

What we know.

$\mu = 100$

$\sigma = 10$

$\bar{X} = 103$

$n = 25$

We need to figure out Z. Next, insert all the numbers in the Z-test formula.

$$Z = \frac{\bar{X} - \mu}{\frac{\sigma}{\sqrt{n}}}$$

$$Z = \frac{(103 - 100)}{10 / \sqrt{25}} = \frac{3}{2} = 1.5$$

Step 4. Make the correct conclusion.

Compare the calculated $Z = 1.5$ with the rejection zone $Z > 1.65$. The calculated Z does not fall in the rejection zone. Therefore, we fail to reject H_0. The evidence is not strong enough to support the claim that the average IQ score of students from wealthy districts is higher than 100 at the $\alpha = .05$ level.

Statistics are widely available in different situations. Besides IQ scores or standardized test scores, life expectancy is a commonly available statistic locally, nationally, and internationally. Let's use life expectancy as an example to conduct a hypothesis test in the next example.

EXAMPLE 7.2

Hawaiians are known to have an active lifestyle, enjoying the fresh air and natural beauty the islands have to offer. The life expectancy of the U.S. population across all 50 states is $\mu = 78.62$ years with a standard deviation $\sigma = 16.51$ years. A randomly selected sample of 100 Hawaiians shows an average life expectancy $\bar{X} = 82.52$. Is Hawaiians' average life expectancy significantly different from 78.62, assuming $\alpha = .01$?

We apply the four-step hypothesis testing process to answer this question.

Step 1. State the pair of hypotheses.

The problem statement asks, "Is Hawaiians' average life expectancy significantly different from 78.62?" The question does not contain any information regarding a particular direction. Therefore, a nondirectional hypothesis is the correct approach. The pair of hypotheses is stated below.

$H_0: \mu = 78.62$

$H_1: \mu \neq 78.62$

Step 2. Identify the rejection zones for the hypothesis test.

From Step 1, we know that we are conducting a two-tailed test. The problem statement specifies $\alpha = .01$. When the tail probability is $\alpha/2 = .01/2 = .005$, according to the Z table, the left tail is $P(Z < -z) = .005$, and the z value is between -2.57 and -2.58. I prefer to use the more conservative approach, so I pick the value of -2.58. Based on the symmetrical nature of the curve, the right tail is $P(Z > z) = .005$, and the z value is 2.58. Therefore, the best way to express the rejection zones for a two-tailed test is $|Z| > 2.58$, as shown in Figure 7.5.

Step 3. Calculate the statistic.

The problem statement asks for a comparison between the average life span of people in Hawaii and the population mean with a known σ. So the Z test is the correct statistic to accomplish this purpose. Let's list all the numbers stated in the problem statement and separate out what we know from what we need to figure out.

Let's list everything we know from the problem statement.

(Continued)

(Continued)

FIGURE 7.5   The Rejection Zones for $|Z| > 2.58$

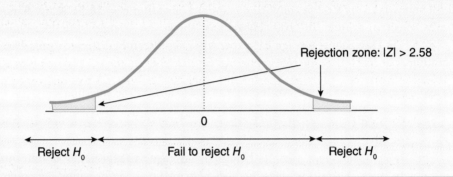

Rejection zone: $|Z| > 2.58$

0

Reject H_0 Fail to reject H_0 Reject H_0

$\mu = 78.62$

$\sigma = 16.51$

$\bar{X} = 82.52$

$n = 100$

We need to figure out the Z. Next, insert all the numbers in the Z-test formula.

$$Z = \frac{\bar{X} - \mu}{\dfrac{\sigma}{\sqrt{n}}}$$

$$Z = \frac{(82.52 - 78.62)}{16.51/\sqrt{100}} = \frac{3.9}{1.65} = 2.36$$

Step 4. Make the correct conclusion.

Compare the calculated $Z = 2.36$ with the rejection zone, $|Z| > 2.58$. The calculated Z does not fall in the rejection zone. Therefore, we fail to reject H_0. The evidence is not strong enough to support the claim that Hawaiians' average life expectancy is significantly different from 78.62.

According to the problem, $\alpha = .01$, which is a very strict standard for a hypothesis test. If we relax the standard to the customary level of $\alpha = .05$, the rejection zone would become $|Z| > 1.96$. With a calculated Z value $= 2.36$, the outcome of a hypothesis test at $\alpha = .05$ would be to reject H_0. It is important for researchers to decide in advance what significance level is appropriate for their research purpose.

After going through a couple of examples, it is clear that the four-step hypothesis testing procedure is a standardized scientific process to test the strength of the empirical evidence on a claim about the population. Let's recap that process.

Step 1. Explicitly state the pair of hypotheses. This means to declare the purpose of the hypothesis test and identify whether it is a directional test or a nondirectional test.

Step 2. Identify the rejection zone for the hypothesis test. Based on the predetermined significance level, the rejection zone can be specified by the critical value of Z. The rejection zone serves as a criterion for decision making on the outcomes of the hypothesis test.

Step 3. Calculate the test statistic. Many different statistical tests will be discussed throughout this book. So far, we have only covered the Z test.

Step 4. Make the correct conclusion. The research conclusion is made by comparing the calculated value of the test statistic and the rejection zone. If the calculated test statistic is within the rejection zone, we reject H_0. When we reject H_0, it means that the evidence is strong enough to claim an effect. If the calculated test statistic is not within the rejection zone, we fail to reject H_0. When we fail to reject H_0, it means that the evidence is not strong enough to support a claim of an effect.

Pop Quiz

1. What values are needed to figure out the rejection zones for Z tests?

   a. The significance level, α

   b. One-tailed test or two-tailed test

   c. Sample size

   d. Both (a) and (b)

   e. All of the above

2. For a two-tailed Z test with $\alpha = .10$, the critical values that set the boundaries for the rejection zones are

   a. $Z > 1.65$

   b. $Z > 1.96$

   c. $|Z| > 1.65$

   d. $|Z| > 1.96$

Answers: 1. d, 2. c

DIRECTIONAL VERSUS NONDIRECTIONAL HYPOTHESIS TESTING

Directional hypothesis tests versus nondirectional hypothesis tests is a topic that needs to be discussed in detail. The most noticeable difference between one-tailed tests and two-tailed tests is the rejection zone. Under a one-tailed test, the probability of committing a Type I error, α, is only on one side of the distribution curve. When conducting a two-tailed test, the probability of committing a Type I error, α, is to be evenly divided into two tails, $\alpha/2$. Assuming $\alpha = .05$, let's examine the rejection zones for these situations.

Right-tailed test

$$\text{Rejection zone: } Z > Z_\alpha$$
$$Z > 1.65$$

Left-tailed test

$$\text{Rejection zone: } Z < -Z_\alpha$$
$$Z < -1.65$$

Two-tailed test

$$\text{Rejection zone: } |Z| > Z_{\alpha/2}$$
$$|Z| > 1.96$$

The critical value is the value that sets the boundary for the rejection zone. Judging by the critical value of Z in each test, the absolute value of Z is higher in a two-tailed test than a one-tailed test, assuming everything else remains the same. A higher critical value of Z means that the strength of the evidence needs to be stronger in a two-tailed test than a one-tailed test to be able to reject H_0. I will illustrate this point by using an example.

EXAMPLE 7.3

Hawaiians are known to have an active lifestyle, enjoying the fresh air and natural beauty the islands have to offer. The life expectancy of the U.S. population across all 50 states is $\mu = 78.62$ years with a standard deviation $\sigma = 16.51$ years. A randomly selected sample of 100 Hawaiians shows an average life expectancy $\bar{X} = 82.52$ years. Is Hawaiians' average life expectancy significantly higher than 78.62 years, assuming $\alpha = .01$?

If you think this example looks familiar, you are correct. This problem uses the same numbers used in Example 7.2. The only difference is the way the question is phrased at the end. It indicates a directional hypothesis test. Let's apply the four-step hypothesis testing procedure to answer this question.

Step 1. State the pair of hypotheses.

According to the problem, "Is Hawaiians' average life expectancy significantly higher than 78.62 years?" The question contains a clear direction indicated by the key word "higher." Therefore, a directional hypothesis, in this case, a right-tailed test, is the correct approach. The pair of hypotheses is stated below.

$H_0: \mu = 78.62$

$H_1: \mu > 78.62$

Step 2. Identify the rejection zone for the hypothesis test.

From Step 1, we know that we are conducting a right-tailed test. The problem statement specifies $\alpha = .01$. When the tail probability is $\alpha = .01$, according to the Z table, the critical value of Z is 2.33. The rejection zone is $Z > 2.33$, as shown in Figure 7.6.

Step 3. Calculate the test statistic.

The statement asks to compare the Hawaiians' average life expectancy with the population mean with a known σ, so the Z test is the correct statistic to accomplish this purpose. It is easy to list all the numbers in the problem statement, so as to separate out what we know and what we need to figure out.

What we know:

$\mu = 78.62$

$\sigma = 16.51$

$M = 82.52$

$n = 100$

FIGURE 7.6   The Rejection Zone for $Z > 2.33$

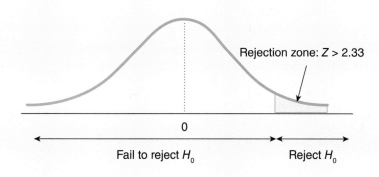

(Continued)

(Continued)

We need to figure out the Z. Next, insert all the numbers in the Z-test formula.

$$Z = \frac{\bar{X} - \mu}{\frac{\sigma}{\sqrt{n}}}$$

$$Z = \frac{(82.52 - 78.62)}{16.51 / \sqrt{100}} = \frac{3.9}{1.65} = 2.36$$

Step 4. Make the correct conclusion.

Compare the calculated $Z = 2.36$ with the rejection zone, $Z > 2.33$. The calculated Z falls in the rejection zone. Therefore, we reject H_0. Hawaiians' life expectancy is significantly higher than 78.62 years.

You probably noticed the different conclusions reached in Examples 7.2 and 7.3 using the same numbers. In Example 7.2, we conducted a two-tailed test but failed to reject H_0. However, in Example 7.3, we conducted a one-tailed test and rejected H_0.

The choice of conducting a one-tailed test or a two-tailed test should not be based on which one is easier to reject H_0 to produce a statistically significant result. When the research topic is fairly new or exploratory and there is no particular theoretical reasoning to suggest a directional test, two-tailed tests are the preferred standard operating procedures.

 Pop Quiz

1. When exploratory research is conducted without extensive prior research or theoretical reasoning to suggest a particular direction of relationship, the preferred hypothesis tests should be _____.

a. two-tailed tests

b. one-tailed tests

c. whichever is easier to produce significant results

d. randomly selected

Answer: a

One-tailed tests are usually reserved for research topics that have been studied repeatedly, for which consistent directional results have been obtained, or in which theoretical reasoning strongly suggests directional outcomes.

EXERCISE PROBLEMS

1. According to the ACT Profile Report-National, the ACT composite scores are normally distributed with $\mu = 21.0$ and $\sigma = 5.4$. Many charter schools receive funding from the state government without providing accountability measures as required by the public schools. A sample of 36 high school seniors is randomly selected from charter schools. Their average ACT composite score is 19.8. Is the average ACT composite score of seniors from charter schools lower than 21.0, assuming $\alpha = .10$?

2. Assume that the heights of a population of adults form a normal distribution with a mean $\mu = 69$ inches and a standard deviation $\sigma = 6$ inches. A village is known to have tall people. A researcher randomly selects a group of 25 people from this village, and their average height is 5 feet 11 inches. Is the average height of people from this village more than 69 inches, assuming $\alpha = .05$?

3. A car manufacturer claims that a new model Q has an average fuel efficiency $\mu = 35$ miles per gallon on the highway, and a standard deviation $\sigma = 5$. The American Automobile Association randomly selects 16 new Qs and measures their fuel efficiency at 33 miles per gallon. Is the car manufacturer truthful in advertising Q's fuel efficiency as being 35 miles per gallon, assuming $\alpha = .10$?

Solutions

1. The problem statement is whether the average ACT composite score of seniors from charter schools is lower than 21.0. "Lower" is a key word for direction; therefore, a left-tailed test is appropriate.

Step 1. State the pair of hypotheses.

Left-tailed test: $H_0: \mu = 21.0$
$H_1: \mu < 21.0$

Step 2. Identify the rejection zone.

For a left-tailed test with $\alpha = .10$, the critical value of Z is 1.28. The rejection zone is $Z < -1.28$, as shown in Figure 7.7.

FIGURE 7.7   Rejection Zone for $Z < -1.28$

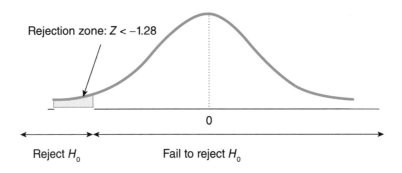

Rejection zone: $Z < -1.28$

0

Reject H_0 Fail to reject H_0

Step 3. Calculate the test statistic.

When comparing the average ACT score of students from charter schools to a population mean with a known σ, the use of a Z statistic is the correct approach.

List all the numbers given in the problem statement.

$\mu = 21.0$
$\sigma = 5.4$
$\overline{X} = 19.8$
$n = 36$

$$Z = \frac{\overline{X} - \mu}{\dfrac{\sigma}{\sqrt{n}}} = \frac{(19.8 - 21.0)}{5.4/\sqrt{36}} = \frac{-1.2}{0.9} = -1.33$$

Step 4. Make a conclusion.

Compare the calculated Z value $= -1.33$ from Step 3 and the rejection zone $Z < -1.28$ from Step 2. The calculated Z is within the rejection zone, so we reject H_0. The evidence is strong enough to support the claim that the average ACT of seniors from charter schools is lower than 21.0 at $\alpha = .10$.

2. According to the problem statement, "Is the average height of people from this village more than 69 inches?" This indicates clear direction, so a one-tailed test (in particular, a right-tailed test) is the correct approach.

Step 1. State the pair of hypotheses.

Right-tailed test: $H_0: \mu = 69$
$H_1: \mu > 69$

Step 2. Identify the rejection zone.

For a right-tailed test with $\alpha = .05$, the critical value of Z is 1.65. The rejection zone is shown in Figure 7.8.

FIGURE 7.8   Rejection Zone for $Z > 1.65$ for Exercise Problem 2

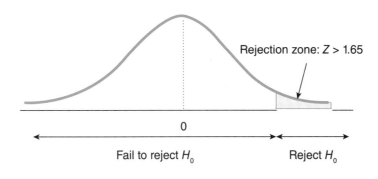

Rejection zone: $Z > 1.65$

0

Fail to reject H_0 Reject H_0

Step 3. Calculate the test statistic.

When comparing the average height of this village to a population mean with a known σ, the use of a Z statistic is the correct approach. Five feet 11 inches is $5 \times 12 + 11 = 71$ inches.

List all the numbers given in the problem statement.

$\mu = 69$
$\sigma = 6$
$\bar{X} = 71$
$n = 25$

$$Z = \frac{\bar{X} - \mu}{\sigma / \sqrt{n}} = \frac{(71 - 69)}{6 / \sqrt{25}} = \frac{2}{1.2} = 1.67$$

Step 4. Make the correct conclusion.

Compare the calculated Z value = 1.67 from Step 3 and the rejection zone $Z > 1.65$ from Step 2. The calculated Z falls in the rejection zone, so we reject H_0. The evidence is strong enough to support the claim that the average height of people in this village is more than 69 inches.

3. The problem statement asks about the truth of an advertisement. Therefore, the H_0 is that we assume the company is telling the truth unless the evidence falsifies the statement. A two-tailed test is appropriate in this case.

Step 1. State the pair of hypotheses.

Two-tailed test: $H_0: \mu = 35$

$H_1: \mu \neq 35$

Step 2. Identify the rejection zone.

For a two-tailed test with $\alpha = .10$, the critical value of Z is 1.65. The rejection zone, $|Z| > 1.65$, is shown in Figure 7.9.

FIGURE 7.9   Rejection Zone for $|Z| > 1.65$ for Exercise Problem 3

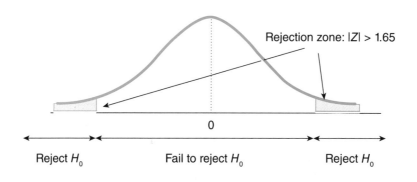

Rejection zone: $|Z| > 1.65$

0

Reject H_0 Fail to reject H_0 Reject H_0

Step 3. Calculate the test statistic.

When comparing the average fuel efficiency with the population mean with a known σ, the use of a Z statistic is the correct approach.

List all the numbers given in the problem statement.

$\mu = 35$

$\sigma = 5$

$$\bar{X} = 33$$
$$n = 16$$

$$Z = \frac{\bar{X} - \mu}{\sigma / \sqrt{n}} = \frac{(33 - 35)}{5 / \sqrt{16}} = \frac{-2}{1.25} = -1.6$$

Step 4. Make a conclusion.

Compare the calculated Z value $= -1.6$ from Step 3 and the rejection zone $|Z| > 1.65$ from Step 2. The calculated Z does not fall in the rejection zone, so we fail to reject H_0. The evidence is not strong enough to reject H_0. The evidence is not strong enough to support the claim that the company is not truthful in its advertisement.

Sharpen your skills with SAGE edge!

Visit edge.sagepub.com/bowen for mobile-friendly quizzes, flashcards, videos, and more!

WHAT YOU LEARNED

Hypothesis testing involves problem-solving skills. At the outset, one must understand the problem statement to determine if any key word indicates a clear direction of the test. If so, a one-tailed test is the correct approach. If not, a two-tailed test is the correct solution. Due to the limited statistical topics covered so far, only the Z test is used to illustrate hypothesis testing. All examples presented in Chapter 7 are used to practice the four-step hypothesis test procedure.

Apply the four-step process to conduct a hypothesis test.

1. State the pair of hypotheses.

   Two-tailed test: $H_0: \mu = xx$

                       $H_1: \mu \neq xx$

Right-tailed test:	$H_0: \mu = xx$
	$H_1: \mu > xx$
Left-tailed test:	$H_0: \mu = xx$
	$H_1: \mu < xx$

Where *xx* is the population parameter stated in the problem.

2. Identify the rejection zone.

Two-tailed test rejection zone:	$\lvert Z \rvert > Z_{\alpha/2}$
Right-tailed test rejection zone:	$Z > Z_{\alpha}$
Left-tailed test rejection zone:	$Z < -Z_{\alpha}$

3. Calculate the statistic. Comparing a sample mean with a population mean with a known σ, the *Z* statistic is the correct approach.

$$Z = \frac{\bar{X} - \mu}{\dfrac{\sigma}{\sqrt{n}}}$$

4. Make the correct conclusion.

Compare the calculated *Z* value from Step 3 and the rejection zone from Step 2. If the calculated *Z* falls in the rejection zone, we reject H_0. If the calculated *Z* does not fall in the rejection zone, we fail to reject H_0. The four-step hypothesis testing procedure will also be applicable in the following chapters with some minor adjustments when needed.

KEY WORDS

Alternative hypothesis, H_1: The hypothesis that researchers turn to when the null hypothesis is rejected. The alternative hypothesis is also called the research hypothesis.

Effect size: The effect size is a standardized measure of the difference between the sample statistic and the hypothesized population parameter in units of standard deviation.

Hypothesis testing: Hypothesis testing is the standardized process to test the strength of scientific evidence for a claim about a population.

Mutually exclusive and collectively exhaustive: Mutually exclusive and collectively exhaustive means that events have no overlap—if one is true, the others cannot be true—and they cover all possible outcomes.

Null hypothesis, H_0: The null hypothesis states that the effect that the researchers are trying to establish does not exist.

One-tailed test (directional test): A one-tailed test is a directional hypothesis test, which is usually conducted when the research topic suggests a consistent directional relationship with either theoretical reasoning or repeated empirical evidence.

Power: Power is defined as the sensitivity to detect an effect when an effect actually exists. The power of the hypothesis test is the probability of correctly rejecting H_0 when H_0 is false. Power is positively correlated with all of the three factors: (1) sample size, (2) significance level, and (3) the standardized effect size.

Rejection zone: The rejection zone is bounded by the critical value of a statistic. When the calculated value falls in the rejection zone, the correct decision is to reject H_0.

Two-tailed test (nondirectional test): A two-tailed test is a nondirectional hypothesis test, which is usually done when the research topic is exploratory or there are no reasons to expect consistent directional relationships from either theoretical reasoning or previous studies.

Type I error: A Type I error is a mistake of rejecting H_0 when H_0 is true. In other words, a Type I error is to claim an effect when the effect actually does not exist. The symbol α represents the probability of making a Type I error.

Type II error: A Type II error is a mistake of failing to reject H_0 when H_0 is false. In other words, a Type II error is failing to claim an effect when the effect actually exists. The symbol β represents the probability of making a Type II error.

LEARNING ASSESSMENT

Multiple Choice: Circle the best answer to every question.

1. The statistical power refers to the sensitivity to
   a. correctly reject the null hypothesis (H_0) when H_0 is actually true.
   b. correctly reject the null hypothesis (H_0) when H_0 is actually false.
   c. correctly accept the null hypothesis (H_0) when H_0 is actually true.
   d. correctly accept the null hypothesis (H_0) when H_0 is actually false.

2. A Type II error refers to
   a. claiming a treatment effect when the effect actually exists.
   b. claiming a treatment effect when the effect actually does not exist.
   c. failing to claim a treatment effect when the effect actually exists.
   d. failing to claim a treatment effect when the effect does not exist.

3. A normal adult population is known to have a mean $\mu = 65$ on the WPA cognitive ability test. A higher score means better cognitive ability. A researcher wants to study the detrimental effects of chemotherapy on brain function, so she randomly selects a group of 16 patients who received chemo in the last month to measure their WPA score. What is the alternative hypothesis for this study?

   a. $H_1: \mu \geq 65$
   b. $H_1: \mu \leq 65$
   c. $H_1: \mu > 65$
   d. $H_1: \mu < 65$

4. In a one-tailed test, $H_0: \mu = 120$, $H_1: \mu < 120$, the rejection zone is

   a. on the right tail of the distribution.
   b. on the left tail of the distribution.
   c. in the middle of the distribution.
   d. evenly split into two tails.

5. Which of the following pairs is usually unknown parameters of the population?

   a. $\bar{X}$ and μ
   b. s and σ
   c. s^2 and σ^2
   d. μ and σ

6. In an one-tailed test, $H_0: \mu = 10$, $H_1: \mu > 10$, the rejection zone is

   a. on the right tail of the distribution.
   b. on the left tail of the distribution.
   c. in the middle of the distribution.
   d. evenly split into two tails.

7. Type I error means that a researcher has

   a. claimed a treatment effect when the effect actually exists.
   b. claimed a treatment effect when the effect actually does not exist.
   c. failed to claim a treatment effect when the effect actually exists.
   d. failed to claim a treatment effect when the effect does not exist.

8. For a two-tailed test with $\alpha = .01$, the critical values that set the boundaries for the rejection zones are

   a. $Z > 1.96$
   b. $Z > 2.58$
   c. $|Z| > 1.96$
   d. $|Z| > 2.58$

9. The starting point of a hypothesis test is the null hypothesis, which

   a. states that an effect does not exist.
   b. is denoted as H_1.
   c. is always stated in terms of sample statistics.
   d. states that the effect exists.

10. A Type I error means that a researcher has

   a. rejected the null hypothesis (H_0) when H_0 is actually true.
   b. rejected the null hypothesis (H_0) when H_0 is actually false.
   c. accepted the null hypothesis (H_0) when H_0 is actually true.
   d. accepted the null hypothesis (H_0) when H_0 is actually false.

11. A researcher is conducting a study to evaluate a program that claims to increase short-term memory capacity. The short-term memory capacity score is normally distributed with $\mu = 7$. Both theoretical reasoning and previous empirical research have shown a strong positive effect of this kind of program. Which of the following is the correct statement of the alternative hypothesis H_1?

    a. $\mu \neq 7$

    b. $\mu = 7$

    c. $\mu > 7$

    d. $\mu < 7$

Free Response Questions

12. Assume that anxiety scores as measured by an anxiety assessment inventory are normally distributed with $\mu = 20$ and $\sigma = 4$. A sample of four patients who are undergoing treatment for anxiety is randomly selected, and their mean anxiety score $\bar{X} = 22$. Is the average anxiety score for patients who are under treatment significantly different from 20? Assume $\alpha = .10$.

13. A normally distributed population has a mean $\mu = 80$ and a standard deviation $\sigma = 8$. Randomly select $n = 16$ from this population. What is the standard error of the mean?

14. National data on student loans indicate that the student loan amount has a mean $\mu = \$30,000$. The distribution of student loans is approximately normal with a standard deviation $\sigma = \$20,000$. A random sample of 25 students from a private university reported a mean student debt load of $\$37,500$. Is the average student loan from this private university higher than $\$30,000$? Assume $\alpha = .05$.

15. According to the National Association of Builders, the average single-family home size in the United States is normally distributed with a mean $\mu = 2,392$ square feet and a standard deviation $\sigma = 760$ square feet. Sixteen single-family houses are randomly selected from Cleveland, and the mean size is 2,025 square feet. Is the average square footage of houses in Cleveland smaller than 2,392 square feet? Assume $\alpha = .05$.

One-Sample *t* Test When σ Is Unknown

After reading and studying this chapter, you should be able to do the following:

- Describe the purpose of a one-sample *t* test, and how it is conducted
- Explain how a *t* test differs from a *Z* test
- Define confidence interval, and describe how the confidence level is calculated
- Name the three pieces of information needed to identify the critical *t* values that set the boundaries of rejection zones in *t* tests

WHAT YOU KNOW AND WHAT IS NEW

In Chapter 7, you learned to conduct a hypothesis test using the *Z* test, to compare a sample

$$Z = \frac{\bar{X} - \mu}{\frac{\sigma}{\sqrt{n}}}$$

mean with the hypothesized population mean when σ is known. The general statistical test formula is expressed as (sample statistic − population parameter)/(standard error of the statistic). In *Z* tests, the population standard deviation, σ, is always readily available in the problem statement to allow the calculation of standard error of the mean, $\sigma/\sqrt{n}$. However, in reality, σ is mostly unknown in a population. Instead of giving up comparing sample means with population means altogether, statisticians figure out how to modify the process to come up with a close-enough process to estimate the significance of differences between a sample mean and a population mean.

The slightly modified tests are called one-sample t tests. In general, one-sample t tests maintain the main features of the Z test to perform comparisons between sample means and population means. Frankly, t tests bring us one step closer to the reality where we can test the significance of the difference between a sample mean and its corresponding population mean when σ is unknown. Since σ is unknown, the sample standard deviation, s, is used as the best estimate of σ. The basic formula for a t test can be expressed as t = (sample statistic − population parameter)/(estimated standard error of the statistic). This generic formula is applicable in this chapter, as well as in Chapters 9 and 10. All the differences between the Z tests and one-sample t tests are clearly documented in the following sections.

THE UNKNOWN σ AND CONDUCTING THE ONE-SAMPLE t TEST

Up to this point in this book, in all the examples and homework problems when a sample mean is compared with the population mean, the population standard deviation, σ, has been readily provided. However, in reality, σ, in most cases, is unknown. To work around this dilemma, s is used as the best estimate of σ. Even though s is a biased estimate of σ because it tends to underestimate the value of σ, there is no formula to correct this underestimation in all cases. Assume, for instance, that the standard deviation of the ACT composite score is σ = 5.5, and that a simple random sample is selected. The sample standard deviation, s, will usually be smaller than 5.5. However, the sample variance, s^2, is an unbiased estimate of the population variance, $σ^2$. There is no systematic underestimate of population variance using the sample variance. The sample variance formula was first discussed in Chapter 3. Let's repeat it here again.

$$s^2 = \frac{\Sigma(X - \bar{X})^2}{df} = \frac{SS}{df} = \frac{SS}{(n-1)}$$

The degrees of freedom for sample variance are $n - 1$ because the sample mean, $\bar{X}$, is used to estimate the population mean in the process of calculating the variance. This restricts the number of values that are free to vary. Accordingly, one degree of freedom is lost. Hence, the degrees of freedom for sample variance are $n - 1$. When s is used to estimate the unknown σ, the estimated standard error of the mean $s_{\bar{X}}$ is calculated simply by replacing σ with s in the standard error of the mean formula, $σ_{\bar{X}} = σ/\sqrt{n}$, and you get $s_{\bar{X}} = s/\sqrt{n}$. This estimated standard error of the mean is the denominator of the one-sample t-test formula. The good news is that the numerator of the one-sample t test is exactly the same as the numerator of the Z test. Putting the numerator and the denominator together, you get the one-sample t-test formula

$$t = \frac{\bar{X} - μ}{s_{\bar{X}}} = \frac{\bar{X} - μ}{\frac{s}{\sqrt{n}}},$$

with $df = n - 1$. The estimated standard error of the mean is the first important distinction between Z tests and one-sample t tests.

The *t* Distribution, a Specific Curve for Every Degree of Freedom

When conducting a hypothesis test for a *Z* test, the calculated *Z* needs to be compared with the critical *Z* value that sets the boundary of the rejection zone, and this critical *Z* value can be found in the *Z* Table as stated in Chapters 5, 6, and 7. The same principle applies to conducting a *t* test. The calculated *t* needs to be compared with the critical *t* value that sets the boundary of the rejection zone. The only difference is that there is only one *Z* curve, but there is a specific *t* curve for every degree of freedom. The critical value of *t* that sets the boundary of the rejection zone varies for every degree of freedom, and the variations are noticeable, especially for small sample sizes, $n < 30$.

Figure 8.1 shows five different *t* curves with five *df*s. The curve with the highest peak represents the standard normal distribution curve, which is the *Z* curve or a *t* curve with $df = \infty$; the other curves with lower peaks represent the *t* curves with $df = 5, 3, 2,$ or 1. The curve with the lowest peak represents the *t* curve with $df = 1$, the curve with the second lowest peak represents the *t* curve with $df = 2$, and the curve with the third lowest peak represents the *t* curve with $df = 3$.

Before we go into examples, let's summarize what you have learned in terms of *t* tests so far. These tests are especially developed to conduct comparisons between sample means

FIGURE 8.1   *t* Curves With Five Different Degrees of Freedom

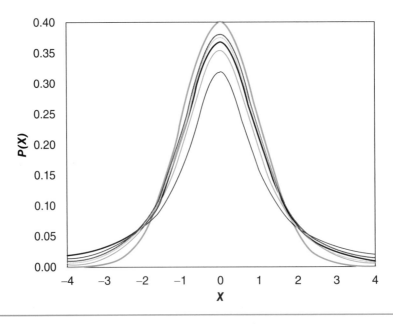

SOURCE: IkamusumeFan (2013).

and population means, particularly when the sample size is small, $n < 30$, and the population standard deviation, σ, is unknown. The slight modifications in t tests as compared with Z tests are listed below.

1. The population standard deviation, σ, is unknown. The sample standard deviation, s, is used as the best estimate of σ.

2. It is important to use the degrees of freedom, $df = n - 1$, to calculate the sample variance and sample standard deviation. The degrees of freedom for the one-sample t test are $n - 1$.

3. There is a unique t-distribution curve for every degree of freedom. It is important especially for small sample sizes, $n < 30$. The critical value that sets the boundary of the rejection zone varies for every degree of freedom.

Here is the formula for a **one-sample t test**, according to these modifications.

$$t = \frac{\overline{X} - \mu}{s_{\overline{X}}} = \frac{\overline{X} - \mu}{\dfrac{s}{\sqrt{n}}} \text{, with } df = n - 1$$

where

$\overline{X}$ = the sample mean

μ = the population mean

n = the sample size

s = the sample standard deviation $= \sqrt{\dfrac{\Sigma(X - \overline{X})^2}{df}} = \sqrt{\dfrac{SS}{df}} = \sqrt{\dfrac{SS}{(n-1)}}$

$s_{\overline{X}}$ = the estimated standard error of the mean $= \dfrac{s}{\sqrt{n}}$

If you put the t-test formula and Z-test formula next to each other, you can see that the only difference is that σ in the Z test is replaced by s in the t test.

$$Z = \frac{\overline{X} - \mu}{\dfrac{\sigma}{\sqrt{n}}} \qquad\qquad t = \frac{\overline{X} - \mu}{\dfrac{s}{\sqrt{n}}}$$

Just as the calculated Z values have to be compared with the critical values of Z that set off the boundaries of the rejection zones to make conclusions about the tests, the calculated t values have to be compared with the critical values of t that set off the boundaries of the rejection zones. The critical values for *t* tests can be found in the *t* Distribution Table or *t* Table in Appendix B. The *t* Table provides critical values of *t* that set the boundaries of rejection zones for *t* tests given three pieces of information: (1) one-tailed or two-tailed tests, (2) *df* of the test, and (3) the α level. The numbers in the top row of the *t* Distribution Table specify various α levels for one-tailed tests and the numbers in the second row specify various α levels for two-tailed tests. The numbers in the first column identify the degrees of freedom (*df*) for the *t* test, and all the numbers inside the *t* Table are critical values that set the boundaries of rejection zones. The shape of *t* curves is symmetric, as in the *Z* distribution, which means that when you cut the *t* curve in half along the peak (i.e., the location of mean, median, and mode), the left side is a mirror image of the right side. In small sample sizes, *n* < 30, *t* curves tend to have lower peaks and higher tails than the *Z* curve. As the sample sizes get bigger and bigger (especially, *n* > 30), *t* curves approximate the *Z* curve, and the differences between the two become less and less noticeable. It is appropriate to conduct *t* tests when the population is normally distributed or when sample size is large (i.e., *n* > 30). Only one of these two conditions needs to be true to appropriately apply *t* tests. Table 8.1 shows a portion of the *t* Table. We will go over some examples to illustrate how to identify critical *t* values that set the boundaries of rejection zones.

TABLE 8.1   A Portion of the *t* Table

df	ONE-TAILED α LEVEL							
	0.25	0.20	0.15	0.10	0.05	0.025	0.01	0.005
	TWO-TAILED α LEVEL							
	0.50	0.40	0.30	0.20	0.10	0.05	0.02	0.01
1	1	1.376	1.963	3.078	6.314	12.71	31.82	63.66
2	0.816	1.061	1.386	1.886	2.92	4.303	6.965	9.925
3	0.765	0.978	1.25	1.638	2.353	3.182	4.541	5.841
4	0.741	0.941	1.19	1.533	2.132	2.776	3.747	4.604
5	0.727	0.92	1.156	1.476	2.015	2.571	3.365	4.032
6	0.718	0.906	1.134	1.44	1.943	2.447	3.143	3.707
7	0.711	0.896	1.119	1.415	1.895	2.365	2.998	3.499
8	0.706	0.889	1.108	1.397	1.86	2.306	2.896	3.355
9	0.703	0.883	1.1	1.383	1.833	2.262	2.821	3.25
10	0.7	0.879	1.093	1.372	1.812	2.228	2.764	3.169
11	0.697	0.876	1.088	1.363	1.796	2.201	2.718	3.106
12	0.695	0.873	1.083	1.356	1.782	2.179	2.681	3.055

EXAMPLE 8.1

Find the critical t value that sets the boundary of the rejection zone in each case.

    a. A two-tailed test with $\alpha = .01$ and $df = 8$

    b. A right-tailed test with $\alpha = .10$ and $df = 11$

    c. A left-tailed test with $\alpha = .05$ and $df = 5$

    a. You must remember that you have to calculate $\alpha/2$ when conducting a two-tailed test using the Z test, because the Z Table only lists one-tailed probability. However, you don't have to do that in the t test. Because the t Table lists both one-tailed α and two-tailed α, you simply need to identify the column with the correct α level and the correct test. Please make a note that one-tailed α is the same column as two-tailed 2α, such as one-tailed $\alpha = .05$ is the same as two-tailed $\alpha = .10$.

In the second row, find the vertical column corresponding to two-tailed $\alpha = .01$, and then find $df = 8$ in the first column; the value in the intersection is 3.355. The rejection zone is expressed as $|t| > 3.355$.

    b. In the top row, find the vertical column corresponding to one-tailed $\alpha = .10$, and then find $df = 11$ in the first column; the value in the intersection is 1.363. The rejection zone for this right-tailed test is $t > 1.363$.

    c. There are only positive t values reported in the t Table. Due to the symmetrical characteristic of the t distribution, negative t values can be identified through the t Table by adding the negative sign to the value reported in the t Table. In the top row, find the vertical column corresponding to one-tailed $\alpha = .05$, and then find $df = 5$ in the first column. The value in the intersection is 2.015. The rejection zone for this left-tailed test is $t < -2.015$.

After learning the t-test formula and finding critical values of t in the t Table, let's conduct some hypothesis tests using t tests. The four-step hypothesis testing procedure, as discussed in Chapter 7, is still applicable in conducting t tests. You will put the four-step hypothesis testing procedure, t-test formula, and t Table into action in the following examples.

EXAMPLE 8.2

ACT composite scores are normally distributed with a $\mu = 21$. A sample of 25 students is randomly selected from a local high school with an $\bar{X} = 23$ and $s = 5.2$. Do the data

(Continued)

(Continued)

support the claim that the average ACT composite score of students from this high school is higher than 21 on the ACT composite score, using $\alpha = .05$?

The population standard deviation, σ, is unknown in this problem statement. It is not possible to conduct a Z test; therefore, a t test is an appropriate alternative. We use the four-step hypothesis testing process to conduct a t test to answer this problem.

Step 1. State the pair of hypotheses.

Based on the problem statement, "the average ACT score of students from this high school is higher than 21," thus the problem indicates a directional hypothesis. The key word "higher" indicates a right-tailed test. It is easy to start with H_1: the alternative hypothesis in which the researchers are interested is $\mu > 21$. Then H_0 covers the equal sign, $\mu = 21$.

$H_0: \mu = 21$

$H_1: \mu > 21$

Step 2. Identify the rejection zone for the hypothesis test.

We need three pieces of information to identify the critical t value that sets the boundary of the rejection zone: (1) one-tailed test or two-tailed test, (2) df, and (3) α level. We know that this is a right-tailed test from Step 1, $\alpha = .05$ and $df = n - 1 = 25 - 1 = 24$ from the problem statement. According to the t Distribution Table, the critical t value is 1.711. The rejection zone for the right-tailed test is $t > 1.711$, as shown in Figure 8.2.

FIGURE 8.2 Using the t Table to Identify Rejection Zone $t > 1.711$

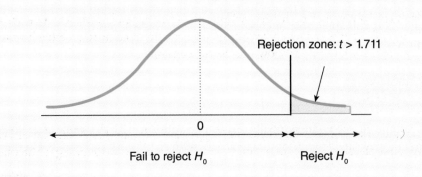

Rejection zone: $t > 1.711$

0

Fail to reject H_0

Reject H_0

Step 3. Calculate the test statistic.

The problem statement asks for a comparison between the average ACT score of students in this high school and the population mean with σ unknown. Therefore, the *t* test is the correct statistic to accomplish this purpose. It is easy to list all the numbers stated in the problem statement, so as to separate out what we know and what we need to figure out.

What we know.

$\mu = 21$

$s = 5.2$

$\overline{X} = 23$

$n = 25$

We need to figure out *t*. Next, insert all the numbers in the *t*-test formula.

$$t = \frac{\overline{X} - \mu}{\frac{s}{\sqrt{n}}}$$

$$t = \frac{23 - 21}{\frac{5.2}{\sqrt{25}}} = \frac{2}{1.04} = 1.923$$

Step 4. Make the correct conclusion.

Compare the calculated $t = 1.923$ with the rejection zone $t > 1.711$. The calculated *t* falls in the rejection zone. Therefore, we reject H_0. At $\alpha = .05$, the evidence is strong enough to support the claim that the average ACT score of students from this high school is higher than 21.

Besides standardized exams, such approaches can also be applied in medical tests, especially using a group of patients with a particular medical condition compared with a known standard (i.e., a population mean) as shown in the next example.

EXAMPLE 8.3

According to WebMD, HDL stands for "high-density lipoprotein." Each bit of HDL is a microscopic blob that consists of a rim of lipoprotein surrounding a cholesterol

(Continued)

(Continued)

center. HDL acts as a maintenance crew for the inner walls of blood vessels (endothelia). HDL chemically scrubs the endothelium clean and keeps it healthy. Assume that the levels of HDL are normally distributed with a $\mu = 50$ mg/dl. A sample of 16 heart attack patients is randomly selected from a large hospital, and their HDL levels are measured with $\bar{X} = 40$ mg/dl and $s = 9$ mg/dl. Do the data support the claim that the average HDL of heart attack patients is lower than 50 mg/dl, using $\alpha = .01$?

The population standard deviation, σ, is unknown in this problem statement. It is not possible to conduct a Z test; therefore, a t test is an appropriate alternative. We use the four-step hypothesis testing process to conduct a t test to answer this problem.

Step 1. State the pair of hypotheses.

The problem statement asks if "the average HDL of heart attack patients is lower than 50 mg/dl." "Lower" is a key word for a left-tailed test.

Left-tailed test: $H_0: \mu = 50$ mg/dl

$H_1: \mu < 50$ mg/dl

Step 2. Identify the rejection zone.

A left-tailed test with $\alpha = .01$ and $df = n - 1 = 16 - 1 = 15$.

Rejection zone: $t < -2.602$ (as shown in Figure 8.3).

Step 3. Calculate the test statistic.

When comparing the average HDL of heart attack patients with the population mean and an unknown σ, using a t test is the correct approach.

List all the numbers given in the problem statement.

$\mu = 50$ mg/dl

$s = 9$ mg/dl

$\bar{X} = 40$ mg/dl

$n = 16$

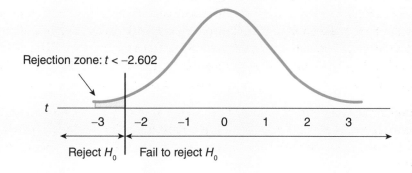

FIGURE 8.3 Using the t Distribution Table to Identify Rejection Zone $t < -2.602$

We need to figure out t. Next, insert all the numbers in the t-test formula.

$$t = \frac{\bar{X} - \mu}{\frac{s}{\sqrt{n}}}$$

$$t = \frac{40 - 50}{\frac{9}{\sqrt{16}}} = \frac{-10}{2.25} = -4.44$$

Step 4. Make the correct conclusion.

Compare the calculated $t = -4.44$ with the rejection zone $t < -2.602$. The calculated t falls in the rejection zone. Therefore, we reject H_0. At $\alpha = .01$, the evidence is strong enough to support the claim that the average HDL of heart attack patients is lower than 50 mg/dl.

The t tests allow us to compare a sample mean $\bar{X}$ with a hypothesized population mean without requiring σ. The sample standard deviation, s, is used as the best estimate of the σ. Both $\bar{X}$ and s can be calculated directly from reported individual scores in a sample. Of course, they require the formulas that were covered in Chapter 3. You'd better refresh your memory on sample mean and sample standard deviation before attempting to solve such problems.

You Must Remember This

The sample mean and standard deviation are basic descriptive statistics that remain important regardless of what statistics are performed. When given all values from a sample, you are able to calculate the sample mean by adding all the values and dividing by the sample size, $\bar{X} = \sum X/n$. Calculating sample standard deviation starts with $SS = \sum (X - \bar{X})^2$, and then $s = \sqrt{SS/df}$.

EXAMPLE 8.4

Reaction time is defined as the time taken to complete a task. Depending on the complexity of the task, each one requires a different reaction time. Assume that the reaction time for seeing a green light and pushing a button is normally distributed with a $\mu = 220$ milliseconds. A group of nine student athletes is randomly selected, and their reaction times are measured at 273, 289, 138, 121, 285, 252, 129, 120, and 130. Do student athletes' reaction times differ from 220 milliseconds, using $\alpha = .10$?

The population standard deviation, σ, is unknown in this problem statement. It is not possible to conduct a Z test; therefore, we use the four-step hypothesis testing process to conduct a t test to answer this problem.

Step 1. State the pair of hypotheses.

The problem statement asks, "Do student athletes' reaction times differ from 220 milliseconds?" This statement does not contain any information regarding direction. Therefore, a nondirectional hypothesis is the correct approach. H_1 is the hypothesis that needs to be established by the evidence, $\mu \neq 220$. And H_0 is $\mu = 220$.

$$H_0: \mu = 220$$

$$H_1: \mu \neq 220$$

Step 2. Identify the rejection zone for the hypothesis test.

From Step 1, we know that we are conducting a two-tailed test. The problem statement specifies $\alpha = .10$, and $df = n - 1 = 9 - 1 = 8$. According to the t Table, the critical t value is 1.86. The rejection zone is $|t| > 1.86$, as shaded in Figure 8.4.

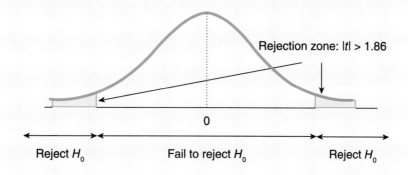

Step 3. Calculate the statistic.

The problem statement asks for a comparison between the average reaction time of student athletes and the population mean with an unknown σ. So the *t* test is the correct statistic to accomplish this purpose. It is easy to list all the numbers stated in the problem statement and to separate what we know from what we need to figure out.

What we know:

   μ = 220 milliseconds

   n = 9

When given all measures in a sample, you can calculate $\bar{X}$ and *s* needed for conducting a *t* test. You need to refresh your memory on what you learned in Chapter 3.

$$\bar{X} = \frac{\sum X}{n}$$

$$SS = \sum (X - \bar{X})^2$$

$$s = \sqrt{\frac{\sum (X - \bar{X})^2}{df}} = \sqrt{\frac{SS}{df}} = \sqrt{\frac{SS}{(n-1)}}$$

Let's put all the measures in a table and demonstrate the step-by-step process in Table 8.2.

(Continued)

(Continued)

First, we need to figure out the sample mean, $\bar{X}$. Then we construct the second column $(X - \bar{X})$, and the third column $(X - \bar{X})^2$, and add all the numbers in the third column to obtain the Sum of Squares, SS.

TABLE 8.2 Nine Student Athletes' Reaction Times

X	$(X - \bar{X})$	$(X - \bar{X})^2$
273	80	6,400
289	96	9,216
138	−55	3,025
121	−72	5,184
285	92	8,464
252	59	3,481
129	−64	4,096
120	−73	5,329
130	−63	3,969
1,737		49,164

$$\bar{X} = \sum X/n = 1737/9 = 193$$

$$SS = \sum(X - \bar{X})^2 = 49164$$

$$s = \sqrt{\frac{\sum(X - \bar{X})^2}{df}} = \sqrt{\frac{SS}{df}} = \sqrt{\frac{SS}{(n-1)}} = \sqrt{\frac{49164}{8}} = \sqrt{6145.5} = 78.4$$

Next, insert all the numbers in the t-test formula.

$$t = \frac{\bar{X} - \mu}{\frac{s}{\sqrt{n}}}$$

$$t = \frac{193 - 220}{\frac{78.4}{\sqrt{9}}} = \frac{-27}{26.1} = -1.03$$

Step 4. Make the correct conclusion.

Compare the calculated $t = -1.03$ with the rejection zone $|t| > 1.86$. The calculated t does not fall in the rejection zone. Therefore, we fail to reject H_0. At $\alpha = .10$, the evidence is not strong enough to support the claim that the average reaction time of student athletes differs from 220 milliseconds.

After going through several examples on conducting t tests, you should get a sense that t tests are more realistic than Z tests because they don't require the population standard deviation, σ. Using the sample standard deviation, s, as the best estimate of σ allows scientists to compare a particular sample mean and a hypothesized population mean to obtain useful information. However, if σ is known or provided, there is no need to estimate its value, so a Z test should apply in such a situation.

It is worth repeating that the t distribution has a special attribute that the Z distribution does not have. For every degree of freedom, there is a specific t curve. That is the reason why it needs three values, (1) one-tailed test versus two-tailed test, (2) α level, and (3) df, to identify the critical values of t that set off the boundaries of rejection zones, whereas it only takes the first two values to identify the critical values of Z that set off the boundaries of rejection zones.

Pop Quiz

1. Which one of the following pieces of information is *not* needed to identify the critical values of t that set off the boundaries of the rejection zones?

   a. The significance level, α

   b. One-tailed test versus two-tailed test

   c. The degrees of freedom for the t test

   d. The population standard deviation, σ

2. When the problem statement provides the population mean, μ, the sample mean, $\bar{X}$, the population standard deviation, σ, the sample standard deviation, s, and the sample size, n, to compare the sample mean with the population mean, which one of the following is the correct approach to conduct hypothesis tests?

   a. $Z = \dfrac{X - \mu}{\sigma}$

   b. $Z = \dfrac{X - \bar{X}}{s}$

   c. $Z = \dfrac{\bar{X} - \mu}{\dfrac{\sigma}{\sqrt{n}}}$

   d. $t = \dfrac{\bar{X} - \mu}{\dfrac{s}{\sqrt{n}}}$

Answers: 1. d, 2. c

CONFIDENCE INTERVALS

Two of the most common types of statistical inferences are hypothesis tests and confidence intervals. You have learned the standard process of conducting hypothesis tests to test the strength of a claim about a population. Now it is time to introduce confidence intervals (CIs). A CI is defined as an interval of values calculated from sample statistics to estimate the values of a population parameter or make inferences about the population parameter. CIs provide additional information on which to base researcher's conclusions. The calculated CIs can convey the quality of the estimation or statistical inference. As an inferential technique, the CI does not require a hypothesis about the population mean and does not have to be used in conjunction with testing a hypothesis. A CI can be appropriately applied when the population is normally distributed or when the sample size is larger than 30. Just to clarify, when the population is normally distributed, there are no sample size restrictions on constructing CIs. Only when the population is not normally distributed does the sample size need to be greater than 30 for the procedure to work properly. Constructing a CI involves two steps: first, obtaining a point estimate, and second, an interval estimate.

POINT ESTIMATE

A point estimate is a single value from the sample used to estimate a population parameter. For example, in estimating a population mean, a sample mean is the best single value for that purpose. When a school district is asked to provide a single value to represent its 12th graders' SAT scores, the best estimate is to randomly select a group of 12th graders in the district to calculate their mean SAT score. The point estimate principle is that the sample mean, $\bar{X}$, is the best estimate of the population mean, μ.

However, this single value does not provide the quality of the estimate. It may be close to or far away from the population parameter. However, such quality information is not available from one single value. Therefore, statisticians extend the point estimate to an interval estimate.

INTERVAL ESTIMATE

An interval estimate, as the term suggests, refers to a range of values used to estimate a population parameter. The width of the interval estimate depends on the confidence level. A confidence level is $(1 - \alpha)$, which is the complement to α, the significance level. When $\alpha = .05$ is used as the default value, a 95% CI is the default width. The confidence level is expressed as a percentage, so it is expressed as $(1 - \alpha)100\%$. CIs are calculated as the point estimate $\pm$ the margin of error, E. The margin of error is calculated by multiplying the critical value of t for a two-tailed test, $t_{\alpha/2}$, by the estimated standard error of the mean, $s / \sqrt{n}$.

$$E = t_{\alpha/2} \left(\frac{s}{\sqrt{n}} \right)$$

The symbol $t_{\alpha/2}$ denotes the critical value of t for a two-tailed test with a significance level = α. The $\alpha/2$ is simply a subscript to identify the critical t value for a two-tailed α. It is not a math operation. Since the margin of error is calculated by the multiplication of $t_{\alpha/2}$ and the estimated standard error of the mean, as α decreases, the confidence level $(1 - \alpha)$ increases, and the CI widens. Therefore, a 99% CI is wider than a 95% CI and a 95% CI is wider than a 90% CI when the estimated standard error of the mean remains the same.

The CIs are put together by taking the point estimate ± the margin of error. In estimating a CI for a population mean, the CI centers at $\bar{X}$. The upper limit of the CI is calculated by adding the margin of error to the sample mean, $\bar{X} + t_{\alpha/2}(s/\sqrt{n})$, and the lower limit of the CI is calculated by subtracting the margin of error from the sample mean, $\bar{X} - t_{\alpha/2}(s/\sqrt{n})$. As you can see, CI always centers at the point estimate, adding the margin of error to reach the upper limit and subtracting the margin of error to reach the lower limit; the two tails outside the CI are evenly split. The probability of each tail is $\alpha/2$. Therefore, the calculation of CIs is very similar to two-tailed tests with a significance level of α.

$$\text{CI of } \mu = \bar{X} \pm t_{\alpha/2} \left(\frac{s}{\sqrt{n}} \right)$$

The rounding rule for constructing a CI is to report the interval lower and upper limits with one more decimal place than reported in the sample mean. I think an example will help clarify how this process works.

EXAMPLE 8.5

Let's use the reaction time example stated in Example 8.4. The reaction time for seeing a green light and pushing a button is normally distributed with a $\mu = 220$ milliseconds. A group of nine student athletes are randomly selected, and their reaction times are measured at 273, 289, 138, 121, 285, 252, 129, 120, and 130.

  a. What is the 90% CI for the student athletes' reaction time?

  b. Interpret the 90% CI.

  c. Compare the 90% CI with the result from the two-tailed hypothesis test with $\alpha = .10$.

(Continued)

(Continued)

    a. When given all measures in a sample, you have to calculate $\bar{X}$ and s before constructing a 90% CI.

$$\bar{X} = \sum X / n = 1737/9 = 193$$

$$SS = \sum (X - \bar{X})^2 = 49164$$

$$s = \sqrt{\frac{\sum (X - \bar{X})^2}{df}} = \sqrt{\frac{SS}{df}} = \sqrt{\frac{SS}{(n-1)}} = \sqrt{\frac{49164}{8}} = 78.4$$

These are the same values as calculated in Table 8.2. A little repetition is good for learning statistics.

    The point estimate of μ is $\bar{X} = 193$.

    The margin of error is $t_{\alpha/2} \left(\dfrac{s}{\sqrt{n}} \right)$.

Let's break the calculation down to $t_{\alpha/2}$ and $\dfrac{s}{\sqrt{n}}$.

With a 90% CI, it means $(1 - \alpha) = .90$; therefore, $\alpha = .10$.

The critical value of t in a two-tailed test with $\alpha = .10$ is the same as a one-tailed test with $\alpha = .05$. The symbol $t_{\alpha/2}$ denotes the critical value of t for a two-tailed test with significance level $= \alpha$. The critical value of t for a two-tailed test, $\alpha = .10$ and $df = 8$, is 1.86.

$$\frac{s}{\sqrt{n}} = \frac{78.4}{\sqrt{9}} = 26.13$$

Now you can insert the margin of error together, $t_{\alpha/2} \dfrac{s}{\sqrt{n}} = 1.86 \dfrac{78.4}{\sqrt{9}} = 48.6$

$$90\% \text{ CI of } \mu = \bar{X} \pm t_{\alpha/2} \frac{s}{\sqrt{n}} = 193 \pm 48.6$$

The lower limit and the upper limit of the 90% CI are reported in brackets [144.4, 241.6] with the lower limit on the left and the upper limit on the right, inside the brackets. The 90% CI [144.4, 241.6] is constructed from the sample of nine student athletes to make an inference about the population mean for all student athletes.

                                                     STRAIGHTFORWARD STATISTICS

b. The correct way to interpret the 90% CI is that we are 90% confident that the population mean for all student athletes, μ, is included in the brackets [144.4, 241.6].

c. The 90% CI [144.4, 241.6] includes the hypothesized population mean under H_0, $\mu = 220$. The evidence is not strong enough to support the claim that there are differences between student athletes' reaction times and the general population's reaction times. Our interests in conducting the hypothesis go beyond the nine student athletes in the sample. The real interest is to compare all student athletes' reaction times with the general population.

The result from the two-tailed hypothesis test with $\alpha = .10$ as reported in Example 8.4 is that the calculated t ($t = -1.03$) does not fall in the rejection zone ($|t| > 1.86$). Therefore, we fail to reject H_0. At $\alpha = .10$, there is not enough evidence to support the claim that student athletes' reaction times differ from 220 milliseconds.

The outcome from a 90% CI is consistent with the result from the two-tailed hypothesis test with $\alpha = .10$. In general, conducting a two-tailed hypothesis test with significance level = α generates the same conclusion as constructing a $(1 - \alpha) \times 100\%$ CI. The range of values of the CI provides additional information for interpretation. When the hypothesized population parameter under H_0 is within the CI, there is no difference between the CI constructed from sample statistics and the hypothesized population parameter. When the hypothesized population parameter is not within the CI, there is a significant difference between the CI and the population parameter.

Let's go through an example when the hypothesized population mean under H_0 is not within the CI.

EXAMPLE 8.6

The licensed drivers' ages in a suburb are normally distributed with a $\mu = 48$. A sample of nine drivers is randomly selected because of their moving violation citations. Their ages are 17, 28, 33, 46, 65, 21, 19, 38, and 40.

a. What is the 95% CI of the average age of drivers who received moving violation citations?

b. Interpret the 95% CI.

(Continued)

(Continued)

a.
$$\bar{X} = \sum X / n$$

$$SS = \sum (X - \bar{X})^2$$

$$s = \sqrt{\frac{\sum (X - \bar{X})^2}{df}} = \sqrt{\frac{SS}{df}} = \sqrt{\frac{SS}{(n-1)}}$$

Let's put all the measures in a table and demonstrate the step-by-step process in Table 8.3.

TABLE 8.3 Nine Drivers' Ages

X	$(X - \bar{X})$	$(X - \bar{X})^2$
17	−17	289
28	−6	36
33	−1	1
45	11	121
65	31	961
21	−13	169
19	−15	225
38	4	16
40	6	36
306		1,854

We calculate $(X - \bar{X})$ in the second column, and $(X - \bar{X})^2$ in the third column, and add all the numbers in the third column to obtain SS.

First, we need to figure out the sample mean $\bar{X} = \sum X / n = 306 / 9 = 34$. The point estimate of μ is $\bar{X} = 34$.

$$SS = \sum (X - \bar{X})^2 = 1854$$

$$s = \sqrt{\frac{\sum(X - \bar{X})^2}{df}} = \sqrt{\frac{SS}{df}} = \sqrt{\frac{SS}{(n-1)}} = \sqrt{\frac{1854}{8}} = \sqrt{231.75} = 15.2$$

The critical t value for a two-tailed test, $\alpha = .05$, $df = 8$ is $t_{\alpha/2} = 2.306$

The margin of error is $t_{\alpha/2}\dfrac{s}{\sqrt{n}} = 2.306\dfrac{15.2}{\sqrt{9}} = 11.7$

95% CI of $\mu = \bar{X} \pm t_{\alpha/2}\dfrac{s}{\sqrt{n}} = 34 \pm 11.7$

The lower limit and the upper limit of the 95% CI are reported in brackets [22.3, 45.7].

b. The 95% CI [22.3, 45.7] for the average age of drivers who are cited for moving violations does not include the hypothesized population mean under H_0, $\mu = 48$. The population mean for all drivers who received moving violations differs from the population mean for all licensed drivers in this suburb. The average age of drivers who received moving violations tends to be younger than the average age of all licensed drivers.

 ## Pop Quiz

1. When the 95% CIs do *not* include the hypothesized population parameter under H_0, the correct conclusion is that

   a. the evidence is strong enough to support the claim that there is an effect at $\alpha = .05$.

   b. the evidence is not strong enough to support the claim that there is an effect at $\alpha = .05$.

   c. we could not reach any conclusion with 95% CIs.

   d. we are 95% confident that the population parameter is not included in the interval.

2. The 90% CIs of t tests provide the same conclusions as

   a. right-tailed t tests with $\alpha = .10$.

   b. two-tailed t tests with $\alpha = .10$.

   c. left-tailed t tests with $\alpha = .10$.

   d. two-tailed t tests with $\alpha = .05$.

Answers: 1. a, 2. b

CIs are another way to make statistical inferences besides hypothesis tests. After both conducting hypothesis tests and constructing CIs using the same examples, you should be very confident that these two approaches provide consistent conclusions. The CI approach provides a range of values to estimate the population parameter. It provides additional information compared with the conclusions of hypothesis tests, where we either reject H_0 or fail to reject H_0.

EXERCISE PROBLEMS

1. A car manufacturer advertises the fuel efficiency of one of its popular models as $\mu = 29$ miles per gallon. Fuel efficiency is normally distributed. Assume that a sample of nine cars is randomly selected by a third-party nonprofit organization, and the cars' fuel efficiency numbers are measured as 17, 28, 33, 35, 30, 21, 19, 29, and 31. Use $\alpha = .05$ to see if there is truth in the advertisement of this car manufacturer.

2. The total cholesterol level for women aged 20 to 30 years is normally distributed with $\mu = 190$ mg/dl. Assume that a large group of women participate in an exercise program and a sample of 25 women in this age-group is randomly selected with $\bar{X} = 181$ mg/dl and $s = 38$ mg/dl. What is the 95% CI of the average total cholesterol level for women aged 20 to 30 years? Interpret the meaning of a 95% CI.

3. Adult male height is normally distributed with $\mu = 70$ inches. Assume that a group of 25 college male swimmers is randomly selected with $\bar{X} = 73$ inches and $s = 5.5$ inches. Use $\alpha = .01$ to conduct a test to find whether the average height of swimmers is more than 70 inches.

Solutions With EXCEL Step-by-Step Instructions

1. The population standard deviation, σ, is unknown in this problem statement; therefore, the four-step hypothesis testing process to conduct a t test is the correct approach to answer this problem.

Step 1. State the pair of hypotheses.

The problem statement asks, "Is there truth in the advertisement?" The question does not contain any information regarding direction. Therefore, a nondirectional hypothesis is the correct approach. H_0 covers the equal sign, $\mu = 29$ miles per gallon, and H_1 is the hypothesis researchers turn to when H_0 is rejected by the evidence.

$H_0: \mu = 29$ miles per gallon

$H_1: \mu \neq 29$ miles per gallon

Step 2. Identify the rejection zone for the test.

From Step 1, we know that we are conducting a two-tailed test. The problem statement specifies $\alpha = .05$ and $df = n - 1 = 9 - 1 = 8$. According to the t Table, the critical t value is 2.306. The rejection zone is $|t| > 2.306$, as shaded in Figure 8.5.

FIGURE 8.5 Using the t Distribution Table to Identify Rejection Zone $|t| > 2.306$

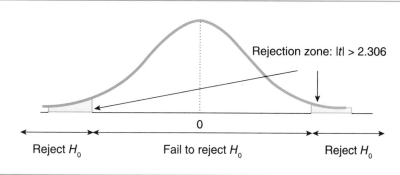

Rejection zone: |t| > 2.306

Reject H_0 Fail to reject H_0 Reject H_0

Step 3. Calculate the test statistic.

Let's list all the numbers stated in the problem statement and separate what we know from what we need to figure out.

What we know:

   $\mu = 29$ miles per gallon

   $n = 9$

When given all measures in a sample, you have to calculate $\bar{X}$ and s before conducting a t test. $\bar{X} = \sum X / n$

$$SS = \sum (X - \bar{X})^2$$

$$s = \sqrt{\frac{\sum (X - \bar{X})^2}{df}} = \sqrt{\frac{SS}{df}} = \sqrt{\frac{SS}{(n-1)}}$$

Let's insert all the measures in a table and demonstrate the step-by-step process in Table 8.4. First, we need to figure out the sample mean, $\bar{X}$.

TABLE 8.4 Nine Cars' Fuel Efficiency

X	$(X - \bar{X})$	$(X - \bar{X})^2$
17	−10	100
28	1	1
33	6	36
35	8	64
30	3	9
21	−6	36
19	−8	64
29	2	4
31	4	16
243		330

Based on the order of operations for $SS = \sum(X - \bar{X})^2$, we calculate $(X - \bar{X})$ in the second column, and $(X - \bar{X})^2$ in the third column, and add all the numbers in the third column to obtain SS. You should refresh your memory and skill on how to construct $(X - \bar{X})$ and $(X - \bar{X})^2$ columns in EXCEL as stated in Chapter 3.

$$\bar{X} = \sum X / n = 243 / 9 = 27$$

$$SS = \sum(X - \bar{X})^2 = 330$$

$$s = \sqrt{\frac{\sum(X - \bar{X})^2}{df}} = \sqrt{\frac{SS}{df}} = \sqrt{\frac{330}{8}} = \sqrt{41.25} = 6.4$$

Such a table helps organize and present your step-by-step work process during an exam when you might have to calculate everything by a handheld calculator. Or, alternatively, you may obtain the sample mean and sample standard deviation by using the prepopulated statistical functions in EXCEL. Enter the values of X in EXCEL, and label **A1** as X; the values go in **A2** to **A10**. To get $\bar{X}$, simply type in the function "=**AVERAGE(A2: A10)**" in a blank cell where **A2** specifies the location of the first value of the sample and **A10** specifies the location of the ninth (also the last) value to calculate the sample mean. Then hit **ENTER**. As shown in Figure 8.6, the answer is 27.

To get the sample standard deviation, s, simply type in "=**STDEV.S(A2:A10)**" in a blank cell to calculate the sample standard deviation. Then hit **ENTER**. As shown in Figure 8.7, the answer is 6.422616. It is rounded off to $s = 6.4$.

Next, insert all the numbers in the t-test formula.

$$t = \frac{\bar{X} - \mu}{\frac{s}{\sqrt{n}}}$$

$$t = \frac{(27 - 29)}{6.4 / \sqrt{9}} = \frac{-2}{2.13} = -0.94$$

Step 4. Make the correct conclusion.

Compare the calculated $t = -0.94$ with the rejection zone $|t| > 2.306$. The calculated t does not fall in the rejection zone. Therefore, we fail to reject H_0. At $\alpha = .05$, the evidence

FIGURE 8.6 Screen Shot of Using "=AVERAGE(A2:A10)" to Create $\bar{X}$

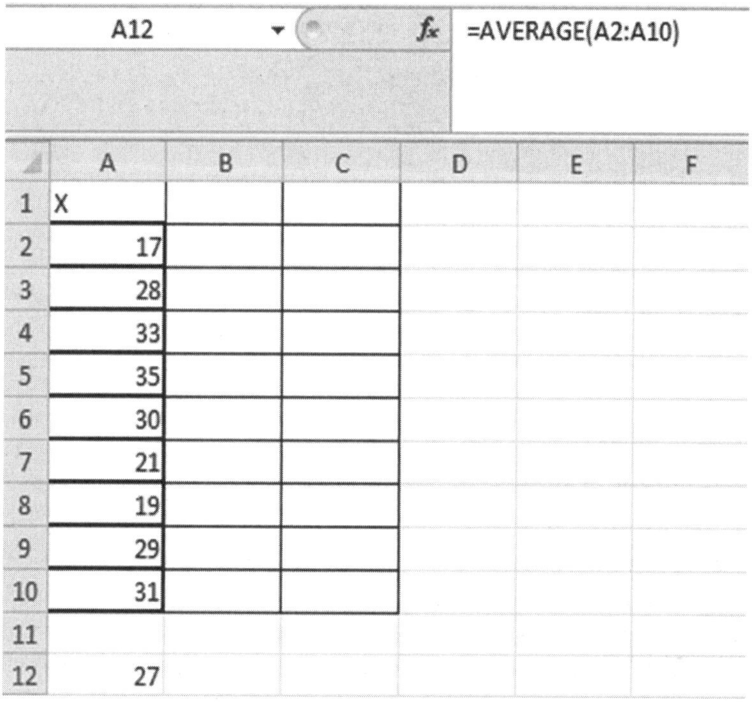

A12			f_x	=AVERAGE(A2:A10)

	A	B	C	D	E	F
1	X					
2	17					
3	28					
4	33					
5	35					
6	30					
7	21					
8	19					
9	29					
10	31					
11						
12	27					

is not strong enough to support the claim that the car manufacturer failed to meet the truth in advertisement standard.

2. The population standard deviation, σ, is unknown in the problem statement; therefore, s is used to estimate σ. The critical t value sets the boundaries of the 95% CI with $df = 24$; two-tailed $\alpha = .05$ is 2.064.

$$95\% \text{ CI of } \mu = \bar{X} \pm t_{\alpha/2}\left(\frac{s}{\sqrt{n}}\right) = 181 \pm 2.064\left(\frac{38}{\sqrt{25}}\right) = 181 \pm 15.7$$

$$95\% \text{ CI of } \mu = [165.3, 196.7]$$

We are 95% confident that the hypothesized population mean, μ, is in the interval [165.3, 196.7]. The average cholesterol level for women participating in the exercise program does not differ from the population mean because 191 is included in the 95% CI.

3. The population standard deviation, σ, is unknown in this problem statement. We use the four-step hypothesis testing process to conduct a t test to answer this problem.

FIGURE 8.7   Screen Shot of Using "=STDEV.S(A2:A10)" to Create *s*

| A13 | | | | f_x | =STDEV.S(A2:A10) |

	A	B	C	D	E	F
1	X					
2	17					
3	28					
4	33					
5	35					
6	30					
7	21					
8	19					
9	29					
10	31					
11						
12	27					
13	6.422616					

Step 1. State the pair of hypotheses.

Based on the problem statement, "the average height of swimmers is taller than 70 inches" indicates a directional hypothesis. The key word "taller" indicates a right-tailed test. It is easy to start with the H_1, the alternative hypothesis that the researchers are interested in establishing, $\mu > 70$ inches. Then H_0 covers the equal sign, $\mu = 70$ inches.

$H_0: \mu = 70$

$H_1: \mu > 70$

Step 2. Identify the rejection zone for the hypothesis test.

We need three pieces of information to identify the critical values that set the boundaries of the rejection zones: (1) one-tailed test or two-tailed test, (2) *df*, and (3) the α level. We know that this is a right-tailed test from Step 1, $\alpha = .01$ and $df = n - 1 = 25 - 1 = 24$ from the problem statement. According to the *t* Distribution Table, the critical *t* value is 2.492. The rejection zone for the right-tailed test is $t > 2.492$, as shown in Figure 8.8.

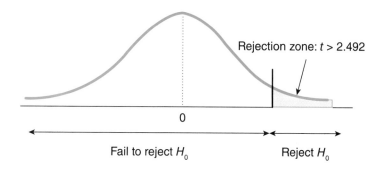

Rejection zone: *t* > 2.492

0

Fail to reject H_0

Reject H_0

Step 3. Calculate the statistics.

It is easy to list all the numbers stated in the problem statement, so as to separate what we know and what we need to figure out.

What we know:

$\mu = 70$ inches

$s = 5.5$ inches

$\overline{X} = 73$ inches

$n = 25$

We need to figure out *t*. Next, insert all the numbers in the *t*-test formula.

$$t = \frac{\overline{X} - \mu}{\dfrac{s}{\sqrt{n}}}$$

$$t = \frac{73 - 70}{\dfrac{5.5}{\sqrt{25}}} = \frac{3}{1.1} = 2.73$$

Step 4. Make the correct conclusion.

Compare the calculated *t* = 2.73 with the rejection zone *t* > 2.492. The calculated *t* falls in the rejection zone. Therefore, we reject H_0. There is enough evidence to support the claim that the average height of swimmers is taller than 70 inches.

SAGE edge™

Sharpen your skills with SAGE edge!

Visit edge.sagepub.com/bowen for mobile-friendly quizzes, flashcards, videos, and more!

WHAT YOU LEARNED

You are one step closer to reality in terms of being able to conduct a proper test between a sample mean and a hypothesized population mean under H_0 when the population standard deviation, σ, is unknown. The t test is appropriate when the population is normally distributed or when $n > 30$. You have also learned that for every degree of freedom, there is a specific t-distribution curve. You need three pieces of information to identify the critical t values that set the boundaries of rejection zones: (1) one-tailed test or two-tailed test, (2) df, and (3) the α level.

The four-step hypothesis testing procedure is still applicable in conducting a t test. The t formula is

$$ t = \frac{\overline{X} - \mu}{s_{\overline{X}}} = \frac{\overline{X} - \mu}{\dfrac{s}{\sqrt{n}}}, \text{ with } df = n - 1. $$

Constructing a CI provides quality evaluation on how good the estimate is. The estimation process uses sample statistics to make inferences about hypothesized population parameters. Constructing a CI with a confidence level $(1 - \alpha)$ is the equivalent of conducting a two-tailed hypothesis test with the significance level $= \alpha$.

A word of caution here: Assume that you encounter a problem statement that asks you to compare a sample mean, $\overline{X}$, with the population mean, μ, and at the same time, provides n, s, and σ. Which test is appropriate to answer this question? Remember that s is used to estimate σ. There is no need for such estimation when σ is provided. Therefore, the correct answer in this tricky scenario is the Z test.

KEY WORDS

Confidence interval: A confidence interval is defined as an interval of values calculated from sample statistics to estimate the value of a population parameter.

Confidence level: Confidence level is expressed as $(1 - \alpha)$, which is the complement to α, the significance level.

Interval estimate: An interval estimate refers to a range of values calculated from sample statistics to estimate a hypothesized population parameter. It is calculated as a point estimate ± the margin of error.

One-sample t test: A one-sample t test is designed to conduct a test between a sample mean and a hypothesized population mean when σ is unknown,

$$t = \frac{\bar{X} - \mu}{s_{\bar{X}}} = \frac{\bar{X} - \mu}{\dfrac{s}{\sqrt{n}}}, \text{with } df = n - 1.$$

Point estimate: A point estimate is to use a single value from the sample to estimate a population parameter.

t Table: The t Distribution Table provides critical values of t that set the boundaries of rejection zones for t tests given three pieces of information: (1) one-tailed test or two-tailed test, (2) the df of the test, and (3) the α level.

LEARNING ASSESSMENT

Multiple Choice: Circle the best answer to every question.

1. The difference between using a Z test and using a t test depends on

   a. whether μ is given in the problem statement.

   b. whether σ is given in the problem statement.

   c. whether $\bar{X}$ is given in the problem statement.

   d. whether n is given in the problem statement.

2. For a two-tailed t test with $\alpha = .01$, $df = 20$. The critical t values that set

the boundaries for the rejection zone are

a. $t > 1.96$.
b. $t > 2.58$.
c. $|t| > 1.96$.
d. $|t| > 2.845$.

3. For a left-tailed t test with $\alpha = .01$, $n = 15$. The rejection zone for this test is expressed as

a. $t < -2.602$.
b. $t < -2.624$.
c. $t > 2.602$.
d. $t > 2.624$.

4. For a right-tailed t test with $\alpha = .01$, $n = 5$. The rejection zone for this test is expressed as

a. $t < -3.747$.
b. $t < -3.365$.
c. $t > 3.747$.
d. $t > 3.365$.

5. Which one of the following scenarios is *not* suitable to conduct a t test?

a. The population is normally distributed and $n > 30$.
b. The population is *not* normally distributed, and sample size is $n > 30$.
c. The population is normally distributed and $n < 30$.
d. The population is *not* normally distributed and $n < 30$.

6. To test whether a sample mean differs from a hypothesized population mean, with $\alpha = .01$, what confidence level should you use if you want to

use a confidence interval to get the same result?

a. 99.5%
b. 99%
c. 97.5%
d. 95%

7. A sample is selected from a population with $\mu = 80$, and a treatment is administered to the sample. If the sample standard deviation is 9, which set of sample characteristics is most likely to lead to a decision to reject H_0?

a. $\bar{X} = 81$ for a sample size $n = 10$
b. $\bar{X} = 81$ for a sample size $n = 100$
c. $\bar{X} = 83$ for a sample size $n = 10$
d. $\bar{X} = 83$ for a sample size $n = 100$

8. When n is small ($n \leq 30$), the t distribution

a. is identical to the normal Z distribution.
b. is flatter, shorter, and more spread out than the normal z distribution.
c. is taller and narrower than the normal z distribution.
d. is a skewed nonsymmetrical distribution.

Free Response Questions

9. A psychologist studies the effect of frequent testing on academic performance. A proficiency exam is used to measure academic performance. The scores on the proficiency exam are normally distributed with a $\mu = 70$. Assume that in a class 49 students are given quizzes three times a week.

At the end of the semester, students take the proficiency exam and their scores have $\bar{X} = 75$ and $s = 14$. This is an exploratory study, and there is not enough information to make a directional hypothesis test. Conduct a proper statistical procedure to test whether giving frequent quizzes has an effect on academic performance, using $\alpha = .05$.

10. Nationwide, the average total amount of student loan debt in 2012 is normally distributed with a $\mu = \$29,400$. Assume that a sample of 36 students is randomly selected from a public university. Their student loans have $\bar{X} = \$27,400$ and $s = \$9,000$. Conduct a proper statistical procedure to test whether the average student loan in this public university is lower than $29,400, using $\alpha = .10$.

11. SAT verbal scores are normally distributed with a $\mu = 500$. A local high school has instituted a new program to engage students in reading. A sample of nine students from this high school is randomly selected following their participation in this reading program, and their SAT verbal scores were reported: 600, 760, 550, 505, 660, 540, 480, 535, and 455.

a. Conduct a proper statistical procedure to test whether the new program has an effect on SAT verbal scores, using $\alpha = .05$.

b. Construct a 95% CI for the average SAT verbal score of students in this high school.

c. Compare the results from 11.a and 11.b.

CHAPTER 9

Independent-Samples t Tests

After reading and studying this chapter, you should be able to do the following:

- Define the independent-samples *t* test and explain when it is used
- Describe the decision rule for equal variances assumed versus equal variances not assumed
- Explain the purpose of the folded-form *F* test and Levene's test in assessing the equality of variances
- Describe the roles of Cohen's *d* and Glass's delta (Δ) in independent *t*-test calculations

WHAT YOU KNOW AND WHAT IS NEW

You have learned the general *t*-test formula,

$$t = \frac{\text{Sample statistic} - \text{Population parameter}}{\text{Estimated standard error of the statistic}}$$

and in particular, you now know that when comparing one sample mean with the population mean and if σ is not known, the one-sample *t* test is appropriate:

$$t = \frac{\bar{X} - \mu}{s_{\bar{X}}} = \frac{\bar{X} - \mu}{\dfrac{s}{\sqrt{n}}}$$

with $df = n - 1$. The same principle is applicable to the independent-samples t test, with minimal modifications. When two samples are independent, simple random samples selected from normally distributed populations, we are interested in using the sample mean differences to make inferences about the population mean differences, the independent-samples t test is the appropriate option. The sample statistic of comparing two sample means is expressed as $(\bar{X}_1 - \bar{X}_2)$, and the difference between two population means is expressed as $(\mu_1 - \mu_2)$. The complicated part is actually in the denominator of the independent-samples t test. Learning to calculate the denominator (i.e., the estimated standard error for the mean difference) is a major task in Chapter 9.

Two important assumptions need to be considered before using the independent-samples t test. First, the observations from each sample are independent. Second, at least one of the two following conditions is met: (1) the two sample sizes are both large ($n > 30$) or (2) both samples are randomly selected from normally distributed populations.

Since the two samples are randomly selected from two separate populations, it is likely that we will have to deal with these two situations: (1) the two populations have equal variances or (2) the two populations have unequal variances. Different sets of formulas are required for these two situations. They will be introduced in separate sections.

INTRODUCING INDEPENDENT SAMPLES AND THE DECISION RULE ON EQUAL VARIANCES

Up to this point in the textbook, all of the statistical tests discussed have required information about the population mean, μ. The information about μ has been readily provided in the problem statement. However, in reality, population parameters are mostly unknown. Population means are not readily provided or easily found when conducting scientific research. In Chapter 9, the focus is on how to compare two sample means randomly selected from two different populations without knowing μ and σ from these two populations. Many cases in scientific research are designed to compare the mean of an experimental group with the mean of a control group to judge whether a particular treatment has an effect. In almost every case, researchers have no information on the population means and standard deviations. For the first time, the independent-samples t-test formulas you learn in this chapter are fully functional without assuming or pretending to know the population parameters.

Let's start by defining the term independent samples. Independent samples are samples selected from different populations where the values from one population are not related or linked with the values from another population. In the scenario of two independent samples, the samples contain different individuals, and there is no overlap between samples. No individual can be in both samples at the same time. Independent samples are also referred to as "between-subject design" in research methods textbooks. For example, researchers are interested in studying married women's psychological stress compared with that of women who are not married. Any female participant in this study can belong to only one of the two groups: "married" versus "not married." There is no overlap between these two groups since no participant can be both "married" and "not married" at the same time. An independent-samples t test is appropriate to conduct the comparison of psychological stress between married and not married women.

Let's examine the evolution of t formulas as we go through the process.

The general t formula:

$$t = \frac{\text{Sample statistic} - \text{Population parameter}}{\text{Estimated standard error of the statistic}}$$

The one-sample t-test formula that you learned in Chapter 8:

$$t = \frac{\bar{X} - \mu}{s_{\bar{X}}} = \frac{\bar{X} - \mu}{\frac{s}{\sqrt{n}}}$$

The independent-samples t-test formula that you will learn in this chapter:

$$t = \frac{(\bar{X}_1 - \bar{X}_2) - (\mu_1 - \mu_2)}{s_{(\bar{X}_1 - \bar{X}_2)}}$$

As indicated in the independent-samples t-test formula, the numerator is simply obtained by calculating the difference between the sample means, $(\bar{X}_1 - \bar{X}_2)$, and comparing it with the theoretical difference between the population means, $(\mu_1 - \mu_2)$, as stated in the H_0. The H_0 is the no-effect hypothesis and is always expressed with the equal sign in both directional and nondirectional hypothesis tests:

$$H_0: \mu_1 - \mu_2 = 0$$

Once $\mu_1 - \mu_2 = 0$ gets into the independent-samples t-test formula, it can be further simplified:

$$t = \frac{(\bar{X}_1 - \bar{X}_2)}{s_{(\bar{X}_1 - \bar{X}_2)}}$$

The only thing new to learn is how to calculate the estimated standard error of the mean difference, as expressed in the denominator of the t formula. In a situation where the population variance, σ^2, is unknown, the sample variance, s^2, is used as the unbiased estimate of σ^2. The estimated standard error of the mean difference has to be logically derived from the two sample variances.

When selecting two samples from two separate populations, it is likely to result in two situations. The first situation occurs when the population variances are similar or equivalent to each other. In this situation, the similar variances should be pooled together to create a pooled variance. Then the pooled variance is used to calculate the estimated standard error of the mean difference. The second situation occurs when the population variances are not similar to each other. In this situation, the variances should be treated as different when calculating the estimated standard error of the mean difference. Distinguishing different formulas and applying the correct set of formulas to solve problems is critically important in this chapter. Therefore, the four-step hypothesis-testing procedure needs to be modified to a five-step hypothesis-testing procedure to include the decision on which set of formulas to use as the first step.

DECISION RULE FOR EQUAL VARIANCES ASSUMED VERSUS EQUAL VARIANCES NOT ASSUMED

When comparing means from two independent samples that contain different individuals, for instance, when comparing men's average salary with women's average salary, you will encounter one of two possible situations: (1) the two variances are equal, similar, or equivalent, or (2) the two variances are not equal, similar, or equivalent. Different formulas are required in these two situations. Deciding whether two variances are equal or not is an empirical question that needs an empirical answer. A hypothesis test on the equality of variances needs to be conducted to answer this question. Since it is a hypothesis test, the four-step process is applicable here.

Step 1. State the pair of hypotheses.

$$H_0: \sigma_1^2 = \sigma_2^2$$

$$H_1: \sigma_1^2 \neq \sigma_2^2$$

Step 2. Identify the rejection zone.

The critical F value that sets the boundary for the rejection zone is determined by two different degrees of freedom, $F_{(df_1, df_2)}$, as stated in the F Table in Appendix C. df_1 is the degrees of freedom for the numerator, which identifies the column. df_2 is the degrees of

*In the independent-samples t test, we
compare means from two different groups.
In each group, the sample mean is used to
estimate the population mean; therefore
1 degree of freedom is lost in the process.
The degrees of freedom for Group 1, df_1, are
calculated as $(n_1 - 1)$, and the degrees of
freedom for Group 2, df_2, are calculated as
$(n_2 - 1)$. This concept of degrees of freedom is
consistent with its introduction in Chapter 3.*

freedom for the denominator, which identifies the row. The intersection between the column and the row provides the critical value for the right-tailed F test. F values have a skewed distribution with a long tail toward the high end of the distribution. F *values are never negative because both the numerator and the denominator are always positive.*

Step 3. Calculate the test statistic.

$$F = \frac{s_1^2}{s_2^2} = \frac{\text{Larger variance}}{\text{Smaller variance}}$$

The reason for designating s_1^2 as the larger variance and s_2^2 as the smaller variance is to create a right-tailed test for the calculated F statistic. This avoids the problem of finding the left-tailed F value. The F Table in most statistics textbooks only reports the right-tailed values. Therefore, in this calculation, the larger variance is placed as the numerator and the smaller variance is placed as the denominator of the F test. When two variances are close to each other, the F value is close to 1. When two variances are far apart from each other, the F value becomes large. When we deliberately force the F formula to only get right-tailed values and completely avoid the left-tailed values, such calculations are labeled as **folded F tests**. The folded F test means that the calculated F value will be larger than 1 to avoid the left-tailed F values. Therefore, the group with the larger variance is labeled as Group 1, and the group with the smaller variance is labeled as Group 2. Such consistent labeling is particularly important when you conduct a directional hypothesis test.

Step 4. Make the correct conclusion.

The decision rule is that when the calculated F value from Step 3 is smaller than or equal to the critical F value identified from Step 2, we fail to reject H_0. Thus, the correct way to conduct an independent-samples t test is to assume equal variances: H_0: $\sigma_1^2 = \sigma_2^2$. On the other hand, when the calculated F value is larger than the critical F value, we reject H_0. Thus, in this situation, the correct way to conduct an independent-samples t test is to use the procedure for equal variances not assumed. Let's use an example to go through the test for equality of variances.

EXAMPLE 9.1

Head circumference is normally distributed for both men and women. A random sample of 14 men's head circumferences generates a standard deviation of 1.42 cm, and a random sample of 25 women's head circumference generates a standard deviation of 3.73 cm. Do men and women have equal variances in head circumference measures?

The four-step hypothesis-testing procedure is still applicable in testing equality of variances.

Step 1. State the pair of hypotheses.

$$H_0 : \sigma_1^2 = \sigma_2^2$$

$$H_0 : \sigma_1^2 \neq \sigma_2^2$$

Step 2. Identify the rejection zone.

The larger standard deviation is s_1, 3.73 cm, and its $df_1 = n_1 - 1 = 25 - 1 = 24$; therefore, the women's group is labeled as Group 1. And s_2 is the smaller standard deviation, 1.42 cm, and its $df_2 = 14 - 1 = 13$; therefore, the men's group is labeled as Group 2.

The critical value of the right-tailed $F_{(df_1, df_2)} = F_{(24,13)} = 2.42$.

Step 3. Calculate the test statistic.

$$F = \frac{s_1^2}{s_2^2} = \frac{3.73^2}{1.42^2} = \frac{13.91}{2.02} = 6.89$$

Step 4. Make the correct conclusion.

The calculated $F = 6.89$ is larger than the critical value of $F_{(24,13)} = 2.42$. Therefore, we reject H_0. There is strong evidence that the two variances are not equal. We should choose the formulas for equal variances not assumed.

This F statistic allows testing for equality of variances from two samples with different sample sizes. The F test is preferable to other similar tests when you have to calculate everything by hand. Most statistics software packages come with built-in tests for equality of variances. It is convenient that you don't have to calculate equality of variances by hand. However, you still need to be able to understand and interpret the printouts from statistical packages. When statistical results are computed by

(Continued)

(Continued)

software packages, users don't have to compare the calculated test statistic with a table full of critical values that set the boundaries of rejection zones. The statistics software packages automatically calculate a p (probability) value associated with the calculated test statistic. This is important for you to know and understand whenever you use a statistical software package: The *p value associated with a test statistic* is defined as the probability of obtaining the magnitude of the calculated test statistic assuming H_0 is true. The calculated p value is compared with a predetermined significance level, α (i.e., .05 or .01). If the calculated p value is less than α, it means that such a magnitude of the calculated test statistic is highly unlikely under the assumption that H_0 is true. Thus, it is logical for researchers to reject H_0 when the calculated p value is less than α. On the other hand, when the calculated p value is larger than or equal to α, researchers fail to reject H_0.

In summary, the p value associated with a test statistic can be used as a criterion for a hypothesis test. The decision rules are as follows:

When $p < \alpha$, we reject H_0.

When $p \geq \alpha$, we fail to reject H_0.

An example using SPSS to run the independent-samples t test will be presented at the end of this chapter, along with detailed explanations of the corresponding printouts.

The result of a hypothesis test on equality of variances is only the beginning of the independent-samples t test. It provides an empirical answer to which set of formulas is appropriate to conduct an independent-samples t test. Different formulas are required when equal variances are assumed versus when equal variances are not assumed. I will present the formulas for equal variances assumed and the formulas for equal variances not assumed in the following sections of this chapter.

Pop Quiz

1. The F test to test for the equality of variances specifies the larger variance as the numerator and the smaller variance as the denominator. Such a process is called a folded F test; therefore, the critical values listed in the F Table are

a. right-tailed values.

b. left-tailed values.

c. positive but can be less than 1.

d. normally distributed.

2. Which degrees of freedom determine the critical values of an F test when conducting a test for equality of variances?

a. n

b. $n - 1$

c. df_1, df_2: df_1 for the numerator and df_2 for the denominator

d. $(r - 1)(c - 1)$, where r is the number of rows and c the number of columns

EQUAL VARIANCES ASSUMED

We start the independent-samples t test in a situation where equal variances are assumed. When two populations have equal variances, $\sigma_1^2 = \sigma_2^2$, we need to pool the variances together by using the pooled variance (s_p^2) formula:

$$\text{Pooled variance} = s_p^2 = \frac{SS_1 + SS_2}{df_1 + df_2}$$

where

SS_1 = the sum of squares from Sample 1

SS_2 = the sum of squares from Sample 2

df_1 = the degrees of freedom from Sample 1

df_2 = the degrees of freedom from Sample 2

Then we use the pooled variance to calculate the estimated standard error of the mean difference, $s_{(\bar{X}_1 - \bar{X}_2)}$, which is the denominator of the independent-samples t-test formula.

$$s_{(\bar{X}_1 - \bar{X}_2)} = \sqrt{\frac{s_p^2}{n_1} + \frac{s_p^2}{n_2}}$$

Now, to put everything together, when $\sigma_1 = \sigma_2$, the independent-samples t-test formula is

$$t = \frac{(\bar{X}_1 - \bar{X}_2)}{s_{(\bar{X}_1 - \bar{X}_2)}}$$

where

$$s_{(\bar{X}_1 - \bar{X}_2)} = \sqrt{\frac{s_P^2}{n_1} + \frac{s_P^2}{n_2}}$$

and

$$s_P^2 = \frac{SS_1 + SS_2}{df_1 + df_2}$$

Since each degree of freedom has its own specific t curve, we need to figure out the degrees of freedom for the independent-samples t test. When equal variances are assumed, you pool the variances together, and you also pool the degrees of freedom together. The degrees of freedom for independent-samples t tests when $\sigma_1^2 = \sigma_2^2$ are obtained by pooling the degrees of freedom from the two groups together. This is done by adding df_1 and df_2. To identify the critical values that set the boundaries of the rejection zones for an independent-samples t test with equal variances, the degrees of freedom for the test will be $df = df_1 + df_2$. You have learned the formula for the independent-samples t test with equal variances assumed condition, and you have learned to calculate the df associated with the t test in order to correctly identify the rejection zone for the test. You are now ready to learn the entire hypothesis-testing process for the independent-samples t test with equal variances assumed.

As discussed earlier, the equality-of-variances test has to be done first to allow you to choose the right set of formulas to conduct the independent-samples t test. Therefore, the four-step hypothesis-testing procedure must be modified to five steps for independent-samples t tests.

Step 1. Conduct the equality-of-variance test.

Step 2. State the pair of hypotheses regarding group means.

Step 3. Identify the rejection zone.

Step 4. Calculate the t statistic.

Step 5. Make the correct conclusion.

We will now use a couple of examples to illustrate this five-step hypothesis-testing procedure on independent-samples t tests.

EXAMPLE 9.2

Adult women's weights and adult men's weights are both normally distributed. Assume that a sample of five men is randomly selected with $\bar{X} = 196$ pounds and $s = 39.59$ pounds and a sample of 15 women is randomly selected with $\bar{X} = 146$ pounds and

$s = 33.31$ pounds. Are there significant differences between men's and women's average weight, using $\alpha = .05$?

Usually, comparisons between a group of randomly selected men and a group of randomly selected women are good examples of comparisons between independent samples that consist of different individuals. Notice that the sizes of these two samples do not need to be the same. First, we need to test for equality of variances.

Step 1. Test for the equality of variances.

We apply the four-step procedure to test for equality of variances.

Substep 1. State the pair of hypotheses regarding variances.

$$H_0: \sigma_1^2 = \sigma_2^2$$

$$H_1: \sigma_1^2 \neq \sigma_2^2$$

Substep 2. Identify the rejection zone for the hypothesis test.

The larger standard deviation is s_1, 39.59 pounds, and its $df_1 = n_1 - 1 = 5 - 1 = 4$; therefore, the men belong to Group 1. And s_2 is the smaller standard deviation, 33.31 pounds, and its $df_2 = 15 - 1 = 14$; therefore, the women belong to Group 2.

The critical value of the right-tailed $F_{(df_1, df_2)} = F_{(4,14)} = 3.11$.

Substep 3. Calculate the F statistic.

$$F = \frac{s_1^2}{s_2^2} = \frac{39.59^2}{33.31^2} = \frac{1567.37}{1109.56} = 1.41$$

Substep 4. Make the correct conclusion.

The calculated $F = 1.41$ is smaller than the critical value of $F_{(4,14)} = 3.11$. Therefore, we fail to reject H_0. The evidence is not strong enough to claim that the two variances are unequal. Therefore, the correct independent-samples t-test approach is to assume equal variances.

Step 2. State the pair of hypotheses regarding population means.

(Continued)

(Continued)

The problem statement asks, "Are there significant differences between men's and women's average weight?" There is no hint of direction. Therefore, a two-tailed test is appropriate.

$H_0: \mu_1 = \mu_2$

$H_1: \mu_1 \neq \mu_2$

Step 3. Identify the rejection zones for the test.

According to the rule, $df = df_1 + df_2 = n_1 + n_2 - 2 = 18$, $\sigma = .05$, it is a two-tailed test, and the critical t value that sets the boundary of the rejection zone is 2.101. The rejection zone is thus $|t| > 2.101$.

Step 4. Calculate the t statistic.

When $\sigma_1^2 = \sigma_2^2$, the variances need to be pooled together.

The problem statement provides sample sizes, n_1 and n_2, and sample standard deviations, s_1 and s_2, so you need to figure out SS_1 and SS_2 to calculate the pooled variance, s_p^2. In Chapter 3, you learned that $s^2 = SS/df$; therefore, $SS = s^2 df$.

$$SS_1 = s_1^2 df_1 = 39.59^2 (5-1) = 6269.47$$

$$SS_2 = s_2^2 df_2 = 33.31^2 (15-1) = 15533.79$$

$$s_p^2 = \frac{SS_1 + SS_2}{df_1 + df_2} = \frac{6269.47 + 15533.79}{4 + 14} = \frac{21803.26}{18} = 1211.29$$

$$s_{(\bar{X}_1 - \bar{X}_2)} = \sqrt{\frac{s_p^2}{n_1} + \frac{s_p^2}{n_2}} = \sqrt{\frac{1211.29}{5} + \frac{1211.29}{15}} = \sqrt{242.26 + 80.75} = \sqrt{323.01} = 17.97$$

$$t = \frac{\bar{X}_1 - \bar{X}_2}{s_{(\bar{X}_1 - \bar{X}_2)}} = \frac{196 - 146}{17.97} = \frac{50}{17.97} = 2.78$$

Step 5. Make the correct conclusion.

The calculated $t = 2.78$ is within the rejection zone. Therefore, we reject H_0. The evidence is strong enough to support the claim that there are significant differences between men's and women's average weights.

The independent-samples t tests are more complicated than the Z tests or one-sample t tests because you have to test for equality of variances first to decide which set of formulas is the appropriate one to use. The more examples you practice, the easier this process becomes. In the next example, we compare the number of driving mistakes displayed by drivers when one group of individuals drive without texting and the other group of individuals drive while texting.

EXAMPLE 9.3

Researchers have long suspected that texting has a detrimental effect on driving behavior. To avoid the unnecessary risk of actual driving on the roads, researchers have measured driving behavior via a simulator. Mistakes such as failing to stay within the lane, driving at least 10 miles over or under the speed limit, failing to stop in front of a stop sign, and/or failing to use the turn signal are automatically recorded by the simulator. Assume that driving mistakes are normally distributed. Participants are randomly assigned into either the experimental group (i.e., texting while driving) or the control group (i.e., driving without texting). There are 9 participants in the experimental group, and their driving mistakes have $\bar{X} = 35.8$ and $s = 7.6$; and there are 10 participants in the control group, and their driving mistakes have $\bar{X} = 23.9$ and $s = 8.1$. Do the data support the claim that texting has a detrimental effect on driving behavior, using $\alpha = .01$?

The participants are randomly assigned to either the experimental group or the control group. The two groups consist of different individuals. Therefore, an independent-samples t test is the appropriate approach to answer this problem. The five-step hypothesis test process needs to be conducted.

Step 1. Test for the equality of variances.

Substep 1. State the pair of hypotheses regarding variances.

$$H_0: \sigma_1^2 = \sigma_2^2$$

$$H_1: \sigma_1^2 \neq \sigma_2^2$$

Substep 2. Identify the criterion for the hypothesis test.

The larger standard deviation is s_1, 8.1 from the control group, and its $df_1 = n_1 - 1 = 10 - 1 = 9$; s_2 is the smaller standard deviation, 7.6 from the experimental group, and its $df_2 = 9 - 1 = 8$. You need to keep the subscripts consistent once you identify the control group as Group 1 due to its larger standard deviation and the experimental group as Group 2.

(Continued)

(Continued)

The critical value of the right-tailed $F_{(df_1, df_2)} = F_{(9,8)} = 3.39$.

Substep 3. Calculate the statistic.

$$F = \frac{s_1^2}{s_2^2} = \frac{8.1^2}{7.6^2} = \frac{65.61}{57.76} = 1.14$$

Substep 4. Make the correct conclusion.

The calculated $F = 1.14$ is smaller than the critical value of $F_{(9,8)} = 3.39$. Therefore, we fail to reject H_0. The evidence is not strong enough to claim that the two variances are unequal. Therefore, the correct independent-samples t-test approach is to assume equal variances.

Step 2. State the pair of hypotheses regarding group means.

The problem statement asks, "Do the data support the claim that texting has a detrimental effect on driving?" "Detrimental effect" is a key word for direction. It means that the experimental group's driving would be worse than the control group's. The measures reflect driving mistakes. As discussed in Step 1, we identify the control group as Group 1. Thus, the mean driving mistakes for the control group (μ_1) should be lower than for the experimental group (μ_2). Take a moment to think about the reasoning process to determine the direction in a one-tailed directional test. You need to make sure the pair of hypotheses expresses the purpose of the test exactly as stated in the problem.

H_0: $\mu_1 = \mu_2$

H_1: $\mu_1 < \mu_2$

Step 3. Identify the rejection zone for the test.

According to the rule, $df = df_1 + df_2 = n_1 + n_2 - 2 = 17$, $\alpha = .01$, it is a left-tailed test, and the critical t value that sets the boundary of the rejection zone is 2.567. The rejection zone is $t < -2.567$.

Step 4. Calculate the t statistic.

When $\sigma_1^2 = \sigma_2^2$, the variances need to be pooled together.

$$SS_1 = s_1^2 df_1 = 8.1^2 (10-1) = 590.49$$

$$SS_2 = s_2^2 df_2 = 7.6^2 (9-1) = 462.08$$

$$s_p^2 = \frac{SS_1 + SS_2}{df_1 + df_2} = \frac{590.49 + 462.08}{9+8} = \frac{1052.57}{17} = 61.92$$

$$s_{(\bar{X}_1 - \bar{X}_2)} = \sqrt{\frac{s_p^2}{n_1} + \frac{s_p^2}{n_2}} = \sqrt{\frac{61.92}{10} + \frac{61.92}{9}} = \sqrt{6.19 + 6.88} = \sqrt{13.07} = 3.62$$

$$t = \frac{\bar{X}_1 - \bar{X}_2}{s_{(\bar{X}_1 - \bar{X}_2)}} = \frac{23.9 - 35.8}{3.62} = \frac{-11.9}{3.62} = -3.29$$

Step 5. Make the correct conclusion.

The calculated $t = -3.29$ is within the rejection zone. Therefore, we reject H_0. The evidence is strong enough to support the claim that texting has a detrimental effect on driving at $\alpha = .01$. Customarily, social sciences studies use $\alpha = .05$ as a standard to keep the risk of committing a Type I error down. This study uses $\alpha = .01$, which is a stricter standard. Even under this stricter standard, the evidence is still strong enough to support the claim that texting has a detrimental effect on driving.

In summary, an independent-samples t test requires the test of equality of variances to be conducted first, so you can select the right set of formulas to conduct the t test. The hypothesis-testing procedure becomes a five-step process. You need to be confident and comfortable with the five-step process by reviewing the examples within this chapter and working out the "Exercise Problems" and "Free-Response Questions."

You need to be aware of the fact that we force the F test for equality of variances to create the right-tailed value only; thus, the larger variance has to be placed in the numerator and is labeled as s_1. The group with the larger variance is labeled as Group 1. Correctly labeling the two groups is very important to conduct a directional hypothesis test using the independent-samples t test.

If the result of the equality-of-variances test is to fail to reject H_0: $\sigma_1^2 = \sigma_2^2$, we have to assume equal variances to complete the hypothesis test on the group means. Pooled variance needs to be calculated.

You Must Remember This

Here is an important reminder. You learned that $s^2 = SS/df$ in Chapter 3. This formula involves three values, s, SS, and df, and when given any two of these values in the problem statement, you will be able to solve the third one. For example, if the problem statement provides df and s, you can figure out SS. If the problem statement provides df and SS, you can figure out the value of s. If the problem statement provides s and SS, you can figure out the df. Of course, you know that df = n − 1. There are a variety of ways in which the problem can be stated. As long as you understand the basic principles of the independent-samples t test, you will be able to solve the problem regardless of how it is stated.

$$\text{Pooled variance} = s_p^2 = \frac{SS_1 + SS_2}{df_1 + df_2}$$

Use the pooled variance to calculate the standard error of the mean difference, $s_{(\bar{X}_1 - \bar{X}_2)}$.

$$s_{(\bar{X}_1 - \bar{X}_2)} = \sqrt{\frac{s_p^2}{n_1} + \frac{s_p^2}{n_2}}$$

$s_{(\bar{X}_1 - \bar{X}_2)}$ is the denominator of the *t* test.

$$t = \frac{\bar{X}_1 - \bar{X}_2}{s_{(\bar{X}_1 - \bar{X}_2)}}$$

The independent-samples *t* tests have $df = df_1 + df_2 = n_1 + n_2 - 2$.

Next, a different set of formulas will be presented to deal with situations where the two populations do not have equal variances. The good news is that the five-step hypothesis test process is still applicable.

Pop Quiz

1. Assume that two samples are randomly selected from two normally distributed populations with equal variances. Sample 1 has $s_1 = 3$ and $SS_1 = 45$, and Sample 2 has $s_2 = 3.4$ and $SS_2 = 104.04$. What is the pooled variance for the two independent samples?

a. $s_p^2 = 10.65$

b. $s_p^2 = 13.87$

c. $s_p^2 = 17.42$

d. $s_p^2 = 23.29$

Answer: a

EQUAL VARIANCES NOT ASSUMED

When $\sigma_1^2 \neq \sigma_2^2$, it is inappropriate to pool the variances. Variances are treated separately, and the estimated standard error of the mean differences is calculated as

$$s_{(\bar{X}_1 - \bar{X}_2)} = \sqrt{\frac{s_1^2}{n_1} + \frac{s_2^2}{n_2}}$$

The formula used to determine the estimated standard error of the mean difference when equal variances are not assumed is actually simpler than the formula used when equal variances are assumed. However, the degrees of freedom for the independent-samples t test with equal variances not assumed needs to be approximated according to the following formula by Satterthwaite (1946).

$$\text{Satterthwaite's approximated } df = \frac{(w_1 + w_2)^2}{\dfrac{w_1^2}{n_1 - 1} + \dfrac{w_2^2}{n_2 - 1}}$$

where

$$w_1 = \frac{s_1^2}{n_1}$$

and

$$w_2 = \frac{s_2^2}{n_2}$$

Such an adjustment results in a smaller df than simply adding df_1 and df_2 together. The smaller df makes the test more conservative. In other words, the critical value goes higher, and the evidence needs to be stronger to reject H_0. It is obvious that the approximated df is not an integer. It needs to be rounded to an integer. If you round it up to the next integer, it goes against the conservative principle, which means picking a higher critical value that sets the boundary of the rejection zone. Therefore, the logical option based on the conservative principle is to round it down. Fortunately, the approximated df is

Author's Aside

As a common practice intended to keep the burden of memorizing a complicated formula to a minimum, some statistics instructors recommend taking the smaller of df_1 and df_2 as an alternative answer for the df for the independent-samples t tests when equal variances are not assumed. Personally, I prefer to allow students to bring a formula sheet to statistics exams. This takes the burden of pure memorization of formulas out of the already stressful statistics exams. I would not object to taking the smaller of df_1 and df_2 as an alternative answer either.

provided in most statistics software packages such as SPSS and SAS. We will use SPSS to run an independent-samples t test in the next section.

Let's illustrate this new set of formulas by going through the five-step hypothesis-testing process for independent-samples t tests using a couple more examples.

EXAMPLE 9.4

Assume that ACT scores are normally distributed. A sample of 25 male college freshmen is randomly selected in a public university, and their ACT scores have $\bar{X} = 22.8$ and $s = 3.1$. A sample of 16 female college freshmen is randomly selected from the same university, and their ACT scores have $\bar{X} = 23.5$ and $s = 5.1$. Is the average ACT score for female freshmen higher than that of the male freshmen, using $\alpha = .05$?

The comparison between the male and female college freshmen's ACT scores calls for an independent-samples t test. Therefore, we need to conduct the five-step hypothesis-testing process.

Step 1. Test for the equality of variances.

Substep 1. State the pair of hypotheses regarding variances.

$$H_0: \sigma_1^2 = \sigma_2^2$$

$$H_1: \sigma_1^2 \neq \sigma_2^2$$

Substep 2. Identify the rejection zone.

The larger standard deviation is s_1, 5.1 for the female college freshmen, and its $df_1 = n_1 - 1 = 16 - 1 = 15$. Therefore, the female group is labeled as Group 1. And s_2 is the smaller standard deviation, 3.1 for male college freshmen, and its $df_2 = n_2 - 1 = 25 - 1 = 24$. Therefore, the male group is labeled as Group 2.

The critical value of the right-tailed $F_{(df_1, df_2)} = F_{(15,24)} = 2.11$.

Substep 3. Calculate the F statistic.

$$F = \frac{s_1^2}{s_2^2} = \frac{5.1^2}{3.1^2} = \frac{26.01}{9.61} = 2.71$$

Substep 4. Make the correct conclusion.

The calculated $F = 2.71$ is larger than the critical value of $F_{(15,24)} = 2.11$. Therefore, we reject H_0. The evidence is strong enough to claim that the two variances are not equal. Therefore, the correct independent-samples t-test approach is to assume unequal variances.

Step 2. State the pair of hypotheses regarding group means.

The problem statement asks, "Is the average ACT score for female freshmen higher than that of male freshmen?" *Higher* is a key word here that indicates a direction. In this problem, the larger s is designated as s_1, so the female freshmen are designated as Sample 1 and males as Sample 2. Therefore, a right-tailed test is appropriate. It is very important to get the direction of the one-tailed hypothesis test stated exactly as in the problem.

$H_0: \mu_1 = \mu_2$

$H_1: \mu_1 > \mu_2$

Step 3. Identify the rejection zone.

$$\text{Satterthwaite's approximated } df = \frac{(w_1 + w_2)^2}{\dfrac{w_1^2}{n_1 - 1} + \dfrac{w_2^2}{n_2 - 1}}$$

where

$$w_1 = \frac{s_1^2}{n_1} = \frac{5.1^2}{16} = \frac{26.01}{16} = 1.63$$

and

$$w_2 = \frac{s_2^2}{n_2} = \frac{3.1^2}{25} = \frac{9.61}{25} = 0.38$$

$$df = \frac{(w_1 + w_2)^2}{\dfrac{w_1^2}{n_1 - 1} + \dfrac{w_2^2}{n_2 - 1}} = \frac{(1.63 + 0.38)^2}{\dfrac{1.63^2}{15} + \dfrac{0.38^2}{24}} = \frac{4.04}{0.183} = 22.08$$

(Continued)

(Continued)

which is rounded down to 22.

According to the t Table, when $df = 22$, $\alpha = .05$; it is a right-tailed test, and the critical t value that sets the boundary of the rejection zone is 1.717. The rejection zone for a right-tailed test is $t > 1.717$.

If you use another commonly used, simplified way to pick the smaller of df_1 and df_2 as the df for the t test, the df is 15. The rejection zone for a right-tailed test under $df = 15$, $\alpha = .05$ is $t > 1.753$. *Caution!* Different methods of calculating the df when $\sigma_1^2 \neq \sigma_2^2$ will lead to different rejection zones for the t test.

Step 4. Calculate the t statistic.

When $\sigma_1^2 \neq \sigma_2^2$, it is inappropriate to pool the variances. So they are left alone.

$$ s_{(\bar{X}_1 - \bar{X}_2)} = \sqrt{\frac{s_1^2}{n_1} + \frac{s_2^2}{n_2}} = \sqrt{\frac{5.1^2}{16} + \frac{3.1^2}{25}} = \sqrt{1.63 + 0.38} = \sqrt{2.01} = 1.42 $$

$$ t = \frac{\bar{X}_1 - \bar{X}_2}{s_{(\bar{X}_1 - \bar{X}_2)}} = \frac{23.5 - 22.8}{1.42} = \frac{0.7}{1.42} = 0.49 $$

Step 5. Make the correct conclusion.

The calculated $t = 0.49$ is not within the rejection zone. Therefore, we fail to reject H_0. The evidence is not strong enough to support the claim that the average of the female freshmen's ACT scores is higher than that for the male freshmen.

This example illustrates the five-step hypothesis-testing process for an independent-samples t test when equal variances are not assumed. This situation requires a complicated approximated df formula but actually has a simpler standard error of the mean difference formula as the denominator of the t test. Overall, the process is manageable as long as students are not burdened with pure memorization of formulas.

Independent-samples t tests are commonly used to make comparisons between two groups: (1) the experimental group and (2) the control group. The experimental group is the group with a particular condition, and the control group is the group without that particular condition. Different individuals are included in those two groups. In the next examples, we compare the BMI measures between runners and nonrunners.

EXAMPLE 9.5

The BMI is the ratio of a person's weight measured in kilograms to the square of his or her height measured in meters. BMI measures are normally distributed. Assume that a group of 20 runners is randomly selected and their BMIs have $\bar{X} = 19.15$ and $s = 3.25$. A group of 21 nonrunners is randomly selected, and their BMIs have $\bar{X} = 26.89$ and $s = 6.01$. Is the average BMI of the runners different from that of the nonrunners, using $\alpha = .01$?

The comparison of BMI between runners and nonrunners requires an independent-samples t test. Therefore, we need to conduct the five-step hypothesis-testing process.

Step 1. Test for equality of variances.

Substep 1. State the pair of hypotheses regarding variances.

$$H_0: \sigma_1^2 = \sigma_2^2$$

$$H_1: \sigma_1^2 \neq \sigma_2^2$$

Substep 2. Identify the criterion for the hypothesis test.

The larger standard deviation is s_1, 6.01 from the nonrunner group, and its $df_1 = n_1 - 1 = 21 - 1 = 20$; therefore, the nonrunner group is labeled as Group 1. And s_2 is the smaller standard deviation, 3.25 from the runner group, and its $df_2 = 20 - 1 = 19$; therefore, the runner group is labeled as Group 2.

The critical value of the right-tailed $F_{(df_1, df_2)} = F_{(20,19)} = 2.16$.

Substep 3. Calculate the F statistic.

$$F = \frac{s_1^2}{s_2^2} = \frac{6.01^2}{3.25^2} = \frac{36.12}{10.56} = 3.42$$

Substep 4. Make the correct conclusion.

The calculated $F = 3.42$ is larger than the critical value of $F_{(20,19)} = 2.16$. Therefore, we reject H_0. The evidence is strong enough to support the claim that the two variances are unequal. Therefore, the correct independent-samples t-test approach is to assume unequal variances.

(Continued)

(Continued)

Step 2. State the pair of hypotheses regarding group means.

The problem statement asks, "Is the average BMI of runners different from that of nonrunners?" There is no hint of direction. Therefore, a two-tailed test is appropriate.

$H_0: \mu_1 = \mu_2$

$H_1: \mu_1 \neq \mu_2$

Step 3. Identify the rejection zones for the test.

$$\text{Satterthwaite's approximated } df = \frac{(w_1 + w_2)^2}{\dfrac{w_1^2}{n_1 - 1} + \dfrac{w_2^2}{n_2 - 1}}$$

where

$$w_1 = \frac{s_1^2}{n_1} = \frac{6.01^2}{21} = \frac{36.12}{21} = 1.72$$

and

$$w_2 = \frac{s_2^2}{n_2} = \frac{3.25^2}{20} = \frac{10.56}{20} = 0.53$$

$$df = \frac{(w_1 + w_2)^2}{\dfrac{w_1^2}{n_1 - 1} + \dfrac{w_2^2}{n_2 - 1}} = \frac{(1.72 + 0.53)^2}{\dfrac{1.72^2}{20} + \dfrac{0.53^2}{19}} = \frac{5.0625}{.1627} = 31.12$$

which is rounded down to 31.

According to the *t* Table for *df* = 31, α = .01; it is a two-tailed test, the closest *df* = 30 on the *t* Table, and the critical value that sets the boundary of the rejection zone is 2.75. The rejection zone for a two-tailed test is $|t| > 2.75$.

If you use another commonly used, simplified way to pick the smaller of df_1 and df_2 as the *df* for the *t* test, the *df* is 19. The rejection zone for a two-tailed test under *df* = 19, α = .01 is $|t| > 2.861$. *Caution!* Different methods of calculating the *df* when $\sigma_1^2 \neq \sigma_2^2$ will lead to different rejection zones for the *t* test.

Step 4. Calculate the *t* statistic.

When $\sigma_1^2 \neq \sigma_2^2$, it is inappropriate to pool the variances, so they are left alone.

$$s_{(\bar{X}_1-\bar{X}_2)} = \sqrt{\frac{s_1^2}{n_1} + \frac{s_2^2}{n_2}} = \sqrt{\frac{6.01^2}{21} + \frac{3.25^2}{20}} = \sqrt{1.72 + 0.53} = \sqrt{2.25} = 1.5$$

$$t = \frac{\bar{X}_1 - \bar{X}_2}{s_{(\bar{X}_1-\bar{X}_2)}} = \frac{26.89 - 19.15}{1.5} = \frac{7.74}{1.5} = 5.16$$

Step 5. Make the correct conclusion.

The calculated $t = 5.16$ is within the rejection zone. Therefore, we reject H_0. The evidence is strong enough to support the claim that the average BMI of the runners is different from that of the nonrunners.

Now you have learned the complete five-step hypothesis-testing process for the independent-samples *t* tests. Such a process actually involves two separate hypothesis tests: (1) the equality of variances and (2) the equality of group means. First, you test for the equality of variances. Based on the outcome of the equality-of-variance test, you select the correct set of formulas to complete the test for the equality of group means. In this five-step process, you are able to handle all the independent-samples *t* tests regardless of whether the two groups have equal variances or not. The five-step process, at times, involves complicated formulas. Whenever calculations get complicated, you can count on computer software to come to the rescue. In the next section, we will learn how to use SPSS to run independent-samples *t* tests and how to interpret the outputs.

 Pop Quiz

1. Which one of the following characteristics is not required to conduct an independent-samples *t* test?

   a. The observations from the two samples must be independent.

   b. The number of groups needs to be two.

   c. Two samples are randomly selected from two populations.

   d. The two samples have equal variances.

   (Continued)

(Continued)

2. When is it appropriate to calculate the pooled variance in conducting an independent-samples *t* test?

   a. When two samples are carefully matched on key variables

   b. When equal variances are assumed

   c. When two samples are randomly selected from two populations

   d. When equal variances are not assumed

Answers: 1. d, 2. b

USING SPSS TO RUN INDEPENDENT-SAMPLES *t* TESTS

SPSS takes care of the calculation process for many statistical procedures by providing drop-down menus, pop-up windows, and point-and-click options. It is very user-friendly. Many times, students wonder, "Why do we still have to learn how to calculate statistical formulas by hand?" It is a good question that deserves a good answer. Let's go through one example using SPSS to run an independent-samples *t* test. Then we will go back to that question.

We will use the personal measures.sav file, which is an SPSS data set that contains the personal measurements of students. The purpose is to compare the height measurements of men versus women. The height measurements are assumed to be normally distributed.

The step-by-step instructions on how to use SPSS to conduct an independent-samples *t* test are shown in Figure 9.1. Once the personal measures.sav file is opened by SPSS, follow these instructions:

Click the **Analyze** tab.

In the drop-down menu, click **Compare Means**.

Then click **Independent-Samples T Test**.

A pop-up window titled **Independent Samples T Test** appears; select **height**, and put it into the **Test Variable(s)** box. The test variable in an independent-samples *t* test is usually an interval or ratio variable that the researchers are interested in comparing between the two groups. Select **sex**, and put it into the **Grouping Variable** box. The grouping variable in an independent-samples *t* test is usually a nominal variable that identifies the groups. Then define **sex** as it is coded in the data set. In this data set, **sex** is coded as 1 and 2 (i.e., 1 = *female*, and 2 = *male*). Once you finish identifying the test variable and the grouping variable in the pop-up window, your screen looks like Figure 9.2, and SPSS is ready to run the independent-samples *t* test. Then hit **OK**.

FIGURE 9.1   Conducting the Independent-Samples *t* Test Using SPSS

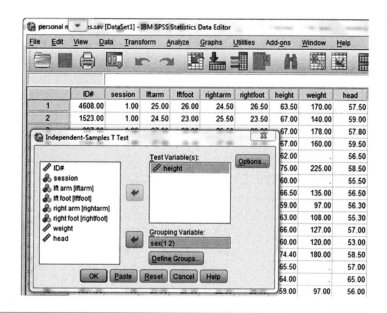

SPSS runs through the programs and generates the results as shown in Tables 9.1 and 9.2.

TABLE 9.1   Descriptive Statistics for the Independent-Samples t Test

Group Statistics

	Sex	N	Mean	Std. Deviation	Std. Error Mean
Height	female	55	63.8545	3.32593	.44847
	male	14	69.6714	3.36096	.89825

TABLE 9.2   Independent-Samples t-Test Results

		Levene's Test for Equality of Variances	
		F	Sig.
Height	Equal variances assumed	.086	.770
	Equal variances not assumed		

t-test for Equality of Means						
				Std. Error	95% Confidence Interval of the Difference	
T	Df	Sig. (2-tailed)	Mean Difference	Difference	Lower	Upper
−5.831	67	.000	−5.81688	.99766	−7.80822	−3.82555
−5.794	19.990	.000	−5.81688	1.00398	−7.91123	−3.72254

Table 9.1 shows the descriptive statistics, including the valid number of observations in each group (or sample size, n), sample mean, sample standard deviation, and standard error of the mean. Table 9.2 shows the results of the independent-samples t test.

In SPSS output, the results of an independent-samples t test include Levene's test for equality of variances and the t test for equality of means, and they are presented in one table from left to right. Due to the limitation of the page orientation of this book, the table is broken into two sections stacked up. The top section of Table 9.2 shows the result of Levene's test for equality of variances. Levene's test, in many respects, does the same thing as we did in the folded-form F-test procedure, but it is a little more sophisticated. When using SPSS, Levene's test for equality of variances is provided before conducting the independent-samples t tests. Levene's test is more robust than the folded-form F test, but Levene's test is too complicated to calculate by hand. We will skip the calculation process of

Levene's test and focus on understanding and interpreting the Levene's test result, so that we can choose the appropriate independent-samples t-test option. The pair of hypotheses for Levene's test is as follows:

$$H_0: \sigma_1^2 = \sigma_2^2$$

$$H_1: \sigma_1^2 \neq \sigma_2^2$$

The top section of Table 9.2 shows that the F value is 0.086 and the p value associated with the F is $p = .770$. Whenever the p value associated with a particular test statistic is reported by statistical packages, users don't have to look up the critical values that set the boundaries of the rejection zones. This is a perfect time to apply the decision rules based on the p value. When the p value associated with a test statistic is used as a criterion for a hypothesis test, the decision rules are as follows:

When $p < \alpha$, we reject H_0.

When $p \geq \alpha$, we fail to reject H_0.

The calculated $p = .770$ is larger than the customary $\alpha = .05$; therefore we fail to reject H_0. The evidence is not strong enough support the claim that the two groups have unequal variances. Therefore, equal variances are assumed.

Move to the bottom section of Table 9.2 for the t test for equality of means. The pair of hypotheses for equality of means in a two-tailed test is as follows:

$$H_0: \mu_1 = \mu_2$$

$$H_1: \mu_1 \neq \mu_2$$

Both "Equal variances assumed" and "Equal variances not assumed" results are presented in the bottom section of Table 9.2. The first row represents the results when equal variances are assumed, and the second row represents the results when equal variances are not assumed. It is easy for programmers to program both sets of formulas for independent-samples t tests into the software package. It is, however, up to end users like you to figure out which row of numbers is relevant for your particular test. Based on Levene's test, equal variances are assumed. In this problem, the numbers in the first row (highlighted in blue) are appropriate, and the numbers in the second row are not relevant and should be ignored. The calculated t value is -5.831, with $df = 67$ and $p = .000$. The calculated $p = .000$ is smaller than $\alpha = .05$; therefore we reject H_0. A special note is needed on $p = .000$, which does not mean the probability is actually zero. It means that the calculated p is so small that the values for the first three places after the decimal point are all zeros but there are nonzero values afterward.

When $p = .000$, the evidence is strong enough to support the claim that there are highly significant differences between men's and women's heights.

Now, let's revisit the question "Why do students still have to learn to calculate statistical formulas by hand when statistics software packages can take care of all the calculation processes?" Through the sex-difference-in-height example, we can clearly demonstrate that not all the numbers reported in a statistical software program are accurate. In the independent-samples t test, it is dangerous not to know the calculations because both sets of results, under equal variances assumed and equal variances not assumed, are presented in the same table. Without adequate understanding of the statistical processes involved, there is a 50% chance that users would choose the wrong results. It is clear that equal variances assumed and equal variances not assumed can't be true at the same time. That is the reason why Levene's test needs to be conducted before the independent-samples t tests. Doing statistical procedures by hand might not be the most efficient way to get to the answers, but it provides a solid foundation that can be used at a later point to accurately interpret the printouts from statistics software packages.

CONFIDENCE INTERVALS OF THE MEAN DIFFERENCE

The last two columns in Table 9.2 display the lower limit and the upper limit of the 95% confidence interval (CI) of the group mean difference. The 95% CI is calculated based on the same principle as that introduced in Chapter 8. That is, CI = point estimate ± margin of error. The margin of error is the multiplicative product between $t_{\alpha/2}$ and the standard error of the statistic. As discussed in Chapter 8, the $t_{\alpha/2}$ denotes the critical t value for a two-tailed α. It is not a math operation. When putting all together, a $(1 - \alpha)100\%$ CI = point estimate ± $t_{\alpha/2}$(standard error of the statistic). The higher the confidence level, the wider is the CI.

When conducting independent-samples t tests, the CI is expressed as

$$(1-\alpha)100\% \text{ CI} = (\bar{X}_1 - \bar{X}_2) \pm t_{\alpha/2}(s_{(\bar{X}_1 - \bar{X}_2)})$$

When equal variances are assumed, $\sigma_1^2 = \sigma_2^2$, the formula is

$$(1-\alpha)100\% \text{ CI} = (\bar{X}_1 - \bar{X}_2) \pm t_{\alpha/2}\left(\sqrt{\frac{s_p^2}{n_1} + \frac{s_p^2}{n_2}}\right)$$

where

$$s_p^2 = \frac{SS_1 + SS_2}{df_1 + df_2}$$

The lower limit of the $(1 - \alpha)100\%$ CI is

$$(\bar{X}_1 - \bar{X}_2) - t_{\alpha/2}\left(\sqrt{\frac{s_p^2}{n_1} + \frac{s_p^2}{n_2}}\right)$$

and the upper limit of the $(1 - \alpha)100\%$ CI is

$$(\bar{X}_1 - \bar{X}_2) + t_{\alpha/2}\left(\sqrt{\frac{s_p^2}{n_1} + \frac{s_p^2}{n_2}}\right)$$

When equal variances are not assumed, $\sigma_1^2 \neq \sigma_2^2$, the CI formula is

$$(1 - \alpha)100\% \text{ CI} = (\bar{X}_1 - \bar{X}_2) \pm t_{\alpha/2}\left(\sqrt{\frac{s_1^2}{n_1} + \frac{s_2^2}{n_2}}\right)$$

The lower limit of the $(1 - \alpha)100\%$ CI is

$$(\bar{X}_1 - \bar{X}_2) - t_{\alpha/2}\left(\sqrt{\frac{s_1^2}{n_1} + \frac{s_2^2}{n_2}}\right)$$

and the upper limit of the $(1 - \alpha)100\%$ CI is

$$(\bar{X}_1 - \bar{X}_2) + t_{\alpha/2}\left(\sqrt{\frac{s_1^2}{n_1} + \frac{s_2^2}{n_2}}\right)$$

In the example of comparing men's and women's heights, Levene's test shows that equal variances are assumed. Therefore, the correct 95% CI for the mean difference is $(-7.808, -3.826)$, as shown in the first row of the last two columns in the bottom section of Table 9.2. The 95% CI supports the claim that significant differences exist between men's and women's heights, because zero is included in the 95% CI for the mean difference.

EFFECT SIZES

This chapter marks the first time you are able to conduct a hypothesis test purely based on sample data, without assuming or pretending to know any population parameters: μ or σ. An independent-samples t test is the procedure utilized by social scientists when they want to study group mean differences among different individuals randomly selected from two different populations. The hypothesis-testing process tells them whether the result of such a study is statistically significant or not. However, when a large sample size is deployed in a study, even a trivial difference can be statistically significant. Indeed, a statistically significant result might not be scientifically or practically meaningful. Therefore, the sixth edition of the *Publication Manual of the American Psychological Association* (APA, 2010) states,

> For the reader to appreciate the magnitude or importance of a study's findings, it is almost always necessary to include some measure of effect size in the Results section. Whenever possible, provide a confidence interval for each effect size reported to indicate the precision of estimation of the effect size. (p. 34)

An effect size is defined as a standardized measure of the strength of a test statistic. In independent-samples t tests, effect sizes are calculated as the standardized difference between two sample means in units of standard deviation. Effect size formulas are different under conditions of equal variances assumed versus equal variances not assumed.

When equal variances are assumed, $\sigma_1^2 = \sigma_2^2$, the effect size is calculated as the sample mean difference divided by the pooled standard deviation (Cohen, 1988) and is referred to as Cohen's *d*.

$$\text{Cohen's } d = \frac{(\bar{X}_1 - \bar{X}_2)}{s_p}$$

where

$$s_p = \sqrt{\frac{SS_1 + SS_2}{df_1 + df_2}}$$

When equal variances are not assumed, $\sigma_1^2 \neq \sigma_2^2$, it is inappropriate to pool the variances. The effect size is calculated by Glass's delta (Δ). Glass's Δ is defined as the sample mean difference divided by the standard deviation of the control group (Glass, McGaw, & Smith, 1981; Hedges, 1981). When there is no distinction between the experimental group and the control group, the larger of s_1 and s_2 should be used as the denominator. This provides a more conservative estimate.

$$\text{Glass's } \Delta = \frac{\bar{X}_1 - \bar{X}_2}{s_{\text{control}}} \text{ or } \frac{\bar{X}_1 - \bar{X}_2}{s_{\text{larger}}}$$

When the effect size equals 1, the interpretation is that two sample means are 1 standard deviation apart from each other. The general interpretation of the magnitude of effect size is that 0.2 is small, 0.5 is moderate, and 0.8 is large (Cohen, 1988). The effect size calculation is meaningful in a single study. In addition, effect size calculation can provide powerful insights in meta-analyses. A meta-analysis is the analysis of analyses. It is the process of synthesizing research results by using rigorous scientific methods to retrieve, select, and statistically analyze the results from previous studies on the same topic. When multiple studies with the same independent and dependent variables are collected, analyzed, and statistically integrated under a meta-analysis, it offers meaningful generalizations or can examine potential factors for inconsistent results. Effect sizes are necessary tools to allow such statistical integration across different studies.

EXAMPLE 9.6

Let's continue working with the height measurements in the SPSS printout. SPSS does not offer effect size calculations, but it is fairly easy to calculate effect size by hand. Use the descriptive statistics in Table 9.1 to calculate the effect size for the comparison of the height measurements between men and women.

According to Levene's test, we fail to reject H_0; therefore equal variances are assumed in this study. Remember the group with larger variance is labeled as Group 1, so male students belong to Group 1 and female students belong to Group 2.

$$SS_1 = s_1^2 df_1 = 3.36^2 \times 13 = 146.76$$

$$SS_2 = s_2^2 df_2 = 3.33^2 \times 54 = 598.80$$

$$s_p = \sqrt{\frac{SS_1 + SS_2}{df_1 + df_2}} = \sqrt{\frac{745.56}{67}} = \sqrt{11.13} = 3.34$$

$$\text{Cohen's } d = \frac{\bar{X}_1 - \bar{X}_2}{s_p} = \frac{69.67 - 63.85}{3.34} = \frac{5.82}{3.34} = 1.74$$

The effect size of the men's and women's height measures turns out to be large, $d = 1.74$, which means that the average men's height measure is 1.74 standard deviations higher than the average women's height measure. The differences are significant and practically meaningful.

Next, let's use an example to go through the process of calculating effect size when equal variances are not assumed.

EXAMPLE 9.7

Let's return to the comparison of the average BMI between runners and nonrunners in Example 9.5. Calculate the effect size for the group mean difference in this study. The essential data are as follows:

Nonrunners: $n_1 = 21$, $\bar{X}_1 = 26.89$, and $s_1 = 6.01$.

Runners: $n_2 = 20$, $\bar{X}_2 = 19.15$, and $s_2 = 3.25$.

The folded-form F test shows that the calculated $F = 3.42$ is larger than the critical value of $F_{(20,19)} = 2.16$. Therefore, we reject H_0. The evidence is strong enough to claim that the two variances are not equal.

When $\sigma_1^2 \neq \sigma_2^2$, it is inappropriate to pool the variances, so the effect size formula should be calculated by Glass's Δ.

$$\text{Glass's } \Delta = \frac{\bar{X}_1 - \bar{X}_2}{s_{\text{control}}}$$

In this problem, we may treat runners as the experimental group and nonrunners as the control group. Or we may simply use the larger standard deviation between the two groups.

$$\text{Glass's } \Delta = \frac{\bar{X}_1 - \bar{X}_2}{s_{\text{larger}}} = \frac{26.89 - 19.15}{6.01} = 1.29$$

Effect size = 1.29 is a large effect. It means that the runners' average BMI is 1.29 standard deviations apart from the nonrunners' average BMI. It shows that the effect size of the BMI difference between the runners and nonrunners is large and practically meaningful.

There are two different sets of formulas for conducting an independent-samples t test. The decision on which set of formulas to choose depends on the outcome of the test for equality of variances. The basic principle is that you only pool the variances together when equal variances are assumed; otherwise you have to treat the variances separately. Such different formulas also apply to effect size calculation. When equal variances are assumed, you use Cohen's $d = (\bar{X}_1 - \bar{X}_2)/s_p$ to calculate the effect size. When equal variances are not assumed, you use Glass's $\Delta = (\bar{X}_1 - \bar{X}_2)/s_{\text{control}}$ to calculate the effect size.

Pop Quiz

1. Which one of the following formulas is appropriate to calculate the effect size when conducting independent-samples t tests with equal variances not assumed?

  a. Cohen's $d = \dfrac{(\bar{X}_1 - \bar{X}_2)}{s_p}$

  b. Glass's $\Delta = \dfrac{(\bar{X}_1 - \bar{X}_2)}{s_{larger}}$

  c. Satterthwaite's approximated $df = \dfrac{(w_1 + w_2)^2}{\dfrac{w_1^2}{n_1 - 1} + \dfrac{w_2^2}{n_2 - 1}}$

  d. $s_{(\bar{X}_1 - \bar{X}_2)} = \sqrt{\dfrac{s_1^2}{n_1} + \dfrac{s_2^2}{n_2}}$

Answer: b

EXERCISE PROBLEMS

1. SAT Critical Reading and SAT Math scores are both normally distributed. Researchers are interested in comparing SAT Critical Reading and SAT Math scores between students who attend public high schools and those who attend private schools. Assume that a sample of public school students and a sample of private school students are randomly selected. Table 9.3 shows the summary descriptive statistics for this study. Use α = .05 to conduct the hypothesis tests.

   a. Is there a significant difference in the average SAT Critical Reading scores between students from public schools and students from private schools?

TABLE 9.3   Descriptive Statistics of SAT Scores of Public and Private School Students

SCHOOL TYPE		n	SAT CRITICAL READING $\bar{X}$	s	SAT MATH $\bar{X}$	s
	PUBLIC SCHOOLS	31	497	115	510	105
	PRIVATE SCHOOLS	30	550	110	574	95

b. Is the average SAT Math score of students from public schools lower than that of students from private schools?

c. What is the effect size for the difference in the average SAT Critical Reading scores between public school students and private school students?

d. What is the effect size for the difference in the average SAT Math scores between public school students and private school students?

e. What is the 95% CI for the difference in the average SAT Critical Reading scores between public school students and private school students?

f. What is the 95% CI for the difference in the average SAT Math scores between public school students and private school students?

2. Assume that a psychologist studies the effect of meditation training on anxiety. Participants in the experimental group are given meditation training before the anxiety assessment. Participants in the control group are given the anxiety assessment without any relaxation training. Each participant is randomly assigned to one of the groups. Conduct a proper statistical procedure to test whether meditation training reduces anxiety level, using $\alpha = .05$. Make sure that you include all the necessary steps in the correct order for your statistical test.

EXPERIMENTAL GROUP	CONTROL GROUP
$s = 7$	$s = 10$
$\bar{X} = 70$	$\bar{X} = 78$
$SS = 686$	$SS = 1,200$

Solutions

1.a.

Step 1. Test for equality of variances.

Substep 1. State the pair of hypotheses regarding variances.

$$H_0: \sigma_1^2 = \sigma_2^2$$

$$H_1: \sigma_1^2 \neq \sigma_2^2$$

Substep 2. Identify the criterion for the hypothesis test.

The larger standard deviation is s_1, 115, and its $df_1 = n_1 - 1 = 31 - 1 = 30$; so the students from public schools are labeled as Group 1. And s_2 is the smaller standard deviation, 110, and its $df_2 = 30 - 1 = 29$; so the students from private schools are labeled as Group 2.

The critical value of the right-tailed $F_{(df_1, df_2)} = F_{(30,29)} = 1.85$.

Substep 3. Calculate the statistic.

$$F = \frac{s_1^2}{s_2^2} = \frac{115^2}{110^2} = \frac{13225}{12100} = 1.09$$

Substep 4. Make the correct conclusion.

The calculated $F = 1.09$ is smaller than the critical value of $F_{(30,29)} = 1.85$. Therefore, we fail to reject H_0. The evidence is not strong enough to claim that the two variances are not equal. Therefore, the correct independent-samples t-test approach is to assume equal variances.

Step 2. State the pair of hypotheses regarding group means.

The problem statement asks, "Is there a significant difference in the average SAT Critical Reading scores between public and private school students?" There is no hint of direction. Therefore, a two-tailed test is appropriate.

$H_0: \mu_1 = \mu_2$

$H_1: \mu_1 \neq \mu_2$

Step 3. Identify the rejection zones for the test.

According to the t Table for $df = df_1 + df_2 = n_1 + n_2 - 2 = 59$, $\alpha = .05$; it is a two-tailed test, and the closest df in the t Table is $df = 60$. Thus, the critical t value that sets the boundary of the rejection zone is 2.00. The rejection zone for a two-tailed test is $|t| > 2.00$.

Step 4. Calculate the t statistic.

When $\sigma_1^2 = \sigma_2^2$, the variances need to be pooled together.

$$SS_1 = s_1^2 df_1 = 115^2 (31 - 1) = 396,750$$

$$SS_2 = s_2^2 df_2 = 110^2 (30 - 1) = 350,900$$

$$s_p^2 = \frac{SS_1 + SS_2}{df_1 + df_2} = \frac{396750 + 350900}{30 + 29} = \frac{747650}{59} = 12{,}672.03$$

$$s_{(\bar{X}_1 - \bar{X}_2)} = \sqrt{\frac{s_p^2}{n_1} + \frac{s_p^2}{n_2}} = \sqrt{\frac{12672.03}{31} + \frac{12672.03}{30}} = \sqrt{408.78 + 422.40} = \sqrt{831.18} = 28.83$$

$$t = \frac{(\bar{X}_1 - \bar{X}_2)}{s_{(\bar{X}_1 - \bar{X}_2)}} = \frac{(497 - 550)}{28.83} = \frac{-53}{28.83} = -1.84$$

Step 5. Make the correct conclusion.

The calculated $t = -1.84$ is not within the rejection zone. Therefore, we fail to reject H_0. The evidence is not strong enough to support the claim that there is a significant difference in the average SAT Critical Reading scores between public and private school students.

1.b.

Step 1. Test for equality of variances.

Substep 1. State the pair of hypotheses regarding variances.

$$H_0: \sigma_1^2 = \sigma_2^2$$

$$H_1: \sigma_1^2 \neq \sigma_2^2$$

Substep 2. Identify the rejection zone.

The larger standard deviation is s_1, 105, and its $df_1 = n_1 - 1 = 31 - 1 = 30$; s_2 is the smaller standard deviation, 95, and its $df_2 = 30 - 1 = 29$.

The critical value of the right-tailed $F_{(df1, df2)} = F_{(30,29)} = 1.85$.

Substep 3. Calculate the test statistic.

$$F = \frac{s_1^2}{s_2^2} = \frac{105^2}{95^2} = \frac{11025}{9025} = 1.22$$

Substep 4. Make the correct conclusion.

The calculated $F = 1.22$ is smaller than the critical value of $F_{(30,29)} = 1.85$. Therefore, we fail to reject H_0. The evidence is not strong enough to claim that the two variances are not equal. Therefore, the correct independent-samples t-test approach is to assume equal variances.

Step 2. State the pair of hypotheses regarding group means.

The problem statement asks, "Is the average SAT Math score of students from public schools lower than that of students from private schools?" *Lower* is a key word for direction. Public school students' SAT Math scores have a larger standard deviation; thus the public school students are assigned to Group 1. The mean of public school students' SAT Math scores is μ_1, and the mean of private school students' SAT Math scores is μ_2. Therefore, a left-tailed test is appropriate. Be aware that the designation of μ_1 and μ_2 needs to be consistent with s_1 and s_2. In a one-tailed test, it is important to state the correct direction in the alternative hypothesis, H_1.

$$H_0: \mu_1 = \mu_2$$

$$H_1: \mu_1 < \mu_2$$

Step 3. Identify the rejection zones for the test.

According to the t Table, when $df = df_1 + df_2 = n_1 + n_2 - 2 = 59$, $\alpha = .05$; it is a left-tailed test, and the closest df is 60. Thus, the critical t value that sets the boundary of the rejection zone is 1.671. The rejection zone for a left-tailed test is $t < -1.671$.

Step 4. Calculate the t statistic.

When $\sigma_1^2 = \sigma_2^2$, the variances need to be pooled together.

$$SS_1 = s_1^2 df_1 = 105^2(31-1) = 330{,}750$$

$$SS_2 = s_2^2 df_2 = 95^2(30-1) = 261{,}725$$

$$s_p^2 = \frac{SS_1 + SS_2}{df_1 + df_2} = \frac{330750 + 261725}{30 + 29} = \frac{592475}{59} = 10{,}041.95$$

$$s_{(\bar{X}_1 - \bar{X}_2)} = \sqrt{\frac{s_p^2}{n_1} + \frac{s_p^2}{n_2}} = \sqrt{\frac{10041.95}{31} + \frac{10041.95}{30}} = \sqrt{323.93 + 334.73} = \sqrt{658.66} = 25.66$$

$$t = \frac{(\bar{X}_1 - \bar{X}_2)}{s_{(\bar{X}_1 - \bar{X}_2)}} = \frac{(510 - 574)}{25.66} = \frac{-64}{25.66} = -2.49$$

Step 5. Make the correct conclusion.

The calculated $t = -2.49$ is within the rejection zone. Therefore, we reject H_0. The evidence is strong enough to support the claim that the average SAT Math score of students from public schools is lower than that of students from private schools.

1.c. When $\sigma_1^2 = \sigma_2^2$, the effect size is calculated as Cohen's $d = (\bar{X}_1 - \bar{X}_2) / s_p$. Based on the answer from 1.a, $s_p = \sqrt{12672.03} = 112.57$.

$$\text{Effect size } d = \frac{(\bar{X}_1 - \bar{X}_2)}{s_p} = \frac{497 - 550}{112.57} = \frac{-53}{112.57} = -0.47$$

The average SAT Critical Reading score of students from public schools is 0.47 standard deviations lower than that of students from private schools. The effect is moderate.

1.d. Based on the answer from 1.b, $s_p = \sqrt{10041.95} = 100.21$.

$$\text{Effect size } d = \frac{(\bar{X}_1 - \bar{X}_2)}{s_p} = \frac{510 - 574}{100.21} = \frac{-64}{100.21} = -0.64$$

The average SAT Math score of students from public schools is 0.64 standard deviations lower than that of students from private schools. The effect is moderate.

1.e. The 95% CI $= (\bar{X}_1 - \bar{X}_2) \pm t_{\alpha/2}(s_{(\bar{X}_1 - \bar{X}_2)})$. When equal variances are assumed, $\sigma_1^2 = \sigma_2^2$, the formula is as follows:

$$95\% \text{ CI} = (\bar{X}_1 - \bar{X}_2) \pm t_{\alpha/2}\left(\sqrt{\frac{s_p^2}{n_1} + \frac{s_p^2}{n_2}}\right)$$

$$s_{(\bar{X}_1 - \bar{X}_2)} = \sqrt{\frac{s_p^2}{n_1} + \frac{s_p^2}{n_2}} = \sqrt{\frac{12672.03}{31} + \frac{12672.03}{30}} = 28.83$$

with $df = 59$, $\alpha = .05$, and $t_{\alpha/2} = 2.00$.

$$95\% \text{ CI} = (\bar{X}_1 - \bar{X}_2) \pm t_{\alpha/2}\left(\sqrt{\frac{s_p^2}{n_1} + \frac{s_p^2}{n_2}}\right) = (497 - 550) \pm 2(28.83) = -53 \pm 57.66$$

The 95% CI for the difference in the average SAT Critical Reading scores of the students from public schools and students from private schools is (−110.66, 4.66). Due to the fact that zero is included in this 95% CI, the difference is not statistically significant.

1.f. The 95% CI $= (\bar{X}_1 - \bar{X}_2) \pm t_{\alpha/2}(s_{(\bar{X}_1 - \bar{X}_2)})$. When equal variances are assumed, $\sigma_1^2 = \sigma_2^2$, the formula is as follows:

$$95\% \text{ CI} = (\bar{X}_1 - \bar{X}_2) \pm t_{\alpha/2}\left(\sqrt{\frac{s_P^2}{n_1} + \frac{s_P^2}{n_2}}\right)$$

$$s_{(\bar{X}_1 - \bar{X}_2)} = \sqrt{\frac{s_P^2}{n_1} + \frac{s_P^2}{n_2}} = \sqrt{\frac{10041.95}{31} + \frac{10041.95}{30}} = 25.66$$

with $df = 59$, $\alpha = .05$, and $t_{\alpha/2} = 2.00$.

$$95\% \text{ CI} = (\bar{X}_1 - \bar{X}_2) \pm t_{\alpha/2}\left(\sqrt{\frac{s_P^2}{n_1} + \frac{s_P^2}{n_2}}\right) = (510 - 574) \pm 2(25.66) = -64 \pm 51.32$$

The 95% CI for the difference in the average SAT Math score for the students from public schools and students from private schools is (−115.32, −12.68). Due to the fact that zero is not included in this 95% CI, the difference is statistically significant.

2.

Step 1. Test for equality of variances.

Substep 1. State the pair of hypotheses regarding variances.

$$H_0: \sigma_1^2 = \sigma_2^2$$

$$H_1: \sigma_1^2 \neq \sigma_2^2$$

Substep 2. Identify the rejection zone.

The larger standard deviation is s_1, 10, and its $df_1 = n_1 - 1$. The control group is labeled as Group 1. However, the problem statement does not provide n_1—well, not directly. The problem statement provides both s and SS for the experimental group and the control group.

You know that $SS = s^2 df$, so if any two values are given, the third one can be determined.

For the control group, $1{,}200 = 10^2 df_1$.

$$df_1 = \frac{SS}{s^2} = \frac{1200}{100} = 12$$

For the experimental group, $686 = 7^2 df_2$.

$$df_2 = \frac{SS}{s^2} = \frac{686}{49} = 14$$

The critical value of F is $F_{(12,14)} = 2.53$. The rejection zone is $F > 2.53$.

Substep 3. Calculate the test statistic.

$$F = \frac{s_1^2}{s_2^2} = \frac{10^2}{7^2} = \frac{100}{49} = 2.04$$

Substep 4. Make the correct conclusion.

The calculated $F = 2.04$ is smaller than the critical value of $F_{(12,14)} = 2.53$. Therefore, we fail to reject H_0. The evidence is not strong enough to claim that the two variances are not equal. Therefore, the correct independent-samples t-test approach is to assume equal variances.

Step 2. State the pair of hypotheses regarding group means.

The problem statement asks, "Can meditation training reduce anxiety?" *Reduce* is a key word for direction. The control group has the larger variance; thus it is designated as Group 1. Therefore, a right-tailed test is appropriate. Be aware that the designation of μ_1 and μ_2 needs to be consistent with s_1 and s_2. In a one-tailed test, it is important to state the correct direction in the alternative hypothesis, H_1.

$H_0: \mu_1 = \mu_2$

$H_1: \mu_1 > \mu_2$

Step 3. Identify the rejection zones for the test.

According to the t Table, when $df = df_1 + df_2 = n_1 + n_2 - 2 = 26$, $\alpha = .05$; it is a right-tailed test; thus the critical t value that sets the boundary of the rejection zone is 1.706. The rejection zone for a right-tailed test is $t > 1.706$.

Step 4. Calculate the t statistic.

When $\sigma_1^2 = \sigma_2^2$, the variances need to be pooled together.

$$s_p^2 = \frac{SS_1 + SS_2}{df_1 + df_2} = \frac{1200 + 686}{12 + 14} = \frac{1886}{26} = 72.54$$

$$s_{(\bar{X}_1 - \bar{X}_2)} = \sqrt{\frac{s_p^2}{n_1} + \frac{s_p^2}{n_2}} = \sqrt{\frac{72.54}{13} + \frac{72.54}{15}} = \sqrt{5.580 + 4.836} = \sqrt{10.416} = 3.23$$

$$t = \frac{(\bar{X}_1 - \bar{X}_2)}{s_{(\bar{X}_1 - \bar{X}_2)}} = \frac{(78 - 70)}{3.23} = \frac{8}{3.23} = 2.48$$

Step 5. Make the correct conclusion.

The calculated $t = 2.48$ is within the rejection zone. Therefore, we reject H_0. The evidence is strong enough to support the claim that meditation training can reduce anxiety levels.

$\circledS$SAGE edge™

Sharpen your skills with SAGE edge!

Visit edge.sagepub.com/bowen for mobile-friendly quizzes, flashcards, videos, and more!

WHAT YOU LEARNED

Chapter 9 demonstrates a practical statistical procedure to compare the means from two groups consisting of different individuals without requiring knowledge of any population parameter, such as μ or σ. Two different situations might occur when comparing two independent samples: either (1) equal variances are assumed or (2) equal variances are not assumed. Tests of the equality of variances need to be performed to determine whether the two groups have equal variances or not. It becomes the first step of the five-step hypothesis-testing process for the independent-samples t test.

Step 1. Test for the equality of variances.

There are four substeps for conducting a *folded-form F test* to test for the equality of variances:

Substep 1. State the pair of hypotheses.

$$H_0: \sigma_1^2 = \sigma_2^2$$

$$H_1: \sigma_1^2 \neq \sigma_2^2$$

Substep 2. Identify the rejection zone.

The larger standard deviation is s_1 and its $df_1 = n_1 - 1$; s_2 is the smaller standard deviation, and its $df_2 = n_2 - 1$. The critical value of the right-tailed F-test is $F_{(df_1, df_2)}$.

Substep 3. Calculate the statistic.

$$F = \frac{s_1^2}{s_2^2} = \frac{\text{Larger variance}}{\text{Smaller variance}}$$

Substep 4. Make the correct conclusion.

If the calculated F is larger than the critical value of $F_{(df_1, df_2)}$, we reject H_0. The evidence is strong enough to support the claim that the two variances are not equal. If the calculated F is smaller than or equal to the critical value of $F_{(df_1, df_2)}$, we fail to reject H_0. In this case, the evidence is not strong enough to support the claim that the two variances are unequal. We have to assume equal variances.

Different sets of formulas for the independent-samples t test are required under different situations. The decision about which set to use is made after the test for the equality of variances is conducted.

When $\sigma_1^2 = \sigma_2^2$, the following hypothesis-testing procedure is appropriate:

Step 2. State the pair of hypotheses regarding group means according to the problem statement.

Two-tailed test:	$H_0: \mu_1 = \mu_2$
	$H_1: \mu_1 \neq \mu_2$
Right-tailed test:	$H_0: \mu_1 = \mu_2$
	$H_1: \mu_1 > \mu_2$
Left-tailed test:	$H_0: \mu_1 = \mu_2$
	$H_1: \mu_1 < \mu_2$

Step 3. Identify the rejection zone.

Use the three pieces of information, $df = df_1 + df_2 = n_1 + n_2 - 2$, α level, and two-tailed test versus one-tailed test, to determine the critical t value that sets the boundary of the rejection zone.

Step 4. Calculate the t statistic.

When $\sigma_1^2 = \sigma_2^2$, the variances need to be pooled together.

$$SS_1 = s_1^2 df_1$$

$$SS_2 = s_2^2 df_2$$

$$s_p^2 = \frac{SS_1 + SS_2}{df_1 + df_2}$$

$$s_{(\bar{X}_1 - \bar{X}_2)} = \sqrt{\frac{s_p^2}{n_1} + \frac{s_p^2}{n_2}}$$

$$t = \frac{(\bar{X}_1 - \bar{X}_2)}{s_{(\bar{X}_1 - \bar{X}_2)}}$$

Step 5. Make the correct conclusion.

If the calculated t value is within the rejection zone, we reject H_0. If the calculated t value is not within the rejection zone, we fail to reject H_0.

When $\sigma_1^2 \neq \sigma_2^2$, the following hypothesis-testing procedure is appropriate.

Step 2. State the pair of hypotheses regarding group means according to the problem statement.

Two-tailed test:	$H_0: \mu_1 = \mu_2$
	$H_1: \mu_1 \neq \mu_2$
Right-tailed test:	$H_0: \mu_1 = \mu_2$
	$H_1: \mu_1 > \mu_2$
Left-tailed test:	$H_0: \mu_1 = \mu_2$
	$H_1: \mu_1 < \mu_2$

Step 3. Identify the rejection zone.

$$\text{Satterthwaite's approximated } df = \frac{(w_1 + w_2)^2}{\dfrac{w_1^2}{n_1 - 1} + \dfrac{w_2^2}{n_2 - 1}}$$

where

$$w_1 = \frac{s_1^2}{n_1}$$

$$w_2 = \frac{s_2^2}{n_2}$$

The calculated Satterthwaite's approximated *df* is not likely to be an integer, and it needs to be rounded down. Use the approximated *df*, α level, and two-tailed versus one-tailed test to determine the critical *t* value that sets the boundary of the rejection zone. Alternatively, you may choose the smaller of df_1 and df_2 as the *df* for the independent-samples *t* test.

Step 4. Calculate the *t* statistic.

When $\sigma_1^2 \neq \sigma_2^2$, it is inappropriate to pool the variances, so they are treated separately.

$$s_{(\bar{X}_1 - \bar{X}_2)} = \sqrt{\frac{s_1^2}{n_1} + \frac{s_2^2}{n_2}}$$

$$t = \frac{(\bar{X}_1 - \bar{X}_2)}{s_{(\bar{X}_1 - \bar{X}_2)}}$$

Step 5. Make the correct conclusion.

If the calculated *t* value is within the rejection zone, we reject H_0. If the calculated *t* value is not within the rejection zone, we fail to reject H_0.

Different formulas also apply to effect size calculations depending on whether equal variances are assumed or not assumed.

When $\sigma_1^2 = \sigma_2^2$, effect size is calculated by Cohen's *d*.

$$\text{Cohen's } d = \frac{(\bar{X}_1 - \bar{X}_2)}{s_p}$$

where

$$s_p = \sqrt{\frac{SS_1 + SS_2}{df_1 + df_2}}$$

$$(1 - \alpha)100\% \text{ CI} = (\bar{X}_1 - \bar{X}_2) \pm t_{\alpha/2}\left(s_{(\bar{X}_1 - \bar{X}_2)}\right)$$

When $\sigma_1^2 \neq \sigma_2^2$, effect size is calculated by Glass's Δ.

$$\text{Glass's } \Delta = \frac{(\bar{X}_1 - \bar{X}_2)}{s_{\text{control}}} \quad \text{or} \quad \Delta = \frac{(\bar{X}_1 - \bar{X}_2)}{s_{\text{larger}}}$$

$$(1-\alpha)100\% \text{ CI} = (\bar{X}_1 - \bar{X}_2) \pm t_{\alpha/2}\left(\sqrt{\frac{s_1^2}{n_1} + \frac{s_2^2}{n_2}}\right)$$

KEY WORDS

Cohen's d: Cohen's d is the formula to calculate effect sizes for independent-samples t tests when equal variances are assumed.

Effect size: An effect size is defined as a standardized measure of a test statistic to determine whether the calculated value is practically meaningful.

Folded F test: The folded F test means that in calculating the F test, the larger variance is designated as the numerator and the smaller variance as the denominator; the calculated F value will always be larger than 1 to avoid the left-tailed F values.

Glass's delta (Δ): Glass's Δ is the formula to calculate effect sizes for independent-samples t tests when equal variances are not assumed.

Independent samples: Independent samples are samples selected from different populations where the values from one population are not related or linked to the values from another population. Independent samples contain different individuals in each sample.

p Value associated with a test statistic: The p value associated with a test statistic is defined as the probability of obtaining the magnitude of the calculated test statistic assuming that H_0 is true.

LEARNING ASSESSMENT

Multiple Choice: Circle the best answer to every question.

1. The folded F test, $F = s_1^2 / s_2^2 = $ Larger variance / Smaller variance, is a test for

   a. equality of means.

   b. equality of variances.

   c. equality of correlations.

   d. equality of probabilities.

2. When $\sigma_1^2 \neq \sigma_2^2$, the correct procedure to compare means is to

   a. pool the variances together.

   b. pool the degrees of freedom together.

   c. leave the variances the way they are when calculating the standard error of the mean difference.

d. pool the means together.

3. When $\sigma_1^2 = \sigma_2^2$, the correct formula for calculating the effect size for the independent-samples t test is

   a. Cohen's d.

   b. Satterthwaite's df.

   c. the folded F test.

   d. Glass's Δ.

4. When $\sigma_1^2 = \sigma_2^2$, the correct df for the independent-samples t test is

   a. $df = df_1 + df_2$.

   b. Satterthwaite's df.

   c. $df = n_1 + n_2 - 1$.

   d. $df = n_1 + n_2$.

5. When $\sigma_1^2 \neq \sigma_2^2$, the correct formula for calculating the effect size for the independent-samples t test is

   a. Cohen's d.

   b. Satterthwaite's df.

   c. the folded F test.

   d. Glass's Δ.

6. With $\alpha = .05$ and $df = 8$, the rejection zone for a right-tailed t test is $t > 1.860$. Assuming that all other factors are held constant, if the df increases to 20, the critical value of t that sets the boundary for the rejection zone would

   a. increase.

   b. decrease.

   c. remain the same.

   d. not be possible to determine based solely on the information provided here.

Free Response Questions

7. Assume that a statistics professor is interested in the effect of frequent quizzes on the retention of statistics knowledge. She teaches two large sections of statistics. In one of the sections, she assigns quizzes three times a week. In the other section, she does not assign quizzes. Everything else remains the same for both sections. Students can only sign up for one or the other section but not both. Statistics exam scores are normally distributed. At the end of the semester, both sections receive the same final exam, and the scores are summarized from a randomly selected sample from each section.

SECTION WITH FREQUENT QUIZZES	SECTION WITHOUT FREQUENT QUIZZES
$n = 15$	$n = 13$
$\bar{X} = 80$	$\bar{X} = 75$
$s = 8.2$	$s = 12.5$

   a. Conduct a proper statistical procedure to test whether giving frequent quizzes increases the retention of statistics knowledge, as demonstrated by the average final exam scores in these two sections, using $\alpha = .05$.

   b. Calculate and interpret the effect size of the difference in the average final exam scores between these two sections.

8. Educators want to evaluate the effect of access to laptop computers on students' grades. Assume that a group of 21 students is randomly selected from a school where every student is given a laptop and teachers assign homework and post notes online. At the end of the semester, the average GPA is 3.4, and SS for the GPA is 12.8. A group of 25 students is randomly selected from a similar school, but the school does not give them laptops; their average GPA is 3.0, and SS for the GPA is 19.44. Use $\alpha = .05$ to answer the following questions:

a. Conduct a proper statistical procedure to test whether having access to a computer has a significant effect on students' GPA.

b. Calculate and interpret the effect size of the difference in students' average GPA between these two schools.

9. An individual's social skills are learned through face-to-face interactions over time. Assume that researchers examine the effect of receiving a cell phone in early childhood on teenagers' social skills. Social skills scores are normally distributed. Higher scores mean better social skills. The researchers measure and compare two groups of teenagers. One group received cell phones before age 5, and the other group received cell phones after age 5. The results are reported below:

USING CELL PHONE BEFORE AGE 5	USING CELL PHONE AFTER AGE 5
$n = 10$	$n = 13$
$\bar{X} = 60.5$	$\bar{X} = 73.8$
$SS = 345.96$	$SS = 1,559.52$

a. Conduct a proper statistical procedure to test whether these two groups of teenagers have different social skills, using $\alpha = .10$.

b. Calculate and interpret the effect size of the difference in the teenagers' social skills between these two groups.

c. Construct a 90% CI of the difference in social skills between these two groups.

Dependent-Sample *t* Test

After reading and studying this chapter, you should be able to do the following:

- Differentiate between the independent-samples *t* test and the dependent-sample *t* test
- Conduct hypothesis tests on dependent-sample *t* tests
- Describe three approaches you can use to conduct a hypothesis test
- Describe what is meant by counterbalance as a step when conducting a dependent-sample *t* test and explain why it is important
- Describe the process of calculating the effect size for a dependent-sample *t* test

WHAT YOU KNOW AND WHAT IS NEW

In Chapter 8, you learned the four-step hypothesis test for the one-sample *t* tests. You learned the five-step hypothesis test for the independent-samples *t* tests in Chapter 9, where you conducted the test by adding a preliminary Step 1 to test the equality of variances in order to choose the correct set of formulas. Since the title of Chapter 10 is "Dependent-Sample *t* Test," the focus is still on *t* tests. Most of the steps in the hypothesis test remain the same as in the four-step hypothesis test, but you will learn a new formula to conduct the dependent-sample *t* test for Step 3.

The new formulas in Chapter 10 actually have roots in Chapter 3. Thus, you need to refresh your memory on the essential part of Chapter 3 about calculating the mean and standard deviation of a variable to master the content in Chapter 10. In Chapter 10, you are going to calculate the difference between a "before" measurement and an "after" measurement from a sample or between two samples with an explicit paired relationship. The focus of Chapter 10 is on the difference between the after-measurement and the before-measurement to show the treatment effect. Once the differences are calculated, you will need to calculate the mean, standard deviation, and standard error of the differences to conduct a hypothesis test for dependent samples.

INTRODUCING DEPENDENT-SAMPLE *t* TESTS

Let's distinguish **dependent samples** from independent samples. Independent samples contain different individuals in each sample, and there are no overlaps between the two samples. No one can be in both samples at the same time. Dependent samples refer to before- and after-measures of the same sample. In rare circumstances, they can refer to different samples with an explicit one-on-one paired relationship. **Dependent-sample *t* tests** are used to calculate the difference in the same sample before and after a treatment or the difference in a variable between two samples with an explicit one-on-one paired relationship.

The dependent-sample *t* test allows comparisons of two interval- or ratio-scale variables from the same sample, such as measuring the score on a science test before and after a group of students go through an experimental teaching method. Since the same group of students is measured repeatedly, this is the reason why dependent-sample *t* tests are also labeled as "within-subject" design or "repeated measures." In some rare cases, dependent-sample *t* tests can be applied to different samples only when variables from the two samples have an explicit one-on-one paired relationship, such as job satisfaction from twins or expressed voting preferences from husband and wife. When dependent-sample *t* tests involve two separate samples, they are also labeled as "paired-sample *t* tests" or "matched-sample *t* tests." The paired nature of the variables allows direct calculation of the difference between them; then, the standard deviation of the difference and standard error of the difference can also be derived.

Let's illustrate the distinction between independent samples and dependent samples by using a study to investigate the effect of a diet program. Researchers conduct an independent-samples *t* test by selecting eight volunteers and randomly assigning each participant to either a control group or an experimental group. The effect of the diet program is shown by comparing the average weight of the control group with the average weight of the experimental group, as shown in Figure 10.1.

FIGURE 10.1 Independent Samples With Different Individuals in the Control and Experimental Groups

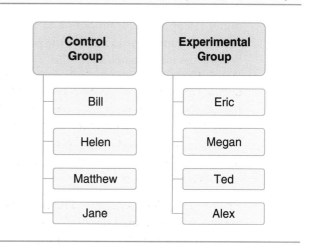

As illustrated in Figure 10.1, Bill, Helen, Matthew, and Jane are assigned to the control group, where they do not receive the diet program. Eric, Megan, Ted, and Alex are assigned to the experimental group, where the diet program is provided. The effectiveness of the diet program will be shown by the difference in the average weight of these two groups. While the difference in the average weight of these two groups may be due to the diet program, it may also be confounded by the preexisting conditions the participants brought along. It is possible that one group's average weight from the start happens to be greater than that of the other group. If so, the effect of the diet plan when tested using an independent-samples t test is likely to be confounded by the individual differences the participants bring along with them.

To avoid the problems associated with confounding effects, the researchers decide to conduct a dependent-sample t test. This is done by randomly selecting four volunteers to participate in the diet program. The four participants' weights are measured before the program, and again after the program. The effect of the diet program is shown by comparing the before- and after-weights of the same people, as shown in Figure 10.2.

Both independent samples and dependent samples are appropriate to conduct scientific research. They simply involve different types of research designs. The research design determines the appropriate procedure to conduct the hypothesis test. The advantage of using dependent samples is to remove the potentially confounding effect of individual differences because the measurements are taken from the same individuals. Taking out the confounding effect of individual differences increases the power of the test. The higher power of the test makes it more likely to detect a significant effect when an effect actually exists. However, it is likely that fatigue, memory, and/or practice effects may influence the results when participants are measured repeatedly. Research participants might not always be available to be measured repeatedly. Attrition in the course of conducting a study using repeated measures can also cause statistical and other problems.

For example, personality questionnaires have been a part of employment selection for quite some time. However, it is known that job applicants can guess the intent of asking particular questions and figure out what are the "best" answers. Giving the best answers instead of honest answers is labeled as "faking," which job applicants resort to, misrepresenting themselves in order to increase the probability of getting hired. Industrial and organizational psychologists want to compare different formats of personality questionnaires on their effectiveness in controlling faking. They design a dependent-sample t test where research participants go through both formats. Without going into the details of these different formats, they are simply labeled as Formats A and B. Thus, the options are either to have the participants complete both formats in one setting or to schedule two sessions and have them complete only one format in each session. Each format of the personality questionnaire requires about 1 hour to complete. There are

FIGURE 10.2 Dependent Samples With the Same Individuals Measured Twice, Before and After the Program

obvious trade-offs in both options. The advantages of one option are the disadvantages of the other. It is unwise to keep research participants for 2 hours to complete both formats in one setting due to the limited attention spans and possible fatigue factor. Participants are not likely to pay close attention to details when they are tired. Researchers might be able to avoid overtaxing participants' attention spans by only giving them one format of the personality questionnaire in one setting and making them come back for the second session 2 weeks later to complete the other format. However, it is always possible that some participants who completed the first session would not come back for the second session. Such attrition would make participants' data from only one session useless in the dependent-sample t test.

 Pop Quiz

1. Which one of the following research studies calls for a dependent-sample t test?

   a. Comparing the psychological stress of married men versus single men

   b. Comparing the happiness of pet owners versus non-pet owners

   c. Comparing cholesterol levels for the same group of patients before and after they take a new drug for 6 months

   d. Comparing the financial savviness of home owners versus renters

Answer: c

CALCULATIONS AND THE HYPOTHESIS-TESTING PROCESS IN DEPENDENT-SAMPLE t TESTS

As mentioned in the "What You Know" section, you will need to refresh your skill in calculating the mean and standard deviation of a variable. That skill only needs slight modification because you need to calculate the mean and standard deviation of the differences between two variables in this chapter. I will make that modification explicit so the connection between what you know and what is new is clear.

MEAN, STANDARD DEVIATION, AND STANDARD ERROR OF THE DIFFERENCES

The explicit one-on-one paired relationship of two measures either from the same sample or from two matched samples allows the direct calculation of the difference scores, $D = X_{after} - X_{before}$, where X_{after} stands for the measurement after the treatment and X_{before} stands for the measurement before the treatment. It is logical to use the after-measurement minus the before-measurement to show the treatment effect. When you add up every difference divided by the sample size, you get the mean difference. This formula is the same as calculating the sample mean:

$$\bar{X} = \frac{\sum X}{n}$$

Actually, when you treat the difference scores, D, as a variable X, the mean, sum of squares (SS), standard deviation, and standard error formulas are exactly the same as the formulas discussed in Chapter 3.

$$\text{Mean difference} = \bar{D} = \frac{\sum D}{n}$$

$$\text{Sum of squares of the differences} = SS_{D} = \sum(D - \bar{D})^2$$

$$\text{Standard deviation of the differences} = s_{D} = \sqrt{\frac{SS_{D}}{df}} = \sqrt{\frac{\sum(D - \bar{D})^2}{(n-1)}}$$

$$\text{Standard error of the differences} = s_{e} = \frac{s_{D}}{\sqrt{n}}$$

Let's use an example to go through these formulas.

EXAMPLE 10.1

Researchers conduct a study to investigate the effect of a diet program. Table 10.1a shows the weights of the four participants—Chris, Robin, Ken, and Adam—before the diet program and after the diet program. Calculate the mean, standard deviation, and standard error of the differences.

The calculation for mean, standard deviation, and standard error of the differences is shown step-by-step in Table 10.1b, where the difference score $D = X_{after} - X_{before}$.

TABLE 10.1a Four Participants' Weights Before and After a Diet Program

PARTICIPANT	BEFORE	AFTER
Chris	140	131
Robin	187	190
Ken	179	162
Adam	210	185

TABLE 10.1b Calculation Process for Mean, Standard Deviation, and Standard Error of the Differences for the Diet Program Participants

PARTICIPANT	BEFORE	AFTER	D	$(D - \bar{D})$	$(D - \bar{D})^2$
Chris	140	131	−9	−9 − (−12) = 3	9
Robin	187	190	3	3 − (−12) = 15	225
Ken	179	162	−17	−17 − (−12) = −5	25
Adam	210	185	−25	−25 − (−12) = −13	169
			−48		**428**

$$\bar{D} = \frac{\sum D}{n} = \frac{-48}{4} = -12$$

$$SS_D = \sum (D - \bar{D})^2 = 9 + 225 + 25 + 169 = 428$$

$$s_D = \sqrt{\frac{\sum (D - \bar{D})^2}{(n-1)}} = \sqrt{\frac{428}{3}} = \sqrt{142.67} = 11.94$$

$$s_e = s_D / \sqrt{n} = 11.94 / \sqrt{4} = 5.97$$

(Continued)

(Continued)

At this point, it should be clear that the same formulas used to calculate the mean, standard deviation, and standard error of a variable apply to the calculation of the mean, standard deviation, and standard error of the differences in a dependent-sample t test.

HYPOTHESIS TESTING FOR DEPENDENT-SAMPLE t TESTS

The purpose of a hypothesis test in dependent samples is to investigate whether there is a significant difference between the measures before and after the treatment. The focus of the test is the differences. The procedure for conducting a hypothesis test for dependent samples is similar to the four-step hypothesis-testing process, because there is only one set of differences. Another way to think about this is that because the same individuals are tested twice or closely matched samples are used in dependent samples, equal variances are assumed automatically.

The four-step hypothesis test for dependent-sample t tests:

Step 1. Explicitly state the pair of hypotheses.

There are two-tailed tests, right-tailed tests, and left-tailed tests for dependent-sample t tests. Based on the problem statement, you need to judge whether a directional hypothesis test or a nondirectional hypothesis test is appropriate. Then choose one of the following three options accordingly.

Two-tailed test:	$H_0: \mu_D = 0$
	$H_1: \mu_D \neq 0$
Right-tailed test:	$H_0: \mu_D = 0$
	$H_1: \mu_D > 0$
Left-tailed test:	$H_0: \mu_D = 0$
	$H_1: \mu_D < 0$

Step 2. Identify the rejection zone.

You need three pieces of information to identify the critical values that set the boundaries of the rejection zone: whether it is a one-tailed test or a two-tailed test, the *df*, and the α level as first introduced in Chapter 8.

Rejection zone for a two-tailed test: $|t| > t_{\alpha/2}$, with $df = n - 1$

Rejection zone for a right-tailed test: $t > t_\alpha$, with $df = n - 1$

Rejection zone for a left-tailed test: $t < -t_\alpha$, with $df = n - 1$

Step 3. Calculate the test statistic.

$$\text{The general principle of a } t \text{ test} = \frac{(\text{Sample statistic} - \text{Population parameter})}{\text{Estimated standard error of the statistic}}$$

In dependent samples,

$$t = \frac{\bar{D} - \mu_D}{s_e}$$

Because $\mu_D = 0$ under the null hypothesis, the t formula can be further simplified to

$$t = \frac{\bar{D}}{s_e} = \frac{\bar{D}}{\dfrac{s_D}{\sqrt{n}}}$$

Step 4. Make the correct conclusion.

If the calculated t from Step 3 is within the rejection zone, we reject H_0. If the calculated t from Step 3 is not within the rejection zone, we fail to reject H_0. Now, it is time to apply the four-step hypothesis-testing procedure of dependent-sample t tests to conduct a test to find out if the diet program really has an effect on participants' weights.

EXAMPLE 10.2

In the previous example, you used the weight measures in Table 10.1a, where the mean difference using after-measures minus before-measures is $\bar{D} = -12$ pounds, and $SS_D = 428$ pounds. You also obtained $s_D = 11.94$ and $s_e = 5.97$. However, these calculated numbers could not provide useful information without completing a hypothesis test. Now, you are able to do just that. Conduct a hypothesis test at $\alpha = .10$ to investigate the effect of the diet program.

(Continued)

(Continued)

Step 1. Explicitly state the pair of hypotheses.

There is no key word to indicate a direction in the problem statement, so a two-tailed hypothesis test is appropriate.

$$H_0: \mu_D = 0$$

$$H_1: \mu_D \neq 0$$

Step 2. Identify the rejection zone.

Based on the problem statement, we use a two-tailed test, $\alpha = .10$, and $df = n - 1 = 4 - 1 = 3$. The critical value in the t Table is 2.353, so the rejection zone for a two-tailed test is $|t| > 2.353$.

Step 3. Calculate the test statistic.

$$t = \frac{\bar{D}}{s_e} = \frac{\bar{D}}{\frac{s_D}{\sqrt{n}}} = \frac{-12}{\frac{11.94}{\sqrt{4}}} = -2.01$$

Step 4. Make the correct conclusion.

The calculated $t = -2.01$ is not within the rejection zone. We thus fail to reject H_0. The evidence is not strong enough to support the claim that the diet program has an effect on weight.

Whenever the problem statements ask whether a program has a significant effect without specifying a direction, such as a positive effect or a negative effect, you have to use a nondirectional hypothesis test (i.e., a two-tailed test). When the problem statements contain key words for a specific direction—either a positive effect, such as improvement, increasing scores, or better performance, or a negative effect, such as a detrimental effect, decreasing scores, or worse performance—you have to use a directional hypothesis test (i.e., a right-tailed test or a left-tailed test). You have to understand exactly what the problem is asking to be able to conduct the correct hypothesis test. Also, you need to know when it is appropriate to use independent-samples t tests and when it is appropriate to use dependent-sample t tests. Let's practice the four-step hypothesis tests by using more examples.

EXAMPLE 10.3

Researchers have long suspected that texting has a detrimental effect on driving behavior. To avoid the unnecessary high risk of actually driving on the roads, driving behavior is measured via a driving simulator. Mistakes such as failing to stay within the lane, driving at least 10 miles above or below the speed limit, and failing to use the turn signal are automatically recorded by the simulator. To avoid individual differences in driving behavior, participants are tested twice: once under the "texting while driving" condition and once under the "driving with-out texting" condition. There are nine participants in the study. Their driving mistakes are reported in Table 10.2a. Do the data support the claim that texting has a detrimental effect on driving behavior, using $\alpha = .05$?

TABLE 10.2a Driving Mistakes When Driving While Texting and Driving Without Texting

PARTICIPANT	TEXTING	NO TEXTING
A	35	23
B	46	39
C	23	12
D	33	10
E	29	14
F	41	29
G	31	17
H	22	13
I	37	23

After you finish reading the problem, you have to decide what kind of t test is appropriate to solve this problem. Table 10.2a provides measures from the same group of people under two different conditions, so you know that the dependent-sample t test is the correct test.

The four-step hypothesis test for dependent sample is appropriate for this question.

Step 1. The problem statement asks "if texting has a detrimental effect on driving." *Detrimental* is a key word to indicate a directional hypothesis. If texting is detrimental to driving, the number of mistakes will be higher under the texting condition. Logically, the effect of texting is calculated by the number of driving mistakes under the texting condition minus the number of driving mistakes under the no-texting condition. The "detrimental" effect is likely to make the difference positive because drivers are likely to make more mistakes when they drive while texting, so a right-tailed test is the correct approach.

Difference = Mistakes under texting − Mistakes under no texting

(Continued)

(Continued)

$$H_0: \mu_D = 0$$

$$H_1: \mu_D > 0$$

Step 2. Identify the rejection zone.

Based on the problem statement, you use a right-tailed test, $\alpha = .05$, and $df = n - 1 = 9 - 1 = 8$. The critical value in the t Table is 1.86, so the rejection zone for the right-tailed test is $t > 1.86$.

Step 3. Calculate the test statistic.

The calculation process for the mean, standard deviation, and standard error of the differences is shown step-by-step in Table 10.2b, where D = Mistakes under texting – Mistakes under no texting.

TABLE 10.2b   Calculation for the Mean, Standard Deviation, and Standard Error of the Differences for the Driving Mistakes

PARTICIPANT	TEXTING	NO TEXTING	D	$(D - \bar{D})$	$(D - \bar{D})^2$
A	35	23	12	$(12 - 13) = -1$	1
B	46	39	7	$(7 - 13) = -6$	36
C	23	12	11	$(11 - 13) = -2$	4
D	33	10	23	$(23 - 13) = 10$	100
E	29	14	15	$(15 - 13) = 2$	4
F	41	29	12	$(12 - 13) = -1$	1
G	31	17	14	$(14 - 13) = 1$	1
H	22	13	9	$(9 - 13) = -4$	16
I	37	23	14	$(14 - 13) = 1$	1
			117		164

$$\bar{D} = \frac{\sum D}{n} = \frac{117}{9} = 13$$

$$SS_D = \sum(D - \bar{D})^2 = 1 + 36 + 4 + 100 + 4 + 1 + 1 + 16 + 1 = 164$$

$$s_D = \sqrt{\frac{\sum(D - \bar{D})^2}{(n-1)}} = \sqrt{\frac{164}{8}} = \sqrt{20.5} = 4.53$$

$$s_e = \frac{s_D}{\sqrt{n}} = \frac{4.53}{\sqrt{9}} = 1.51$$

$$t = \frac{\bar{D}}{s_e} = \frac{\bar{D}}{\frac{s_D}{\sqrt{n}}} = \frac{13}{\frac{4.53}{\sqrt{9}}} = 8.61$$

Step 4. Make the correct conclusion.

The calculated $t = 8.61$ is within the rejection zone. We reject H_0. The evidence is very strong in supporting the claim that texting has a detrimental effect on driving behavior.

As mentioned previously, the result of a dependent-sample t test is not confounded by individual differences, because the same individuals are used in both before- and after-measures. However, fatigue, learning, memory, practice, or other time-related factors are likely to influence the results when participants are measured repeatedly. One thing that might improve the design of a study using dependent samples is to counterbalance the order of presentations. Counterbalance is a cautionary step in conducting repeated measures of the same sample to make sure that the order of presentation of conditions is balanced out. In a research study where participants are exposed to both Conditions A and B, half of the research participants receive Condition A first and the other half receive Condition B first. In this case, a good way to counterbalance is to randomly assign half of the participants to the "driving while texting" condition first and the other half to the "driving without texting" first. The counterbalancing makes sure that any improvements in the "driving without texting" condition cannot be attributed to learning or practice factors.

CONFIDENCE INTERVAL OF THE DIFFERENCES

A confidence interval (CI) provides an interval of values calculated from sample statistics to estimate the values of a population parameter or make inferences about the population parameter. CIs provide additional information on which to base the researcher's conclusions. The calculated CIs can convey the quality of the estimation or statistical inference. The CI of the differences for dependent samples applies the same principle of calculating a CI from previous chapters: CI = point estimate ± margin of error.

When putting $(1 - \alpha)100\%$ CI together, the higher the confidence level, the wider is the CI. In conducting dependent-sample t tests, the procedure is modified to

$$(1 - \alpha)100\% \, CI = \bar{D} \pm t_{\alpha/2} s_e$$

Let's use a familiar example to practice the CI formula for the dependent-sample t test. It also allows us to compare and contrast the result from a hypothesis test with the result from a CI using the same numbers.

EXAMPLE 10.4

Calculate a 95% CI on the difference in driving mistakes made by the same group of research participants under different driving conditions, as reported in Table 10.2a, with $n = 9$, $\bar{D} = 13$, and $SS_D = 164$. Also, construct a 90% CI on the difference in driving mistakes, and comment on the width of the CI under different confidence levels.

According to the step-by-step process reported in Table 10.2a, we obtain the following numbers.

$$\bar{D} = 13$$

$$s_D = \sqrt{\frac{SS_D}{df}} = \sqrt{\frac{164}{8}} = 4.53$$

$$s_e = \frac{s_D}{\sqrt{n}} = \frac{4.53}{\sqrt{9}} = 1.51$$

$(1 - \alpha)100\% = 95\%$, $\alpha = .05$, and $df = n - 1 = 9 - 1 = 8$;
the two-tailed critical value of $t_{\alpha/2} = 2.306$.

$$95\% \text{ CI of the differences} = \bar{D} \pm t_{\alpha/2}s_e = 13 \pm 2.306(1.51) = 13 \pm 3.48 = [9.52, 16.48]$$

The difference is significant because zero is not included in the 95% CI.

Construct a 90% CI for the difference in driving mistakes using the same sample statistics.

$(1 - \alpha)100\% = 90\%$, $\alpha = .10$, and $df = n - 1 = 9 - 1 = 8$;
the two-tailed critical value of $t_{\alpha/2} = 1.86$.

$$90\% \text{ CI of the differences} = \bar{D} \pm t_{\alpha/2}s_e = 13 \pm 1.86(1.51) = 13 \pm 2.81 = [10.19, 15.81]$$

The 95% CI is wider than the 90% CI and contains a bigger margin of error.

It is noteworthy to point out that a one-tailed hypothesis test with $\alpha = .05$ generates the same result as a 90% CI. Because the CI starts with the point estimate and adds the margin of error to reach the upper limit of the interval and subtracts the margin of error to reach the lower limit of the interval, the CI always generates a two-tailed situation. A one-tailed test with $\alpha = .05$ has the same critical value as a two-tailed test with $\alpha = .10$. The conclusion from the right-tailed test with $\alpha = .05$ is to reject H_0 and support the claim that texting has a detrimental effect on driving. The 90% CI says that we are 90% confident that the differences between driving while texting and driving without texting are between 10.19 and 15.81. Zero is not included in the 90% CI, so the difference between these two conditions is significant. If zero is included in the CI, the difference between the two conditions is not significant.

EFFECT SIZE FOR THE DEPENDENT-SAMPLE t TEST

An effect size is a standardized measure of the strength of a test statistic. In independent-samples t tests, effect sizes are calculated as the standardized differences between two sample means in units of standard deviation. When equal variances are assumed, $\sigma_1^2 = \sigma_2^2$, Cohen's d is calculated as the sample mean difference divided by the pooled sample standard deviation, as shown in Chapter 9.

$$\text{Cohen's } d = \frac{\text{Mean difference}}{\text{Estimated standard deviation of the differences}}$$

The same principle of the effect size still applies in Chapter 10, but it needs to be modified slightly to calculate the effect size for a dependent-sample t test:

$$\text{Cohen's } d = \frac{\bar{D}}{s_D}$$

The effect size for a dependent-sample t test expresses the standardized difference in units of standard deviation of the differences. Let's look at an example for calculating effect size in a dependent-sample t test.

EXAMPLE 10.5

Using the data in Table 10.2a from Example 10.3, calculate the effect size for the difference in driving mistakes under a texting condition versus under a no-texting condition. The important values from Example 10.3 are $n = 9$, $\bar{D} = 13$, and $SS_D = 164$.

(Continued)

(Continued)

We obtained the following information from Table 10.2b.

$$\bar{D} = \frac{\Sigma D}{n} = \frac{117}{9} = 13$$

$$SS_D = \Sigma(D - \bar{D})^2 = 164$$

$$s_D = \sqrt{\frac{\Sigma(D - \bar{D})^2}{(n-1)}} = \sqrt{\frac{164}{8}} = \sqrt{20.5} = 4.53$$

$$\text{Cohen's } d = \frac{\bar{D}}{s_D} = \frac{13}{4.53} = 2.87$$

The effect size for the difference in driving mistakes between driving under texting versus driving under no texting is 2.87. The effect size is very large.

We have covered the four-step hypothesis-testing procedure, CIs, and effect sizes for dependent-sample t tests. Although the process starts with two variables, the explicit pairing relationship of these variables allows direct calculation of the differences between these two variables. The focus of the dependent-sample t test is on the differences. Then you apply the same formulas you learned in Chapter 3 to calculate the mean difference, the standard deviation of the differences, and the standard error of the differences. The reason the four-step hypothesis-testing procedure is applicable is because a dependent-sample t test deals with one set of the difference scores so you don't have to worry about equal variances assumed or not. The same principle that you learned in Chapters 8 and 9—$(1 - \alpha)100\%$ CI = point estimate ± margin of error—is still applicable in calculating the CI for the dependent-sample t tests; the procedure is expressed as $(1-\alpha)100\%\,\text{CI} = \bar{D} \pm t_{\alpha/2} s_e$. The same principle that you learned in Chapter 9 on the effect size as a standardized measure of sample mean difference is still applicable in the effect size for the dependent-sample t tests; the procedure is expressed as

$$\text{Cohen's } d = \frac{\bar{D}}{s_D}$$

1. The alternative hypothesis for a right-tailed test of a dependent-sample t test is expressed as

   a. $\mu_1 - \mu_2 = 0$.

   b. $\mu_D = 0$.

   c. $\mu_1 - \mu_2 > 0$.

   d. $\mu_D > 0$.

2. The correct formula to calculate the effect size for dependent-sample t tests is

   a. Cohen's $d = \dfrac{\bar{D}}{s_D}$.

   b. Cohen's $d = \dfrac{(\bar{X}_1 - \bar{X}_2)}{s_p}$.

   c. Glass's $\Delta = \dfrac{(\bar{X}_1 - \bar{X}_2)}{s_{control}}$.

   d. Glass's $\Delta = \dfrac{(\bar{X}_1 - \bar{X}_2)}{s_{larger}}$.

Answers: 1. d, 2. a

USING SPSS TO RUN DEPENDENT-SAMPLE t TESTS

Let's proceed with one example using SPSS to run a dependent-sample t test. We will use the personal measures.sav file, which is an SPSS data set containing personal measures from students. The purpose is to test whether there are significant differences between the measures of the right foot and left foot from the same individuals. Assume that the foot measures are normally distributed. It is obvious that right- and left-foot measures have an explicitly one-on-one pairing relationship, so a dependent-sample t test is appropriate.

Here is how to use SPSS to conduct a dependent-sample t test, as shown in Figure 10.3.

Click the **Analyze** tab in the drop-down menu.

Click **Compare Means**.

Then, click **Paired-Samples T Test**.

A pop-up window (Figure 10.4) appears to ask you to identify the "**Paired Variables**." Select **lftfoot** (i.e., the measures of the left foot) and **rightfoot** (i.e., the measures of the right foot), and put them into the **Paired Variables** box. The selection can be done by clicking on the variables and moving them to the box, one at a time, or you can click on **lftfoot** and hold down the CRTL key and click on **rightfoot** and move both variables to the box at the same time; then hit **OK**.

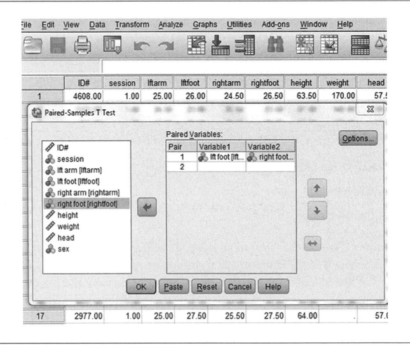

FIGURE 10.4   An SPSS Pop-Up Window for Identifying the Paired Variables

SPSS runs through the programs and generates the results as shown in Tables 10.3 and 10.4.

Table 10.3 shows the original output generated by SPSS. It shows the descriptive statistics including the sample mean in each group; sample size, n; sample standard deviation; and standard error of the mean. Please note the correct symbol for the sample size is a lowercase n instead of the uppercase N as shown in the SPSS output.

TABLE 10.3 Descriptive Statistics for the Paired-Samples t Test

Paired Samples Statistics

		Mean	N	Std. Deviation	Std. Error Mean
Pair 1	lft foot	24.8333	69	2.41574	.29082
	right foot	24.8783	69	2.23422	.26897

Table 10.4 shows the results of the paired-sample t test, including the mean difference $(\bar{D})$, standard deviation of the differences (s_D), standard error of the differences (s_e), 95% CI of the difference, calculated t value, df of the t test, and p value associated with a two-tailed test. SPSS refers to the p values as the significance levels (shortened to **Sig**), as shown in the last column of Table 10.4.

TABLE 10.4 Paired-Samples t-Test Results

Paired Samples Test

	Paired Differences							
	Mean	Std. Deviation	Std. Error Mean	95% Confidence Interval of the Difference		T	df	Sig. (2-tailed)
				Lower	Upper			
Pair 1 lft foot - right foot	−.04493	.84775	.10206	−.24858	.15873	−.440	68	.661

You may verify the result by plugging the numbers into the dependent-samples t-test formula,

$$t = \frac{\bar{D}}{s_e} = \frac{\bar{D}}{\dfrac{s_D}{\sqrt{n}}} = \frac{-0.04493}{\dfrac{0.84775}{\sqrt{69}}} = -0.440$$

The closest critical value of t for $\alpha = .05$ and $df = 68$ is $t = 2$. The rejection zone is $|t| > 2$. The calculated $t = -.440$ is not in the rejection zone. We fail to reject H_0.

As discussed in Chapter 9, the p value associated with a test statistic can be used as a criterion for a hypothesis test. The decision rules are as follows:

When $p < \alpha$, reject H_0.

When $p \geq \alpha$, fail to reject H_0.

The p value for the paired-samples t test is calculated as $p = .661$. When the p value is larger than .05, we fail to reject H_0. In this case, $.661 > .05$, so we fail to reject H_0. The evidence is not strong enough to support the claim that there are significant differences between left-foot and right-foot measures.

The 95% CI is $[-0.24858, 0.15873]$. The differences are not significant because zero is included in the 95% CI of the differences.

All three approaches (i.e., rejection zone, p value, and 95% CI) indicate the same result, that the evidence is not strong enough to support the claim that there are significant differences between the left-foot and right-foot measures of the same individuals.

EXERCISE PROBLEMS

In the beginning of this chapter, we emphasized the distinctions between independent samples and dependent samples. The advantage of using dependent samples is to avoid or eliminate the potential confounding effects of individual differences. Eliminating individual differences increases the statistical power of the hypothesis test. Increasing statistical power makes it more likely to detect an effect when the effect actually exists. Let's demonstrate what this means mathematically by using identical hypothetical numbers in an independent-samples t test in Exercise 1 and a dependent-sample t test in Exercise 2.

TABLE 10.5a   Cholesterol Levels for the Control Group and Experimental Group

CONTROL GROUP	EXPERIMENTAL GROUP
240	210
198	183
267	240
211	203

1. Pharmaceutical Company A designed a study to test a new drug's effect in lowering cholesterol. Researchers selected eight volunteers and randomly assigned them to either the control group or the experimental group. The control group received a placebo, and the experimental group received the new drug for 2 months. The participants' cholesterol levels were measured at the end of the 2 months; they are reported in Table 10.5a. The cholesterol levels were normally distributed.

    a. Is the new drug effective in lowering cholesterol at $\alpha = .05$?

    b. What is the effect size for the difference in cholesterol levels between the control group and the experimental group?

c. What is the 90% CI for the difference in cholesterol levels between the control group and the experimental group?

2. Pharmaceutical Company B designed a study to test a new drug's effect in lowering cholesterol. Researchers randomly selected four volunteers and measured their cholesterol before they started taking the new drug and again measured their cholesterol after they had taken the new drug for 2 months. The participants' cholesterol levels are reported in Table 10.6a. Assume that the cholesterol levels were normally distributed.

TABLE 10.6a Cholesterol Levels of Participants Before and After Taking the New Drug

BEFORE	AFTER
240	210
198	183
267	240
211	203

a. Is the new drug effective in lowering cholesterol at $\alpha = .05$?

b. What is the effect size for the difference in cholesterol levels before and after taking the new drug?

c. What is the 90% CI for the difference in cholesterol levels before and after taking the new drug?

Solutions

1.a. Eight participants are randomly assigned to either the control group or the experimental group so that different individuals are assigned to different groups. These two groups are independent samples. Here is the five-step procedure to conduct an independent-samples t test.

Step 1. Test the equality of variances.

Substep 1. State the pair of hypotheses regarding variances.

$$H_0: \sigma_1^2 = \sigma_2^2$$

$$H_1: \sigma_1^2 \neq \sigma_2^2$$

Substep 2. Identify the rejection zone.

Both groups have equal df, $df_1 = n_1 - 1 = 4 - 1 = 3$ and $df_2 = 4 - 1 = 3$. The critical value of the right-tailed $F_{(df_1, df_2)} = F_{(3,3)} = 9.03$. The rejection zone of the F test is $F > 9.03$.

Substep 3. Calculate the statistic.

We need to use the mean and standard deviation formulas in Chapter 3 to calculate means and standard deviations for the control and the experimental groups: $\bar{X}_C$ and $\bar{X}_E$, s_C and s_E, respectively, from Table 10.5a. Step-by-step calculations are shown in Table 10.5b. Columns such as $(X_C - \bar{X}_C)$, $(X_C - \bar{X}_C)^2$, $(X_E - \bar{X}_E)$, and $(X_E - \bar{X}_E)^2$ are created to calculate s_C and s_E.

TABLE 10.5b Step-by-Step Calculation for Cholesterol Levels Between the Control Group and the Experimental Group

CONTROL GROUP, X_C	EXPERIMENTAL GROUP, X_E	$(X_C - \bar{X}_C)$	$(X_C - \bar{X}_C)^2$	$(X_E - \bar{X}_E)$	$(X_E - \bar{X}_E)^2$
240	210	11	121	1	1
198	183	−31	961	−26	676
267	240	38	1,444	31	961
211	203	−18	324	−6	36
$\bar{X}_C = 229$	$\bar{X}_E = 209$		2,850		1,674

$$\bar{X}_C = \frac{\Sigma X_C}{n_C} = \frac{(240 + 198 + 267 + 211)}{4} = 229$$

$$\bar{X}_E = \frac{\Sigma X_E}{n_E} = \frac{(210 + 183 + 240 + 203)}{4} = 209$$

$$s_C^2 = \frac{SS_C}{df_C} = \frac{2850}{3} = 950$$

$$s_E^2 = \frac{SS_E}{df_E} = \frac{1674}{3} = 558$$

The control group has the larger variance, so it is labeled as Group 1.

The experimental group has the smaller variance, so it is labeled as Group 2.

$$F = \frac{s_1^2}{s_2^2} = \frac{950}{558} = 1.70$$

Substep 4. Make the correct conclusion.

The calculated $F = 1.70$ is not within the rejection zone $F > 9.03$. Therefore, we fail to reject H_0. The evidence is not strong enough to claim that the two variances are unequal. Therefore, the correct independent-samples t-test approach is to assume equal variances.

Step 2. State the pair of hypotheses regarding group means.

The problem statement asks, "Is the drug effective in lowering cholesterol at $\alpha = .05$?" *Lowering* is a key word for direction. Therefore, a one-tailed test is appropriate. It is important to get the direction in the H_1 correct. The control group has the larger s, so the control group is labeled as Group 1. If the new drug is effective in lowering cholesterol, the mean for the control group, μ_1, will be higher than the mean for the experimental group, μ_2. It is a right-tailed test for $\mu_1 > \mu_2$.

$H_0: \mu_1 = \mu_2$

$H_1: \mu_1 > \mu_2$

Step 3. Identify the rejection zone for the test.

According to the t Table, when $df = df_1 + df_2 = n_1 + n_2 - 2 = 6$, $\alpha = .05$; it is a right-tailed test, and the critical t value that sets the boundary of the rejection zone is 1.943. The rejection zone is $t > 1.943$.

Step 4. Calculate the t statistic.

When $\sigma_1^2 = \sigma_2^2$, the variances need to be pooled together.

$$SS_1 = 2850$$

$$SS_2 = 1674$$

$$s_p^2 = \frac{SS_1 + SS_2}{df_1 + df_2} = \frac{2850 + 1674}{3 + 3} = 754$$

$$s_{(\bar{X}_1 - \bar{X}_2)} = \sqrt{\frac{s_p^2}{n_1} + \frac{s_p^2}{n_2}} = \sqrt{\frac{754}{4} + \frac{754}{4}} = \sqrt{188.5 + 188.5} = \sqrt{377} = 19.42$$

$$t = \frac{(\bar{X}_1 - \bar{X}_2)}{s_{(\bar{X}_1 - \bar{X}_2)}} = \frac{(229 - 209)}{19.42} = \frac{20}{19.42} = 1.03$$

Step 5. Make the correct conclusion.

The calculated $t = 1.03$ is not within the rejection zone. Therefore, we fail to reject H_0. The evidence is not strong enough to support the claim that the new drug is effective in lowering cholesterol.

1.b. When equal variances are assumed, $\sigma_1^2 = \sigma_2^2$, the effect size is calculated as

$$\text{Cohen's } d = \frac{(\bar{X}_1 - \bar{X}_2)}{s_p}$$

where

$$s_p = \sqrt{\frac{SS_1 + SS_2}{df_1 + df_2}} = \sqrt{754} = 27.46$$

$$\text{Cohen's } d = \frac{(\bar{X}_1 - \bar{X}_2)}{s_p} = \frac{229 - 209}{27.46} = \frac{20}{27.46} = 0.73$$

The effect size is 0.73, which is almost large according to Cohen's interpretation.

1.c. The 90% CI for the difference between the control and experimental groups is calculated as point estimate ± margin of error $= (\bar{X}_1 - \bar{X}_2) \pm t_{\alpha/2} s_{(\bar{X}_1 - \bar{X}_2)}$.

$$90\% \text{ CI} = (229 - 209) \pm 1.943(19.42) = 20 \pm 37.73 = [-17.73, 57.73]$$

Because the 90% CI for the mean difference includes zero, the evidence is not sufficient enough to claim that the difference between the control group and the experimental group is significant.

2.a.

Step 1. The problem statement asks "if the new drug is effective in lowering cholesterol." *Lowering* is a key word to indicate a directional hypothesis. When we calculate the difference as the cholesterol level after taking the new drug minus the cholesterol level before taking the new drug, the differences are likely to be negative, so a left-tailed test is the correct approach.

$$\text{Difference} = X_{\text{after}} - X_{\text{before}}$$

$$H_0: \mu_D = 0$$

$$H_1: \mu_D < 0$$

Step 2. Identify a criterion for the hypothesis test.

Based on the problem statement, we use a left-tailed test, $\alpha = .05$, and $df = n - 1 = 4 - 1 = 3$. The critical value in the t Table is 2.353, so the rejection zone for the left-tailed test is $t < -2.353$.

Step 3. Calculate the test statistic.

The calculation process for the mean, standard deviation, and standard error of the differences is shown step-by-step in Table 10.6b, where $D = X_{after} - X_{before}$.

TABLE 10.6b   Step-by-Step Calculation for the Cholesterol Level of Participants Before and After Taking the New Drug

BEFORE	AFTER	D	$(D - \bar{D})$	$(D - \bar{D})^2$
240	210	−30	−10	100
198	183	−15	5	25
267	240	−27	−7	49
211	203	−8	12	144
		−80		318

$$\bar{D} = \frac{\Sigma D}{n} = \frac{-80}{4} = -20$$

$$SS_D = \Sigma(D - \bar{D})^2 = 100 + 25 + 49 + 144 = 318$$

$$s_D = \sqrt{\frac{\Sigma(D - \bar{D})^2}{(n-1)}} = \sqrt{\frac{318}{3}} = \sqrt{106} = 10.30$$

$$s_e = \frac{s_D}{\sqrt{n}} = \frac{10.30}{\sqrt{4}} = 5.15$$

$$t = \frac{\bar{D}}{s_e} = \frac{\bar{D}}{\frac{s_D}{\sqrt{n}}} = \frac{-20}{\frac{10.30}{\sqrt{4}}} = -3.88$$

Step 4. Make the correct conclusion.

The calculated $t = -3.88$ is within the rejection zone. We reject H_0. The evidence is strong enough to support the claim that the new drug is effective in lowering cholesterol levels.

2.b.   The effect size for the dependent-sample t test is calculated as

$$\text{Cohen's } d = \frac{\text{Mean difference}}{\text{Standard deviation of the differences}} = \frac{\bar{D}}{s_D}$$

$$\text{Cohen's } d = \frac{\bar{D}}{s_D} = \frac{-20}{10.30} = -1.94$$

The effect size is −1.94, which is large according to Cohen's interpretation. The new drug's cholesterol-lowering effect is practically meaningful.

2.c.   The 90% CI for the mean difference is calculated as point estimate ± margin of error $= \bar{D} \pm t_{a/2} s_e$.

$$90\% \text{ CI} = (-20) \pm 2.353(5.15) = -20 \pm 12.12 = [-32.12, -7.88]$$

Because the 90% CI does not include zero, the evidence is enough to claim that the difference in cholesterol levels before and after taking the new drug is significant.

Exercise 1, utilizing an independent-samples t test, and Exercise 2, utilizing a dependent-sample t test, demonstrate the impact of research designs by arriving at different conclusions based on identical numbers used to conduct different hypothesis tests. You might think of the old adage that one can make statistics say anything one wants, which implies that statistical conclusions are all arbitrary. This is certainly not true because there are always limits set by the data and the research design. Exercises 1 and 2 illustrate that the results of a statistical hypothesis test depend on the research design and the appropriate statistical procedure that can be used in the study.

Take a close look at the numerator of the independent-samples t test, $(\bar{X}_1 - \bar{X}_2) = 20$, which turns out to be identical in magnitude but opposite in sign to the numerator of the dependent-sample t test, $\bar{D} = -20$. But the denominator of the independent-samples t test,

$$s_{(\bar{X}_1 - \bar{X}_2)} = \sqrt{\frac{s_p^2}{n_1} + \frac{s_p^2}{n_2}} = 19.42$$

turns out to be larger than the denominator of the dependent-sample t test,

$$s_e = \frac{s_D}{\sqrt{n}} = 5.15$$

Eliminating individual differences makes the standard error of the differences smaller, thus making the calculated t value larger. The larger calculated t value makes it more likely to reject H_0. Eliminating individual differences also makes the effect size of the dependent-sample t test larger than that of the independent-samples t test.

Exercises 1 and 2 both require the calculation of mean differences, standard deviation of the differences, and standard error of the differences. Such calculations require the formulas from Chapters 3 and 7. These two exercises demonstrate the accumulative nature of learning statistics.

SAGE edge™

Sharpen your skills with SAGE edge!

Visit edge.sagepub.com/bowen for mobile-friendly quizzes, flashcards, videos, and more!

WHAT YOU LEARNED

Dependent-sample t tests usually involve the same group of research participants being measured twice—once before the treatment and once after the treatment. On some rare occasions, dependent-sample t tests are applied to two closely matched or paired samples. The before and after or the unique pairing procedure allows the calculation of difference scores, mean of the differences, standard deviation of the differences, and standard error of the differences. The general principle of t tests applies here.

$$t = \frac{(\text{Sample statistic} - \text{Population parameter})}{\text{Estimated standard error of the statistic}}$$

The four-step hypothesis test procedure also applies in the dependent-sample t tests.

Step 1. Explicitly state the pair of hypotheses.

Two-tailed test: $H_0: \mu_D = 0$

   $H_1: \mu_D \neq 0$

Right-tailed test: $H_0: \mu_D = 0$

   $H_1: \mu_D > 0$

Left-tailed test: $H_0: \mu_D = 0$

   $H_1: \mu_D < 0$

Step 2. Identify the rejection zone.

Rejection zone for a two-tailed test: $|t| > t_{\alpha/2}$, with $df = n - 1$

Rejection zone for a right-tailed test: $t > t_{\alpha}$, with $df = n - 1$

Rejection zone for a left-tailed test: $t < -t_{\alpha}$, with $df = n - 1$

Step 3. Calculate the test statistic.

$$t = \frac{\bar{D}}{s_e} = \frac{\bar{D}}{\frac{s_D}{\sqrt{n}}}$$

Step 4. Make the correct conclusion.

Compare the calculated t value in Step 3 with the rejection zone in Step 2. If the calculated t falls within the rejection zone, we reject H_0. If the calculated t is not within the rejection zone, we fail to reject H_0.

There are three different approaches to conduct the hypothesis test that provide consistent results: (1) the rejection zone, (2) the p value, and (3) the CI. The effect size for the dependent-sample t test provides a standardized measure of the sample mean difference in units of standard deviation. The effect size offers insight as to whether the difference is practically meaningful.

There are two assumptions of dependent-sample t tests.

1. Dependent-sample t tests can only be conducted on interval or ratio variables. This allows the calculation of differences, the standard deviation of the differences, and the standard error of the differences.

2. The distribution of differences needs to be normal. Fortunately, dependent-sample t tests remain valid with a large sample size (i.e., $n > 30$), even when the variables have a moderate divergence from the normal distribution.

KEY WORDS

Counterbalance: Counterbalance is a cautionary step in conducting repeated measures of the same sample to make sure that the order of presentation of conditions is balanced out.

Dependent samples: Dependent samples usually refer to the same group of research participants who go through different conditions of a study, such as before and after a treatment. Sometimes, dependent samples apply to samples with an explicit one-on-one pairing relationship.

Dependent-sample t tests: Dependent-sample t tests are used to test the differences between two variables from the same sample before and after a treatment or the difference between two variables from two samples with an explicit one-on-one paired relationship.

Multiple Choice: Circle the best answer to every question.

1. Everything else being equal, which of the following hypothesis tests is likely to have the highest statistical power?

   a. Independent-samples t test with equal variances assumed

   b. Independent-samples t test with equal variances not assumed

   c. Dependent-sample t test

   d. The statistical power remains the same as long as the degrees of freedom are the same.

2. Which one of the following studies calls for a dependent-sample t test?

   a. A group of 20 men rate women's attractiveness before and after having two servings of beer.

   b. A comparable pay study compares salaries between male and female workers on the same position in the same company.

   c. A comparison of learning outcomes from two classes of sixth graders is made, one class using lectures and the other using student-centered inquiry.

   d. A comparison of job satisfaction is made between married workers and unmarried workers.

3. Which of the following terms is *not* the same as the dependent-sample t test?

   a. Paired-sample t test

   b. Between-subject design

   c. Matched-sample t test

   d. Repeated measures

4. A researcher would like to determine if relaxation training is effective in reducing the number of headaches for chronic headache sufferers. The researcher records the number of headaches suffered by 10 participants both before and after the relaxation training. Which statistical procedure is appropriate for this study?

   a. Independent-samples t test with equal variances assumed

   b. Independent-samples t test with equal variances not assumed

   c. One-sample t test

   d. Dependent-sample t test

5. In a dependent-sample t test, researchers want to have 10 people's ratings of female attractiveness both before and after the participants consume two servings of beer. How many research participants do the researchers need?

   a. $n = 10$

   b. $n = 20$

   c. $n = 30$

   d. $n = 40$

6. A psychologist wants to investigate the impact of study-abroad programs on students' openness to experience. A group of students are measured on their openness to experience before and after they have studied abroad.

Which statistical procedure is appropriate for this study?

a. Independent-samples t test with equal variances assumed

b. Independent-samples t test with equal variances not assumed

c. One-sample t test

d. Dependent-sample t test

Free Response Questions

7. Assume that a researcher wants to find out if relaxation training is effective in reducing the number of headaches for chronic headache sufferers. For a week prior to training, each participant records the number of headaches suffered. The participants then receive the relaxation training. A week after the training, the participants record the number of headaches suffered again. The differences in the number of headaches are normally distributed. The numbers are given in Table 10.7.

TABLE 10.7 Number of Headaches Reported by Participants Before and After Relaxation Training

BEFORE TRAINING	AFTER TRAINING
15	9
10	8
16	12
11	8
17	11
20	12
13	13
5	6
8	9

a. Do the data support the claim that the relaxation training is effective in reducing the number of headaches, using $\alpha = .01$? Make sure you include all the necessary steps in the hypothesis test.

b. What is the effect size for the difference in the number of headaches before and after the relaxation training?

c. What is the 98% CI for the difference in the number of headaches before and after the relaxation training?

8. Assume that a researcher would like to investigate if beer consumption changes males' ratings of female attractiveness. Nine male participants are randomly selected and given a set of 10 pictures of females before and after they have consumed two servings of beer. To mask the purpose of the study, only one picture is identified as

TABLE 10.8 Ratings of Female Attractiveness Before and After Consuming Two Servings of Beer

BEFORE	AFTER
5	5
6	5
6	7
7	9
2	4
4	7
8	8
7	8
8	9

the target picture, and it is presented in both settings. Eighteen other pictures are presented only once to the participants. Assume that the differences in the attractiveness ratings are normally distributed. The ratings of the target picture both before and after beer consumption are given in Table 10.8.

a. Do the data support the claim that beer consumption has a significant effect on the ratings of female attractiveness, using $\alpha = .10$? Make sure you include all the necessary steps in the right order for your statistical test.

b. What is the effect size for the difference in attractiveness ratings before and after beer consumption?

c. What is the 80% CI for the difference in attractiveness ratings before and after beer consumption?

9. Assume that a researcher is interested in finding out whether exercise raises body temperature. Eight participants are asked to run on a treadmill for 30 minutes. Their body temperature is measured both before

TABLE 10.9 Body Temperature Before and After 30 Minutes on a Treadmill

BEFORE	AFTER
98.2	98.3
97.1	97.6
96.3	96.5
97.5	98.5
98.3	99.3
99.5	98.9
98.9	98.5
98.7	99.3

and after the run. The body temperatures are reported in Table 10.9.

a. Do the data support the claim that exercise raises body temperature, using $\alpha = .05$? Make sure you include all the necessary steps in the hypothesis test.

b. What is the effect size for the exercise on body temperature?

c. What is the 90% CI for the difference in body temperature before and after exercise?

Correlation

After reading and studying this chapter, you should be able to do the following:

- Define and explain the purpose of Pearson's product moment correlation
- Conduct a hypothesis test on Pearson's *r*
- Explain the coefficient of determination
- Explain Spearman's rank correlation
- Describe how to purify the relationship between two primary variables by keeping the third variable constant using partial correlation
- Describe point biserial correlation
- Distinguish among different types of correlation methods: Pearson's correlation, Spearman's rank correlation, partial correlation, and point biserial correlation

What You Know and What Is New

In this chapter, it makes sense to introduce the concept of *correlation* first because it is different from the various *t* tests that we have covered so far. The *t* tests are used to compare two group means, the test variable is an interval or ratio variable, and the grouping variable is a nominal variable to identify the groups (i.e., pet owners vs. non–pet owners, control group vs. experimental group, or before-measures vs. after-measures). However, the correlation is a statistical tool to measure the strength and direction of the relationship between two interval or ratio variables. Correlations allow us to see if these two variables are moving in the same direction (i.e., when one goes up, the other also goes up) or moving in opposite directions (i.e., when one goes up, the other goes down). The "up" or "down" is relative to the sample mean of that particular variable. For example, let's say you want to study the relationship between hours spent on a treadmill and calories burned. It is logical to expect that the more hours spent on a treadmill, the more calories burned. If you spent more than average hours on a treadmill, you were likely to burn higher than average calories. If you spent less than average hours on a treadmill, you were likely to burn lower than average calories. Therefore, before you calculate a correlation, you need to calculate the means for the two variables first. Once you understand correlation conceptually, the calculation is easy.

In Chapter 3, you learned to calculate means and sum of squares (*SS*), which sets the foundation for Chapter 11. Calculating the relationship between two interval or ratio variables involves figuring out means and *SS* for both variables. The means and *SS* are the very basic statistics you already learned. Now, you simply need to know how to put means and *SS* together to show if two variables are moving in the same direction or in opposite directions. Detailed formulas for the correlation are described in the next section.

PEARSON'S CORRELATION

The *Pearson product moment correlation coefficient*, or simply called Pearson's correlation, *r*, is a statistical procedure that calculates a linear relationship between two interval or ratio variables. This is the formal name for the measure most often referred to as the "correlation." The Pearson's correlation formulas provide objective mathematical operations to measure the strength and direction of the linear relationship between two interval or ratio variables. Because any two interval or ratio variables can generate a correlation coefficient, it is important to report a correlation coefficient with the pair of variables involved in the calculation clearly identified. We will introduce two different formulas to calculate Pearson's *r*, describe and interpret Pearson's *r*, and use examples to demonstrate the entire process.

PEARSON'S CORRELATION FORMULAS

Pearson's correlation is logically simple and mathematically designed to measure the strength and direction of the relationship between two variables, *X* and *Y*. We will explain the formulas and everything that goes into them.

$$\text{Pearson's correlation } r = \frac{\text{SP}}{\sqrt{SS_X SS_Y}}$$

where

SP is the sum of cross products $= \sum (X - \bar{X})(Y - \bar{Y})$

$SS_X = \sum (X - \bar{X})^2$ is the sum of squares of X

$SS_Y = \sum (Y - \bar{Y})^2$ is the sum of squares of Y

The SS_X and SS_Y are familiar terms from earlier chapters, and both are always positive. Therefore, the denominator in the r formula is always positive. Only SP $= \sum (X - \bar{X})(Y - \bar{Y})$ is a new term. SP stands for the sum of cross products, also called covariance. The multiplication of $(X - \bar{X})$ and $(Y - \bar{Y})$ provides the indication of whether the variables X and Y are moving in the same direction or in opposite directions. When X and Y are moving in the same direction, they are likely to be above $\bar{X}$ and $\bar{Y}$ at the same time or below $\bar{X}$ and $\bar{Y}$ at the same time; therefore, the cross products $(X - \bar{X})(Y - \bar{Y})$ are likely to be positive. When X and Y are moving in opposite directions, one is likely to be above its mean (i.e., positive difference) and the other is likely to be below its mean (i.e., negative difference); therefore, the cross products $(X - \bar{X})(Y - \bar{Y})$ are likely to be negative. The summation ($\sum$) sums up the cross products for every data point and provides an overall trend of the relationship between X and Y. When SP is positive, it means that X and Y are mostly moving in the same direction; therefore, the correlation r is positive. When SP is negative, it means that X and Y are mostly moving in opposite directions; therefore, the correlation r is negative.

Let's use two graphs as shown in Figures 11.1a and b to illustrate the SP. When you want to investigate the relationship between X and Y, you can put the data points (X_i, Y_i) on a two-dimensional graph with each dot showing the values of the variables on both X and Y axes. Now calculate $\bar{X}$ and $\bar{Y}$; then draw a line on the graph to mark the mean value on each axis. The graph is divided into four quadrants by the $\bar{X}$ and $\bar{Y}$. Let's label them as $+ +, + -, - -,$ and $- +$ based on the outcome of $(X - \bar{X})$ and $(Y - \bar{Y})$. When most data points are in the $+ +$ or $- -$ quadrants, the SP is positive and Pearson's r is positive as shown in Figure 11.1a. When most data points are in the $+ -$ or $- +$ quadrants, the SP is negative and Pearson's r is negative as shown in Figure 11.1b.

You may also calculate Pearson's correlation from Z scores (which you learned in Chapter 4). This formula is mathematically the same as the first Pearson's r formula just presented in a slightly different format. First, transform the raw scores X and Y into Z scores: Z_X and Z_Y.

Given Z scores, the Pearson correlation formula is

$$r = \frac{\sum Z_X Z_Y}{(n - 1)}$$

where $n =$ the number of paired variables, X and Y.

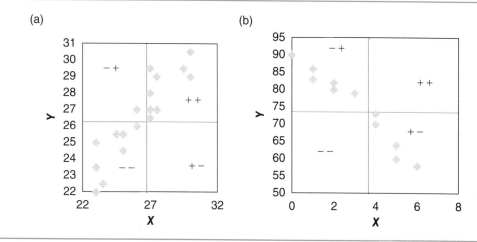

As discussed in Chapter 4, the Z score provides the exact location of each data point in the distribution. When the Z scores are positive, the raw values are above the mean. When the Z scores are negative, the raw values are below the mean. When calculating the correlation between variables X and Y, simply convert X and Y into Z scores, Z_X and Z_Y, multiply them to create $Z_X Z_Y$, and then sum them up and divide it by $(n-1)$.

Pearson's r is used to investigate the linear relationship between two interval or ratio variables. Even strong correlations do not imply causation. Strong correlation shows that the two variables have a tendency of showing up together and they have shared variances. One of the most important applications of Pearson's r in psychological research is to calculate *reliability* and *validity* of a newly designed instrument (test or assessment) to measure a specific psychological concept or construct. Reliability and validity are central concepts in research methods. However, the focus of this book is not research methods. I will only provide a very brief introduction about these two important concepts and show how correlations can be used in this context.

Reliability measures the stability, consistency, and replicability of an instrument. When a psychological instrument is reliable, it is supposed to produce the same result repeatedly when used to measure the same person. One of the most commonly used methods to measure reliability is *test–retest reliability*. Test–retest reliability is measured by giving the instrument to a group of people once and giving the same instrument to the same group of people again, and then calculating the correlation between scores from the first test and the scores from the second test. *Validity* refers to the extent that the instrument actually measures what it is supposed to measure. One of the most commonly used validity measures that actually requires empirical evidence is criterion-related validity.

Criterion-related validity is used to demonstrate the accuracy of a new measure by correlating its results with a well-established and validated measure. Assume that a newly designed 10-minute screening instrument for depression is given to a group of volunteers with different levels of depression symptoms and the same group is also given a comprehensive depression diagnostic test that is well-established with high validity. The correlation between the results from the 10-minute screening tool and the comprehensive depression diagnostic test can be used to demonstrate the validity of the 10-minute screening tool. We will have more discussions on the interpretation of correlation in the next section.

Let's use an example to demonstrate how to conduct a Pearson's correlation. Suppose that we are curious about the relationship between adults' height and weight. Height and weight are both ratio variables. We don't expect that there is a cause-and-effect relationship between height and weight, but we suspect that height and weight are related. Assume that a group of 20 adults are randomly selected and their height and weight measures are reported in Table 11.1.

TABLE 11.1   Height and Weight Measures From 20 Adults

ADULT #	HEIGHT (INCHES)	WEIGHT (POUNDS)
1	63.5	170
2	67	140
3	67	178
4	67	160
5	75	225
6	66.5	135
7	59	97
8	63	108
9	66	127
10	60	120
11	74.5	180
12	74	200
13	69	170
14	64.5	118
15	68	170
16	66.5	130
17	63	170
18	64.5	130
19	53	110
20	55	134

STRAIGHTFORWARD STATISTICS

It is not possible to figure out the relationship between height and weight by staring at this table. It is not wise to jump right into the Pearson's r formula and start crunching numbers. Although Pearson's r is one of the statistical tools to measure the relationship between two interval or ratio variables, it is not applicable in all situations. Obviously, when the relationship between two variables does not form a straight line, Pearson's r would not be the appropriate option to measure the relationship. Therefore, we are putting off the urge to jump into calculating Pearson's r until we discuss how to evaluate the appropriateness of applying Pearson's r to measure the relationship between two variables. It is also crucial to learn how to interpret the results of Pearson's r.

DESCRIBING AND INTERPRETING PEARSON'S r

A scatterplot is commonly used as a preliminary tool to evaluate whether the relationship between two interval or ratio variables is linear or not. A scatterplot between two variables is defined as a graph of dots plotted in a two-dimensional space. Each dot contains a pair of values on the X and Y axes. In this case, simply use height as the X-axis and weight as the Y-axis. Plot the pairs of values reported in Table 11.1 in a scatterplot as shown in Figure 11.2a. The step-by-step instructions on how to create a scatterplot in EXCEL are provided later in this chapter.

After creating a scatterplot for two variables, you need to learn to extract information out of it. In other words, you need to interpret the scatterplot.

FIGURE 11.2a Scatterplot of Height and Weight Measures of 20 Adults

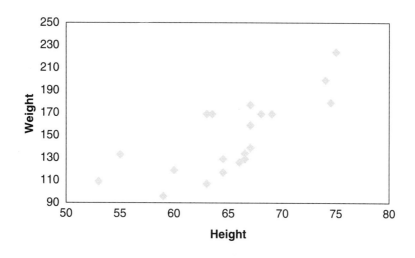

The Shape of the Relationship: Linear or Curvilinear

The way the data points spread across the plot tells you whether a straight line or a curve will fit the data better. Pearson's correlation measures assume a linear relationship between two variables. They are not the appropriate statistics to use when the relationship is curvilinear. How do we know when the relationship is curvilinear? When you draw a straight line to fit the dots in the graph, at best, the line fits some dots in a particular location of the distribution really well but is far away from dots in other locations. Let's examine Figure 11.2a on the shape of the relationship. Draw a straight line to fit the dots as shown in Figure 11.2b.

FIGURE 11.2b Draw a Straight Line to Fit the Scatterplot of Height and Weight Measures of 20 Adults

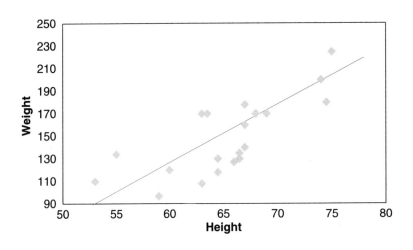

Intuitively we can see that the straight line fits the dots in the entire distribution well. This implies that a linear relationship exists between height and weight. Scatterplots can convey a variety of information about the relationship between two variables, but you have to know what you are looking at. Let's look at what information can be conveyed by a number of scatterplots in the next example.

EXAMPLE 11.1

Assume that researchers gathered measures of left arm and right arm from a randomly selected sample. Most people's left-arm measures are closely matched with their right-arm measures. The scatterplot of these two measures were closely clustered around a straight line as shown in Figure 11.3a. Assume that another group of researchers gathered numbers on the hours of sleep students got the night before an exam and their exam grades. Exam grades could be influenced by many factors such as students' intelligence, study skills, test-taking skills, and a good night's sleep. Therefore, it is unlikely that there is a strong relationship between the hours of sleep and exam grades. The scatterplot of these two variables is shown in Figure 11.3b. Which one of the scatterplots shown in Figures 11.3a and b indicates that correlation is an appropriate statistic to investigate the relationship between the two variables?

FIGURE 11.3a–d Linear or Curvilinear Relationship

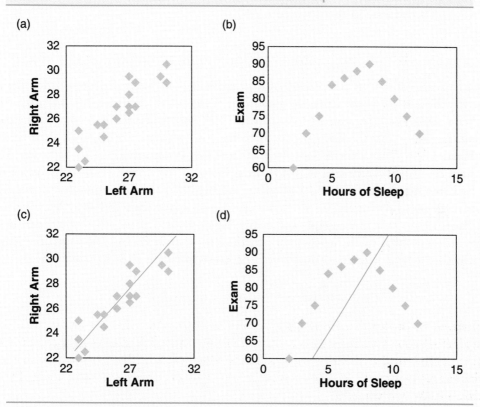

Judging by the scatterplot Figure 11.3a, the dots all lined up pretty well. People who have a long left arm also have a long right arm, and people who have a short left arm also have a short right arm. When you draw a straight line to fit the dots, the line fits the dots in the entire distribution well, as shown in Figure 11.3c. Therefore, correlation is an appropriate statistic to use to characterize the relationship between left-arm and right-arm measures.

(Continued)

(Continued)

Figure 11.3b shows a curvilinear pattern because the straight line fits the dots well only when hours of sleep are less than eight. The line is far away from the dots when hours of sleep are higher than eight as shown in Figure 11.3d. The exam scores go up with the hours of sleep until it reaches about 8 hours; then the exam scores drop with more sleep. Therefore, Figure 11.3b indicates that correlation is not an appropriate statistic to characterize the relationship between hours of sleep and the exam scores.

If you wonder how the straight line that best fits the data points is determined, then you have to wait until you read Chapter 12 (Simple Regression) to satisfy your curiosity, where it is discussed in detail.

The Direction of the Relationship: Positive (+) or Negative (−)

Once a linear pattern has been established, we can judge the direction of the relationship by the way the dots are spread across the graph. The direction of the relationship is expressed by either a positive or a negative sign. A positive correlation depicts an uptrend, with the data points spreading from the lower left corner to the upper right corner of the graph, as shown in Figure 11.3a. When a person has a long left arm, the person also has a long right arm. The positive correlation can be seen in that as the X values increase, the Y values tend to increase as well. In other words, the X and Y values are moving in the same direction. A negative correlation depicts a downtrend in which the data points spread from the upper left corner to the lower right corner of the graph, as shown in Figure 11.3e. The negative correlation can be seen in that as the X values increase, the Y values tend to decrease. In other words, the X and Y values are moving in opposite directions. The X-axis in Figure 11.3e represents the number

FIGURE 11.3e, f   Strong Negative r (e) and Weak r (f)

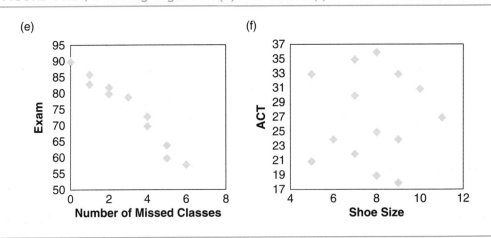

STRAIGHTFORWARD STATISTICS

of missed classes, and the Y-axis is the exam score. Each dot in the scatterplot represents a student. The negative correlation shows that students who missed higher numbers of classes tended to get lower exam scores.

The Strength of the Relationship

Without actually calculating the correlation coefficient, the strength of the relationship can be roughly seen in the scatterplots by considering the aggregated distance from the data points to the straight line: The smaller the aggregated distance between the dots to the line, the stronger the correlation. In other words, when dots are close to the line, the correlation is strong. When dots are far away from the line, the correlation is weak. In Figure 11.3e, the dots fall either right on the line or very close to it. This is a strong correlation. In Figure 11.3f, the dots are spread out in every direction and almost form a circle. When you draw a line to fit the dots, the aggregated distance between the dots to the line is large. The correlation in Figure 11.3f is weak.

Author's Aside

This negative correlation between number of classes missed and exam grades has been observed in statistics courses repeatedly, due to the accumulative nature of the course material. Once a student misses a class or two, it creates a gap in his or her knowledge. He or she is likely to feel lost and falls behind in the following class sessions. The impact of missed classes shows in the exam scores. Don't blame Murphy's law that the day you miss a class is the day when the professor presents key concepts that are covered in the next exam.

The range of correlation is $-1 \leq r \leq 1$. The strength of the correlation can be defined as the absolute value of the correlation. Compare Figures 11.3e and f. Figure 11.3e has a stronger correlation than Figure 11.3f, so its absolute value is closer to 1. Conversely, Figure 11.3f has a weaker correlation than Figure 11.3e, so its correlation is closer to 0. The strongest correlation occurs when $r = 1$ or $r = -1$, and the weakest correlation occurs when $r = 0$.

The Presence of Outliers

Correlation can be heavily influenced by outliers. For example, Figures 11.3g and h are identical data except for one outlier shown by a large star ( ) in the graphs. However, the location of the outlier has a huge impact on the correlation coefficients. Without the outlier, the correlation is close to 0. Figure 11.3g with the outlier on the lower left-hand side creates a positive correlation, but Figure 11.3h with the outlier on the lower right-hand side creates a negative correlation.

It is prudent to visually inspect the scatterplot to identify potential outliers. If outliers are due to data entry errors, remove those outliers before calculating correlations. The effect of other outliers can be identified by calculating the correlation with outliers first and calculating the correlation again without outliers. The difference between these two calculations is due to the effect of outliers.

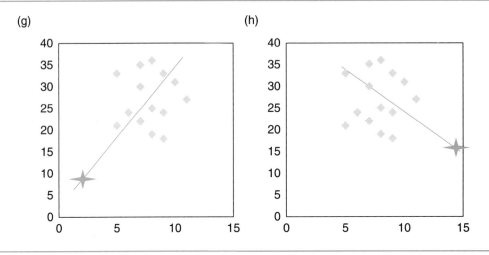

(g)   (h)

SHOWING PEARSON'S CORRELATION IN ACTION

We now have covered the Pearson's correlation r formula, learned how to evaluate whether it was appropriate to apply the formula in each situation, and interpreted its results. We are ready to use an example to go through the entire process.

EXAMPLE 11.2

A statistics course instructor is curious about the relationship between the number of students' missed classes and their final exam scores. Assume that a group of 11 students is randomly selected. Students' missed classes and final exam scores are reported in Table 11.2a.

Use Table 11.2a to answer the following questions.

  a. Is correlation appropriate to measure the relationship between number of missed classes and final exam scores?

  b. What is the Pearson correlation between number of missed classes and final exam scores?

Questions (a) and (b) require different procedures.

  a. You need to construct a scatterplot to answer Part a. The scatterplot of missed classes and final exam scores is presented in Figure 11.4. According to Figure

TABLE 11.2a The Number of Classes Missed and Final Exam Scores

STUDENT	MISSED CLASSES, X	FINAL EXAM SCORE, Y
1	0	90
2	1	83
3	1	86
4	2	82
5	2	80
6	3	79
7	4	70
8	4	73
9	5	60
10	5	64
11	6	58

11.4, a straight line fits the data points in the entire distribution very well, and there are no outliers. Outliers can be visually spotted by a data point that is far away from the rest of the data points. There is no outlier in this case. Correlation is thus appropriate to measure the relationship between number of missed classes and final exam scores.

b. Pearson's correlation $r = \dfrac{SP}{\sqrt{SS_X SS_Y}}$

where

$$SP = \sum(X - \bar{X})(Y - \bar{Y})$$

$$SS_X = \sum(X - \bar{X})^2$$

$$SS_Y = \sum(Y - \bar{Y})^2$$

According to Pearson's r formula, we need to add the following five columns to Table 11.2a, $(X - \bar{X})$, $(Y - \bar{Y})$, $(X - \bar{X})(Y - \bar{Y})$, $(X - \bar{X})^2$, and $(Y - \bar{Y})^2$, to demonstrate the step-by-step process. The results are shown in Table 11.2b. The step-by-step instruction to calculate Pearson's r using EXCEL will be provided in a later section of this chapter. You

(Continued)

(Continued)

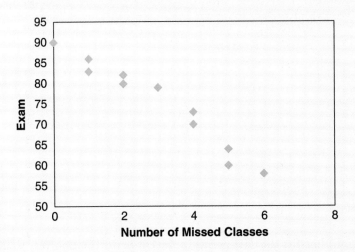

should refresh your memory and skill on how to construct added columns in EXCEL and calculate $\bar{X}$ as stated in Chapter 3.

There are 11 students in the table, $n = 11$. The first step is to calculate $\bar{X}$ and $\bar{Y}$ to construct the additional five columns, and the last row of every column is the total of that column.

$$\bar{X} = \sum X/n = 33/11 = 3$$

$$\bar{Y} = \sum Y/n = 825/11 = 75$$

$$SP = \sum(X - \bar{X})(Y - \bar{Y}) = -205$$

$$SS_X = \sum(X - \bar{X})^2 = 38$$

$$SS_Y = \sum(Y - \bar{Y})^2 = 1164$$

$$r = \frac{SP}{\sqrt{SS_X SS_Y}} = \frac{-205}{\sqrt{(38)(1164)}} = -.975$$

TABLE 11.2b **Step-by-Step Calculation of Pearson's *r* Between the Number of Classes Missed and Final Exam Scores**

MISSED CLASSES, X	FINAL EXAM SCORE, Y	$(X - \bar{X})$	$(Y - \bar{Y})$	$(X - \bar{X})(Y - \bar{Y})$	$(X - \bar{X})^2$	$(Y - \bar{Y})^2$
0	90	−3	15	−45	9	225
1	83	−2	8	−16	4	64
1	86	−2	11	−22	4	121
2	82	−1	7	−7	1	49
2	80	−1	5	−5	1	25
3	79	0	4	0	0	16
4	70	1	−5	−5	1	25
4	73	1	−2	−2	1	4
5	60	2	−15	−30	4	225
5	64	2	−11	−22	4	121
6	58	3	−17	−51	9	289
Total 33	825			**−205**	**38**	**1,164**

The Pearson correlation between the number of missed classes and final exam scores is −.975. This means that as the number of missed classes increases, the final exam scores tend to decrease in an almost perfect linear manner.

As you see, the differences in the ranges of variables X and Y can be large, as shown in Example 11.2. This is attributable in part to differences in the units in which their values are observed and reported. One missed class is not the same thing—not the same unit—as one missed point on an exam. However, when both variables are converted into standardized Z scores, differences in the ranges or units in which the raw variables are reported simply do not matter. We can demonstrate this by applying another form of the Pearson correlation formula

$$r = \frac{\Sigma Z_X Z_Y}{(n - 1)}$$

to the data reported in Table 11.2a. Based on the calculation from Table 11.2b, we already know the following sample statistics.

$$\bar{X} = \sum X/n = 33/11 = 3$$

$$\bar{Y} = \sum Y/n = 825/11 = 75$$

$$SS_X = \sum(X - \bar{X})^2 = 38$$

$$SS_Y = \sum(Y - \bar{Y})^2 = 1164$$

We need to calculate s_X and s_Y to convert the raw variables X and Y into standardized Z scores.

$$s = \sqrt{\frac{SS}{(n-1)}}$$

$$s_X = \sqrt{\frac{SS_X}{(n-1)}} = \sqrt{\frac{38}{10}} = 1.95$$

$$s_Y = \sqrt{\frac{SS_Y}{(n-1)}} = \sqrt{\frac{1164}{10}} = 10.79$$

Let's use $\bar{X}$, $\bar{Y}$, S_X, and S_Y to calculate the standardized Z_X and Z_Y and create $Z_X Z_Y$ in Table 11.2c.

Let me do a slow-motion walk-through on the process of calculating Z_X and Z_Y. For the first student who missed $X = 0$ classes and got $Y = 90$ on the final exam, the Z_X and Z_Y are calculated as follows:

$$Z_X = \frac{(X - \bar{X})}{s_X} = \frac{(0-3)}{1.95} = -1.538$$

$$Z_Y = \frac{(Y - \bar{Y})}{s_Y} = \frac{(90-75)}{10.79} = 1.390$$

Continue the process and calculate the Z_X and Z_Y for the rest of the sample. Their Z_X and Z_Y are recorded in Table 11.2c. Multiply Z_X and Z_Y to create $Z_X Z_Y$; then add them up to get the summation $\sum Z_X Z_Y$. Now you are ready to calculate Pearson's r from the standard Z scores.

$$r = \frac{\sum Z_X Z_Y}{(n-1)} = \frac{-9.743}{10} = -.974$$

TABLE 11.2c Calculation of Pearson's *r* From *Z* Scores of Number of Classes Missed and Final Exam Scores

MISSED CLASSES, *X*	FINAL EXAM SCORE, *Y*	Z_X	Z_Y	$Z_X Z_Y$
0	90	−1.538	1.390	−2.139
1	83	−1.026	0.741	−0.760
1	86	−1.026	1.019	−1.046
2	82	−0.513	0.649	−0.333
2	80	−0.513	0.463	−0.238
3	79	0.000	0.371	0.000
4	70	0.513	−0.463	−0.238
4	73	0.513	−0.185	−0.095
5	60	1.026	−1.390	−1.426
5	64	1.026	−1.019	−1.046
6	58	1.538	−1.576	−2.424
Total **33**	**825**			**−9.743**

The slight difference in the two Pearson's *r* values at the third place after the decimal point is due to rounding. If the computations could be carried out in a large number of places to the right of the decimal point, both formulas for Pearson's *r* would provide the exact same answer.

Pop Quiz

1. Both test-retest reliability and criterion-related validity can be calculated by

   a. *t* tests.

   b. *Z* tests.

   c. *F* tests.

   d. Pearson's *r*.

2. The direction of Pearson's *r* is determined by

   a. $SS_X = \sum (X - \bar{X})^2$

   b. $SS_Y = \sum (Y - \bar{Y})^2$

   c. $SP = \sum (X - \bar{X})(Y - \bar{Y})$

   d. the coefficient of determination, r^2

Answers: 1. d, 2. c

Hypothesis Testing for Pearson's Correlation

The four-step process for conducting a hypothesis test as discussed in Chapter 7 is still applicable in this chapter. We will apply the same basic process to conduct hypothesis tests on Pearson's correlations.

Step 1. Explicitly state the pair of hypotheses.

Step 2. Identify the rejection zone.

Step 3. Calculate the test statistic.

Step 4. Make the correct conclusion.

Let's explain this four-step hypothesis testing for Pearson's *r* step by step.

Step 1. Explicitly state the pair of hypotheses.

Hypothesis tests are conducted by using sample statistics to make inferences about the population parameters. In hypothesis tests of Pearson's correlation, the main focus is on whether a relationship between two variables exists in the population. The population correlation is expressed as ρ (rho, the 17th letter of the Greek alphabet), and the sample correlation is expressed as *r*. Here is a list of hypotheses for all possible hypothesis tests of Pearson's correlation.

Two-tailed test:	$H_0: \rho = 0$
	$H_1: \rho \neq 0$
Right-tailed test:	$H_0: \rho = 0$
	$H_1: \rho > 0$
Left-tailed test:	$H_0: \rho = 0$
	$H_1: \rho < 0$

Step 2. Identify the rejection zone.

When conducting a hypothesis test for a Pearson's correlation, the calculated *r* needs to be compared with the critical value of *r* that sets the boundary of the rejection zone using the same principle stated in Chapter 7. The critical values for Pearson's *r* can be found in the Pearson's Correlation Table, or *r* Table, in Appendix D. The numbers in the top row of the *r* Table stipulate the α level for one-tailed tests, and the numbers in the second row stipulate the α level for two-tailed tests. The numbers in the first column identify the degrees of freedom ($df = n - 2$) for Pearson's *r*, and all the numbers inside the *r* Table are critical values that set the boundaries of the rejection zones. We first discussed the degrees of freedom in the context of identifying the rejection zone back in Chapter 8, one-sample

t test when σ is unknown. The df for one-sample t tests is $(n-1)$ because the one-sample statistic is used to estimate one population, and so 1 df is lost in the process, and we are left with $df = (n-1)$ in a one-sample t test. Pearson's correlation formula requires calculation of both $\bar{X}$ and $\bar{Y}$ to estimate μ_X and μ_Y, so 2 df are lost in the process, and we are left with $df = (n-2)$ for Pearson's correlation.

Notice that there are no negative numbers in the Pearson's r Table. Therefore, you should compare the absolute value of the calculated r with the critical values listed in the r Table as shown in Table 11.3. You will need to know three pieces of information to identify the critical value of r to conduct a hypothesis test: (1) a one-tailed versus two-tailed test, (2) the df of the test, and (3) the α level.

Rejection zone for a two-tailed test: $|r| > r_{\alpha/2}$, with $df = n - 2$

Rejection zone for a right-tailed test: $r > r_\alpha$, with $df = n - 2$

Rejection zone for a left-tailed test: $r < -r_\alpha$, with $df = n - 2$

Step 3. Calculate the test statistic.

$$\text{Pearson's correlation } r = \frac{SP}{\sqrt{SS_X SS_Y}}$$

where

$$SP = \Sigma(X - \bar{X})(Y - \bar{Y})$$

$$SS_X = \Sigma(X - \bar{X})^2$$

$$SS_Y = \Sigma(Y - \bar{Y})^2$$

The rounding rule for calculating Pearson's correlation is to stop at the third place after the decimal point so as to conform to the way correlation coefficients are listed in the r Table.

Step 4. Make the correct conclusion.

The decision rules are that if the calculated r is within the rejection zone, we reject H_0. In this case, we conclude that a linear relationship exists between the paired variables. If the calculated r is not within the rejection zone, we fail to reject H_0. In this case, we conclude that the evidence is not enough to support the claim that a linear relationship exists between the paired variables.

When the p value associated with the calculated r is reported by a statistical software package, there is no need to use the r Table to determine the conclusion. The decision rules can be based on the p value. If the p value associated with the calculated r is less than the predetermined α level, we reject H_0 and conclude that a linear relationship exists between the paired

TABLE 11.3 A Portion of the Critical Values for the Pearson Correlations

	LEVEL OF SIGNIFICANCE FOR ONE-TAILED TEST			
	.05	.025	.01	.005
	LEVEL OF SIGNIFICANCE FOR TWO-TAILED TEST			
$df = n - 2$	.10	.05	.02	.01
1	.988	.997	.9995	.9999
2	.900	.950	.980	.990
3	.805	.878	.934	.959
4	.729	.811	.882	.917
5	.669	.754	.833	.874
6	.622	.707	.789	.834
7	.582	.666	.750	.798
8	.549	.632	.716	.765
9	.521	.602	.685	.735
10	.497	.576	.658	.708
11	.476	.553	.634	.684
12	.458	.532	.612	.661
13	.441	.514	.592	.641
14	.426	.497	.574	.628
15	.412	.482	.558	.606
16	.400	.468	.542	.590
17	.389	.456	.528	.575
18	.378	.444	.516	.561

variables. If the p value associated with the calculated r is not less than the predetermined α level, we fail to reject H_0 and conclude that the evidence is not enough to support the claim of a linear relationship between the paired variables. These are the same decision rules about a p value associated with a test statistic as were first introduced in Chapter 9.

When the p value associated with a test statistic is used as a criterion for a hypothesis test, the decision rules are as follows:

When $p < \alpha$, we reject H_0.

When $p \geq \alpha$, we fail to reject H_0.

Now you have learned the entire hypothesis test for Pearson's correlation. Let's go through the process by using a few examples. First, we will demonstrate how to conduct the process when you have to calculate the numbers by hand, so we specifically select an example with a small sample size to make the calculation manageable. Later on, we will demonstrate how to conduct the process by using EXCEL, so you can calculate Pearson's correlation in a large sample size without being overwhelmed by the tedious calculation procedure.

EXAMPLE 11.3

A sample of 10 adults is randomly selected and their height and weight measures are reported in Table 11.4a. Is there a positive linear relationship between height and weight, assuming $\alpha = .05$?

TABLE 11.4a Height and Weight of 10 Adults

HEIGHT	WEIGHT
67	178
67	160
59	97
63	108
66	127
60	120
74.5	180
69	170
68	170
66.5	130

You should visually inspect the scatterplot of height and weight as shown in Figure 11.5 to make sure that a linear relationship exists between height and weight measures.

According to Figure 11.5, there are no obvious outliers and a straight line fits all data points well. We decide that it is appropriate to apply the four-step hypothesis test for a Pearson's r between height and weight measures.

Step 1. Explicitly state the pair of hypotheses.

The problem statement asks you to conduct a hypothesis test for a positive linear relationship between the paired variables. Therefore, a right-tailed hypothesis test is appropriate.

Right-tailed test: $H_0: \rho = 0$

$H_1: \rho > 0$

Step 2. Identify the rejection zone for the hypothesis test.

According to the r Table with a one-tailed test, $df = n - 2 = 10 - 2 = 8$, $\alpha = .05$, and the critical value of r is $r = .549$. The rejection zone for a right-tailed test is $r > .549$.

(Continued)

(Continued)

FIGURE 11.5 Scatterplot of Height and Weight of 10 Adults

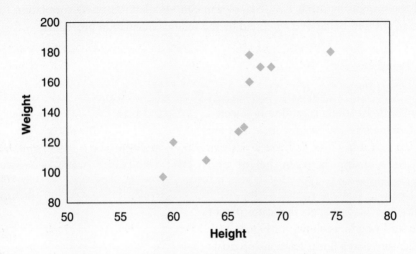

Step 3. Calculate the test statistic.

According to the Pearson's *r* formula, we need to add the following five columns to what was included earlier as Table 11.4a, $(X - \bar{X})$, $(Y - \bar{Y})$, $(X - \bar{X})(Y - \bar{Y})$, $(X - \bar{X})^2$, and $(Y - \bar{Y})^2$, to demonstrate the step-by-step process. The results are shown in Table 11.4b.

There are 10 adults in the table, $n = 10$. The first steps are to figure out $\bar{X}$ and $\bar{Y}$ to construct the additional five columns, and to calculate the total of the column in the last row when necessary.

$$\bar{X} = \sum X/n = 660/10 = 66$$

$$\bar{Y} = \sum X/n = 1440/10 = 144$$

$$SP = \sum(X - \bar{X})(Y - \bar{Y}) = 1060$$

$$SS_X = \sum(X - \bar{X})^2 = 181.5$$

$$SS_Y = \sum(Y - \bar{Y})^2 = 8626$$

$$r = \frac{SP}{\sqrt{SS_X SS_Y}} = \frac{1060}{\sqrt{(181.5)(8626)}} = .847$$

TABLE 11.4b Step-by-Step Process to Conduct a Hypothesis Test for a Positive Linear Relationship Between Height and Weight Measures

HEIGHT, X (INCHES)	WEIGHT, Y (POUNDS)	$(X - \bar{X})$	$(Y - \bar{Y})$	$(X - \bar{X})(Y - \bar{Y})$	$(X - \bar{X})^2$	$(Y - \bar{Y})^2$
67	178	1	34	34	1	1,156
67	160	1	16	16	1	256
59	97	−7	−47	329	49	2,209
63	108	−3	−36	108	9	1,296
66	127	0	−17	0	0	289
60	120	−6	−24	144	36	576
74.5	180	8.5	36	306	72.25	1,296
69	170	3	26	78	9	676
68	170	2	26	52	4	676
66.5	130	0.5	−14	−7	0.25	196
Total **660**	**1,440**			**1,060**	**181.5**	**8,626**

The Pearson correlationbetween height and weight measures is .847.

Step 4. Make a conclusion.

The calculated $r = .847$ is within the rejection zone. Therefore, we reject H_0. The evidence is strong enough to support the claim that there is a positive correlation between height and weight measures.

It is important to emphasize that a strong correlation such as $r = .847$ does not suggest a causal relationship. It only suggests that as a rule, height and weight usually go together. Taller people usually weigh more than shorter people though there are exceptions to the rule, but assuming a cause-and-effect relationship between two variables can be illogical or simply wrong. The next example shows the danger or fallacy of assuming causation between two variables due to strong positive correlations.

EXAMPLE 11.4

A group of sociologists is interested in the relationship between the number of Boy Scout troops and annual number of violent crimes in each municipality. The number of Boy Scout troops in a municipality is a ratio variable because it has an absolute zero. Annual number of violent crimes is also a ratio variable. Both numbers can be obtained from official records of each municipality. Assume that a group of 12 municipalities is randomly selected. The pairs of numbers from each municipality are organized and reported in Table 11.5a.

1. Visually inspect the data to see if there is a linear relationship between number of Boy Scout troops and annual violent crimes.

2. Conduct a hypothesis test on the relationship between number of Boy Scout troops and annual violent crimes reported in each municipality, using $\alpha = .05$.

TABLE 11.5a Number of Boy Scout Troops and Annual Number of Violent Crimes in Each Municipality

MUNICIPALITY	BOY SCOUT TROOPS	CRIMES
A	15	2,601
B	22	1,150
C	17	5,871
D	70	1,799
E	59	8,380
F	49	3,813
G	83	6,958
H	87	8,535
I	63	2,970
J	50	2,229
K	25	1,020
L	12	454

1. Construct a scatterplot with number of Boy Scout troops as the X-axis and annual crimes as the Y-axis. The scatterplot is shown in Figure 11.6. The relationship is not very strong; however, there is a trend from lower left side to upper right and no outliers in this graph. We can assume that a linear relationship exists between the number of Boy Scout troops and annual violent crimes.

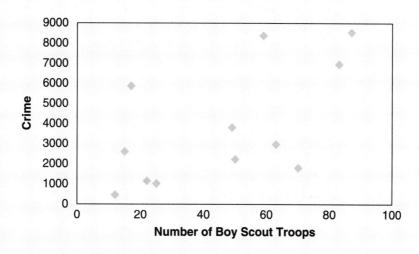

FIGURE 11.6 Scatterplot of Number of Boy Scout Troops and Annual Crimes

2. The four-step hypothesis test for a Pearson's r between number of Boy Scout troops and annual crimes.

Step 1. Explicitly state the pair of hypotheses.

The problem statement asks to conduct a hypothesis test for the relationship between the paired variables. There is no indication of any direction. Therefore, a two-tailed hypothesis is appropriate.

Two-tailed test: $H_0: \rho = 0$

$H_1: \rho \neq 0$

Step 2. Identify the rejection zone for the hypothesis test.

According to the r Table, with a two-tailed test, $df = n - 2 = 12 - 2 = 10$, $\alpha = .05$, and the critical value of r is .576. The rejection zone for a two-tailed test, $df = 10$ and $\alpha = .05$, is $|r| > .576$.

Step 3. Calculate the test statistic.

According to the Pearson's r formula, we need to add the following five columns to Table 11.5a, $(X - \bar{X})$, $(Y - \bar{Y})$, $(X - \bar{X})(Y - \bar{Y})$, $(X - \bar{X})^2$, and $(Y - \bar{Y})^2$, to demonstrate the step-by-step process. The results are shown in Table 11.5b.

(Continued)

(Continued)

TABLE 11.5b Step-by-Step Process to Calculate Pearson's r Between Number of Boy Scout Troops and Annual Number of Violent Crimes

	BOY SCOUT TROOPS	CRIMES	$(X - \bar{X})$	$(Y - \bar{Y})$	$(X - \bar{X})(Y - \bar{Y})$	$(X - \bar{X})^2$	$(Y - \bar{Y})^2$
	15	2,601	−31	−1,214	37,634	961	1,473,796
	22	1,150	−24	−2,665	63,960	576	7,102,225
	17	5,871	−29	2,056	−59,624	841	4,227,136
	70	1,799	24	−2,016	−48,384	576	4,064,256
	59	8,380	13	4,565	59,345	169	20,839,225
	49	3,813	3	−2	−6	9	4
	83	6,958	37	3,143	116,291	1,369	9,878,449
	87	8,535	41	4,720	193,520	1,681	22,278,400
	63	2,970	17	−845	−14,365	289	714,025
	50	2,229	4	−1,586	−6,344	16	2,515,396
	25	1,020	−21	−2,795	58,695	441	7,812,025
	12	454	−34	−3,361	114,274	1,156	11,296,321
Total	**552**	**45,780**			**514,996**	**8,084**	**92,201,258**

There are 12 municipalities in the table, $n = 12$. The first step is to figure out $\bar{X}$ and $\bar{Y}$, and then to construct the additional five columns. The last row of every column is the total of that column when appropriate.

$$\bar{X} = \sum X/n = 552/12 = 46$$

$$\bar{Y} = \sum Y/n = 45780/12 = 3815$$

$$SP = \sum(X - \bar{X})(Y - \bar{Y}) = 514996$$

$$SS_X = \sum(X - \bar{X})^2 = 8084$$

$$SS_Y = \sum(Y - \bar{Y})^2 = 92201258$$

$$r = \frac{SP}{\sqrt{SS_X SS_Y}} = \frac{514996}{\sqrt{(8084)(92201258)}} = .597$$

The Pearson correlation between number of Boy Scout troops and annual number of violent crimes is .597.

Step 4. Make a conclusion.

The calculated $r = .597$ is within the rejection zone. Therefore, we reject H_0. The evidence is strong enough to support the claim that there is a significant correlation between the number of Boy Scout troops and annual number of violent crimes.

The strong correlation between the number of Boy Scout troops and annual number of violent crimes only suggests that in a city, these two variables seem to go together. When the number of Boy Scout troops goes up, the number of violent crimes also goes up. It would be a very unfortunate mistake to say that participating in Boy Scout activities causes violent behaviors. The apparent correlation between two variables may be caused by a third variable, which may or may not be included in the study. We will address the interpretations and assumptions of Pearson's correlation in the next section.

Pop Quiz

1. The degrees of freedom for a Pearson's *r* is

   a. *n*.

   b. *n* – 1.

   c. *n* – 2.

   d. *n* – 3.

Answer: c

INTERPRETATIONS AND ASSUMPTIONS OF PEARSON'S CORRELATION

Strong correlations are commonly and mistakenly interpreted as cause-and-effect connections. They are not. Establishing causality requires strict control over all other variables. It also requires systematic manipulation and random assignment of different levels of the independent variable, so as to isolate and to observe its effect on the dependent variable. The distinction between independent variable and dependent variable is not pertinent in calculating Pearson's correlation. For example, a correlation can be calculated between number of sun spots and the Dow Jones Industrial Average in a given day over several months. Sun spots are natural astronomical phenomena and the Dow Jones Industrial Index is a human-made economic index based on the changes in trading prices of selected stocks. These two numbers can go in the same direction or in opposite directions, and it may even be statistically significant. It would be a big stretch for anyone to suspect that there is a cause-and-effect relationship between these two variables. Or a correlation can be calculated between income and monthly fee paid on a cell phone plan, where both variables are simply obtained by participants' self-reports. There are no controls and/or manipulation on these two variables. There are many other variables that may have an impact on the income or monthly cell phone bill but may not have been measured or reported in a survey or an observational study. Therefore, it is impossible to make an assertion of causality based on a correlation.

INTERPRETATIONS OF PEARSON'S CORRELATION

Correlation can also be used to measure the percentage of variance that overlaps between X and Y. The coefficient of determination, r^2, which is defined as the percentage of the variance in Y that overlap with X, is shown in Figure 11.7.

Strong correlations do not imply causality. As in Example 11.4, it simply does not make sense to interpret that the number of Boy Scout troops in a city causes the number of violent crimes. No reasonable person would think that participating in Boy Scout activities causes people to commit violent crimes. In this case, researchers simply record the values of both variables as reported in each city without any attempt to manipulate the values of these variables. Causality can only be achieved by strict experimental design to allow randomly assigning research participants to different levels of the independent variable, manipulating the independent variable, and controlling all other variables. Such a research design makes it possible to isolate the effect of the independent variable on the dependent variable to reflect the proper cause-and-effect relationship. However, a calculated positive correlation simply reflects the numerical fact that two variables move in the same direction. As the number of Boy Scout troops increases, so does the number of violent crimes. What is a potential explanation for this positive correlation? Is there a third variable that might explain why these two variables move in the same direction?

FIGURE 11.7 Coefficient of Determination, r^2

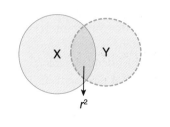

Scientific studies are usually done with careful planning in research designs. The more variables that get considered and measured, the fewer surprises researchers encounter at the end. Oftentimes, studies are conducted to test particular models with complicated and complex relationships among many variables. If a third variable can be found to have a significant relationship with both variables involved in the correlation, this third variable is a confounding variable. A confounding variable is an extraneous variable in a study that correlates with both the independent variable and the dependent variable. Or if there is no pertinent distinction between independent and dependent variables in a given situation, then the confounding variable is one that correlated with the two primary variables of interest. The population of a city might be a confounding variable for the strong correlation between the number of Boy Scout troops and number of violent crimes. All else held equal, it seems reasonable to expect to find more Boy Scout troops *and* more violent crimes in cities with larger populations.

ASSUMPTIONS OF PEARSON'S CORRELATION

When using sample correlation to make inferences about the population correlation, the following assumptions need to be considered.

1. Variables X and Y form a bivariate normal distribution, which means that X values are normally distributed, Y values are normally distributed, and for every value of X, Y values are normally distributed.

2. The scatterplot confirms the existence of a linear relationship between two variables.

3. The scatterplot does not show obvious outliers. If outliers are attributed to data entry errors, remove those outliers before calculating correlations. The effect of other outliers can be identified by first calculating correlations with the outliers and calculating correlation again without outliers. The difference between these two calculations is attributable to outliers.

4. Besides the regular normal distribution for the paired variables X and Y, there is an additional requirement called *homoscedasticity*. Try saying that 10 times in a row fast! Homoscedasticity is defined as the condition in which the variance of Y for any given value of X is the same across all possible values of X. There is equal spread of Y values for every value of X.

If any of these four assumptions is violated, Pearson's r is not an appropriate measure of association for the paired variables.

Pop Quiz

1. The coefficient of determination measures

   a. the percentage of overlap between the variables X and Y.

   b. the cause-and-effect relationship between X and Y.

   c. the mean difference between X and Y.

   d. the pooled variance of X and Y.

Answer: a

SPECIAL TYPES OF CORRELATION

Pearson's correlation is designed for interval and ratio variables. A special correlation formula is designed to calculate correlation between two ordinal variables: Spearman's rank correlation. Spearman's rank correlation is a nonparametric alternative to Pearson's correlation where the data are not interval or ratio variables. Nonparametric statistics can be applied when the data do not have equal units or are not normally distributed. Spearman's rank correlation is similar to Pearson's r in that it also characterizes the association between two variables. But it does not fulfill the linearity, or normality, assumptions as Pearson's r does.

SPEARMAN'S RANK CORRELATION

Spearman's rank correlation, r_S, calculates the relationship between two ordinal variables, where values represent rankings. The subscript S on the r_S is meant to distinguish Spearman's rank correlation from Pearson's correlation. Usually subscripts are used to make the symbol special and to distinguish it from other similar symbols. However, the formula for Spearman's rank correlation looks the same as Pearson's correlation.

Tied ranks happen when two values are identical and should be assigned identical ranks. Tied ranks are handled by averaging the ranks that those values should have been assigned. For example, when the identical values happen on Ranks 4 and 5 of the variable, the assigned tied ranks for both should be $(4 + 5)/2 = 4.5$.

$$r_S = \frac{SP}{\sqrt{SS_X SS_Y}}$$

However, there is also a special simplified formula for Spearman's rank correlation when there are no tied ranks.

$$r_S = 1 - \frac{6 \sum d^2}{n(n^2 - 1)}$$

where

d = the difference between the X rank and the Y rank

n = number of paired variables

Let's use an example to illustrate the outcomes of these two different formulas for Spearman's rank correlation.

EXAMPLE 11.5

It is a common saying that you pay for the quality of goods. However, it is unclear whether more expensive products always deliver higher quality. Assume that a non-profit consumer organization tested many models of gas range. Their investigators came up with a list of the quality rankings of recommended stand-alone gas ranges and ovens with the prices as shown in Table 11.6a.

1. Apply both formulas for Spearman's rank correlation to compare the outcomes.

2. Conduct a hypothesis test on the positive association between quality rankings and price rankings according to the common belief that you pay for the quality, using $\alpha = .05$.

1. The prices of the gas ranges and ovens first need to be converted to rankings with the most expensive one ranked as 1 as shown in Table 11.6b. Then the step-by-step calculations are demonstrated by the additional columns of $(X - \bar{X})$, $(Y - \bar{Y})$, $(X - \bar{X})(Y - \bar{Y})$, $(X - \bar{X})^2$, and $(Y - \bar{Y})^2$ for the first Spearman's rank correlation formula as well as d and d^2 for the second Spearman's rank correlation formula.

TABLE 11.6a Quality Ranking and Price of Stand-Alone Gas Range and Oven

BRAND	QUALITY RANKING	PRICE (IN $)
A	1	799.99
B	2	3,799.99
C	3	1,799.99
D	4	2,200
E	5	1,200
F	6	900
G	7	1,400

$$\bar{X} = \frac{\sum X}{n} = \frac{28}{7} = 4$$

$$\bar{Y} = \frac{\sum Y}{n} = \frac{28}{7} = 4$$

$$r_S = \frac{SP}{\sqrt{SS_X SS_Y}} = \frac{3}{\sqrt{(28)(28)}} = \frac{3}{28} = .107$$

$$r_S = 1 - \frac{6\sum d^2}{n(n^2 - 1)} = 1 - \frac{6(50)}{7(49 - 1)} = .107$$

(Continued)

(Continued)

TABLE 11.6b Calculation Process of Quality Ranking and Price Ranking of Stand-Alone Gas Range and Oven

QUALITY RANKING, X	PRICE RANKING, Y	$(X - \bar{X})$	$(Y - \bar{Y})$	$(X - \bar{X})(Y - \bar{Y})$	$(X - \bar{X})^2$	$(Y - \bar{Y})^2$	D	D^2
1	7	−3	3	−9	9	9	6	36
2	1	−2	−3	6	4	9	−1	1
3	3	−1	−1	1	1	1	0	0
4	2	0	−2	0	0	4	−2	4
5	5	1	1	1	1	1	0	0
6	6	2	2	4	4	4	0	0
7	4	3	0	0	9	0	−3	9
Total 28	28			3	28	28		50

Both formulas arrive at the same outcome.

2. Conduct a hypothesis test on the positive association between quality rankings and price rankings. The four-step hypothesis test is applicable for Spearman's rank correlation.

Step 1. State the pair of hypotheses.

The problem statement asks you to test for a positive association between quality rankings and price rankings. Therefore, a right-tailed test is appropriate.

Right-tailed test: $H_0: \rho_S = 0$

$H_1: \rho_S > 0$

Step 2. Identify the rejection zone.

When the sample size is small (i.e., $n \leq 30$), the critical values that set the boundaries of the rejection zones can be found in the Critical Values for Spearman's Rank Correlation Table in Appendix E. When the sample size is large (i.e., $n > 30$), the critical values of r_S can be identified by the $r_S = \pm z / \sqrt{n - 1}$ formula, where the calculated z corresponds to significance level. Refer to the Z Table in Appendix A to obtain the p value.

When $n = 7$, for one-tailed test with $\alpha = .05$, the critical value of Spearman's rank correlation is .714. The rejection zone is $r_s > .714$.

Step 3. Calculate the test statistic.

According to Part A of the question, $r_s = .107$.

Step 4. Make a conclusion.

The calculated r_s is not within the rejection zone; therefore, we fail to reject H_0. The evidence is not strong enough to support the claim that there is a positive relationship between price and quality. In plain English, it means that more expensive products do not necessarily deliver higher quality.

PARTIAL CORRELATION FORMULA

We have seen that Pearson's r correlation can be calculated between any two interval or ratio variables. Using the techniques we've considered so far, it is simple to examine the relationship between two variables at a time. However, in reality, the relationship between two variables does not happen in isolation. Oftentimes, there are other variables overlapping with the two variables of interest as shown in Figure 11.8. Wouldn't it be great if we could purify the relationship between two variables by eliminating the impact of a third variable? A partial correlation is the appropriate statistical tool to accomplish that goal.

A **partial correlation** is defined as the purified correlation between two variables that one gets while controlling a third variable by holding it constant.

Figure 11.8 shows the relationships among three variables: X, Y, and Z. Due to the fact that two variables can generate a correlation, there are three different correlations that can be generated by three variables: r_{XY}, r_{XZ}, and r_{YZ}.

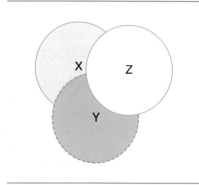

FIGURE 11.8 Relationships Among Three Variables

The partial correlation between X and Y, while keeping Z constant, is expressed as $r_{XY.Z}$.

$$r_{XY.Z} = \frac{r_{XY} - (r_{XZ}r_{YZ})}{\sqrt{(1 - r_{XZ}^2)(1 - r_{YZ}^2)}}$$

All variables involved in the partial correlations still need to meet the assumptions of Pearson's r. Let's go back to Example 11.4, where the number of Boy Scout troops and number of violent crimes show significant positive correlation. It seems to be odd that these two variables move in the same direction. Whenever two variables display a surprising positive correlation, it is highly likely that a third variable is making these two variables move in the same direction. I will explore that in the next example.

EXAMPLE 11.6

We calculated the correlation between number of Boy Scout troops (X) and number of violent crimes (Y), $r_{XY} = .597$ in Example 11.4. It seems highly unlikely that participating in Boy Scout activities has any direct relationship with violent crimes. However, there must be a logical explanation for such a positive correlation between these two variables. Therefore, more variables are explored in this study. One such variable is the population in each city. The population in each city, Z, is obtained, and the correlation between the number of Boy Scout troops and the city population is calculated as $r_{XZ} = .751$. It makes sense that when the population goes up in the city, the number of Boy Scout troops also goes up. The correlation between the number of violent crimes and the city population is also calculated, and it is $r_{YZ} = .768$. It also makes sense that when the population goes up in the city, the number of violent crimes goes up. What is the partial correlation between the number of Boy Scout troops and the number of violent crimes, while holding city population constant?

The city population is highly correlated with both the number of Boy Scout troops $r = .751$ and the number of violent crimes $r = .768$.

To purify the relationship between the number of Boy Scout troops and violent crimes while keeping city population constant, the partial correlation is as follows:

$$r_{XY.Z} = \frac{r_{XY} - (r_{XZ}r_{YZ})}{\sqrt{(1 - r_{XZ}^2)(1 - r_{YZ}^2)}} = \frac{.597 - (.751)(.768)}{\sqrt{(1 - .751^2)(1 - .768^2)}} = \frac{.597 - .577}{\sqrt{(.436)(.410)}} = \frac{.02}{.423} = .047$$

Once the city population is held constant, the correlation between the number of Boy Scout troops and the number of violent crimes becomes .047, and it is a very weak relationship. Therefore, the city population is a confounding variable that causes both the number of Boy Scout troops and the number of violent crimes to move in the same direction. Now, the supporters of the Boy Scouts can heave a sigh of relief. Once the city population is kept constant, there is no relationship between the number of Boy Scout troops and the number of violent crimes. Partial correlation is a great tool that might shed some light into particularly puzzling correlations you might encounter in the future.

In the next section, I will present another useful correlation, the point biserial correlation that connects back to what you learned in Chapter 9, the independent-samples t tests.

POINT BISERIAL CORRELATION

Another kind of correlation with slight modification to the assumptions of Pearson's correlation is the *point biserial correlation*. The **point biserial correlation,** r_{pbi}, is applicable when one variable has interval or ratio properties but the other variable is a naturally occurring dichotomous variable coded as 0 or 1. Naturally occurring dichotomous variables include, for instance, males versus females, married versus not married, success versus failure, hired versus not hired, or guilty versus not guilty. As long as the dichotomous variable is coded as 0 or 1, the point biserial correlation's calculation and interpretation are very similar to Pearson's r.

$$r_{pbi} = \frac{SP}{\sqrt{SS_X SS_Y}}$$

There is another statistical procedure that is suitable for investigating the relationship between an interval or a ratio variable and a dichotomous variable. The independent-samples t test as discussed in Chapter 9 can be applicable when an interval or ratio variable is compared between two groups. Actually, the result of a point biserial correlation is identical to the result of an independent-samples t test with equal variance assumed.

$$r_{pbi}^2 = \frac{t^2}{t^2 + df}$$

where $df = (n - 2)$, the degrees of freedom of the t test.

The critical values of the point biserial correlation are listed in Appendix F. When the absolute value of the calculated point biserial correlation is greater than the critical value, we reject H_0. Otherwise, we fail to reject H_0.

We contrast the results from both a point biserial correlation and an independent-samples t test in Example 11.7. This example provides a direct connection between what you learned in Chapter 9 and this chapter.

EXAMPLE 11.7

Assume that a group of 16 professors is randomly selected from a Midwestern urban university. Their annual salary and sex are reported in Table 11.7a. The unit for the annual salary is in thousands of dollars and professor's sex is coded as *male* = 1 and *female* = 0. Is there a relationship between professor's sex and annual salary, at $\alpha = .05$? Use both the point biserial correlation and independent-samples t test to test the hypothesis.

(Continued)

(Continued)

1. First, use the point biserial correlation to calculate the relationship between professor's sex and annual salary. The four-step hypothesis test for the point biserial correlation is needed to accomplish this purpose.

TABLE 11.7a   Professor's Sex and Salary

SALARY	SEX
86	1
67	1
75	1
91	1
89	1
77	1
94	1
61	1
55	0
67	0
71	0
83	0
79	0
63	0
69	0
73	0

Step 1. The problem statement does not specify a direction, so a two-tailed test is appropriate.

$$Two\text{-}tailed\ test: \quad H_0: \rho_{pbi} = 0$$
$$H_1: \rho_{pbi} \neq 0$$

Step 2. Identify the rejection zone.

According to the Critical Values for the Point Biserial Correlation Table in Appendix F, the critical value for a two-tailed test, $n = 16$, and $\alpha = .05$ is $r_{pbi} = .49$. The rejection zone for a two-tailed test is $|r_{pbi}| > .49$.

Step 3. Calculate the test statistic.

The point biserial correlation formula can be calculated by

$$r_{pbi} = \frac{SP}{\sqrt{SS_X SS_Y}}$$

Table 11.7b shows the step-by-step process to calculate $\bar{X}$ and $\bar{Y}$ and to construct the additional five columns, and the last row of every column is the total of that column.

$$\bar{X} = \sum X / n = 1200/16 = 75$$

$$\bar{Y} = \sum Y / n = 8/16 = .5$$

$$r_{pbi} = \frac{SP}{\sqrt{SS_X SS_Y}} = \frac{40}{\sqrt{(1942)(4)}} = \frac{40}{88.136} = .454$$

TABLE 11.7b Step-by-Step Calculation for the Point Biserial Correlation Between Professor's Sex and Salary

SALARY	SEX	$(X - \bar{X})$	$(Y - \bar{Y})$	$(X - \bar{X})(Y - \bar{Y})$	$(X - \bar{X})^2$	$(Y - \bar{Y})^2$
86	1	11	0.50	5.5	121	0.25
67	1	−8	0.50	−4	64	0.25
75	1	0	0.50	0	0	0.25
91	1	16	0.50	8	256	0.25
89	1	14	0.50	7	196	0.25
77	1	2	0.50	1	4	0.25
94	1	19	0.50	9.5	361	0.25
61	1	−14	0.50	−7	196	0.25
55	0	−20	−0.50	10	400	0.25
67	0	−8	−0.50	4	64	0.25
71	0	−4	−0.50	2	16	0.25
83	0	8	−0.50	−4	64	0.25
79	0	4	−0.50	−2	16	0.25
63	0	−12	−0.50	6	144	0.25
69	0	−6	−0.50	3	36	0.25
73	0	−2	−0.50	1	4	0.25
1,200	**8**			**40**	**1,942**	**4**

Step 4. Make the correct conclusion.

The calculated r_{pbi} = .454 is not within the rejection zone. Therefore, we fail to reject the null hypothesis. The data are not strong enough to support the claim that there is a significant relationship between professor's sex and annual salary.

2. Second, use the independent-samples t test to compare male professors' salary with female professors' salary. The values of male and female professors' salary are reported in different columns in Table 11.7c.

(Continued)

(Continued)

TABLE 11.7c Male and Female Professors' Salary in Thousands of Dollars

MALE	FEMALE	$(X - \bar{X}_m)$	$(X - \bar{X}_m)^2$	$(X - \bar{X}_f)$	$(X - \bar{X}_f)^2$
86	55	6	36	−15	225
67	67	−13	169	−3	9
75	71	−5	25	1	1
91	83	11	121	13	169
89	79	9	81	9	81
77	63	−3	9	−7	49
94	69	14	196	−1	1
61	73	−19	361	3	9
640	560		998		544

$$\text{Mean of male professors' salary } \bar{X}_m = \frac{\sum X_m}{n} = \frac{640}{8} = 80$$

$$\text{Mean of female professors' salary } \bar{X}_f = \frac{\sum X_f}{n} = \frac{560}{8} = 70$$

$$SS \text{ for male professors } SS_m = \sum(X - \bar{X}_m)^2 = 998$$

$$SS \text{ for female professors } SS_f = \sum(X - \bar{X}_f)^2 = 544$$

The five-step hypothesis test for the independent-samples t test is shown below.

Step 1. Test equality of variances.

Substep 1. State the pair of hypotheses regarding variances.

$$H_0: \sigma_1^2 = \sigma_2^2$$

$$H_1: \sigma_1^2 \neq \sigma_2^2$$

Substep 2. Identify the rejection zone.

Males are designated as Group 1 because s_1 is the larger standard deviation, $\sqrt{SS / df} = \sqrt{998 / 7} = 11.94$ and its $df_1 = n_1 - 1 = 8 - 1 = 7$, and s_2 is the smaller standard deviation, $\sqrt{SS / df} = \sqrt{544 / 7} = 8.82$ and its $df_2 = 8 - 1 = 7$.

The critical value of the right-tailed $F_{(df_1, df_2)} = F_{(7,7)} = 3.79$

Substep 3. Calculate the statistic.

$$F = \frac{s_1^2}{s_2^2} = \frac{11.94^2}{8.82^2} = \frac{142.56}{77.79} = 1.83$$

Substep 4. Make the correct conclusion

The calculated $F = 1.83$ is smaller than the critical value of $F_{(7,7)} = 3.79$. Therefore, we fail to reject H_0. The evidence is not strong enough to claim that two variances are not equal. Therefore, the correct independent-samples t-test approach is to assume equal variances.

Step 2. State the pair of hypotheses regarding group means.

The problem statement does not indicate any direction. Therefore, a two-tailed test is appropriate.

$H_0: \mu_1 = \mu_2$

$H_1: \mu_1 \neq \mu_2$

Step 3. Identify the rejection zones for the test.

According to the rule, $df = df_1 + df_2 = n_1 + n_2 - 2 = 14$, $\alpha = .05$, and for a two-tailed test, the critical t value that sets the boundary of the rejection zone is 2.415. The rejection zone for a two-tailed test is $|t| > 2.415$.

Step 4. Calculate the t statistic.

When $\sigma_1^2 = \sigma_2^2$, the variances need to be pooled together.

$$s_p^2 = \frac{SS_1 + SS_2}{df_1 + df_2} = \frac{998 + 544}{7 + 7} = \frac{1542}{14} = 110.14$$

(Continued)

(Continued)

$$s_{(\bar{X}_1 - \bar{X}_2)} = \sqrt{\frac{s_p^2}{n_1} + \frac{s_p^2}{n_2}} = \sqrt{\frac{110.14}{8} + \frac{110.14}{8}} = \sqrt{13.7675 + 13.7675} = \sqrt{27.535} = 5.25$$

$$t = \frac{(\bar{X}_1 - \bar{X}_2)}{s_{(\bar{X}_1 - \bar{X}_2)}} = \frac{(80 - 70)}{5.25} = \frac{10}{5.25} = 1.905$$

Step 5. Make the correct conclusion.

The calculated $t = 1.905$ is not within the rejection zone. Therefore, we fail to reject H_0. The evidence is not strong enough to support the claim that there is a significant difference between male and female professors' annual salary.

Let's use the formula between the point biserial correlation and t value to verify the results in Example 11.7.

$$r_{pbi}^2 = \frac{t^2}{t^2 + df}$$

$$r_{pbi}^2 = .454 \quad \text{and} \quad t = 1.905$$

The left side of the equation is $.454^2 = .206$; the right side of the equation is $1.905^2/(14 + 1.905^2) = .206$. Using the point biserial correlation generates results identical to those found using the independent-samples t test with equal variance assumed.

This is a good time to summarize what you learned in the special types of correlations. In Spearman's rank correlation, you learned how to calculate the correlation between two ordinal variables where values represent rankings. This procedure can be applied to variables that do not have equal units or are not normally distributed. As you have done many times before, with a new test statistic, you need a new table of the critical values to identify the rejection zones. Then apply the four-step hypothesis test procedure to conduct the test.

The partial correlation allows you to purify the relationship between two variables, especially when these two variables display a surprising or puzzling relationship. Two interval or ratio variables can produce a correlation. However, the two variables might overlap with other variables. Partial correlation can purify the correlation between two variables while eliminating the influence of the third variable by keeping it constant.

The point biserial correlation applies to calculate the correlation between an interval or a ratio variable and a naturally dichotomous variable. With this new test statistic, you need a new table of the critical values to identify the rejection zone. Then apply the four-step hypothesis test procedure to conduct the test. The naturally dichotomous variable can be treated as a grouping variable; therefore, an independent-samples t test is also applicable in this case. When more than one statistical procedure is applicable in a situation, they should produce identical results, as demonstrated in Example 11.7.

Pop Quiz

1. Which one of the following correlations is used to measure the relationship between two ordinal variables?

   a. Pearson's r

   b. Spearman's rank correlation

   c. Partial correlation

   d. Point biserial correlation

2. Which one of the following correlations is used to purify the relationship between two variables while keeping the third variable constant?

   a. Pearson's r

   b. Spearman's rank correlation

   c. Partial correlation

   d. Point biserial correlation

3. Which one of the following correlations can produce a result identical to that produced by an independent-samples t test with equal variance assumed?

   a. Pearson's r

   b. Spearman's rank correlation

   c. Partial correlation

   d. Point biserial correlation

Answers: 1. b, 2. c, 3. d

EXCEL STEP-BY-STEP INSTRUCTION FOR CONSTRUCTING A SCATTERPLOT

The EXCEL step-by-step instruction is designed to provide extra help for you to either construct a graph or do number crunching. EXCEL is very useful when dealing with a large sample size. For illustration purposes, we use EXCEL to analyze the height and weight measures from 20 adults as shown in Table 11.1. First you have to enter the data in EXCEL as shown in Figure 11.9.

FIGURE 11.9 EXCEL Screenshot for Height and Weight of 20 Adults

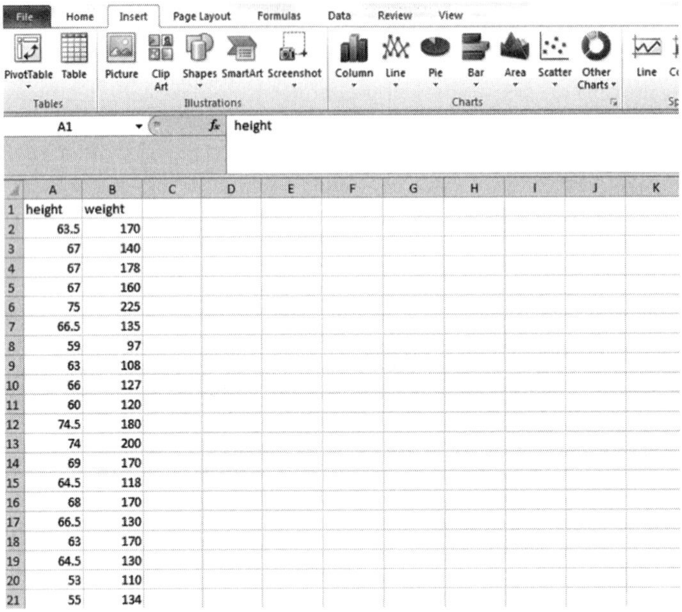

	A	B	C	D	E	F	G	H	I	J	K
1	height	weight									
2	63.5	170									
3	67	140									
4	67	178									
5	67	160									
6	75	225									
7	66.5	135									
8	59	97									
9	63	108									
10	66	127									
11	60	120									
12	74.5	180									
13	74	200									
14	69	170									
15	64.5	118									
16	68	170									
17	66.5	130									
18	63	170									
19	64.5	130									
20	53	110									
21	55	134									

To create a scatterplot in EXCEL, highlight the columns where the two variables are located. To highlight the **height** variable, move the cursor to the location where the first value of **height** is found, **A2**, and left click. Hold down the **Shift** key, go down to the last value of **height**, **A21.** Then click the right arrow → to highlight all the values of weight in **Column B** as well. Once both columns are highlighted, click on the **Insert** tab, and click **Scatter;** then select the first option in the drop-down menu of **Scatter**. A scatterplot appears inside the EXCEL worksheet as shown in Figure 11.10. You may fine-tune the scatterplot by clicking on the first option in **Chart Layouts** to modify the chart title and axes titles to create a scatterplot of height and weight of 20 adults.

The scatterplot looks empty on the left side for the height and weight measures of 20 adults because the default graph starts at the origin (0, 0). You can modify the default by directly *double clicking* on the *X*-axis in the EXCEL graph. When you do this, a **Format Axis** menu appears as shown in Figure 11.11. Under **Axis Options**, change the **Minimum** from **Auto** to **Fixed** by clicking the radio button. Change the number from **0.0** to **50.0** inside the input box. Repeat the same procedure for the *Y*-axis by directly double clicking on the *Y*-axis in the EXCEL graph. Under **Axis Options** change the **Minimum** from **Auto** to **Fixed** by clicking the radio button. Change the number from **0.0** to **90.0** inside the input box. Changing the minimum on the axes allows us to get rid of the empty space and zoom in on the actual data dots as shown in Figure 11.12.

FIGURE 11.10   Scatterplot of Height and Weight Measurements of 20 Adults

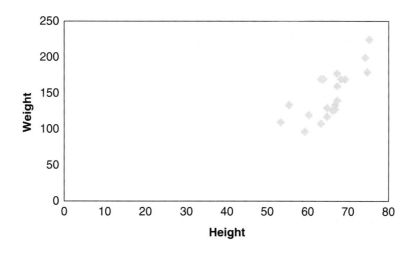

FIGURE 11.11   Format Axis Menu Under Scatterplot

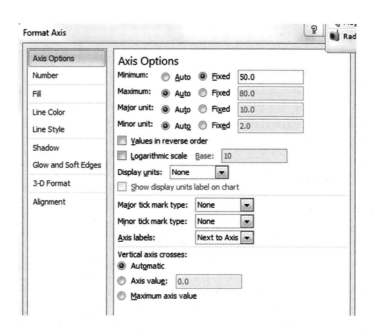

FIGURE 11.12 Scatterplot of Height and Weight Measures of 20 Adults After Changing the Minimum on Both Axes

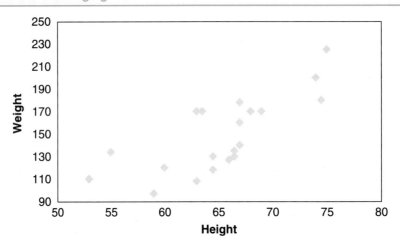

EXCEL STEP-BY-STEP INSTRUCTION FOR CALCULATING PEARSON'S r

First, it is important to show how to get all the numbers needed in a formula in EXCEL. Once you learn the skill to program math operations in EXCEL, you can program any statistical formula in EXCEL. Therefore, let's go through the step-by-step process to calculate Pearson's $r = SP/\sqrt{SS_X SS_Y}$. According to the formula, you need to add the $(X - \bar{X})$, $(Y - \bar{Y})$, $(X - \bar{X})(Y - \bar{Y})$, $(X - \bar{X})^2$, and $(Y - \bar{Y})^2$ columns to demonstrate the step-by-step process.

Type the number of classes missed and final exam scores from Table 11.2a (p. 339) in EXCEL as shown in Figure 11.13. The following instructions refer to the EXCEL screenshot shown in Figure 11.13.

1. Move the cursor to **B13**, and type =**SUM(B2:B12)**. Then hit **Enter**. The answer for the total missed classes grades is $\sum X = 33$. In **B14**, type in =**B13/11** to calculate Mean $\bar{X} = \sum X/n = 33/11 = 3$. Move the cursor to **C13**, and type =**SUM(C2:C12)**. Then hit **Enter**. The answer for the total final exam grades is $\sum Y = 825$. In **C14**, type in =**B13/11** to calculate Mean $\bar{Y} = \sum Y/n = 825/11 = 75$.

2. In **D1**, label the column as $(X - \bar{X})$. In **D2**, type in =**B2-B$14**, which shows the operation of first $(X - \bar{X})$. The $ in the Excel program allows the operation to fix the value of $\bar{X}$ in **B14** for the subsequent operations. Then, it is possible to copy the operation to produce the rest of $(X - \bar{X})$. Move the cursor to the lower right corner of **D2** until **+** shows up. Hold the left click and move the mouse to drag it to **D12**; then release the mouse. You will see the rest of $(X - \bar{X})$ automatically show up in **D3** to **D12**.

3. In **E1**, label the column as $(Y - \bar{Y})$. In **E2**, type in =**C2-C$14**, which shows the operation of first $(Y - \bar{Y})$ as shown in Figure 11.13. The $ in the Excel program allows the operation to fix the value of $\bar{Y}$ in **C14** as you move from row to row down the column for the subsequent operations. Then, it is possible to copy the operation to produce the rest of $(Y - \bar{Y})$. Move the cursor to the lower right corner of **E2** until **+** shows up. Hold the left click and move the mouse to drag it to **E12**; then release the mouse. You will see the rest of $(Y - \bar{Y})$ automatically show up in **E3** to **E12**.

4. The following instructions refer to the EXCEL screenshot shown in Figure 11.14. In **F1**, label the column as $(X - \bar{X})(Y - \bar{Y})$. In **F2**, type in =**D2*E2**, which shows the operation of first $(X - \bar{X})(Y - \bar{Y})$. Then move the cursor to the lower right corner of **F2** until **+** shows up. Hold the left click and move the mouse to drag it to **F12**; then release the mouse. You will see the rest of $(X - \bar{X})(Y - \bar{Y})$ automatically show up in **F3** to **F12**.

FIGURE 11.13 Screenshot for the First Two Added Columns: $(X - \bar{X})$ and $(Y - \bar{Y})$

	A	B	C	D	E
1	Student	Missed classes, X	Final exam, Y	$(X-\bar{X})$	$(Y-\bar{Y})$
2	1	0	90	-3	15
3	2	1	83	-2	
4	3	1	86	-2	
5	4	2	82	-1	
6	5	2	80	-1	
7	6	3	79	0	
8	7	4	70	1	
9	8	4	73	1	
10	9	5	60	2	
11	10	5	64	2	
12	11	6	58	3	
13	Total	33	825		
14		3	75		

5. In **G1**, label the column as $(X - \bar{X})^2$. In **G2**, type in =**D2^2**, which shows the operation of first $(X - \bar{X})^2$. The "^" symbol can be created by holding down the **Shift** key and **6** at the same time. Then move the cursor to the lower right corner of **G2** until **+** shows up. Hold the left click and move the mouse to drag it to **G12**; then release the mouse. You will see the rest of $(X - \bar{X})^2$ automatically show up in **G3** to **G12**.

6. In **H1**, label the column as $(Y - \bar{Y})^2$. In **H2**, type in =**E2^2**, which shows the operation of first $(Y - \bar{Y})^2$. Then move the cursor to the lower right corner of **H2** until **+** shows up. Hold the left click and move the mouse to drag it to **H12**; then release the mouse. You will see the rest of $(Y - \bar{Y})^2$ automatically show up in **H3** to **H12**.

FIGURE 11.14 Screenshot for the Last Three Added Columns: $(X - \bar{X})(Y - \bar{Y})$, $(X - \bar{X})^2$, and $(Y - \bar{Y})^2$, as Well as the Calculations for SP, SS_X, and SS_Y

F13 f_x =SUM(F2:F12)

	A	B	C	D	E	F	G	H
1	Student	Missed classes, X	Final exam, Y	$(X-\bar{X})$	$(Y-\bar{Y})$	$(X-\bar{X})(Y-\bar{Y})$	$(X-\bar{X})^2$	$(Y-\bar{Y})^2$
2	1	0	90	-3	15	-45	9	225
3	2	1	83	-2	8	-16	4	64
4	3	1	86	-2	11	-22	4	121
5	4	2	82	-1	7	-7	1	49
6	5	2	80	-1	5	-5	1	25
7	6	3	79	0	4	0	0	16
8	7	4	70	1	-5	-5	1	25
9	8	4	73	1	-2	-2	1	4
10	9	5	60	2	-15	-30	4	225
11	10	5	64	2	-11	-22	4	121
12	11	6	58	3	-17	-51	9	289
13	Total	33	825			-205	38	1164
14		3	75					

FIGURE 11.15 Screenshot for Using EXCEL Built-In Formula to Obtain Pearson's r

C16 f_x =PEARSON(B2:B12,C2:C12)

	A	B	C	D	E	F	G	H
1	Student	Missed classes, X	Final exam, Y	$(X-\bar{X})$	$(Y-\bar{Y})$	$(X-\bar{X})(Y-\bar{Y})$	$(X-\bar{X})^2$	$(Y-\bar{Y})^2$
2	1	0	90	-3	15	-45	9	225
3	2	1	83	-2	8	-16	4	64
4	3	1	86	-2	11	-22	4	121
5	4	2	82	-1	7	-7	1	49
6	5	2	80	-1	5	-5	1	25
7	6	3	79	0	4	0	0	16
8	7	4	70	1	-5	-5	1	25
9	8	4	73	1	-2	-2	1	4
10	9	5	60	2	-15	-30	4	225
11	10	5	64	2	-11	-22	4	121
12	11	6	58	3	-17	-51	9	289
13	Total	33	825			-205	38	1164
14		3	75					
15								
16		Pearson's	-0.97473					

7. SP is the sum of prodcts of deviations $= \Sigma (X - \bar{X})(Y - \bar{Y})$. To get this value, move the cursor to **F13** and type in =**SUM(F2:F12)**; then hit **Enter**. The calculation for SP shows up at the bottom of the column as −205. Move the cursor to the lower right corner of **F13** until **+** shows up. Hold down the left click key and drag it across **G13** and **H13**; then let go. The calculation for $SS_X = \Sigma (X - \bar{X})^2$ shows up in **G13**, and the calculation for $SS_Y = \Sigma (Y - \bar{Y})^2$ shows up in **H13** as shown in Figure 11.14.

Now, you have all the numbers you need to calculate Pearson's r.

$$r = \frac{SP}{\sqrt{SS_X SS_Y}} = \frac{-205}{\sqrt{(38)(1164)}} = -.975$$

8. You may verify your answer with the EXCEL built-in formula by moving the cursor to a blank EXCEL cell such as **C16** (Figure 11.15) and typing in =**PEARSON (B2:B12,C2:C12)**; then hit **Enter**. This command specifies for EXCEL to calculate the Pearson correlation between the number of missed classes and final exam. The answer −.975 appears. This shortcut is easy and convenient, but it does not show the step-by-step process as demonstrated from Steps 1 to 7.

EXERCISE PROBLEMS

1. Are cell phones used as productivity tools? If so, people who have higher incomes are likely to spend more money on cell phone bills. Assume that a group of 14 people is randomly selected and their cell phone bills and monthly income are reported in Table 11.8a.

   a. Construct a scatterplot to see if there is a linear relationship between cell phone bill and monthly income.

   b. Conduct a hypothesis test for a positive relationship between cell phone bill and monthly income, using $\alpha = .05$.

2. Beach resorts have annual reports on numbers of drowning accidents, ice cream sales, and numbers of visitors. Assume that the

TABLE 11.8a   Cell Phone Bill and Monthly Income

CELL PHONE BILL	MONTHLY INCOME
101	2,450
65	4,167
90	1,007
105	1,750
33	202
95	1,506
55	3,000
44	2,101
49	1,943
87	4,784
79	3,556
84	3,025
106	2,877
85	2,450

TABLE 11.9a Results From the 10-Minute Screening and the Comprehensive Diagnostic Test

10-MINUTE SCREENING TEST	COMPREHENSIVE DIAGNOSTIC TEST
20	47
21	46
19	54
22	45
22	50
23	45
23	43
24	49
24	63
25	60
26	69
27	65

numbers of drowning accidents, ice cream sales, and visitors are all normally distributed. The Pearson correlation between drowning accidents and ice cream sales is .678, the Pearson correlation between drowning accidents and number of visitors is .895, and the Pearson correlation between ice cream sales and number of visitors is .743. What is the correlation between drowning accidents and ice cream sales while keeping number of visitors constant?

3. Assume that a newly designed 10-minute screening instrument for depression is given to a group of 12 volunteers with different levels of depression symptoms, and the same group is also given a comprehensive depression diagnostic test that is well-established with high validity. The results of these tests for the 12 volunteers on both the screening instrument and the comprehensive diagnostic test are reported in Table 11.9a, with higher numbers reflecting more symptoms. Assume the scores of the 10-minute screening instrument and the comprehensive diagnostic test are normally distributed. Conduct a hypothesis test to see if there is a positive relationship between these two measures.

Solutions

1.a. Construct a scatterplot between cell phone bill and monthly income as shown in Figure 11.16. According to the scatterplot, it is reasonable to assume a weak linear relationship between cell phone bill and monthly income.

1.b. Assume that cell phone bills and monthly income are normally distributed. The four-step hypothesis test for Pearson's r is appropriate to answer this question.

Step 1. State the pair of hypotheses.

The problem statement asks you to test a positive relationship between cell phone bill and monthly income. A right-tailed test is the appropriate test.

Right-tailed test: $H_0: \rho = 0$

$H_1: \rho > 0$

FIGURE 11.16   A Scatterplot of Cell Phone Bills and Monthly Income

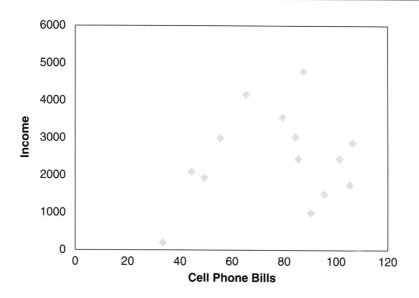

Step 2. Identify the rejection zone.

The critical value of Pearson's *r* for a right-tailed test with $df = n - 2 = 14 - 2 = 12$ and α = .05 is .458. The rejection zone is $r > .458$.

Step 3. Calculate the statistic.

$$r = \frac{SP}{\sqrt{SS_X SS_Y}}$$

The step-by-step calculation is shown in Table 11.8b with added columns $(X - \bar{X})$, $(Y - \bar{Y})$, $(X - \bar{X})(Y - \bar{Y})$, $(X - \bar{X})^2$, and $(Y - \bar{Y})^2$.

$$\bar{X} = \sum X / n = 1078 / 14 = 77$$

$$\bar{Y} = \sum Y / n = 34818 / 14 = 2487$$

$$SP = \sum (X - \bar{X})(Y - \bar{Y}) = 78530$$

$$SS_X = \sum (X - \bar{X})^2 = 7348$$

TABLE 11.8b Calculation of Pearson's *r* Between Cell Phone Bill and Monthly Income

CELL PHONE CHARGE	MONTHLY INCOME	$(X - \bar{X})$	$(Y - \bar{Y})$	$(X - \bar{X})(Y - \bar{Y})$	$(X - \bar{X})^2$	$(Y - \bar{Y})^2$
101	2,450	24	−37	−888	576	1,369
65	4,167	−12	1,680	−20,160	144	2,822,400
90	1,007	13	−1,480	−19,240	169	2,190,400
105	1,750	28	−737	−20,636	784	543,169
33	202	−44	−2,285	100,540	1,936	5,221,225
95	1,506	18	−981	−17,658	324	962,361
55	3,000	−22	513	−11,286	484	263,169
44	2,101	−33	−386	12,738	1,089	148,996
49	1,943	−28	−544	15,232	784	295,936
87	4,784	10	2,297	22,970	100	5,276,209
79	3,556	2	1,069	2,138	4	1,142,761
84	3,025	7	538	3,766	49	289,444
106	2,877	29	390	11,310	841	152,100
85	2,450	8	−37	−296	64	1,369
1,078	34,818			78,530	7,348	19,310,908

$$SS_Y = \sum(Y - \bar{Y})^2 = 19310908$$

$$r = \frac{SP}{\sqrt{SS_X SS_Y}} = \frac{78530}{\sqrt{(7348)(19310908)}} = .208$$

Step 4. Make the correct conclusion.

The calculated Pearson $r = .208$, which is not within the rejection zone. Therefore, we fail to reject the null hypothesis. The evidence is not strong enough to support the claim that a positive relationship exists between cell phone bill and monthly income.

2. The partial correlation calculates the relationship between X and Y, while keeping Z constant.

$$r_{XY.Z} = \frac{r_{XY} - (r_{XZ} r_{YZ})}{\sqrt{(1 - r_{XZ}^2)(1 - r_{YZ}^2)}}$$

$$r_{XY} = .678$$

$$r_{XZ} = .895$$

$$r_{YZ} = .743$$

$$r_{XY.Z} = \frac{r_{XY} - (r_{XZ}r_{YZ})}{\sqrt{(1 - r_{XZ}^2)(1 - r_{YZ}^2)}} = \frac{.678 - (.895)(.743)}{\sqrt{(1 - .895^2)(1 - .743^2)}} = \frac{.678 - .665}{\sqrt{(.199)(.488)}} = \frac{.013}{.299} = .043$$

The partial correlation between drowning accidents and ice cream sales, while keeping number of visitors constant, is .043. The relationship is very weak.

3. The four-step hypothesis test for Pearson's r is appropriate to answer this question.

Step 1. State the pair of hypotheses.

The problem statement asks you to test a positive relationship between the 10-minute screening and the comprehensive diagnostic test. A right-tailed test is the appropriate test.

Right-tailed test: $H_0: \rho = 0$
   $H_1: \rho > 0$

Step 2. Identify the rejection zone.

The critical value of Pearson's r for a right-tailed test with $df = n - 2 = 12 - 2 = 10$ and $\alpha = .05$ is .497. The rejection zone is $r > .497$.

Step 3. Calculate the statistic.

$$r = \frac{\text{SP}}{\sqrt{SS_X SS_Y}}$$

The step-by-step calculation is shown in Table 11.9b with added columns $(X - \bar{X})$, $(Y - \bar{Y})$, $(X - \bar{X})(Y - \bar{Y})$, $(X - \bar{X})^2$, and $(Y - \bar{Y})^2$.

$$\bar{X} = \sum X/n = 276/12 = 23$$

$$\bar{Y} = \sum Y/n = 636/12 = 53$$

$$\text{SP} = \sum(X - \bar{X})(Y - \bar{Y}) = 155$$

TABLE 11.9b Calculation of Pearson's *r* Between the 10-Minute Screening and the Comprehensive Diagnostic Test

10-MINUTE SCREENING	COMPREHENSIVE TEST	$(X - \bar{X})$	$(Y - \bar{Y})$	$(X - \bar{X})(Y - \bar{Y})$	$(X - \bar{X})^2$	$(Y - \bar{Y})^2$
20	47	−3	−6	18	9	36
21	46	−2	−7	14	4	49
19	54	−4	1	−4	16	1
22	45	−1	−8	8	1	64
22	50	−1	−3	3	1	9
23	45	0	−8	0	0	64
23	43	0	−10	0	0	100
24	49	1	−4	−4	1	16
24	63	1	10	10	1	100
25	60	2	7	14	4	49
26	69	3	16	48	9	256
27	65	4	12	48	16	144
276	636			155	62	888

$$SS_X = \sum(X - \bar{X})^2 = 62$$

$$SS_Y = \sum(Y - \bar{Y})^2 = 888$$

$$r = \frac{SP}{\sqrt{SS_X SS_Y}} = \frac{155}{\sqrt{(62)(888)}} = .661$$

Step 4. Make the correct conclusion.

The calculated Pearson *r* = .661, which is within the rejection zone. Therefore, we reject the null hypothesis. The evidence is strong enough to support the claim that a positive relationship exists between the 10-minute screening and the comprehensive diagnostic test. As we discussed before, the correlation between the 10-minute screening and the well-established and validated comprehensive diagnostic test is the criterion-related validity for the 10-minute screening.

Sharpen your skills with SAGE edge!

Visit edge.sagepub.com/bowen for mobile-friendly quizzes, flashcards, videos, and more!

WHAT YOU LEARNED

Pearson's correlation is a statistical procedure that quantifies the extent that two variables move in the same direction or opposite directions. Pearson's r provides both the direction and strength of the relationship. The range of Pearson's r is $-1 \leq r \leq 1$.

$$\text{Pearson correlation } r = \frac{SP}{\sqrt{SS_X SS_Y}}$$

or

$$\text{Pearson's } r = \frac{\sum Z_X Z_Y}{(n-1)}$$

The four-step hypothesis test procedure applies to Pearson's r, Spearman's rank correlation, and the point biserial correlation.

Spearman's rank correlation is a nonparametric alternative to Pearson's correlation, where the data do not have equal units or are not normally distributed. Spearman's correlation is calculated based on the rankings of the paired variables.

$$r_S = \frac{SP}{\sqrt{SS_X SS_Y}}$$

However, there is also a special simplified formula for Spearman's rank correlation when there are no tied ranks.

$$r_S = 1 - \frac{6\sum d^2}{n(n^2 - 1)}$$

where

   d = the difference between the X rank and the Y rank

   n = number of paired variables

A partial correlation is defined as the purified correlation between two variables while controlling a third variable by holding it constant.

$$r_{XY.Z} = \frac{r_{XY} - (r_{XZ} r_{YZ})}{\sqrt{(1 - r_{XZ}^2)(1 - r_{YZ}^2)}}$$

The point biserial correlation is applicable when one variable is interval or ratio but the other variable is a naturally occurring dichotomous variable coded as 0 or 1.

$$r_{\text{pbi}} = \frac{SP}{\sqrt{SS_X SS_Y}}$$

The point biserial correlation generates results that are identical to those obtained using the independent-samples t test with equal variance assumed.

$$r_{\text{pbi}}^2 = \frac{t^2}{t^2 + df}$$

KEY WORDS

Coefficient of determination: The coefficient of determination is defined as r^2, which is the percentage of variance overlap between X and Y or the percentage of variance in Y that is explained by X.

Confounding variable: A confounding variable is an extraneous variable in a study that correlates with both the independent variable and the dependent variable.

Homoscedasticity: Homoscedasticity is the condition under which the variance in Y is the same across all possible values of X. In other words, there is equal spread of Y for every value of X.

Partial correlation: A partial correlation is the purified correlation between two variables while controlling a third variable by holding it constant.

STRAIGHTFORWARD STATISTICS

Pearson's correlation, *r*: Pearson's *r* is a statistical procedure that quantifies the extent that two variables move in the same direction or opposite directions. It provides direction and strength of the relationship.

Point biserial correlation, r_{pbi}: The point biserial correlation measures the correlation between an interval or ratio variable and a naturally occurring dichotomous variable coded as 0 or 1.

Scatterplot: A scatterplot between two variables is a graph of dots plotted in a two-dimensional space. Each data point contains a pair of values on the *X* and *Y* axes.

Spearman's rank correlation, r_s: Spearman's rank correlation measures the relationship between two ordinal variables where values represent rankings.

LEARNING ASSESSMENT

Multiple Choice: Circle the best answer to every question.

1. Which of the following pairs of variables is most likely to be positively correlated?

   a. Years after retirement and bank account amount

   b. Age and running speed

   c. Number of hours in the sun and severity of sunburn

   d. Number of missed classes and exam grades

2. Which of the following pairs of variables is most likely to be negatively correlated?

   a. Years on the job and salary

   b. Educational attainment and income

   c. Number of hours in the sun and severity of sunburn

   d. Number of missed classes and exam grades

3. What is the most likely direction of the relationship between time running on a treadmill and calories burned?

   a. Positive correlation

   b. Negative correlation

   c. No relationship

   d. None of the above

4. How is the strength of Pearson's product moment correlation coefficient, *r*, expressed?

   a. The calculated value of Pearson's *r*

   b. The absolute value of Pearson's *r*

   c. The square of Pearson's *r*

   d. The square root of Pearson's *r*

5. What is the range of Pearson's product moment correlation coefficient, *r*?

   a. $-1 < r < 1$

   b. $0 < r < 1$

c. $-1 \leq r \leq 1$

d. $0 \leq r \leq 1$

6. The Pearson r between age and reaction time is .784. What is the percentage of variance in reaction time that is overlapped with age?

a. 78.4%

b. 21.6%

c. 4.6%

d. 61.5%

7. The partial correlation is calculated

a. to show association between an interval or ratio variable and a dichotomous variable.

b. to show association between two dichotomous variables.

c. to show association between two primary variables while keeping a third variable constant.

d. to show association between two interval or ratio variables.

8. The coefficient of determination is defined as

a. the direction of Pearson's r.

b. the absolute value of Pearson's r.

c. the absolute value of Spearman's rank correlation.

d. the square of Pearson's r.

9. Spearman's rank correlation is specifically designed to calculate the relationship between

a. one nominal variable and one ratio variable.

b. two ordinal variables.

c. one nominal variable and one interval variable.

d. three variables.

Free Response Questions

10. Assume that a group of 10 incoming freshmen is randomly selected. Their ACT composite scores and SAT scores are reported in Table 11.10. Assume that ACT and SAT scores are normally distributed.

a. Construct a scatterplot to visually inspect the data to see if there is a linear relationship between ACT and SAT scores.

b. Conduct a hypothesis test to see whether there is a significant relationship between ACT and SAT scores, using $\alpha = .05$.

TABLE 11.10   ACT and SAT Scores of 10 Incoming Freshmen

ACT	SAT
27	1,890
26	1,450
31	2,050
34	2,150
30	2,250
21	1,380
20	1,450
19	1,600
18	1,350
24	1,680

11. A group of eight adult males is randomly selected. Their exercise logs record hours of exercise over a 2-month period. The total hours of exercise are calculated from their exercise logs, and their weight changes are measured at the end of 2 months as reported in Table 11.11. Assume that weight changes and hours of exercise are normally distributed.

a. Construct a scatterplot to visually inspect the data to see if a linear relationship exists between exercise and weight change.

b. Conduct a hypothesis test to see whether there is a significant relationship between exercise and weight change, using $\alpha = .10$.

TABLE 11.11 Hours of Exercise and Weight Change for Eight Adult Males

EXERCISE	WEIGHT CHANGE
27	–7
52	–18
39	18
58	–25
21	41
54	–29
20	3
49	–39

12. The National Highway Traffic Safety Administration does front crash, side crash, and rollover tests to rate a car's crash safety. Here is a list of small to midsize sedans with their crash safety ranking and their weight as shown in Table 11.12. Conduct a hypothesis test to see whether there is a significant relationship between the crash safety ranking and weight.

TABLE 11.12 Crash Safety Ranking and Weight

CAR	CRASH SAFETY RANKING	WEIGHT (POUNDS)
A	1	3,676
B	2	3,399
C	3	3,386
D	4	2,438
E	5	3,588
F	6	3,139
G	7	2,618

Simple Regression

After reading and studying this chapter, you should be able to do the following:

- Describe how the slope and *Y*-intercept are mathematically determined
- Explain how to identify the regression equation by calculating slope and *Y*-intercept
- Identify the four-step hypothesis test for the significance of a simple regression
- Describe the statistical assumptions for regression
- Distinguish and explain the differences between correlations and regression

What You Know and What Is New

You learned how to calculate different types of correlations in Chapter 11. The most commonly used correlation is Pearson's *r*, which is designed to estimate a linear relationship between two interval or ratio variables. It does not specify which one is the independent variable (i.e., predictor) or the dependent variable (i.e., criterion).

$$\text{Pearson's correlation formula } r = \frac{\text{SP}}{\sqrt{SS_X SS_Y}}$$

Although the linear relationship in Pearson's *r* is indicated by the direction and strength of the correlation coefficient, it does not explicitly identify a line that will fit the scatterplot of *X* and Y. Locating the line that best fits the X and Y values is the main focus of this chapter, in which we cover *simple regression*.

In a simple regression, there is only one independent variable (or predictor), X, and one dependent variable (or criterion), Y. We explicitly identify the line that fits the scatterplot of X and Y with the smallest sum of the squared vertical distances between the individual data points and the line. We will study what this sum means and the details on how to calculate it in this chapter. One of the main purposes of regression is prediction. This is what we will focus on in this chapter. It is possible to draw many lines to fit the data points but there is only one best fitting line. The best fitting line is depicted by a straight line that goes through $(\bar{X}, \bar{Y})$ to minimize the vertical distances between the actual Y values and the predicted value of Y, which is denoted as $\hat{Y}$. The value of $\hat{Y}$ is calculated based on the relationship between X and Y to figure out how Y changes when X increases by one unit. Such predictions are the essential differences between regression and correlation.

Y-INTERCEPT AND SLOPE

Simple regression is the most commonly used linear predictive analysis when making quantitative predictions of the dependent variable, Y, based on the values of the independent variable, X. Many straight lines could be drawn to fit the data points. Each line might have a slightly different slope or intercept. The best fitting straight line is the regression line. Figure 12.1 shows two such lines, but only one produces the minimal sum of squared distances. The solid line in Figure 12.1 is the regression line, while the dotted line is not. The vertical black line represents the distance between the data point and the straight line. The vertical distance is error $= Y - \hat{Y}$ as shown in Figure 12.1. An error can be calculated for every data point. Errors (or residuals) are defined as the differences between the actual Y and the predicted $\hat{Y}$.

The "best fitting" is mathematically defined by the smallest sum of squared errors, $\Sigma(Y - \hat{Y})^2$ across all data points. The regression equation is the equation for the regression line, which is expressed as $\hat{Y} = a + bX$, where a is labeled as the Y-intercept and b is labeled as the slope. The Y-intercept is the value of Y when $X = 0$. The slope is the value change in Y when X increases by one unit. They are mathematically determined by the following formulas.

$$b = \frac{\text{SP}}{SS_X}$$

$$a = \bar{Y} - b\bar{X}$$

This method of estimating a regression line is referred to as the ordinary least squares (OLS). OLS depicts the best fitting line by a straight line that goes through $(\bar{X}, \bar{Y})$ and minimizes the vertical distances between the actual Y values and the predicted $\hat{Y}$.

FIGURE 12.1 Straight Lines to Fit the Scatterplot of X and Y

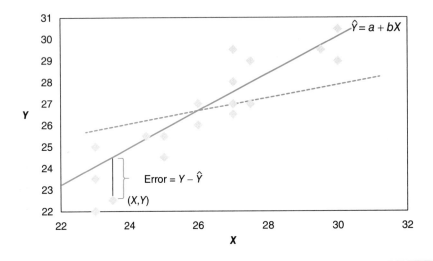

Let's use an example to illustrate how to calculate the Y-intercept and slope from the two variables X and Y.

$$b = \frac{SP}{SS_X}$$

$$a = \bar{Y} - b\bar{X}$$

where

$$SP = \sum(X - \bar{X})(Y - \bar{Y})$$

$$SS_X = \sum(X - \bar{X})^2$$

Both SP and SS_X are familiar terms from Chapter 11. You should feel confident with these calculations.

EXAMPLE 12.1

Physical activities burn calories. The relationship between hours of exercise and calories burned can be analyzed. Assume that a group of 10 adults is randomly selected. Their hours of exercise and calories burned are reported in Table 12.1a. What is the regression line to predict calories burned by using hours spent on exercising?

Similar to calculating Pearson's r, we need to figure out the $\bar{X}$ and $\bar{Y}$ and then add the following four columns in Table 12.1b: $(X - \bar{X})$, $(Y - \bar{Y})$, $(X - \bar{X})(Y - \bar{Y})$, and $(X - \bar{X})^2$. These demonstrate the step-by-step calculation process.

$$\bar{X} = \sum X / n = 37 / 10 = 3.7$$

$$\bar{Y} = \sum Y / n = 7100 / 10 = 710$$

$$SP = \sum (X - \bar{X})(Y - \bar{Y}) = 2575$$

$$SS_X = \sum (X - \bar{X})^2 = 23.1$$

$$b = \frac{SP}{SS_X} = \frac{2575}{23.1} = 111.47$$

$$a = \bar{Y} - b\bar{X}$$

$$a = 710 - 111.47(3.7) = 297.55$$

TABLE 12.1a Hours of Exercise and Calories Burned for 10 Adults

HOURS OF EXERCISE, X	CALORIES BURNED, Y
1	300
3	460
6	990
2.5	850
4.5	940
5	1,100
4	750
2	610
3.5	450
5.5	650

TABLE 12.1b Step-by-Step Calculation for Regression Line Between Hours of Exercise and Calories Burned for 10 Adults

HOURS OF EXERCISE, X	CALORIES BURNED, Y	$(X - \bar{X})$	$(Y - \bar{Y})$	$(X - \bar{X})(Y - \bar{Y})$	$(X - \bar{X})^2$
1	300	−2.7	−410	1,107	7.29
3	460	−0.7	−250	175	0.49
6	990	2.3	280	644	5.29
2.5	850	−1.2	140	−168	1.44
4.5	940	0.8	230	184	0.64
5	1,100	1.3	390	507	1.69
4	750	0.3	40	12	0.09
2	610	−1.7	−100	170	2.89
3.5	450	−0.2	−260	52	0.04
5.5	650	1.8	−60	−108	3.24
37	7,100			2,575	23.1

(Continued)

(Continued)

The regression line between the hours of exercise and calories burned is
$\hat{Y} = 297.55 + 111.47X$.

$\hat{Y}$ is the estimated value of Y, which is calculated from the regression equation. For every value of X, the corresponding $\hat{Y}$ can be calculated by plugging in the value of X into the regression equation. The sum of squared distance between every $\hat{Y}$ and the actual Y value, $\sum(Y - \hat{Y})^2$, is minimized by the regression line.

When we draw the regression line to fit the scatterplot of hours of exercise and calories burned, the result is shown in Figure 12.2.

FIGURE 12.2   Regression Line and Scatterplot of Hours of Exercise and Calories Burned

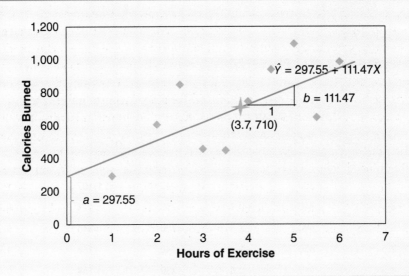

In Figure 12.2, the Y-intercept 297.55 is the value of Y when $X = 0$. The slope is the value change in Y when X increases by one unit. In Example 12.1, for every additional hour exercised, 111.47 more calories are burned. The blue star in the middle of Figure 12.2 is the data point representing $(\bar{X}, \bar{Y}) = (3.7, 710)$. The regression line always goes through $(\bar{X}, \bar{Y})$. This is true for all simple regressions.

Pop Quiz

1. Which one of the following data points is always on the regression line?

   a. (0, 0)

   b. (a, b)

   c. (10, 10)

   d. $(\bar{X}, \bar{Y})$

HYPOTHESIS TESTING WITH SIMPLE REGRESSION

Predictions are used in everyday activities. Educators want to predict students' academic performance, corporations want to predict the market trends, and employers want to predict new hires' job performance, just to name a few examples. Not all predictions are created equal. You need to know how to judge whether the independent variable really helps predicting the values of the dependent variable; therefore, you need to learn how to conduct hypothesis tests on regressions. Simple regression is to predict the values of Y by using the values of X. The focus of regression is the dependent variable Y. The independent variable X is used in a supporting role to provide information, so you can do a better job of predicting Y. Without any information on X, the best prediction for Y is $\bar{Y}$. As you will recall from Chapter 3, the mean is the most frequently used central tendency measure for representing the center of a distribution, assuming there are no extreme outliers. By using the values of X, you can calculate a regression line $\hat{Y} = a + bX$ to predict Y based on X. With the information on X, the best prediction for Y is $\hat{Y}$. Thus, the difference between $\hat{Y}$ and $\bar{Y}$, $(\hat{Y} - \bar{Y})$, could be viewed as the contribution from regression. Let's contrast the differences among Y, $\bar{Y}$, and $\hat{Y}$.

$$\text{Deviation of } Y = (Y - \bar{Y})$$

$$\text{Explained deviation by regression} = (\hat{Y} - \bar{Y})$$

$$\text{Unexplained deviation by regression} = (Y - \hat{Y})$$

Putting all three deviations together, you get

Deviation of Y = Explained deviation by regression + Unexplained deviation by regression

$$(Y - \bar{Y}) = (\hat{Y} - \bar{Y}) + (Y - \hat{Y})$$

The unexplained deviation is what is missed by the regression. It is also referred to as error or residual. Some books use these two terms interchangeably. I prefer to use error throughout this book. Errors represent the difference or distance between the actual Y and the predicted $\hat{Y}$. Errors do not mean mistakes are made. It means the predicted values $\hat{Y}$ are not exactly the same as the actual Y values. The smaller the errors, the better the predictions.

$$\text{Error} = (Y - \hat{Y})$$

Sometimes the actual Y is higher than $\hat{Y}$ (positive error), and sometimes the actual Y is lower than $\hat{Y}$ (negative error). To avoid positive errors completely canceling out the negative errors, we square the errors, $\text{squared errors} = (Y - \hat{Y})^2$. This is the same method as discussed in Chapter 3 where we squared the deviations and then added them up to create the useful sum of squares.

To figure out the total squared errors across all values, simply add them up. When the slope and intercept are calculated the way we just learned, the sum of the squared errors is known as the least squares. This is because of all the possible lines that could be used to predict Y given X, the slope and intercept calculated this way produce the smallest (or least) amount of errors.

$$\text{Sum of squared errors} = \text{SSE} = \sum (Y - \hat{Y})^2$$

Apply the same principle to $(\hat{Y} - \bar{Y})$. You square the $(\hat{Y} - \bar{Y})$ and then add them up. You get a new term, which is labeled the *sum of squares due to regression*, $\text{SSR} = \sum (\hat{Y} - \bar{Y})^2$.

Again, apply the same principle to $(Y - \bar{Y})$. You square $(Y - \bar{Y})^2$ and then add them up. You get a familiar sum of squared deviations of Y, $SS_Y = \sum (Y - \bar{Y})^2$. Since Y is the main focus of a regression analysis, the SS_Y is also labeled as SST or the sum of squares total. The relationship among all three sum of squared terms in regression is $\text{SST} = \text{SSR} + \text{SSE}$.

Your head might be spinning at this point. A visual presentation of what I just covered might help. In Figure 12.3, SST is the Y circle, SSR is the overlap between X circle and Y circle, and SSE is the part of Y that does not overlap with X. The overlap between X and Y can be calculated by one simple formula, the coefficient of determination r^2, as first introduced in Chapter 11, where r is the Pearson's correlation between X and Y. The total variation of Y is SS_Y and the overlap between X and Y is r^2. Therefore, the explained variation of Y is $\text{SSR} = r^2 SS_Y$. The unexplained variation of Y is $\text{SSE} = (1 - r^2) SS_Y$. When we add the explained variation with the unexplained variation of Y, we get the total variation of Y.

$$\text{SSR} = r^2 SS_Y$$

$$\text{SSE} = (1 - r^2) SS_Y$$

Total variation of Y = Explained variation in Y + Unexplained variation in Y

$$SS_Y = r^2 SS_Y + \left(1 - r^2\right) SS_Y$$

$$SST = SSR + SSE$$

To evaluate whether the X values help predict the Y values, we partition the total variances of Y into two separate parts: (1) variances due to regression and (2) variances due to errors.

Variance was first introduced in Chapter 3, and it is calculated as $s^2 = SS/df$. This formula is still relevant in this chapter. Partitioning variances due to different sources is called the **analysis of variances (ANOVA)**, which is discussed in-depth in Chapter 13. In simple regression, we construct an ANOVA summary table to test the significance of the regression model. The idea is to compare and contrast the variances due to regression and the variances due to error. If the variances due to regression are much bigger than the variances due to error, the model is effective. If the variances due to regression are not much bigger than the variances due to error, the model is not effective. We will go over all the formulas to construct the ANOVA summary table for regression.

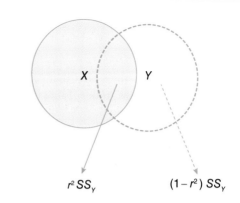

FIGURE 12.3 Explained and Unexplained Variation of Y

$r^2 SS_Y$ $\qquad$ $(1 - r^2) SS_Y$

You know variance $s^2 = SS/df$. We already learned SS terms in regression: SST, SSR, and SSE. Now, we need to figure out degrees of freedom for these terms. The **degrees of freedom due to regression** are defined as the number of predictors in the regression equation. There is only one predictor in a simple regression. Therefore, the degree of freedom for a simple regression is 1. In the language of ANOVA, variances are also labeled as mean squares (MS). Therefore, the variances due to regression are also labeled as mean squares due to regression, MSR.

$$\text{MSR} = \frac{\text{SSR}}{df_R} = \frac{\text{SSR}}{1}$$

The **degrees of freedom due to error** are defined as $(n - 2)$. This is because in the process of calculating a simple regression, $\bar{X}$ and $\bar{Y}$ are used to estimate two population parameters, μ_X and μ_Y. Every time you estimate a parameter, you lose 1 df. Estimating two parameters means losing 2 df. The variances due to error are also labeled as mean squares error, or MSE.

$$MSE = \frac{\text{SSE}}{df_E} = \frac{\text{SSE}}{(n - 2)}$$

The significance of the regression is calculated by an F test. The calculated F value demonstrates the ratio of variance explained by the regression to the variance left unexplained by the errors.

$$F = \frac{MSR}{MSE}$$

The critical values of F that set the boundaries of the rejection zones can be found using $F_{(df_1, df_2)}$ in the same F Table you used to determine whether equal variances are assumed in Chapter 9. This table is provided in Appendix C. Each critical F value is determined by two different degrees of freedom, where df_1 is the degrees of freedom from the numerator and df_2 is the degrees of freedom from the denominator. In the case of a simple regression, df_1 is the degrees of freedom due to regression, $df_1 = df_R = 1$ and df_2 is the degrees of freedom due to errors, $df_2 = df_E = (n-2)$. Therefore, the critical values of F can be identified by $F_{(1, n-2)}$ in the F Table for simple regression.

Now, you are ready to put everything together and conduct the four-step hypothesis test for a simple regression.

Step 1. State the pair of hypotheses.

The purpose of a simple regression is to use the values of X to predict the values of Y. Therefore, one of the most important parts of the regression equation is the slope, which describes how the value of Y changes when X increases by one unit. The slope is also called the regression coefficient. It is denoted as b when the data are from a sample and as β when describing a population. The hypotheses always describe the population parameters. If knowing the values of X do not help predict the values of Y, $\beta = 0$. On the other hand, if knowing the values of X better predict the values of Y, $\beta \neq 0$. Accordingly, the pair of hypotheses for a simple regression is expressed as follows:

$H_0: \beta = 0$

$H_1: \beta \neq 0$

The test statistic for a simple regression is an F test, calculated as $F = MSR/MSE$. MSR is derived from SSR, and MSE is derived from SSE. These numbers are always positive. Therefore, the calculated F values are always positive. Unlike the Z tests or t tests in previous chapters, F tests only produce positive values. This makes it impossible to use F for one-tailed tests. One-tailed or directional tests are *possible* only when the test statistics can show either positive or negative values. Therefore, hypothesis tests for simple regression are two-tailed or nondirectional tests when using F tests.

Step 2. Identify the rejection zone.

The critical values of F that set off the boundaries of the rejection zones are identified by $F_{(1,n-2)}$ in the F Table. The rejection zone is identified as calculated $F > F_{(1,n-2)}$.

Step 3. Calculate the test statistic.

The process of calculating F for a simple regression as discussed earlier can be summarized in Table 12.2.

TABLE 12.2 The ANOVA Summary Table for Calculating F for a Simple Regression

SOURCE	SS	df	MS	F
Regression	$SSR = r^2 SS_Y$	1	$MSR = \dfrac{SSR}{1}$	$\dfrac{MSR}{MSE}$
Error	$SSE = (1 - r^2)SS_Y$	$n - 2$	$MSE = \dfrac{SSE}{(n-2)}$	
Total	SS_Y or SST	$n - 1$		

A large F value indicates that the variances explained by the regression are relatively large compared with the variances left unexplained (i.e., error variances). A small F value indicates that the variances explained by the regression are relatively small compared with the variances left unexplained (i.e., error variances). However, the standard to judge what is considered to be "large" is in the critical values from the F Table as specified in Step 2.

Step 4. Make the correct conclusion.

If the calculated F from Step 3 is within the rejection zone, we reject H_0. If the calculated F is not within the rejection zone, we fail to reject H_0.

Finally, the process of conducting a hypothesis test on a simple regression is complete. It is time to use an example to go through the four-step hypothesis test for a simple regression. In Example 12.1, we calculated the regression line, and the results are shown in Table 12.1b. Now we can complete the process by conducting a hypothesis test on the overall significance of the simple regression, using $\alpha = .05$.

$$\bar{X} = \sum X / n = 37 / 10 = 3.7$$

$$\bar{Y} = \sum Y / n = 7100 / 10 = 710$$

Step 1. State the pair of hypotheses.

$$H_0: \beta = 0$$

$$H_1: \beta \neq 0$$

Step 2. Identify the rejection zone.

The critical value of F under $\alpha = .05$ is $F_{(1,8)} = 5.32$. The rejection zone is $F > 5.32$.

Step 3. Calculate the statistic.

Conducting a hypothesis test on a simple regression requires r^2. Therefore, one additional column, $(Y - \bar{Y})^2$, needs to be added to Table 12.1b to complete this process. This is shown in Table 12.1c.

$$r = \frac{SP}{\sqrt{SS_X SS_Y}} = \frac{2575}{\sqrt{(23.1)(616400)}} = .682$$

$$r^2 = .682^2 = .466$$

TABLE 12.1c Step-by-Step Calculation for Conducting a Hypothesis Test on a Simple Regression Between Hours of Exercise and Calories Burned for 10 Adults

HOURS OF EXERCISE, X	CALORIES BURNED, Y	$(X - \bar{X})$	$(Y - \bar{Y})$	$(X - \bar{X})(Y - \bar{Y})$	$(X - \bar{X})^2$	$(Y - \bar{Y})^2$
1	300	−2.7	−410	1107	7.29	168,100
3	460	−0.7	−250	175	0.49	62,500
6	990	2.3	280	644	5.29	78,400
2.5	850	−1.2	140	−168	1.44	19,600
4.5	940	0.8	230	184	0.64	52,900
5	1,100	1.3	390	507	1.69	152,100
4	750	0.3	40	12	0.09	1,600
2	610	−1.7	−100	170	2.89	10,000
3.5	450	−0.2	−260	52	0.04	67,600
5.5	650	1.8	−60	−108	3.24	3,600
37	7,100			2,575	23.1	616,400

$$SS_Y = 616,400$$

$$SSR = r^2 SS_Y = .466(616,400) = 287242.4$$

$$SSE = (1 - r^2)SS_Y = (1 - .466)(616,400) = 329157.6$$

Put all the numbers into the ANOVA summary table for a simple regression, as shown in Table 12.1d.

TABLE 12.1d The ANOVA Summary Table for the Simple Regression Between Hours of Exercise and Calories Burned

SOURCE	SS	df	MS	F
Regression	287242.4	1	287242.4	6.98
Error	329157.6	8	41144.7	
Total	616,400	9		

Step 4. Make the correct conclusion.

The calculated $F = 6.98$ is within the rejection zone; therefore, we reject H_0. The evidence is strong enough to support the claim that using hours of exercise helps predict calories burned by this simple regression line $\hat{Y} = 297.55 + 111.47X$.

Once you reject H_0, you know that using X values helps predict Y values. You may use the regression equation to calculate $\hat{Y}$ for any value of X within the value range in the sample. For example, you can calculate the predicted calories burned, $\hat{Y}$, when the hours of exercise is 4 by plugging $X = 4$ into the regression equation.

$$\hat{Y} = 297.55 + 111.47(4) = 743.43$$

The predicted calories burned with 4 hours of exercise are 743.43 according to the regression equation. Such predictions work well for X values within the range of the original X values in the sample but might not work for X values outside the range of X in the sample.

There is a quick and easy way to double-check your calculations in this summary table by using the basic principle SST = SSR + SSE. In this example, SSR = 287242.4 and SSE = 329157.6. If and only if these two add up to be SST = 616,400 are all of your calculations correct. In this case, they do add up, so the calculations are correct. The process to conduct a hypothesis test for the simple regression is quite complicated. You can certainly benefit from doing more practice. There are discussions and debates about whether education is a worthy investment for the future. Let's use an example to predict annual salary from education.

EXAMPLE 12.2

It would be interesting to find out the relationship between education and annual salary. Assume that a group of ten 28-year-olds is randomly selected. Their years of schooling and annual salaries (in thousands of dollars) are reported in Table 12.3a. Use the values in Table 12.3a to address the following considerations.

TABLE 12.3a Years of Schooling and Annual Salaries for 28-Year-Olds

YEARS OF SCHOOLING	ANNUAL SALARY ($1,000)
12	25
13.5	19
14	61
15	27
16.5	35
17	34
18.5	36
19	33
20.5	75
21	55

a. Construct a scatterplot to verify if a linear relationship exists between years of schooling and annual salaries.

b. Identify the best fitting line for years of schooling and annual salaries.

c. Conduct a hypothesis test to verify if years of schooling help predict annual salaries.

Answers

a. The scatterplot of years of schooling and annual salaries is shown in Figure 12.4.

FIGURE 12.4 A Scatterplot of Years of Schooling and Annual Salaries

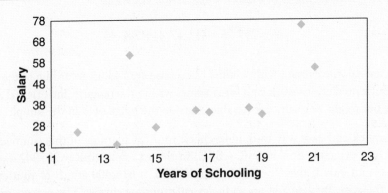

According to the scatterplot, a linear relationship exists between years of schooling and annual salaries. There are no obvious outliers.

b. According to the formulas for the slope and Y-intercept for the regression line,

$$a = \bar{Y} - b\bar{X}$$

$$b = \frac{SP}{SS_X}$$

We need to figure out the $\bar{X}$ and $\bar{Y}$.

$$\bar{X} = \sum X / n = 167 / 10 = 16.7$$

$$\bar{Y} = \sum Y / n = 400 / 10 = 40$$

Then add the following five columns to Table 12.3a, $(X - \bar{X})$, $(Y - \bar{Y})$, $(X - \bar{X})(Y - \bar{Y})$, $(X - \bar{X})^2$, and $(Y - \bar{Y})^2$, to demonstrate the step-by-step calculation process as shown in Table 12.3b.

$$SP = \sum(X - \bar{X})(Y - \bar{Y}) = 276.5$$

$$SS_X = \sum(X - \bar{X})^2 = 84.1$$

TABLE 12.3b Step-by-Step Calculation to Predict Annual Salaries Using Years of Schooling for 28-Year-Olds

YEARS OF SCHOOLING	ANNUAL SALARY, $1,000	$(X - \bar{X})$	$(Y - \bar{Y})$	$(X - \bar{X})(Y - \bar{Y})$	$(X - \bar{X})^2$	$(Y - \bar{Y})^2$
12	25	−4.7	−15	70.5	22.09	225
13.5	19	−3.2	−21	67.2	10.24	441
14	61	−2.7	21	−56.7	7.29	441
15	27	−1.7	−13	22.1	2.89	169
16.5	35	−0.2	−5	1	0.04	25
17	34	0.3	−6	−1.8	0.09	36
18.5	36	1.8	−4	−7.2	3.24	16
19	33	2.3	−7	−16.1	5.29	49
20.5	75	3.8	35	133	14.44	1,225
21	55	4.3	15	64.5	18.49	225
167	400			276.5	84.1	2,852

(Continued)

(Continued)

$$b = \frac{SP}{SS_X} = \frac{276.5}{84.1} = 3.288$$

$$a = \bar{Y} - b\bar{X} = 40 - 3.288(16.7) = -14.910$$

Therefore, the regression line to predict annual salary using years of schooling is

$$\hat{Y} = -14.910 + 3.288X$$

On average, for every additional year of schooling, annual salary increases by 3.288 thousand dollars.

c.

Step 1. State the pair of hypotheses.

$H_0: \beta = 0$

$H_1: \beta \neq 0$

Step 2. Identify the rejection zone.

The critical value of F in the F Table under $\alpha = .05$ is $F_{(1,8)} = 5.32$. The rejection zone is $F > 5.32$.

Step 3. Calculate the statistic.

$$SS_Y = \Sigma(Y - \bar{Y})^2 = 2852$$

$$r = \frac{SP}{\sqrt{SS_X SS_Y}} = \frac{276.5}{\sqrt{(84.1)(2852)}} = .565$$

$$r^2 = .565^2 = .319$$

$$SSR = r^2 SS_Y = .319(2{,}852) = 909.788$$

$$SSE = (1 - r^2)SS_Y = (1 - .319)(2{,}852) = 1942.212$$

Put all the numbers into the ANOVA summary table for a simple regression to predict annual salary using years of schooling as shown in Table 12.3c.

Step 4. Make the correct conclusion.

The calculated F is not within the rejection zone; therefore, we fail to reject H_0. The evidence is not strong enough to support the claim that the years of schooling can help predict the annual salary.

TABLE 12.3c   The ANOVA Summary Table for the Simple Regression Between Annual Salary and Years of Schooling

SOURCE	SS	df	MS	F
Regression	909.788	1	909.788	3.747
Error	1942.212	8	242.777	
Total	2,852	9		

STANDARD ERROR OF THE ESTIMATE

Another way to demonstrate the accuracy of the regression line is to measure the standard error of the estimate. The standard error of the estimate is defined as the standard deviation of the prediction errors $(Y - \hat{Y})$. In other words, the standard error of the estimate measures the standard distance between the regression line and the actual Y values. If the standard error of the estimate is large, it means that $\hat{Y}$ is very far away from the actual value of Y. If the standard error of the estimate is small, it means that $\hat{Y}$ is very close to the actual value of Y. To obtain the standard error of the estimate, follow the same operation as you do to create standard deviation (s) from sum of squared (SS) deviations for a sample,

$$s^2 = \frac{SS}{df} \text{ and } s = \sqrt{\frac{SS}{df}}$$

The sum of squared deviations of estimate is $\sum (Y - \hat{Y})^2$; therefore,

$$\text{The standard error of estimate} = \sqrt{\frac{\Sigma(Y - \hat{Y})^2}{df}} = \sqrt{\frac{\text{SSE}}{(n-2)}} = \sqrt{MSE}$$

The degrees of freedom for standard error of estimate are $n - 2$ because in the process of estimating $\hat{Y}$, you need to estimate two parameters. Every time you estimate a parameter, you lose 1 df. Estimating two parameters means losing 2 df. Therefore, the degrees of freedom for the standard error of estimate are $n - 2$.

THE MATHEMATICAL RELATIONSHIP BETWEEN PEARSON'S r AND THE REGRESSION SLOPE, b

Pearson's r formula is $r = SP / \sqrt{SS_X SS_Y}$. The regression slope is $b = SP / SS_X$.

You can see that they are very similar to each other. Indeed, there is a simple mathematical relationship between r and b.

$$b = r \frac{\sqrt{SS_Y}}{\sqrt{SS_X}}$$

Because $s_X = \sqrt{SS_X / df}$ and $s_Y = \sqrt{SS_Y / df}$, the mathematical relationship between r and b can be simplified to

$$b = r \frac{s_Y}{s_X}$$

This means that the regression slope b is equal to Pearson's r multiplied by the standard deviation of Y, then divided by the standard deviation of X. Pearson's r is calculated based on the standard scores (Z scores) of both X and Y variables; thus, both variables are on the same Z scale. Therefore, Pearson's r has a definite range of $-1 \leq r \leq 1$. In contrast, the regression slope, b, is calculated on the original scales of the variables X and Y, which may vary dramatically. Thus, there is no definite range for a regression slope. A regression slope is defined as the value change in Y when X increases by one unit. As demonstrated in previous examples, the regression slope can be the calories burned for each additional hour of exercise or the added annual salary for each additional year of schooling. The values of the calculated regression slopes do not confine themselves within a certain range. The bridge between the Z scale and the original scale is the standard deviation of the variable, so it makes perfect sense that the regression slope b equals Pearson's r multiplied by the standard deviation of Y and divided by the standard deviation of X.

1. The *F* test is used to evaluate the quality of the simple regression model, $F = MSR / MSE$. What is the relationship between the calculated *F* value and the standard error of the estimate $\sqrt{MSE}$?

   a. The larger the *F* value, the smaller the standard error of the estimate

   b. The larger the *F* value, the larger the standard error of the estimate

   c. The *F* value is the square of the standard error of the estimate.

   d. The *F* value is the square root of the standard error of the estimate.

Answer: a

Assumptions for Simple Regression

There are a few assumptions you need to pay attention to in order to ensure that results of a regression analysis are accurate. These assumptions are commonly referred to as Gauss-Markov assumptions, named after two mathematicians, Carl Friedrich Gauss and Andrey Markov, who were credited with developing the OLS method to come up with the best linear unbiased estimator, abbreviated BLUE.

1. There is a linear relationship between variables X and Y. If the relationship between X and Y is not linear, regression analysis will produce biased estimates of the actual relationship. A scatterplot of X and Y can verify whether the relationship is linear.

2. Error (or residual) is calculated by the distance between the predicted $\hat{Y}$ and the actual Y values, $(Y - \hat{Y})$. The variances of errors are the same across all values of X. The variances of Y are also the same across all values of X. This is denoted as $\mathrm{Var}(\varepsilon) = \mathrm{Var}(Y) = \sigma^2$, which is commonly referred to as the **homoscedasticity** in regression. Homoscedasticity is defined as homogeneity of variances. It is a good word to throw around to impress people with your knowledge in statistics. Being able to say homoscedasticity is much more impressive than saying homogeneity of variances. Being able to see homoscedasticity will probably help learning this concept. A scatterplot of errors and $\hat{Y}$ can verify whether the homoscedasticity is violated, as shown in Figure 12.5. In Figure 12.5, you can see a roughly even spread of residuals (i.e., errors) across all $\hat{Y}$, and most errors are within -100 and $+100$. There is a slightly larger range of errors on the left side of the graph than on the right side of the graph. Such a slight variation of homoscedasticity has little effect on the significance test, but a severe violation of homoscedasticity will lead to serious distortion of the results.

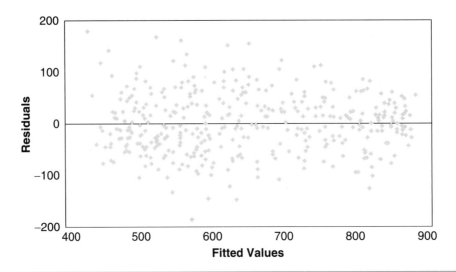

SOURCE: Chen, X., Ender, P., Mitchell, M., & Wells, C. (2003). *Regression With Stata*. Institute for Digital Research and Education, University of California at Los Angeles. http://www.ats.ucla.edu/stat/stata/web books/reg/chapter2/statareg2.htm. Reprinted with permission.

When the scatterplot of errors and $\hat{Y}$ assumes a funnel shape with errors on one side of the graph significantly larger than errors on the other side of the graph, as shown in Figure 12.6, it is called heteroscedasticity. Figure 12.6 shows that the errors on the left side of the graph are spread out much further (i.e., between 10 and −10) than the errors on the right side (i.e., between 1 and −1). It is a funnel shape with the larger opening to the left. The homogeneity of error variances assumption is violated. If the errors on the left side of the graph are much smaller than the errors on the right side, the larger opening of the funnel is to the right. It is also called heteroscedasticity.

3. The mean (or expected value) of the error term is zero. This is denoted as $E(\varepsilon) = 0$. This is due to one of the mathematical constraints that the sum of all error terms adds to zero; it is denoted as $\sum(\varepsilon) = \sum(Y - \hat{Y}) = 0$. All positive errors cancel out the negative errors.

4. Error terms are independent of one another. They are not correlated.

Applying the same principle of simple regression, but extending the principles further, you may consider multiple predictors at the same time to predict the criterion when you conduct multiple regressions. For example, in evaluating student applicants for a graduate program admission, multiple pieces of information can be considered in the decision-making process, such as GPA from undergraduate degrees, GRE scores, the quality of recommendation letters,

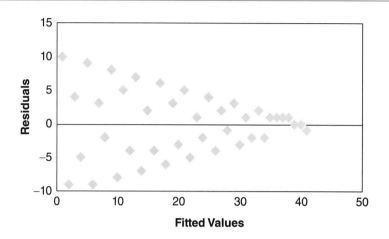

and the relevance of the personal statement to the program's curriculum. The calculations of multiple regressions are usually done by statistical software packages, which provide the significance test for every predictor included in the regression analysis and evaluate the effectiveness of the entire regression model. In this book, I assume that most instructors are teaching students introductory statistics by using calculators. The materials on EXCEL and SPSS are additional instructional resources for those instructors who teach EXCEL and SPSS. They are not meant to be required class material. I decided that multiple regression belongs to advanced statistics, so I will not cover its formulas, hypothesis test, and interpretation in this book. However, I want to point out the proper scales of measurement for the predictors in multiple regressions. The predictors in a multiple regression can be either interval or ratio variables or dichotomous variables coded as 0 or 1. Although a dichotomous variable when coded as 0 or 1 can be considered as a predictor in a simple regression, this is rarely done. A simple regression using a dichotomous predictor generates the same result as one would get when conducting a t test. Most statisticians would opt to conduct a t test instead of conducting a simple regression with a dichotomous predictor.

Another cautionary note on regression is that outliers have a strong impact on regressions,

Author's Aside

Students who are interested in getting more details on the assumptions of regression can do so by reading Berry (1993).

Berry, W. D. (1993). Understanding regression assumptions. (Sage University Paper Series on Quantitative Applications in the Social Sciences, 07-092). Newbury Park, CA: Sage.

the same way as they do on correlations. Remove outliers that are known to be caused by mistakes in measurement or data collection procedures. Examining the impact of remaining outliers can be conducted by running regression analysis with and without outliers.

To make it clear, a simple regression analysis reveals the relationship between the independent variable (X) and the dependent variable (Y) by specifying how the Y value changes when X increases by one unit. A significant simple regression does not imply causation. It is the same situation as discussed in correlations. Causation can only be established by strict experimental designs, not by statistical procedures.

STEP-BY-STEP INSTRUCTIONS ON SPSS

You may follow the exact same EXCEL step-by-step instruction shown in Chapter 11 to calculate SP, SS_X, and SS_Y. Then calculate the slope and Y-intercept for the regression line by using the OLS formulas. Or you can use SPSS to conduct a simple regression.

We use school ratings data to conduct a simple regression in SPSS. Public school districts are mandated by law to provide students' proficiency test results on social studies, language, and math from selected grades in K–12 schools. Proficiency tests along with other performance criteria are included in the school report cards every year. To demonstrate a simple regression, we use the median household income as the independent variable and the number of standards met by the school districts as the dependent variable in a school rating data set. Assume that a random sample of 31 school districts is selected. The number of standards met by the school district is in the first column and the median household income is reported in thousands of dollars, in the second column as shown in Figure 12.7.

Here are the steps to use SPSS to conduct a simple regression using median household income to predict number of standards met for a school district.

Click the **Analyze** tab.

In the drop-down menu, click **Regression**.

Then, click **Linear**.

After you complete these three steps, your screen should look like Figure 12.7.

A pop-up window appears to ask you to identify the **Dependent** and **Independent(s)** variables in the **Linear Regression**. The pop-up window asks for the **Dependent** variable first. Therefore, you click on **Number of standards met**.

Click on ⮕ to move the **Number of standards met** into the **Dependent** variable box.

Click on **median**.

Click on ➡ to move the **median** into the **Independent(s)** variable box, after you put both variables in the right places, your pop-up window should look like Figure 12.8.

Then, click **OK**.

After you hit **OK**, SPSS will run the simple regression that you've requested. It will generate the following tables in the printout. We will go through them one by one.

The first table in the SPSS printout under simple regression shows the independent variable that enters into the regression equation. The **Enter** method includes the independent variable specified by the user. There is only one independent variable in simple regression. The dependent variable (number of standards met) is specified at the bottom of the table as a footnote, as shown in Table 12.4.

The second table provides the model summary that includes important statistics, as shown in Table 12.5. The first number, **R**, is the Pearson correlation coefficient between the median household income and number of standards met. **R Square** is simply calculated by $R \times R$, which gives the percent of variance from the dependent variable explained by the independent variable. It is also called the coefficient of determination, as discussed in Chapter 11. There is no need to pay attention to the **Adjusted R Square** in a simple regression, because there is only one independent variable. The adjusted R^2 adjusts the R^2 by taking number of predictors in the model into consideration. The adjusted R^2 is a modified R^2 and only relevant to multiple regression. When you add a predictor in the model, the R^2 always goes up,

FIGURE 12.8   SPSS Linear Regression With "Number of Standards Met" as the
Dependent Variable and Median Household Income as the
Independent Variable

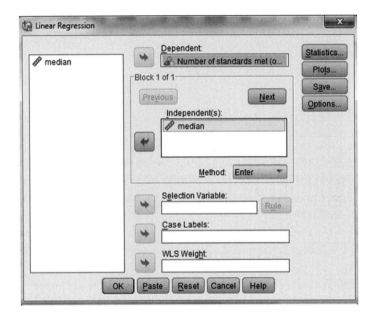

TABLE 12.4   Variables Entered as Reported by SPSS

Variables Entered/Removed[b]

Model	Variables Entered	Variables Removed	Method
1	median[a]		Enter

a. All requested variables entered.

b. Dependent Variable: Number of standards met (out of 25)

TABLE 12.5   Model Summary Table for the Simple Regression Between Median
Household Income and Number of Standards Met

Model Summary

Model	R	R Square	Adjusted R Square	Std. Error of the Estimate
1	.727[a]	.528	.512	5.511

a. Predictors: (Constant), median.

but you run into the risk of making the model too complicated to interpret or overfitting the model. The adjusted R^2 takes the cost of adding a new predictor and compares it with the benefit and then reports the efficiency of the new model. The adjusted R^2 does not always go up as the number of predictors goes up.

The last number is the

$$\text{Standard error of the estimate} = \sqrt{\frac{\Sigma(Y - \hat{Y})^2}{df}} = \sqrt{\frac{\text{SSE}}{(n-2)}} = \sqrt{MSE}$$

which reflects the accuracy of the prediction as discussed earlier in this chapter.

The third table presents the ANOVA summary table, which forms the foundation of the hypothesis test of the simple regression, as shown in Table 12.6. The calculated F value demonstrates the ratio of variance explained by the regression to the variance left unexplained by the errors. The calculated $F = 32.486$, which indicates that the variance explained by the regression is 32.486 times the variance left unexplained by the errors. The $Sig.$ value in the last column is the calculated p value associated with the F test. The p value provides the exact level of significance of the test. The p value gives the probability of obtaining the observed test statistic assuming that the null hypothesis is true. When the p value associated with a test statistic is used as a standard for a hypothesis test, the decision rules are as follows:

When the $p < \alpha$, we reject H_0.

When the $p \geq \alpha$, we fail to reject H_0.

This is the same set of decision rules as discussed in Chapter 9. The decision rules for a hypothesis test using p values are the same across all statistical procedures. In this example, the calculated $p = .000$ and the default $\alpha = .05$; therefore, we reject H_0. The median household income can predict the number of standards met in the school district very well. Please

TABLE 12.6 The ANOVA Summary Table for the Simple Regression Between the Median Household Income and the Number of Standards Met

ANOVA[b]

Model		Sum of Squares	Df	Mean Square	F	Sig.
1	Regression	986.645	1	986.645	32.486	.000[a]
	Residual	880.775	29	30.372		
	Total	1867.419	30			

a. Predictors: (Constant), median

b. Dependent Variable: Number of standards met (out of 25)

note that $p = .000$ means that the calculated probability is very small. For example, the calculated $p = .000123$; when it is rounded to three places after the decimal, it becomes $p = .000$.

The fourth table provides the regression coefficients needed to specify the regression equation, $\hat{Y} = a + bX$. We use the unstandardized coefficients to specify the regression equation, since these are stated in the same units as those in which the variables are measured. The standardized coefficients, or beta values, are stated in terms of Z scores. The first row in the table gives the constant, which refers to the intercept a, and the second row gives the unstandardized regression coefficient for median household income, which refers to the slope. Therefore, the regression line is $\hat{Y} = -3.619 + .608X$ as shown in Table 12.7.

TABLE 12.7 Regression Coefficients as Calculated by SPSS

Coefficients[a]

Model		Unstandardized Coefficients		Standardized Coefficients	t	Sig.
		B	Std. Error	Beta		
1	(Constant)	−3.619	4.052		−.893	.379
	Median	.608	.107	.727	5.700	.000

a. Dependent Variable: Number of standards met (out of 25)

The correct way to interpret this regression equation is that for every one-thousand dollar increase in the median household income in a school district, the number of standards met increases by .608. The t column indicates the t test for each predictor in the model. The pair of hypotheses for the two-tailed t test in SPSS are as follows:

$H_0: \beta_1 = 0$

$H_1: \beta_1 \neq 0$

There is only one predictor in the simple regression. The t is calculated by

$$t = \frac{\text{Unstandardized coefficient}}{\text{Standard error of the coefficient}} = \frac{.608}{.107} = 5.682$$

It is slightly different from the 5.700 as reported in Table 12.7 due to rounding. The computer keeps many digits after the decimal point during the calculation, but reports only three places after the decimal point for the final answer, so the 5.700 is more accurate than the 5.682. The last column, $Sig.$, shows that the p value associated with the t test is .000. We reject H_0. The median household income is highly significant in predicting number of standards met.

Both the ANOVA table (Table 12.6) and the regression coefficient table (Table 12.7) provide the identical results with $p = .000$. The F test in ANOVA provides significance for the entire model. Because there is only one predictor in the simple regression, the pair of hypotheses in the F test is the same as the t test. Thus, a unique mathematical relationship exists between the F test and the t test under the simple regression: $F = t^2$. Let's verify this relationship with the reported t and F values. When you square the t value $5.700^2 = 32.49$ and compare it with the reported F value 32.486, the slight discrepancy is due to rounding.

EXERCISE PROBLEMS

1. A car dealer specializing in used Corvettes has a large inventory on the lot. Assume that a group of 10 used Corvettes is randomly selected. Ages of the cars and their prices are reported in Table 12.8a. Use the values in Table 12.8a to answer the following questions.

Author's Aside

Although I have already indicated that this chapter is limited to simple regression, I would like to point out a useful connection between a simple regression and a multiple regression. The t statistics as reported in the SPSS regression coefficients table are particularly useful in multiple regressions, because a separate t test is conducted for each predictor in the multiple regression, and it represents each predictor's contribution to the overall regression model above and beyond all other predictors. The interpretation of each predictor in multiple regressions follows the same principle. When the p value associated with a t test is used as a standard for a hypothesis test, the decision rules are as follows:

When the $p < \alpha$, we reject H_0. The predictor is significant.

When the $p \geq \alpha$, we fail to reject H_0. The predictor is not significant.

   a. Construct a scatterplot of age and price of used Corvettes to see if a linear relationship exists between these two variables.

   b. Identify the regression line using used Corvette's age to predict its price.

   c. What is the predicted price for a 6-year-old Corvette?

   d. Use $\alpha = .05$ to evaluate if using the ages of the cars helps predict the prices of used Corvettes.

2. Assume that a group of nine students is randomly selected from statistics courses. Their number of hours of studying for an exam and grades from the exam are reported in Table 12.9a.

   a. Construct a scatterplot of hours of studying and grades to see if a linear relationship exists between these two variables.

TABLE 12.8a	Age and Price of Used Corvettes
AGE, X	PRICE, Y ($1,000)
1	62.8
2	58.5
4	46.2
5	45
7	35.4
10	43.5
11	40.3
12	33
13	25.3
15	26

TABLE 12.9a	Hours of Studying and Exam Grades
HOURS OF STUDYING, X	GRADE, Y
2	60
3	71
3	83
4	72
4	75
4	65
5	83
5	74
6	92

b. Identify the regression line using the hours of studying to predict grades.

c. Use $\alpha = .05$ to evaluate if hours of studying help predict grades.

3. Assume that a group of 20 employees is randomly selected from a large company. Employees' years of experience on the job and performance ratings are reported in Table 12.10. Higher ratings mean better job performance.

a. Construct a scatterplot of years of experience and performance ratings to see if a linear relationship exists between these two variables.

b. Identify the regression line using years of experience to predict job performance.

Solutions

1.a. The scatterplot of age and price of used Corvettes is shown in Figure 12.9. According to the scatterplot, a straight line with downhill trend fits the data points well. Therefore, a linear relationship exists between the age and price of used Corvettes.

1.b. We need to figure out the $\bar{X}$ and $\bar{Y}$ and then add the following five columns to Table 12.8b, $(X - \bar{X})$, $(Y - \bar{Y})$, $(X - \bar{X})(Y - \bar{Y})$, $(X - \bar{X})^2$, and $(Y - \bar{Y})^2$, to demonstrate the step-by-step process.

$$\bar{X} = \sum X / n = 80 / 10 = 8$$

$$\bar{Y} = \sum Y / n = 416 / 10 = 41.6$$

$$SP = \sum (X - \bar{X})(Y - \bar{Y}) = -497.4$$

$$SS_X = \sum (X - \bar{X})^2 = 214$$

$$b = \frac{SP}{SS_X} = \frac{-497.4}{214} = -2.32$$

$$a = \bar{Y} - b\bar{X}$$

$$a = 41.6 - (-2.32)(8) = 60.16$$

The regression line for using age to predict price is $\hat{Y} = 60.16 - 2.32X$. For each additional year of the used Corvette, the price decreases by 2.32 thousand dollars.

1.c. When $X = 6$, the predicted $\hat{Y} = 60.16 - 2.32(6) = 46.24$. The predicted price for a 6-year-old Corvette is 46.24 thousand dollars.

1.d. Here is the four-step hypothesis test for a simple regression.

Step 1. State the pair of hypotheses.

$$H_0: \beta = 0$$

$$H_1: \beta \neq 0$$

Step 2. Identify the rejection zone.

The critical value of F in the F Table under $\alpha = .05$ is $F_{(1,8)} = 5.32$. The rejection zone is $F > 5.32$.

Step 3. Calculate the statistic.

Conducting a hypothesis test on a simple regression requires r^2 and SS_Y.

$$r = \frac{SP}{\sqrt{SS_X SS_Y}} = \frac{-497.4}{\sqrt{(214)(1394.52)}} = -.910$$

$$r^2 = (-.910)^2 = .828$$

TABLE 12.10 Employees' Years of Experience and Job Performance Ratings

YEARS, X	PERFORMANCE, Y
1	51
3	75
4	57
5	63
7	69
9	75
10	80
12	88
13	88
15	90
16	70
17	90
18	87
19	84
21	81
23	77
24	74
26	70
27	87
29	60

FIGURE 12.9　Scatterplot of Age and Price of Used Corvettes

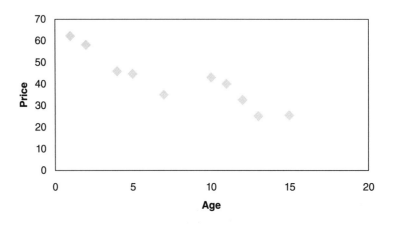

TABLE 12.8b　Step-by-Step Calculation Using Age to Predict Price of Used Corvettes

AGE, X	PRICE, Y ($1,000)	$(X - \bar{X})$	$(Y - \bar{Y})$	$(X - \bar{X})(Y - \bar{Y})$	$(X - \bar{X})^2$	$(Y - \bar{Y})^2$
1	62.8	−7	21.2	−148.4	49	449.44
2	58.5	−6	16.9	−101.4	36	285.61
4	46.2	−4	4.6	−18.4	16	21.16
5	45	−3	3.4	−10.2	9	11.56
7	35.4	−1	−6.2	6.2	1	38.44
10	43.5	2	1.9	3.8	4	3.61
11	40.3	3	−1.3	−3.9	9	1.69
12	33	4	−8.6	−34.4	16	73.96
13	25.3	5	−16.3	−81.5	25	265.69
15	26	7	−15.6	−109.2	49	243.36
80	**416**			**−497.4**	**214**	**1,394.52**

$$SS_Y = 1394.52$$

$$SSR = r^2 SS_Y = .828(1394.52) = 1154.66$$

$$SSE = (1 - r^2)SS_Y = (1 - .828)(1394.52) = 239.86$$

　　　　　　　　　　　　　　　　　　　　STRAIGHTFORWARD STATISTICS

Put all the numbers into the ANOVA summary table for age and price of used Corvettes as shown in Table 12.8c.

TABLE 12.8c   ANOVA Summary Table for the Simple Regression Between the Age and Price of Used Corvettes

SOURCE	SS	df	MS	F
Regression	1154.66	1	1154.66	38.514
Error	239.86	8	29.98	
Total	1394.52	9		

Step 4. Draw the correct conclusion.

The calculated $F = 38.514$ is within the rejection zone, so we reject H_0. The ages of the cars help predict the prices of used Corvettes.

2.a.   The scatterplot of hours of studying and grades is shown in Figure 12.10. According to the scatterplot, a straight line with uphill trend fits the data points well. Therefore, a linear relationship exists between these two variables.

2.b.   We need to figure out the $\bar{X}$ and $\bar{Y}$ and then add the following five columns to Table 12.9b, $(X - \bar{X})$, $(Y - \bar{Y})$, $(X - \bar{X})(Y - \bar{Y})$, $(X - \bar{X})^2$, and $(Y - \bar{Y})^2$, to demonstrate the step-by-step calculation for the regression line.

FIGURE 12.10   Scatterplot of Hours of Studying and Exam Grades

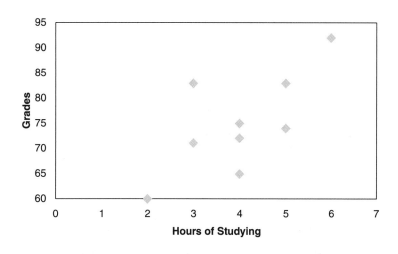

TABLE 12.9b   Step-by-Step Calculation Using Hours of Studying to Predict Exam Grades

HOURS OF STUDYING, X	GRADE, Y	$(X - \bar{X})$	$(Y - \bar{Y})$	$(X - \bar{X})(Y - \bar{Y})$	$(X - \bar{X})^2$	$(Y - \bar{Y})^2$
2	60	−2	−15	30	4	225
3	71	−1	−4	4	1	16
3	83	−1	8	−8	1	64
4	72	0	−3	0	0	9
4	75	0	0	0	0	0
4	65	0	−10	0	0	100
5	83	1	8	8	1	64
5	74	1	−1	−1	1	1
6	92	2	17	34	4	289
36	**675**			**67**	**12**	**768**

$$\bar{X} = \sum X / n = 36 / 9 = 4$$

$$\bar{Y} = \sum Y / n = 675 / 9 = 75$$

$$SP = \sum (X - \bar{X})(Y - \bar{Y}) = 67$$

$$SS_X = \sum (X - \bar{X})^2 = 12$$

$$b = \frac{SP}{SS_X} = \frac{67}{12} = 5.58$$

$$a = \bar{Y} - b\bar{X}$$

$$a = 75 - (5.58)(4) = 52.68$$

The regression line for using hours of studying to predict exam grade is $\hat{Y} = 52.68 + 5.58X$. For each additional hour of studying, the exam grade increases by 5.58. The lesson learned here is that you need to study longer to get higher grades.

2.c.   Here is the four-step hypothesis test for a simple regression.

Step 1. State the pair of hypotheses.

$H_0: \beta = 0$

$H_1: \beta \neq 0$

Step 2. Identify the rejection zone.

The critical value of F in the F Table under $\alpha = .05$ is $F_{(1,7)} = 5.59$. The rejection zone is $F > 5.59$.

Step 3. Calculate the statistic.

Conducting a hypothesis test on a simple regression requires r^2 and SS_Y.

$$r = \frac{SP}{\sqrt{SS_X SS_Y}} = \frac{67}{\sqrt{(12)(768)}} = .698$$

$$r^2 = (.698)^2 = .487$$

$$SS_Y = 768$$

$$SSR = r^2 SS_Y = .487(768) = 374.016$$

$$SSE = (1 - r^2)SS_Y = (1 - .487)(768) = 393.984$$

Put all the numbers into the ANOVA summary table between the hours of studying and grades as shown in Table 12.9c.

TABLE 12.9c ANOVA Summary Table for the Simple Regression Between the Hours of Studying and Grades

SOURCE	SS	df	MS	F
Regression	374.016	1	374.016	6.645
Error	393.984	7	56.283	
Total	768	8		

Step 4. Draw the correct conclusion.

The calculated $F = 6.645$ is within the rejection zone, so we reject H_0. The hours of studying help predict the exam grades.

3.a. The scatterplot of the years of experience and performance ratings is shown in Figure 12.11. According to the scatterplot, it is impossible for a straight line to fit all data points across the entire distribution equally well. The relationship between the years of experience and performance ratings seems to vary at different stages. At the beginning of one's career, performance tends to increase with years of experience. In the range 1 to 15

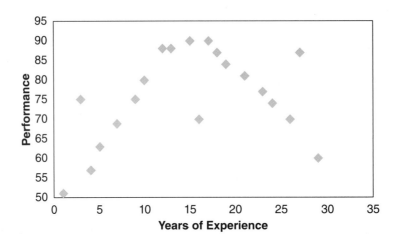

years, the relationship between years of experience and performance is positively correlated. Near the middle, around 17 years of experience, the performance goes down with increasing years of experience. In the range 17 to 30 years, the relationship between years of experience and performance switches to a negative correlation. Although this is a general trend, there are always exceptions to the rules.

3.b. You would have a hard time trying to fit a straight line to the data points in the scatterplot. The relationship between years of experience and job performance starts in a positive direction up to 15 to 20 years; then it switches to a negative direction. A linear relationship does not change direction. A relationship between two variables that changes directions is not a linear relationship. Thus, it is not appropriate to use the simple linear regression equation as discussed in this chapter to describe a nonlinear relationship.

$SAGE edge™

Sharpen your skills with SAGE edge!

Visit edge.sagepub.com/bowen for mobile-friendly quizzes, flashcards, videos, and more!

What You Learned

There are a couple of important distinctions between correlation and regression.

1. A correlation coefficient can be generated by any two interval or ratio variables without distinguishing between an independent variable and a dependent variable; because $r_{XY} = r_{YX}$, there is no need for such a distinction. Regression, on the other hand, requires a clearly explicit label on both the independent variable and the dependent variable. The purpose of regression is to predict the values of Y using the values of X. Therefore, Y is the main variable and X is the supporting variable; they are not interchangeable.

2. All correlation coefficients fall within the range of -1 and 1, $-1 \leq r \leq 1$. There is no range for the unstandardized regression coefficients.

An OLS regression line is mathematically determined to produce the smallest squared distance between the line $\hat{Y}$ and the actual Y values.

$$\text{Regression line } \hat{Y} = a + bX$$

$$b = \frac{\text{SP}}{SS_X}$$

$$a = \bar{Y} - b\bar{X}$$

where

$$\text{SP} = \sum(X - \bar{X})(Y - \bar{Y})$$

$$SS_X = \sum(X - \bar{X})^2$$

The four-step hypothesis test for a simple regression is as follows.

Step 1. State the pair of hypotheses.

$$H_0: \beta = 0$$

$$H_1: \beta \neq 0$$

Step 2. Identify the rejection zone.

The critical values of F that set off the boundaries of the rejection zones are identified by $F_{(1, n-2)}$ in the F Table. The rejection zone is identified as calculated $F > F_{(1, n-2)}$.

Step 3. Calculate the test statistic.

The process of calculating the F test for a simple regression is summarized and shown in Table 12.2, which includes all the operations that lead to the calculated F.

$$F = \frac{MSR}{MSE}$$

Step 4. Make the correct conclusion.

If the calculated F from Step 3 is within the rejection zone, we reject H_0. If the calculated F is not within the rejection zone, we fail to reject H_0.

KEY WORDS

Adjusted R^2: The adjusted R^2 is only relevant in multiple regression. It adjusts the R^2 by taking the number of predictors in the model into consideration.

Analysis of variance (ANOVA): ANOVA is a statistical procedure that partitions variances due to different sources.

Degrees of freedom due to error: The degrees of freedom due to error in a simple regression are defined as $(n - 2)$.

Degrees of freedom due to regression: The degrees of freedom due to regression are the number of predictors in the regression equation. In simple regression, the degree of freedom due to regression is 1.

Error: Error in regression is the difference between the actual Y and the predicted $\hat{Y}$, Error $= (Y - \hat{Y})$.

Heteroscedasticity: Heteroscedasticity refers to the condition when the variances of the errors are not the same across all values of X or across all $\hat{Y}$. This is commonly referred to as violations to the homogeneity of variances.

Homoscedasticity: Homoscedasticity refers to the condition when the variances of the errors are the same across all values of X or across all $\hat{Y}$. This is commonly referred to as the homogeneity of variances.

Ordinary least squares (OLS): OLS depicts the best fitting line by a straight line that goes through $(\bar{X}, \bar{Y})$ and minimizes the vertical distances between the actual Y values and the predicted $\hat{Y}$.

Regression equation: The regression equation is the equation for the regression line, which is expressed as $\hat{Y} = a + bX$, where a is labeled as the Y-intercept and b is labeled as the slope.

Simple regression: The simple regression is the most commonly used linear predictive analysis when making quantitative predictions of the dependent variable, Y, based on the values of the independent variable, X.

Slope: The regression slope is the value change in Y when X increases by one unit.

Standard error of the estimate: The standard error of the estimate is the standard deviation of the prediction errors. It is to measure the standard distance between the regression line and the actual Y values.

Y-intercept: The Y-intercept is the value of Y when X equals 0.

LEARNING ASSESSMENT

Multiple Choice: Circle the best answer to every question.

1. The simple regression equation is expressed as $\hat{Y} = a + bX$. $\hat{Y}$ is the predicted value of Y according to the regression. Errors are defined as the differences between actual Y values and the predicted $\hat{Y}$. Therefore, the sum of squared errors is expressed as

   a. $SSE = \sum(Y - \hat{Y})^2$
   b. $SSE = \sum(\hat{Y} - \bar{Y})^2$
   c. $SSE = \sum(Y - \bar{Y})^2$
   d. $SSE = \sum(X - \bar{X})^2$

2. In a simple regression, the degrees of freedom due to error are

   a. $(n - 1)$
   b. $(n - 2)$
   c. $(n - 3)$
   d. $(n - 4)$

3. The regression line is $\hat{Y} = a + bX$. The intercept a is defined as

   a. the value of Y when $X = 0$.
   b. the value of X when $Y = 0$.
   c. the value changes in Y when X increases by one unit.
   d. the value changes in X when Y increases by one unit.

4. Which one of the following statements is correct?

   a. The correct range for the correlation coefficient is $-1 \leq r \leq 1$.
   b. The correct range for the regression coefficient is $-1 \leq b \leq 1$.
   c. The correct range for probability is $-1 \leq p \leq 1$.
   d. The correct range for the probability of committing a Type I error is $-1 \leq \alpha \leq 1$.

5. The coefficient of determination measures the percentage of variance from the dependent variable Y that can be explained by the independent variable X, and is calculated by

   a. r.

   b. r^2.

   c. b.

   d. b^2.

6. What are the degrees of freedom when conducting an F test for a simple regression analysis?

   a. $(1, n - 1)$

   b. $(1, n - 2)$

   c. $(2, n - 1)$

   d. $(2, n - 2)$

7. Which of the following statistics will always be positive?

   a. t tests

   b. Z tests

   c. Pearson correlations

   d. F tests

8. What is the coefficient that describes the value changes in Y when X increases by one unit?

   a. Intercept

   b. Slope

   c. F value

   d. Pearson's r

Free Response Questions

9. The car curb weight measures the weight of a car in pounds without including cargo, driver, passengers, or any other item. When comparing cars with the same type of engine, the lighter the car weight, the more fuel efficient the car is. Fuel efficiency is measured by averaging highway and city driving. The number is reported as miles per gallon, usually abbreviated as mpg. Assume that a group of 15 cars is randomly selected. Their weights and fuel efficiency numbers are reported in Table 12.11.

   a. Construct a scatterplot of car weight and fuel efficiency to see if a linear relationship exists between these two variables.

   b. Identify the regression line using weight to predict fuel efficiency.

   c. What is the predicted fuel efficiency when a car weighs 4,500 pounds?

TABLE 12.11   Car Weight and Fuel Efficiency

WEIGHT (POUNDS)	FUEL EFFICIENCY (mpg)
3,190	28.8
3,572	23
2,888	28.5
3,777	20
3,208	18.5
3,393	25.6
4,653	20
3,495	25
3,208	24
4,345	22.5
2,616	31.5
5,950	14
2,235	31.5
4,039	15.7
6,500	13.4

d. Use $\alpha = .05$ to evaluate if car weights help predict fuel efficiency.

10. A retail company wants to investigate the relationship between number of customers' complaints and number of sales transactions among its sales associates. Assume that a group of 10 sales associates is randomly selected from this company. Their number of sales and number of customers' complaints are reported in Table 12.12.

    a. Construct a scatterplot of the number of sales and number of customers' complaints to see if a linear relationship exists between these two variables.

    b. Identify the regression line using the number of customers' complaints to predict the number of sales transactions.

    c. Use $\alpha = .05$ to evaluate if customers' complaints help predict number of sales.

TABLE 12.12   Number of Customers' Complaints and Number of Sales Transactions

CUSTOMERS' COMPLAINTS	SALES TRANSACTIONS
12	126
13	298
19	444
20	277
16	356
17	340
26	361
30	482
25	384
22	582

One-Way Analysis of Variance

After reading and studying this chapter, you should be able to do the following:

- Define one-way analysis of variance (ANOVA)
- Describe the sources of between-group variance and within-group variance
- Calculate sum of squares total (SST), sum of squares between (SSB), and sum of squares within (SSW)
- Construct and interpret an ANOVA summary table
- Conduct the hypothesis test for ANOVA
- Conduct post hoc comparisons after a significant ANOVA result with three or more groups
- Calculate and interpret the effect size for ANOVA

WHAT YOU KNOW AND WHAT IS NEW

Over the course of earlier chapters of this textbook, you have learned different types of *t* tests that are suitable in different situations. Independent-samples *t* tests are used to compare means from two different groups. Dependent-sample *t* tests are applied to compare pretest and posttest scores from the same group or to compare paired samples. *ANOVA*, which is the focus of this chapter, can also be applied to independent samples as well as dependent samples.

In ANOVA terms, the distinction between comparisons among groups consisting of different people versus comparisons among the same group of individuals measured repeatedly is referred to as "*between-subject*" design versus "*within-subject*" design. The **between-subject design** refers to research in which participants are assigned to different groups based on different levels of the independent variables. Every participant is assigned to only one group. For example, marital status is used as an independent variable to study happiness. Research participants are classified into "single," "married," and "divorced" groups. Then their reported levels of happiness are measured and compared. In this case, different groups consist of different individuals; therefore, this is research with a between-subject design.

The **within-subject design** is used when research participants are assigned to all levels of the independent variables. Every participant experiences all levels of the independent variable and is measured repeatedly. The within-subject design is also referred to as *repeated measures*. For example, researchers want to study the effect of texting while driving compared with other impairments such as driving under the influence of alcohol. Participants' driving mistakes are measured repeatedly via a driving simulator under all three conditions: (1) driving without distraction, (2) texting while driving, and (3) driving under the influence of alcohol.

Mastering the ability to distinguish within-subject designs from between-subject designs is a vital first step in learning ANOVA, because different statistical formulas are required to calculate them. The focus of this chapter is on between-subject ANOVA. Although ANOVA is closely connected with t tests, your knowledge and skills in regression are highly relevant. In a simple regression, an F test is used to evaluate the effectiveness of the regression model, and an ANOVA summary table is calculated to facilitate the hypothesis test for the simple regression. In the ANOVA table, the variances due to regression and the variances due to errors are partitioned separately, and the ratio of variances due to regression to variances due to error is the calculated F value. Similarly, in ANOVA, the variances due to between-group factors and the variances due to within-group factors are partitioned separately, and the ratio of variances due to between-group factors to variances due to within-group factors is the calculated F in ANOVA. The details are provided in the next section.

INTRODUCING ANOVA

ANOVA is a statistical method to test the equality of group means by partitioning variances due to different sources. You might have noticed that both independent-samples t tests and ANOVA are statistical methods to test the equality of group means. The only difference between the independent-samples t tests and ANOVA is that t tests are only applied to comparison between two groups while ANOVA is applied to comparisons between two or more groups. When ANOVA is used in comparing means from two populations, it generates identical results to those from t tests, $F = t^2$. Therefore, to demonstrate the unique utility of ANOVA, we are going to use it to compare means in three or more populations.

We will discuss single-factor ANOVA (one-way ANOVA) in this chapter. The "single" factor refers to one independent variable. Therefore, single-factor ANOVA is defined as an ANOVA method that uses only one factor to classify data into different groups. Not to go too wild about how many groups we can compare, the examples in this chapter are mostly applied to three groups, as illustrated in Table 13.1. Keep in mind that comparisons among more groups are logically and practically possible. The subscript i refers to individuals in each group, and the subscript j refers to j groups. When comparing means among three groups, $j = 1, 2,$ or 3. In Table 13.1, $\bar{X}_1$, $\bar{X}_2$, and $\bar{X}_3$ (as shown in the last row) symbolize the mean for Group 1, the mean for Group 2, and the mean for Group 3, respectively. $\bar{\bar{X}}$ at the lower-right corner refers to the mean for the entire sample. The number of participants in each group is denoted by n_1, n_2, and n_3. The entire sample size is equal to the sum of the three group sizes, $n = n_1 + n_2 + n_3$. The number of participants in each group does not need to be the same. Let's lay out all the numbers for an ANOVA with three groups in Table 13.1 to visualize the sum of squared total deviations (SST), $\text{SST} = \sum\sum(X_{ij} - \bar{\bar{X}})^2$. The first subscript refers to the row and the second to the column, as is conventional. The different styles of dash and solid blue lines all converge on the mean for the entire sample, $\bar{\bar{X}}$. The blue spiderweb–like lines show how the SST is obtained. First, calculate the difference between every individual value in every group, X_{ij}, and the overall sample mean, $\bar{\bar{X}}$. That is why all the lines point to $\bar{\bar{X}}$. As we discussed in Chapter 3, deviations are calculated by the difference between the individual values and the sample mean. To avoid positive deviations completely canceling out the negative deviations, the deviations need to be squared. When you add up all the squared deviations, you create $\text{SST} = \sum\sum(X_{ij} - \bar{\bar{X}})^2$.

$$\text{SST} = \sum\sum(X_{ij} - \bar{\bar{X}})^2$$

It is not difficult to understand how to calculate SST conceptually. In practice, however, it might take a while to conduct such a calculation by hand. Out of consideration for you, I

TABLE 13.1 Visualization of Sum of Squares Total (SST) in Three Groups

INDIVIDUAL i	GROUP 1	GROUP 2	GROUP 3
1	X_{11}	X_{12}	X_{13}
2	X_{21}	X_{22}	X_{23}
3	X_{31}	X_{32}	X_{33}
...			
i	X_{i1}	X_{i2}	X_{i3}
	$\bar{X}_1$	$\bar{X}_2$	$\bar{X}_3$	$\bar{\bar{X}}$

am providing the values of SST in the examples, exercise problems, and learning assessment questions in this chapter. It is far more important for you to understand the concept of SST than to painstakingly calculate the difference between every individual value and the sample mean, square the difference, and then add up all the squared differences to create $SST = \sum\sum(X_{ij} - \bar{\bar{X}})^2$.

In simple regression, we construct an ANOVA summary table to evaluate the effectiveness of the regression model by partitioning the total sum of squared deviations or sum of squares total (SST) into the sum of squares due to regression (SSR) and the sum of squares due to error (SSE). It is denoted as SST = SSR + SSE. The focus of a regression is on predicting Y; therefore, SS_Y is also labeled as SST. To refresh your memory, the ANOVA summary table is shown in Table 13.2.

TABLE 13.2 The ANOVA Summary Table for Calculating F for a Simple Regression

SOURCE	SS	df	MS	F
Regression	$SSR = r^2 SS_Y$	1	$MSR = \dfrac{SSR}{1}$	$\dfrac{MSR}{MSE}$
Error	$SSE = (1 - r^2)SS_Y$	$n - 2$	$MSE = \dfrac{SSE}{(n-2)}$	
Total	SS_Y or SST	$n - 1$		

Similarly, in an ANOVA, we partition the total sum of squares into the SSB groups and the SSW groups, SST = SSB + SSW. Both SSB and SSW will be discussed in detail in the next section.

BETWEEN-GROUP VARIANCE AND WITHIN-GROUP VARIANCE

You learned in Chapter 3 that $variance = \dfrac{SS}{df}$. When you calculate the variance of a variable, you need the SS (Sum of Squares) and the degrees of freedom (df) of that particular variable. The reason to square the deviations when calculating the SS is to avoid negative differences completely canceling out the positive differences. When we partition the total variances into variances due to different sources, we need to know the SS and df for each source as shown in Table 13.2. The ANOVA summary table in simple regression shows that the total variance is partitioned into different sources: variance due to regression and variance due to error. Then the calculated F value shows the ratio of variance due to regression to the variance due to error. Similarly, in ANOVA, the variances are partitioned into different sources: the between-group variance and the within-group variance. The discussions will involve identifying SSB, SSW, the degrees of freedom from between groups (df_B), and the degrees of freedom from within groups (df_W). The conceptual meanings and mathematical formulas of SSB, SSW, df_B, and df_W will be clearly explained in the next subsections one by one.

SUM OF SQUARES BETWEEN

The **sum of squares between groups (SSB)** is the focus of this subsection. SSB shows the variability between different groups. Different people are assigned to different groups. The group assignment is based on different levels of the independent variables. In a one-way ANOVA, there is only one independent variable. Different levels of the independent variable reflect different treatment conditions in experimental designs. Thus, SSB is sometimes referred to as SSTR, Sum of Squares due to Treatment, in some other statistics textbooks. Since not all research uses strictly experimental designs, we stick with the term *SSB* throughout this chapter. The differences between group means are largely attributable to systematic differences due to group effects. Mathematically, SSB is calculated by taking the squared differences between individual group means, $\bar{X}_j$, and the sample mean, $\bar{\bar{X}}$, multiplied by the number of participants in each group, and then summing them up.

$$SSB = \sum n_j (\bar{X}_j - \bar{\bar{X}})^2$$

where

$\bar{X}_j$ is the mean in Group j

n_j is the number of participants in Group j

$\bar{\bar{X}}$ is the sample mean

Let's visualize the $SSB = \sum n_j (\bar{X}_j - \bar{\bar{X}})^2$ in Table 13.3. The SSB is the sum of the multiplicative products between the number of participants in Group j and the squared differences between Group j mean and the entire sample mean.

$$SSB = \sum n_j (\bar{X}_j - \bar{\bar{X}})^2$$

Let's illustrate the calculation of SSB with an example. Assume that a software company designs a new application to conduct electronic financial transactions without using a credit card. The new application can be used in PCs, tablets, or smartphones. The company wants to find out whether there are differences in user satisfaction among the three types of devices. The company randomly selects 30 people and assigns 10 of them into each group to pilot test the application in PCs, tablets, or smartphones. The levels of user satisfaction are

TABLE 13.3　Visualization of Sum of Squares Between (SSB) in Three Groups

INDIVIDUAL i	GROUP 1	GROUP 2	GROUP 3	
1	X_{11}	X_{12}	X_{13}	
2	X_{21}	X_{22}	X_{23}	
3	X_{31}	X_{32}	X_{33}	
...				
i	X_{i1}	X_{i2}	X_{i3}	
	$\bar{X}_1$	$\bar{X}_2$	$\bar{X}_3$	$\bar{\bar{X}}$
	n_1	n_2	n_3	

measured and reported as $\bar{X}_1 = 3.4$, $\bar{X}_2 = 4$, and $\bar{X}_3 = 4.3$, respectively. In a three-group situation, SSB can be calculated easily.

$$\text{SSB} = n_1(\bar{X}_1 - \bar{\bar{X}})^2 + n_2(\bar{X}_2 - \bar{\bar{X}})^2 + n_3(\bar{X}_3 - \bar{\bar{X}})^2$$

where $n_1 = n_2 = n_3 = 10$ and $\bar{\bar{X}}$ is the entire sample mean, which is calculated as mean of all group means.

$$\bar{\bar{X}} = (3.4 + 4 + 4.3)/3 = 3.9$$

$$\text{SSB} = 10(3.4 - 3.9)^2 + 10(4 - 3.9)^2 + 10(4.3 - 3.9)^2 = 4.2$$

It is easy to see that when there are large differences between group means and the sample mean, the SSB is large. When group size is large, SSB is large. However, the magnitude of SSB provides useful information only when it is compared with the variability from the other source, SSW.

SUM OF SQUARES WITHIN

The **sum of squares within groups (SSW)** reflects the variability within groups, which is the focus of this subsection. The SSW is largely attributable to the random individual differences or unsystematic measurement errors that are beyond the control of the researchers. Mathematically, the calculation is done within each group. The SSW is calculated by computing the squared differences between the individual scores, X_{ij}, within a group and its corresponding group mean, $\bar{X}_j$, and then summing them up.

$$\text{SSW} = \sum\sum(X_{ij} - \bar{X}_j)^2$$

Random individual differences are the preexisting conditions research participants bring along with them. In the example of the new software application for financial transactions introduced above, such differences would include technology savviness, social economic status, family structure, occupation, personality traits, past experience with electronic transactions, and so on. Measurement errors are unsystematic errors that happen sometimes to some people. The sources for the unsystematic measurement errors can be due to the questionnaire, the data collection procedures, or the research participants. Some of these random individual differences and unsystematic measurement errors might have unknown effects on the target variable X. Let's visualize the $SSW = \sum\sum(X_{ij} - \bar{X}_j)^2$ in Table 13.4. The SSW is the sum of the squared differences between individual scores in Group j and the Group j mean.

$$SSW = \sum\sum(X_{ij} - \bar{X}_j)^2$$

TABLE 13.4   Visualization of Sum of Squares Within (SSW) in Three Groups

INDIVIDUAL i	GROUP 1	GROUP 2	GROUP 3	
1	X_{11}	X_{12}	X_{13}	
2	X_{21}	X_{22}	X_{23}	
3	X_{31}	X_{32}	X_{33}	
...				
i	X_{i1}	X_{i2}	X_{i3}	
	$\bar{X}_1$	$\bar{X}_2$	$\bar{X}_3$	$\bar{\bar{X}}$

Judging from the number of blue lines involved in calculating SSW, it is a tedious process to get all the values calculated. However, you can easily calculate the value of SSW if SST and SSB are known.

$$SST = SSB + SSW$$

$$SSW = SST - SSB$$

Since ANOVA is a statistical procedure for testing the equality of group means by partitioning variances into different sources, we need to calculate variances from different sources. We have discussed SSB and SSW. Next, we need to figure out both df_B and df_W in order to calculate the variance between groups and variance within groups.

DEGREES OF FREEDOM FOR BETWEEN GROUPS (df_B) AND WITHIN GROUPS (df_W)

ANOVA is a statistical measure to partition variances due to different sources. As we mentioned earlier, variance $= SS/df$. When the total variability is partitioned to the variability between groups and the variability within a group, you get SST = SSB + SSW. Every SS has a df particularly linked with it. The partition of the df follows the same pattern as the partition of the SS, and we get $df_T = df_B + df_W$. The df represents the number of values that are free to vary. The df linked with a particular SS is calculated by the number of values that go into the calculation minus 1.

For example, $\text{SST} = \sum\sum(X_{ij} - \bar{\bar{X}})^2$, so there are j groups in the entire sample. The sample size $n = n_1 + n_2 + n_3 + \cdots + n_j$, so n values go into the calculation of SST hence the $df_T = n - 1$.

Similarly, we can figure out the df between groups by $\text{SSB} = \sum n_j(\bar{X}_j - \bar{\bar{X}})^2$.

The SSB is calculated by squaring the differences between each group mean and the sample mean, multiplying by the group size, and then adding them up. The number of values that goes into the calculation of SSB equals the number of groups. The df_B is defined as the number of groups minus 1. Assume that the number of groups is k; then df_B is $k - 1$. Apply the general formula for variance = SS / df in this particular situation, and you get the **between-group variance** (also referred to as the mean squares between groups, MSB in ANOVA terminology).

$$\text{MSB} = \frac{\text{SSB}}{df_B} = \frac{\text{SSB}}{(k-1)}$$

Next, we can identify the df_W by $\text{SSW} = \sum\sum(X_{ij} - \bar{X}_j)^2$. The SSW is calculated within each group by squaring the differences between individual values and their group mean and then adding them up. Assume that the number of groups is k; then the df within the group for Group 1 is $(n_1 - 1)$, for Group 2 is $(n_2 - 1)$, for Group 3 is $(n_3 - 1)$, ... and for Group k is $(n_k - 1)$. The df_W is the sum of df for each group.

$$\begin{aligned} df_W &= (n_1 - 1) + (n_2 - 1) + (n_3 - 1) + \cdots + (n_k - 1) \\ &= (n_1 + n_2 + n_3 + \cdots + n_k) - k \\ &= n - k \end{aligned}$$

The degrees of freedom within groups (df_W) are defined as sample size minus k, which is $(n - k)$. Once we know the degrees of freedom within groups, we can calculate the **within-group variance** (also referred to as the mean squares within groups, MSW, in ANOVA terminology).

$$\text{MSW} = \frac{\text{SSW}}{df_W} = \frac{\text{SSW}}{(n-k)}$$

When SSB and SSW add to be SST, the dfs associated with these terms also add up.

$$df_T = df_B + df_W$$

$$(n - 1) = (k - 1) + (n - k)$$

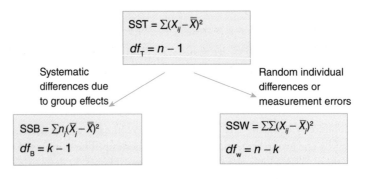

Now, we can summarize everything in this section into one figure and one table. In summary, ANOVA is a statistical method that tests the equality of group means by partitioning variances into different sources. The partitioning process is shown in Figure 13.1. Such partitioning applies to both the *SS* and the *df*.

Similar to the hypothesis test for regression $F = \text{MSR} / \text{MSE}$, the hypothesis test for ANOVA is calculated as $F = \text{MSB} / \text{MSW}$. We will discuss the four-step hypothesis test for ANOVA in more detail in the next session.

We can also organize and summarize the results of partitioning *SS*, *df*, and MS from different sources in the ANOVA summary table as shown in Table 13.5. The ANOVA summary table shows in a streamlined manner the process of calculating the *F* value.

TABLE 13.5 The ANOVA Summary Table

SOURCE	SS	df	MS	F
Between groups	SSB	$df_B = k - 1$	$MSB = \dfrac{SSB}{(k-1)}$	$F = \dfrac{MSB}{MSW}$
Within groups	SSW	$df_w = n - k$	$MSW = \dfrac{SSW}{(n-k)}$	
Total	SST	$df_T = n - 1$		

Pop Quiz

Researchers study the effect of distracted driving on driving behavior. Driving behavior is measured by the number of mistakes recorded on a simulator. There are 36 participants who are randomly assigned to one of the three groups: (1) driving while eating, (2) driving while texting, or (3) normal driving without distraction. Each group has 12 participants, and the group means are 22, 25, and 16, respectively, SST = 2,016. Use this information to answer the following three questions.

1. What is the SSB based on the information provided here?

   a. 504

   b. 1,008

   c. 1,512

   d. 2,015

2. What is the SSW based on the information provided here?

   a. 504

   b. 1,008

   c. 1,512

   d. 2,015

3. What are the degrees of freedom within groups (df_w)?

   a. 2

   b. 3

   c. 33

   d. 35

Answers: 1. a, 2. c, 3. c

HYPOTHESIS TESTING WITH ANOVA

We have discussed all the elements such as *SS*, *df*, and *MS* involved in the ANOVA summary table. It is time to put all elements together to conduct hypothesis tests with ANOVA. The general principles of the four-step hypothesis testing procedure with ANOVA are explicitly stated first, followed by several examples to illustrate the process.

Step 1. State the pair of hypotheses for ANOVA.

$H_0: \mu_1 = \mu_2 = \mu_3 = \cdots = \mu_k$

$H_1:$ Not all μ_k are equal.

The null hypothesis, H_0, states that all group means are the same. The alternative hypothesis, H_1, states that not all group means are the same. At least one of the equal signs in the null hypothesis is not true. If the outcome of an ANOVA is to fail to reject H_0, no further analysis needs to be done. If the outcome of an ANOVA is to reject H_0, additional **post hoc comparisons** need to be done in order to identify exactly where the significant difference comes from.

Step 2. Identify the rejection zone.

The critical values of F that set the boundaries of the rejection zones can be found using the $F_{(df_1, df_2)}$ in the same F table you used to determine whether equal variances are assumed, in Chapter 9, and whether a regression analysis is significant, in Chapter 12. This table is provided in Appendix C. Each critical F value is determined by two different dfs, where df_1 is the df from the numerator and df_2 is the df from the denominator. In the case of ANOVA, df_1 is the degrees of freedom between groups, $df_B = k - 1$, and df_2 is the degrees of freedom within groups, $df_W = (n - k)$. Therefore, the critical values of F can be identified by $F_{(k-1, n-k)}$ in the F Table for ANOVA. The rejection zone is identified as the calculated $F > F_{(k-1, n-k)}$.

Step 3. Calculate the F test for the ANOVA.

The F test can be easily calculated by completing Table 13.5 with all the SS terms and dfs associated them. Once the ANOVA summary table is complete,

$$F = \frac{MSB}{MSW}$$

Step 4. Make the correct conclusion.

If the calculated F is within the rejection zone, we reject H_0. If the calculated F is not within the rejection zone, we fail to reject H_0. In the case of failing to reject H_0, no additional analysis is needed. In the case of rejecting H_0, you need to conduct post hoc comparisons to identify exactly where the significant differences come from.

Conceptually, post hoc comparisons are conducted by making all possible pairwise comparisons to identify exactly which equal sign in the null hypothesis does not hold true. In the case of $k = 3$, there are three groups: Groups 1, 2, and 3. When the calculated $F > F_{(k-1, n-k)}$, we reject H_0. Now, we have to compare all possible pairwise comparisons. The formula to calculate the number of all possible pairs is $k(k - 1)/2$. Thus, when there are three groups, $k = 3$, there are three possible pairwise comparisons because $k(k - 1)/2 = 3(3 - 1)/2 = 3$.

These are all of the possible pairwise comparisons: μ_1 versus μ_2, μ_1 versus μ_3, and μ_2 versus μ_3. These comparisons need to be conducted simultaneously. Assume that the risk of committing a Type I error is α in each pairwise comparison. When conducting the same type of tests $k(k - 1)/2$ times, the Type I error rate accumulates. The accumulated Type I error rate from conducting similar comparisons multiple times is called the **familywise error rate (FWER)**. The FWER is the probability of committing a Type I error after conducting $k(k - 1)/2$ possible pair comparisons at the same time. Assume that the Type I error for one individual pairwise comparison is α, the FWER is calculated as committing one or more Type I errors in the multiple comparisons.

$$FWER = 1 - (1 - \alpha)^{\frac{k(k-1)}{2}}$$

Assume that $\alpha = .05$ and $k = 3$; then $k(k-1)/2 = 3$, so the FWER $= 1 - (1 - .05)^3 = .1426$.

The point is that when the Type I error rate for each pairwise comparison is $\alpha = .05$, you conduct three pairwise comparisons simultaneously, and you have inflated the FWER. An inflated FWER may increase the risk of Type I error, which is to falsely claim an effect when it actually does not exist.

Several methods may be used in post hoc comparisons to ensure simultaneous correctness of a set of hypothesis tests while keeping the FWER under control. We will illustrate these post hoc comparisons via SPSS when the situation arises.

EXAMPLE 13.1

Assume that a software company designs a new application to conduct electronic financial transactions without using a credit card. The new application can be used in PCs, tablets, or smartphones. The company wants to find out whether there are differences in user satisfaction among these three types of devices. The company randomly selects 30 people and assigns 10 of them into one group to pilot test the application in PCs, another 10 on tablets, and another 10 on smartphones. The user's satisfaction is measured on a Likert scale of 1 to 5, with 1 = "*very dissatisfied*" and 5 = "*very satisfied*," and reported in Table 13.6.

$$SST = \sum\sum(X_{ij} - \bar{\bar{X}})^2 = 38.7$$

TABLE 13.6   User Satisfaction in Three Groups

PC	TABLET	SMARTPHONE
3	5	5
4	4	4
5	3	3
2	3	5
4	4	4
5	4	5
5	5	3
1	3	4
1	4	5
4	5	5
$\bar{X}_1 = 3.4$	$\bar{X}_2 = 4$	$\bar{X}_3 = 4.3$

(*Continued*)

(Continued)

Conduct a hypothesis test to verify the equality of user satisfaction on the new application across three types of devices. Are there significant differences in user satisfaction across PCs, tablets, and smartphones?

As discussed before, calculating the SST is a tedious process to square the differences between every individual value and the sample mean and then add them up. I see no reason to have you go through this process with 30 individual values; therefore, SST = 38.7 is provided in the problem statement.

Step 1. State the pair of hypotheses.

$$H_0: \mu_1 = \mu_2 = \mu_3 = \cdots = \mu_k$$

H_1: Not all μ_k are equal.

Step 2. Identify the rejection zone.

There are three groups, $k = 3$, 10 people in each group, $n_1 = n_2 = n_3 = 10$, and the sample size $n = 30$. The critical value of F is identified by $F_{(2,27)} = 3.35$ in the F Table for ANOVA. The rejection zone is identified as the calculated $F > 3.35$.

Step 3. Calculate the F test.

Although the overall sample mean is not provided in this example, there is enough information for you to figure it out. Under equal group size in all three groups, the sample mean is

$$\bar{\bar{X}} = (3.4 + 4 + 4.3)/3 = 3.9$$

$$SSB = \sum n_j (\bar{X}_j - \bar{\bar{X}})^2 = 10(3.4 - 3.9)^2 + 10(4 - 3.9)^2 + 10(4.3 - 3.9)^2 = 4.2$$

$$SSW = SST - SSB = 38.7 - 4.2 = 34.5$$

Now we have all the numbers to complete the ANOVA summary table as shown in Table 13.7.

Step 4. Make the correct conclusion.

The calculated $F = 1.64$ is not within the rejection zone, so we fail to reject H_0. The evidence is not strong enough to claim that there are significant differences in user satisfaction for the electronic financial transaction application across three types of devices. No further analysis needs to be conducted.

TABLE 13.7 The ANOVA Summary Table for User Satisfaction on a New Application Across Three Types of Devices

SOURCE	SS	df	MS	F
Between groups	4.2	$df_B = 2$	MSB = 2.1	F = 1.64
Within groups	34.5	$df_W = 27$	MSW = 1.28	
Total	**38.7**	$df_T = 29$		

When the calculated F value is not significant, the evidence is not strong enough to claim inequality among group means. Since no difference in group means can be inferred from the data, no further analyses are needed. In the following example, we are going to demonstrate, after the calculated F value in ANOVA turns out to be significant, what we should do next.

EXAMPLE 13.2

Assume that a food manufacturing company conducts three focus groups to test different advertising strategies on customers' perceptions of food quality. Three advertising strategies are tested in this study: (1) weight control, (2) all natural ingredients, and (3) organic/environmental friendliness. The participants are randomly selected from a large panel and offered compensation for their time. All participants are provided exactly the same food product. The differences in food quality ratings are assumed to be influenced by the different advertising strategies. There are eight participants in each focus group. The company wants to find out whether significant differences exist in the evaluation of the food quality among the three groups. The ratings of the food quality are measured and reported in Table 13.8, with higher values representing better quality.

$$SST = 47.833$$

Conduct a hypothesis test to verify the equality of the food quality ratings among three focus groups. Are there significant differences in food quality ratings based on the three advertising strategies?

Step 1. State the pair of hypotheses.

H_0: $\mu_1 = \mu_2 = \mu_3 = \cdots = \mu_k$

H_1: Not all μ_k are equal.

(Continued)

(Continued)

TABLE 13.8 Food Quality Ratings in Three Focus Groups

WEIGHT CONTROL	ALL NATURAL	ORGANIC/ENVIRONMENTAL FRIENDLINESS
6	9	9
5	8	8
3	6	8
7	7	7
8	7	9
6	8	6
6	6	7
7	5	8
$\bar{X}_1 = 6$	$\bar{X}_2 = 7$	$\bar{X}_3 = 7.75$

Step 2. Identify the rejection zone.

There are three groups, $k = 3$, with eight people in each group, $n_1 = n_2 = n_3 = 8$, and the sample size $n = 24$. The critical value of F is identified by $F_{(2,21)} = 3.47$ in the F Table for ANOVA. The rejection zone is identified as the calculated $F > 3.47$.

Step 3. Calculate the F test.

Under equal group size, the sample mean is

$$\bar{\bar{X}} = (6 + 7 + 7.75)/3 = 6.917$$

$$\text{SSB} = \sum n_j (\bar{X}_j - \bar{\bar{X}})^2 = 8(6 - 6.917)^2 + 8(7 - 6.917)^2 + 8(7.75 - 6.917)^2 = 12.333$$

$$\text{SSW} = \text{SST} - \text{SSB} = 47.833 - 12.333 = 35.5$$

Now we have all the numbers to complete the ANOVA summary table as shown in Table 13.9.

Step 4. Make the correct conclusion.

The calculated $F = 3.649$ is within the rejection zone, so we reject H_0. The evidence is strong enough to claim that significant differences exist in the food quality ratings

TABLE 13.9 The ANOVA Summary Table for the Food Quality Ratings in Three Focus Groups

SOURCE	SS	df	MS	F
Between groups	12.333	$df_B = 2$	MSB = 6.167	F = 3.649
Within groups	35.5	$df_W = 21$	MSW = 1.690	
Total	47.833	$df_T = 23$		

across the three focus groups. However, a significant F test does not tell us exactly where the difference occurs. Thus, further analysis needs to be conducted to identify the sources of significant difference. Post hoc comparisons are designed to fulfill this purpose.

POST HOC COMPARISONS

Post hoc means "after the fact." After the calculated F value in ANOVA turns out to be within the rejection zone, $F > F_{(k-1, n-k)}$, you reject H_0. You conclude that not all group means are equal. But at this point, a significant F test does not tell you exactly where the significant difference comes from. Your answer is incomplete until you can clearly and definitely identify exactly where the significant difference occurs.

You don't have to worry about post hoc comparisons in two groups because you are sure that the significant ANOVA can only mean $\mu_1 \neq \mu_2$ in two groups. In case of three or more groups, there are multiple possibilities with regard to where the significant differences may come from. Specifically, in Example 13.2, the calculated $F = 3.649$ is within the rejection zone. We concluded that not all group means are equal. To identify exactly where the source of the significant difference is located, you will have to do the comparisons on all possible pairs simultaneously: μ_1 versus μ_2, μ_1 versus μ_3, and μ_2 versus μ_3. There are three possible pairwise comparisons that need to be conducted. If $\alpha = .05$ is set for an individual pairwise hypothesis test, conducting three separate hypothesis tests will inflate the FWER.

We will discuss three different methods to conduct post hoc comparisons and identify whether they keep the familywise risk of committing a Type I error under control: **least significant difference (LSD)**, Tukey's **honestly significant difference (HSD)**, and the Bonferroni adjustment. We will start with discussing the formula for each method. Then we will use the formulas to conduct post hoc comparisons after the significant F test in Example 13.2. Afterward, we will use SPSS to analyze the same numbers as shown in Example 13.2 to go through the one-way ANOVA with post hoc comparisons using the SPSS printouts that appear later in the chapter.

Least Significant Difference

The first post hoc method was developed by Fisher in 1935 to calculate the LSD between two group means using the equivalent of multiple t tests (Williams & Abdi, 2010). Any difference between two group means greater than LSD is significant. Any group mean difference equal to or less than LSD is not significant.

$$LSD = t\sqrt{MSW\left(\frac{1}{n_1} + \frac{1}{n_2}\right)}$$

When two groups have an equal number of participants, $n_1 = n_2$, the LSD formula can be simplified as

$$LSD = t\sqrt{\frac{2MSW}{n_1}}$$

where t is the critical value of t from a t table with a $df = (n - k)$, the same df as MSW of the F test in ANOVA, and the same two-tailed α level.

The n_1 and n_2 refer to the number of participants in Group 1 and Group 2, respectively.

In Example 13.2, we already calculated MSW = 1.69 with $df = 21$, and $n_1 = n_2 = 8$.

The critical t value for a two-tailed $\alpha = .05$ with $df = 21$ is 2.08.

$$LSD = 2.08\sqrt{\frac{2(1.69)}{8}} = 1.352$$

The mean difference between Group 1 and Group 2 is $\bar{X}_2 - \bar{X}_1 = 7 - 6 = 1$.

The difference is smaller than LSD, so it is not significant.

The mean difference between Group 1 and Group 3 is $\bar{X}_3 - \bar{X}_1 = 7.75 - 6 = 1.75$.

The difference is larger than LSD, so it is significant. We can, therefore, infer from our example that there are significant differences in food quality ratings between an advertising strategy based on organic/environmental friendliness and one based on weight control.

The mean difference between Group 2 and Group 3 is $\bar{X}_3 - \bar{X}_2 = 7.75 - 7 = 0.75$.

The difference is smaller than LSD, so it is not significant.

A special caution to keep in mind is that LSD does not keep the FWER under control when conducting multiple t tests simultaneously. Therefore, it has an inflated risk of committing a Type I error.

Tukey's Honestly Significant Difference Test

Tukey's HSD is named after John W. Tukey, who developed the HSD test formula to calculate a critical value for group mean differences while keeping the familywise risk of committing a Type I error under control (Abdi & Williams, 2010).

$$\text{HSD} = q\sqrt{\frac{\text{MSW}}{n}}$$

where n is the number of participants in each group and all groups have the same number of participants, $n = n_1 = n_2 = n_3 \ldots = n_k$.

We know that ANOVA formulas do not require group sizes to be equal. You need to know how to handle unequal group sizes when calculating HSD. Since the HSD formula requires the reciprocal of n, that is, $1/n$, the best way to deal with unequal group sizes is to calculate the harmonic mean of the group sizes before applying the HSD formula (Lane, 2010). Where there are k groups in the comparison and the number of participants in each group are $n_1, n_2, n_3, \ldots, n_k$.

$$\text{The harmonic mean for the group sizes } n_h = \frac{k}{\dfrac{1}{n_1} + \dfrac{1}{n_2} + \dfrac{1}{n_3} + \cdots + \dfrac{1}{n_k}}$$

When conducting pairwise comparisons, there are two groups involved in the comparison. Let's assume that the group sizes are n_1 and n_2; the harmonic mean for the group sizes is

$$n_h = \frac{2}{\dfrac{1}{n_1} + \dfrac{1}{n_2}}$$

Then replace n_h with n in the HSD formula to calculate the value.

$$\text{HSD} = q\sqrt{\frac{\text{MSW}}{n_h}}$$

Any group mean difference greater than HSD is significant, and any group mean difference equal to or less than HSD is not significant. Similar to the t value from the LSD test, a q value needs to be found in a table. The values of q are shown in Appendix G, the Critical Values of **Studentized Range Distribution** (q). The Studentized range distribution is used to test the difference between the largest and the smallest group means measured in units of standard deviation of sample means when applying to three or more groups.

The q is a basic statistic that is applicable to post hoc comparisons to identify a significant difference between any two groups after rejecting the null hypothesis that all groups' means are equal by the ANOVA. The critical value of q can be identified by the same α level as the ANOVA and two values: (1) k = number of groups and (2) df for the MSW is $(n - k)$.

To conduct a Tukey's HSD test in Example 13.2, we need to identify the critical q value from the q Table. If a particular df is not shown in the table, you should find the closest df. The q value is identified by three numbers: (1) α level, (2) k, and (3) $(n - k)$. They are .05, 3, and 21 in this example. However, the table only lists $(n - k)$ from 1 to 20, and then jumps to 24. The closest df for MSW is 20 in the q Table; therefore, the closest q value shown in the table is 3.58.

$$HSD = 3.58\sqrt{\frac{1.69}{8}} = 1.645$$

The mean difference between Group 1 and Group 2 is $\bar{X}_2 - \bar{X}_1 = 7 - 6 = 1$.

The difference is smaller than HSD, so it is not significant.

The mean difference between Group 1 and Group 3 is $\bar{X}_3 - \bar{X}_1 = 7.75 - 6 = 1.75$.

The difference is larger than HSD, so it is significant.

The mean difference between Group 2 and Group 3 is $\bar{X}_3 - \bar{X}_2 = 7.75 - 7 = 0.75$.

The difference is smaller than HSD, so it is not significant.

You might have noticed that the HSD is higher than LSD. Because HSD controls for the familywise risk of committing a Type I error, the critical value is set higher than LSD, which does not control for the familywise risk, HSD > LSD. Therefore, in some cases, it is possible to find post hoc comparisons significant using LSD but not significant using HSD.

Bonferroni Adjustment

The **Bonferroni adjustment** is named after an Italian mathematician, Carlo Emilio Bonferroni. This method does not involve a new formula to calculate a critical value of the group mean difference. The Bonferroni correction simply adjusts the α level of the individual pairwise comparison to a new level in order to control the familywise α level at .05 or another predetermined value.

The Bonferroni adjustment formula is stated below.

$$\alpha_B = \frac{\alpha_{FW}}{\dfrac{k(k-1)}{2}}$$

where

α_B is the newly adjusted α level for the individual pairwise comparison

α_{FW} is the predetermined acceptable familywise α level, the default is .05

$k(k-1)/2$ is the number of all possible pairwise comparisons

For example, in comparing three group means, you will have $3(3-1)/2 = 3$ possible pair comparisons. Assume that the familywise α level $= .05$, the new α_B for the individual pair comparison is $0.5/3 = .017$.

Conceptually, the Bonferroni adjustment is simple and easy to understand: calculating the significance level of each pairwise comparison, and then comparing those to a nonstandard α level. Unfortunately, you won't be able to find the critical values for such a nonstandard α level in the appendices of statistics textbooks, including this one. It is much easier to use SPSS or other statistical software when the p value associated with each test statistic is automatically reported. You may simply use the decision rules based on the p value associated with the t test to identify the source of significant difference. The step-by-step instructions for using SPSS to run an ANOVA on the data in Example 13.2 are presented in an upcoming section of this chapter.

Pop Quiz

1. Which one of the following post hoc comparisons fails to keep the FWER under control?

   a. Tukey's HSD

   b. LSD

   c. Bonferroni adjustment

   d. All of the post hoc comparisons mentioned above keep the FWER under control.

Answer: b

STATISTICAL ASSUMPTIONS OF AN ANOVA

An accurate ANOVA result relies on the fact that the variables involved in the ANOVA do not violate the following statistical assumptions.

1. We assume that all k populations have equal variance. In SPSS, Levene's test for homogeneity of variances (discussed in Chapter 9) provides a way to verify this assumption. If Levene's test generates a significant result with a calculated $p < .05$, the homogeneity of variance is violated.[a] If Levene's test generates a nonsignificant result with a calculated $p \geq .05$, the homogeneity of variance is upheld.

2. All k populations are normally distributed. Normal distribution is a basic requirement when group means are compared.

3. All k samples are randomly selected and independent from one another. In one-way ANOVA, we only deal with between-subject factors. Therefore, each research participant is assigned to only one group. Each group consists of different individuals.

If these assumptions are not met, the accuracy of the F test might be distorted. This can lead to an arbitrarily increased risk of committing a Type I error.

EFFECT SIZE FOR ONE-WAY ANOVA

The most common measure of effect size for the one-way ANOVA is η^2, pronounced as eta squared. Conceptually, η^2 measures the percentage of the total variance of the dependent variable explained by the independent variable or the between-group factor. Mathematically, η^2 is calculated using the formula $\eta^2 = \text{SSB} / \text{SST}$.

The hypothesis test can tell you whether the ratio of the between-group variance to the within-group variance is statistically significant. However, when a large sample size is involved, even small, trivial between-group variance can lead to a statistically significant F value. A statistically significant outcome does not tell you how large the difference is or whether the difference is practically meaningful. The calculation of effect size (eta squared) in one-way ANOVA tells you what percentage of the total variance of the dependent variable is explained by the independent variable.

---

a. When Levene's test shows that the equal variances are not assumed, it shows that the populations where the samples are selected from are not identical. The results of the ANOVA are distorted and you should stop. Or you may run some mathematical transformation on the dependent variable to possibly fix the unequal variances. Usually logarithms or reciprocals can be used to restore equal variances.

Let's use the numbers in Example 13.2 to calculate an effect size of three advertising strategies: (1) weight control, (2) all natural ingredients, and (3) organic/environmental friendliness on customers' perceptions of the food quality. The ANOVA summary table is reprinted in Table 13.9, and it provides all the numbers you need to calculate the effect size.

TABLE 13.9   The ANOVA Summary Table for the Food Quality Ratings in Three Focus Groups

SOURCE	SS	df	MS	F
Between groups	12.333	$df_B = 2$	MSB = 6.167	F = 3.649
Within groups	35.5	$df_W = 21$	MSW = 1.690	
Total	47.833	$df_T = 23$		

$$\text{The effect size } \eta^2 = \frac{\text{SSB}}{\text{SST}} = \frac{12.333}{47.833} = .258$$

Although the hypothesis test generates a significant F value, the effect size for the three advertising strategies on customers' perceptions of the food quality is .258. There is 25.8% of the total variance in the food quality ratings that can be explained by the different advertising strategies.

Pop Quiz

1. There are 36 participants who are randomly assigned to one of the three groups: (1) driving while eating, (2) driving while texting, or (3) normal driving without distraction. Each group has 12 participants, and the ANOVA summary table is shown below.

SOURCE	SS	df	MS	F
Between groups	504	$df_B = 2$	MSB = 252	F = 5.500
Within groups	1512	$df_W = 33$	MSW = 45.82	
Total	2016	$df_T = 35$		

(Continued)

(Continued)

What is the effect size for the distracted
driving conditions on driving behavior?

The effect size for the driving conditions on driving behavior is .25. There is 25% of the
variance of driving behavior that can be explained by the different driving conditions.

Answer: **The effect size** $\eta^2 = \dfrac{SSB}{SST} = \dfrac{504}{2016} = .25$

STEP-BY-STEP INSTRUCTIONS FOR USING SPSS TO RUN AN ANOVA

Let's use the data in Example 13.2 to demonstrate the process of running an ANOVA using SPSS. The food quality rating is entered as a variable in the first column, and group membership is entered as a variable in the second column. It is conventional to treat each column as a variable and each row as a case or a research participant.

Open IBM SPSS Statistics 22 and enter the values of the variables as shown on the screen.

Click the **Analyze** tab.

In the drop-down menu, click **Compare Means**.

Then, click **One-Way ANOVA** as shown in Figure 13.2.

A pop-up window appears to ask you to identify the **Dependent variable** and **Factor** in the ANOVA. The dependent variable is the variable that you want to compare across three focus groups. The factor is the independent variable or grouping variable that you use to classify participants into different groups.

Click on **Foodrating**.

Click on ⬇ to move the **Foodrating** into the **Dependent variable** box.

Click on **Group**.

Click on ⬇ to move the **Group** into the **Factor** box; after you put both variables in the right places, your pop-up window should look like Figure 13.3.

You see three blue buttons on the right-hand side in Figure 13.3. Click on the middle one Post Hoc... . You will see a menu option for Post Hoc Multiple Comparisons pop up as shown in Figure 13.4.

FIGURE 13.2 Running One-Way ANOVA on SPSS

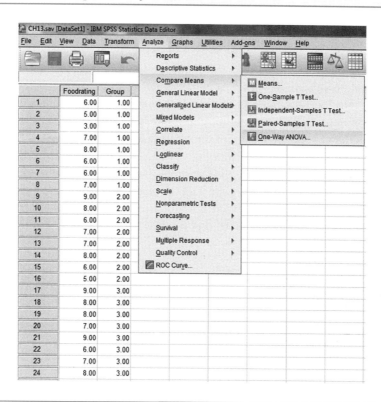

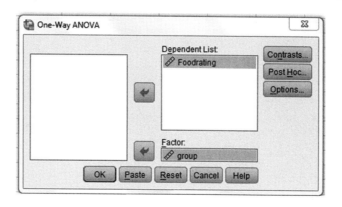

Click on the three options that we discussed in a previous section: (1) LSD, (2) Bonferroni, and (3) Tukey in the top portion of the menu labeled **Equal Variance Assumed**. Once you complete the step, your pop-up window looks like Figure 13.4.

As you can see in Figure 13.4, there are many options you may choose to conduct post hoc comparisons. The top part presents options when equal variances are assumed, and the bottom part presents options when equal variances are not assumed. You know whether equal variances are assumed or not by the outcome of Levene's test of equality of variances. LSD, Tukey's HSD, and Bonferroni are three of the most commonly used post hoc options under equal variances assumed. Other methods present similar ways to conduct post hoc comparisons with slightly modified formulas. Due to the introductory nature of this book, I choose to cover only three such formulas in this book. The post hoc options when equal variances are not assumed are beyond the scope of this book. They are likely to be covered in advanced statistics.

After you are done with selecting post hoc comparisons, click on **CONTINUE** to close the window.

Your screen looks like Figure 13.3 again. Click on Options... on the right-hand side. You see a menu option for One-Way ANOVA Options pop up as shown in Figure 13.5. The top section of the Option menu provides Statistics.

Check **Descriptive** and **Homogeneity of variance test**. Once you complete the step, your pop-up window looks like Figure 13.5.

Click **Continue** to close the window.

Click **OK**.

FIGURE 13.4   One-Way ANOVA: Post Hoc Multiple Comparisons

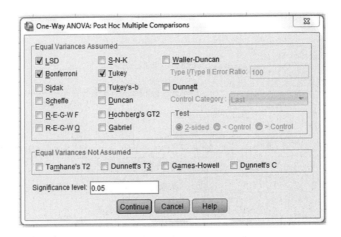

STRAIGHTFORWARD STATISTICS

FIGURE 13.5   One-Way ANOVA: Options Menu

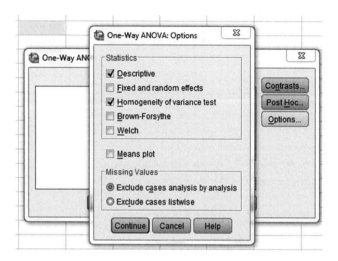

After you hit **OK**, SPSS will run the one-way ANOVA that you've requested. It generates many tables in the output file. We will go through them one by one. The first table you need to pay attention to in SPSS after running an ANOVA is the Descriptives as shown in Table 13.10. It shows the number of participants, mean, standard deviation, standard error, and 95% confidence interval (CI) for the mean, minimum, and maximum in each group. These constitute the basic statistical information, which might come in handy.

The second table is the result from Levene's test of homogeneity of variances as shown in Table 13.11. Levene's test is designed to verify that all groups have equal variances. A conclusion is

TABLE 13.10   Descriptive Statistics Table for an ANOVA

Descriptives

Foodrating

	N	Mean	Std. Deviation	Std. Error	95% Confidence Interval for Mean		Minimum	Maximum
					Lower Bound	Upper Bound		
Weight control	8	6.0000	1.51186	.53452	4.7361	7.2639	3.00	8.00
All natural	8	7.0000	1.30931	.46291	5.9054	8.0946	5.00	9.00
Organic/Environmental friendliness	8	7.7500	1.03510	.36596	6.8846	8.6154	6.00	9.00
Total	24	6.9167	1.44212	.29437	6.3077	7.5256	3.00	9.00

TABLE 13.11   Result of Levene's Test of Homogeneity of Variances in an ANOVA

Test of Homogeneity of Variances

Foodrating

Levene Statistic	df1	df2	Sig.
.138	2	21	.871

drawn based on the calculated p value associated with Levene's statistic as reported in the last column of the table (Sig.), $p = .871$. When the p value associated with a test statistic is used as a criterion for a hypothesis test, the decision rules are the following.

When the $p < \alpha$, we reject H_0.

When the $p \geq \alpha$, we fail to reject H_0.

The decision rules involved in the calculated p values associated with test statistics are universal, exactly as they were first discussed in Chapter 9.

The pair of hypotheses for Levene's test of homogeneity of variances is stated as

$H_0: \sigma_1^2 = \sigma_2^2 = \sigma_3^2$

H_1: Not all three population variances are equal.

Assume that $\alpha = .05$, $p = .871$ is greater than .05; therefore, we fail to reject H_0. The equal variances assumption is not violated in this case.

Table 13.12 presents the ANOVA summary table with SS, df, MS, F, and the p value associated with the F statistic. We can verify all the values in Table 13.12 with Table 13.9. They are identical except there is no p value reported in Table 13.9. The significance level (Sig.) associated with the $F = 3.648$ is $p = .044$.

TABLE 13.12   The ANOVA Summary Table for the Food Ratings in Three Focus Groups as Shown in SPSS

ANOVA

Foodrating

	Sum of Squares	Df	Mean Square	F	Sig.
Between Groups	12.333	2	6.167	3.648	.044
Within Groups	35.500	21	1.690		
Total	47.833	23			

The pair of hypotheses for the ANOVA F test is stated as the following.

H_0: $\mu_1 = \mu_2 = \mu_3$

H_1: Not all three population means are equal.

Assume that $\alpha = .05$, $p = .044$ is less than .05; therefore, we reject H_0. The evidence is strong enough to support the claim that not all group means are equal. We come to the same conclusion with either the critical value of the F test or the calculated p value associated with the F test.

The last table shows the outcomes of post hoc comparisons after a significant F test. You select Tukey's HSD, LSD, and Bonferroni to conduct the post hoc comparisons. When pairwise comparisons are significant at $\alpha = .05$, they are flagged with "*" (asterisk) in Table 13.13.

TABLE 13.13 Post Hoc Comparisons Using Tukey's HSD, LSD, and Bonferroni

Multiple Comparisons

Dependent Variable:Foodrating

	(I) Group	(J) Group	Mean Difference (I-J)	Std. Error	Sig.	95% Confidence Interval Lower Bound	95% Confidence Interval Upper Bound
Tukey HSD	Weight	Natural	-1.00000	.65009	.294	-2.6386	.6386
		Organic	-1.75000*	.65009	.035	-3.3886	-.1114
	Natural	Weight	1.00000	.65009	.294	-.6386	2.6386
		Organic	-.75000	.65009	.493	-2.3886	.8886
	Organic	Weight	1.75000*	.65009	.035	.1114	3.3886
		Natural	.75000	.65009	.493	-.8886	2.3886
LSD	Weight	Natural	-1.00000	.65009	.139	-2.3519	.3519
		Organic	-1.75000*	.65009	.014	-3.1019	-.3981
	Natural	Weight	1.00000	.65009	.139	-.3519	2.3519
		Organic	-.75000	.65009	.262	-2.1019	.6019
	Organic	Weight	1.75000*	.65009	.014	.3981	3.1019
		Natural	.75000	.65009	.262	-.6019	2.1019
Bonferroni	Weight	Natural	-1.00000	.65009	.417	-2.6911	.6911
		Organic	-1.75000*	.65009	.041	-3.4411	-.0589
	Natural	Weight	1.00000	.65009	.417	-.6911	2.6911
		Organic	-.75000	.65009	.785	-2.4411	.9411
	Organic	Weight	1.75000*	.65009	.041	.0589	3.4411
		Natural	.75000	.65009	.785	-.9411	2.4411

*The mean difference is significant at the 0.05 level.

Note: HSD = honestly significant difference, LSD = least significant difference.

In Table 13.13, there are six pairs of post hoc comparisons reported for each post hoc method. With three groups, there are three distinct pairs, as explained earlier. However, although SPSS reported six pairs, three of the pairs have the same magnitudes but different signs in comparison to the other three pairs: that is, $(\bar{X}_2 - \bar{X}_1) = -(\bar{X}_1 - \bar{X}_2)$; $(\bar{X}_1 - \bar{X}_3) = -(\bar{X}_3 - \bar{X}_1)$; and $(\bar{X}_2 - \bar{X}_3) = -(\bar{X}_3 - \bar{X}_2)$. Judging by the values in Table 13.13, all three post hoc methods (Tukey's HSD, LSD, and Bonferroni) provide identical outcomes. All indicate that there is a significant difference in food quality ratings between weight control and organic/environmental friendliness advertising strategies but no significant differences in the two other pairs.

The significant pairwise comparisons in Table 13.13 can also be identified via the 95% CIs of the respective mean differences. If zero is included in the 95% CI of the mean difference, the difference is not significant. When the lower bound of the 95% CI is a negative value and the upper bound is a positive value, zero is included in the 95% CI. If zero is not included in the 95% CI of the mean difference, the difference is significant. For example, in the last two columns of the Bonferroni adjustment, the 95% CI between organic/environmental friendliness and weight control is [.0589, 3.4411]. Both lower bound and upper bound are positive numbers. Zero is not included in this CI; therefore, the mean difference is significant.

You have a lot of information to interpret from conducting an ANOVA analysis. In summary, the overall ANOVA analysis shows that focus group participants rate the food quality significantly differently based on different advertising strategies. The post hoc comparisons identify exactly where the significant difference comes from. The pair comparison between weight control and organic/environmental friendliness groups generates significant difference. The differences from the two other pairs—weight control versus all natural and organic/environmental friendliness versus all natural—are not significant.

EXERCISE PROBLEMS

1. Assume that a beverage company wants to compare customer preferences on the color of a sports drink: red, orange, and yellow. The company randomly selects 30 participants. They then randomly assign 10 participants to each group. The customers' preferences are measured and reported in Table 13.14. The preferences are measured by the sum of four questions with a 5-point response scale, higher numbers representing more favorable ratings.

$$SST = 96.8$$

a. Conduct a hypothesis test to verify the equality of the customers' preference of the sports drinks across three different colors. Are there significant differences in the customers' preferences for the sports drink across three different colors?

b. Calculate the effect size for customers' preferences across three different colors.

2. Many people lose their jobs during economic downturns. Assume that an industrial and organizational psychologist is studying the degree of psychological stress of job seekers. A sample of 63 job seekers is randomly selected. Their ages are classified into three levels: (1) younger than 40 years, (2) 40 to 55 years, and (3) older than 55 years. The descriptive statistics of psychological stress scores for all three groups are reported in Table 13.15. Higher numbers mean higher reported psychological stress.

$$SST = 2524.4$$

TABLE 13.14 Customers' Preference of Color of the Sports Drink

RED	ORANGE	YELLOW
19	14	13
18	13	14
16	13	17
17	15	15
15	15	17
14	17	18
17	15	19
18	16	18
19	16	17
17	18	16
$\bar{X}_1 = 17$	$\bar{X}_2 = 15.2$	$\bar{X}_3 = 16.4$

a. Conduct a hypothesis test to verify the equality of the psychological stress across three different age-groups. Are there significant differences in the job seekers' psychological stress across different age-groups?

b. Calculate the effect size of job seekers' psychological stress across different age-groups.

TABLE 13.15 Descriptive Statistics of Psychological Stress Scores for All Three Groups

AGE	n	$\bar{X}$	s
Younger than 40 years	20	41.3	5.34
40 to 55 years	20	43.7	5.97
Older than 55 years	23	48.8	5.68
Total	63		

Solutions

1.a. The four-step hypothesis test for an ANOVA:

Step 1. State the pair of hypotheses.

$H_0: \mu_1 = \mu_2 = \mu_3 = \cdots = \mu_k$

$H_1:$ Not all μ_k are equal.

Step 2. Identify the rejection zone.

There are three groups, $k = 3$, 10 people in each group, $n_1 = n_2 = n_3 = 10$, and the sample size $n = 30$. The critical value of F is identified by $F_{(2,27)} = 3.35$ in the F Table for ANOVA. The rejection zone is identified as the calculated $F > 3.35$.

Step 3. Calculate the F test.

Under equal group size, the sample mean is

$$\bar{\bar{X}} = \left(17 + 15.2 + 16.4\right) / 3 = 16.2$$

$$\text{SSB} = \sum n_j (\bar{X}_j - \bar{\bar{X}})^2 = 10(17 - 16.2)^2 + 10(15.2 - 16.2)^2 + 10(16.4 - 16.2)^2 = 16.8$$

$$\text{SSW} = \text{SST} - \text{SSB} = 96.8 - 16.8 = 80$$

Now we have all the numbers to complete the ANOVA summary table as shown in Table 13.16.

Step 4. Make the correct conclusion.

The calculated $F = 2.835$ is not within the rejection zone, so we fail to reject H_0. The evidence is not strong enough to claim that significant differences exist among sports drinks with three different colors. No further analysis is needed.

1.b. The effect size for the ANOVA is $\eta^2 = \dfrac{\text{SSB}}{\text{SST}} = \dfrac{16.8}{96.8} = .174$.

The effect size of customers' preferences of different color sports drinks is .174. There is only 17.4% of the variance explained by the different colors.

TABLE 13.16 The ANOVA Summary Table for the Customers' Preferences of Different Color Sports Drinks

SOURCE	SS	df	MS	F
Between groups	16.8	$df_B = 2$	MSB = 8.4	F = 2.835
Within groups	80	$df_W = 27$	MSW = 2.963	
Total	96.8	$df_T = 29$		

2.a. The four-step hypothesis test for an ANOVA is as follows:

Step 1. State the pair of hypotheses.

$H_0: \mu_1 = \mu_2 = \mu_3 = \cdots = \mu_k$

H_1: Not all μ_k are equal.

Step 2. Identify the rejection zone.

There are three groups, $k = 3$, $n_1 = 20$, $n_2 = 20$, $n_3 = 23$, and the sample size $n = 63$. The critical value of F is identified by $F_{(2,60)}$. The critical value is $F_{(2,60)} = 3.15$. The rejection zone is identified as the calculated $F > 3.15$.

Step 3. Calculate the F test.

Due to the fact that the group sizes are not the same, the sample mean needs to be calculated as a weighted mean, which was covered in Chapter 3. The weighted sample mean for three groups with different group sizes is calculated as the sum of each group mean weighted by its group size and divided by the sum of all group sizes, which is the sample size.

The weighted sample mean $\bar{\bar{X}} = \left(n_1 \bar{X}_1 + n_2 \bar{X}_2 + n_3 \bar{X}_3 \right) / \left(n_1 + n_2 + n_3 \right)$

$$\bar{\bar{X}} = \left(20(41.3) + 20(43.7) + 23(48.8) \right) / 63 = 44.8$$

$$\text{SSB} = \sum n_j \left(\bar{X}_j - \bar{\bar{X}} \right)^2 = 20(41.3 - 44.8)^2 + 20(43.7 - 44.8)^2 + 23(48.8 - 44.8)^2 = 637.2$$

$$\text{SSW} = \text{SST} - \text{SSB} = 2524.4 - 637.2 = 1887.2$$

Now we have all the numbers to complete the ANOVA summary table as shown in Table 13.17.

TABLE 13.17   The ANOVA Summary Table for the Job Seekers' Psychological Stress Among Three Age-Groups

SOURCE	SS	df	MS	F
Between groups	637.2	$df_B = 2$	MSB = 318.6	F = 10.129
Within groups	1887.2	$df_W = 60$	MSW = 31.453	
Total	2524.4	$df_T = 62$		

Step 4. Make the correct conclusion.

The calculated $F = 10.129$ is within the rejection zone, so we reject H_0. The evidence is strong enough to claim that not all job seekers experience the same level of psychological stress. However, a significant F test does not inform us exactly where the significant difference occurs. Thus, post hoc pairwise comparisons need to be conducted to identify the sources of difference.

Let's use Tukey's HSD post hoc comparisons to fulfill this purpose.

$$HSD = q\sqrt{\frac{MSW}{n}}$$

Group 1 and Group 2 have the same group size, $n_1 = n_2 = 20$. The critical value of q in these three group comparisons is identified as $q_{(3,60)}$. According to the q Table, the critical value of $q_{(3,60)} = 3.40$.

$$HSD = q\sqrt{\frac{MSW}{n}} = 3.40\sqrt{\frac{31.453}{20}} = 4.264$$

The difference between Group 1 and Group 2 = 43.7 – 41.3 = 2.4

Compared with the calculated HSD = 4.264, the difference between Groups 1 and 2 $\bar{X}_2 - \bar{X}_1 <$ HSD; the difference is not significant.

Group 1 and Group 3 have different group sizes, so we need to calculate the harmonic mean for the group sizes:

$$n_h = \frac{2}{\dfrac{1}{20} + \dfrac{1}{23}} = 21.51$$

When dealing with unequal group sizes in ANOVA, some adjustment needs to be done before applying the HSD formula. Replace n with n_h to calculate the HSD.

$$HSD = q\sqrt{\frac{MSW}{n_h}} = 3.40\sqrt{\frac{31.453}{21.51}} = 4.111$$

The difference between Group 1 and Group 3 = 48.8 – 41.3 = 7.5.

Compared with the calculated HSD = 4.111, the difference between Groups 1 and 3 $\bar{X}_3 - \bar{X}_1 >$ HSD; the difference is significant.

Group 2 and Group 3 also have different group sizes, $n_2 = 20$ and $n_3 = 23$, so the harmonic mean for the group sizes is 21.51. The difference between Group 2 and Group 3 = 48.8 – 43.7 = 5.1.

Compared with the calculated HSD = 4.111, the difference between Groups 2 and 3 $\bar{X}_3 - \bar{X}_2 > \text{HSD}$; the difference is significant.

Therefore, we conclude that there are significant differences in job seekers' psychological stress between the group younger than 40 years and the group older than 55 years. There are also significant differences in job seekers' psychological stress between the group older than 55 years and the group between 40 and 55 years. There is not, however, enough evidence to claim significant difference between the two younger groups. It seems that job seekers who are older than 55 years experience significantly higher levels of psychological stress than the two younger groups.

2.b. The effect size for the ANOVA is $\eta^2 = \dfrac{\text{SSB}}{\text{SST}} = \dfrac{637.2}{2524.4} = .252$.

The effect size of job seekers' psychological stress across different age-groups is .252. There is 25.2% of the variance of the psychological stress explained by the different age-groups.

$\circledS$SAGE edge™

Sharpen your skills with SAGE edge!

Visit edge.sagepub.com/bowen for mobile-friendly quizzes, flashcards, videos, and more!

WHAT YOU LEARNED

Conducting a hypothesis test with ANOVA is a multiple-stage process. First, you partition the variances into different sources; then, gather all the *SS*, *df*, and MS to construct an ANOVA summary table. The *F* test in the ANOVA summary table calculates the ratio of the between-group variance to the within-group variance. The between-group variance is largely attributable to the systematic group effects that are deliberately designed by the researchers, and the within-group variance is largely attributable to random individual differences or unsystematic measurement errors. The *F* test informs you of the calculated ratio of the between-group variance to the within-group variance. The critical values in the *F* Table provide the standards to judge whether the evidence is strong enough to reject H_0 in the hypothesis-testing process.

The four-step hypothesis test process for ANOVA is stated as follows.

Step 1. State the pair of hypotheses for ANOVA.

$H_0: \mu_1 = \mu_2 = \mu_3 = \cdots = \mu_k$

H_1: Not all μ_k are equal.

Step 2. Identify the rejection zone.

The critical values of F can be identified by $F_{(k-1,\, n-k)}$ in the F Table for ANOVA. The rejection zone is identified as the calculated $F > F_{(k-1,\, n-k)}$.

Step 3. Calculate the F test for ANOVA.

The F test can be easily calculated by completing Table 13.5. Once the ANOVA summary table is complete, you can calculate $F = \text{MSB}/\text{MSW}$.

Step 4. Make the correct conclusion.

If the calculated F is not within the rejection zone, we fail to reject H_0. No additional analysis is needed. If the calculated F is within the rejection zone, we reject H_0. After rejecting H_0 in an ANOVA with three or more groups, you need to conduct post hoc pairwise comparisons to identify exactly where the significant differences come from. LSD, Tukey's HSD, and Bonferroni adjustment are commonly used post hoc comparison methods.

KEY WORDS

Analysis of variance (ANOVA): ANOVA is a statistical method to test the equality of group means by partitioning variances into different sources.

Between-subject design: The between-subject design refers to research in which participants are assigned to different groups based on different levels of the independent variables. Every participant is assigned to only one group.

Between-subject factor: In an ANOVA, the independent variable of a research study with a between-subject design is referred to as the between-subject factor.

Between-group variance: The between-group variance is calculated as the SSB divided by the df_B; in a special ANOVA term, the between-group variance is also called the mean squares between groups, $\text{MSB} = \text{SSB}/df_B$.

Bonferroni adjustment: The Bonferroni adjustment simply adjusts the α level of the individual pairwise comparison to a new level in order to control the familywise error rate.

Familywise error rate (FWER): The FWER refers to the probability of making a Type I error in a set of similar multiple comparisons.

Honestly significant difference (HSD): The HSD is a post hoc method to calculate a critical value for group mean differences while keeping the familywise risk of committing a Type I error under control.

Least significant difference (LSD): The LSD is the first post hoc method developed to calculate the difference between any two group means using the equivalent of multiple t tests, but without controlling the familywise error rate.

One-way ANOVA: One-way ANOVA is an ANOVA that uses only one factor to classify sample data into different groups.

Post hoc comparisons: Post hoc comparisons are used after a significant ANOVA F test to identify exactly where the significant difference comes from.

Sum of squares between groups (SSB): SSB is the sum of squares between groups and is defined by the squared differences between individual group means, $\bar{X}_j$, and the sample mean, $\bar{\bar{X}}$, multiplied by the number of participants in each group; then, add them up. It is calculated as $SSB = \sum n_j (\bar{X}_j - \bar{\bar{X}})^2$.

Sum of squared total deviations (SST): SST is the total sum of squared difference between individual scores, X_{ij}, and the sample mean, $\bar{\bar{X}}$. It is calculated as $SST = \sum\sum (X_{ij} - \bar{\bar{X}})^2$.

Sum of squares within groups (SSW): SSW is the sum of squares within groups and is defined by the squared differences between individual scores, X_{ij}, within a group relative to its corresponding group mean, $\bar{X}_j$; then, add them up. It is calculated as $SSW = \sum\sum (X_{ij} - \bar{X}_j)^2$.

Studentized Range Distribution: The Studentized range distribution is used to test the difference between the largest and the smallest group means measured in units of sample standard deviations when applying to three or more groups.

Within-subject design: The within-subject design indicates that research participants are assigned to all levels of the independent variables. Every participant experiences all levels of the independent variable and is measured repeatedly.

Within-group variance: The within-group variance is calculated as the SSW divided by the df_W; in a special ANOVA term, the within-group variance is also called the mean squares within groups, $MSW = SSW / df_W$.

Multiple Choice: Circle the best answer to every question.

1. Which one of the following statistical procedures is appropriate to compare means across three different groups?

   a. Independent-samples t tests

   b. Dependent-samples t tests

   c. ANOVA

   d. Correlation

2. Which one of the following statements is true in terms of LSD, HSD, and the Critical Values of Studentized Range Distribution (q)?

   a. LSD is larger than HSD.

   b. HSD is larger than LSD.

   c. LSD is larger than q.

   d. HSD is larger than q.

3. When do you need to conduct post hoc comparisons to identify exactly where the difference comes from?

   a. After conducting an ANOVA for three or more groups

   b. After conducting an ANOVA for two groups

   c. After a significant ANOVA result for three or more groups

   d. After a significant ANOVA result for two groups

4. What are the df for the between-group variance, df_B, in ANOVA?

   a. $df_B = k$, where k = number of groups

   b. $df_B = k - 1$, where k = number of groups

   c. $df_B = n - k$, where n = sample size and k = number of groups

   d. $df_B = n - 1$, where n = sample size

5. What are the df for the within-group variance, df_W, in ANOVA?

   a. $df_W = k$, where k = number of groups

   b. $df_W = k - 1$, where k = number of groups

   c. $df_W = n - k$, where n = sample size and k = number of groups

   d. $df_W = n - 1$, where n = sample size

6. What are the df for the total variance, df_T, in ANOVA?

   a. $df_T = k$, where k = number of groups

   b. $df_T = k - 1$, where k = number of groups

   c. $df_T = n - k$, where n = sample size and k = number of groups

   d. $df_T = n - 1$, where n = sample size

7. Which one of the following variances is largely attributable to systematic group effects that are deliberately designed by the researchers?

   a. The total variance

   b. The between-group variance

   c. The within-group variance

   d. The subject variance

8. Which one of the following variances is largely attributable to random individual differences or unsystematic measurement errors?

   a. The total variance

   b. The between-group variance

   c. The within-group variance

   d. The variance due to regression

9. The dependent variable in an ANOVA needs to be

   a. a nominal, ordinal, interval, or ratio variable.

   b. an ordinal, interval, or ratio variable.

   c. an interval or ratio variable.

   d. a ratio variable.

10. When conducting multiple post hoc comparisons without keeping FWER under control,

    a. The FWER is larger than the individual pairwise comparison error rate.

    b. The FWER is smaller than the individual pairwise comparison error rate.

    c. The FWER is the same as the individual pairwise comparison error rate.

    d. There is no relationship between the individual pairwise comparison error rate and the FWER.

Free Response Questions

11. Assume that the Insurance Institute for Highway Safety conducted crash safety tests on small SUVs, midsize SUVs, and large SUVs. Five SUVs in each type are randomly selected. The crash safety ratings for each type of SUV are reported in Table 13.18. The ratings are reported on a scale of 1 to 10, higher numbers representing better safety results.

TABLE 13.18 Crash Safety Ratings for Three Types of SUVs

SMALL SUV	MIDSIZE SUV	LARGE SUV
6	7	9
5	8	6
7	8	8
6	6	8
7	7	7
$\bar{X}_1 = 6.2$	$\bar{X}_2 = 7.2$	$\bar{X}_3 = 7.6$

$$\text{SST} = 16$$

   a. Conduct a hypothesis test to verify the equality of the crash safety ratings across three types of SUVs. Are there significant differences in the crash safety ratings across three different types of SUVs?

   b. Calculate the effect size of the different types of SUVs on the crash safety ratings.

12. Assume that a team of psychologists wants to compare college students' ability to concentrate under different noise conditions: constant background noise, unpredictable noise, and no noise. Psychologists randomly select 30 participants and split them into three groups. They then randomly place each group under one of the three conditions. The ability to concentrate is measured by a speed test that consists of a large number of easy questions. Higher scores mean better concentration. The speed test scores from each group are reported in Table 13.19.

TABLE 13.19 Speed Test Scores in Three Groups

CONSTANT NOISE	UNPREDICTABLE NOISE	NO NOISE
21	16	15
20	15	16
18	15	19
19	17	17
17	17	19
16	14	20
19	17	21
20	18	20
21	18	19
19	19	18
$\bar{X}_1 = 19$	$\bar{X}_2 = 16.6$	$\bar{X}_3 = 18.4$

$$SST = 110$$

a. Conduct a hypothesis test to verify the equality of the speed test scores across three different types of noise conditions. Are there significant differences in the ability to concentrate under three different types of noise conditions?

13. Assume that the College Board collects information about the total annual cost of tuition, room, and board from small private universities, midsize private universities, and large private universities. The tuition, room, and board from different private universities are reported in thousands of dollars, in Table 13.20.

TABLE 13.20 Tuition, Room, and Board for Private Universities

SMALL PRIVATE	MIDSIZE PRIVATE	LARGE PRIVATE
62	61	64
63	62	67
64	64	62
65	63	63
60	65	66
	66	64
		62
$\bar{X}_1 = 62.8$	$\bar{X}_2 = 63.5$	$\bar{X}_3 = 64$

$$SST = 58.5$$

a. Conduct a hypothesis test to verify the equality of the tuition, room, and board across three different sizes of private universities. Are there significant differences in the tuition, room, and board charged by the private universities with different sizes?

STRAIGHTFORWARD STATISTICS

CHAPTER 14

Chi-Square Tests for Goodness of Fit and Independence

LEARNING OBJECTIVES

After reading and studying this chapter, you should be able to do the following:

- Describe the difference between parametric statistics and nonparametric statistics

- Describe the formula for calculating expected frequencies for one-way frequency tables and two-way contingency tables

- Identify the degrees of freedom for chi-square tests

- Describe how to use the Chi-square Table to identify the critical values of chi-square

- Conduct goodness-of-fit tests using one-way frequency tables

- Conduct independence tests using two-way contingency tables

- Conduct hypothesis tests using chi-square

WHAT YOU KNOW AND WHAT IS NEW

You learned the four-step hypothesis-testing procedure in Chapter 7, continued to apply it in Chapter 8, slightly modified it to a five-step hypothesis-testing procedure in Chapter 9, and maintained the four-step procedure in Chapters 10 to 13. The good news is that the four-step hypothesis is still applicable in Chapter 14. The major difference is that all the previous topics from Chapter 7 to Chapter 13 are *parametric statistics* but the chi-square test is a *nonparametric statistic*.

Parametric statistics are defined as statistical procedures that make assumptions about the shape of the population distribution and also about certain population parameters such as μ, σ, and σ^2. Such assumptions allow sample statistics to be used to estimate the population parameters. Parametric statistics require variables to be interval or ratio scales of measurement. Different types of *t* tests, correlation, regression, and ANOVA are all examples of parametric statistics.

In contrast, nonparametric statistics are defined as statistical procedures that make no assumptions about the shape of population distributions. They are also called distribution-free statistics. Nonparametric statistics can be applied to nominal or ordinal scales of measurement as well as interval or ratio variables that are not normally distributed. In this chapter, the focus is on the *chi-square test*. The chi-square (χ^2) is the first nonparametric statistic you have encountered so far. You will learn to like it. One of the most useful applications of the chi-square is to test the fairness of employment decisions such as hiring, promotion, and layoff. Specifically, the Civil Rights Act of 1964 prohibits discrimination on the basis of race, color, sex, religion, or national origin in employment decisions. The chi-square test is a perfect tool to verify whether female employees are promoted at the same rate as males or whether employees from different ethnic backgrounds are laid off at the same rate when the company goes through a workforce reduction.

THE CHI-SQUARE

If I am asked to pick my favorite statistical analysis, the answer has to be the chi-square. The chi-square formula is simple, logical, and easy to understand, and it generates stable results. I will use many examples and one story to demonstrate the reasons why chi-square is my favorite statistical procedure. But first, let's introduce the concepts and formulas of chi-square tests.

The basic concept of a chi-square test is to calculate the difference between the observed frequency of a particular value of a variable and a theoretically expected frequency of that value, square the difference, and divide by the expected value. This procedure is repeated for every cell of the table, and then the results are summed up as follows.

observed frequencies and expected frequencies are vital when conducting hypothesis tests, as will be shown later in the chapter.

EXPECTED FREQUENCY UNDER A TWO-WAY CONTINGENCY TABLE

Besides one-way frequency tables, the chi-square can also be applied to measure the relationship between two nominal/ordinal variables. The chi-square test is based on the frequency distribution of the variables. When there are two variables, each participant can be classified based on two variables at the same time. For example, assume that a study examines the relationship between sex and smoking behavior. Assume for the moment that there are two ways to classify smoking behavior, smoker versus nonsmoker, and two ways to classify sex, male versus female. When research participants are classified based on these two variables at the same time, it leads to four ways to classify the participants: (1) male smoker, (2) male nonsmoker, (3) female smoker, and (4) female nonsmoker. The chi-square is used to test the independence of these two variables. Therefore, it is referred to as the chi-square test for independence or a two-way contingency table.

When two variables are independent of each other, it means that there is no relationship between these two variables. The frequency distribution of one variable does not depend on the values of the other variable. Let's use a true story to illustrate how to calculate the expected frequencies for the chi-square test for independence.

A company specializing in medical devices underwent a workforce reduction in its sales force. In the process of making the layoff decisions, one female employee—who was laid off despite her impressive sales records—decided to sue the company for sex discrimination. The company's attorney made the following comment: "Two thirds of the sales force were women; of course, we would lay off more women in the workforce reduction process." This comment sounded reasonable at first. However, it deserves to be carefully scrutinized.

The outcome of a workforce reduction for an individual employee can be classified as either "laid off" or "not laid off." The other variable is the employee's sex, and it can be classified as either "male" or "female." Every salesperson in the company can be classified based on these two variables. Assume that all salespeople are classified based on layoff decision and sex; the results are reported in Table 14.1, a 2 × 2 contingency table. The reported numbers are slightly modified to make the calculations easier than with the real numbers. There are 5 male salespeople who were laid off, 25 female salespeople who were laid off, 28 male salespeople who were not laid off, and 42 female salespeople who were not laid off. The row totals show that there were 33 male salespeople and 67 female salespeople in the company before the layoff decisions. The column totals show that there were 30 salespeople who were laid off and 70 salespeople who were not laid off.

TABLE 14.1 A 2 × 2 Contingency Table for Layoff Decision and Sex

	LAID OFF	NOT LAID OFF	ROW TOTAL
MALE	5	28	33
FEMALE	25	42	67
COLUMN TOTAL	30	70	100

Females constitute two thirds of the salesforce. The company trims 30% of the salesforce in the workforce reduction. If the layoff decision and sex are independent, it implies that employee's sex is not considered when the layoff decision is made. Thus, if there is no relationship between layoff decision and sex, the proportion of female employees should remain the same in the category of "laid off" employees as well in as the category of "not laid off" employees, both of which should be the same as the proportion of females in the company's salesforce.

There are four cells in this 2 × 2 contingency table. The number of cells in a contingency table does not include the row totals and column totals. The expected frequency for each cell is calculated under the independence assumption,

$$E = \frac{\text{Row total} \times \text{Column total}}{n}$$

Such a calculation is mathematically designed to make the expected frequency in each cell have the same proportion as the row total and column total relative to its sample size. The expected frequency for each cell is reported in Table 14.2. The expected frequencies need not necessarily be integers. The row totals and column totals remain the same in both the observed frequency table and the expected frequency table.

Let's scrutinize the company attorney's comment: "Two thirds of the sales force were women; of course, we would lay off more women in the workforce reduction process." This statement is half true. The devil is in the details. The company's attorney tried to justify the fact that more women were laid off by asserting that there were more women in the sales positions to begin with. The real issue, however, is *how many more*. If the proportion of women who got laid off is the same as the proportion of women who did not get laid off, and both are the same as two thirds, then I would agree that there is no relationship between layoff decision and sex.

The expected frequency table is calculated based on the independence assumption between the two variables. The expected frequency table presents what the numbers would be were the proportion of women the same in the "laid off" category as in the "not laid off" category. More generally, the expected frequencies state the theoretically predicted frequencies under the assumption that the variables are distributed exactly the same as stipulated by the null hypothesis that layoff decisions and employees' sex are independent. The expected frequencies show what the numbers in each cell should look like if there is no relationship between layoff

TABLE 14.2 Expected Frequency for the 2 × 2 Contingency Table Between Layoff Decision and Sex

	LAID OFF	NOT LAID OFF	ROW TOTAL
MALE	$\dfrac{33 \times 30}{100} = 9.9$	$\dfrac{33 \times 70}{100} = 23.1$	33
FEMALE	$\dfrac{67 \times 30}{100} = 20.1$	$\dfrac{67 \times 70}{100} = 46.9$	67
COLUMN TOTAL	30	70	100

decision and sex. The differences between the observed frequencies and the expected frequencies show the strength of the relationship between the two variables.

Comparing the observed frequencies with the expected frequencies, you can see that the company should have laid off 9.9 salesmen and 20.1 saleswomen, but it laid off 5 salesmen and 25 saleswomen. The company should have kept 23.1 salesmen and 46.9 saleswomen, but it kept 28 salesmen and 42 saleswomen.

Judging by the discrepancies between the observed frequencies and expected frequencies, on the face of things it is doubtful whether the layoff decisions were carried out without considering the employees' sex. A hypothesis test using the chi-square can answer the question as to the probability of getting such observed frequencies if the workforce reduction decisions were independent of employees' sex. The outcome of such a chi-square test can show whether the company is biased against women in its workforce reduction decisions. The hypothesis test with the chi-square test for independence will be discussed in a later section.

Pop Quiz

1. The row totals and column totals from a contingency table can be calculated from

a. only the observed frequencies of the two variables.

b. only the expected frequencies of the two variables.

c. either the observed frequencies or the expected frequencies; they produce the same row totals and column totals.

d. the sum of the observed frequencies and the expected frequencies.

Answer: c

GOODNESS-OF-FIT TESTS

Chi-square goodness-of-fit tests refer to using one categorical variable to investigate whether the sample distribution of the values in this variable fits with a particular theoretical distribution. Knowing how to calculate the expected frequency is a vital part of conducting a chi-square test. Once the expected frequencies are calculated, everything else simply falls into place through easy calculation and the use of chi-square tables. The chi-square formula is

$$\text{Chi-square} = \chi^2 = \sum \frac{(O - E)^2}{E}$$

Based on the formula, if there are large discrepancies between the observed frequencies and the expected frequencies, the calculated χ^2 will be large. If there are small discrepancies between the observed frequencies and the expected frequencies, the calculated χ^2 will be small. Small χ^2 indicates that the sample frequencies (i.e., the observed frequencies) fit well with the theoretical frequencies (i.e., the expected frequencies) under the null hypothesis. This is the reason why the one-way chi-square test is also called the *goodness-of-fit* test.

Every time we introduce a new test statistic, we need to know how to judge its statistical significance. When we introduced the Z test, the t test, Pearson's r, regression, and the ANOVA in previous chapters, we introduced the Z Table, the t Table, critical values for Pearson's r Table, and the F Table to identify the critical values that set off the boundaries of the rejection zones for these test statistics. It is the same way with chi-square tests. The degrees of freedom for the chi-square goodness-of-fit test are determined by $(c - 1)$, where c is the number of columns or categories in the one-way frequency table. There is a specific chi-square curve for every degree of freedom, the same way as there is a specific t curve for every degree of freedom in t tests. The critical values of chi-square that set off the boundaries of the rejection zones are presented in Appendix H. The rejection zone for the chi-square goodness-of-fit test is identified as $\chi^2 > \chi^2_{(c-1)}$. It is important to point out that the critical value that sets off the rejection zone is on the right side of the distribution.

We have already established the chi-square formula and the critical values of chi-square. Now we are ready to put everything together to conduct a hypothesis test with the chi-square goodness-of-fit test. It is important to point out that chi-square values can only be positive numbers. Large calculated χ^2 indicates a lack of fit between the observed frequencies and the expected frequencies.

HYPOTHESIS TESTING WITH THE CHI-SQUARE GOODNESS-OF-FIT TEST

Even though chi-square is a nonparametric statistic, the four-step hypothesis-testing procedure you learned in the previous chapters on parametric statistics still applies. The four-step hypothesis-testing procedure with the chi-square goodness-of-fit test includes the same four steps as in previous hypothesis tests but with slight modifications:

1. State the pair of hypotheses.

2. Identify the rejection zone.

3. Calculate the test statistic.

4. Draw the correct conclusion.

Step 1. State the pair of hypotheses.

Due to the fact that chi-square is a nonparametric statistic, the hypotheses do not describe a population parameter as in the previous parametric statistics. The pair of hypotheses in chi-square tests is a simple description of whether a particular sample distribution fits its theoretical distribution.

H_0: A particular (empirical) variable distribution fits its theoretical distribution (i.e., uniform distribution, binominal distribution, etc.).

H_1: A particular variable distribution does not fit its theoretical distribution.

Step 2. Identify the rejection zone.

Each degree of freedom has its own chi-square curve. The degrees of freedom for chi-square are calculated as $df = (c - 1)$. According to the critical values found in the Chi-square Table, the rejection zone for a chi-square test is identified as $\chi^2 > \chi^2_{(c-1)}$.

Assume that $\alpha = .05$, with $df = 1$; the rejection zone for a chi-square test is $\chi^2 > 3.841$.

Assume that $\alpha = .05$, with $df = 2$; the rejection zone for a chi-square test is $\chi^2 > 5.991$.

Assume that $\alpha = .05$, with $df = 3$; the rejection zone for a chi-square test is $\chi^2 > 7.815$.

Step 3. Calculate the test statistic.

$$\text{Chi-square} = \chi^2 = \sum \frac{(O - E)^2}{E}$$

Step 4. Draw the correct conclusion.

Compare the calculated χ^2 value with the rejection zone. If the calculated χ^2 is within the rejection zone, we reject H_0. If the calculated χ^2 is not within the rejection zone, we fail to reject H_0. Several examples are used throughout the remainder of this chapter to illustrate this four-step hypothesis test with chi-square tests.

EXAMPLE 14.2

Assume that you suspect that a die has been tampered with. You throw the die 36 times and record the number of times each value on the die occurs in Table 14.3. Conduct a hypothesis test to see if this die is a fair die, assuming $\alpha = .05$.

TABLE 14.3   Observed Frequency (O) of the Number of Dots of a Die

X	1	2	3	4	5	6
O	9	5	7	4	3	8

The probability theory tells us that if this die is a fair die, each number of dots has a uniform probability, $p = 1/6$. The expected frequency for each number of dots when you throw the die 36 times is $E = np = 36(1/6) = 6$. This fulfills the requirement that the expected frequency in each of the cells of the table should be at least 5. If more than 20% of the cells contain an expected frequency less than 5, it is not appropriate to use the chi-square test. Here is an important reminder. Although some of the observed frequencies fell below 5, as stated before, there are no requirements for the observed frequencies to be at least 5. This would not pose any threat to the accuracy of the chi-square for goodness-of-fit test.

At first glance, none of the observed frequencies match the expected frequencies $E = 6$. You might have the impulse to jump to the conclusion that this die is not a fair die. I would strongly encourage you to temporarily control that impulse until after the hypothesis test is finished.

TABLE 14.4   Observed Frequency (O) and Expected Frequency (E) of the Number of Dots on a Die

X	1	2	3	4	5	6
O	9	5	7	4	3	8
E	6	6	6	6	6	6

Let's include the expected frequencies in the table as shown in Table 14.4.

It is time to put all the numbers together to conduct a hypothesis test to see if this die is a fair die.

Step 1. State the pair of hypotheses.

H_0: The die produces the same frequencies as the expected frequencies for all six values.

H_1: The die does not produce the same frequencies as the expected frequencies for all six values.

Step 2. Identify the rejection zone.

When $\alpha = .05$, with $df = (c - 1) = 6 - 1 = 5$, the rejection zone for the chi-square test is $\chi^2 > 11.07$.

Step 3. Calculate the test statistic.

$$\chi^2 = \sum \frac{(O - E)^2}{E} = \frac{(9 - 6)^2}{6} + \frac{(5 - 6)^2}{6} + \frac{(7 - 6)^2}{6} + \frac{(4 - 6)^2}{6} + \frac{(3 - 6)^2}{6} + \frac{(8 - 6)^2}{6} = 4.667$$

Step 4. Draw the correct conclusion.

The calculated $\chi^2 = 4.667$ is not within the rejection zone. Therefore, we fail to reject H_0. The evidence is not strong enough to claim that the die is not a fair die. Although the observed frequencies appear to be different from the expected frequencies, the differences are, on balance of all the numbers considered together, not large enough to be statistically significant.

In this example, the expected frequency for every value on the die is the same due to the fact that the number of dots on a die has a uniform probability distribution. We are going to discuss a different kind of probability distribution in the next example.

EXAMPLE 14.3

Assume that a school psychologist randomly selects 100 families with three children to conduct a study on the middle child's academic achievement. The psychologist describes the sample as 17 families with three girls, 30 families with two girls and one boy, 35 families with one girl and two boys, and 18 families with three boys. Conduct a hypothesis test to see if this sample of 100 families with three children have the same distribution of boys and girls as in the population of families with three children, assuming $\alpha = .05$.

(Continued)

(Continued)

Let's use probability theory to figure out the distribution of boys and girls in a family of three children in the population. The probability of having a girl is $p(g) = .5$. The probability of having a boy is $p(b) = .5$ This is the binominal probability distribution as discussed in Chapter 5.

The binomial probability formula is

$$P(r) = \frac{n!}{(n-r)!r!} p^r q^{(n-r)} \quad \text{for } r = 0, 1, 2, 3, \ldots, n$$

In this case, let r be the number of girls in the family; $r = 0, 1, 2,$ or 3. The probability of having zero girls and three boys is

$$P(0) = \frac{3!}{(3-0)!0!} (.5)^0 (.5)^3 = .125$$

The expected frequency for having three boys in a sample of 100 families is $np = 100 \times .125 = 12.5$.

The probability of having one girl and two boys is

$$P(1) = \frac{3!}{(3-1)!1!} (.5)^1 (.5)^2 = .375$$

The expected frequency for having one girl and two boys in a sample of 100 families is $np = 100 \times .375 = 37.5$.

The probability of having two girls and one boy is

$$P(2) = \frac{3!}{(3-2)!2!} (.5)^2 (.5)^1 = .375$$

The expected frequency for having two girls and one boy in a sample of 100 families is $np = 100 \times .375 = 37.5$.

The probability of having three girls is

$$P(3) = \frac{3!}{(3-3)!3!} (.5)^3 (.5)^0 = .125$$

The expected frequency for having three girls in a sample of 100 families is $np = 100 \times .125 = 12.5$.

None of the expected frequencies is lower than 5; therefore, it is appropriate to proceed with the chi-square test. Let's organize both the observed and the expected frequencies in Table 14.5.

TABLE 14.5   Number of Boys and Girls in 100 Families With Three Children

FAMILY WITH THREE CHILDREN	THREE GIRLS	TWO GIRLS, ONE BOY	ONE GIRL, TWO BOYS	THREE BOYS
O	17	30	35	18
E	12.5	37.5	37.5	12.5

Step 1. State the pair of hypotheses.

H_0: The sample distribution of boys or girls in a family with three children is the same as the binomial probability distribution for a family with three children.

H_1: The sample distribution of boys or girls in a family with three children is not the same as the binomial probability distribution for a family with three children.

Step 2. Identify the rejection zone.

When $\alpha = .05$, with $df = (c - 1) = 4 - 1 = 3$, the rejection zone for the chi-square test is $\chi^2 > 7.815$.

Step 3. Calculate the test statistic.

$$\chi^2 = \sum \frac{(O - E)^2}{E} = \frac{(17 - 12.5)^2}{12.5} + \frac{(30 - 37.5)^2}{37.5} + \frac{(35 - 37.5)^2}{37.5} + \frac{(18 - 12.5)^2}{12.5} = 5.707$$

Step 4. Draw a conclusion.

The calculated $\chi^2 = 5.707$ is not within the rejection zone, so we fail to reject H_0. The evidence is not strong enough to claim that the sample distribution for a family with three children differs from the theoretical binomial probability distribution for a family with three children. The sample distribution fits the theoretical binomial probability distribution well.

We have finished the chi-square test that applies to the one-way frequency table or the goodness-of-fit test. Now we are ready to move on to the chi-square test for independence between two nominal or ordinal variables. In the next section, I will demonstrate the reason why the chi-square test for independence is one of my favorite statistics.

1. Chi-square $= \chi^2 = \sum (O - E)^2 / E$; the larger the calculated χ^2,

   a. the greater are the discrepancies between the observed frequencies and the expected frequencies.

   b. the smaller are the discrepancies between the observed frequencies and the expected frequencies.

   c. the greater is the variance of the expected frequencies.

   d. the greater is the variance of the observed frequencies.

Answer: a

CHI-SQUARE TEST FOR INDEPENDENCE

The **chi-square test for independence** is a nonparametric statistical procedure to measure the relationship between two nominal or ordinal variables. The chi-square test for independence is based on what is called a **contingency table**. A contingency table is defined as a frequency table where each individual is classified based on the column variable and the row variable at the same time. The observed frequency table presents the frequency count based on two variables. The expected frequency table presents the theoretical predicted frequency count under the H_0, which means that the frequency distribution of one variable does not depend on the values of the other variable. The expected frequency is calculated as

$$E = \frac{\text{Row total} \times \text{Column total}}{n}$$

Such a formula is mathematically designed to make sure that the expected frequencies are calculated in proportion to the row total and column total relative to the sample size.

Once the expected frequencies are figured out, the chi-square formula is calculated simply as

$$\text{Chi-square} = \chi^2 = \sum \frac{(O - E)^2}{E}$$

The degrees of freedom for the chi-square test for independence are calculated as $(r - 1)(c - 1)$, where r is the number of rows and c the number of columns in the contingency table. The rejection zone for a chi-square test for independence is identified as $\chi^2 > \chi^2_{(r-1)(c-1)}$. The critical values of chi-square tests are always on the right side of the distribution.

We have already established the chi-square formula and the critical values of chi-square. It seems that we are ready to put everything together to conduct a hypothesis test with chi-square in order to test the relationship between two nominal or ordinal variables.

HYPOTHESIS TESTING WITH THE CHI-SQUARE TEST FOR INDEPENDENCE

You should feel relieved that the same four-step hypothesis-testing procedure can also be applied to the chi-square test for independence:

1. State the pair of hypotheses.

2. Identify the rejection zone.

3. Calculate the test statistic.

4. Draw the correct conclusion.

Step 1. State the pair of hypotheses.

Due to the fact that chi-square is a nonparametric statistic, the hypotheses do not describe a population parameter. The pair of hypotheses in the chi-square test for independence is a simple description of whether two variables are independent of each other.

H_0: Two variables are independent of each other.

H_1: Two variables are not independent of each other.

Step 2. Identify the rejection zone.

Each degree of freedom has its own chi-square curve. The degrees of freedom for the chi-square test for independence are $df = (r - 1)(c - 1)$. According to the critical values in the Chi-Square Table, the rejection zone for a chi-square test is identified as $\chi^2 > \chi^2_{(r-1)(c-1)}$.

Step 3. Calculate the test statistic.

$$\text{Chi-square} = \chi^2 = \sum \frac{(O - E)^2}{E}$$

Step 4. Draw the correct conclusion.

Compare the calculated χ^2 value with the rejection zone. If the calculated χ^2 is within the rejection zone, we reject H_0. If the calculated χ^2 is not within the rejection zone, we fail to reject H_0. Examples are used to illustrate this four-step hypothesis test with chi-square tests for independence.

The time has come to finish the story about the medical device company being sued for sex discrimination in its layoff decisions by conducting a hypothesis test with the chi-square test for independence. All the relevant information is presented in Example 14.4.

EXAMPLE 14.4

A company specializing in medical devices underwent workforce reduction in its sales force. The outcome of a workforce reduction for an individual employee can be classified as either "laid off" or "not laid off." The employee's sex can be classified as either "male" or "female." Every salesperson in the company can be classified based on these two variables. The results of the workforce reduction decisions were reported in Table 14.1, in a 2 × 2 contingency table. Here is the table again, for your convenience.

TABLE 14.1 A 2 × 2 Contingency Table for Layoff Decision and Sex

	LAID OFF	NOT LAID OFF	ROW TOTAL
MALE	5	28	33
FEMALE	25	42	67
COLUMN TOTAL	30	70	100

Conduct a hypothesis test to see if layoff decision and employee's sex are independent, using $\alpha = .05$.

Step 1. State the pair of hypotheses.

H_0: The layoff decision and employee's sex are independent.

H_1: The layoff decision and employee's sex are not independent.

Step 2. Identify the rejection zone.

When $\alpha = .05$, with $df = (r - 1)(c - 1) = (2 - 1)(2 - 1) = 1$, the rejection zone for the chi-square test is $\chi^2 > 3.841$.

Step 3. Calculate the test statistic.

The expected frequencies are calculated by

$$E = \frac{\text{Row total} \times \text{Column total}}{n}$$

The expected frequency for the "laid-off male" is $(33 \times 30) / 100 = 9.9$.

The expected frequency for the "laid-off female" is $(67 \times 30) / 100 = 20.1$.

The expected frequency for the "not laid-off male" is $(33 \times 70) / 100 = 23.1$.

The expected frequency for the "not laid-off female" is $(67 \times 70) / 100 = 46.9$.

$$\chi^2 = \sum \frac{(O - E)^2}{E} = \frac{(5 - 9.9)^2}{9.9} + \frac{(28 - 23.1)^2}{23.1} + \frac{(25 - 20.1)^2}{20.1} + \frac{(42 - 46.9)^2}{46.9} = 5.171$$

Step 4. Draw the correct conclusion.

The calculated $\chi^2 = 5.171$ is within the rejection zone, so we reject H_0. The evidence is strong enough to support the claim that the layoff decision and employee's sex are not independent. The probability of obtaining such observed frequencies is pretty small ($p < .05$) under the assumption that layoff decisions are independent of employees' sex. Therefore, the conclusion based on the chi-square test for independence is that it is unlikely that the company did not consider the employee's sex when it went through the workforce reduction process. The evidence is strong enough to support the claim that layoff decisions and employees' sex were not independent.

It is amazing that such a simple chi-square test for independence can provide solid statistical evidence to discredit the medical device company attorney's statement that "two thirds of the sales force were women; of course, we would lay off more women in the workforce reduction process." The problem is that the company has laid off too many women and not enough men to reach the fair proportion of two thirds of women in both the "laid-off" category and the "not laid off" category.

In a very similar context, you might have heard that a big-box retailer has been accused of unfair employment practices and has many lawsuits pending against it. The next example is a demonstration of how the chi-square test for independence can be applied in such a situation.

EXAMPLE 14.5

Assume that a large big-box retailer is accused of sex discrimination in promotion decisions. The personnel files in the company's Midwest region show that there were 3,300 male employees and among them 960 were promoted in the past 6 months. During the same time, there were 2,700 female employees, and among them, 700 were promoted.

(Continued)

(Continued)

Do the data substantiate the claim that this large big-box retailer discriminated against female workers in promotion decisions? Conduct a four-step hypothesis-testing procedure to test if promotion decisions and employee's sex are independent, using $\alpha = .05$.

Step 1. State the pair of hypotheses.

H_0: The promotion decision and employee's sex are independent.

H_1: The promotion decision and employee's sex are not independent.

Step 2. Identify the rejection zone.

When $\alpha = .05$, with $df = (r - 1)(c - 1) = (2 - 1)(2 - 1) = 1$, the rejection zone for the chi-square test is $\chi^2 > 3.841$.

Step 3. Calculate the test statistic.

It is important to be able to extract the numbers from the problem statement and accurately construct the observed frequency table with mutually exclusive categories. There are two categories in the outcomes of the promotion decision: "promoted" and "not promoted." The problem statement specifies that "there were 3,300 male employees and among them 960 were promoted in the past 6 months"; so it means that 960 males were promoted and 2,340 males were not promoted out of 3,300 male employees. The same reasoning applies to the female employees; so you know that 700 female employees were promoted and 2,000 female employees were not promoted out of 2,700 female employees. The observed frequency table is constructed in Table 14.6.

The expected frequency for each cell is calculated under the independence assumption,

$$E = \frac{\text{Row total} \times \text{Column total}}{n}$$

TABLE 14.6 Observed Frequency for the 2 × 2 Contingency Table Between Promotion Decision and Employee's Sex

	PROMOTED	NOT PROMOTED	ROW TOTAL
MALE	960	2,340	3,300
FEMALE	700	2,000	2,700
COLUMN TOTAL	1,660	4,340	6,000

The expected frequency for the "promoted male" is $\dfrac{3,300 \times 1,660}{6,000} = 913$

The expected frequency for the "promoted female" is $\dfrac{2,700 \times 1,660}{6,000} = 747$

The expected frequency for the "not promoted male" is $\dfrac{3,300 \times 4,340}{6,000} = 2,387$

The expected frequency for the "not promoted female" is $\dfrac{2,700 \times 4,340}{6,000} = 1,953$

The expected frequency table is constructed in Table 14.7.

TABLE 14.7 Expected Frequency for the 2 × 2 Contingency Table Between Promotion Decision and Employee's Sex

	PROMOTED	NOT PROMOTED
MALE	913	2,387
FEMALE	747	1,953

$$\chi^2 = \sum \frac{(O-E)^2}{E} = \frac{(960-913)^2}{913} + \frac{(2340-2387)^2}{2387} + \frac{(700-747)^2}{747} + \frac{(2000-1953)^2}{1953} = 7.433$$

Step 4. Draw the correct conclusion.

The calculated $\chi^2 = 7.433$ is within the rejection zone, so we reject H_0. The evidence is strong enough to support the claim that the promotion decision and employee's sex are not independent. The probability of obtaining such observed frequencies is pretty small (i.e., $p < .05$) under the assumption that the promotion decision and employee's sex are independent. Therefore, the conclusion based on the chi-square test for independence is that it was highly unlikely that the big-box retailer did not consider employee's sex when the promotion decisions were made.

The chi-square test for independence is a powerful statistic for investigating the relationship between two nominal or ordinal variables. It does not make assumptions about the shape of the population distribution or the population parameters. The calculation of chi-square only requires a frequency count based on the variables involved. As long as the expected frequencies are at least 5, the results of chi-square tests are accurate and reliable.

The Civil Rights Act of 1964 makes it illegal for employers to discriminate against any individual due to race, sex, color, religion, or national origin. These variables are all nominal variables. Any one of these variables can be used to investigate whether there is discrimination in various employment practices such as hiring, promotion, or layoff decisions. As an industrial and organizational psychologist, I have been involved in discrimination litigations as an expert witness who provides statistical evidence to show, overall, if a company's employment decisions are made fairly. Fair decisions are supposed to be made without considering the employee's race, sex, color, religion, or national origin. Chi-square tests use the discrepancies between observed frequencies and expected frequencies to show how far apart a company's practice is from a truly fair decision-making process. That is the reason why my favorite statistical procedure is the chi-square test.

Besides discrimination in the workplace, chi-square tests can also be applied to investigate the relationship between two nominal or ordinal variables in medical fields. The next examples illustrate such uses.

EXAMPLE 14.6

Assume that a medical insurance company wants to evaluate the effectiveness of cardiac rehabilitation (rehab) in terms of whether heart patients return for repeat procedures within 12 months of their original one. Cardiac rehab is a professionally supervised program to help patients recover from heart attacks, heart surgery, stenting, or angioplasty. Cardiac rehab programs usually provide education and counseling services to help heart patients increase physical fitness, reduce cardiac symptoms, improve health, and reduce the risk of future heart problems. A group of patients is randomly selected from a large hospital's cardio rehab center. Each patient is classified based on two variables: (1) whether the patient completed the cardiac rehab and (2) whether the patient has had a repeat heart procedure within 12 months of the original procedure. The frequency counts for both variables are reported in Table 14.8. Conduct a hypothesis test to investigate the relationship between cardiac rehab and whether the patient repeated a heart procedure within 12 months, assuming $\alpha = .05$.

TABLE 14.8 Observed Frequency for the Contingency Table Between Cardiac Rehab and Repeat Heart Procedure Within 12 Months

	COMPLETED CARDIAC REHAB	DID NOT COMPLETE CARDIAC REHAB	ROW TOTAL
REPEATED HEART PROCEDURE	15	20	35
DID NOT REPEAT HEART PROCEDURE	102	63	165
COLUMN TOTAL	117	83	200

Step 1. State the pair of hypotheses.

H_0: The completion of cardiac rehab and a repeat heart procedure are independent.

H_1: The completion of cardiac rehab and a repeat heart procedure are not independent.

Step 2. Identify the rejection zone.

When $\alpha = .05$, with $df = (r-1)(c-1) = (2-1)(2-1) = 1$, the rejection zone for the chi-square test is $\chi^2 > 3.841$.

Step 3. Calculate the test statistic.

We need to construct the expected frequencies before we can calculate the chi-square. The expected frequency for each cell is calculated under the independence assumption,

$$E = \frac{\text{Row total} \times \text{Column total}}{n}$$

The expected frequency table is reported in Table 14.9.

$$\chi^2 = \sum \frac{(O-E)^2}{E} = \frac{(15-20.475)^2}{20.475} + \frac{(20-14.525)^2}{14.525} + \frac{(102-96.525)^2}{96.525} + \frac{(63-68.475)^2}{68.475} = 4.276$$

Step 4. Draw the correct conclusion.

The calculated $\chi^2 = 4.276$ is within the rejection zone, so we reject H_0. The evidence is strong enough to infer that completion of cardiac rehab and a repeat heart procedure

(Continued)

(Continued)

TABLE 14.9 Expected Frequency for the 2 × 2 Contingency Table Between Cardiac Rehab and Repeat Heart Procedure

	COMPLETED CARDIAC REHAB	DID NOT COMPLETE CARDIAC REHAB
REPEATED HEART PROCEDURE	20.475	14.525
DID NOT REPEAT HEART PROCEDURE	96.525	68.475

are not independent. The probability of obtaining such observed frequencies is pretty small ($p < .05$) under the assumption that the two variables are independent of each other. Therefore, the conclusion is that whether the patient completed the cardiac rehab is related to whether the patient had repeat heart procedures. In other words, patients who completed the cardiac rehab are less likely to have repeat heart procedures within 12 months. Such information can be extracted from the differences between the observed frequency and the expected frequency in the cells. Patients who completed the cardiac rehab have a lower than expected number of repeated heart procedures and a higher than expected number of instances of not having repeat heart procedures. Patients who did not complete the cardiac rehab had a higher than expected number of repeat heart procedures and a lower than expected number of instances of not having repeat heart procedures. Health insurance companies should provide incentives to encourage heart patients to complete cardiac rehab by switching to an active and healthy lifestyle in order to reduce the risk of undergoing repeat heart procedures in the future.

Many situations in which the use of chi-square is appropriate involve dichotomous nominal variables, such as gender, layoff decisions, promotion decisions, whether patients complete cardiac rehab, and whether patients have repeat heart procedures. But chi-square can also be used with many levels or categories of each nominal or ordinal variable. The next example describes a situation where each variable can be classified into multiple levels or categories.

EXAMPLE 14.7

In 2012, the Office for National Statistics in Great Britain conducted a national Opinions and Lifestyle Survey to study the smoking habits of people of age 16 years and older. In this survey, a smoking habit is classified into three categories: (1) current smoker, (2) ex-smoker, and (3) never smoked. Economic activity is also classified into three categories: (1) employed, (2) unemployed, and (3) economically inactive (e.g., students or retired people). The frequency counts based on these two variables are reported in Table 14.10. Conduct a hypothesis test to investigate whether smoking habit and economic status are independent, assuming $\alpha = .05$.

TABLE 14.10 Observed Frequency for the Contingency Table Between Smoking Habit and Economic Activity

	EMPLOYED	UNEMPLOYED	ECONOMICALLY INACTIVE	ROW TOTAL
SMOKER	1,390	250	913	2,553
EX-SMOKER	1,192	90	1,396	2,678
NEVER SMOKED	4,038	300	3,061	7,399
COLUMN TOTAL	6,620	640	5,370	12,630

SOURCE: Data retrieved from Office for National Statistics (2013).

Step 1. State the pair of hypotheses.

H_0: Smoking habit and economic activity are independent.

H_1: Smoking habit and economic activity are not independent.

Step 2. Identify the rejection zone.

When $\alpha = .05$, with $df = (r - 1)(c - 1) = (3 - 1)(3 - 1) = 4$, the rejection zone for the chi-square test is $\chi^2 > 9.488$.

Step 3. Calculate the test statistic.

We need to construct the expected frequencies before we can calculate the chi-square. The expected frequency for each cell is calculated under the independence assumption,

$$E = \frac{\text{Row total} \times \text{Column total}}{n}$$

(Continued)

(Continued)

The expected frequency table is reported in Table 14.11.

TABLE 14.11 Expected Frequency for the 3 × 3 Contingency Table Between Smoking Habit and Economic Activity

	EMPLOYED	UNEMPLOYED	ECONOMICALLY INACTIVE
SMOKER	1,338.15	129.37	1,085.48
EX-SMOKER	1,403.67	135.70	1,138.63
NEVER SMOKED	3,878.18	374.93	3,145.89

$$\chi^2 = \sum \frac{(O-E)^2}{E} = \frac{(1390-1338.15)^2}{1338.15} + \frac{(1192-1403.67)^2}{1403.67} + \frac{(4038-3878.18)^2}{3878.18} +$$

$$\frac{(250-129.37)^2}{129.37} + \frac{(90-135.70)^2}{135.70} + \frac{(300-374.93)^2}{374.93} + \frac{(913-1085.48)^2}{1085.48} + \frac{(1396-1138.63)^2}{1138.63} +$$

$$\frac{(3061-3145.89)^2}{3145.89} = 271.24$$

Step 4. Draw a conclusion.

The calculated $\chi^2 = 271.24$ is within the rejection zone, so we reject H_0. The evidence is strong enough to support the claim that smoking habit and economic activity are not independent. The probability of obtaining such observed frequencies is very small ($p < .05$) under the assumption that these two variables are independent of each other. Therefore, the conclusion is that smoking habit and economic activity are related. For each level of economic activity, some large contributors to the overall chi-square may be seen by examining the squared discrepancy between the observed frequency and the expected frequency divided by the expected frequency in each cell. Employed people have a much lower number of ex-smokers than expected. Similarly, unemployed people have a higher number of smokers than expected. Economically inactive people have a much greater number of ex-smokers than expected. This shows that people have different smoking habits across different levels of economic activity.

The simple and straightforward nature of the chi-square test for independence allows students to handle realistic numbers from a large, national-scale survey with tens of thousands of participants without any problem.

Pop Quiz

1. A significant chi-square test for independence means that

   a. there is a causal relationship between the two variables.

   b. we can predict the dependent variable with the information on the independent variable.

   c. the two variables move in the same direction.

   d. it is highly unlikely that we would obtain the observed frequencies if the two variables were independent of each other.

Answer: d

EXERCISE PROBLEMS

1. Assume that a university classifies students' academic performance into the following five categories: (1) academic warning (GPA $\leq$ 2.00), (2) academic watch (GPA 2.01–2.50), (3) continuing improvement (GPA 2.51–3.00), (4) good performance (GPA 3.01–3.50), and (5) academic excellence (GPA 3.51–4.00). It is believed that students are evenly divided into these five categories. A sample of 100 students is randomly selected from the university, and their GPAs are reported in Table 14.12. Conduct a hypothesis test to see if there is a uniform distribution among students' academic performance in this university, assuming $\alpha = .05$.

TABLE 14.12 Number of Students in Each Academic Performance Category

GPA $\leq$ 2.00	GPA 2.01–2.50	GPA 2.51–3.00	GPA 3.01–3.50	GPA 3.51–4.00	TOTAL
12	16	17	31	24	100

2. Assume that a researcher tests a randomly selected sample of 606 people for color vision and then classifies them according to their sex and color vision status (normal, red–green color blindness, other color blindness). The result is reported in Table 14.13. Conduct a hypothesis test to investigate if color blindness and sex are independent, assuming $\alpha = .05$.

3. A medical supply company is accused of age discrimination in its decisions on workforce reduction. The personnel files indicate that there were 51 employees aged 40 years and older, and among them, 22 were laid off in the past 2 months. During the

TABLE 14.13 Observed Frequency for Sex and Color Vision Category

GENDER	NORMAL	RED-GREEN COLOR BLINDNESS	OTHER COLOR BLINDNESS	ROW TOTAL
MALE	192	42	12	246
FEMALE	348	6	6	360
COLUMN TOTAL	540	48	18	606

same time, there were 37 employees younger than 40 years, and among them, 8 were laid off. Conduct a hypothesis test to investigate if the reduction in workforce decision and employee's age are independent, assuming $\alpha = .05$.

Solutions

1.

Step 1. State the pair of hypotheses.

H_0: Students' GPAs are uniformly distributed across the five categories.

H_1: Students' GPAs are not uniformly distributed across the five categories.

Step 2. Identify the rejection zone.

When $\alpha = .05$, with $df = (c - 1) = 5 - 1 = 4$, the rejection zone for the chi-square test is $\chi^2 > 9.488$.

Step 3. Calculate the test statistic.

The expected frequency for a uniform distribution in the five categories is $E = np = 100(.20) = 20$.

$$\chi^2 = \sum \frac{(O - E)^2}{E} = \frac{(12 - 20)^2}{20} + \frac{(16 - 20)^2}{20} + \frac{(17 - 20)^2}{20} + \frac{(31 - 20)^2}{20} + \frac{(24 - 20)^2}{20} = 11.30$$

Step 4. Draw the correct conclusion.

The calculated $\chi^2 = 11.30$ is within the rejection zone. Therefore, we reject H_0. The evidence is strong enough to claim that students' GPAs are not uniformly distributed in this university across the five academic performance categories. The frequency counts are higher than expected for the two high-GPA categories but lower than expected for the low-GPA categories.

2.

Step 1. State the pair of hypotheses.

H_0: Sex and color blindness are independent.

H_1: Sex and color blindness are not independent.

Step 2. Identify the rejection zone.

When $\alpha = .05$, with $df = (r - 1)(c - 1) = 2$, the rejection zone for the chi-square test is $\chi^2 > 5.991$.

Step 3. Calculate the test statistic.

The expected frequency is

$$E = \frac{\text{Row total} \times \text{Column total}}{n}$$

The expected frequency table is reported in Table 14.14.

TABLE 14.14   Expected Frequency for Sex and Color Blindness

GENDER	NORMAL	RED-GREEN COLOR BLINDNESS	OTHER COLOR BLINDNESS
MALE	219.21	19.49	7.31
FEMALE	320.79	28.51	10.69

$$\chi^2 = \sum \frac{(O - E)^2}{E} = \frac{(192 - 219.21)^2}{219.21} - \frac{(42 - 19.49)^2}{19.49} + \frac{(12 - 7.31)^2}{7.31} + \frac{(348 - 320.79)^2}{320.79} +$$

$$\frac{(6 - 28.51)^2}{28.51} + \frac{(6 - 10.69)^2}{10.69} = 54.523$$

Step 4. Draw the correct conclusion.

The calculated $\chi^2 = 54.523$ is within the rejection zone. Therefore, we reject H_0. The evidence is strong enough to claim that sex and color vision status are not independent. Males have higher numbers than expected in red–green color blindness and other color blindness. Females have lower numbers than expected in red–green color blindness and other color blindness.

3. It is important to correctly translate the problem statement into a two-way contingency table. The problem statement identifies two nominal variables: (1) age and (2) layoff decisions. Although age is usually treated as an interval variable, in this problem statement, age is reported as a nominal variable. The categories of age are "age 40 and older" or "younger than 40." The categories of layoff decision are "laid off" or "not laid off." The categories in each variable are mutually exclusive.

The observed frequencies for age and layoff decision are reported in Table 14.15.

TABLE 14.15 Observed Frequency for Age and Layoff Decision

	LAID OFF	NOT LAID OFF	ROW TOTAL
AGE $\geq$ 40	22	29	51
AGE $<$ 40	8	29	37
COLUMN TOTAL	30	58	88

Step 1. State the pair of hypotheses.

H_0: Age and layoff decision are independent.

H_1: Age and layoff decision are not independent.

Step 2. Identify the rejection zone.

When $\alpha = .05$, with $df = (r - 1)(c - 1) = 1$, the rejection zone for the chi-square test is $\chi^2 > 3.841$.

Step 3. Calculate the test statistic.

The expected frequency is

$$E = \frac{\text{Row total} \times \text{Column total}}{n}$$

The expected frequency table is reported in Table 14.16.

$$\chi^2 = \sum \frac{(O - E)^2}{E} = \frac{(22 - 17.39)^2}{17.39} + \frac{(29 - 33.61)^2}{33.61} + \frac{(8 - 12.61)^2}{12.61} + \frac{(29 - 24.39)^2}{24.39} = 4.411$$

TABLE 14.16 Expected Frequency for Age and Layoff Decision

	LAID OFF	NOT LAID OFF
AGE ≥ 40	17.39	33.61
AGE < 40	12.61	24.39

Step 4. Draw the correct conclusion.

The calculated $\chi^2 = 4.411$ is within the rejection zone. Therefore, we reject H_0. The evidence is strong enough to claim that age and layoff decision are not independent. Employees who are 40 years and older have higher numbers than expected in the category of being laid off. In contrast, employees who are younger than 40 years have lower numbers than expected in the category of being laid off.

⑤SAGE edge™

Sharpen your skills with SAGE edge!

Visit edge.sagepub.com/bowen for mobile-friendly quizzes, flashcards, videos, and more!

WHAT YOU LEARNED

You now have learned your first nonparametric statistic: the chi-square. Chi-square tests can be used to evaluate goodness-of-fit or independence tests. The chi-square test is a distribution-free test and only requires frequency counts of the variables involved in the tests.

The basic component of a chi-square test is to calculate the expected frequency. The expected frequency for the goodness-of-fit test is simply $E = np$, where n is the sample size and p is the theoretical probability according to the null hypothesis. The expected frequency for the independence test is

$$E = \frac{\text{Row total} \times \text{Column total}}{n}$$

Each cell in the table has an observed frequency and an expected frequency. Chi-square tests are calculated as $\chi^2 = \sum (O - E)^2 / E$. Larger calculated χ^2 values indicate larger discrepancies between the observed frequencies and the expected frequencies. Expected frequencies are based on the null hypothesis. The critical value of χ^2 depends on its degrees of freedom. The degrees of freedom for goodness-of-fit tests are $(c - 1)$, where c is the number of columns or categories for the variable. The degrees of freedom for independence tests are $(c - 1)(r - 1)$, where c is the number of columns and r is the number of rows.

The four-step hypothesis-testing procedure for the goodness-of-fit test is stated below.

Step 1. State the pair of hypotheses.

H_0: A particular variable distribution fits its theoretical distribution (i.e., uniform distribution, binominal distribution, etc.).

H_1: A particular variable distribution does not fit its theoretical distribution.

Step 2. Identify the rejection zone.

Each degree of freedom has its own chi-square curve. The degrees of freedom for chi-square are calculated as $df = (c - 1)$. According to the critical values found in the chi-square table, the rejection zone for a chi-square test is identified as $\chi^2 > \chi^2_{(c-1)}$.

Step 3. Calculate the test statistic.

$$\text{Chi-square} = \chi^2 = \sum \frac{(O - E)^2}{E}$$

Step 4. Draw the correct conclusion.

The four-step hypothesis-testing procedure for the independence tests is stated below.

Step 1. State the pair of hypotheses.

H_0: The two variables are independent of each other.

H_1: The two variables are not independent of each other.

Step 2. Identify the rejection zone.

Each degree of freedom has its own chi-square curve. The degrees of freedom for the chi-square test for independence are $df = (r - 1)(c - 1)$. According to the critical values found in the chi-square table, the rejection zone for a chi-square test is identified as $\chi^2 > \chi^2_{(r-1)(c-1)}$.

Step 3. Calculate the test statistic.

$$\text{Chi-square} = \chi^2 = \sum \frac{(O - E)^2}{E}$$

Step 4. Draw the correct conclusion.

Chi-square goodness-of-fit tests: Chi-square goodness-of-fit tests refer to using one categorical variable to investigate whether the sample distribution of the values in this variable fits with a particular theoretical distribution.

Chi-square tests: Chi-square tests investigate the differences between the observed frequencies and the expected frequencies. When the calculated chi-square values are larger than the critical values in the Chi-square Table, the results are statistically significant.

Chi-square tests for independence: Chi-square tests for independence are statistics applied to investigate the relationship between two nominal or ordinal variables.

Contingency table: A contingency table refers to a two-way frequency table where frequency counts are based on two nominal or ordinal variables at the same time.

Expected frequency: Expected frequency is the theoretically predicted frequency that assumes that the variable is distributed exactly as stated in the null hypothesis.

Nonparametric statistics: Nonparametric statistics are statistical procedures that make no assumptions about the shape of the population distribution. They are also called distribution-free statistics.

Observed frequency: Observed frequency is the frequency count of a particular value of a variable that we observe in a sample.

Parametric statistics: Parametric statistics are statistical procedures that make assumptions about the shape of the population distribution and also about certain population parameters such as μ, σ, and σ^2.

LEARNING ASSESSMENT

Multiple Choice: Circle the best answer to every question.

1. The degrees of freedom for the chi-square goodness-of-fit test are

    a. $(c - 1)$, where c is the number of columns.

    b. $(r - 1)(c - 1)$, where r is the number of rows and c is the number of columns.

    c. $(n - 2)$, where n is the sample size.

    d. $(n - 1)$, where n is the sample size.

2. The degrees of freedom for the chi-square test for independence are

    a. $(c - 1)$, where c is the number of columns.

b. $(r-1)(c-1)$, where r is the number of rows and c is the number of columns.

c. $(n-2)$, where n is the sample size.

d. $(n-1)$, where n is the sample size.

3. The observed frequencies for a two-way contingency table

   a. are the expected number under the independence assumption.

   b. need to be greater than 5.

   c. have to be integers (i.e., whole numbers).

   d. carry fractions or a decimal point.

4. The expected frequencies for a two-way contingency table

   a. are the observed number from the sample.

   b. need to be greater than 5, or no more than 20% of the expected frequencies may be less than 5.

   c. have to be integers (i.e., whole numbers).

   d. may not add up to the same row totals as the observed frequencies.

5. Which one of the following statistics is appropriate to test the relationship between two nominal or ordinal variables?

   a. Regression

   b. Pearson's r

   c. ANOVA

   d. Chi-square

6. Which pair of distributions has a different curve for every degree of freedom?

   a. t distribution and χ^2 distribution

   b. Z distribution and t distribution

   c. Z distribution and F distribution

   d. Z distribution and χ^2 distribution

7. The rejection zone for a χ^2 test

   a. is located on the right side of the distribution.

   b. is located on the left side of the distribution.

   c. is located on both tails of the distribution.

   d. depends on what hypotheses are being tested.

Free Response Questions

8. The results of the male and female students' grades from multiple statistics classes are reported in Table 14.17.

TABLE 14.17   Male and Female Students' Grades From Multiple Statistics Classes

	A	B	C	D	F
MALE	25	37	44	15	7
FEMALE	31	55	66	7	5

Conduct a hypothesis test to verify if statistics grades and students' sex are independent.

9. A large retail chain is under attack for racial discrimination in promotions. The personnel files in the corporate headquarters show that 3,215 white employees were hired and among them 966 were promoted in the past 6 months. During the same time, 288 black employees were hired, and among them, 74 were promoted; 317 Hispanic employees were hired, and among them, 81 were promoted; 39 employees whose racial background was classified as other were hired, and among them, 5 were promoted. Conduct a hypothesis test to see if employees' racial background and promotion decisions are independent in this large retail chain.

10. The Type A personality is known to be related to some health problems. Type A personality is characterized as competitive, achievement oriented, talking fast, eating fast, impatient with a painful awareness of time urgency, and free-floating hostility. Assume that researchers study the Type A personality and heart health. They randomly select 200 adults aged 40 years and older. The 200 adults are classified by their Type A personality and history of heart problems, as reported in Table 14.18. Conduct a hypothesis test to see if Type A personality and heart problems are independent.

TABLE 14.18   Type A Personality and Heart Problems

	HEART PROBLEMS	NO HEART PROBLEMS	ROW TOTAL
TYPE A PERSONALITY	25	55	80
NOT TYPE A PERSONALITY	22	98	120
COLUMN TOTAL	47	153	200

Appendix A

The Standard Normal Distribution Table (Z Table)

The values inside the table represent the areas under the curve to the left of the Z values *or* the probability of Z values smaller than the specified z value, $P(Z < z)$. The column represents Z values to one place after the decimal point and the row represents Z values to the second place after the decimal point. The intersection of the column and the row show the probability associated with that Z value, as shown in Figure A.1.

$$1.\ P(Z < 2) = .9772$$

When the question asks for the areas to the right of the Z values *or* the probability of Z values larger than the specified z value, $P(Z > z)$, the probability under the curve is 1, $P(Z > z)$ can be calculated by $1 - P(Z < z)$, as shown in Figure A.2.

$$2.\ P(Z > -1) = 1 - P(Z < -1) = 1 - .1587 = .8413$$

FIGURE A.1 The Z Table Provides Probability to the Left of the Specified Value

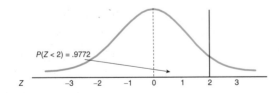

FIGURE A.2 The Area to the Right of the Specified Z Value, $P(Z > z)$ Is Calculated as $1 - P(Z < z)$

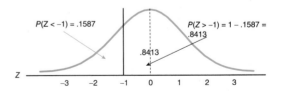

STANDARD NORMAL DISTRIBUTION TABLE: Z TABLE

Z	0.00	0.01	0.02	0.03	0.04	0.05	0.06	0.07	0.08	0.09
0.0	0.5000	0.5040	0.5080	0.5120	0.5160	0.5199	0.5239	0.5279	0.5319	0.5359
0.1	0.5398	0.5438	0.5478	0.5517	0.5557	0.5596	0.5636	0.5675	0.5714	0.5753
0.2	0.5793	0.5832	0.5871	0.5910	0.5948	0.5987	0.6026	0.6064	0.6103	0.6141
0.3	0.6179	0.6217	0.6255	0.6293	0.6331	0.6368	0.6406	0.6443	0.6480	0.6517
0.4	0.6554	0.6591	0.6628	0.6664	0.6700	0.6736	0.6772	0.6808	0.6844	0.6879
0.5	0.6915	0.6950	0.6985	0.7019	0.7054	0.7088	0.7123	0.7157	0.7190	0.7224
0.6	0.7257	0.7291	0.7324	0.7357	0.7389	0.7422	0.7454	0.7486	0.7517	0.7549
0.7	0.7580	0.7611	0.7642	0.7673	0.7704	0.7734	0.7764	0.7794	0.7823	0.7852
0.8	0.7881	0.7910	0.7939	0.7967	0.7995	0.8023	0.8051	0.8078	0.8106	0.8133
0.9	0.8159	0.8186	0.8212	0.8238	0.8264	0.8289	0.8315	0.8340	0.8365	0.8389
1.0	0.8413	0.8438	0.8461	0.8485	0.8508	0.8531	0.8554	0.8577	0.8599	0.8621
1.1	0.8643	0.8665	0.8686	0.8708	0.8729	0.8749	0.8770	0.8790	0.8810	0.8830
1.2	0.8849	0.8869	0.8888	0.8907	0.8925	0.8944	0.8962	0.8980	0.8997	0.9015
1.3	0.9032	0.9049	0.9066	0.9082	0.9099	0.9115	0.9131	0.9147	0.9162	0.9177
1.4	0.9192	0.9207	0.9222	0.9236	0.9251	0.9265	0.9279	0.9292	0.9306	0.9319
1.5	0.9332	0.9345	0.9357	0.9370	0.9382	0.9394	0.9406	0.9418	0.9429	0.9441
1.6	0.9452	0.9463	0.9474	0.9484	0.9495	0.9505	0.9515	0.9525	0.9535	0.9545
1.7	0.9554	0.9564	0.9573	0.9582	0.9591	0.9599	0.9608	0.9616	0.9625	0.9633
1.8	0.9641	0.9649	0.9656	0.9664	0.9671	0.9678	0.9686	0.9693	0.9699	0.9706
1.9	0.9713	0.9719	0.9726	0.9732	0.9738	0.9744	0.9750	0.9756	0.9761	0.9767
2.0	0.9772	0.9778	0.9783	0.9788	0.9793	0.9798	0.9803	0.9808	0.9812	0.9817
2.1	0.9821	0.9826	0.9830	0.9834	0.9838	0.9842	0.9846	0.9850	0.9854	0.9857
2.2	0.9861	0.9864	0.9868	0.9871	0.9875	0.9878	0.9881	0.9884	0.9887	0.9890
2.3	0.9893	0.9896	0.9898	0.9901	0.9904	0.9906	0.9909	0.9911	0.9913	0.9916
2.4	0.9918	0.9920	0.9922	0.9925	0.9927	0.9929	0.9931	0.9932	0.9934	0.9936
2.5	0.9938	0.9940	0.9941	0.9943	0.9945	0.9946	0.9948	0.9949	0.9951	0.9952
2.6	0.9953	0.9955	0.9956	0.9957	0.9959	0.9960	0.9961	0.9962	0.9963	0.9964
2.7	0.9965	0.9966	0.9967	0.9968	0.9969	0.9970	0.9971	0.9972	0.9973	0.9974
2.8	0.9974	0.9975	0.9976	0.9977	0.9977	0.9978	0.9979	0.9979	0.9980	0.9981
2.9	0.9981	0.9982	0.9982	0.9983	0.9984	0.9984	0.9985	0.9985	0.9986	0.9986
3.0	0.9987	0.9987	0.9987	0.9988	0.9988	0.9989	0.9989	0.9989	0.9990	0.9990

STANDARD NORMAL DISTRIBUTION TABLE: Z TABLE

Z	0.00	−0.01	−0.02	−0.03	−0.04	−0.05	−0.06	−0.07	−0.08	−0.09
0.0	0.5	0.496	0.492	0.488	0.484	0.4801	0.4761	0.4721	0.4681	0.4641
−0.1	0.4602	0.4562	0.4522	0.4483	0.4443	0.4404	0.4364	0.4325	0.4286	0.4247
−0.2	0.4207	0.4168	0.4129	0.409	0.4052	0.4013	0.3974	0.3936	0.3897	0.3859
−0.3	0.3821	0.3783	0.3745	0.3707	0.3669	0.3632	0.3594	0.3557	0.352	0.3483
−0.4	0.3446	0.3409	0.3372	0.3336	0.33	0.3264	0.3228	0.3192	0.3156	0.3121
−0.5	0.3085	0.305	0.3015	0.2981	0.2946	0.2912	0.2877	0.2843	0.281	0.2776
−0.6	0.2743	0.2709	0.2676	0.2643	0.2611	0.2578	0.2546	0.2514	0.2483	0.2451
−0.7	0.242	0.2389	0.2358	0.2327	0.2296	0.2266	0.2236	0.2206	0.2177	0.2148
−0.8	0.2119	0.209	0.2061	0.2033	0.2005	0.1977	0.1949	0.1922	0.1894	0.1867
−0.9	0.1841	0.1814	0.1788	0.1762	0.1736	0.1711	0.1685	0.166	0.1635	0.1611
−1.0	0.1587	0.1562	0.1539	0.1515	0.1492	0.1469	0.1446	0.1423	0.1401	0.1379
−1.1	0.1357	0.1335	0.1314	0.1292	0.1271	0.1251	0.123	0.121	0.119	0.117
−1.2	0.1151	0.1131	0.1112	0.1093	0.1075	0.1056	0.1038	0.102	0.1003	0.0985
−1.3	0.0968	0.0951	0.0934	0.0918	0.0901	0.0885	0.0869	0.0853	0.0838	0.0823
−1.4	0.0808	0.0793	0.0778	0.0764	0.0749	0.0735	0.0721	0.0708	0.0694	0.0681
−1.5	0.0668	0.0655	0.0643	0.063	0.0618	0.0606	0.0594	0.0582	0.0571	0.0559
−1.6	0.0548	0.0537	0.0526	0.0516	0.0505	0.0495	0.0485	0.0475	0.0465	0.0455
−1.7	0.0446	0.0436	0.0427	0.0418	0.0409	0.0401	0.0392	0.0384	0.0375	0.0367
−1.8	0.0359	0.0351	0.0344	0.0336	0.0329	0.0322	0.0314	0.0307	0.0301	0.0294
−1.9	0.0287	0.0281	0.0274	0.0268	0.0262	0.0256	0.025	0.0244	0.0239	0.0233
−2.0	0.0228	0.0222	0.0217	0.0212	0.0207	0.0202	0.0197	0.0192	0.0188	0.0183
−2.1	0.0179	0.0174	0.017	0.0166	0.0162	0.0158	0.0154	0.015	0.0146	0.0143
−2.2	0.0139	0.0136	0.0132	0.0129	0.0125	0.0122	0.0119	0.0116	0.0113	0.011
−2.3	0.0107	0.0104	0.0102	0.0099	0.0096	0.0094	0.0091	0.0089	0.0087	0.0084
−2.4	0.0082	0.008	0.0078	0.0075	0.0073	0.0071	0.0069	0.0068	0.0066	0.0064
−2.5	0.0062	0.006	0.0059	0.0057	0.0055	0.0054	0.0052	0.0051	0.0049	0.0048
−2.6	0.0047	0.0045	0.0044	0.0043	0.0041	0.004	0.0039	0.0038	0.0037	0.0036
−2.7	0.0035	0.0034	0.0033	0.0032	0.0031	0.003	0.0029	0.0028	0.0027	0.0026
−2.8	0.0026	0.0025	0.0024	0.0023	0.0023	0.0022	0.0021	0.0021	0.002	0.0019
−2.9	0.0019	0.0018	0.0018	0.0017	0.0016	0.0016	0.0015	0.0015	0.0014	0.0014
−3.0	0.0013	0.0013	0.0013	0.0012	0.0012	0.0011	0.0011	0.0011	0.001	0.001

Appendix B

The *t*-Distribution Table (*t* Table)

	ONE-TAILED α LEVEL							
	0.25	0.20	0.15	0.10	0.05	0.025	0.01	0.005
	TWO-TAILED α LEVEL							
df	0.50	0.40	0.30	0.20	0.10	0.05	0.02	0.01
1	1	1.376	1.963	3.078	6.314	12.71	31.82	63.66
2	0.816	1.061	1.386	1.886	2.92	4.303	6.965	9.925
3	0.765	0.978	1.25	1.638	2.353	3.182	4.541	5.841
4	0.741	0.941	1.19	1.533	2.132	2.776	3.747	4.604
5	0.727	0.92	1.156	1.476	2.015	2.571	3.365	4.032
6	0.718	0.906	1.134	1.44	1.943	2.447	3.143	3.707
7	0.711	0.896	1.119	1.415	1.895	2.365	2.998	3.499
8	0.706	0.889	1.108	1.397	1.86	2.306	2.896	3.355
9	0.703	0.883	1.1	1.383	1.833	2.262	2.821	3.25
10	0.7	0.879	1.093	1.372	1.812	2.228	2.764	3.169
11	0.697	0.876	1.088	1.363	1.796	2.201	2.718	3.106
12	0.695	0.873	1.083	1.356	1.782	2.179	2.681	3.055
13	0.694	0.87	1.079	1.35	1.771	2.16	2.65	3.012
14	0.692	0.868	1.076	1.345	1.761	2.145	2.624	2.977
15	0.691	0.866	1.074	1.341	1.753	2.131	2.602	2.947

(Continued)

(Continued)

	ONE-TAILED α LEVEL							
	0.25	0.20	0.15	0.10	0.05	0.025	0.01	0.005
	TWO-TAILED α LEVEL							
df	0.50	0.40	0.30	0.20	0.10	0.05	0.02	0.01
16	0.69	0.865	1.071	1.337	1.746	2.12	2.583	2.921
17	0.689	0.863	1.069	1.333	1.74	2.11	2.567	2.898
18	0.688	0.862	1.067	1.33	1.734	2.101	2.552	2.878
19	0.688	0.861	1.066	1.328	1.729	2.093	2.539	2.861
20	0.687	0.86	1.064	1.325	1.725	2.086	2.528	2.845
21	0.686	0.859	1.063	1.323	1.721	2.08	2.518	2.831
22	0.686	0.858	1.061	1.321	1.717	2.074	2.508	2.819
23	0.685	0.858	1.06	1.319	1.714	2.069	2.5	2.807
24	0.685	0.857	1.059	1.318	1.711	2.064	2.492	2.797
25	0.684	0.856	1.058	1.316	1.708	2.06	2.485	2.787
26	0.684	0.856	1.058	1.315	1.706	2.056	2.479	2.779
27	0.684	0.855	1.057	1.314	1.703	2.052	2.473	2.771
28	0.683	0.855	1.056	1.313	1.701	2.048	2.467	2.763
29	0.683	0.854	1.055	1.311	1.699	2.045	2.462	2.756
30	0.683	0.854	1.055	1.31	1.697	2.042	2.457	2.75
40	0.681	0.851	1.05	1.303	1.684	2.021	2.423	2.704
50	0.679	0.849	1.047	1.299	1.676	2.009	2.403	2.678
60	0.679	0.848	1.045	1.296	1.671	2	2.39	2.66
80	0.678	0.846	1.043	1.292	1.664	1.99	2.374	2.639
100	0.677	0.845	1.042	1.29	1.66	1.984	2.364	2.626
120	0.677	0.845	1.041	1.289	1.658	1.98	2.358	2.617
∞	0.674	0.842	1.036	1.282	1.645	1.96	2.326	2.576

Appendix C
The F Table

df1 / df2	1	2	3	4	5	6	7	8	9	10	11	12	15	20	24	30	40	60	100
1	161.4	199.5	215.7	224.6	230.2	234.0	236.8	238.9	240.5	241.9	243.0	243.9	245.9	248.0	249.1	250.1	251.1	252.2	253.0
2	18.51	19.0	19.16	19.25	19.30	19.33	19.35	19.37	19.38	19.40	19.40	19.41	19.43	19.45	19.45	19.46	19.47	19.48	19.49
3	10.13	9.55	9.28	9.12	9.01	8.94	8.89	8.85	8.81	8.79	8.76	8.74	8.7	8.66	8.64	8.62	8.59	8.57	8.56
4	7.71	6.94	6.59	6.39	6.26	6.16	6.09	6.04	6.00	5.96	5.94	5.91	5.86	5.80	5.77	5.75	5.72	5.69	5.66
5	6.61	5.79	5.41	5.19	5.05	4.95	4.88	4.82	4.77	4.74	4.70	4.68	4.62	4.56	4.53	4.50	4.46	4.43	4.41
6	5.99	5.14	4.76	4.53	4.39	4.28	4.21	4.15	4.10	4.06	4.03	4.00	3.94	3.87	3.84	3.81	3.77	3.74	3.71
7	5.59	4.74	4.35	4.12	3.97	3.87	3.79	3.73	3.68	3.64	3.60	3.57	3.51	3.44	3.41	3.38	3.34	3.30	3.27
8	5.32	4.46	4.07	3.84	3.69	3.58	3.50	3.44	3.39	3.35	3.31	3.28	3.22	3.15	3.12	3.08	3.04	3.01	2.97
9	5.12	4.26	3.86	3.63	3.48	3.37	3.29	3.23	3.18	3.14	3.10	3.07	3.01	2.94	2.90	2.86	2.83	2.79	2.76
10	4.96	4.10	3.71	3.48	3.33	3.22	3.14	3.07	3.02	2.98	2.94	2.91	2.85	2.77	2.74	2.70	2.66	2.62	2.59
11	4.84	3.98	3.59	3.36	3.20	3.09	3.01	2.95	2.90	2.85	2.82	2.79	2.72	2.65	2.61	2.57	2.53	2.49	2.46
12	4.75	3.89	3.49	3.26	3.11	3.00	2.91	2.85	2.80	2.75	2.72	2.69	2.62	2.54	2.51	2.47	2.43	2.38	2.35
13	4.67	3.81	3.41	3.18	3.03	2.92	2.83	2.77	2.71	2.67	2.63	2.60	2.53	2.46	2.42	2.38	2.34	2.30	2.26
14	4.60	3.74	3.34	3.11	2.96	2.85	2.76	2.70	2.65	2.60	2.57	2.53	2.46	2.39	2.35	2.31	2.27	2.22	2.19
15	4.54	3.68	3.29	3.06	2.90	2.79	2.71	2.64	2.59	2.54	2.51	2.48	2.40	2.33	2.29	2.25	2.20	2.16	2.12
16	4.49	3.63	3.24	3.01	2.85	2.74	2.66	2.59	2.54	2.49	2.46	2.42	2.35	2.28	2.24	2.19	2.15	2.11	2.07
17	4.45	3.59	3.20	2.96	2.81	2.70	2.61	2.55	2.49	2.45	2.41	2.38	2.31	2.23	2.19	2.15	2.10	2.06	2.02
18	4.41	3.55	3.16	2.93	2.77	2.66	2.58	2.51	2.46	2.41	2.37	2.34	2.27	2.19	2.15	2.11	2.06	2.02	1.98
19	4.38	3.52	3.13	2.90	2.74	2.63	2.54	2.48	2.42	2.38	2.34	2.31	2.23	2.16	2.11	2.07	2.03	1.98	1.94
20	4.35	3.49	3.10	2.87	2.71	2.60	2.51	2.45	2.39	2.35	2.31	2.28	2.20	2.12	2.08	2.04	1.99	1.95	1.91

(Continued)

(Continued)

df1 / df2	1	2	3	4	5	6	7	8	9	10	11	12	15	20	24	30	40	60	100
21	4.32	3.47	3.07	2.84	2.68	2.57	2.49	2.42	2.37	2.32	2.28	2.25	2.18	2.10	2.05	2.01	1.96	1.92	1.88
22	4.30	3.44	3.05	2.82	2.66	2.55	2.46	2.40	2.34	2.30	2.26	2.23	2.15	2.07	2.03	1.98	1.94	1.89	1.85
23	4.28	3.42	3.03	2.80	2.64	2.53	2.44	2.37	2.32	2.27	2.24	2.20	2.13	2.05	2.01	1.96	1.91	1.86	1.82
24	4.26	3.40	3.01	2.78	2.62	2.51	2.42	2.36	2.30	2.25	2.22	2.18	2.11	2.03	1.98	1.94	1.89	1.84	1.80
25	4.24	3.39	2.99	2.76	2.60	2.49	2.40	2.34	2.28	2.24	2.20	2.16	2.09	2.01	1.96	1.92	1.87	1.82	1.78
26	4.23	3.37	2.98	2.74	2.59	2.47	2.39	2.32	2.27	2.22	2.18	2.15	2.07	1.99	1.95	1.90	1.85	1.80	1.76
27	4.21	3.35	2.96	2.73	2.57	2.46	2.37	2.31	2.25	2.20	2.17	2.13	2.06	1.97	1.93	1.88	1.84	1.79	1.74
28	4.20	3.34	2.95	2.71	2.56	2.45	2.36	2.29	2.24	2.19	2.15	2.12	2.04	1.96	1.91	1.87	1.82	1.77	1.73
29	4.18	3.33	2.93	2.70	2.55	2.43	2.35	2.28	2.22	2.18	2.14	2.10	2.03	1.94	1.90	1.85	1.81	1.75	1.71
30	4.17	3.32	2.92	2.69	2.53	2.42	2.33	2.27	2.21	2.16	2.13	2.09	2.01	1.93	1.89	1.84	1.79	1.74	1.70
40	4.08	3.23	2.84	2.61	2.45	2.34	2.25	2.18	2.12	2.08	2.04	2.00	1.92	1.84	1.79	1.74	1.69	1.64	1.59
50	4.03	3.18	2.79	2.56	2.40	2.29	2.20	2.13	2.07	2.03	1.99	1.95	1.87	1.78	1.74	1.69	1.63	1.58	1.52
60	4.00	3.15	2.76	2.53	2.37	2.25	2.17	2.10	2.04	1.99	1.95	1.92	1.84	1.75	1.70	1.65	1.59	1.53	1.48
80	3.96	3.11	2.72	2.49	2.33	2.21	2.13	2.06	2.00	1.95	1.91	1.88	1.79	1.70	1.65	1.60	1.54	1.48	1.43
100	3.94	3.09	2.70	2.46	2.31	2.19	2.10	2.03	1.97	1.93	1.89	1.85	1.77	1.68	1.63	1.57	1.52	1.45	1.39

NOTE: Critical values of the F distribution for $\alpha = 0.05$; $P\{F > F.05 \, (df_1, df_2)\} = 0.05$. Numerator degrees of freedom $= df_1$; denominator degrees of freedom $= df_2$.

Appendix D

The Critical Values of Pearson's Correlation Table (*r* Table)

	LEVEL OF SIGNIFICANCE FOR ONE-TAILED TEST			
	.05	.025	.01	.005
	LEVEL OF SIGNIFICANCE FOR TWO-TAILED TEST			
$df = n - 2$	.10	.05	.02	.01
1	.988	.997	.9995	.9999
2	.900	.950	.980	.990
3	.805	.878	.934	.959
4	.729	.811	.882	.917
5	.669	.754	.833	.874
6	.622	.707	.789	.834
7	.582	.666	.75	.798
8	.549	.632	.716	.765
9	.521	.602	.685	.735
10	.497	.576	.658	.708
11	.476	.553	.634	.684
12	.458	.532	.612	.661
13	.441	.514	.592	.641

(Continued)

(Continued)

	LEVEL OF SIGNIFICANCE FOR ONE-TAILED TEST			
	.05	.025	.01	.005
	LEVEL OF SIGNIFICANCE FOR TWO-TAILED TEST			
$df = n - 2$	.10	.05	.02	.01
14	.426	.497	.574	.628
15	.412	.482	.558	.606
16	.400	.468	.542	.590
17	.389	.456	.528	.575
18	.378	.444	.516	.561
19	.369	.433	.503	.549
20	.360	.423	.492	.537
21	.352	.413	.482	.526
22	.344	.404	.472	.515
23	.337	.396	.462	.505
24	.330	.388	.453	.495
25	.323	.381	.445	.487
26	.317	.374	.437	.479
27	.311	.367	.430	.471
28	.306	.361	.423	.463
29	.301	.355	.416	.456
30	.296	.349	.409	.449
35	.275	.325	.381	.418
40	.257	.304	.358	.393
45	.243	.288	.338	.372
50	.231	.273	.322	.354
60	.211	.250	.295	.325
70	.195	.232	.274	.302
80	.183	.217	.256	.284
90	.173	.205	.242	.267
100	.164	.195	.23	.254

Appendix E

The Critical Values for Spearman's Rank Correlation Table (r_s Table)

	LEVEL OF SIGNIFICANCE FOR ONE-TAILED TEST			
	0.05	0.025	0.01	0.005
	LEVEL OF SIGNIFICANCE FOR TWO-TAILED TEST			
n	0.10	0.05	0.02	0.01
5	0.90	*	*	*
6	0.829	0.886	0.943	*
7	0.714	0.786	0.893	0.929
8	0.643	0.738	0.833	0.881
9	0.6	0.7	0.783	0.883
10	0.564	0.648	0.745	0.794
11	0.536	0.618	0.709	0.755
12	0.503	0.587	0.678	0.727
13	0.484	0.56	0.648	0.703
14	0.464	0.538	0.626	0.679
15	0.446	0.521	0.604	0.654
16	0.429	0.503	0.582	0.635
17	0.414	0.488	0.566	0.618
18	0.401	0.472	0.55	0.6

(Continued)

(Continued)

	LEVEL OF SIGNIFICANCE FOR ONE-TAILED TEST			
	0.05	0.025	0.01	0.005
	LEVEL OF SIGNIFICANCE FOR TWO-TAILED TEST			
n	0.10	0.05	0.02	0.01
19	0.391	0.46	0.535	0.584
20	0.38	0.447	0.522	0.57
21	0.37	0.436	0.509	0.556
22	0.361	0.425	0.497	0.544
23	0.353	0.416	0.486	0.532
24	0.344	0.407	0.476	0.521
25	0.337	0.398	0.466	0.511
26	0.331	0.39	0.457	0.501
27	0.324	0.383	0.449	0.492
28	0.318	0.375	0.441	0.483
29	0.312	0.368	0.433	0.475
30	0.306	0.362	0.425	0.467
40	0.264	0.313	0.368	0.405
45	0.248	0.294	0.347	0.382
50	0.235	0.279	0.329	0.363
55	0.224	0.266	0.314	0.346
60	0.214	0.255	0.301	0.331

NOTE: Asterisks indicate missing values.

Appendix F
The Critical Values for the Point Biserial Correlation Table (r_{pbi} Table)

	LEVEL OF SIGNIFICANCE FOR ONE-TAILED TEST			
	0.05	0.025	0.01	0.005
	LEVEL OF SIGNIFICANCE FOR TWO-TAILED TEST			
n	0.1	0.05	0.02	0.01
5	0.76	0.83	0.89	0.92
6	0.70	0.77	0.84	0.88
7	0.65	0.73	0.80	0.84
8	0.60	0.69	0.76	0.81
9	0.57	0.65	0.73	0.78
10	0.54	0.62	0.70	0.75
11	0.51	0.59	0.67	0.72
12	0.49	0.57	0.65	0.69
13	0.47	0.55	0.62	0.67
14	0.45	0.53	0.60	0.65
15	0.44	0.51	0.59	0.63
16	0.42	0.49	0.57	0.62
17	0.41	0.48	0.55	0.60
18	0.40	0.47	0.54	0.58

(Continued)

(Continued)

	LEVEL OF SIGNIFICANCE FOR ONE-TAILED TEST			
	0.05	0.025	0.01	0.005
	LEVEL OF SIGNIFICANCE FOR TWO-TAILED TEST			
n	0.1	0.05	0.02	0.01
19	0.39	0.45	0.52	0.57
20	0.38	0.44	0.51	0.56
21	0.37	0.43	0.50	0.54
22	0.36	0.42	0.49	0.53
23	0.35	0.41	0.48	0.52
24	0.34	0.40	0.47	0.51
25	0.34	0.39	0.46	0.50
26	0.33	0.39	0.45	0.49
27	0.32	0.38	0.44	0.48
28	0.32	0.37	0.44	0.48
29	0.31	0.37	0.43	0.47
30	0.31	0.36	0.42	0.46
40	0.26	0.31	0.37	0.40
60	0.21	0.25	0.30	0.33
120	0.15	0.18	0.21	0.23
200	0.12	0.14	0.16	0.18

Appendix G

The Critical Values of the Studentized Range Distribution Table (q Table)

df FOR MSW	k = NUMBER OF GROUPS								
	2	3	4	5	6	7	8	9	10
5	3.64	4.60	5.22	5.67	6.03	6.33	6.58	6.80	6.99
6	3.46	4.34	4.90	5.30	5.63	5.90	6.12	6.32	6.49
7	3.34	4.16	4.68	5.06	5.36	5.61	5.82	6.00	6.16
8	3.26	4.04	4.53	4.89	5.17	5.40	5.60	5.77	5.92
9	3.20	3.95	4.41	4.76	5.02	5.24	5.43	5.59	5.74
10	3.15	3.88	4.33	4.65	4.91	5.12	5.30	5.46	5.60
11	3.11	3.82	4.26	4.57	4.82	5.03	5.2	5.35	5.49
12	3.08	3.77	4.20	4.51	4.75	4.95	5.12	5.27	5.39
13	3.06	3.73	4.15	4.45	4.69	4.88	5.05	5.19	5.32
14	3.03	3.70	4.11	4.41	4.64	4.83	4.99	5.13	5.25
15	3.01	3.67	4.08	4.37	4.59	4.78	4.94	5.08	5.20
16	3.00	3.65	4.05	4.33	4.56	4.74	4.90	5.03	5.15
17	2.98	3.63	4.02	4.30	4.52	4.70	4.86	4.99	5.11
18	2.97	3.61	4.00	4.28	4.49	4.67	4.82	4.96	5.07
19	2.96	3.59	3.98	4.25	4.47	4.65	4.79	4.92	5.04

(Continued)

(Continued)

df FOR MSW	k = NUMBER OF GROUPS								
	2	3	4	5	6	7	8	9	10
20	2.95	3.58	3.96	4.23	4.45	4.62	4.77	4.9	5.01
24	2.92	3.53	3.90	4.17	4.37	4.54	4.68	4.81	4.92
30	2.89	3.49	3.85	4.10	4.30	4.46	4.60	4.72	4.82
40	2.86	3.44	3.79	4.04	4.23	4.39	4.52	4.63	4.73
60	2.83	3.40	3.74	3.98	4.16	4.31	4.44	4.55	4.65
120	2.80	3.36	3.68	3.92	4.10	4.24	4.36	4.47	4.56
∞	2.77	3.31	3.63	3.86	4.03	4.17	4.29	4.39	4.47

NOTE: MSW = mean square within, df = degrees of freedom.

Appendix H

The Critical Values for the Chi-Square Tests (χ^2 Table)

df	RIGHT-TAILED α LEVEL				
	0.1	0.05	0.025	0.01	0.005
1	2.706	3.841	5.024	6.635	7.879
2	4.605	5.991	7.378	9.210	10.597
3	6.251	7.815	9.348	11.345	12.838
4	7.779	9.488	11.143	13.277	14.86
5	9.236	11.07	12.833	15.086	16.75
6	10.645	12.592	14.449	16.812	18.548
7	12.017	14.067	16.013	18.475	20.278
8	13.362	15.507	17.535	20.09	21.955
9	14.684	16.919	19.023	21.666	23.589
10	15.987	18.307	20.483	23.209	25.188
11	17.275	19.675	21.920	24.725	26.757
12	18.549	21.026	23.337	26.217	28.300
13	19.812	22.362	24.736	27.688	29.819
14	21.064	23.685	26.119	29.141	31.319
15	22.307	24.996	27.488	30.578	32.801
16	23.542	26.296	28.845	32.000	34.267
17	24.769	27.587	30.191	33.409	35.718

(Continued)

(Continued)

		RIGHT-TAILED α LEVEL			
df	0.1	0.05	0.025	0.01	0.005
18	25.989	28.869	31.526	34.805	37.156
19	27.204	30.144	32.852	36.191	38.582
20	28.412	31.410	34.170	37.566	39.997
21	29.615	32.671	35.479	38.932	41.401
22	30.813	33.924	36.781	40.289	42.796
23	32.007	35.172	38.076	41.638	44.181
24	33.196	36.415	39.364	42.980	45.559
25	34.382	37.652	40.646	44.314	46.928
26	35.563	38.885	41.923	45.642	48.290
27	36.741	40.113	43.195	46.963	49.645
28	37.916	41.337	44.461	48.278	50.993
29	39.087	42.557	45.722	49.588	52.336
30	40.256	43.773	46.979	50.892	53.672
40	51.805	55.758	59.342	63.691	66.766
50	63.167	67.505	71.420	76.154	79.490
60	74.397	79.082	83.298	88.379	91.952
70	85.527	90.531	95.023	100.425	104.215
80	96.578	101.879	106.629	112.329	116.321
90	107.565	113.145	118.136	124.116	128.299
100	118.498	124.342	129.561	135.807	140.169

Answers to the Learning Assessments

CHAPTER 1

1. d

2. a

3. c

4. d

5. a

6. c

7. d

8. d

Free Response Questions

9. $\sum X = 19$,

$(\sum X)^2 = 19^2 = 361$, and

$\sum X^2 = 99$

10.

X	X − 1	(X − 1)²	X²
−3	−4	16	9
0	−1	1	0
1	0	0	1
2	1	1	4
0		18	14

$\sum X = 0$,

$\sum (X − 1)^2 = 18$, and

$\sum X^2 − 3 = 14 − 3 = 11$

11.

X	Y	X Y
3	−1	−3
4	0	0
5	1	5
7	2	14
		16

$\sum XY = 16$, and

$(\sum XY)^2 = 16^2 = 256$

12.

X	Y	X^2	Y^2	X^2Y^2	$(X - 2)$	$(Y - 3)$	$(X - 2)(Y - 3)$
3	−1	9	1	9	1	−4	−4
4	0	16	0	0	2	−3	−6
5	1	25	1	25	3	−2	−6
7	2	49	4	196	5	−1	−5
				230			**−21**

$\sum X^2Y^2 = 230$, and

$\sum (X - 2)(Y - 3) = -21$

13.

X	Y	Y^2	$X - 5$	$Y + 1$	$(X - 5)(Y + 1)$
4	−1	1	−1	0	0
5	−1	1	0	0	0
6	1	1	1	2	2
9	2	4	4	3	12
		7			**14**

$\sum Y^2 = 7$, and

$\sum (X - 5)(Y + 1) = 14$

14. Equation 1: $2X + 3Y = 21$

Equation 2: $3X - Y = 4$

(Equation 1) + 3 × (Equation 2)

$2X + 3Y = 21$

+) $9X - 3Y = 12$
_____

$11X \quad = 33$

$X = 3$ insert this value into Equation 2

$3(3) - Y = 4$

$Y = 5$

15. Equation 1: $X - 2Y = -8$

Equation 2: $3X - Y = 6$

(Equation 1 × 3) − (Equation 2)

$3X - 6Y = -24$

−) $3X - Y = 6$
_____

$-5Y = -30$

$Y = 6$ put this value into Equation 1.

$X - 2(6) = -8$

$X - 12 = -8$

$X = 4$

CHAPTER 2

1. a

2. b

3. b

4. d

5. c

6. d

Free Response Questions

7. To estimate the total amount (in dollars) of the traffic citations, you have to calculate the midpoint in each interval, and then conduct the $\sum fX_{midpoint}$ as shown in Table 2.10a for the answer.

TABLE 2.10a Frequency Table of Traffic Citations With Midpoint

X (CITATION AMOUNT IN DOLLARS)	f (FREQUENCY)	$X_{midpoint}$	$fX_{midpoint}$
90-109	12	99.5	1194
110-129	53	119.5	6333.5
130-149	104	139.5	14508
150-169	290	159.5	46255
170-189	405	179.5	72697.5
190-209	852	199.5	169974
210-229	907	219.5	199086.5
230-249	981	239.5	234949.5
			744998

The total traffic citation amounts to $744,998 in this small city.

The histogram of the citation amount is shown in Figure 2.25.

FIGURE 2.25 Histogram of Traffic Citation Amount

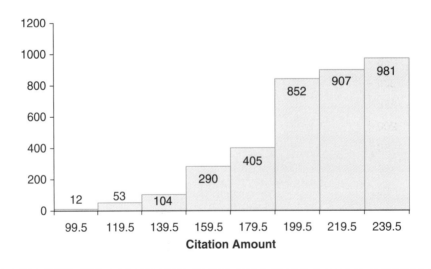

Based on the histogram of the citation amount, most of the traffic citation amounts pile up on the high end of the distribution with a tail to the low end of the distribution. The citation amount is negatively skewed in this small city.

8. To estimate the total days absent, you have to calculate the midpoint in each interval, and then conduct the $\sum fX_{midpoint}$ as shown in Table 2.11a for the answer.

TABLE 2.11a Frequency Table of Days Absent With Midpoint

X (DAYS ABSENT)	f (FREQUENCY)	$X_{midpoint}$	$fX_{midpoint}$
0-1	329	0.5	164.5
2-3	342	2.5	855
4-5	198	4.5	891
6-7	60	6.5	390
8-9	13	8.5	110.5
10-11	3	10.5	31.5
12-13	2	12.5	25
14-15	1	14.5	14.5
			2482

The total number of days absent for all employees is 2482 days.

The histogram of days absent is shown in Figure 2.26.

FIGURE 2.26 Histogram of Days Absent

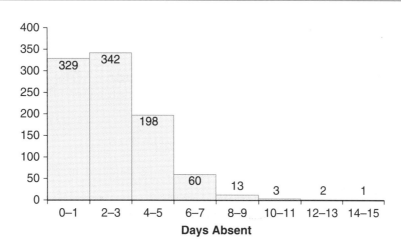

Based on the histogram of the days absent, most employees had a small number of days absent and a few of them had a high number of days absent. The number of days absent concentrates on the low end of the distribution with a long tail on the high end of the distribution. It is positively skewed.

CHAPTER 3

1. a	7. b
2. b	8. c
3. c	9. a
4. b	10. a
5. c	11. b
6. a	12. a

Free Response Questions

13.a. Mode is the value with the highest frequency, mode = 8.

Median is the midpoint of a sorted dataset. When $n = 50$, there are two midpoints in locations $L = n/2 = 50/2 = 25$ and the next one, 26. The value for the 25th position is 8, and the value for the 26th position is 8. The average of these two values is 8, which is the median.

Mean formula in a frequency table needs to be modified to $\bar{X} = \Sigma fX/n$. According to Table 3.18a, $\bar{X} = \Sigma fX/n = 390/50 = 7.8$. The mean shoe size for women is 7.8.

13.b. Based on the locations of mode = 8, median = 8, and mean = 7.8, the mode is the same as the median, and the mean is very close to it. The distribution of women's shoes is similar to a normal distribution.

13.c. The range = maximal value − minimal value = 11 − 5 = 6.

The SS formula in a frequency table needs to be modified to $SS = \Sigma f(X - \bar{X})^2$. According to Table 3.18a, $SS = 86$.

Sample variance $s^2 = SS/(n-1) = 86/(50-1) = 86/49 = 1.8$

Sample standard deviation $s = \sqrt{\text{variance}} = \sqrt{1.8} = 1.3$

TABLE 3.18a Women's Shoe Sizes With Columns of fX, $X - \bar{X}$, $(X - \bar{X})^2$, and $f(X - \bar{X})^2$

X (SHOE SIZE)	f (FREQUENCY)	fX	$X - \bar{X}$	$(X - \bar{X})^2$	$f(X - \bar{X})^2$
5	2	10	−2.8	7.84	15.68
6	5	30	−1.8	3.24	16.2
7	14	98	−0.8	0.64	8.96
8	16	128	0.2	0.04	0.64
9	7	63	1.2	1.44	10.08
10	5	50	2.2	4.84	24.2
11	1	11	3.2	10.24	10.24
	50	390			86
	Mean	7.8			

13.d. The minimal = 5

The maximal = 11

Q_1: $L = \dfrac{k}{100} \times n = \dfrac{25}{100} \times 50 = 12.5$, round it up to 13. The value of 13th position is 7.

Median = Q_2 = 8

Q_3: $L = \dfrac{k}{100} \times n = \dfrac{75}{100} \times 50 = 37.5$, round it up to 38. The value of 38th position is 9 (Figure 3.9).

FIGURE 3.9 Boxplot for 50 Women's Shoe Sizes

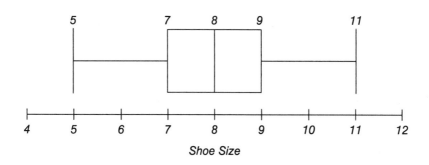

Shoe Size

14.a. Mode is the value with the highest frequency. The highest frequency is 20, and the value is the mode, mode = 121–150 seconds.

Median is the midpoint of a sorted dataset. When $n = 55$, there is one midpoint in positions $(n)/2 = (55)/2 = 27.5$, which rounds up to 28. The value for the 28th position is 121–150, median = 121–150 seconds.

The estimated mean formula in a frequency table with equal intervals needs to be modified to $\bar{X} = \sum fx_{midpoint} / n$. According to Table 3.19a, $\bar{X} = \sum fx_{midpoint} / n = 8352.5 / 55 = 151.9$. The mean fast-food drive-through time is 151.9 seconds.

TABLE 3.19a Fast-Food Drive-Through Times With $X_{midpoint}$ and $fX_{midpoint}$ Columns

X (SECONDS)	f (FREQUENCY)	$X_{midpoint}$	$fX_{midpoint}$
61-90	2	75.5	151
91-120	6	105.5	633
121-150	20	135.5	2710
151-180	17	165.5	2813.5
181-210	7	195.5	1368.5
211-240	3	225.5	676.5
	55		8352.5

14.b. Based on the locations of mode (121–150 seconds), median (121–150 seconds), and mean (151.9 seconds), mode is the same as median, and mean is very close to it. The distribution of the fast-food drive-through time is similar to a normal distribution.

CHAPTER 4

1. d

2. c

3. a

4. c

5. c

6. b

7. c

8. c

9. a

10. d

Free Response Questions

11. Two equations can solve two unknowns.

From Megan's scores $Z = \dfrac{X - \bar{X}}{s}$

$1.5 = \dfrac{97.5 - \bar{X}}{s}$

Equation 1: $1.5s = 97.5 - \bar{X}$

From Jenny's score $Z = \dfrac{X - \bar{X}}{s}$

$-1 = \dfrac{60 - \bar{X}}{s}$

Equation 2: $-s = 60 - \bar{X}$

Using elimination principle, (Equation 1) − (Equation 2), you get $2.5s = 37.5$

$s = 37.5/2.5 = 15$

Put $s = 15$ back in (Equation 2)

$-15 = 60 - \bar{X}$

$\bar{X} = 75$

The mean for the high school girls' fitness test is 75, and the standard deviation is 15.

12. Convert raw scores to Z scores to make this comparison.

For the English test $Z = \dfrac{(X - \bar{X})}{s} = \dfrac{(40 - 30)}{8} = 1.25$

For the Math test $Z = \dfrac{(X - \bar{X})}{s} = \dfrac{(50 - 55)}{5} = -1$

Robin scores 1.25 standard deviations above the mean in English and 1 standard deviation below the mean in Math. Robin performs better in English than Math.

13. Convert raw scores to Z scores to make the judgment.

SAT Critical Reading $Z = \dfrac{(X - \mu)}{\sigma} = \dfrac{(730 - 497)}{115} = 2.03$

SAT Math $Z = \dfrac{(760 - 513)}{120} = \dfrac{247}{120} = 2.06$

Both Ted's SAT Critical Reading Z score and SAT Math Z score are higher than two standard deviations above the mean. They are both unusually high scores.

14. Convert raw score to Z score to make the judgment.

ACT composite score $Z = \dfrac{29 - 21.0}{5.2} = \dfrac{8}{5.2} = 1.54$

Hanna's ACT Z score is 1.54. It is not an unusual score.

Chapter 5

1. a

2. c

3. b

4. c

5. b

6. c

Free Response Questions

7. The question asks for $P(31 < X < 41)$. There is no direct connection between raw scores and probabilities.

Use the Z formula to transform raw scores to Z scores.

$$Z = \frac{X - \mu}{\sigma} = \frac{31 - 27.1}{6.5} = 0.6$$

$$Z = \frac{X - \mu}{\sigma} = \frac{41 - 27.1}{6.5} = 2.14$$

$P(31 < X < 41) = P(0.6 < Z < 2.14)$

$P(0.6 < Z < 2.14)$ can be calculated as $P(Z < 2.14) - P(Z < 0.6) = .9838 - .7257 = .2581$

The proportion of adult females with BMI between 31 and 41 is 25.81% (Figure 5.15).

FIGURE 5.15 Using the Z Table to Figure Out $P(0.6 < Z < 2.14)$

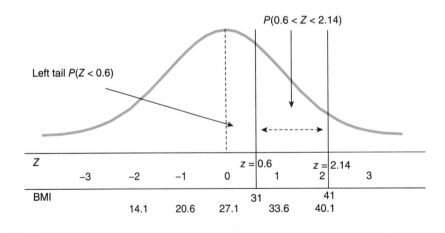

NOTE: **BMI** = body mass index.

8. The values of the sum of the dots on two dice and their probabilities are listed in Table 5.5a. The event of throwing two dice to get a number of dots that is an even number greater than six is given by {8, 10, 12}, and the probability for the event is

$$\frac{5}{36} + \frac{3}{36} + \frac{1}{36} = \frac{9}{36} = .25$$

9.

$$P(\text{Winning the jackpot of Classic Lotto}) = \frac{6 \times 5 \times 4 \times 3 \times 2 \times 1}{49 \times 48 \times 47 \times 46 \times 45 \times 44} = \frac{720}{10068347520} = \frac{1}{13983816}$$

10. $P(X < 60) = P(Z < (60 - 68)/19) = P(Z < -0.42) = .3372$

The probability of randomly selecting a patient with a heart rate less than 60 is .3372 (Figure 5.16).

11. The question asks for the top 30%, $P(Z > z) = .30$.

$P(Z > z) = 1 - P(Z < z) = .30$

$P(Z < z) = .70$

According to the Z Table, the probability closest to .70 is .6985, and its corresponding Z value is 0.52.

$$Z = \frac{X - \mu}{\sigma}$$

FIGURE 5.16   Using the Z Table to Figure Out $P(Z < -0.42)$

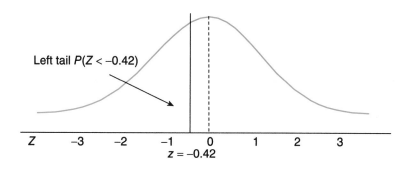

Left tail $P(Z < -0.42)$

$z = -0.42$

$$0.52 = \frac{X - 21}{5.4}$$

$$X = 23.81$$

$Z = 0.52$ is linked to the raw score through the Z formula, and the calculated X is 23.81. The ACT composite score that separates the top 30% from the rest of the distribution is roughly 24 (Figure 5.17).

FIGURE 5.17 Using the Z Table to Figure Out $P(Z < z) = .70$

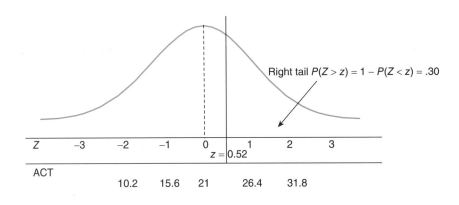

NOTE: ACT = American College Test.

CHAPTER 6

1. b

2. d

3. b

4. a

5. d

6. b

7. c

8. c

9. c

10. a

11. d

Free Response Questions

12. The weight limit is 3,200; with 1 male driver and 15 male passengers to overload the water taxi, the $\bar{X}$ needs to be greater than 3200/16 = 200.

The correct mathematical expression according to the question is $P(\bar{X} > 200)$. There is no direct connection between sample mean and probability, so the $\bar{X}$ needs to be converted to a Z value.

$$Z = \frac{\bar{X} - \mu}{\frac{\sigma}{\sqrt{n}}} = \frac{200 - 182.5}{\frac{40.8}{\sqrt{16}}} = \frac{17.5}{10.2} = 1.72$$

$$P(\bar{X} > 200) = P(Z > 1.72)$$

Draw and identify this area under the standard normal distribution curve, $P(Z > 1.72)$ (Figure 6.8).

FIGURE 6.8   Using the Z Table to Figure Out $P(Z > 1.72)$

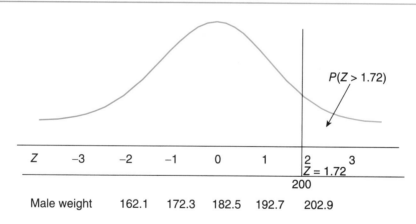

$$P(Z > 1.72) = 1 - P(Z < 1.72) = 1 - .9573 = .0427$$

The probability of the water taxi getting overloaded with 16 males is .0427 or 4.27%. Setting the maximal number of passengers in the water taxi at 16 is wise. Due to the fact that the average weight of women is lighter than the average weight of men, when the water taxi is carrying 16 passengers, including both men and women, the probability of overloading is lower than 4.27%.

13. The question asks for $P(\bar{X} > 17)$. There is no direct connection between the sample mean and probability, so the $\bar{X}$ needs to be converted to a Z value.

$$Z = \frac{\bar{X} - \mu}{\frac{\sigma}{\sqrt{n}}} = \frac{17 - 15}{\frac{5}{\sqrt{16}}} = \frac{2}{1.25} = 1.6$$

$$P(\bar{X} > 17) = P(Z > 1.6)$$

Draw and identify this area under the standard normal distribution curve, $P(Z > 1.6)$ (Figure 6.9).

FIGURE 6.9   Using the Z Table to Figure Out $P(Z > 1.6)$

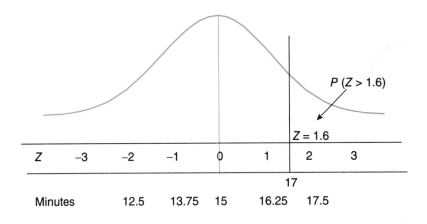

$$P(Z > 1.6) = 1 - P(Z < 1.6) = 1 - .9452 = .0548$$

The probability of this random sample of 16 customers who spent longer than 17 minutes on the company's website to get an insurance quote is .0548 or 5.48%. Such a result is a low probability event if the average time to get an insurance quote on the company's website is truly 15 minutes as advertised.

14. The question asks for $P(\bar{X} < 15)$. There is no direct connection between the sample mean and probability, so the $\bar{X}$ needs to be converted to a Z value.

$$Z = \frac{\bar{X} - \mu}{\frac{\sigma}{\sqrt{n}}} = \frac{15 - 16}{\frac{1.5}{\sqrt{9}}} = \frac{-1}{0.5} = -2$$

$$P(\bar{X} < 15) = P(Z < -2)$$

Draw and identify this area under the standard normal distribution curve, $P(Z < -2)$ (Figure 6.10).

FIGURE 6.10   Using the Z Table to Figure Out $P(Z < -2)$

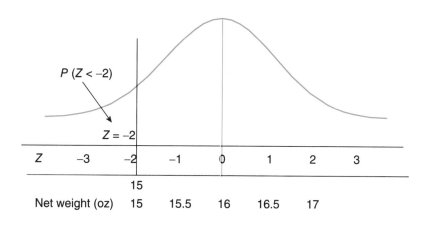

$$P(Z < -2) = .0228$$

The probability of randomly selecting nine bags of chicken and vegetable dumplings weighing less than 15 ounces is .0228 or 2.28%. Such a result is unusual if the average net weight of the chicken and vegetable dumplings is truly 16 ounces as labeled.

CHAPTER 7

1. b

2. c

3. d

4. b

5. d

6. a

7. b

8. d

9. a

10. a

11. c

12. *Step 1.* State the pair of hypotheses.

$$\text{Two-tailed test:} \quad H_0: \mu = 20$$
$$H_1: \mu \neq 20$$

Step 2. Identify the rejection zone.

A two-tailed test with $\alpha = .10$

Rejection zone: $|Z| > 1.65$

Step 3. Calculate the test statistic.

When comparing the average anxiety score of patients with the population mean with a known σ, the Z statistic is the correct approach.

List all the numbers given in the problem statement.

$\mu = 20$

$\sigma = 4$

$\bar{X} = 22$

$n = 4$

$$Z = \frac{\bar{X} - \mu}{\frac{\sigma}{\sqrt{n}}} = \frac{(22 - 20)}{4/\sqrt{4}} = \frac{2}{2} = 1$$

Step 4. Make the correct conclusion.

Compare the calculated $Z = 1$ from Step 3 to the rejection zone $|Z| > 1.65$ from Step 2. The calculated Z is not within the rejection zone; therefore, we fail to reject H_0. The evidence is not strong enough to support the claim that patients' anxiety score is significantly different from that of the population.

13. $\sigma_{\bar{X}} = \sigma/\sqrt{n} = 8/\sqrt{16} = 2$.

14. *Step 1.* State the pair of hypotheses.

$$\text{Right-tailed test:} \quad H_0: \mu = \$30{,}000$$
$$H_1: \mu > \$30{,}000$$

Step 2. Identify the rejection zone.

A right-tailed test with α = .05

Rejection zone: Z > 1.65

Step 3. Calculate the statistic.

When comparing the average student loan in this private university to a population mean with a known σ, the use of a Z statistic is the correct approach.

List all the numbers given in the problem statement.

μ = $30,000

σ = $20,000

$\bar{X}$ = $37,500

n = 25

$$Z = \frac{\bar{X} - \mu}{\frac{\sigma}{\sqrt{n}}} = \frac{(37,500 - 30,000)}{20,000 / \sqrt{25}} = \frac{7,500}{4,000} = 1.88$$

Step 4. Make the correct conclusion.

Compare the calculated Z value = 1.88 from Step 3 and the rejection zone Z > 1.65 from Step 2. The calculated Z is within the rejection zone, so we reject H_0. The evidence is strong enough to support the claim that the average student loan from this private university is higher than $30,000.

15. *Step 1.* State the pair of hypotheses.

Left-tailed test: H_0: μ = 2,392 square feet

H_1: μ < 2,392 square feet

Step 2. Identify the rejection zone.

A left-tailed test with α = .05

Rejection zone: Z < −1.65

Step 3. Calculate the statistic.

When comparing the average square footage of houses in Cleveland with the population mean with a known σ, the use of a Z statistic is the correct approach.

List all the numbers given in the problem statement.

$\mu = 2{,}392$ square feet

$\sigma = 760$ square feet

$\bar{X} = 2{,}025$ square feet

$n = 16$

$$Z = \frac{\bar{X} - \mu}{\dfrac{\sigma}{\sqrt{n}}} = \frac{(2025 - 2392)}{760 / \sqrt{16}} = \frac{-367}{190} = -1.93$$

Step 4. Make the correct conclusion.

Compare the calculated Z value $= -1.93$ from Step 3 and the rejection zone $Z < -1.65$ from Step 2. The calculated Z falls in the rejection zone, so we reject H_0. The evidence is strong enough to support the claim that the average square footage of houses in Cleveland is smaller than 2,392 square feet.

CHAPTER 8

1. b

2. d

3. b

4. c

5. d

6. b

7. d

8. b

Free Response Questions

9. This is an exploratory study, and there is not enough information to make a directional hypothesis test. Therefore, the correct procedure is to conduct a two-tailed test.

Step 1. State the pair of hypotheses.

$H_0: \mu = 70$

$H_1: \mu \neq 70$

Step 2. Identify the rejection zone for the hypothesis test.

From Step 1, we know that we are conducting a two-tailed test. The problem statement specifies $\alpha = .05$, and $df = n - 1 = 49 - 1 = 48$. There is no $df = 48$ listed in the t Table.

The closest *df* is 50. According to the *t* Table, the closest critical *t* value is 2.009. The rejection zone is $|t| > 2.009$, as shaded in Figure 8.9.

FIGURE 8.9   Use the *t* Table to Identify the Rejection Zone $|t| > 2.009$

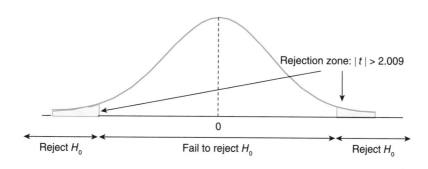

Step 3. Calculate the test statistic.

It is easy to list all the numbers stated in the problem statement and to separate what we know from what we need to figure out.

What we know.

   $\mu = 70$

   $n = 49$

   $\bar{X} = 75$

   $s = 14$

Next, insert all the numbers in the *t*-test formula.

$$t = \frac{\bar{X} - \mu}{\frac{s}{\sqrt{n}}}$$

$$t = \frac{(75 - 70)}{14 / \sqrt{49}} = \frac{5}{2} = 2.5$$

Step 4. Make the correct conclusion.

Compare the calculated $t = 2.5$ with the rejection zone $|t| > 2.009$. The calculated *t* falls within the rejection zone. Therefore, we reject H_0. At $\alpha = .05$, the evidence is strong enough to support the claim that frequent quizzes have an effect on academic performance.

10. The problem asks to test whether the average student loan in this public university is lower than the national average of $29,400. This is a left-tailed test.

Step 1. State the pair of hypotheses.

H_0: $\mu = \$29,400$

H_1: $\mu < \$29,400$

Step 2. Identify the rejection zone for the hypothesis test.

From Step 1, we know that we are conducting a left-tailed test. The problem statement specifies $\alpha = .10$, and $df = n - 1 = 36 - 1 = 35$. According to the t Table, 35 is exactly halfway between 30 and 40; I suggest using the more conservative (i.e., difficult to reach) critical value as reported by the $df = 30$. The critical t value in the t Table is 1.310. The rejection zone is $t < -1.310$, as shaded in Figure 8.10.

FIGURE 8.10 Use the t Table to Identify the Rejection Zone $t < -1.310$

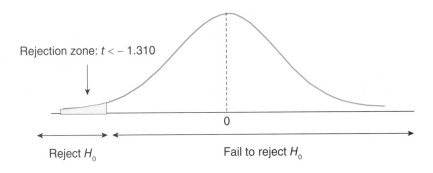

Step 3. Calculate the test statistic.

It is easy to list all the numbers stated in the problem statement and to separate what we know from what we need to figure out.

What we know.

$\mu = \$29,400$

$n = 36$

$\bar{X} = \$27,400$

$s = \$9,000$

Next, insert all the numbers in the t-test formula.

$$t = \frac{\bar{X} - \mu}{\frac{s}{\sqrt{n}}}$$

$$t = \frac{(27400 - 29400)}{9000 / \sqrt{36}} = \frac{-2000}{1500} = -1.33$$

Step 4. Make a conclusion.

Compare the calculated $t = -1.33$ with the rejection zone $t < -1.310$. The calculated t is in the rejection zone. Therefore, we reject H_0. At $\alpha = .10$, the evidence is strong enough to support the claim that the average student loan in this public university is lower than \$29,400.

11.a. The population standard deviation, σ, is unknown in this problem statement; therefore, the four-step hypothesis testing process to conduct a t test is the correct approach to answer this problem.

Step 1. State the pair of hypotheses.

The problem statement asks "whether the new program has an effect on SAT verbal scores." The question does not contain any information regarding a direction. Therefore, a nondirectional hypothesis test is the correct approach. H_0 covers the equal sign, $\mu = 500$, and H_1: $\mu \neq 500$ is the hypothesis that researchers turn to when H_0 is rejected by the evidence.

H_0: $\mu = 500$

H_1: $\mu \neq 500$

Step 2. Identify the rejection zone.

From Step 1, we know that we are conducting a two-tailed test. The problem statement specifies $\alpha = .05$, and $df = n - 1 = 9 - 1 = 8$. According to the t Table, the critical t value is 2.306. The rejection zone is $|t| > 2.306$, as shaded in Figure 8.11.

Step 3. Calculate the test statistic.

It is easy to list all the numbers stated in the problem statement and to separate what we know from what we need to figure out.

What we know.

$\mu = 500$

$n = 9$

FIGURE 8.11 Use the *t* Table to Identify the Rejection Zone $|t| > 2.306$

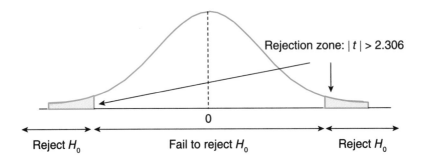

When given all measures in a sample, you have to calculate $\bar{X}$ and s before conducting a *t* test.

$$\bar{X} = \sum X/n$$

$$SS = \sum(X - \bar{X})^2$$

$$s = \sqrt{\frac{\sum(X - \bar{X})^2}{df}} = \sqrt{\frac{SS}{df}} = \sqrt{\frac{SS}{(n-1)}}$$

Let's insert all the measures in a table and demonstrate the step-by-step process in Table 8.5.

First, we need to figure out the sample mean, $\bar{X}$. Then we construct $(X - \bar{X})$ in the second column, and $(X - \bar{X})^2$ in the third column, and add all the numbers in the third column to obtain SS.

$$\bar{X} = \sum X/n = 5085/9 = 565$$

$$SS = \sum(X - \bar{X})^2 = 72950$$

$$s = \sqrt{\frac{\sum(X - \bar{X})^2}{df}} = \sqrt{\frac{SS}{df}} = \sqrt{\frac{SS}{(n-1)}} = \sqrt{\frac{72950}{8}} = 95.5$$

Next, insert all the numbers in the *t*-test formula.

$$t = \frac{\bar{X} - \mu}{\dfrac{s}{\sqrt{n}}}$$

TABLE 8.5 Nine SAT Verbal Scores

X	$(X - \bar{X})$	$(X - \bar{X})^2$
600	35	1225
760	195	38025
550	−15	225
505	−60	3600
660	95	9025
540	−25	625
480	−85	7225
535	−30	900
455	−110	12100
5085		**72950**

$$t = \frac{(565 - 500)}{95.5/\sqrt{9}} = \frac{65}{31.83} = 2.04$$

Step 4. Make the correct conclusion.

Compare the calculated $t = 2.04$ with the rejection zone $|t| > 2.306$. The calculated t does not fall in the rejection zone. Therefore, we fail to reject H_0. At $\alpha = .05$, the evidence is not strong enough to support the claim that the new program has an effect on SAT verbal scores.

11.b. The population standard deviation, σ, is unknown in the problem statement; therefore, s is used to estimate σ. The critical t value sets the boundaries of the 95% CI with $df = 8$, two-tailed, and $\alpha = .05$ is $t = 2.306$.

$$95\% \text{ CI of } \mu = \bar{X} \pm t_{\alpha+2}\left(\frac{s}{\sqrt{n}}\right) = 565 \pm 2.306\left(\frac{95.5}{\sqrt{9}}\right) = 565 \pm 73.40$$

95% CI of μ is [491.60, 638.40]. We are 95% confident that the average SAT Verbal for this high school is included in the interval [491.60, 638.40].

11.c. The result of the hypothesis test in 11.a is that we fail to reject H_0. The evidence is not strong enough to support the claim that the new program has an effect on SAT verbal scores. Using the sample data to construct the 95% CI for the average SAT verbal score of the high school, the result is [491.60, 638.40]. The population mean, $\mu = 500$, is included in the 95% CI. Therefore, the effect for the new program is not significant.

CHAPTER 9

1. b

2. c

3. a

4. a

5. d

6. b

Free Response Questions

7.a.

Step 1. Test for equality of variances.

Substep 1. State the pair of hypotheses regarding variances.

$$H_0: \sigma_1^2 = \sigma_2^2$$

$$H_1: \sigma_1^2 \neq \sigma_2^2$$

Substep 2. Identify the rejection zone.

The larger standard deviation is s_1, 12.5, and its $df_1 = n_1 - 1 = 13 - 1 = 12$; s_2 is the smaller standard deviation, 8.2, and its $df_2 = 15 - 1 = 14$.

The critical value of the right-tailed $F_{(df_1, df_2)} = F_{(12,14)} = 2.53$.

Substep 3. Calculate the statistic.

$$F = \frac{s_1^2}{s_2^2} = \frac{12.5^2}{8.2^2} = \frac{156.25}{67.24} = 2.32$$

Substep 4. Make the correct conclusion.

The calculated $F = 2.32$ is smaller than the critical value of $F_{(df_1, df_2)} = 2.53$. Therefore, we fail to reject H_0. The evidence is not strong enough to claim that the two variances are not equal. Therefore, the correct independent-samples t-test approach is to assume equal variances.

Step 2. State the pair of hypotheses regarding group means.

The problem statement asks, "Does giving frequent quizzes increase the retention of statistics knowledge as demonstrated by the average final exam scores?" *Increase* is a key word for direction. Since the group without frequent quizzes has a larger sample standard deviation, it is designated as Group 1. The group with frequent quizzes is labeled as Group 2. The alternative hypothesis is to test whether μ_1 is less than μ_2. A left-tailed test is appropriate. Many students automatically associate the key word *increase* with a right-tailed test without paying attention to which sample is labeled as Sample 1 due to the larger sample standard deviation. In a one-tailed test, it is important to state the correct direction in the alternative hypothesis, H_1.

$$H_0: \mu_1 = \mu_2$$

$$H_1: \mu_1 < \mu_2$$

Step 3. Identify the rejection zone.

According to the t Table, when $df = df_1 + df_2 = n_1 + n_2 - 2 = 26$, $\alpha = .05$; it is a left-tailed test, and the critical t value that sets the boundary of the rejection zone is 1.706. The rejection zone for a left-tailed test is $t < -1.706$.

Step 4. Calculate the t statistic.

When $\sigma_1^2 = \sigma_2^2$, the variances need to be pooled together.

$$SS_1 = s_1^2 df_1 = 12.5^2 (13 - 1) = 1875$$

$$SS_2 = s_2^2 df_2 = 8.2^2 (15 - 1) = 941.36$$

$$s_P^2 = \frac{SS_1 + SS_2}{df_1 + df_2} = \frac{1875 + 941.36}{12 + 14} = \frac{2816.36}{26} = 108.32$$

$$s_{(\bar{X}_1 - \bar{X}_2)} = \sqrt{\frac{s_P^2}{n_1} + \frac{s_P^2}{n_2}} = \sqrt{\frac{108.32}{13} + \frac{108.32}{15}} = \sqrt{8.33 + 7.22} = \sqrt{15.55} = 3.94$$

$$t = \frac{(\bar{X}_1 - \bar{X}_2)}{s_{(\bar{X}_1 - \bar{X}_2)}} = \frac{(75 - 80)}{3.94} = \frac{-5}{3.94} = -1.27$$

Step 5. Make the correct conclusion.

The calculated $t = -1.27$ is not within the rejection zone. Therefore, we fail to reject H_0. The evidence is not strong enough to support the claim that frequent quizzes increase the retention of statistics knowledge.

7.b. When $\sigma_1^2 = \sigma_2^2$, the effect size is calculated by Cohen's $d = (\bar{X}_1 - \bar{X}_2) / s_P$.

Based on the answer from 7.a, $s_p = \sqrt{108.32} = 10.41$.

$$\text{Effect size } d = \frac{(\bar{X}_1 - \bar{X}_2)}{s_p} = \frac{75 - 80}{10.41} = \frac{-5}{10.41} = -0.48$$

The average score of students without frequent quizzes is 0.48 standard deviations lower than that of students with frequent quizzes. The effect is moderate.

8.a.

Step 1. Test for equality of variances.

Substep 1. State the pair of hypotheses regarding variances.

$$H_0: \sigma_1^2 = \sigma_2^2$$

$$H_1: \sigma_1^2 \neq \sigma_2^2$$

Substep 2. Identify the criterion for the hypothesis test.

The group without laptops has a larger SS than the group with laptops, $SS_1 = 19.44$, $df_1 = 24$, and $s_1 = \sqrt{SS_1 / df_1} = \sqrt{19.44 / 24} = 0.9$. The group with laptops has $df_2 = 21 - 1 = 20$, and its standard deviation is $s_2 = \sqrt{SS_2 / df_2} = \sqrt{12.8 / 20} = 0.8$.

The critical value of the right-tailed $F_{(df_1, df_2)} = F_{(24,20)} = 2.08$.

Substep 3. Calculate the statistic.

$$F = \frac{s_1^2}{s_2^2} = \frac{0.81}{0.64} = 1.27$$

Substep 4. Make the correct conclusion.

The calculated $F = 1.27$ is smaller than the critical value of $F_{(24,20)} = 2.08$. Therefore, we fail to reject H_0. The evidence is not strong enough to claim that the two variances are not equal. Therefore, the correct independent-samples t-test approach is to assume equal variances.

Step 2. State the pair of hypotheses regarding group means.

The problem statement asks, "Does having access to a laptop computer have a significant effect on students' GPA?" There is no key word to indicate a direction in the problem statement. A two-tailed test is appropriate.

$$H_0: \mu_1 = \mu_2$$

$$H_1: \mu_1 \neq \mu_2$$

Step 3. Identify the rejection zone.

According to the *t* Table, when $df = df_1 + df_2 = n_1 + n_2 - 2 = 44$, $\alpha = .05$; it is a two-tailed test, and the closest critical *t* value that sets the boundary of the rejection zone is 2.021. The rejection zone for a two-tailed test is $|t| > 2.021$.

Step 4. Calculate the *t* statistic.

When $\sigma_1^2 = \sigma_2^2$, the variances need to be pooled together.

$$SS_1 = 19.44$$

$$SS_2 = 12.8$$

$$s_p^2 = \frac{SS_1 + SS_2}{df_1 + df_2} = \frac{19.44 + 12.8}{24 + 20} = \frac{32.24}{44} = 0.733$$

$$s_{(\bar{X}_1 - \bar{X}_2)} = \sqrt{\frac{s_p^2}{n_1} + \frac{s_p^2}{n_2}} = \sqrt{\frac{0.733}{25} + \frac{0.733}{21}} = \sqrt{0.029 + 0.35} = \sqrt{0.064} = 0.253$$

$$t = \frac{(\bar{X}_1 - \bar{X}_2)}{s_{(\bar{X}_1 - \bar{X}_2)}} = \frac{(3.0 - 3.4)}{0.253} = \frac{-0.4}{0.253} = -1.581$$

Step 5. Make the correct conclusion.

The calculated $t = -1.581$ is not within the rejection zone. Therefore, we fail to reject H_0. The evidence is not strong enough to support the claim that having laptops has a significant effect on students' GPA.

8.b. When $\sigma_1^2 = \sigma_2^2$, the effect size is calculated by Cohen's $d = (\bar{X}_1 - \bar{X}_2)/s_p$.

Based on the answer from 8.a, $s_p = \sqrt{0.733} = 0.856$.

$$\text{Effect size } d = \frac{(\bar{X}_1 - \bar{X}_2)}{s_p} = \frac{3.0 - 3.4}{0.856} = \frac{-0.4}{0.856} = -0.467$$

The average GPA of students without laptops at school is 0.467 standard deviation lower than that of students with laptops at school. The effect is moderate.

9.a.

Step 1. Test for equality of variances.

Substep 1. State the pair of hypotheses regarding variances.

$$H_0: \sigma_1^2 = \sigma_2^2$$

$$H_1: \sigma_1^2 \neq \sigma_2^2$$

Substep 2. Identify the rejection zone.

The sample standard variance, s^2, was not provided directly in the problem statement, so you have to calculate $s^2 = SS/df$.

The variance for the group that received cell phones after age 5 is

$$s^2 = \frac{SS}{df} = \frac{1559.52}{12} = 129.96$$

The variance for the group that received cell phones before age 5 is

$$s^2 = \frac{SS}{df} = \frac{345.96}{9} = 38.44$$

Therefore, the group that received cell phones after age 5 is labeled as Group 1, with $df_1 = 12$. The other group is Group 2, with $df_2 = 9$.

The critical value of the right-tailed $F_{(df_1, df_2)} = F_{(12,9)} = 3.07$.

Substep 3. Calculate the statistic.

$$F = \frac{s_1^2}{s_2^2} = \frac{129.96}{38.44} = 3.38$$

Substep 4. Make the correct conclusion.

The calculated $F = 3.38$ is larger than the critical value of $F_{(12,9)} = 3.07$. Therefore, we reject H_0. The evidence is strong enough to claim that the two variances are not equal. Therefore, the correct independent-samples t-test approach is not to assume equal variances.

Step 2. State the pair of hypotheses regarding group means.

The problem statement asks, "Do these two groups have different social skills?" There is no key word to indicate a direction in the problem statement. A two-tailed test is appropriate.

$H_0: \mu_1 = \mu_2$

$H_1: \mu_1 \neq \mu_2$

Step 3. Identify the rejection zone.

$$\text{Satterthwaite's approximated } df = \frac{(w_1 + w_2)^2}{\dfrac{w_1^2}{n_1 - 1} + \dfrac{w_2^2}{n_2 - 1}}$$

where

$$w_1 = \frac{s_1^2}{n_1} = \frac{129.96}{13} = 9.997$$

and

$$w_2 = \frac{s_2^2}{n_2} = \frac{38.44}{10} = 3.844$$

$$df = \frac{(w_1 + w_2)^2}{\dfrac{w_1^2}{n_1 - 1} + \dfrac{w_2^2}{n_2 - 1}} = \frac{(9.997 + 3.844)^2}{\dfrac{9.997^2}{12} + \dfrac{3.844^2}{9}} = \frac{191.57}{9.97} = 19.21$$

rounded down to 19.

According to the *t* Table, when *df* = 19, α = .10; it is a two-tailed test, and the critical *t* value that sets the boundary of the rejection zone is 1.729. The rejection zone for a two-tailed test is $|t| > 1.729$.

Step 4. Calculate the *t* statistic.

When $\sigma_1^2 \neq \sigma_2^2$, the variances need to be left alone. We do not pool the variances.

$$s_{(\bar{X}_1 - \bar{X}_2)} = \sqrt{\frac{s_1^2}{n_1} + \frac{s_2^2}{n_2}} = \sqrt{\frac{129.96}{13} + \frac{38.44}{10}} = \sqrt{9.997 + 3.844} = \sqrt{13.841} = 3.72$$

$$t = \frac{(\bar{X}_1 - \bar{X}_2)}{s_{(\bar{X}_1 - \bar{X}_2)}} = \frac{(73.8 - 60.5)}{3.72} = \frac{13.3}{3.72} = 3.58$$

Step 5. Make the correct conclusion.

The calculated $t = 3.58$ is within the rejection zone. Therefore, we reject H_0. The evidence is strong enough to support the claim that these two groups of teenagers have different levels of social skills.

9.b.   When $\sigma_1^2 \neq \sigma_2^2$, the effect size is calculated as

$$\text{Glass's } \Delta = \frac{(\bar{X}_1 - \bar{X}_2)}{s_{control}} \quad \text{or} \quad \Delta = \frac{(\bar{X}_1 - \bar{X}_2)}{s_{larger}}$$

$$\text{Effect size } \Delta = \frac{(\bar{X}_1 - \bar{X}_2)}{s_{larger}} = \frac{73.8 - 60.5}{11.4} = \frac{13.3}{11.4} = 1.17$$

The average social skills of teenagers who received cell phones after age 5 is 1.17 standard deviations higher than the average social skills of teenagers who received cell phones before age 5. The effect is large.

9.c.   Construct a 90% CI for the difference in social skills between these two groups.

When equal variances are not assumed, $\sigma_1^2 \neq \sigma_2^2$, the 90% CI is

$$(\bar{X}_1 - \bar{X}_2) \pm t_{\alpha/2}\left(\frac{s_1^2}{n_1} + \frac{s_2^2}{n_2}\right)$$

The point estimate is $(\bar{X}_1 - \bar{X}_2) = 73.8 - 60.5 = 13.3$. The margin of error is

$$t_{\alpha/2}\left(\sqrt{\frac{s_1^2}{n_1} + \frac{s_2^2}{n_2}}\right) = 1.729(3.72) = 6.43$$

Therefore, the 90% CI is 13.3 ± 6.43, that is, $[6.87, 19.73]$. We are 90% confident that the difference in average social skills between these two groups is between 6.87 and 19.73, with the teenagers who were given cell phones after age 5 having better social skills.

Caution! The answers for Question 9 are slightly different if you use the smaller of df_1 and df_2 as the df when $\sigma_1^2 \neq \sigma_2^2$. Here are the alternative answers.

9.a.

Step 1. Test for equality of variances.

Substep 1. State the pair of hypotheses regarding variances.

$$H_0: \sigma_1^2 = \sigma_2^2$$

$$H_1: \sigma_1^2 \neq \sigma_2^2$$

Substep 2. Identify the rejection zone.

The sample standard variance, s^2, was not provided directly in the problem statement, so you have to calculate $s^2 = SS/df$.

The variance for the group that received cell phones after age 5 is

$$s^2 = \frac{SS}{df} = \frac{1559.52}{12} = 129.96.$$

The variance for the group that received cell phones before age 5 is

$$s^2 = \frac{SS}{df} = \frac{345.96}{9} = 38.44.$$

Therefore, the group that received cell phones after age 5 is Group 1, with $df_1 = 12$. The other group is Group 2, with $df_2 = 9$.

The critical value of the right-tailed $F_{(df_1, df_2)} = F_{(12,9)} = 3.07$.

Substep 3. Calculate the statistic.

$$F = \frac{s_1^2}{s_2^2} = \frac{129.96}{38.44} = 3.38$$

Substep 4. Make the correct conclusion.

The calculated $F = 3.38$ is larger than the critical value of $F_{(12,9)} = 3.07$. Therefore, we reject H_0. The evidence is strong enough to claim that the two variances are not equal. Therefore, the correct independent-samples t-test approach is not to assume equal variances.

Step 2. State the pair of hypotheses regarding group means.

The problem statement asks, "Do these two groups have different social skills?" There is no key word to indicate a direction in the problem statement. A two-tailed test is appropriate.

$$H_0: \mu_1 = \mu_2$$

$$H_1: \mu_1 \neq \mu_2$$

Step 3. Identify the rejection zone.

According to the *t* Table, when $df = 9$, $\alpha = .10$; it is a two-tailed test, and the critical *t* value that sets the boundary of the rejection zone is 1.833. The rejection zone is $|t| > 1.833$.

Step 4. Calculate the *t* statistic.

When $\sigma_1^2 \neq \sigma_2^2$, the variances need to be left alone. We do not pool the variances.

$$s_{(\bar{X}_1 - \bar{X}_1)} = \sqrt{\frac{s_1^2}{n_1} + \frac{s_1^2}{n_2}} = \sqrt{\frac{129.96}{13} + \frac{38.44}{10}} = \sqrt{9.997 + 3.844} = \sqrt{13.841} = 3.72$$

$$t = \frac{(\bar{X}_1 - \bar{X}_2)}{s_{(\bar{X}_1 - \bar{X}_2)}} = \frac{(73.8 - 60.5)}{3.72} = \frac{13.3}{3.72} = 3.58$$

Step 5. Make the correct conclusion.

The calculated $t = 3.58$ is within the rejection zone. Therefore, we reject H_0. The evidence is strong enough to support the claim that these two groups of teenagers have different levels of social skills.

9.b. When $\sigma_1^2 \neq \sigma_2^2$, the effect size is calculated as

$$\text{Glass's } \Delta = \frac{(\bar{X}_1 - \bar{X}_2)}{s_{\text{control}}} \quad \text{or} \quad \Delta = \frac{(\bar{X}_1 - \bar{X}_2)}{s_{\text{larger}}}$$

$$\text{Effect size } \Delta = \frac{(\bar{X}_1 - \bar{X}_2)}{s_{\text{larger}}} = \frac{73.8 - 60.5}{11.4} = \frac{13.3}{11.4} = 1.17$$

The average social skills of teenagers who received cell phones after age 5 is 1.17 standard deviations higher than the average social skills of teenagers who received cell phones before age 5. The effect is large.

9.c. Construct a 90% CI for the difference in social skills between these two groups.

When equal variances are not assumed, $\sigma_1^2 \neq \sigma_2^2$, the 90% CI is

$$(\bar{X}_1 - \bar{X}_2) \pm t_{\alpha/2} \left(\sqrt{\frac{s_1^2}{n_1} + \frac{s_2^2}{n_2}} \right)$$

The point estimate is $(\bar{X}_1 - \bar{X}_2) = 73.8 - 60.5 = 13.3$. The margin of error is

$$t_{\alpha/2}\left(\sqrt{\frac{s_1^2}{n_1}+\frac{s_2^2}{n_2}}\right)=1.833(3.72)=6.82$$

Therefore, the 90% CI is 13.3 ± 6.82, that is, [6.48, 20.12]. We are 90% confident that the difference in social skills between these two groups is between 6.48 and 20.12, with the teenagers who were given cell phones after age 5 having better social skills.

CHAPTER 10

1. c		4. d	
2. a		5. a	
3. b		6. d	

Free Response Questions

7.a.

Step 1. The problem statement asks "if the relaxation training is effective in reducing the number of headaches." *Reducing* is a key word to indicate a directional hypothesis. When we calculate the difference as the number of headaches after the relaxation training minus the number of headaches before the relaxation training, the differences are likely to be negative, so a left-tailed test is the correct approach.

$$\text{Difference} = \text{After training} - \text{Before training}$$

$H_0: \mu_D = 0$

$H_1: \mu_D < 0$

Step 2. Identify the rejection zone.

Based on the problem statement, we use a left-tailed test, $\alpha = .01$, and $df = 9 - 1 = 8$.

The critical value in the t Table is 2.896, so the rejection zone for a left-tailed test is $t < -2.896$.

Step 3. Calculate the test statistic.

The calculation process for mean, standard deviation, and standard error of the differences is shown step-by-step in Table 10.7a.

TABLE 10.7a Step-by-Step Calculation for the Number of Headaches Reported by the Participants Before and After Relaxation Training

BEFORE TRAINING	AFTER TRAINING	D	$(D - \bar{D})$	$(D - \bar{D})^2$
15	9	−6	−3	9
10	8	−2	1	1
16	12	−4	−1	1
11	8	−3	0	0
17	11	−6	−3	9
20	12	−8	−5	25
13	13	0	3	9
5	6	1	4	16
8	9	1	4	16
		−27		**86**

$$\bar{D} = \frac{\sum D}{n} = \frac{-27}{9} = -3$$

$$SS_D = \sum(D - \bar{D})^2 = 9 + 1 + 1 + 0 + 9 + 25 + 9 + 16 + 16 = 86$$

$$s_D = \sqrt{\frac{\sum(D - \bar{D})^2}{(n-1)}} = \sqrt{\frac{86}{8}} = \sqrt{10.75} = 3.28$$

$$s_e = \frac{s_D}{\sqrt{n}} = \frac{3.28}{\sqrt{9}} = 1.09$$

$$t = \frac{\bar{D}}{s_e} = \frac{\bar{D}}{\frac{s_D}{\sqrt{n}}} = \frac{-3}{\frac{3.28}{\sqrt{9}}} = -2.75$$

Step 4. Make the correct conclusion.

The calculated $t = -2.75$ is not within the rejection zone. We fail to reject H_0. The evidence is not strong enough to support the claim that the relaxation training is effective in reducing the number of headaches at $\alpha = .01$.

7.b. The effect size for the dependent-sample t test is calculated as

$$\text{Cohen's } d = \frac{\text{Mean difference}}{\text{Standard deviation of the differences}} = \frac{\bar{D}}{s_D}$$

$$\text{Cohen's } d = \frac{\bar{D}}{s_D} = \frac{-3}{3.28} = -0.91$$

The effect size is –.91, which is large according to Cohen's interpretation. The effect size for the relaxation training in reducing the number of headaches is practically meaningful.

7.c. The 98% CI for the mean difference is calculated as

$$\text{Point estimate} \pm \text{Margin of error} = \bar{D} \pm t_{\alpha/2} s_e.$$

$$98\% \text{ CI} = (-3) \pm 2.896(1.09) = -3 \pm 3.16 = [-6.16, 0.16]$$

Because the 98% CI includes zero, the evidence is not strong enough to support the claim that the differences in the number of headaches before and after the relaxation training are significant at $\alpha = .02$.

8.a.

Step 1. The problem statement asks "if beer consumption has any significant effect on female attractiveness ratings." There is no key word to indicate a directional hypothesis, so a two-tailed test is the correct approach.

$$\text{Difference} = \text{After training} - \text{Before training}$$

$H_0: \mu_D = 0$

$H_1: \mu_D \neq 0$

Step 2. Identify the rejection zone.

Based on the problem statement, we use a two-tailed test, $\alpha = .10$, and $df = 9 - 1 = 8$.

The critical value in the t Table is 1.86, so the rejection zone is $|t| > 1.86$.

Step 3. Calculate the test statistic.

The calculation process for the mean, standard deviation, and standard error of the differences is shown step-by-step in Table 10.8a.

TABLE 10.8a Step-by-Step Calculation for Female Attractiveness Ratings Before and After Beer Consumption

BEFORE CONSUMPTION	AFTER CONSUMPTION	D	$(D - \bar{D})$	$(D - \bar{D})^2$
5	5	0	−1	1
6	5	−1	−2	4
6	7	1	0	0
7	9	2	1	1
2	4	2	1	1
4	7	3	2	4
8	8	0	−1	1
7	8	1	0	0
8	9	1	0	0
		9		12

$$\bar{D} = \frac{\Sigma D}{n} = \frac{9}{9} = 1$$

$$SS_D = \Sigma(D - \bar{D})^2 = 1 + 4 + 0 + 1 + 1 + 4 + 1 + 0 + 0 = 12$$

$$s_D = \sqrt{\frac{\Sigma(D - \bar{D})^2}{(n-1)}} = \sqrt{\frac{12}{8}} = \sqrt{1.5} = 1.22$$

$$s_e = \frac{s_D}{\sqrt{n}} = \frac{1.22}{\sqrt{9}} = 0.41$$

$$t = \frac{\bar{D}}{s_e} = \frac{\bar{D}}{\frac{s_D}{\sqrt{n}}} = \frac{1}{\frac{1.22}{\sqrt{9}}} = 2.45$$

Step 4. Make the correct conclusion.

The calculated $t = 2.45$ is within the rejection zone. We reject H_0. The evidence is strong enough to support the claim that the beer consumption had a significant effect on female attractiveness ratings at $\alpha = .10$.

8.b.   The effect size for the dependent-sample t test is calculated as

$$\text{Cohen's } d = \frac{\text{Mean difference}}{\text{Standard deviation of the differences}} = \frac{\bar{D}}{s_D}$$

$$\text{Cohen's } d = \frac{\bar{D}}{s_D} = \frac{1}{1.22} = 0.82$$

The effect size is 0.82, which is large according to Cohen's interpretation.

8.c.   The 80% CI for the difference in female attractiveness ratings before and after beer consumption is calculated as Point estimate $\pm$ Margin of error $= \bar{D} \pm t_{\alpha/2} s_e$.

$$80\% \text{ CI} = 1 \pm 1.397(0.41) = 1 \pm 0.57 = [0.43, 1.57]$$

Because the 80% CI does not include zero, the evidence is strong enough to claim that there is a significant difference in female attractiveness ratings before and after beer consumption at $\alpha = .20$.

9.a.

Step 1. The problem statement asks "if exercise raises body temperature." *Raise* is a key word to indicate a directional hypothesis, so a right-tailed test is the correct approach.

$$\text{Difference} = \text{After} - \text{Before}$$

$H_0: \mu_D = 0$

$H_1: \mu_D > 0$

Step 2. Identify the rejection zone.

Based on the problem statement, you use a right-tailed test, $\alpha = .05$, and $df = n - 1 = 8 - 1 = 7$. The critical value in the t Table is 1.895, so the rejection zone for the right-tailed test is $t > 1.895$.

Step 3. Calculate the test statistic.

The calculation process for mean, standard deviation, and standard error of the difference is shown step-by-step in Table 10.9a.

$$\bar{D} = \frac{\Sigma D}{n} = \frac{2.4}{8} = 0.30$$

$$SS_D = \Sigma(D - \bar{D})^2 = 2.46$$

TABLE 10.9a   Body Temperature Before and After 30 Minutes on a Treadmill

BEFORE	AFTER	D	$(D - \bar{D})$	$(D - \bar{D})^2$
98.2	98.3	0.1	−0.2	0.04
97.1	97.6	0.5	0.2	0.04
96.3	96.5	0.2	−0.1	0.01
97.5	98.5	1	0.7	0.49
98.3	99.3	1	0.7	0.49
99.5	98.9	−0.6	−0.9	0.81
98.9	98.5	−0.4	−0.7	0.49
98.7	99.3	0.6	0.3	0.09
		2.4		2.46

$$s_D = \sqrt{\frac{\Sigma(D - \bar{D})^2}{(n-1)}} = \sqrt{\frac{2.46}{7}} = \sqrt{0.351} = 0.593$$

$$s_e = \frac{s_D}{\sqrt{n}} = \frac{0.593}{\sqrt{8}} = 0.210$$

$$t = \frac{\bar{D}}{s_e} = \frac{\bar{D}}{\frac{s_D}{\sqrt{n}}} = \frac{0.30}{\frac{0.593}{\sqrt{8}}} = 1.429$$

Step 4. Make the correct conclusion.

The calculated $t = 1,429$ is not within the rejection zone. We fail to reject H_0. The evidence is not strong enough to support the claim that exercise raises body temperature, at $\alpha = .05$.

9.b.   The effect size for the dependent-sample t test is calculated as

$$\text{Cohen's } d = \frac{\text{Mean difference}}{\text{Standard deviation of the differences}} = \frac{\bar{D}}{s_D}$$

$$\text{Cohen's } d = \frac{\bar{D}}{s_D} = \frac{0.30}{0.593} = 0.51$$

The effect size is 0.51, which is moderate according to Cohen's interpretation. The difference in body temperature before and after exercise is practically meaningful.

9.c. The 90% CI for the mean difference in body temperature before and after exercise is calculated as Point estimate $\pm$ Margin of error $= \bar{D} \pm t_{\alpha/2} s_e$.

$$90\% \text{ CI} = 0.30 \pm 1.895(0.210) = 0.30 \pm .40 = [-0.10, 0.70]$$

Because the 90% CI for the difference includes zero, the evidence is not strong enough to claim that exercise raises body temperature at $\alpha = .10$.

CHAPTER 11

1. c

6. d

2. d

7. c

3. a

8. d

4. b

9. b

5. c

Free Response Questions

10.a. Construct a scatterplot between ACT and SAT scores as shown in Figure 11.17. The scatterplot shows that there is a linear relationship between ACT and SAT scores.

FIGURE 11.17 A Scatterplot of ACT and SAT Scores

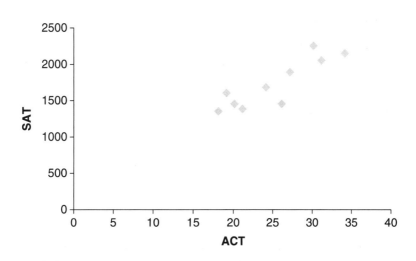

10.b.

Step 1: Explicitly state the pair of hypotheses.

The problem statement asks to conduct a hypothesis test for a relationship between ACT and SAT scores. Therefore, a two-tailed hypothesis is appropriate.

Two-tailed test: $\qquad$ $H_0: \rho = 0$

$\qquad\qquad\qquad\qquad\qquad$ $H_1: \rho \neq 0$

Step 2: Identify the rejection zone.

According to the r Table, with a two-tailed test, $df = n - 2 = 10 - 2 = 8$, $\alpha = .05$, the critical value of r is $r = .632$. The rejection zone for a two-tailed test is $|r| > .632$.

Step 3: Calculate the test statistic.

According to the Pearson's r formula, we need to add the following five columns to Table 11.10, $(X - \bar{X})$, $(Y - \bar{Y})$, $(X - \bar{X})(Y - \bar{Y})$, $(X - \bar{X})^2$, and $(Y - \bar{Y})^2$, to demonstrate the step-by-step process as shown in Table 11.10a.

The first step is to figure out $\bar{X}$ and $\bar{Y}$ to construct the additional five columns, and the last row of every column is the total of that column.

TABLE 11.10a Calculation of the Correlation Between ACT and SAT Scores of 10 Incoming Freshmen

ACT	SAT	$(X - \bar{X})$	$(Y - \bar{Y})$	$(X - \bar{X})(Y - \bar{Y})$	$(X - \bar{X})^2$	$(Y - \bar{Y})^2$
27	1,890	2	165	330	4	27,225
26	1,450	1	−275	−275	1	75,625
31	2,050	6	325	1,950	36	105,625
34	2,150	9	425	3,825	81	180,625
30	2,250	5	525	2,625	25	275,625
21	1,380	−4	−345	1,380	16	119,025
20	1,450	−5	−275	1,375	25	75,625
19	1,600	−6	−125	750	36	15,625
18	1,350	−7	−375	2,625	49	140,625
24	1,680	−1	−45	45	1	2,025
250	17,250			14,630	274	1,017,650

$$\bar{X} = \sum X/n = 250/10 = 25$$

$$\bar{Y} = \sum Y/n = 17250/10 = 1725$$

$$SP = \sum (X - \bar{X})(Y - \bar{Y}) = 14630$$

$$SS_X = \sum (X - \bar{X})^2 = 274$$

$$SS_Y = \sum (Y - \bar{Y})^2 = 1017650$$

$$r = \frac{SP}{\sqrt{SS_X SS_Y}} = \frac{14630}{\sqrt{(274)(1017650)}} = .876$$

Step 4: Make the correct conclusion.

The calculated $r = .876$ is within the rejection zone, so we reject H_0. The evidence is strong enough to support the claim that there is a significant relationship between ACT and SAT scores.

11.a. Construct a scatterplot between hours of exercise and weight change as shown in Figure 11.18. The scatterplot shows that there is a linear relationship between hours of exercise and weight change.

FIGURE 11.18 A Scatterplot of Hours of Exercise and Weight Change

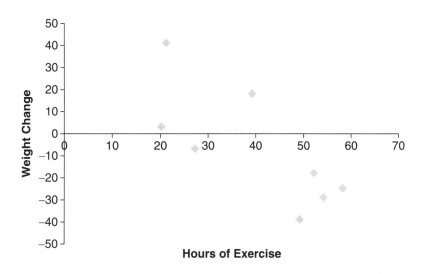

11.b.

Step 1: Explicitly state the pair of hypotheses.

The problem statement asks you to conduct a hypothesis test for a relationship between hours of exercise and weight change. Since no direction is indicated, a two-tailed hypothesis is appropriate.

Two-tailed test: $H_0: \rho = 0$

$H_1: \rho \neq 0$

Step 2: Identify the rejection zone.

According to the *r* Table, with a two-tailed test, $df = n - 2 = 8 - 2 = 6$, and $\alpha = .10$, the critical value of *r* is $r = .622$. The rejection zone for a two-tailed test is $|r| > .622$.

Step 3: Calculate the test statistic.

According to the Pearson's *r* formula, we need to add the following five columns to Table 11.11, $(X - \bar{X})$, $(Y - \bar{Y})$, $(X - \bar{X})(Y - \bar{Y})$, $(X - \bar{X})^2$, and $(Y - \bar{Y})^2$, to demonstrate the step-by-step process as shown in Table 11.11a.

The first step is to figure out $\bar{X}$ and $\bar{Y}$ to construct the additional five columns, and the last row of every column is the total of that column.

TABLE 11.11a Calculation of the Correlation Between Hours of Exercise and Weight Change Among Eight Adult Males

EXERCISE	WEIGHT CHANGE	$(X - \bar{X})$	$(Y - \bar{Y})$	$(X - \bar{X})(Y - \bar{Y})$	$(X - \bar{X})^2$	$(Y - \bar{Y})^2$
27	−7	−13	0	0	169	0
52	−18	12	−11	−132	144	121
39	18	−1	25	−25	1	625
58	−25	18	−18	−324	324	324
21	41	−19	48	−912	361	2,304
54	−29	14	−22	−308	196	484
20	3	−20	10	−200	400	100
49	−39	9	−32	−288	81	1,024
320	−56			−2,189	1,676	4,982

$$\bar{X} = \sum X/n = 320/8 = 40$$

$$\bar{Y} = \sum Y/n = 56/8 = -7$$

$$SP = \sum(X - \bar{X})(Y - \bar{Y}) = -2189$$

$$SS_X = \sum(X - \bar{X})^2 = 1676$$

$$SS_Y = \sum(Y - \bar{Y})^2 = 4982$$

$$r = \frac{SP}{\sqrt{SS_X SS_Y}} = \frac{-2189}{\sqrt{(1676)(4982)}} = -.758$$

Step 4: Make the correct conclusion.

The calculated $r = -.758$ is within the rejection zone, so we reject H_0. The evidence is strong enough to support the claim that there is a significant relationship between hours of exercise and weight change.

12. The crash safety is expressed by rankings; therefore, the weight of the car also needs to be expressed as rankings as shown in Table 11.12a. Spearman's rank correlation is appropriate to calculate the relationship between rankings.

The four-step hypothesis test is applicable for Spearman's rank correlation.

Step 1: State the pair of hypotheses.

The problem statement asks you to test the relationship between crash safety rankings and weight rankings. Therefore, a two-tailed test is appropriate.

Two-tailed test: $H_0: \rho_S = 0$

$H_1: \rho_S \neq 0$

Step 2: Identify the rejection zone.

When $n = 7$, a two-tailed test, $\alpha = .05$, the critical value of Spearman's rank correlation is .786. The rejection zone for a two-tailed test is $|r_S| > .786$.

Step 3: Calculate the test statistic.

$$r_S = 1 - \frac{6\Sigma d^2}{n(n^2 - 1)} = 1 - \frac{6(22)}{7(49 - 1)} = .607$$

TABLE 11.12a Crash Safety Rankings and Weight Rankings

CAR	CRASH SAFETY RANKING	WEIGHT (POUNDS)	WEIGHT RANKING	D	D²
A	1	3,676	1	0	0
B	2	3,399	3	−1	1
C	3	3,386	4	−1	1
D	4	2,438	7	−3	9
E	5	3,588	2	3	9
F	6	3,139	5	1	1
G	7	2,618	6	1	1
					22

Step 4: Make the correct conclusion.

The calculated $r_S = .607$ is not in the rejection zone, so we fail to reject H_0. Therefore, the evidence is not strong enough to support the claim that there is a relationship between crash safety and weight of the car.

CHAPTER 12

1. a   5. b

2. b   6. b

3. a   7. d

4. a   8. b

Free Response Questions

9.a. The scatterplot of car weight and fuel efficiency is shown in Figure 12.12. There is a linear relationship between car weight and fuel efficiency according to Figure 12.12.

9.b. We need to figure out the $\bar{X}$ and $\bar{Y}$ and then add the following five columns to Table 12.11a, $(X - \bar{X})$, $(Y - \bar{Y})$, $(X - \bar{X})(Y - \bar{Y})$, $(X - \bar{X})^2$, and $(Y - \bar{Y})^2$, to demonstrate the step-by-step calculation to identify the regression line.

FIGURE 12.12 Scatterplot of Car Weight and Fuel Efficiency

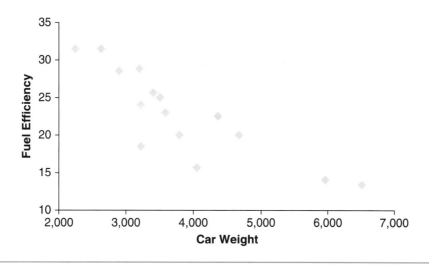

TABLE 12.11a Car Weight and Fuel Efficiency

WEIGHT (POUNDS)	FUEL EFFICIENCY (MPG)	$(X - \bar{X})$	$(Y - \bar{Y})$	$(X - \bar{X})(Y - \bar{Y})$	$(X - \bar{X})^2$	$(Y - \bar{Y})^2$
3,190	28.8	−614.6	6	−3,687.60	377,733.16	36
3,572	23	−232.6	0.2	−46.52	54,102.76	0.04
2,888	28.5	−916.6	5.7	−5,224.62	840,155.56	32.49
3,777	20	−27.6	−2.8	77.28	761.76	7.84
3,208	18.5	−596.6	−4.3	2,565.38	355,931.56	18.49
3,393	25.6	−411.6	2.8	−1,152.48	169,414.56	7.84
4,653	20	848.4	−2.8	−2,375.52	719,782.56	7.84
3,495	25	−309.6	2.2	−681.12	95,852.16	4.84
3,208	24	−596.6	1.2	−715.92	355,931.56	1.44
4,345	22.5	540.4	−0.3	−162.12	292,032.16	0.09
2,616	31.5	−1,188.6	8.7	−10,340.82	1,412,769.96	75.69
5,950	14	2,145.4	−8.8	−18,879.52	4,602,741.16	77.44
2,235	31.5	−1,569.6	8.7	−13,655.52	2,463,644.16	75.69
4,039	15.7	234.4	−7.1	−1,664.24	54,943.36	50.41
6,500	13.4	2,695.4	−9.4	−25,336.76	7,265,181.16	88.36
57,069	**342**			**−81,280.10**	**19,060,977.60**	**484.50**

$$\bar{X} = \Sigma X / n = 57069 / 15 = 3804.6$$

$$\bar{Y} = \Sigma Y / n = 342 / 15 = 22.80$$

$$SP = \Sigma(X - \bar{X})(Y - \bar{Y}) = -81280.10$$

$$SS_X = \Sigma(X - \bar{X})^2 = 19060977.60$$

$$b = \frac{SP}{SS_X} = \frac{-81280.1}{19060977.60} = -0.00426$$

$$a = \bar{Y} - b\bar{X}$$

$$a = 22.80 - (-0.00426)(3,804.6) = 39.01$$

The regression line for using car weight to predict fuel efficiency is $\hat{Y} = 39.01 - 0.00426X$. For each additional pound the car weighs, the fuel efficiency decreases by 0.00426 mpg.

9.c. The predicted fuel efficiency for a car that weighs 4,500 pounds is $\hat{Y} = 39.01 - 0.00426(4500) = 19.84$ mpg.

9.d. Here is the four-step hypothesis test for a simple regression.

Step 1. State the pair of hypotheses.

$$H_0: \beta = 0$$

$$H_1: \beta \neq 0$$

Step 2. Identify the rejection zone.

The critical value of F in the F Table under $\alpha = .05$ is $F_{(1,13)} = 4.67$. The rejection zone is $F > 4.67$.

Step 3. Calculate the test statistic.

Conducting a hypothesis test on a simple regression requires r^2 and SS_Y.

$$r = \frac{SP}{\sqrt{SS_X SS_Y}} = \frac{-81280.10}{\sqrt{(19060977.68)(484.5)}} = -.846$$

$$r^2 = (-.846)^2 = .715$$

$$SS_Y = 484.5$$

$$\text{SSR} = r^2 SS_Y = .715(484.5) = 346.42$$

$$\text{SSE} = (1 - r^2)SS_Y = (1 - .715)(484.5) = 138.08$$

Put all the numbers into the summary hypothesis test table for car weight and fuel efficiency as shown in Table 12.11b.

TABLE 12.11b ANOVA Summary Table for the Simple Regression Between the Car Weight and Fuel Efficiency

SOURCE	SS	df	MS	F
Regression	346.42	1	346.42	32.620
Error	138.08	13	10.62	
Total	**484.5**	**14**		

Step 4. Draw the correct conclusion.

The calculated F is 32.620, which is within the rejection zone, so we reject H_0. Car weights help predict fuel efficiency.

10.a. The scatterplot of number of customers' complaints and sales transactions is shown in Figure 12.13. There is a linear relationship between these two variables according to Figure 12.13.

FIGURE 12.13 Scatterplot of Number of Customers' Complaints and Sales Transactions

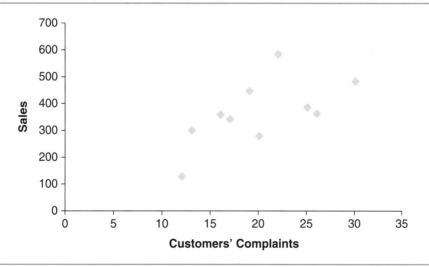

10.b. We need to figure out the $\bar{X}$ and $\bar{Y}$ and then add the following five columns to Table 12.12a, $(X - \bar{X})$, $(Y - \bar{Y})$, $(X - \bar{X})(Y - \bar{Y})$, $(X - \bar{X})^2$, and $(Y - \bar{Y})^2$, to demonstrate the step-by-step calculation to identify the regression line.

$$\bar{X} = \sum X/n = 200/10 = 20$$

$$\bar{Y} = \sum Y/n = 3650/10 = 365$$

$$SP = \sum(X - \bar{X})(Y - \bar{Y}) = 4088$$

$$SS_X = \sum(X - \bar{X})^2 = 304$$

$$b = \frac{SP}{SS_X} = \frac{4,088}{304} = 13.45$$

$$a = \bar{Y} - b\bar{X}$$

$$a = 365 - (13.45)(20) = 96$$

TABLE 12.12a Number of Customers' Complaints and Number of Sales Transactions

CUSTOMERS' COMPLAINTS	SALES TRANSACTIONS	$(X - \bar{X})$	$(Y - \bar{Y})$	$(X - \bar{X})(Y - \bar{Y})$	$(X - \bar{X})^2$	$(Y - \bar{Y})^2$
12	126	−8	−239	1,912	64	57,121
13	298	−7	−67	469	49	4,489
19	444	−1	79	−79	1	6,241
20	277	0	−88	0	0	7,744
16	356	−4	−9	36	16	81
17	340	−3	−25	75	9	625
26	361	6	−4	−24	36	16
30	482	10	117	1,170	100	13,689
25	384	5	19	95	25	361
22	582	2	217	434	4	47,089
200	3,650			4,088	304	137,456

The regression line obtained when using the number of customers' complaints to predict number of sales transactions is $\hat{Y} = 96 + 13.45X$. For each additional complaint from a customer, the number of sales transactions increases by 13.45. This result suggests that the higher the number of customers' complaints, the higher the number of sales transactions made by the salesperson.

10.c. Here is the four-step hypothesis test for a simple regression.

Step 1. State the pair of hypotheses.

$$H_0: \beta = 0$$
$$H_1: \beta \neq 0$$

Step 2. Identify the rejection zone.

The critical value of F in the F Table under $\alpha = .05$ is $F_{(1,8)} = 5.32$. The rejection zone is $F > 5.32$.

Step 3. Calculate the statistic.

Conducting a hypothesis test on a simple regression requires r^2 and SS_Y.

$$r = \frac{SP}{\sqrt{SS_X SS_Y}} = \frac{4088}{\sqrt{(304)(137456)}} = .632$$

$$r^2 = (.632)^2 = .399$$

$$SS_Y = 137,456$$

$$SSR = r^2 SS_Y = .399(137,456) = 54,844.944$$

$$SSE = (1 - r^2)SS_Y = (1 - .399)(137,456) = 82,611.056$$

Put all the numbers into the summary hypothesis test table for customers' complaints and sales transactions as shown in Table 12.12b.

TABLE 12.12b   ANOVA Summary Table for the Simple Regression Between the Number of Customers' Complaints and Sales Transactions

SOURCE	SS	df	MS	F
Regression	54,844.944	1	54,844.944	5.31
Error	82,611.056	8	10,326.382	
Total	137,456	9		

Step 4. Draw the correct conclusion.

The calculated $F = 5.31$ is not within the rejection zone, so we fail to reject H_0. The evidence is not enough to support the claim that number of customers' complaints predict the number of sales transactions.

CHAPTER 13

1. c

2. b

3. c

4. b

5. c

6. d

7. b

8. c

9. c

10. a

Free Response Questions

11.a. The four-step hypothesis test for an ANOVA:

Step 1. State the pair of hypotheses.

$$H_0: \mu_1 = \mu_2 = \mu_3 = \cdots = \mu_k$$
$$H_1: \text{Not all } \mu_k \text{ are equal.}$$

Step 2. Identify the rejection zone.

There are three groups, $k = 3$, five SUVs in each group, $n_1 = n_2 = n_3 = 5$, and the sample size, $n = 15$. The critical value of F is identified by $F_{(2,12)} = 3.89$ in the F Table for ANOVA. The rejection zone is identified as the calculated $F > 3.89$.

Step 3. Calculate the F test.

Under equal group size, the sample mean is

$$\bar{\bar{X}} = (6.2 + 7.2 + 7.6) / 3 = 7$$

$$\text{SSB} = \sum n_j (\bar{X}_j - \bar{\bar{X}})^2 = 5(6.2 - 7)^2 + 5(7.2 - 7)^2 + 5(7.6 - 7)^2 = 5.2$$

$$\text{SSW} = \text{SST} - \text{SSB} = 16 - 5.2 = 10.8$$

Now we have all the numbers to complete the ANOVA summary table as shown in Table 13.21.

TABLE 13.21 The ANOVA Summary Table for the Crash Safety Ratings in Three Types of SUVs

SOURCE	SS	df	MS	F
Between groups	5.2	$df_B = 2$	MSB = 2.6	F = 2.889
Within groups	10.8	$df_W = 12$	MSW = 0.9	
Total	16	$df_T = 14$		

Step 4. Make the correct conclusion.

The calculated $F = 2.889$ is not within the rejection zone, so we fail to reject H_0. The evidence is not strong enough to claim that there are significant differences in crash safety ratings among the three different types of SUVs. No further analysis is needed.

11.b.

$$\text{The effect size for the ANOVA is } \eta^2 = \frac{\text{SSB}}{\text{SST}} = \frac{5.2}{16} = .325$$

There are 32.5% of the variance of the crash safety ratings that can be explained by the different types of SUVs.

12. The four-step hypothesis test for an ANOVA is as follows:

Step 1. State the pair of hypotheses.

$$H_0: \mu_1 = \mu_2 = \mu_3 = \cdots = \mu_k$$
$$H_1: \text{Not all } \mu_k \text{ are equal.}$$

Step 2. Identify the rejection zone.

There are three groups, $k = 3$, 10 people in each group, $n_1 = n_2 = n_3 = 10$, and the sample size, $n = 30$. The critical value of F is identified by $F_{(2,27)} = 3.35$ in the F Table for ANOVA. The rejection zone is identified as the calculated $F > 3.35$.

Step 3. Calculate the F test.

Under equal group size, the sample mean is

$$\bar{\bar{X}} = (19 + 16.6 + 18.4) / 3 = 18$$

$$\text{SSB} = \Sigma n_j (\bar{X}_j - \bar{\bar{X}})^2 = 10(19 - 18)^2 + 10(16.6 - 18)^2 + 10(18.4 - 18)^2 = 31.2$$

$$\text{SSW} = \text{SST} - \text{SSB} = 110 - 31.2 = 78.8$$

Now we have all the numbers to complete the ANOVA summary table as shown in Table 13.22.

TABLE 13.22 The ANOVA Summary Table for the Speed Test Scores in Three Groups

SOURCE	SS	df	MS	F
Between groups	31.2	$df_B = 2$	$MSB = 15.6$	$F = 5.345$
Within groups	78.8	$df_W = 27$	$MSW = 2.919$	
Total	110	$df_T = 29$		

Step 4. Make the correct conclusion.

The calculated $F = 5.345$ is within the rejection zone, so we reject H_0. The evidence is strong enough to claim that there are significant differences in speed test scores among three different noise conditions. Further analysis is needed to identify exactly where the differences come from.

Tukey's HSD is used to identify the source of the significant differences. To conduct a Tukey's HSD test, we need to identify the critical q value from the q table. If a particular df is not shown in the table, you should find the closest df. The q value is identified by three numbers: (1) α level, (2) k, and (3) $(n - k)$. They are .05, 3, and 27 in this example. However, the table only lists $(n - k)$ from 1 to 20 and then jumps to 24, 30, 40, and so on. Both 24 and 30 have equal distance to 27. In this case, you need to use the one that gives you the higher critical value. The critical value for the three groups with $df = 24$ is 3.53, and the critical value for groups with $df = 30$ is 3.49. Therefore, the critical value is 3.53.

$$HSD = q\sqrt{\frac{MSW}{n}}$$

$$HSD = 3.53\sqrt{\frac{2.919}{10}} = 1.907$$

The mean difference between Group 1 and Group 2 is $\bar{X}_2 - \bar{X}_1 = 19 - 16.6 = 2.4$.

The difference is larger than HSD, so it is significant.

The mean difference between Group 1 and Group 3 is $\bar{X}_3 - \bar{X}_1 = 19 - 18.4 = 0.6$.

The difference is smaller than HSD, so it is not significant.

The mean difference between Group 2 and Group 3 is $\bar{X}_3 - \bar{X}_2 = 18.4 - 16.6 = 1.8$.

The difference is smaller than HSD, so it is not significant.

The significant difference comes from the group with constant noise and the group with unpredictable noise. Those in the group with constant noise score higher than those in the group with unpredictable noise. The differences in the two other pairs—constant noise versus no noise and no noise versus unpredictable noise—are not significant.

13. The four-step hypothesis test for an ANOVA is as follows:

Step 1. State the pair of hypotheses.

$$H_0: \mu_1 = \mu_2 = \mu_3 = \cdots = \mu_k$$

$H_1:$ Not all μ_k are equal.

Step 2. Identify the rejection zone.

There are three groups, $k = 3$, a different group size in each group, $n_1 = 5$, $n_2 = 6$, and $n_3 = 7$, and the sample size $n = 18$. The critical value of F is identified by $F_{(2,15)} = 3.69$ in the F Table for ANOVA. The rejection zone is identified as the calculated $F > 3.69$.

Step 3. Calculate the F test.

Under unequal group size, the weighted sample mean is

$$\bar{\bar{X}} = \left(5(62.8) + 6\ (63.5) + 7(64)\right) / 18 = 63.5$$

$$\text{SSB} = \sum n_j (\bar{X}_j - \bar{\bar{X}})^2 = 5(62.8 - 63.5)^2 + 6(63.5 - 63.5)^2 + 7(64 - 63.5)^2 = 4.20$$

$$\text{SSW} = \text{SST} - \text{SSB} = 58.5 - 4.20 = 54.30$$

Now we have all the numbers to complete the ANOVA summary table as shown in Table 13.23.

Step 4. Make a correct conclusion.

The calculated $F = 0.580$ is not within the rejection zone, so we fail to reject H_0. The evidence is not strong enough to claim that there are significant differences in tuition, room, and board in private universities with different sizes. No further analysis is needed.

TABLE 13.23 The ANOVA Summary Table for the Tuition, Room, and Board in Three Different Sizes of Private Universities

SOURCE	SS	df	MS	F
Between groups	4.20	$df_B = 2$	$\text{MSB} = 2.10$	$F = 0.580$
Within groups	54.30	$df_W = 15$	$\text{MSW} = 3.62$	
Total	58.5	$df_T = 17$		

CHAPTER 14

1. a

5. d

2. b

6. a

3. c

7. a

4. b

Free Response Questions

8.

Step 1. State the pair of hypotheses.

H_0: Statistics grades and student's sex are independent.

H_1: Statistics grades and student's sex are not independent.

Step 2. Identify the rejection zone.

When $\alpha = .05$, with $df = (r - 1)(c - 1) = 4$, the rejection zone for the chi-square test is $\chi^2 > 9.488$.

Step 3. Calculate the test statistic.

The expected frequency is

$$E = \frac{\text{Row total} \times \text{Column total}}{n}$$

The expected frequency table is reported in Table 14.19.

$$\chi^2 = \frac{(O-E)^2}{E} = \frac{(25-24.55)^2}{24.55} + \frac{(37-40.33)^2}{40.33} + \frac{(44-48.22)^2}{48.22} + \frac{(15-9.64)^2}{9.64} + \frac{(7-5.26)^2}{5.26} +$$
$$\frac{(31-31.45)^2}{31.45} + \frac{(55-51.67)^2}{51.67} + \frac{(66-61.78)^2}{61.78} + \frac{(7-12.36)^2}{12.36} + \frac{(5-6.74)^2}{6.74} = 7.491$$

TABLE 14.19 Expected Frequency for Statistics Grades and Student's Sex

	A	B	C	D	F
MALE	24.55	40.33	48.22	9.64	5.26
FEMALE	31.45	51.67	61.78	12.36	6.74

Step 4. Draw the correct conclusion.

The calculated $\chi^2 = 7.491$ is not within the rejection zone. Therefore, we fail to reject H_0. The evidence is not strong enough to support the claim that statistics grades and student's sex are not independent. Male and female students have similar grades.

9. It is important to correctly translate the problem statement into a two-way contingency table with mutually exclusive categories, as shown in Table 14.20. The problem stated that 3,215 white employees were hired over the past 6 months and 966 out of them were promoted. This means that the rest of the white employees were not promoted. A simple subtraction shows that the number of white employees who were not promoted is 2,249. Applying the same logic, you get the number of black employees who were not promoted as 214, the number of Hispanic employees who were not promoted as 236, and the number of employees whose racial background was classified as other and who were not promoted as 34.

TABLE 14.20   Observed Frequency for Promotion Decision and Race

	PROMOTED	NOT PROMOTED	ROW TOTAL
WHITE	966	2,249	3,215
BLACK	74	214	288
HISPANIC	81	236	317
OTHER	5	34	39
COLUMN TOTAL	1,126	2,733	3,859

Once the observed frequency table is set, the four-step hypothesis-testing procedure can be carried out.

Step 1. State the pair of hypotheses.

> H_0: Promotion and employee's race are independent.
>
> H_1: Promotion and employee's race are not independent.

Step 2. Identify the rejection zone.

When $\alpha = .05$, with $df = (r - 1)(c - 1) = 3$, the rejection zone for the chi-square test is $\chi^2 > 7.815$.

Step 3. Calculate the test statistic.

The expected frequency is

$$E = \frac{\text{Row total} \times \text{Column total}}{n}$$

The expected frequency table is reported in Table 14. 21.

TABLE 14.21   Expected Frequency for Promotion Decisions and Race

	PROMOTED	NOT PROMOTED
WHITE	938.09	2,276.91
BLACK	84.03	203.97
HISPANIC	92.50	224.50
OTHER	11.38	27.62

$$\chi^2 = \sum \frac{(O-E)^2}{E} = \frac{(966-938.09)^2}{938.09} + \frac{(2249-2276.91)^2}{2276.91} + \frac{(74-84.03)^2}{84.03} + \frac{(214-203.97)^2}{203.97} +$$

$$\frac{(81-92.50)^2}{92.50} + \frac{(236-224.50)^2}{224.50} + \frac{(5-11.38)^2}{11.38} + \frac{(34-27.62)^2}{27.62} = 9.932$$

Step 4. Draw the correct conclusion.

The calculated $\chi^2 = 9.932$ is within the rejection zone. Therefore, we reject H_0. The evidence is strong enough to suggest that promotion decisions and employee's race are not independent. It is highly unlikely that we would obtain these observed frequencies in Table 14.20 if the promotion decisions were made without considering employees' race.

10.

Step 1. State the pair of hypotheses.

H_0: Type A personality and heart problems are independent.

H_1: Type A personality and heart problems are not independent.

Step 2. Identify the rejection zone.

When $\alpha = .05$, with $df = (r - 1)(c - 1) = 1$, the rejection zone for the chi-square test is $\chi^2 > 3.841$.

Step 3. Calculate the test statistic.

The expected frequency is

$$E = \frac{\text{Row total} \times \text{Column total}}{n}$$

The expected frequency table is reported in Table 14.22.

TABLE 14.22   Expected Frequency for Type A Personality and Heart Problems

	HEART PROBLEMS	NO HEART PROBLEMS
TYPE A PERSONALITY	18.8	61.2
NOT TYPE A PERSONALITY	28.2	91.8

$$\chi^2 = \sum \frac{(O - E)^2}{n} = \frac{(25 - 18.8)^2}{18.8} + \frac{(55 - 61.2)^2}{61.2} + \frac{(22 - 28.2)^2}{28.2} + \frac{(98 - 91.8)^2}{91.8} = 4.455$$

Step 4. Draw the correct conclusion.

The calculated $\chi^2 = 4.455$ is within the rejection zone. Therefore, we reject H_0. The evidence is strong enough to suggest that Type A personality and heart problems are not independent. Type A personality is related to heart problems. People with Type A personality have a higher number of heart problems than expected, so they need to take precautions to eat right, exercise regularly, and learn stress reduction strategies in order to maintain a heart-healthy lifestyle.

Glossary

Absolute zero: Absolute zero means a complete absence of the attribute that you are measuring. It is not an arbitrarily assigned number.

Addition Rule 1 of probability: When Event A and Event B are mutually exclusive, the probability of either Event A or Event B happening is the sum of the probabilities of each event: $P(A \text{ or } B) = P(A) + P(B)$.

Addition Rule 2 of probability: When Event A and Event B are not mutually exclusive, the probability of either Event A or Event B, or both, happening is the sum of the probabilities of each event minus the overlapping part of the two events: $P(A \text{ or } B) = P(A \cup B) = P(A) + P(B) - P(A \cap B)$.

Adjusted R^2: The adjusted R^2 is only relevant in multiple regression. It adjusts the R^2 by taking the number of predictors in the model into consideration.

Alternative hypothesis, H_1: The hypothesis that researchers turn to when the null hypothesis is rejected. The alternative hypothesis is also called the research hypothesis.

Analysis of variance (ANOVA): ANOVA is a statistical method to test the equality of group means by partitioning variances into different sources.

Bar graph: A bar graph uses bars of equal width to show frequency or relative frequency of discrete categorical data (i.e., nominal or ordinal data). Adjacent bars are not touching each other.

Between-group variance: The between-group variance is calculated as the SSB divided by the df_B; in a special ANOVA term, the between-group variance is also called the mean squares between groups $MSB = SSB / df_B$.

Between-subject design: The between-subject design refers to research in which participants are assigned to different groups based on different levels of the independent variables. Every participant is assigned to only one group.

Between-subject factor: In an ANOVA, the independent variable of a research study with a between-subject design is referred to as the between-subject factor.

Binomial probability distribution: A binomial probability distribution is a probability distribution that applies to variables with only two possible outcomes (i.e., success vs. failure) in each trial. The trials are independent of one another. The probability of a success and the probability of a failure remain the same in all trials.

Bonferroni adjustment: The Bonferroni adjustment simply adjusts the α level of the individual pairwise comparison to a new level in order to control the familywise error rate.

Boxplot: A boxplot is a graphic tool that presents five quantitative attributes of a sample: (1) the minimum, (2) Q_1, (3) Q_2, (4) Q_3, and (5) the maximum.

Central limit theorem: The central limit theorem states that when the same random sampling procedure is repeated to produce many sample means, the sample means form a normal distribution with a mean of μ and a standard deviation of $\sigma_{\bar{X}} = \sigma / \sqrt{n}$ as long as the samples are selected from a normally distributed population or the sample size $n > 30$.

Central tendency: Central tendency is defined as utilizing a single value to represent the center of a distribution. There are three commonly used measures for central tendency: (1) mean, (2) median, and (3) mode.

Chi-square goodness-of-fit tests: Chi-square goodness-of-fit tests refer to using one categorical variable to investigate whether the sample distribution of the values in this variable fits with a particular theoretical distribution.

Chi-square tests: Chi-square tests investigate the differences between the observed frequencies and the expected frequencies. When the calculated chi-square values are larger than the critical values in the Chi-square Table, the results are statistically significant.

Chi-square tests for independence: Chi-square tests for independence are statistics applied to investigate the relationship between two nominal or ordinal variables.

Cluster sampling: Cluster sampling works best when "natural" grouping (clustering) occurs in the population. Random sampling is conducted to select which clusters are included in the sample. Once a cluster is selected in the sample, all individuals in the cluster are included in the sample.

Coefficient of determination: The coefficient of determination is defined as r^2, which is the percentage of variance overlap between X and Y or the percentage of variance in Y that is explained by X.

Cohen's d: Cohen's d is the formula to calculate effect sizes for independent-samples t tests when equal variances are assumed.

Confidence interval: A confidence interval is defined as an interval of values calculated from sample statistics to estimate the value of a population parameter.

Confidence level: Confidence level is expressed as $(1 - \alpha)$, which is the complement to α, the significance level.

Confounding variable: A confounding variable is an extraneous variable in a study that correlates with both the independent variable and the dependent variable.

Contingency table: A contingency table refers to a two-way frequency table where frequency counts are based on two nominal or ordinal variables at the same time.

Continuous variables: Continuous variables are values that do not have separation from one integer to the next. Continuous variables usually are expressed with decimals or fractions.

Convenience sample: A convenience sample is one in which researchers use anyone who is willing to participate in the study. A convenience sample is created based on easy accessibility.

Counterbalance: Counterbalance is a cautionary step in conducting repeated measures of the same sample to make sure that the order of presentation of conditions is balanced out.

Cumulative relative frequency: Cumulative relative frequency is defined as the accumulation of the relative frequency for a particular value and all the relative frequencies of lower values.

Data: Data are defined as factual information used as a basis for reasoning, discussion, or calculation, so that meaningful conclusions can be drawn.

Degrees of freedom: The degrees of freedom in a statistical procedure are defined as the number of values involved in the calculation that can vary freely in the sample.

Degrees of freedom due to error: The degrees of freedom due to error in a simple regression are defined as $(n - 2)$.

Degrees of freedom due to regression: The degrees of freedom due to regression are the number of predictors in the regression equation. In simple regression, the degree of freedom due to regression is 1.

Dependent samples: Dependent samples usually refer to the same group of research participants who go through different conditions of a study, such as before and after a treatment. Sometimes, dependent samples apply to samples with an explicit one-on-one pairing relationship.

Dependent-sample *t* tests: Dependent-sample *t* tests are used to test the differences between two variables from the same sample before and after a treatment or the difference between two variables from two samples with an explicit one-on-one paired relationship.

Dependent variable: A dependent variable is the variable that is the focus of researchers' interests and is affected by the different levels of an independent variable.

Descriptive statistics: Descriptive statistics are statistical procedures used to describe, summarize, organize, and simplify relevant characteristics of sample data.

Discrete variables: Discrete variables are values that have clear separation from one integer to the next. The answers for discrete variables can only be integers (i.e., whole numbers).

Disjoint events: Disjoint events are the same things as mutually exclusive events.

Distribution: Distribution is the arrangement of values of a variable as it occurs in a sample or a population.

Effect size: The effect size is a standardized measure of the difference between the sample statistic and the hypothesized population parameter in units of standard deviation.

Empirical rule: The empirical rule describes the following attributes for variables with a normal distribution: About 68% of the values fall within 1 standard deviation of the mean, about 95% of the values fall within 2 standard deviations of the mean, and about 99.7% of the values fall within 3 standard deviations of the mean.

Equal intervals: Equal intervals are created in a frequency table by including the same number of values in each interval.

Error: Error in regression is the difference between the actual Y and the predicted $\hat{Y}$, Error $= (Y - \hat{Y})$.

Event: An event is defined as a set of outcomes from an experiment or a procedure.

Expected frequency: Expected frequency is the theoretically predicted frequency that assumes that the variable is distributed exactly as stated in the null hypothesis.

Experimental research: Experimental research is usually conducted in a tightly controlled environment (i.e., research laboratories). The three important features in experimental research are (1) control, (2) manipulation, and (3) random assignment.

Extraneous variable: The extraneous variables are variables that are not included in the study but might have an impact on the relationship between variables included in the study.

Familywise error rate (FWER): The FWER refers to the probability of making Type I error in a set of similar multiple comparisons.

Folded F test: The folded F test means that in calculating the F test, the larger variance is designated as the numerator and the smaller variance as the denominator; the calculated F value will always be larger than 1 to avoid the left-tailed F values.

Frequency: Frequency is a simple count of a particular value or category occurring in a sample or a population.

Frequency distribution table: A frequency distribution table lists all values or categories arranged in an orderly fashion in a table, along with a tally count for each value or category in a data set.

Glass's delta (Δ): Glass's Δ is the formula to calculate effect sizes for independent-samples t tests when equal variances are not assumed.

Heteroscedasticity: Heteroscedasticity refers to the condition when the variances of the errors are not the same across all values of X or across all $\hat{Y}$. This is commonly referred to as violations to the homogeneity of variances.

Histogram: A histogram is a graphical presentation of a continuous variable. The bars of a histogram are touching each other to illustrate that the values are continuous.

Homoscedasticity: Homoscedasticity is the condition under which the variance in Y for any given value of X is the same across all possible values of X. In other words, there is equal spread of Y for every value of X.

Honestly significant difference (HSD): The HSD is a post hoc method to calculate a critical value for group mean differences while keeping the familywise risk of committing a Type I error under control.

Hypothesis testing: Hypothesis testing is the standardized process to test the strength of scientific evidence for a claim about a population.

Independent events: Two events A and B are independent when the occurrence of one event does not affect the probability of the occurrence of the other event.

Independent samples: Independent samples are samples selected from different populations where the values from one population are not related or linked to the values from the other population. Independent samples contain different individuals in each sample.

Independent variable: An independent variable is the variable that is deliberately manipulated by the researchers in a study.

Inferential statistics: Inferential statistics are statistical procedures that use sample statistics to generalize to or make inferences about a population.

Interval estimate: An interval estimate refers to a range of values calculated from sample statistics to estimate a hypothesized population parameter.

Interval scale: An interval scale not only arranges observations according to their magnitudes but also distinguishes the ordered arrangement in equal units.

Law of large numbers: The law of large numbers is a probability theorem describing the relationship between sample means and population means. When the number of trials approaches infinity, the observed sample mean approaches the population mean $E(X) = \mu = np$.

Least significant difference (LSD): The LSD is the first post hoc method developed to calculate the difference between any two group means using the equivalent of multiple t tests, but without controlling the familywise error rate.

Likert scales: Likert scales are often used to measure people's opinions, attitudes, or preferences. Likert scales measure attributes along a continuum of choices such as 1 = *strongly disagree*, 2 = *somewhat disagree*, 3 = *neutral*, 4 = *somewhat agree*, or 5 = *strongly agree* with each individual statement.

Line graph: A line graph is a graphical display of quantitative information with a line or curve that connects a series of adjacent data points.

Mean: The mean is defined as the arithmetic average of all values in a data distribution.

Mean squared deviation: The mean squared deviation is another term for the variance.

Measures of variability: There are three commonly used measures for variability: (1) range, (2) variance, and (3) standard deviation.

Median: The median is defined as the value in the middle position of a sorted variable arranged from the lowest value to the highest value.

Mode: The mode is defined as the value or category with the highest frequency in a data distribution.

Multiplication rule for independent events: When Event A and Event B are independent, the probability of both events happening is $P(AB) = P(A) \times P(B)$.

Mutually exclusive and collectively exhaustive: Mutually exclusive and collectively exhaustive means that events have no overlap—if one is true, the others cannot be true—and they cover all possible outcomes.

Mutually exclusive events: When Event A and Event B are mutually exclusive, it means that only one of the events can happen: If one happens, the other does not.

Negatively skewed distribution: When the data points mostly concentrate on the high-end values with a long tail to the low-end values, the distribution is negatively skewed.

Nominal scale: In a nominal scale, measurements are used as identifiers, such as your student identification number, phone number, or social security number.

Nonexperimental research: Nonexperimental research is conducted to observe and study research participants in their natural settings without deliberately controlling the environment or manipulating their behaviors or preferences.

Nonparametric statistics: Nonparametric statistics are statistical procedures that make no assumptions about the shape of the population distribution. They are also called distribution-free statistics.

Normal distribution: A normal distribution curve peaks at the mean of the values, and then symmetrically tapers off on both sides with 50% of the data points above the mean and 50% of the data points below the mean. Draw a line straight through the mean, and the left side and the right side are mirror images of each other.

Null hypothesis, H_0: The null hypothesis states that the effect that the researchers are trying to establish does not exist.

Observed frequency: Observed frequency is the frequency count of a particular value of a variable that we observe in a sample.

One-sample t test: A one-sample t test is designed to conduct a test between a sample mean and a hypothesized population mean when σ is unknown,

$$t = \frac{\bar{X} - \mu}{s_{\bar{X}}} = \frac{\bar{X} - \mu}{\frac{s}{\sqrt{n}}}, \text{ with } df = n - 1.$$

One-tailed test (directional test): A one-tailed test is a directional hypothesis test, which is usually conducted when the research topic suggests a consistent directional relationship with either theoretical reasoning or repeated empirical evidence.

One-way ANOVA: One-way ANOVA is an ANOVA that uses only one factor to classify sample data into different groups.

Ordinal scale: In an ordinal scale, measurements not only are used as identifiers but also carry orders in a particular sequence.

Ordinary least squares (OLS): OLS depicts the best fitting line by a straight line that goes through $(\bar{X}, \bar{Y})$ and minimizes the vertical distances between the actual Y values and the predicted $\hat{Y}$.

Outliers: Outliers refer to extreme values in a distribution. These are usually far away from the rest of the data points.

p value associated with a test statistic: The p value associated with a test statistic is defined as the probability of obtaining the magnitude of the calculated test statistic assuming that H_0 is true.

Parameter: Parameters are defined as numerical characteristics of a population.

Parametric statistics: Parametric statistics are statistical procedures that make assumptions about the shape of the population distribution and also about certain population parameters such as μ, σ, and σ^2.

Partial correlation: A partial correlation is the purified correlation between two variables while controlling a third variable by holding it constant.

Pearson's correlation, r: Pearson's r is a statistical procedure that quantifies the extent that two variables move in the same direction or the opposite directions. It provides direction and strength of the relationship.

Pie chart: A circular graph that utilizes slices to show different categories. The size of each slice is proportional to the frequency or relative frequency of each category.

Point biserial correlation, r_{pbi}: The point biserial correlation measures the correlation between an interval or ratio variable and a naturally occurring dichotomous variable coded as 0 or 1.

Point estimate: A point estimate is to use a single value from the sample to estimate a population parameter.

Population: A population is defined as an entire collection of everything or everyone that researchers are interested in studying or measuring.

Positively skewed distribution: When the data points mostly concentrate on the low-end values with a long tail to the high-end values, the distribution is positively skewed.

Post hoc comparisons: Post hoc comparisons are used after a significant ANOVA F test to identify exactly where the significant difference comes from.

Power: Power is defined as the sensitivity to detect an effect when an effect actually exists. Power is positively correlated with all of the three factors: (1) sample size, (2) significance level, and (3) the standardized effect size.

Probability density function: A probability density function describes the probability for a continuous, random variable to be in a given range of values.

Probability distribution: There are three requirements for a probability distribution:

Probability of Event A = $P(A)$ =

$$\frac{\text{Number of ways A can happen}}{\text{Total number of all possible outcomes}}$$

1. The variable X is a discrete, random, numerical variable. The number of possible values of X is finite. Each value is associated with a probability.

2. The probability of each value needs to be within 0 and 1, inclusive. This is expressed as $0 \leq P(X) \leq 1$.

3. The sum of the probabilities of all the values equals 1. It is expressed as $\sum P(X) = 1$.

Quasi-experimental research: Quasi-experimental research has some but not all of the features of experimental research. More specifically, if one or more of the control, manipulation, and random assignment features are not feasible but others remain intact, the research becomes quasi-experimental.

Random sample: A random sample is an ideal way to select participants for scientific research. A random sample occurs when every member in the population has an equal chance of being selected.

Range: The range is defined as the maximum minus the minimum in a variable.

Ratio scale: A ratio scale contains every characteristic that lower-level scales of measurement have, such as identifiers, ranking order, equal units, and something extra: an absolute zero.

Real limits: Real limits cover a range of possible values that may be reflected by a single continuous measure. The lower limit is the value minus ½ of the unit and the upper limit is the value plus ½ of the unit.

Regression equation: The regression equation is the equation for the regression line, which is expressed as $\hat{Y} = a + bX$, where a is labeled as the Y-intercept and b is labeled as the slope.

Rejection zone: The rejection zone is bounded by the critical value of a statistic. When the calculated value falls in the rejection zone, the correct decision is to reject H_0.

Relative frequency: Relative frequency is defined as the frequency of a particular value or category divided by the total frequency (or sample size). Relative frequency is also called proportion.

Sample: A sample is defined as a subset of the population from which measures are actually obtained.

Sample space: A sample space is a complete list of all possible outcomes.

Sample statistics: Sample statistics are defined as numerical attributes of a sample.

Sampling distribution of the sample means: The sampling distribution of the sample means is defined as the distribution of all sample means from all samples of a particular sample size, n, randomly selected from the same population (i.e., $\bar{X}_1, \bar{X}_2, \bar{X}_3, \dots$).

Sampling error: A sampling error is defined as when a sample is randomly selected, a natural divergence, difference, distance, or error occurs between sample statistics and population parameters.

Scales of measurement: Scales of measurement illustrate different ways that variables are defined and measured. Each scale of measurement has certain mathematical properties that determine the appropriate application of statistical procedures.

Scatterplot: A scatterplot between two variables is a graph of dots plotted in a two-dimensional space. Each data point contains a pair of values on the X and Y axes.

Simple event: A simple event is defined as an elementary event that cannot be broken into simpler parts.

Simple random sample: A simple random sample is a subset of individuals (a sample) chosen from a larger set (a population). Each individual is chosen randomly and entirely by chance and each subset of k individuals has the same probability of being chosen for the sample as any other subset of k individuals.

Simple regression: The simple regression is the most commonly used linear predictive analysis when making quantitative predictions of the dependent variable, Y, based on the values of the independent variable, X.

Skewed distribution: A skewed distribution happens when data points are not symmetrical, and they concentrate more on one side of the mean than the other.

Slope: The regre ssion slope is the value change in Y when X increases by one unit.

Spearman's rank correlation, r_S: Spearman's rank correlation measures the relationship between two ordinal variables where values represent rankings.

Standard deviation: Standard deviation is a commonly used measure for variation, and it is mathematically defined as $\sigma = \sqrt{\text{variance}}$ for a population or $s = \sqrt{\text{variance}}$ for a sample.

Standard error of the estimate: The standard error of the estimate is the standard deviation of the prediction errors. It is to measure the standard distance between the regression line and the actual Y values.

Standard error of the mean: The standard error of the mean is defined as the standard deviation of all sample means. Its calculation is the standard deviation of the population divided by the square root of the sample size, $\sigma_{\bar{X}} = \sigma / \sqrt{n}$.

Statistics: Statistics is a science that deals with the collection, organization, analysis, and interpretation of numerical data.

Stratified sampling: Stratified sampling is the process of grouping members of the population into relatively homogeneous subgroups before sampling. A random sample from each stratum is independently taken in the same proportion as the stratum's size to the population. These subsets of the strata are then pooled to form a random sample.

Studentized Range Distribution: The Studentized range distribution is used to test the difference between the largest and the smallest group means measured in units of sample standard deviations when applying to three or more groups.

Sum of squared deviations (SS): SS is the acronym for sum of squared deviations, population $SS = \sum(X - \mu)^2$, and sample $SS = \sum(X - \bar{X})^2$. SS is an important step in calculating variance and standard deviation. It is also called sum of squares.

Sum of squared total deviations (SST): SST is the total sum of squared difference between individual scores, X_{ij}, and the sample mean, $\bar{\bar{X}}$. It is calculated as $SST = \sum\sum(X_{ij} - \bar{\bar{X}})^2$.

Sum of squares between groups (SSB): SSB is the sum of squares between groups and is defined by the squared differences between individual group means, $\bar{X}_j$, and the sample mean, $\bar{\bar{X}}$, multiplied by the number of participants in each group; then, add them up. It is calculated as $SSB = \sum n_j(\bar{X}_j - \bar{\bar{X}})^2$.

Sum of squares within groups (SSW): SSW is the sum of squares within groups and is defined by the squared differences between individual scores, X_{ij}, within a group relative to its corresponding group mean, $\bar{X}_j$; then, add them up. It is calculated as $SSW = \sum\sum(X_{ij} - \bar{X}_j)^2$.

Systematic sample: A systematic sample is achieved by selecting a sample from a population using a random starting point and a fixed interval. Typically, every "kth" member is selected from the total population for inclusion in the sample.

t Table: The t Distribution Table provides critical values of t that set the boundaries of rejection zones for t tests given three pieces of information: (1) one-tailed test or two-tailed test, (2) the df of the test, and (3) the α level.

Two-tailed test (nondirectional test): A two-tailed test is a nondirectional hypothesis test, which is usually done when the research topic is exploratory or there are no reasons to expect consistent directional relationships from either theoretical reasoning or previous studies.

Type I error: A Type I error is a mistake of rejecting H_0 when H_0 is true. In other words, a Type I error is to claim an effect when the effect actually does not exist. The symbol α represents the probability of making a Type I error.

Type II error: A Type II error is a mistake of failing to reject H_0 when H_0 is false. In other words, a Type II error is failing to claim an effect when the effect actually exists. The symbol β represents the probability of making a Type II error.

Uniform distribution: In a uniform distribution, every value appears with similar frequency, proportion, or probability.

Variability: Variability describes the extent to which observed values from a variable are dispersed, spread out, or scattered.

Variable: A variable refers to a measurable attribute. These measures have different values from one person to another, or the values change over time.

Variance: Variance is a commonly used measure for variability, and it is mathematically defined as the mean squared deviation, population variance, $\sigma^2 = SS / N$, and sample variance $s^2 = SS / (n-1)$.

Weighted mean: The weighted mean is defined as calculating the mean when data values are assigned different weights, w. The formula for weighted mean is $\bar{X} = \sum wX / \sum w$.

Within-subject design: The within-subject design indicates that research participants are assigned to all levels of the independent variables. Every participant experiences all levels of the independent variable and is measured repeatedly.

Within-group variance: The within-group variance is calculated as the SSW divided by the df_{W}; in a special ANOVA term, the within-group variance is also called the mean squares within groups $MSW = SSW / df_{\mathrm{W}}$.

Y-intercept: The Y-intercept is the value of Y when X equals 0.

Z scores: Z scores are standard scores that describe the differences of individual raw scores from the mean in numbers of standard deviation units.

Z test: A Z test measures the difference between a sample statistic and its known or hypothesized population parameter in units of standard error, $Z = (\bar{X} - \mu) / (\sigma/\sqrt{n})$.

References

Abdi, H., & Williams, L. J. (2010). Tukey's honestly significant difference (HSD) test. In N. J. Salkind (Ed.), *Encyclopedia of research design* (pp. 583–585). Thousand Oaks, CA: Sage.

The ACT. (2014). *ACT profile report–National: Graduating class 2014.* Retrieved from http://www.act.org/newsroom/data/2014/pdf/profile/National2014.pdf

American Psychological Association. (2010). *Publication manual of the American Psychological Association* (6th ed.). Washington, DC: Author.

Berry, W. D. (1993). *Understanding regression assumptions* (Sage University Paper Series on Quantitative Applications in the Social Sciences, 07-092). Newbury Park, CA: Sage.

Blackwell, D. L. (2010). *Family structure and children's health in the United States: Findings From the National Health Interview Survey, 2001–2007.* Hyattsville, MD: Department of Health and Human Services, Centers for Disease Control and Prevention, National Center for Health Statistics: *Vital Health Statistics 10*(246). (DHHS Publication No: [PHS] 2011-1574). Retrieved from http://www.cdc.gov/nchs/data/series/sr_10/sr10_246.pdf

Cohen, J. (1988). *Statistical power analysis for the behavioral sciences* (2nd ed.). Hillsdale, NJ: Erlbaum.

The College Board. (2014). *SAT percentile ranks.* New York, NY: Author. Retrieved from https://secure-media.collegeboard.org/digitalServices/pdf/sat/sat-percentile-ranks-crit-reading-math-writing-2014.pdf

Glass, G. V., McGaw, B., & Smith, M. L. (1981). *Meta-analysis in social research.* Beverly Hills, CA: Sage.

Hedges, L. V. (1981). Distribution theory for Glass' estimator of effect size and related estimators. *Journal of Educational Statistics, 6*(2), 107–128. doi:10.3102/10769986006002107

IkamusumeFan. (2013). *File:T distribution 5df enhanced.svg.* Retrieved from http://en.wikipedia.org/wiki/File:T_distribution_5df_enhanced.svg#filelinks

Irwin, J. O. (1968). Gosset, William Sealy—Works by Gosset: Supplementary bibliography. *International Encyclopedia of the Social Sciences.* Retrieved from http://www.encyclopedia.com/doc/1G2-3045000476.html

Jones, J. (1996). The effects of non-response on statistical inference. *Journal of Health Social Policy, 8*(1), 49–62. Retrieved from http://www.ncbi.nlm.nih.gov/pubmed/10162904

Lane, D. M. (2010). Tukey's honestly significant difference (HSD). In N. J. Salkind (Ed.), *Encyclopedia of research design* (pp. 1565–1570). Thousand Oaks, CA: Sage.

Miller, G. A. (1956). The magical number seven, plus or minus two: Some limits on our capacity for processing information. *Psychological Review, 63*, 81–97. doi:10.1037/h0043158

Office for National Statistics. (2013). *Opinions and lifestyle survey, smoking habits amongst adults, 2012.* London, England: Author. Retrieved from http://www.ons.gov.uk/ons/dcp171776_328041.pdf

Park, H. M. (2010). *Hypothesis testing and statistical power of a test.* Bloomington, IN:

University Information Technology Services, Indiana University. Retrieved from http://iu.edu/~statmath/stat/all/power/power.pdf

Rocori Middle School. (2014). *Bullying survey process and results*. Cold Spring, MN: Author. Retrieved from http://www.rocori.k12.mn.us/sites/default/files/2014%20RMS%20Bullying%20Survey%20Results.pdf

Satterthwaite, F. W. (1946). An approximate distribution of estimates of variance components. *Biometrics Bulletin, 2*(6), 110–114. Retrieved from http://www.jstor.org/stable/3002019

Williams, L. J., & Abdi, H. (2010). Fisher's least significant difference (LSD) test. In N. J. Salkind (Ed.), *Encyclopedia of research design* (pp. 492–495). Thousand Oaks, CA: Sage.

Index